ArtScroll Series™

Rabbi Nosson Scherman / Rabbi Meir Zlotowitz

General Editors

OSHER CHAIM LEVENE

With
RABBI YEHOSHUA HARTMAN

Published by

Mesorah Publications, ltd

JEWISH WISDOM IN THE NUMBERS

FIRST EDITION
First Impression ... February 2013
Second Impression ... February 2018
Third Impression ... July 2020

Published and Distributed by
MESORAH PUBLICATIONS, Ltd.
313 Regina Avenue / Rahway, N.J. 07065

Distributed in Europe by
LEHMANNS
Unit E, Viking Business Park
Rolling Mill Road
Jarrow, Tyne & Wear NE32 3DP
England

Distributed in Australia & New Zealand by
GOLDS WORLD OF JUDAICA
3-13 William Street
Balaclava, Melbourne 3183
Victoria Australia

Distributed in Israel by
SIFRIATI / A. GITLER — BOOKS
POB 2351
Bnei Brak 51122

Distributed in South Africa by
KOLLEL BOOKSHOP
Northfield Centre, 17 Northfield Avenue
Glenhazel 2192, Johannesburg, South Africa

THE ARTSCROLL® SERIES
JEWISH WISDOM IN THE NUMBERS
© *Copyright 2013, by* MESORAH PUBLICATIONS, Ltd.
313 Regina Avenue / Rahway, N.J. 07065 / (718) 921-9000 / www.artscroll.com

---

ISBN 10: 1-4226-1344-5 / ISBN 13: 978-1-4226-1344-3

Typography by CompuScribe at ArtScroll Studios, Ltd.

Printed in the United States of America
Bound by Sefercraft, Quality Bookbinders, Ltd., Rahway, N.J. 07065

לעילוי נשמות

אבי שהיה לי למורה
הרב יחזקאל ב"ר שלום הרטמן זצ"ל

אשר שימש ברבנות וכל ימיו היוו דוגמא לשרשרת
אחת ואחידה של תורה וגמ"ח לכלל ולפרט

שחל"ח י"ח כסלו התשל"ז

מורי שהיה לי לאב
מרן הרב רבי יצחק ב"ר חיים יואל הוטנר
זצוקללה"ה

אשר הטעימני בטעם החיים ומכלל הטעמה זו –
הכניסני לתוך עולמו הקדוש של המהר"ל מפראג

שחל"ח כ' כסלו התשמ"א

ת.נ.צ.ב.ה

יהושע דוד הרטמן

ציון לנפש חיה

לעילוי נשמת

רבי מרדכי ווייס ז"ל
R' Mordechai Weisz z'l

מראשי קהילת מנשסטר יצ"ו

אשר עסק כל ימיו בעשיית חסד בגופו ובממונו, מגדולי
תמכי דאורייתא, גריס באורייתא תדירא מזכה את
הרבים, וראש וראשון לכל דבר שבקדושה

נלב"ע כ"א אלול תשס"ט

ת.נ.צ.ב.ה

מאת משפחתו

לעילוי נשמת ידיד נפשי

ר' גדליה חנוך ב"ר אברהם פסח קליין ז"ל
R' Gadya Klyne z'l

י"ד סיון תשע"ב

ת.נ.צ.ב.ה

מאת אשר חיים לוין

TABLE OF CONTENTS

PREFACE

BOOKS HAVE EDUCATED, ENTERTAINED, AND ENTHRALLED ME EVER since I learned to read. It is likely that I suffer the not-so-rare Jewish condition of "bibliophilia" — the love of books. My state became far more acute after my bar mitzvah, when I became the proud recipient of a new library of *sefarim*.

There was one particular English volume that held a special magnetic grip over me. Again and again I returned to its pages, mesmerized by every insight and idea. I did not know it at the time but **The Wisdom in the Hebrew Alphabet**, by Rabbi Michael Munk *zt"l* (Mesorah Publications: 1983) would be my first exposure to the brilliant Torah insights of the Maharal of Prague. And this book would later serve as the template for writing this present work.

Jewish Wisdom in the Numbers is based upon the notion that numbers are more than just units of counting. Numbers are symbolic of spiritual truths that span the full length and breadth of *Yiddishkeit*. So much of Jewish life can be brilliantly viewed through the prism of the number system that can serve as a guide to Jewish thought.

These essays showcase the symbolism and qualities contained within numbers that find multiple expressions within Torah. They are equivalent to "biographical sketches" about the "personalities" of numbers — but stop short of purporting to provide a definitive "portrait." I hope that, like me, you find the material compelling and fascinating.

The Maharal's teachings about numbers serve as the primary source material for this work. Other sources used to complement the "portraits" include *Baal HaTurim, Rokeach, Shelah HaKadosh, Sefas Emes, Shem MiShmuel, R' Tzadok HaKohen,* and *Vilna Gaon*.

The bulk of research was gleaned from the acclaimed Machon Yerushalayim editions of the Maharal with the commentary and annotations by my close friend, rebbe, mentor, and confidant, Rabbi Yehoshua Hartman *shlita*. Our friendship began upon R' Yehoshua's arrival in London to take up the position of Rosh Beis HaMedrash at Hasmonean High School and his kind acceptance to give a late Thursday evening Maharal *chabura* at my house — one that I am still enjoying every week 5 years later!

R' Yehoshua was introduced to the Torah of the Maharal by his rebbe, HaGaon HaRav Yitzchak Hutner *zt"l*, famed author of the *Pachad Yitzchak*, and has dedicated so much of his energies elucidating the Maharal's works to the Torah world. In a prolific writing career, his multivolume Hebrew annotated editions include (to date) *Gur Aryeh, Netzach Yisrael, Tiferes Yisrael, Be'er HaGolah, Ner Mitzvah, Derech Chaim, Nesiv HaTeshuvah,* and *Nesiv HaTorah,* which are widely acclaimed for their scholarship, comprehensiveness, and lucidity.

Our discussions about this topic, his penetrating critique, wide-ranging insights, sharp observations, and perceptive suggestions proved indispensable in our collaboration in the writing of this work. I drew upon his encyclopedic notes and indexes. Many key ideas were crystallized in our discussions, *shiurim,* and *chaburas.* His important foreword masterfully frames the Maharal's approach to numbers within Torah literature. Despite R' Yehoshua's protests to the contrary, I could not have written this work without him. Nevertheless, I take full responsibility for the final presentation of the material.

Many ideas heard from the penetrating *shiurim* of HaGaon HaRav Moshe Shapiro *shlita* were incorporated into this work. My approach to the area of Torah *hashkafah* and *mussar* was indelibly shaped by my late rebbe, Rabbi Mordechai Miller *zt"l*, Principal of Gateshead Seminary, one of Rav Dessler's earliest and closest talmidim, to whom I will always be indebted.

Other sources that proved helpful were the reference book *Otzar HaMisparim, Treasury of Numbers,* a comprehensive listing of the appearance of numbers in Torah and rabbinic literature (Rabbi Yisrael Zeligman: 1942), Rabbi Shimshon Pincus' short book *Brachos B'Cheshbon* (2003) on the Pesach song *Echad Mi Yodea,* and Rabbi Moshe Tzuriel's 2-part article, "Numbers: Their Implication and Symbolism according to the Maharal" (*HaMayan Journal* 1978: No. 183-184).

I am further indebted to my *chavrusas, chaverim,* and mentors for their critiques of individual essays or large parts of the manuscript. Particular mention is due to Rabbi Daniel Rowe and Rabbi Saul Zneimer in England, and to Rabbi Yehoshua Pfeffer and Rabbi Zave Rudman in *Eretz Yisrael.* Rabbi Akiva Tatz was kind enough to look over some early sections of the manuscript.

Special thanks to R' Shmuel Blitz and Mrs. Miriam Zakon for their interest in this project from its inception. I am exceptionally grateful to Mrs. Zakon for her skillful editing of the manuscript, her infectious enthusiasm, and her care and concern to present the material in the clearest manner possible. Thanks to Mendy Herzberg who coordinated the book in New York, Mrs. Judi Dick for her many suggestions and insights and Mrs. Frimy Eisner for her careful reading, commenting and editing, as well as to Mrs. Estie Dicker who entered the many comments, Rivky Plittman who designed and laid out the book, and Eli Kroen for designing the cover.

Rabbi Pinchas Waldman deserves extra special thanks for his meticulous check of all the sources, for clarifying many concepts, and for correcting mistakes that crept in.

Thanks to Rabbi Nosson Scherman, Rabbi Meir Zlotowitz, Rabbi Avraham Biderman, and the whole ArtScroll team for their expertise and professionalism in shepherding this work to light. It is a great privilege to be able to disseminate Torah through their publishing house.

I thank my dear parents R' Pinchas (Paul) and Miriam Levene and my wonderful in-laws, Mr. and Mrs. Shmuel Tesler, for their love, support, and enthusiasm for all my endeavors. They should be blessed with *nachas* and *berachos*.

My *eishes chayil* Chavi may not have directly contributed to the content of this work, but she made the many hours of writing it possible. May the Torah learned in this work be a *zechus* for the development of our lovely children Avigayil, Sari, Shifra, Yaakov Sholom, and Yehoshua, so that they grow up to be *ehrlich, yorei shamayim,* and a source of *nachas* to the *Ribbono Shel Olam.*

FOREWORD

by Rabbi Yehoshua Hartman

JEWISH WISDOM IN THE NUMBERS EXAMINES THE SYMBOLISM IN THE numbers that appear in so many areas of Jewish life.

Insofar as the main principles of this work are rooted in the ideas formulated by the Maharal, it is appropriate to introduce the book with a few brief opening comments about the Maharal's writings in general and the Maharal's approach to numerology in particular.

The Maharal of Prague needs hardly any introduction.

Rabbi Yehudah ben Betzalel Loewe was a brilliant Talmud scholar, halachic authority, highly influential teacher, and outspoken Jewish leader in Bohemia. He passed away just over 400 years ago. His most outstanding and enduring legacy, however, were his trail-blazing writings, which established him as one of the seminal figures of Jewish thought in the last 500 years.

The Maharal's most outstanding and enduring legacy were his trail-blazing writings.

When originally published, the works of the Maharal were not widely circulated. For a fairly long stretch of time, his books remained relatively obscure. Only upon their subsequent republishing would the Maharal's illuminating ideas gain wide currency and spread throughout the Jewish world.

In due course, his teachings greatly influenced proponents of the Chasidic and Mussar movements alike. He pioneered an innovative course to brilliantly reveal the concealed areas of Torah that came to shape Jewish thought and philosophy. In the last century, the Maharal's works have become phenomenally popular. Today, more than any time in history, there is an unquenchable thirst by Jews for the Torah thought of the Maharal.

His teachings greatly influenced proponents of the Chasidic and Mussar movements alike. They provided an innovative course to brilliantly reveal the concealed areas of Torah that came to shape Jewish thought.

Perhaps the main obstacle facing the contemporary Jew learning the Maharal's works is the struggle to grasp the abstruse concepts mentioned.

It is not uncommon for a reader to excitedly delve into the Maharal's writings only to grow increasingly frustrated at his inability to fully comprehend the concepts found within the Maharal's in-depth explanations.

In truth, the real barrier lies with the concepts themselves. Most of the ideas that the Maharal reveals seem foreign because they originate in the esoteric portion of Torah. My rebbe, HaGaon Rabbi Yitzchak Hutner zt"l, famously noted that the genius of the Maharal's writings lies in his rare ability to frame Torah through the medium of *nistar belashon nigleh*, the Hidden in the language of the Revealed.

The Maharal pulls back the curtain. He unveils the depth of meaning within G-d's world and the multilayered teachings of Chazal. He brilliantly formulates his explanations by cloaking these ideas using distinctive non-kabbalistic terms. Consequently, the Maharal brings to light many profound concepts to a far broader audience — even those not exposed to or well-versed in the teachings of the hidden portion of Torah.

Nevertheless, the Maharal takes special care never to divulge more than what he considers to be absolutely necessary. Often, the Maharal confesses his reluctance to elaborate. He may curtail his explanation by remarking that a fuller treatment of the concept is reserved for "the masters of truth."

So there is a difficult balancing act going on in the Maharal's writings — one in which the relationship to the hidden portion of Torah is "touching but not touching," "connected but unconnected," "overt yet covert."

This principle is especially pertinent in the genre of "the Torah of Numbers." It is quite clear that the origins of the Maharal's theory regarding numbers are drawn from kabbalistic sources. Consider the following example from the Maharal's comments to the fifth chapter in *Pirkei Avos*, where he addresses why the rabbinic adages are respectively grouped into statements associated with the numbers 10, 7, and 4:

> I have elaborated to explain the words of the "wise [men of] truth" [a phrase meaning "kabbalists"] as alluded to in the continuous mentioning of these 3 numbers [10, 7, and 4]. It is impossible to write about this — more than a drop in the ocean — because these matters are deep. They emanate from the inner, higher wisdom .... All these words are known in the higher wisdom. It is impossible to expound further. Man should comprehend these matters to their truthful [end point]. One cannot elaborate .... Place your eyes and heart to these matters .... I have expanded discussions about these matters [of numerology] so that man does not dismiss the words of the Sages as theories

or speculations. Everything about these matters is of the higher wisdom ...

Maharal, *Derech Chaim* 5:15

Throughout his many works, the Maharal pays close attention to the appearance of numbers in the Written Torah and within the words of Chazal. This is in line with his thorough treatment of all details within aggadic material. Nothing is haphazard or accidental; everything is meaningful and exact. This principle equally applies to numbers, whose symbolism beautifully ties in with illuminating the specific teachings being conveyed.

Throughout his many works, the Maharal pays close attention to the appearance of numbers.

Nowhere in the Maharal's writings, however, is the reader given a formal, systematic treatment of numerology. Nor is he clearly presented with an all-encompassing framework for dealing with other numbers.

It gives me great pleasure to strengthen and support the efforts of my dear friend R' Osher Chaim Levene. He has taken it upon himself to clarify the "Torah of the Numbers" based upon the ground rules established by the Maharal. He has diligently labored to collect this information from the Maharal's writings, whose explanations of the symbolism of numbers are scattered through the length and breadth of his works. He has complemented this with the teachings of other Torah giants, such as the Baal HaTurim, Rokeach, Vilna Gaon, Sefas Emes, and R' Tzadok HaKohen, among others. Through his efforts, he endeavors to present a thorough, coherent picture that addresses the essence of each number.

In truth, those who learn the Maharal's writings can be broadly divided into two camps. There are the elite few who are knowledgeable in the esoteric areas of Torah. These exceptional individuals understand the Maharal according to the *ta'am elyon*, higher meaning. They discern how the Maharal's discussions relate to the exalted hidden wisdom. But the Maharal was *not* written exclusively for the masters of kabbalah. His audience includes *any* Jew whose soul yearns to taste the wholeness and profundity of Torah. Such a reader can savor the words of the Maharal according to its *ta'am tachton*, lower meaning.

But the Maharal was not written exclusively for the masters of kabbalah. His audience includes any Jew whose soul yearns to taste the wholeness and profundity of Torah.

This double-layered reading similarly applies to the Maharal's discussions regarding numbers. Much of the symbolism within numbers truly belongs to the hidden portion of Torah. Still, there remains a wealth of information that is readily accessible to every Jew — even for the majority of people who lack knowledge of the exalted portions of Torah. They are able to drink the waters starting with its

There remains a wealth of information that is readily accessible to every Jew.

"lower meaning" and to begin ascending the ladder to reach higher and higher levels. This work will certainly enable the reader to initiate the climb.

May the profound thought of the Maharal into the symbolism of numbers enable us to plumb the richness of Torah and may it inspire us to see the brilliance of G-d's word and grow in our *avodas Hashem*.

Rabbi Yehoshua Hartman
Erev Succos 5773

OVERVIEW
JUDAISM BY THE NUMBERS

I. THE PERSONALITY OF A NUMBER

Numbers are man's essential tool to interact with the many plural forms around him.

WE LIVE IN A WORLD OF NUMBERS.
Numbers are man's essential tool to interact with the many plural forms around him. He uses numbers to measure, count, or sequence the dazzling array of phenomena within the universe.

In mathematics and science, numbers are used to investigate the complex structure of the cosmos. In the field of sports, numbers record athletic feats and triumphs. And in the world of commerce, numbers are the foremost measure of business activities in terms of profits or losses. But numbers also regularly feature in man's daily affairs — anything from timepieces to timetables, home addresses to telephone contacts, pin numbers to passwords, salaries to state benefits.

Life without them would be inconceivable. This is why the "language of numbers" is the undisputed universal language of the world.

Life without them would be inconceivable. This is why the "language of numbers" is the undisputed universal language of the world.

The widespread application of numbers is certainly not restricted to mundane matters. It similarly fulfills an important spiritual role within Jewish life.

GIVE ME A NUMBER

When we explore the relationship between numbers and Torah, we discover manifold examples of numbers present in all walks of Jewish life.

The popular Seder song: אֶחָד מִי יוֹדֵעַ, *Who Knows One?*, pairs the first 13 numbers with well-known Jewish concepts: G-d is 1; 2 are the Tablets; 3 are the Patriarchs; 4 are the Matriarchs; 5 are the Books of the Torah, and so on.

This deceptively simple folk-song is not a playful game. It actually points to the great significance that is invested into numbers when they are framed within a Torah setting. When we explore the relationship between numbers and Torah, we discover manifold examples of numbers present in all walks of Jewish life.

Numbers play an important role in recounting historical details (e.g., lifespan of the Biblical Personalities, timelines, the duration of events). They are absolutely indispensable within the practical realm of *mitzvah* observance (e.g., calculations of dates in the calendar, the age at which a child is deemed an adult, the formation of a *minyan* for prayer, the dimensions of a *succah*, the measurement of an *eiruv*, just to mention a handful of examples).

Other offshoots that further emphasize the significance of numbers include the use of *gematria*, numerical value, where each letter of the Hebrew alphabet is attributed a value based upon its sequential positioning (i.e., א, the first letter = 1; ב, the second letter = 2, etc.), with many important insights derived from the comparison between a word and its numerical value. The number of letters or words found in Scriptural sentences or Jewish prayers (e.g., 248 words in *Shema*[1] or 18 blessings in the *Amidah*[2]) also have their significance.

What is the mysterious nature of "numbers"? Why are they important? And what is their pivotal role in the presentation of Torah?

What is the mysterious nature of "numbers"?

NUMBERS: WHAT ARE THEY?

Philosophers have long debated whether or not numbers exist outside the human experience. Do numbers exist independent of man? Or are they simply man's necessary response to the multiplicity in the world around him? This argument revolves around the answer to the central question: Were numbers invented or were they discovered?

Were numbers invented or were they discovered?

One school of thought sees mathematics as a man-made innovation; an abstract entity introduced as a practical tool to make sense of the quantity within the universe. This view rejects numbers as being innately meaningful or possessing intrinsic characteristics. The second school of thought adopts the opposite stance. Dismissing the theory of numbers as a human invention, this view adulates mathematics as the measure of all things; they see numbers as "the language of nature itself."[3]

What is the Torah perspective on this? Clearly, numbers feature extensively both in the world of creation and in the world of Torah. Indeed, creation and Torah are inextricably related: Torah is the Divine blueprint for creation.[4] The presence of numbers in Torah underscores the extent that numbers relate to the Divine design embedded within creation. This does not, however, imbue numbers with any innate magical qualities. Nor does it give them an independent will of their own. Like all of nature's wonders, their significance is exclusively derived from *their role as Divine tools within the cosmos.*

Numbers relate to the Divine design embedded within creation.

NUMBERS: WHAT THEY DO

Judaism invests numbers with metaphysical meaning — *not because of "what they are" but because of "what they do."* The sig-

Judaism invests numbers with metaphysical meaning — not because of what they are but because of what they do.

nificance of numbers comes from their role as the instrument that conveys the spiritual nature of the concept they help quantify.

The innate characteristics of a specific number brilliantly embody the spiritual truths to which it gives expression.

Within a Torah framework, the mathematical properties of numbers are effectively used to illuminate the universal truths of Torah. The innate characteristics of a specific number brilliantly embody the spiritual truths to which it gives expression.

The following example illustrates this point. The Jewish nation was established by the illustrious *Avos*, Patriarchs: Avraham, Yitzchak, and Yaakov. Particular stress is placed upon their number: "there were *only* 3 Avos."[5] There is no need for a rabbinic statement to teach us basic arithmetic! Rather, this statement comes to explain why there *had* to be 3 *Avos* — no more and no less. It comes to describe the exclusivity of this group. Additionally, the spiritual truth behind this physical reality taps into the symbolism of 3 as the epitome of foundation, permanence, and continuity — the basic building blocks forming the indestructible G-dly nation of Israel.[6]

NUMBER: FULL OF PERSONALITY

A helpful analogy is to view each number as a distinct "personality."

A particularly helpful analogy to relate to the symbolism of numbers is *to view each number as a distinct "personality."*

A number, like a person, can be subject to a biographical sketch. Typically, a biography details the essential facts of the subject, such as his background, context, and setting. But it also includes an in-depth analysis of the subject's personality — one extrapolated from his life experiences within the milieu in which he finds himself. This portrait will explore his relationship with family members and associates, it will trace his influence and legacy, and highlight some of his main qualities — both those that he shares with others but also those that are uniquely his own.

These same principles apply to study the unique "personality" of a number.

The main distinctiveness of a number lies in its numeric quantity. In this respect, every number is absolutely unique.

The main distinctiveness of a number lies in its numeric quantity. In this respect, every number is absolutely unique; 6 basketballs are not the same as 7. Nevertheless, numbers *do* share mathematical qualities with other numbers, almost like family members share related genetic properties and certain attributes.

Some examples of numeric relationship are apparent in the square or square root of numbers that links them; how multiples of 10, 100, etc. are connected; and how one number can be composed of two smaller ones. In addition, "earlier" numbers can be viewed as "ancestors" and "later" numbers as their "descendants." The innate qualities of the number 60 can be traced back to 6 and also find further expression in 600,000.[7]

Relationships between numbers may be direct or indirect.

Relationships between numbers may be direct or indirect. They may contain multiple similarities, indicating many common features. Or they may be remote, with the most minimal resemblance: similar to distant human relatives.[8] Seeing the interplay or relationship between a person and his family, like that between numbers, offers valuable insights into its true nature.

Much is revealed into the inner world of a person by examining his life experiences. The same analogy holds true with numbers. One can discover much about the rich, unique personality of a number by exploring its application in Torah and *mitzvah* observance. Conversely, many features of a number find exquisite expression as they are manifest in all areas of Jewish thought and practice.

It is essential to get to know the distinct "personalities" of the numbers.

Consequently, it is essential to get to know the distinct "personalities" of the numbers. This will give us a new appreciation of how numbers are the tools that embody the timeless concepts and principles of Judaism. And they are the key to unlocking the all-inclusive and integrated system that permeates Jewish life.

II. WHY EVERY NUMBER COUNTS

The basic idea of a count is to quantify a given set of items.

A KEY USE OF NUMBERS IS AS A MEASURE OF QUANTITY.
The basic idea of a count is to quantify a given set of items by tallying the number of units and placing them into a single, defining group.

IN FOR THE COUNT

Several highly prominent examples of counting feature in Judaism. There is the count of 49 days of the *Omer,* arranged into 7 weeks of 7 days or its parallel arrangement found in the 7 sets of Sabbatical yearly cycles.[9] There is the count of kosher animals passing under a rod through an opening in a pen for the farmer to specify every 10th animal as *ma'aser,* tithe.[10] There is the notable manner in which the *Kohen* sprinkled the sacrificial blood on Yom Kippur: 7 times downward and 1 time upward.[11] And then there was the census of the Israelites in the Wilderness.

The presence of counting within Judaism clearly indicates that there is more to counting than just numbering.

The presence of counting within Judaism clearly indicates that there is more to *counting* than just *numbering*. Why should the practice of using numbers to quantify items into a grouping carry any religious significance? Is there anything distinctively "Jewish" in the counting process?

The Build-up

A count is conceptually equivalent to the act of building.

The traditional Torah perspective does not consider a count as just a simple, numeric summation. A count is conceptually equivalent to the act of *building*.

Consider the manner in which a builder operates. Working from the intricate plans conceived by the architect, a builder must assemble the requisite materials and fabrics — concrete, wooden beams, bricks and mortar, etc. — piece by piece, carefully arranging them in a structured and orderly fashion. Every component is marked to play an essential role in the building process. *Everything must relate to, and build upon, what came before and what follows after.* In this manner, the individual parts are sequentially assembled into a single, defining group to enable the builder to complete the construction of the whole structure.

Everything must relate to, and build upon, what came before and what follows after.

The dynamics of the counting process involve two stages — both of which are beautifully encapsulated within the Hebrew word מִסְפָּר, *number.*

The first stage of counting is how a number imposes limitations upon those items to be included or excluded in the count.

First and foremost, a number quantifies a given set of items as the definite amount. It naturally imposes limitations upon those items to be included or excluded in the count. מִסְפָּר relates to the word סְפַר, *boundary.* Borders form the demarcations of a country.[12]

But there is an important second stage — *where numbers come to defy their natural limitations.* Here the counting process realizes the state where many different components join together to construct one whole. Like the diverse materials available to a builder, all the parts are assembled to construct a fully functional building. This concept is also contained within the term מִסְפָּר, whose root letters form the word סֵפֶר, *book.* By "confining" specific information within its covers, the author skillfully assembles letters, words, sentences, paragraphs and chapters in this defined space to construct a well-crafted book consisting of one סִפּוּר, *narrative.*[13] The details are not left as isolated or disparate entities; they come together to build up and create one unified picture.[14]

There is an important second stage — where many different components join together to construct one whole.

CREATION: MAKE IT COUNT

This concept of counting and building up numbers is central to the existence and functionality of the universe.

Numbers are the building blocks used in the construction of physical matter.[15] Both the origin of the cosmos and its development must be viewed as part of a meaningful process — one that is similarly counting and building up toward the realization of its destiny.

Numbers are the building blocks used in the construction of physical matter.

G-d fashioned the universe in stages. Creation was built, so to speak, through the unfolding of the first 6 Days of Creation. Each day introduced a new, distinct, and additional element. Similar to how a count joins and builds one element to another, the sequential numbered days count up to merge together culminating in the 7th Day, Shabbos.

Every component of existence, like every number, is individually significant. Nothing is superfluous or redundant. Every object in creation therefore has its specific and integral contribution to play. Its uniqueness is fully realized where it neatly fits into the construction of the cosmos — where it is framed in terms of the construction of something far bigger, grander, and all-encompassing.

Every component of existence, like every number, is individually significant.

Parallel to the 6 Days of Creation in the original creation of the universe is the development of world history that would pass through 6 millennia.[16] Like the actual creation itself, this involves a spiritual act of building. All the myriad creatures spanning the time continuum count. Moreover, they join together, building up to finally realize G-d's purpose of the universe. World history unfolds towards the coming of Mashiach and the attainment of the World to Come. The Chosen Nation, charged with the task of building up the universe, are the people whose lives have much to do with the symbolism of counting.

All the myriad creatures spanning the time continuum count.

The Chosen Nation, charged with the task of building up the universe, are the people whose lives have much to do with the symbolism of counting.

The Exodus: The COUNT IS ON

There is an act of counting in the Jewish calendar that is marked immediately after the period when the Children of Israel celebrated their nationhood.

For over two centuries, Yaakov's descendants were enslaved in the land of מִצְרַיִם, *Egypt*, whose Hebrew name implies a state of מְצָרִים, *straits*.[17] In fact, the numerical value of מִצְרַיִם is identical to the word מִסְפָּר, *number* (380).[18] We have seen that the basic function of a number count is to quantify a given set of items. It imposes limitations or parameters upon those items that are incorporated into the count.

One aspect of the Israelites' servitude was subservience to Egyptian ideology in relation to their view of the natural world. The physical world is subject to quantity and limitations, in contrast to the spiritual world, which as the realm of the infinite transcends all limitation. The "straits" of Egypt depicted a man-made environment where G-d did not — and indeed could not — feature. Consequently, there was no attempt to find meaning or purpose in such a world.

Breaking free of Egypt released the Children of Israel from this outlook. The Exodus meant that they could now go beyond the basic function of a number to quantify a given set of items. They could progress onto the second stage of a count: *to integrate the numbers toward completion of an all-inclusive construction.* Creating a meaningful structure bespeaks a Divine design — which is directed toward connecting to the All-Infinite Creator.

Significantly, the *Omer* counting in the Jewish calendar begins on the morrow *after* the Israelites left Egypt. Here they started the count in the knowledge that each day and week carries within it its unique or specific task. No day exists in isolation. Once it has been defined on its own individual terms, it is counted and assembled.[19] The departure from Egypt began a counting process that built up to Shavuos, when the Torah was given.[20] This 49-day period in the Jewish calendar records the original passage of the Children of Israel as they were built into one national entity — ultimately encamping *like one man with one heart.*[21] This was the point when the ultimate purpose and conclusion of the Exodus would be realized.[22]

ISRAEL: STAND UP AND BE COUNTED

Reflecting on how a count integrates diverse components into one whole entity, we see the extraordinary phenomenon of the Children of Israel themselves being subject to a count in the national census.[23]

In our earlier analogy, we noted that a builder must ensure that he has all the requisite materials and the necessary quantities available in order to complete his construction. This calls for every individual component to be properly accounted for, in the knowledge that every component serves a specific but absolutely vital purpose. Nothing must be missing.

So too, every individual Jew — within the stated parameters — had to be included in the national census. First, this census accentu-

The physical world is subject to quantity and limitations, in contrast to the spiritual world.

The Exodus meant that they could progress onto the second stage of a count: to integrate the numbers toward completion of an all-inclusive construction.

They started the count in the knowledge that no day exists in isolation. Once it has been defined on its own individual terms, it is counted and assembled.

This calls for every individual component to be properly accounted for as it serves a specific but absolutely vital purpose.

ated that each person was entrusted with a Divinely appointed task — one that was uniquely his. Second, it determined how his identity was best framed in the context of the national whole.

COUNTING: CALLED TO ACCOUNT

The counting of every individual Jew in the national census simultaneously highlights his distinctiveness and his contribution to the national persona.

This concept is wonderfully hinted at in two words that both mean *counting*: מִנְיָן and פְּקִידָה. In truth, they can be respectively related to the words מְמוּנֶּה, *appointed*,[24] and תַּפְקִיד, *designated task*.[25] Counting stresses the importance of each individual. It confirms, so to speak, his "Divine appointment." At the same time, it also demands accountability, so that he fulfills his designated, personal charge.[26]

This explains the inherent danger of a count. Singling out an individual, by proclaiming his distinctiveness, rightly draws attention to him. Within the cosmos, he has some measure of uniqueness that no one else shares. No one else can do what he has to do. Consequently, if he is not for himself, who else will be there for him?[27] Differentiating him sets him apart. But at the same time it may cast judgment upon him and lead to a Heavenly indictment. This is because *the very process of "a count" means that it "calls him to account."* It comes to determine whether or not he has actually lived up to his charge.[28]

THE COUNT TO INFINITY

The significance of the national census meant that individual Jews were not left as disparate, disconnected units. Having defined his individuality, the individual was now ready to be counted and to be integrated into a broader context. In the Wilderness, the Jew was counted as a member of his family, of his tribe, and finally, of his nation.[29] Here the enumerated individuals, like different military divisions in an army, would come together to construct an integrated entity.[30] Every Jew finds his true vocation through his unique contribution to building his nation. He wants to be associated with the collective national identity of Israel that is so beloved to G-d.[31] Indeed, the objective of the national census was in order to draw attention to the cherished nature of G-d's Chosen Nation — in which every individual member counts.[32]

Every individual Jew — within the stated parameters — had to be included in the national census.

Counting confirms a Jew's "Divine appointment" and also demands his accountability to fulfill his designated, personal charge.

The very process of "a count" means that it "calls him to account."

Every Jew finds his true vocation through his unique contribution to building his nation.

This is why, despite their finite properties as the smallest of the nations,[33] the Jewish People are often compared to the dust, sand, and stars — prominent symbols of the uncountable.[34] They are not confined to the restricted, Egyptian-like quantifiable nature of numbers. They would continuously see G-d as the Creator of numbers. And they *rightly count and construct numbers, building them up until they finally realize the destiny of creation* — to proclaim the Glory of G-d Who is the All-Infinite.

The Jewish People rightly count and construct numbers, building them up until they finally realize the destiny of creation.

Every number has its unique personality. And it has its particular task.

It counts. It gathers. It inhabits the finite physical world of מִסְפָּר, *numbers*. Nonetheless, it builds up and will finally reach the ultimate infinite spiritual world of אֵין מִסְפָּר, *beyond numbers.*[35]

NOTES

1. See "248: In Action."
2. See "18: The Lifeline."
3. Galileo said, "The book of nature is written in mathematical language." The Greek philosophers constructed an entire theory of the universe based upon numbers. Modern mathematical physics retains the ancient Greek assumption that the universe is rationally ordered according to mathematical principles. Similarly, numbers play an important role in music — such as length of strings in instruments — and in astronomy.
4. *Zohar, Terumah* 161a.
5. "Only 3 [men] are called *Avos*, Patriarchs" (*Berachos* 16b).
6. See "3: Three-Dimensional".
7. See "6: It's Only Natural," "60: In Principle," and "600,000: The Jewish People."
8. Some numbers are "related" by sharing common qualities or stand as variations of the same theme (e.g., 4 and 6 as expansions of directions into 2 or 3 dimensions of the physical world. See "4: Finding the Place" and "6: It's Only Natural."
9. See "7: A Holy Spark" and "49: Full Measure."
10. *Vayikra* 27:32.
11. Mishnah, *Yoma* 5:3.
12. Border towns are termed *arei s'far*, cities of the edge (or *yishuvei s'far* in the modern vernacular) see *Rashi, Devarim* 33:25. They are similar to the coastline, which is defined by the seashore (*Rashi, Yehoshua* 24:11).
13. The story of our redemption from Egypt is called *sipur yetzias Mitzrayim*, story of the departure from Egypt. It is noteworthy that a writ of divorce is called *sefiras devarim* (*Gittin* 21b) insofar as, like a *sefer*, the document must narrate what is taking place.
14. The verse, *to count our days so teach us, then we should acquire a heart of wisdom* (*Tehillim* 90:12) means that the manner to reach wisdom is where the individual points are plotted to create a pathway heading in a true direction.

15. One can readily note the etymological similarities between the term סְפִירָה, *Divine Emanation*, and the word מִסְפָּר, *number*.
16. See "6000: The End of the World."
17. *Eichah* 1:3.
18. This is attributed to the Arizal (cited in *Mavo L'Chochmas HaKabbalah* 2:3).
19. Indeed, the word עֹמֶר relates to מְעַמֵר, *gathering or binding together*, fruit or grain as in sheaf-making, which denotes the symbol of assembly. See *Rambam, Hilchos Shabbos* 8:6.
20. *Vayikra* 23:9-16. See "49: The Full Measure."
21. *Rashi, Shemos* 19:2.
22. See "50: All the Way."
23. See *Bamidbar Rabbah* 2:11 which states that there were a total of 10 censuses throughout Israel's history. One count was conducted in the aftermath of the Golden Calf. Another was carried out in the second year after leaving Egypt, after constructing the Mishkan (*Bamidbar* 1:1 and *Rashi* ad loc.). Later, prior to the new generation entering the Holy Land, another census was taken. In fact, the count was reserved to Jewish males between the ages of 20 and 60 years old who were suitable to serve in the army (*Bamidbar* 1:3) — to the exclusion of women, the elderly, and the young. (The Levites were subject to a separate census with different criteria.) Each person was counted as a member of his respective tribe (*Bamidbar* 1:21).
24. See, e.g., *Sotah* 42a. See *Malbim, Bereishis* 15:5 for the difference between *manah* and *safer* to mean *counting*.
25. See *Bereishis* 41:34, I *Melachim*, 11:28, *Mishnah, Eidios* 5:7.
26. This is the reason that the count at the beginning of *Sefer Bamidbar* was conducted by the *number of names* (*Bamidbar* 1:2), where a name defines the essence of the respective individual. See *Tehillim* 147:4 about how G-d counts the stars that represent spiritual forces in the universe. This indicates their innate worth and function within the universe.
27. *Pirkei Avos* 1:14.
28. The obligation to count the people by collecting a half-shekel from each person was so that *there be no plague among them* (*Shemos* 30:12). This transferred the count onto coins rather than the heads of individuals. See *Rashi, Shemos* 30:12 how counting causes an "evil eye." See *Rambam Hilchos Temidim U-Musafim* 4:4 and *Magen Avraham, Orach Chaim* 156:2 about the general prohibition of counting a group of Jews.
29. The Jewish nation was organized into its respective families and tribal divisions (that would typically share the same general mission) and strategically positioned in the encampments around the Sanctuary. See *Zohar, Ki Sisa* 187b and *Shelah HaKadosh, Parshas Bamidbar* for how the reason they were counted was in order that the *Shechinah* would dwell in their midst.
30. The qualification to be included in the census were men within the 20 -60 age range who were eligible to serve in the *tzava*, army (*Bamidbar* 1:3), that was itself synonymous of a collective group (See *Ramban, Bamidbar* 1:2-3).
31. The special level of Divine providence and protection afforded to Israel as G-d's cherished nation is not extended to one who has disconnected himself from his people (*Rabbeinu Bachya, Shemos* 30:12).
32. *Rashi, Bamidbar* 1:1.
33. *Devarim* 7:7.
34. *Bereishis* 13:16, 15:5, 22:17, 26:4, 28:14; *Bamidbar* 23:10.
35. *Sfas Emes, Bamidbar* 5637.

THE ONE AND ONLY 1

1 refers to the Oneness and Unity
of G-d, Creator of the universe.

Events or objects that, like the number 1,
come at the beginning as the "first" in a series
often possess a special holiness.
These "firsts" signify a purposeful life in
the service of the One G-d.

ONE OF A KIND

1 does not consist of anything other than itself.

THE NUMBER 1 IS UNIQUE AS IT IS THE FIRST OF THE WHOLE NUMBERS. As a single entity, 1 is the only number that is not plural. There are no multiple elements in it that can be counted or measured. This is because 1 does not consist of anything other than itself. This is the only reason that 1 cannot be classified as a *number* in the conventional sense of the word. It can be broken down as a fraction, but never as a function of other numbers.[1]

The Oneness of G-d is the Oneness of an indivisible Unity.

Standing apart and in a class of its own, the number 1 is naturally used to describe the Oneness of G-d.

The Oneness of G-d is the Oneness of an indivisible Unity Who is not subject to multiplicity or divisibility.[2] There is nothing else that is truly One. By extension, this Unity also means that in truth nothing really exists outside of Him.

1: ONENESS OF G-D

The number 1 has unique mathematical properties that in some way reflect the Unity of G-d. Unlike all other numbers, whether you multiply 1 by itself or divide it by itself, the answer remains 1.

$$1 \times 1 = 1$$
$$1 \div 1 = 1$$

Indivisibility cannot be a property of anything that possesses a body, shape, or form. Any physical entity can be subdivided into different parts, all the way down to its atomic substructure. But this does not apply to G-d, Who does not have any body, shape, or form, and Whose Oneness is unchanging and constant.

He is the Source of everything and existence revolves around Him.

The eternal declaration of Jewish faith is שְׁמַע יִשְׂרָאֵל ה׳ אֱלֹקֵינוּ ה׳ אֶחָד, *Hear O Israel, HASHEM is our G-d, HASHEM is the One and Only.*[3] It is recited at least twice daily. It is one of the first verses we are taught as children and the statement we make with our last dying breath: our mortal testimony to G-d, the immortal Source of all existence.

Jewish life centers upon the awe-inspiring realization that He is the Source of everything and existence revolves around Him.

FIRST OF ALL: BEGINNINGS

The uniqueness of 1 is seen in a related quality. It is the first of all the numbers and is therefore synonymous with the "beginning" or "point of origin."

The beginning often reflects an object's essence. This is because the basis or the defining feature of an object is encoded at the point that it comes into being. We can liken this to laying down foundations, the first phase in the construction of a building. In Aramaic, the term מֵעִיקָרָא, *at the outset*, comes from the word עִיקָר, *primary*, conveying that this is the most decisive moment *because it all starts from here.* Due to its leading position, 1 is similarly the root of all the other numbers.[4]

This concept is integral to the opening word of Torah: *bereishis*, "in the beginning of" or "at first."[5] The meaning of existence, its essence, is to be realized by Israel and the Torah, both of whom are or can be called *reishis*, first.

The initiation point sets the tone: הַכֹּל הוֹלֵךְ אַחַר הָרֹאשׁ, *everything follows after the beginning [literally, head].*[6] The opening stage is an important guide of what is likely to unfold. This is best illustrated in the Jewish year, which starts on Rosh Hashanah (literally, the head or beginning of the year). As the Day of Judgment, it determines what the rest of the year holds. (This gives rise to the ancient custom of not "sleeping away" the first day of Rosh Hashanah as a portent for a sleepy year.[7]) Another example is the marital obligation during *shanah rishonah*, first year [of marriage], during which a husband is exempt from communal duties such as going to the army, because that is the foundation for the new couple's entire married life.[8]

First impressions are said to count because similarly they shape a man's perspective.[9]

The initiation point sets the tone.

IN THE FIRST PLACE

BY DEFINITION, ONLY 1 THING CAN BE FIRST IN ANY PROCESS.[10] IN this respect, the first entity that comes into existence is uniquely placed to be considered the most elevated.

The first is naturally predestined to embrace holiness, which, by its very nature, implies elevation.[11] The reason the formative "first portion" is *kadosh*, holy, is because it taps into the symbolism of G-d as the One Creator and First Cause.[12] Once the first stage of a process is dedicated toward G-d, everything else is likely to follow suit.[13]

Some examples of "firsts" being sanctified to G-d are *mitzvos* regarding the first fruits, the first of the farmer's crops, the firstborn son, and the firstborn animal.

1ST: FIRST FRUITS, FIRST CROPS

The farmer in Israel had to identify and set aside *bikkurim*, the first-ripening fruits of the seven species growing each year in his field. These fruits were joyously taken up to the Temple. After a waving ceremony,[14] these were given to the *Kohen*, priest.[15]

Terumah, the first portion of the crop (literally, lifted apart), was the sanctified tithe separated from agricultural produce. Once designated, the tithes were given as a gift to a *Kohen* to be eaten in a state of purity.[16] Related to this was *challah*, first of the dough, which was also given to a *Kohen*.[17]

Additionally, there was the obligation of *reishis hageiz*, the first wool shearing. Again, this was not for the farmer's personal use but was a gift to the *Kohen*.[18]

1ST: FIRSTBORN

The firstborn son, whose birth makes his father into a father, is entitled to a double portion of his father's inheritance.[19] It was the special qualities associated with a *bechor*, firstborn, that Yaakov sought from Eisav by purchasing the birthright.[20]

The Jewish firstborn males originally were the nation's priests.[21]

Due to the sin of the Golden Calf, *Kehunah*, the priesthood, was transferred to Aharon and his descendants from the Tribe of Levi. Aharon and the *Kohanim* led the service in the Temple. They were accorded the privilege to be *first* in all *devarim sheb'kedushah*, holy matters.[22] In the *mitzvah* ceremony of *pidyon haben*, the redemption of the [firstborn] son, the innate holiness of the firstborn is recognized 30 days after his birth by the actions of the *bechor's* father, who presents 5 pieces of silver to a *Kohen* to redeem his son.[23]

The firstborn male offspring of a kosher animal born to a Jewish farmer is also consecrated.[24] This means it cannot be worked nor can its fleece be shorn for the benefit of the owner.[25] Where unblemished, it was brought as an offering, with its innards burnt on the Altar, and its meat eaten by the *Kohen*.[26] A similar law applies to only one type of nonkosher firstborn animal — a donkey, which must be redeemed with a lamb or a kid.[27]

All this relates to the sanctified stature of Israel, nationally identified as the firstborn.

1ST: FIRSTBORN NATION

G-d lovingly called His nation בְּנִי בְכֹרִי יִשְׂרָאֵל, *My firstborn son, Israel*.[28] Historically, other nations emerged before the formation of the Jewish people at the Exodus. Still, this designation alludes to Israel's primacy in terms of fulfilling the spiritual purpose of the universe.[29] Just as a son is an extension of the father, so too, *Israel is the beginning of G-d's revelation of His power in the world*.[30]

G-d's redemption of His firstborn son, Israel, resonates within the *mitzvah* of *pidyon haben*, where the father similarly takes steps to redeem his beloved firstborn.[31] When G-d struck the Egyptians with Ten Plagues, the coup de grace was *Makkas Bechoros*, Plague of the Firstborn,[32] targeting the Egyptian firstborns whose lives were dedicated to idolatrous worship[33] and, most specifically, Pharaoh, himself a firstborn.[34]

Starting in the first month of the Jewish calendar (Nissan),[35] the Children of Israel were set on course to live a sanctified existence — both nationally and individually — and to become one, unique nation.

THE CHOSEN ONE

HISTORICALLY, THE ONENESS OF G-D'S FIRSTBORN FINDS ITS ROOTS in their originating founding father, Avraham.

AVRAHAM THE ONE

Introducing a new world order, Avraham is credited as the 1 individual to realize the purpose of Creation.[36] First of the Patriarchs, the

All this relates to the sanctified stature of Israel, nationally identified as the firstborn.

Starting in the first month, the Children of Israel were set on course to live a sanctified existence.

founding forefather of the Jewish nation is associated with the number 1: "… for when he was yet 1 alone did I summon him."[37]

The forefather who single-handedly fought the world, Avraham was "1 individual" versus the rest of civilization.[38] G-d came to his rescue, saying: "I am Unique in My world; He [Avraham] is unique in his world. It is only befitting for the 'Unique One' to save the 'unique one.'"[39] As the first human being to proclaim G-d as Master of the Universe,[40] Avraham preached the Oneness and Unity of G-d to a pagan world that denied His Supremacy and allowed for the false belief in multiple independent forces within existence. Avraham set into motion the genesis of Israel, whose national psyche is similarly bound together with the number 1.

Avraham set into motion the genesis of Israel.

pesach: 1 Little Lamb

Prior to leaving Egypt, Israel declared the Oneness of G-d as the first and Only Power, as repeatedly symbolized within the *mitzvah* of *korban pesach*, the paschal lamb.

This offering consisted of a lamb up to 1 year old (not older); eaten in 1 group;[41] its roasted meat unified it into 1 piece;[42] no bone was allowed to be broken from the *korban pesach* to fracture its oneness. In truth, the original *korban pesach* was the landmark point of Israel's national formation in the Exodus. In this respect, it attests to G-d's Oneness by the Jews forever turning their backs on Egyptian idolatry.[43]

The original korban pesach was the point of Israel's national formation.

One People; One Community

The number 1 is an underlying feature of Jewish life: "The other nations have many rites, many clergy, and many houses of worship. We, the Jewish people, have but 1 G-d, 1 Ark, 1 Torah, 1 Altar, and 1 High Priest."[44] That is why the whole Torah was given by 1 Shepherd (G-d) and taught by 1 leader (Moshe).[45]

Always, the Jewish people are "a nation that dwells alone."[46] Compared to all the other nations, they are truly distinct.[47] Other groups of people may share a common country, language, nationality, or culture; but only Israel is intrinsically one. Their national unified affinity is by virtue of the Torah.[48] In contrast to the diverse non-Jewish nations, Israel is exclusively one entity; one "man" pulsating to the same heartbeat.[49] When a Jew in Paris suffers, the Jew in New

Only Israel is intrinsically one.

York grieves. And wherever a Jew travels, his brethren around the globe routinely open their doors and their hearts to him.

The Jews' ideology and identity — a legacy given over from generation to generation — revolve around their commitment to G-d's Torah as given at Sinai, where Israel nationally embraced it "as one man with one heart."[50] Herein lies their implicit declaration: "We have no independent self — other than what G-d asks us. Our life and death exist exclusively to perform His Will. Other than this, we have no reason to exist!" Israel mirrors their Creator: "You [G-d] are 1; Your Name is 1; Who is like your people Israel, 1 nation in the land?"[51]

In the future Messianic era, the world will universally proclaim His Oneness: "On that day, G-d will be One and His Name will be One."[52]

Who is like your people Israel, 1 nation in the land?

NOTES

1. *Maharal, Derech HaChaim* 5:17. See *Maharal, Gevuros Hashem* 54, for how the number 1 is used in the context of comparing it to subsequent numbers 2, 3, 4, etc.
2. See *Rambam, Hilchos Yesodei HaTorah* 1:7.
3. *Devarim* 6:4. The danger that any compromise of the Unity of G-d poses is evident from the distinction in the slight variance of the respective last letters of the words אֶחָד, 1, and אַחֵר, other.
4. *Maharal, Gevuros Hashem* 29.
5. *Bereishis* 1:1.
6. *Pirkei DeRebbi Eliezer* 42; *Eruvin* 41a. See *Maharal, Tiferes Yisrael* 33; *Netzach Yisrael* 43. Every action originates from the head, seat of the human intellect, which signals everything that will ensue.
7. See *Shulchan Aruch, Orach Chaim* 583:2 and *Mishnah Berurah* 9.
8. *Devarim* 24:5. There are special laws governing the first year of a marriage, for it forms the bedrock and foundation for the relationship.
9. "The first [to make his point] in a quarrel is held to be right" (*Mishlei* 18:17). The judge may listen only where both litigants are present or he faces compromising his impartiality (*Sanhedrin* 7b; *Shulchan Aruch, Choshen Mishpat* 17:5, 8).
10. See "2: Opposite and Equal."
11. See *Havdalah* blessing "... Who separates between holy and mundane ...."
12. *Maharal: Netzach Yisrael* 3; *Gevuros Hashem* 38; *Derech HaChaim* 6:10.
13. The relationship with G-d is equated with essence and is always at the fore. In comparison, everything else is, at best, of secondary significance (see R' Samson Raphael Hirsch, *Bereishis* 4:4).
14. *Menachos* 61a
15. *Shemos* 23:19, 34:26; *Devarim* 26: 1-11. See *Mishnah, Bikkurim.*
16. *Bamidbar* 18:11; *Devarim* 18:4. See *Mishnah, Terumos.*
17. *Bamidbar* 15:17-21.
18. *Devarim* 18:4; see *Chullin* 135a.
19. *Devarim* 21:17.
20. *Bereishis* 25:31-34. Reuven, the firstborn child of Yaakov, did not live up to the exalted role of the firstborn; due to his impulsiveness, he forfeited his firstborn rights (*Bereishis* 49:3-4; *Rashi* ad loc.).

21. *Zevachim* 112b. See also *Rashi, Shemos* 24:5; *Sforno, Shemos* 13:2.
22. In lieu of the firstborn, a *Kohen* is elevated and accorded the first rights. So, for example, the *Kohen* is the first person called up to the Torah reading and the first one invited to lead the blessings at a meal (*Nedarim* 62a-b, based *on Vayikra* 21:8).
23. *Shemos* 13:2, 12-13 and *Bamidbar* 18:15-16.
24. *Shemos* 13:2.
25. *Devarim* 15:19.
26. Nowadays a *bechor* is consecrated as well. The proper thing to do is to have a non-Jew become a partner, even only if for a minimal share, before the animal is born; this renders the animal unsanctified (*Bechoros* 13a; *Shulchan Aruch, Yoreh Deah* 320:6).
27. *Shemos* 13:13. This redemption applies nowadays as well. See *Shulchan Aruch, Yoreh Deah* 321:1.
28. Ibid. 4:22. See also *Rabbeinu Bachya, Shemos* 34:19.
29. *Maharal, Gur Aryeh, Bereishis* 1 and R' Yitzchak Hutner, *Pachad Yitzchak, Pesach* 74.
30. *Maharal, Gevuros Hashem* 29. Whereas Israel was the nation related to the concept of *reishis*, first, with its association to Torah and to the purpose of existence, their foremost antagonist was Amalek. This brazen nation audaciously attacked the Jewish nation in the aftermath of the miraculous Exodus. Ideologically, Amalek challenged G-d as the First Cause and, by extension, Israel, the "firstborn of G-d" (see *Shemos* 17:8-16 and *Devarim* 25:17-19). But Amalek's efforts to present themselves as an alternative *reishis*, first, will ultimately be for naught: "Amalek was the first of the nations; but his end shall come to destruction" (*Bamidbar* 24:20). The Glory of G-d and His Heavenly Throne will be complete with the eradication of Amalek. See "26: In the Name of G-d."
31. *Bamidbar Rabbah* 17:1.
32. *Shemos* 12:29.
33. See *Malbim, Shemos* 11:5.
34. Pharaoh arrogantly deified himself (*Mechilta, Shemos* 13) and audaciously declared, "Mine is the River and I have made myself" (*Yechzekel* 29:3, *Malbim* ad loc.).
35. The first *mitzvah* given by G-d to the Jewish people was *Kiddush HaChodesh*, the sanctification of the months, starting with Nissan, the first month (*Shemos* 12:1-2 and *Maharal, Gevuros Hashem* 37).
36. The word בְּהִבָּרְאָם, *when they were created* (*Bereishis* 2:4), rearranges to read בְּאַבְרָהָם, *[created] for the sake of Avraham* (*Bereishis Rabbah* 12:4). Additionally, Avraham was the focal point of the world (*Bereishis Rabbah* 42:11), which was why he was the target of the 4 Kings. See "4: In Place."
37. *Yeshayah* 51:2. See *Maharal, Derech Hashem* 6:10 and *Gevuros Hashem* 36. Before the Dispersion, world civilization was 1 nation and 1 language (*Bereishis* 11:6). Whereas the Generation of the Dispersion lost their unity and their ability to speak of the glory of G-d, only Avraham survived intact. Avraham alone had the ability to replicate the oneness and unified communication (*Maharal, Chidushei Aggados, Nedarim* p. 10).
38. His name Ivri from *eiver,* the other side, depicts Avraham as on the "other side," one lone individual in contradistinction to the rest of human civilization.
39. *Pesachim* 118a.
40. *Berachos* 7b.
41. One should preferably have at least two people designated for the *korban pesach.* However, if it was slaughtered even for 1 individual it is still kosher (*Pesachim* 91a, *Rambam, Hilchos Korban Pesach* 2:2). But as there must be no leftovers, the person must then be able to eat all the meat by himself. Moreover, 1 single *korban pesach,* if it was offered on behalf of the Jewish nation in its entirety, though it should not be done, is still kosher according to some opinions (*Kiddushin* 41b-42a, *Rambam* ibid 2:2-4).
42. This is unlike cooking, which breaks it down into several components.
43. *Maharal, Gevuros Hashem* 36. The Jewish people were to specifically slaughter the lamb, an Egyptian god, which corresponds to Aries, the zodiac sign of the first month, Nissan (*Zohar, Pinchas*).

44. *Rashi, Bamidbar* 16:6. See ibid. 15:29, where Torah is referred to by the number 1 (i.e., תּוֹרָה אַחַת, *a single teaching*).
45. *Chagigah* 3b.
46. *Bamidbar* 23:9.
47. Whereas the 70 oxen of Succos parallel the 70 non-Jewish nations, the single ox of Shemini Atzeres relates to the uniqueness of Israel. See *Bamidbar* 29:13-36 and "70: The Sum of the Parts."
48. It is through Torah that the Jewish people are 1 (*Maharal, Netzach Yisrael* 10). See *Maharal, Nesiv HaTorah* 1 which explains how Torah, that organizes and unites, is also 1.
49. *Maharal, Gevuros Hashem* 69.
50. See *Shemos* 19:2 and *Rashi* ad loc.
51. *Shabbos Minchah,* based on *I Divrei HaYamim* 17:21 and *II Shmuel* 7:23.
52. *Zechariah* 14:9.

2
OPPOSITE
AND EQUAL

2 introduces blessing and abundance
into a world in which opposites
must relate to and complement each other.

It also opens up the possibility of conflict
and, even more dangerously,
a movement away from the unity
of G-d and His Will.

Ideally, 2 should become the symmetrical
mirror image of 1, so 2 entities become consistent
and loyal reflections of each other.

THE NUMBER 2 IS THE INTRODUCTION TO THE WORLD OF *MANY*.
The plural starts with 2.[1] Whenever the Torah speaks in the plural without specifying a number, it is understood to refer to the lowest possible plural number: 2.[2] One cannot begin to count with fewer than 2 objects. That 2 is the first number to represent "many" is hinted at in the Hebrew word for 2, שְׁנַיִם. Of all the single-digit numbers, 2 is the only one that carries the suffix ים, which is otherwise used to denote larger numbers, such as multiple units of 10 (e.g., עֶשְׂרִים, 20, שְׁלֹשִׁים, 30).[3]

The presence of 2 parties opens up the possibility of a "relationship" — one in which the first subject interacts with the second. This, of course, could begin only with the creation of the universe. Before then, there was only the Unity of G-d. After Creation, the prototype and ultimate relationship possible is that between G-d and His creations.

The prototype and ultimate relationship possible is that between G-d and His creations.

2: G-Ò AND HIS CREATIONS

We have noted that 1 symbolizes G-d, the One Creator.[4] In comparison, the number 2 can be said to represent His multifaceted creations.

G-d gave Creation its existence. He then invited the crown of Creation — mankind — to enter into a relationship with Him. Both the act of creation and this proposition reflect the altruistic act of *chesed*, kindness, on G-d's part.[5] This was exclusively enacted for the benefit of man; it is not for G-d's benefit. This is because *the ultimate goodness is the relationship that each individual human being forges with G-d* — one that is developed continuously throughout a lifetime of Torah learning and *mitzvah* observance.[6]

The ultimate goodness is the relationship that each human being forges with G-d.

2: THE BLESSING OF CREATION

While the Creator is 1, His creations are many.[7] The concept of בְּרָכָה, *blessing*, is founded upon the number 2, whose characteristic is the start of growth, increase, proliferation, and abundance. The out-pouring of G-d's bounty within existence is indeed a blessing.[8] Hence the Torah narrative recounts the Creation events by opening with בּ, the 2nd letter of the Hebrew alphabet (בְּרֵאשִׁית).[9]

The essential relationship between G-d and His creations is that of the master *Mashpia*, Giver, Who showers blessing upon every one of His creations, each of which is a *mekabel*, recipient.[10] G-d is self-contained and perfect; His creatures are neither. It is for this reason that they must engage in give-and-take interactions with others.[11] Perfection cannot come from within them, only from without. This key principle lies at the center of the man-woman relationship.

The essential relationship between G-d and His creations is that of the master Giver, Who showers blessing upon His creations.

2: MALE AND FEMALE

The existence of 2 primary forces permeates the universe: "Everything G-d created in His universe, male and female He created them."[12] Though it is not exclusive to human relationships, the optimal pairing of male and female is found within the marriage of husband and wife.

Man himself is a microcosm of the universe.[13] But the human being was fashioned as 2 interrelating parts: "male and female He created them."[14] Separately, each party is incomplete: "It is not good that man be alone; let Me [G-d] make him a helper opposite him."[15] Together, husband and wife complement each other in a union of blessing; a man without a wife, for example, is said to live without blessing.[16] Furthermore, their marital union can lead man and woman to become partners with G-d in the creation of new life. Indeed, the first *mitzvah* mentioned in the Torah is the obligation for man to pro-create. This is itself the epitome of blessing and relates, again, to 2 as the opening number of abundance.[17]

Husband and wife complement each other in a union of blessing.

OPPOSITES: THIS VERSUS THAT

THE NUMBER 2 CAN REFER TO THE PAIRS OF OPPOSITES WITHIN Creation. The very existence of opposites can become a source of conflict caused by their antithetical characteristics.

2: COUNTERPARTS

Some well-known counterparts within Creation include life and death, truth and falsehood, left and right, up and down.

There are many opposing forces within the universe. The verse states, "G-d has made the one as well as the other."[18] There is the universal principle that "everything G-d created, He created something else corresponding to it."[19] Some of the well-known counterparts within Creation include life and death, truth and falsehood, left and right, up and down.

In the laws of physics, forces occur in pairs that are opposite in direction and equal in magnitude. There are the positive and negative polarities of electrical charges and the opposite poles of north and south in magnetic fields. In the spiritual realm, there are counterparts in areas such as ritual purity and ritual impurity, what is forbidden and what is permitted, objects that are sacred and objects that are mundane.

DAY 2: DIVISION

The existence of opposites often results in a clash between 2 counterparts standing on contrary sides. This leads to division and to a breakdown in the relationship — with the number 2 reflecting the conflict.[20]

The first example of such division was Day 2 of Creation, when G-d divided the waters in the formation of the Heavens above and the oceans below.[21] The phrase "it was good," used to describe G-d's assessment of the other days of creation,[22] is glaringly absent on Day 2,[23] when conflict and division first appeared.

Disputes in human relationships can be readily traced back to the schism of 2.

Disputes in human relationships can be readily traced back to the schism of 2. The first historic quarrel between Adam's 2 sons, Kayin and Hevel, tragically led to murder.[24] The conflict between Yaakov's sons, the catalyst to the Egyptian exile, was attributed to their jealousy of Yosef's special coat, which weighed 2 *sela*.[25] On the 2nd day after Moshe left Pharaoh's palace in Egypt to observe the fate of his persecuted brethren, he intervened upon witnessing 2 Jews fighting.[26] And the first unresolved rabbinic dispute in the transmission of *Mesorah*, Oral Tradition, was between the *zugos*, pairs, of leading scholars in the Court.[27]

2: CONFLICT OF INTEREST

Of all conflicts, the most serious is that which assaults the ultimate relationship in the universe: the relationship between man and his Creator.

Man is supposed to align his personal will with the Will of G-d — so that they are one and the same.[28] This is the dynamic of *mitzvah* observance, where man becomes G-d's "partner."[29] Sin ruins this relationship. The sinner ideologically moves away from the Oneness of G-d. His behavior makes it appear that there are actually 2 separate and independent entities that come to assert their respective wills: first, the Will of G-d and second, the will of man.

Sin itself leads to a major conflict of interest. This dichotomy was first played out in the primordial sin. Adam and Chavah defied G-d's command in favor of their own desire to eat from the Tree of Knowledge of Good and Evil.[30]

Furthermore, *sin implies a departure from what came before.* In the ideological shift from 1 to 2, sin deviates from G-d's plan by introducing something seemingly new or foreign. This unwelcome change is reflected in the word שְׁנַיִם, 2, related to the words שְׁנִיּוֹת, *alternatives* or *secondary*; or שִׁנּוּי, *change.*[31] Here man deviates from the path of halachah (literally, *walking* — in the pathway defined by G-d), by opting to undertake an alternative option.

Sin implies a departure from what came before.

2: BATTLE OF THE INCLINATIONS

Man's life decisions are formed by the pair of conflicting forces waging a moral battle inside him. Man is able to exercise his independence via the use of *bechirah*, free choice. Typically, he must select from a minimum of 2 alternatives: right and wrong, good and evil.

The spiritual component within man, his soul, is pulled toward the יֵצֶר טוֹב, Good Inclination, urging him to choose *tov*, good. Its goal is to purify the body by elevating it toward G-dliness and the World to Come. At the same time, the physical part of man, his body, is influenced by the יֵצֶר הָרַע, Evil Inclination, which is drawn after *ra*, evil. Its pursuit of worldly pleasures means the rejection of anything spiritual or G-dly. Each presents itself as an equally viable and compelling choice — "this" versus "that."[32] And it is up to the individual to make the right choice: "See, I [G-d] have placed before you on this day, life and good, and death and evil …. Choose life."[33]

The spiritual component is pulled toward the יֵצֶר טוֹב.

Every individual must imagine that the merits and demerits of the world are very finely balanced. This precarious state of equilibrium is waiting for something to tip the scales in one direction. One good deed or one evil deed can determine the world's fate.[34] The actions of man are the forces that can build or destroy the world.[35]

One good deed or one evil deed can determine the world's fate.

What a person becomes is essentially shaped by his choices. Like the divergence of the 2 identical goats on Yom Kippur (one sacrificed to G-d, the other thrown from a cliff to Azazel),[36] man's choices in life define which 1 of 2 pathways his life follows: a righteous life leading to sublime paradise of delighting with G-d in *Gan Eden*, Garden of Eden, or a sinful life that distances man from G-d and that ultimately necessitates the painful purification experience of *Gehinnom*, Purgatory.[37]

MIRROR IMAGE

W E HAVE SEEN THAT THE INTRODUCTION OF PLURALITY INTO Creation — through the number 2 — enables parties to enter into a relationship. Furthermore, the duality of 2 often leads to a schism where there is separation and conflict. There is, however, a way to repair the relationship between 2 and 1. This calls for the 2 parties (or opposites) to become the mirror image of each other.

2: MATCHING PAIRS

The spectacular symmetries within the natural world can be seen in plant leaves, the wings of a butterfly, the structure of crystals, and the formation of snowflakes.[38] Perhaps the most intricate projection of symmetry is the anatomical design of the human being. The numerous pairs of limbs and organs in the body include the eyes, eyebrows, nostrils, ears, cheeks, lips, shoulders, arms, hands, legs, ankles, and feet. Here the corresponding pairs within Creation need not be considered contradictory; the opposites become the amazing reflection of the other.

The symmetries in nature are symbolic of the spiritual symmetries within existence.

The symmetries in nature are symbolic of the spiritual symmetries within existence. Some examples of the symmetries of interrelated pairs include the following:

- Partners in Creation: G-d and His creations, when they follow His instruction[39]
- Worlds: the spiritual and physical worlds[40]
- Realms: Heaven and Earth[41]
- Jerusalem: the supernal and earthly Jerusalem[42]
- The human being: the inner soul and the outer body[43]
- Inclinations: the *Yetzer Tov* and the *Yetzer Hara*[44]
- Realization: potential and actual
- Mankind: man and woman
- Torah: the *Torah She'Bichsav*, the Written Law, and *Torah She'Be'al Peh*, the Oral Law[45]
- Tablets of Stone: *Shnei Luchos HaBris*, Two Tablets of the Covenant[46]
- Commandments: positive and prohibitive commandments[47]
- Tefillin: head-tefillin and hand-tefillin

2: REPETITION AND CONSISTENCY

When man bends his personal will to mirror the Will of G-d, he demonstrates his fierce loyalty. *Here his 2, so to speak, perfectly reflects G-d's 1.* Just as an angel, as the representative of G-d, is exclusively defined in terms of its singular mission — "1 angel cannot perform 2 missions, nor do 2 angels perform 1 mission"[48] — the Jew is consistent in his timeless commitment to G-d through his continuous adherence to Torah values.[49]

The Jew is consistent in his timeless commitment to G-d through his continuous adherence to Torah values.

This means the Jew faithfully follows through. He duplicates the word of G-d. Here the word שְׁנַיִם, 2, is no longer related to שִׁינוּי, change, but is affiliated to the verb לִשְׁנוֹת, to repeat something.[50] This is thematically related to the repetitive cycle of a שָׁנָה, year, that repeatedly follows an annually set course. So, too, is the conduct of a Jew the physical replication of that which G-d demands.

2: DOUBLING UP

But there is a deeper dimension that goes beyond mere repetition. It is not just that a Jew comes to reflect the Will of G-d by pledging his allegiance. *By emulating G-d, man transforms himself into a G-dly being.*

He aligns himself to the extent that a human creation can actually be said to "double up" to the Divine Creator. This does not mean, of course, that man resembles G-d in every respect — he cannot and will not. Still, it does mean that the relationship between Israel and G-d is intertwined to the degree that there is a mirror-image reflection.

Some partnerships see the respective parties individually undertake different activities. They complement each other by being united in a common cause — even though they are not necessarily doing the same thing. Other partnerships are organized such that each is undertaking the very same activity as his partner. The "doubling up" here is in the sense that "double" refers *to the same object twice*.[51]

This concept applies to the twinning of G-d and Israel in the unbreakable בְּרִית, covenant, where the 2 parties become 1.[52] Theirs is a partnership belonging to the second category: Israel partners G-d in the identical endeavor of moving Creation toward realizing its ultimate purpose.[53] It is not just a complementary role; it is double role such that G-d credits their contribution in Creation as being on par with His! In this respect, Israel is allegorically termed a "twin" of G-d.[54]

The state of the covenantal relationship between G-d and Israel was symbolized by the interaction of the two *keruvim*, cherubs, upon the *Aron*, Ark, which were molded from a single piece of gold. When the cherubs were facing each other, the Jewish People knew that the relationship was favorable. When the cherubs miraculously turned away from each other, it signified a fractured association.[55]

The mission of Israel in Creation is the mirror image of the mission that G-d wants in Creation. They are not two different things; one is the double of the other. The objective within the heart of Israel is exactly what G-d desires.[56] This mirror image must filter through in other areas — for example, man's inner potential must be duplicated in his outer actual,[57] the spiritual finding expression in the physical, his work in This World must earn him eternal worlds in the future.[58]

A DOUBLE ACT

This, then, is the implicit challenge within the number 2 of achieving a double act.

In a multiple world that lends itself to conflict and friction, a Jew must actively pursue the partnership between opposites. He must make sure that 2 conceptually mirrors 1. He looks for the symmetries within existence to align this with that. So the program for Creation unfolding with the number 2 tells the story of interrelating and matching pairs.

In every set of forces, the optimal relationship is not one that is conflicted or antagonistic. Rather than pursue the dangerous path associated with change or divergence, he opts for the principles of consistency, loyalty, and repetition. Throughout life, the Jew follows through on his commitment to G-d. And he exercises his free will so that diametric opposites coalesce to become a mirror reflection of each other.

The Jew follows through on his commitment to G-d.

NOTES

1. See *Maharal, Gevuros Hashem* 8, who explains how the number 2 is the prototype of plurality.
2. *Niddah* 38b and *Rashi* ad loc.
3. *Maharal, Derech Chaim* 3:3. Indeed, there is no oneness within the number 2.
4. See "1: The One and Only."
5. "The world is built upon [Your] *chesed*, kindness" (*Tehillim* 89:3). "*Chesed* declared 'Let the world be created!'" (*Bereishis Rabbah* 8:5). The Torah, the blueprint of creation, begins and ends with kindness (*Sotah* 14a).
6. The goal is for man to cleave to G-d by elevating himself and all of existence with him to reach a state of perfection (*Ramchal, Mesillas Yesharim* 1).
7. *Maharal, Tiferes Yisrael* 34.
8. *Maharal, Netzach Yisrael* 45. The word *berachah*, blessing, is innately related to the number 2, as in the 2nd letter of the Hebrew alphabet (ב) with which Creation starts. Here the universe was expanding continuously, like 2 unravelling balls of warp thread, until G-d halted it (*Chagigah* 12a). Conversely, 1 symbolizes confinement or restrictions — the antithesis of expansiveness, prosperity, and fruitfulness.
9. See *Maharal, Tiferes Yisrael* 34, who responds to the *Ibn Ezra's* question of why the letter ב should refer to blessing.
10. *Ramchal, Derech Hashem* 2:2.
11. See *Shemos Rabbah* 31:15 as to how all the world's creations "borrow from" and "lend to" one another; for example, day and night.
12. *Bava Basra* 74b; *Pesachim* 56a.
13. See R' Chaim Volozhin, *Nefesh HaChaim* 1:4. See also "613: At Your Command."
14. *Bereishis* 1:27.
15. Ibid. 2:18.
16. *Yevamos* 62b.
17. The relationship with the number 2 can be seen in the integration of the genders through the *mitzvah* of *pirya v'rivya*, procreation, which is fulfilled once the couple bear both male and female children (1 boy and 1 girl) — namely, a minimum of 2 children (*Yevamos* 61b, *Rambam, Hilchos Ishus* 15:4).
18. *Koheles* 7:14.
19. *Chagigah* 15a.
20. See *Maharal, Netzech Yisrael* 45, who explains that 2 is the most powerful example of plurality as there can be never be a unity between two opposites, which, like two parallel lines, never converge.

Reconciliation is possible only with the introduction of a 3rd element. See "3: Three-Dimensional."

21. *Bereishis* 1:6.
22. The phrase "it was good" is found with regard to the other days of Creation (*Bereishis* 1:4, 1:10, 1:25).
23. *Bereishis Rabbah* 4:6. Though there was a division between light and darkness on the first day, darkness can be considered just an absence of light (not an opposite, such as the dry atmosphere separating waters on the second day), which in essence was existing even before creation. Moreover, light is considered an absolute good, in comparison with darkness and emptiness, which existed beforehand; see *Sfas Emes, Miketz* 634; *Pri Tzaddik Korach* 5.
24. *Bereishis* 4:1-8. See *Tanchuma, Bereishis* 9, as to how Kayin and Hevel respectively divided the world into 2 parts: Kayin claimed all real estate and fixed property while Hevel chose all movable goods. This led to their disputation — each claiming the other was infringing upon his territory.
25. *Shabbos* 10b.
26. *Shemos* 2:13.
27. In the transmission of the *Mesorah*, Oral Tradition, it passed from mouth to mouth until the Men of the Great Assembly. Thereafter, it was transmitted through *zugos*, pairs, who were the leaders of the Sanhedrin (Supreme Court of 71 judges) in the capacity of *Nasi* and *Av Beis Din*, which is the point at which it broke down, laying the foundation for disputations (see *Chagigah* 16a and *Tosafos* ad loc.). In contrast, a legal dispute between 2 parties, for example, is dealt with in a local *beis din*, courthouse, consisting of only three judges, that sat twice each week starting with Monday, the 2nd day of the week (*Mishnah Kesubos* 1:1; *Mishnah Sanhedrin* 1:1).
28. *Pirkei Avos* 2:4.
29. See "613: At Your Command."
30. *Bereishis* 3:1-24.
31. *Maharal, Gevuros Hashem* 9.
32. *Ramchal, Derech Hashem* 1:3:1-1:3:2. Nevertheless, the Sages teach us that the greater the person, the stronger the *Yetzer Hara*'s opposition to counteract him (*Succah* 52a).
33. *Devarim* 30:15, 19. See *Rambam, Hilchos Teshuvah* 5:3.
34. *Kiddushin* 40b. See *Rambam, Hilchos Teshuvah* 3:4.
35. Adam was urged by G-d, "Contemplate that you not ruin and destroy My world" (*Koheles Rabbah* 7:28).
36. *Vayikra* 16:5-10. Yitzchak's twin sons parallel the two identical goats taken on Yom Kippur. Originally placed side by side and identical in every respect, the eventual fate of Yaakov and Eisav, like that of the goats, could not have been more different. One goat was to attain the apex of holiness, being slaughtered as an offering *l'HASHEM*, to G-d; the other was dispatched to the rocky wilderness, *l'Azazel*, and thrown from a cliff to its death.
37. The creation of *Gehinnom* on Day 2 (*Pesachim* 54a) ties in with 2's association with sin and divergence from G-d, and with retribution meted out to those whose actions deviate from the dictates of the One G-d.
38. The eye revels in the aesthetic beauty of symmetry. Even in the arts, symmetry creates a highly visual impression, as is evident in architecture, pottery, sculpture.
39. G-d created man "in the image of G-d" — to emulate His attributes. On his part, man has to "go in all His ways" (*Devarim* 10:12). Just as He is Merciful, so should [man] also be merciful; just as He is Compassionate, so should [man] also be compassionate" (*Sofrim* 3:17; *Sifri, Eikev* 49). Conversely, "Whoever has mercy on [G-d's] creatures, Heaven will be merciful to him" (*Shabbos* 151b).
40. The Sovereignty in the Heavenly realm is reflected in the sovereignty of the earthly realm (*Berachos* 58a).
41. Heaven and Earth are interdependent. It is impossible to have Heaven without Earth or vice versa (*Rabbeinu Bachya, Vayikra* 1:1).
42. *Bava Basra* 75b, *Taanis* 5a. See also *Tanchuma, Mishpatim* 18. See *Mechilta*, cited by *Rashi, Shemos*

15:17, who explains how the Heavenly Throne of Glory is directly above the Temple on Earth.

43. The inside of a Torah scholar must match his outside (*Yoma* 72b).

44. The inner forces of the *Yetzer Tov* and *Yetzer Hara* are in sync in serving G-d (*Berachos* 54a).

45. *Gittin* 60b. Israel's commitment at Sinai was affirmed by their 2-word formula: "*naaseh v'nishma*," we will do and we will observe (*Shemos* 24:7), for which each individual was awarded 2 crowns (*Shabbos* 88a).

46. The 10 Commandments on 2 stones were divided into מִצְוֹת בֵּין אָדָם לַחֲבֵירוֹ, *the interpersonal precepts* on the left Tablet, and מִצְוֹת בֵּין אָדָם לַמָּקוֹם, *the man-to-G-d laws* on the right Tablet.

47. The 248 *mitzvos asei*, Positive Commandments, actively build a relationship with G-d by one observing G-d's Will. The 365 *mitzvos lo saaseh*, Prohibitive Commandments, are safeguards to preserve this relationship. See "248: In Action" and "365: For Your Protection."

48. *Bereishis Rabbah* 50:2; see *Rashi, Bereishis* 18:2.

49. See *Ein Yaakov*, Introduction, quoting a Midrash stating that the most encompassing principle of the Torah is the verse, "You shall bring one lamb in the morning and one lamb in the evening" (*Bamidbar* 28:4) — as a reference to the consistent routine of *mitzvah* observance.

50. The word "Mishnah" is related to the word *sheini*, second, because it embodies the Oral Torah, which was the 2nd Torah revealed to Moshe (the first being the Written Torah).

51. This is illustrated in contractual conditions, which should be identical to the *tenai kaful*, double stipulation, in the vow of the Tribes of Gad and Reuven when they pledged to fight alongside the other Tribes before being granted their share in the Trans-Jordan (*Bamidbar* 32:20-23) (*Kiddushin* 61a).

52. In ancient times, entering into a covenant necessitated that the parties deposit an indispensable part of themselves into the hands of their beloved (*Vilna Gaon, Sefer Yetzirah*).

53. The existence of man is itself based on a covenant with G-d. The *Targum* translates *bris*, covenant, as *k'yam*, existence (see e.g., *Targum, Bereishis* 9:16).

54. "Do not read G-d calls Israel, 'My dove My perfect one (תַמָּתִי)' (*Shir HaShirim* 5:2) but rather 'My twin' (תְאוֹמָתִי)." Here G-d, so to speak, equates His contribution to theirs (*Shir HaShirim Rabbah* 5:2, quoted by *Ramchal, Daas Tevunos* 158). See the similar statement "Do not read '*ami atah*' (you are My people), but '*imi atah*' (you [Israel] are together in partnership with Me) (*Zohar* Introduction 5a; R' Chaim Volozhin, *Nefesh HaChaim* 2:10). In fact, the righteous are destined in the future to be called by the Name of G-d (*Bava Basra* 75b).

55. *Yoma* 54a. See also *Zohar, Terumah* 152b and *Achrei Mos* 59b; R' Chaim Volozhin, *Nefesh HaChaim* 1, 8.

56. One elegant example of doubling up that becomes one is found in the laws of *arba minim*, 4 Species. The middle top leaf of the *lulav* is called the *teyomes*. This is related to the word *te'umim*, twins (*Rashi, Succah* 32a), as the *teyomes* is comprised of a double-leaf that must be joined. Should it be split, this would render the *lulav* invalid (*Shulchan Aruch, Orach Chaim* 645:3).

57. That which was "first in thought" finds expression in the "end in action" (*Lechah Dodi*).

58. The earthly remains of the Jewish ancestors were interred in *Mearas HaMachpeilah*, the Double Cave. The simple meaning of this name is a reference to the married couples buried within or to the double chambers of the tomb (*Eruvin* 53a, quoted by *Rashi, Bereishis* 23:9). Symbolically, this marks how *their spiritual lives lived out on Earth would create and define their eternal lives in the hereafter*. Their eternal achievements were earned in their lives here. The holiness of Heaven was mirrored in their sanctification here on Earth. Moreover, this mirror image was reflected in the Jewish ancestors, who exemplified the ideal relationship between a husband and wife — as one single, shared identity that was lived out through both of their respective bodies. The woman's role is as the *ezer kenegdo*, a helper opposite him (*Bereishis* 2:18). She protects her husband from harm and prevents him from sinning. In the well-known words of the Talmud, "If he is deserving, then she will be his *ezer*, helper; but if not, she will be his *kenegdo*, opponent (*Yevamos* 63a). Originally, Adam and Chavah were created as part of the same entity. Through marriage, spouses lives their partner's life as an actual

extension of their own life. This is the principle *ishto k'gufo*, his wife is like himself (*Berachos* 24a). Their relationship is not simply a partnership but one in which the parties retain their separate, independent identities, yet with the same aims and goals of holiness.

3

THREE DIMENSIONAL

3 denotes a state of equilibrium,
the midway point between 1 and 2
that brings harmony between opposites.

As illustrated by the founding fathers
of the Jewish People, 3 forms the essential
pillars in building a new reality.

The sequence of 3 sets up a chain of continuity —
one destined to endure for all eternity.

THE BASIS OF JEWISH LIFE

IN TERMS OF ITS SUM AND POSITION, 3 CREATES A SOLID, FIRM BASIS. It establishes the necessary foundations and, by doing so, rightfully lies at the center of Jewish living.

3: The process

Every process can be divided into 3 stages. There is the beginning point, which articulates the objective at the very outset. This clearly defines the direction in which one is heading. Next, there is the middle or interim phase, when man sets out into motion using all the tools at his disposal to actively pursue his goal. Lastly, there is the final phase, when man reaches his destination. Here he celebrates having attained his goal by arriving at the end.[1]

This World is subject to the characteristics of space and time that can be broken down into 3 components.

This 3-fold process operates within the confines of the physical universe. This World is subject to the characteristics of space and time that can themselves be broken down into 3 components. In terms of space, the human eye views the world through the 3 spatial dimensions of length, width, and height. And the framework of time can similarly be divided into 3 tenses: the past, the present, and the future.[2]

3: STATE OF EQUILIBRIUM

We have noted the very different qualities between the first two numbers, 1 and 2. While the number 1 is symbolic of the One and Only G-d, the number 2 represents the duality of Creation, as either a force of division or of symmetry.[3]

The third number is perfectly poised to address the contradictory natures of its two predecessors.

Along comes the number 3. Its positioning as the third number means it is perfectly poised to address the contradictory natures of its two predecessors. Typically, 3 is not associated with extremities but with the midway position or golden mean position.[4] This is the reason that the nature of 3 is capable of successfully harmonizing contradictory parts. The interrelationship of 2 opposites can combine to create a new 3rd reality. This course of action integrates opposites, but at the same time, does not require them to lose their respective identities in the process.[5]

Consider the following examples that illustrate this phenomenon.

- When facing 2 seemingly conflicting statements, the 3rd statement is expertly positioned to provide clarification or to offer a peaceful resolution. In the words of the famous rule of biblical exegesis, "Where there are 2 [conflicting passages], let the 3rd [passage] comes to reconcile them."[6]

- A stool with 2 legs at opposite sides cannot stand. But place a 3rd leg equidistant to the two extremities (forming a triangle) and now you have solidity in a sturdy piece of furniture. The third leg has brought stability.

- In a dispute between 2 feuding parties, the appointment of a 3rd party acting as an independent, unbiased arbitrator can result in a resolution in a binding decision.[7]

Due to its standing as the exemplary symbol of peace, of balance, and of equilibrium,[8] 3 contains many of the qualities to be classified as the ideal number.[9] It stamps certainty onto a world of uncertainty. It introduces stability into a world of instability. And it attains peace by unifying matters in a world of conflicts.[10] As famously put, the thesis of 1, the antithesis of 2, integrate in the synthesis of 3.

The thesis of 1, the antithesis of 2, integrate in the synthesis of 3.

This synthesis is exemplified in mankind. Man performs a balancing act to fuse his spiritual and physical natures, his soul and his body. His task is not to push these opposites further apart. His goal is as peacemaker to facilitate their coexistence. He fulfills the purpose of Creation when he successfully integrates his physical and spiritual components into a new, higher reality.

The fusion of 1 and 2 through the number 3 finds important expression in the model of a family. The opposite natures of man and woman join together as "one flesh," combining in the conception of new life in the birth of a child.[11] They retain their differing personalities whilst creating a new, integrated 3rd reality that is conceived through their combined contribution.[12]

The opposite natures of man and woman join to create a 3rd reality conceived through their combined contribution.

FOUNDATIONS

THE FOUNDATIONS OR BUILDING BLOCKS NECESSARY IN CREATION ARE conceptually identified with the number 3.[13] The most powerful example of this is the origin of the Jewish People. They were founded by their 3 forefathers. By extension, this phenomenon is reflected within some of the most essential foundations of Jewish living — Jewish belief, the festivals, Torah, and *mitzvos* — that are similarly established based upon the number 3.

3 AVOS: FOUNDING FATHERS

The founding *Avos*, forefathers, of the Jewish People were Avraham, Yitzchak, and Yaakov. Particular stress is placed on their number: "Only 3 were called *Avos*."[14]

Not merely genealogical ancestors, the 3 Patriarchs established the principles for Jewish living and implanted them into the psyche of their descendants. Indeed, the word *Avos* is more widely used to connote an essential set of fundamentals or principles.[15] In fact, the Jewish forefathers respectively parallel the 3 central pillars upon which the world stands: *gemilus chassadim*, acts of kindness (Avraham); *avodah*, Divine service (Yitzchak); and Torah (Yaakov).[16] So too, each one of the *Avos* emphasized an essential quality of the Divine: *chesed*, loving-kindness; *gevurah*, justice; and *tiferes*, beauty.

The forefathers parallel the 3 central pillars upon which the world stands.

But the process of setting up the rock-solid foundations of the Chosen Nation also required excluding all their unworthy offshoots (Avraham's son Yishmael, Yitzchak's son Eisav). The building of Israel was rightly attributed to the combined forces of all 3 forefathers. Together, their qualities provided the timeless template of what it would mean to be a Jew.[17] Only after the 3rd generation were all of Yaakov's sons worthy of becoming the Children of Israel.[18] His spiritual vantage point as the 3rd of the *Avos* meant Yaakov was "the choicest."[19] Through him, 3 being the final stage of a process, all 3 essential parts converged into 1 cohesive unit.[20]

The forces of all 3 forefathers provide the template of what it means to be a Jew.

3: JEWISH BELIEF

The theological foundation of Judaism can be organized into 3 central tenets. The first is (a) מְצִיאוּת ה׳, existence of G-d, as the Singular, Eternal Creator. The second is (b) תּוֹרָה מִן הַשָּׁמַיִם, Divinity of Torah, as the immutable laws transmitted to the Jewish People through Moshe, the greatest of the prophets. The third is (c)שָׂכָר וָעוֹנֶשׁ, reward and punishment, where every individual is accountable for his conduct and its far-reaching consequences.[21]

The theological foundation of Judaism can be organized into 3 central tenets.

These exactly parallel the 3 stages of a process. The first and essential beginning point is belief in the existence of G-d. Everything originates from the Creator and Master of the Universe.[22] A Jew prays only to G-d and knows that no other force in Creation has any independent power. The second, middle, phase deals with how man goes about developing a relationship with G-d. This revolves around Torah as the Divine set of instructions given by G-d to man at Sinai. Study and observing its laws are the guaranteed means for getting the maximum out of life. Finally, the third stage is the concept of reward and punishment that awaits man upon reaching his final destination. The eternal World to Come is formed by how he has lived his life in This World.[23]

The eternal World to Come is formed by how one has lived in This World.

3: FESTIVALS

The שָׁלֹשׁ רְגָלִים, 3 Pilgrimage Festivals, within the Jewish calendar were occasions when a Jew was obligated to ascend to Jerusalem to bring at least 3 offerings in the Temple.[24] פֶּסַח, Passover, commemorates the Exodus from Egypt when the Jewish nation was liberated from slavery. שָׁבוּעוֹת, Pentecost, marks the giving of Torah on Mount Sinai 50 days after the Exodus. סֻכּוֹת, Tabernacles, celebrates the booths/Clouds of Glory that protected the Israelites in the Wilderness.[25]

The celebrations of the 3 Festivals are not simply commemorations of historic events that occurred on the same calendar dates; through them, the Jewish People actually relive the illumination of these past events, to undergo the same elevated spiritual experience. Thus, on Pesach they relive the spiritual freedom of the Exodus; on Shavuos they reaccept the Torah; and on Succos they live in booths under the protection of G-d.[26]

The celebrations of the 3 Festivals are not simply commemorations of historic events.

Following the sequence of the agricultural year, the 3 Festivals open with Pesach in the springtime, with the beginning of the growth of produce in the fields. Shavuos is the "Festival of harvesting" the crops, while Succos is the "Festival of gathering" into the storehouses.[27] Naturally, the 3 Festivals correspond to the 3 *Avos*: Avraham relates to Pesach, Yitzchak to Shavuos, and Yaakov to Succos.[28] One allusion to Pesach in Avraham's life was the baking of cakes for his guests on Pesach, a reference to matzah.[29] The blowing of the shofar at Sinai in the giving of Torah[30] is evocative of the ram whose horns were entangled in the bush and brought as an offering in lieu of Yitzchak.[31] Finally, there is an allusion of Succos associated with Yaakov, who constructed booths for his flocks.[32]

The 3 Festivals correspond to the 3 Avos.

Furthermore, the festival of Pesach can relate to the first tenet, the existence of G-d insofar as G-d proclaimed His Name and Divine Providence through the miracles of the Exodus.[33] The festival of Shavuos, when the Torah was given, parallels Torah given from Heaven. Finally, the ingathering of produce on Succos, when the farmer sees his "reward" at the end of the agricultural year, relates to reward and punishment.

3: TORAH AND MITZVOS

The basis of Jewish life revolves upon the Jews' fidelity to G-d through observance of Torah. There is an inseparable bond between the destinies of 3 intertwined parties: (1) G-d, (2) Torah, and (3) Israel.[34] Whether in the structure of Scripture or the fulfillment of its laws, the foundations of Torah and organization of *mitzvos* are often arranged into 3.

The Talmud records that "G-d gave the 3-fold Torah to a 3-fold people through the 3rd-born child on the 3rd day in the 3rd Jewish month."[35] The 3-fold Torah refers to the Written Torah that is called תנ"ך (Tanach), an acronym for תּוֹרָה, [Five] Books of the Torah; נְבִיאִים, Prophets; and כְּתוּבִים, Writings.[36] The 3-fold people are the nation of Israel that consists of 3 categories — *Kohen*, priest; *Levi*, Levite; and *Yisrael*, ordinary Jew.[37] The Torah was transmitted via Moshe, the 3rd of his parent's children.[38] It was given at Sinai after 3 days of sanctification,[39] in Sivan, the 3rd month of the Jewish calendar.[40] *Krias HaTorah*, public Torah reading, was arranged to ensure that 3 days do not elapse without the congregation hearing the holy words of Torah.[41] A minimum of 3 people must be called up to the Torah reading and each passage read must contain at least 3 verses.[42]

The nation of Israel consists of 3 categories.

Torah study translates into a lifetime of mitzvah observance. This enters and sanctifies the 3 spiritual realms.

In turn, Torah study translates into a lifetime of *mitzvah* observance. This enters and sanctifies the 3 spiritual realms: עוֹלָם, *space*; שָׁנָה, *time*; and נֶפֶשׁ, *spirit*.[43] The dimensions of space, of time, and of the spirit within man are dedicated in the loving worship of G-d.[44] As we have stated before, each of these realms can itself be subdivided into 3: space can be expressed 3-dimensionally (length, width, height), time can be split into 3 tenses (past, present, and future), and the spirit is also divided into 3 *elementary* components (נֶפֶשׁ, *spirit*; רוּחַ, *wind* or *life*[45]; and נְשָׁמָה, *soul*).[46]

Mitzvah observance is composed of 3 essential human endeavors: מַחֲשָׁבָה, *thought*; דִּבּוּר, *speech*; and מַעֲשֶׂה, *action*.[47] Each stage entails an additional dimension of revelation into the physical world.

Human thought is concealed from everyone else. Speech is articulating one's thoughts to others. And action connotes the human body in operation in the outside world. In *mitzvah* performance, man must sanctify all 3 endeavors. He starts with his intention to serve G-d, follows through with his recitation of the blessing prior to starting any action, and finally physically puts his observance into practice.

Several *mitzvah* groupings are arranged into sets of 3. While Judaism strongly upholds the preservation of life, there are 3 cardinal sins that may not be violated even under pain of death: *avodah zarah*, idolatry; *gilui arayos*, adultery; *shefichas damim*, murder.[48] There are 3 commandments traditionally reserved for the Jewish woman: *challah*, separating a portion of dough for the *Kohen*; *niddah*, laws of family purity; and *ner*, kindling the Shabbos lights.[49] The Talmud mentions the 3 specific *mitzvos* that offer the Jew a measure of protection: the *mezuzah* scroll on his door post, the *tzitzis* on his garment, and the *tefillin* on his body.[50]

Mitzvah observance is composed of thought, speech, and action.

3 mitzvos offer protection: the mezuzah, the tzitzis, and the tefillin.

A MATTER OF GREAT IMPORTANCE

WE HAVE SEEN THAT THE PILLARS OF JEWISH LIVING — STARTING from the Jewish forefathers — are arranged into 3 essential, interrelated parts. These foundations are to be joined together to form 1 integrated whole. Here the grouping into 3 introduces something prominent or distinctive, whose importance is underscored by the emergence of a pattern.

3 introduces something whose importance is underscored by the emergence of a pattern.

NOT LESS THAN 3

Many halachic rulings convey the principle that matters of importance are only accorded to units of 3 or more, but lesser numbers are deemed insignificant.

Some famous applications of this concept in Jewish law include:

❖ A distance of up to 3 handbreadths between two surfaces is not deemed to constitute a gap or break.[51]

❖ The volume of 3 *log* of drawn water invalidates a *mikveh* (ritual immersing pool) under certain conditions.[52]

❖ In harvesting a field, 1 or 2 stalks of grain or grapes that fall during the harvesting belong to the poor and not to the farmer; the 3rd that falls belongs to the farmer.[53]

3: Chazakah

The grouping of 3 is responsible for creating a new order or reality. The Jewish nation left Egypt in the 1st month (Nissan) and received the Torah in Sivan, the 3rd month.[54] A legal ruling is determined by a *beis din*, Jewish court of law, composed of a minimum of 3 male judges.[55] And the requisite number of men eating together that join for *zimun*, invitation to *Birchas HaMazon*, Grace after Meals, is 3.[56]

The grouping of 3 defines something new and distinctive.

The grouping of 3 defines something new and distinctive. It is truly deserving of a separate classification.[57] Some illustrations of this phenomenon: Once an animal gores 3 times, a *shor tam*, timid ox, assumes a new identity as a *shor muad*, forewarned ox, with the owner now liable for full indemnity.[58] In halachah, nighttime is determined when 3 stars are visible to the naked eye.[59] And a public declaration would be proclaimed 3 times.[60]

Perhaps the most famous example of the power of 3 is the principle of חֲזָקָה, confirmation or presumption.[61] One who occupies a plot of land for 3 successive years gains the presumption of title, under certain conditions.[62]

3 Days

3 consecutive days provide the ideal phase leading up to an event of profound significance.

In many historical events, 3 consecutive days provide the ideal phase leading up to an event of profound significance. The journey of Avraham en route to the Binding of Yitzchak took 3 days.[63] Pharaoh refused the Israelites' request to leave Egypt and travel 3 days into the Wilderness.[64] There were 3 national preparatory days prior to receiving the Torah at Sinai.[65] Yehoshua similarly readied the people for 3 days before crossing the Jordan into the Holy Land.[66] And in preparation for risking her life for the Jewish people, Queen Esther fasted 3 days and 3 nights.[67]

By extension, the arrival of the 3rd day as the culmination of 3 successive days carries within it great importance. 3 angelic guests visited Avraham on the 3rd day after his circumcision.[68] It was on the 3rd day after the citizens of Shechem were circumcised that Shimon and Levi killed the menfolk and rescued their sister, Dinah.[69] Lavan was informed on the 3rd day that Yaakov had fled.[70] And on the 3rd day Esther donned royalty to go before the king to plead for the salvation of the Jewish people.[71]

THE UNBROKEN CHAIN

FINALLY, ONCE A PROCESS HAS UNDERGONE THE 3 REQUISITE STAGES for a solid foundation, the 3 pillars themselves become transformed into the immovable template for permanence and guaranteed continuity.[72]

3-ply cord

In the words of the wisest of men, "a 3-ply cord is not easily severed."[73] This symbolically refers to the Children of Israel as descended from *all* 3 forefathers: Avraham, Yitzchak, and Yaakov. Their qualification as Chosen Nation (forged by their triple ancestral merits)[74] guarantees their continued existence throughout the millennia.

The number שָׁלֹשׁ, 3, relates to the word שַׁלְשֶׁלֶת, chain.[75] This is because each new generation adds a link to a chain that is an evocative symbol of continuity.

Each generation adds a link to a chain evocative of continuity.

The treasured heritage of Torah is timelessly passed on from the past to the present and then into the future. Torah transmission is said to pass through 3 generations: "from your mouth, from the mouth of your seed, and from the mouth of the seed of your seed. So says G-d, from now until forever."[76] Indeed, the existence of 3 successive generations of Torah scholars provides the assurance that Torah will never depart from this lineage.[77]

3 successive generations of Torah scholars assure that Torah will never depart from this lineage.

3: forever after

With their foundations firmly established and running deep, the eternity of the Jew is guaranteed. He continues in the footsteps of his illustrious 3 forefathers. He is stalwart in his beliefs. Even when faced with the despair of exile and the relentless oppression from antagonists, he tenaciously soldiers on.

This everlasting strength of Israel is marked by their affiliation to the number 3.[78] It is contained within their name יִשְׂרָאֵל, from the phrase יָשָׁר אֵ־ל, *straight ones of G-d*, that sees the Jewish People pursue the straight and central path of truth: of halachah,[79] of Torah,[80] and of life.[81] They refuse to deviate to either of the 2 extremes, not to the left and not to the right, from the straight path set by God.[82]

Here the Jewish People use all the aforementioned essential foundations of Jewish living arranged in sets of 3 in an uninterrupted chain of continuity that is successfully transmitted from father to son down the generations. It is this that will continue to endure forever after.

The Jewish People use all the essential foundations of Jewish living arranged in sets of 3.

NOTES

1. *Maharal, Chiddushei Aggados, Sanhedrin* 97a p. 208. See also *Maharal, Gevuros Hashem* 9.
2. Time is also subject to 3 phases — beginning, middle, and end (*Maharal, Gur Aryeh, Bamidbar* 22:28). In fact, tradition divides Jewish history into 3 epochs of 2,000 years: a period of emptiness, a period of Torah, and a period [that leads up to] Mashiach (*Sanhedrin* 97a). See "2000: The Borderline" and "6000: The End of the World."
3. See "1: The One and Only" and "2: Opposite and Equal."
4. *Maharal, Gevuros Hashem* 54.
5. *Maharal, Tiferes Yisrael* 25.
6. Rabbi Yishmael's *Baraisa*, Introduction to *Sifra*.
7. The number 3 is a midway point as the medium to synthesize opposites (*Maharal, Derashah al HaTorah*).
8. *Maharal, Gevuros Hashem* 9.
9. See ibid. 31, where he explains that 3 is the "ideal/optimal number" insofar as it has plurality not evident in 1, but it is more than just a pair as in the number 2.
10. See "2: Opposite and Equal."
11. *Bereishis* 2:24 and *Rashi* ad loc.
12. *Maharal, Netzech Yisrael* 45. The 3 partners in this enterprise are G-d, the father, and the mother (*Niddah* 31a). The parents are the 2 partners who provide the physical component. And it is G-d Who joins forces as the 3rd party to contribute the spiritual soul (ibid).
13. Modern science notes that the basic unit of matter is the atom, whose constituent particles consist of 3: proton, neutron, and electron. The subatomic protons and neutrons are both composed of elementary particles called quarks. Never found in isolation but only as composite particles, quarks are grouped into 3, with both the proton and neutron consisting of 3 high-energy quarks.
14. *Berachos* 16b.
15. See, for example, *Avos Neizikim*, Principal Damages (*Bava Kamma* 2a), or *Avos Melachos*, Principal Labors forbidden on Shabbos. See *Ramchal, Derech Hashem* 2:4:3-6.
16. *Pirkei Avos* 1:2. These famously parallel the 3 *Avos* (*Maharal, Derech Chaim* 1:2). An alternative set of 3 principles upon which the world is to endure is also given: *din*, justice; *emes*, truth; and *shalom*, peace (*Pirkei Avos* 1:18).
17. *Ramban*, Introduction, *Sefer Shemos*. See also *Maharal, Gur Aryeh, Bereishis* 32 [4] and *Gevuros*

Hashem 16. The Avos were also the "forefathers" for a Jewish convert (*Sfas Emes, Lech Lecha* 5648). That millions of Jews through the millennia have found the strength to die as martyrs rather than renounce their G-d, for example, is all due to the precedent set by Avraham (R' Chaim Volozhin, *Ruach Chaim* 5:3; R' Dessler, *Michtav MeiEliyahu* 1, p. 10).

18. *Shabbos* 146a. See "12: Tribes of Israel."
19. *Maharal, Gevuros Hashem* 9.
20. See *Maharal, Tiferes Yisrael* 18 and *Derech Chaim* 3:3 about the unity of 3.
21. *Sefer Halkkarim* 1:4. The *Rambam*'s famous 13 Principles of Faith can be arranged around these 3 main categorizations. See also, "13: Eternal Love."
22. See "1: The One and Only."
23. See "310: Worlds Apart."
24. The 3 sacrifices were *olas reiyah*, pilgrimage offering; *shalmei Chagigah*, Festival peace-offering; and *shalmei simchah*, rejoicing peace-offering (*Chagigah* 2a, *Rambam, Hilchos Chagigah* 1:1).
25. *Shemos* 23:14, 17; *Devarim* 16:16.
26. *Ramchal, Derech Hashem* 4:7-8.
27. *Shemos* 23:14-17.
28. *Tur, Orach Chaim* 417.
29. See *Bereishis* 18:6.
30. *Shemos* 19:16, 19.
31. *Bereishis* 22:13.
32. Ibid. 33:17.
33. *Shemos* 6:3 and *Rashi* ad loc.
34. *Zohar* 3, 73a. Each party is, so to speak, defined in respect to the others. G-d created the universe for Israel using Torah as the blueprint. G-d identifies Himself through His beloved nation, with the grand purpose of existence resting upon their shoulders. That means Israel must live exclusively for G-d as they readily define their lives through Torah.
35. *Shabbos* 88a.
36. Often, the Talmud proves a point by adducing threefold support from Torah, *Neviim*, and *Kesuvim* (e.g. *Avodah Zarah* 19b; *Megillah* 31a). In Rosh Hashanah *Mussaf*, the Scriptural verses for the 3 central themes each contains at least 3 verses from each of the 3 sections of Torah, *Neviim*, and *Kesuvim*. Just as the Written Torah is divided into 3 sections, so too can the Oral Torah be subdivided into 3 sections: Talmud, Halachah, Aggadah (*Tanchuma, Yisro* 10). Elsewhere, man's studies are supposed to be split into 3 areas: *Tanach*, Mishnah, and Talmud (*Avodah Zarah* 19b).
37. The 3-fold people can also refer to the 3 hereditary characteristics of the Jewish People: *rachmanim*, people of compassion; *beishanim*, a shame-faced people; and *gomlei chassadim*, benefactors of kindness (*Yevamos* 79a). The Mishnah depicts the disciples of Avraham as having 3 positive traits (a good eye, a humble spirit, and an undemanding soul) compared to the followers of Bilaam who exhibit the 3 opposite traits: an evil eye, a vain spirit, and a grasping soul (*Pirkei Avos* 5:19).
38. The 3 miraculous gifts in the Wilderness were the *be'er*, well; *ananei hakavod*, Clouds of Glory; and *mon*, manna, and they were given in the respective merits of the 3 siblings, Miriam, Aharon, and Moshe (*Taanis* 9a).
39. *Shemos* 19:11.
40. In all, there were 3 stages in Moshe's teaching of Torah in the Wilderness: Sinai; the Ohel Moed, Tent of Meeting; and the plains of Moav (*Chagigah* 6b).
41. *Bava Kamma* 82a. This is based on the Children of Israel wandering for 3 days in the Wilderness without finding water (*Shemos* 15:22). — water being a euphemism for Torah. "Have I not written for you 3-fold things of counsel and knowledge?" (*Mishlei* 22:20). This parallels 3 books of *Tanach* and 3 days between the reading of the Torah (*Bava Kamma* 82a; *Midrash Tanchuma Yisro* 10). In the Wilderness, the Ark traveled 3 days before Israel (*Bamidbar* 10:33). See *Maharal, Netzach Yisrael* 26.

Today's custom is to annually complete the Five Books of the Torah, but in Talmudic times, there were some places in Israel that had a 3-year-cycle (*Megillah* 29b; *Nachal Eshkol* II 19;2).

42. *Rambam*, *Hilchos Tefillah* 12:3; see also *Mishnah Berurah, Orach Chaim* 137:1-2. The minimum of 3 people standing around the Torah Scroll parallels the 3 parties at Sinai: G-d (the Torah-Giver), Children of Israel (the recipient), and Moshe (the intermediary). See *Mishnah Berurah, Orach Chaim* 141:16

43. *Sefer Yetzirah* 3:4-8.

44. The loving service of G-d must be conveyed in 3 ways: "with all your heart, with all your soul, and with all your resources" (*Devarim* 6:5).

45. See *Maharsha Berachos* 3a.

46. See *Bereishis Rabbah* 14:9; *Zohar* 3, 25a and *Nefesh HaChaim* 2:17. In the language of the *Maharal*, the 3 primary parts of the soul are labeled the *guf*, body; *nefesh*, spirit; and *sechel*, intellect (*Maharal, Nesiv HaAvodah* 1). The 3 parts of the soul are said to parallel the 3 vital organs in the human body: *moach*, brain; *lev*, heart; *koveid*, liver. See *Shelah HaKadosh, Toldos Adam, Beis Yisrael* 21 for how the word *melech*, king, is an acronym for these organs. See also *Shem MiShmuel, Vayikra* 5675.

47. See *Ramban, Vayikra* 1:9. This theme is often found in the writings of the *Shelah HaKadosh, Shem MiShmuel*, and *Sfas Emes*. It is attributed to the *Arizal, Sefer Likkutim, Eikev* 8.

48. *Sanhedrin* 74a; *Shulchan Aruch, Yoreh Deah* 157:1 These 3 commandments cannot be violated under pain of death inasmuch as they undermine the basic fabric of Judaism.

49. *Shabbos* 31b.

50. The Jew is promised a 3-fold protection by being surrounded by these 3 *mitzvos* (*Menachos* 43b).

51. See *Maharal, Ohr Chadash*, Introduction, p. 57. This is the reason that the Chanukah menorah should be placed above 3 handbreadths from the ground so that it would not be considered as if it was placed on the ground (*Shulchan Aruch, Orach Chaim* 671:6).

52. Mishnah, *Mikvaos* 2:4.

53. *Vayikra* 19:9-10; *Rambam Matnos Aniyim* 4:1, 15.

54. *Maharal, Tiferes Yisrael* 25.

55. *Sanhedrin* 2a.

56. Mishnah, *Berachos* 7:1.

57. *Maharal, Chiddushei Aggados, Sanhedrin* 96a Vol. 3, p. 202.

58. See *Bava Kamma* 23b.

59. *Shulchan Aruch, Orach Chaim* 293:2.

60. See Mishnah, *Parah* 3:10 and *Tosafos Yom Tov*, which discuss the fact that wherever the Rabbis instituted a public declaration, they customarily said it 3 times. See *Menachos* 65a regarding the procedure for reaping the *omer*, where the declarations were made 3 times. The 13 Divine Attributes are recited 3 times on Yom Tov before removing the Torah Scroll from the Ark. Among other declarations repeated thrice is *Kol Nidrei* on Yom Kippur night.

61. While there is a Talmudic dispute whether *chazakah* may already be established after the second time (*Yevamos* 64b), there is a universal acceptance that this state is definitely achieved upon the 3rd occurrence.

62. *Bava Basra* 28a-29a. There has to be a reason that he is occupying the land, such as sale, gift, inheritance, etc.; not just merely occupying for 3 years. Moreover, even if it is occupied, but the previous or real owner can prove that he protested against the occupation, then the 3 years of occupation without any other proof are not enough to maintain ownership.

63. *Bereishis* 22:4.

64. *Shemos* 5:3.

65. Ibid. 19:11, 15.

66. *Yehoshua* 1:11.

67. *Esther* 4:16.

68. *Bereishis* 18:2.
69. Ibid. 34:25.
70. Ibid. 31:22.
71. *Esther* 5:1.
72. *Maharal, Chiddushei Aggados, Kiddushin* 30a, p. 134.
73. *Koheles* 4:12.
74. *Rashi, Devarim* 32:9.
75. *Maharal, Chiddushei Aggados, Bava Basra* 73b Vol. 3 p. 88.
76. *Yeshayah* 59:21.
77. *Bava Metzia* 85a. See also *Bereishis* 50:23 for how Yosef merited seeing 3 generations through his son Ephraim.
78. *Maharal, Netzach Yisrael* 5. Conversely, the opposition by Israel's antagonists also uses this number.
79. *Maharal, Chiddushei Aggados, Sanhedrin* 106b, p. 250.
80. *Maharal, Tiferes Yisrael* 11.
81. *Maharal, Gur Aryeh Bereishis* 49:33. This alludes to the axiom, "Our ancestor Yaakov did not die" (*Taanis* 5b).
82. *Maharal, Gevuros Hashem* 9 and 54.

4
FINDING THE PLACE

It is within the context of 4 that a "place" is created and defined in the physical realm.

It takes 4 to build a place around a central mid-point.

Conversely, the negative counterpart of 4 represents the divergence away from the central point, as man journeys away from his true place.

IN PLACE

THE NUMBER 4 IS THE "PLACE" IN WHICH EXISTENCE FINDS EXPRESSION. We have seen 3 as symbolic of the essential foundation necessary for building a permanent structure.[1] We now require the medium wherein that foundation can be built. The perfect forum for this lies in the next number: 4.

One of the basic mathematical properties of the number 4 is as the double expression of 2. Whether by adding or multiplying by itself, the number 2 transfers to 4.

$$2 + 2 = 4$$
$$2 \times 2 = 4$$

The function of 4 is to expand the concept of plural until it has a fuller expression in the physical realm.

The principle of plural was first manifest in the number 2.[2] The function of 4 is to now expand this concept until it has a fuller expression in the physical realm.[3] This concept reverts to the origin of space and to the essence of what "place" represents.

well placed

One of the most unusual Divine Names is הַמָּקוֹם, the Place.[4] The word מָקוֹם, place, relates to מְקַיֵּם, to give existence.[5] Nothing in the physical realm can exist independent of "place." Indeed, the human mind finds it impossible to grasp the notion of a universe that exists outside the confines of place. "Place" is the domain where Creation exists.[6]

With the creation of "place," G-d provides the circumstances and space within which to exist.

The designation הַמָּקוֹם testifies to the constant reliance upon G-d that every object within existence has. *He is the Place of the world; the world is not His place.*[7] With the creation of "place," G-d provides Creation with the circumstances and space within which to exist. He is similarly responsible for supporting life that, in turn, has to find its place within His Creation.[8] The objective is to ensure that Creation fulfills its purpose so that His Glory fills the expanses of the universe: "All the land is filled with your Glory."[9]

4 X 4

G-d creates space. And man occupies it. The definitive number that represents space or place is the number 4.[10] The manifold applications of this include: (a) 4 as a depiction of space; (b) 4 as a basic unit of measurement; (c) 4 showing movement in all directions; and (d) 4 symbolizing the parameters of man's personal space.

(A) DEPICTING SPACE

In itself, a point lacks dimension. A line drawn between 2 points has length, yet its form is 1-dimensional. A surface that extends in both length and width provides a depiction into 4 directions.[11] The physical plane opens to the 4 points of a compass: North, South, East, and West.[12] Alternatively, using Biblical terminology, this opens up to the "4 corners of the world."[13] Symbolically, these reflect a set of 4 constant, objective points that serve as references for man's directions in life.[14]

The physical plane opens to the 4 points of a compass.

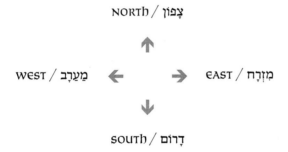

NORTH / צָפוֹן

WEST / מַעֲרָב   EAST / מִזְרָח

SOUTH / דָּרוֹם

(B) MEASUREMENT

In terms of the halachic units of measurement, a *parsah* is equal to 4 *mil*.[15] A *tefach* (handbreadth) is equal in length to the width of 4 thumbs.[16] And there is the ubiquitous dimension of ד׳ אַמּוֹת, 4 cubits.

(C) MOVEMENT

The definitive distance of "going places" in terms of movement to or from a place is 4 cubits. In the laws of Shabbos, a Jew is forbidden to carry or transport an object a distance of 4 cubits in the public domain.[17] Matters of holiness may not be recited within a distance of 4 cubits from something ritually impure or repugnant.[18] A person

The definitive distance in terms of movement to or from a place is 4 cubits.

must stand up for a Torah scholar passing within 4 cubits from him.[19] Furthermore, a Jew is not meant to walk 4 cubits without a head covering or to walk this same distance with a haughty posture.[20]

(D) PRIVATE DOMAIN

Every individual occupies 4 square cubits; this spatial area is said to belong to him.

The minimum space classified as a separate and private domain, when partners divide a home or yard, must occupy an area of 4 square cubits.[21] Whatever lies inside the 4 x 4 is halachically classified as being of the same domain.[22] Every individual *occupies* a space of 4 square cubits;[23] this spatial area is said to *belong* to him.[24]

The principle underlying the notion of space is that *everything in the universe is designated its rightful place in which to fulfill its assigned purpose*: "There is nothing that does not have its place."[25]

An individual's task is to realize his mission within the exclusive space allocated to him.

Typically, the raison d'être of an object is bound up with the place in which it finds itself. This constitutes the habitat where it truly belongs.[26] Indeed, every person carries a natural affinity to his locality and is often even called after his town or area.[27] An individual's task is to realize his mission within the exclusive space allocated to him. The term *makom* is thus also used to conceptually define a person's position and standing.[28]

We have seen 4 as the dimension of place. A person's life has meaning only to the degree that he "finds his place." In other words, man must correctly use the designated space G-d gives him to fulfill the Divine Will. This requires man to go from potential to actual to realize his true self. As an extension of place, 4 is the forum in which something is allowed to develop and fulfill its destiny.[29]

4 is the forum in which something is allowed to develop and fulfill its destiny.

THE 4-LETTER NAME OF G-D

The *Shem HaMeforash* (יהוה), Explicit Name, is the Ineffable 4-Letter Name of G-d (or Tetragrammaton, from the Latin meaning 4 Letters). Whereas all other Divine Names refer to how man views or perceives G-d in the world through His Attributes, the *Shem HaMeforash* is considered His definitive Name.[30] This Name relates to G-d as the eternal Master of the universe, "the One Who is, Who was, and Who will be."[31] It also signifies G-d as the "One who brings all of existence into being." He is the Source of all existence whose essence fills His Creation.

The 4-Letter Name of G-d is considered His definitive Name.

In the mystical tradition, the composition of the *Shem HaMeforash* is a 4-Letter Name; that number of letters is not incidental but highly significant. It finds expression in the structure of Creation.

CREATION: 4 WORLDS

Creation unfolds to take shape within the physical realm. In the creation process, an amorphous state of Divine potential takes on a definitive shape using the number 4 to find its physical expression. The descent from the united higher realm of G-dliness into the lower world of space is symbolized by the move from the singularity of 1 to the multiplicity of 4.[32]

The development of the universe was shaped through the following 4 spiritual worlds.[33]

1.	אֲצִילוּת	Emanation
2.	בְּרִיאָה	Creation
3.	יְצִירָה	Formation
4.	עֲשִׂיָּה	Completion

In relation to everything that follows it, the world of אֲצִילוּת (from the root אֵצֶל, meaning "nearness") is closest to the Divine. It is best characterized as that level of reality that does not yet exist. Here the Divine qualities that will be used within Creation are undifferentiated. The world below this is בְּרִיאָה, which refers to the creation process as the transition of "something from nothing." Below this is יְצִירָה, in the shaping of what exists whereby it is given a definitive form. Finally, the lowest world of עֲשִׂיָּה is where a formed object finds its final realization to reach its completed state. The Divine influence descends through these worlds until its ultimate revelation in the lowest world.

The Divine influence descends until its ultimate revelation in the lowest world.

THE 4 ELEMENTS

The 4 primary forces are earth, water, spirit, and fire.

The essential forces within Creation similarly find their expression opening up into 4. The 4 primary forces, referred in medieval terms by the term *elements* (not to be confused with the chemical elements), are עָפָר, *earth*; מַיִם, *water*; רוּחַ, *spirit* or *air*; and אֵשׁ, *fire*.[34] A modern variation of this could be expressed through the 4 corresponding states of matter: solid, liquid, gas, and energy.

The 4 elements exactly parallel the categorization of 4 types of creations in the universe: דּוֹמֵם, *inert matter*; צוֹמֵחַ, *vegetation*; חַי, *living creatures*; and מְדַבֵּר, *articulate man*. The lowest creation of inert matter is parallel to earth, vegetation connects to water necessary for plant growth, living creatures contain spirit and a basic life force, and man's distinctive soul is akin to fire and the spiritual flame burning within him.[35]

1.	עָפָר, earth	דּוֹמֵם, inert matter
2.	מַיִם, water	צוֹמֵחַ, vegetation
3.	רוּחַ, spirit	חַי, living creatures
4.	אֵשׁ, fire	מְדַבֵּר, articulate man

BIRTH OF ISRAEL: 4 MOTHERS

Creation takes shape in 4 worlds whose primary forces are the 4 elements. This has its parallel in the national expression of Israel as a people "built" by the 4 *Imahos*, Matriarchs: Sarah, Rivkah, Rachel, and Leah. Their union with the 3 *Avos*, Patriarchs, resulted in the 12 Tribes of Israel.[36]

3 provides the foundation; 4, the edifice, the place.

The progression from 3 to 4 is where theory becomes practice. The necessary foundations (3 *Avos*) open out to find full expression into the 4 directions of the physical (4 *Imahos*). The Jewish Mothers played a pivotal role in bearing, educating, and rearing those who would develop into the Children of Israel. Once again, 3 provides the foundation; 4, the edifice, the place.

PESACH SEDER: 4 CUPS OF WINE

The birth of Israel as a nation was through their redemption on Pesach. Their emergence into a newly founded Jewish people at the Exodus was completed through 4 stages in their liberation.

There are 4 renowned expressions,[37] as celebrated in the 4 cups of wine at the Seder:

1.	וְהוֹצֵאתִי	I will take you out.
2.	וְהִצַּלְתִּי	I will save you.
3.	וְגָאַלְתִּי	I will redeem you.
4.	וְלָקַחְתִּי	I will take you.

This has several parallels in other appearances of the number 4 in the lead-up to Pesach and in the Haggadah.

- There are אַרְבַּע פָּרָשִׁיּוֹת, 4 Torah portions, read on 4 weeks in the lead-up to Pesach. (a) *Shekalim* (the counting of the Jews through donations of a half-*shekel*), (b) *Zachor* (remembrance of the attack by Amalek in the Wilderness), (c) *Parah* (the preparation of the *parah adumah*, Red Cow, used for ritual purification) and (d) *HaChodesh* (sanctification of the Jewish calendar prior to the Exodus).
- According to many versions of the Haggadah, and in the text universally adopted today, there are the 4 renowned questions of מַה נִּשְׁתַּנָּה, Why is this night different?[38]
- The Exodus story is retold to 4 sons: חָכָם, the wise son; רָשָׁע, the wicked son; תָּם, the simpleton; and שֶׁאֵינוֹ יוֹדֵעַ לִשְׁאוֹל, the child who does not know how to ask.
- The word *baruch*, blessed, appears 4 times in the *Baruch HaMakom* passage.
- The Exodus came after 4 generations of Israel sojourning in Egypt.[39]
- In the Exodus G-d revealed His 4-Letter Ineffable Name to mankind.[40]

The birth of the nation using 4 stages mirrors the role of the 4 Matriarchs in the development of Israel. The Exodus was the event that brought the template of Israel created by the 3 *Avos* into full fruition.

The birth of the nation using 4 stages mirrors the role of the 4 Matriarchs in the development of Israel.

4: The Jewish Camp

The Jewish people were able to express their true selves in the aftermath of the Exodus. They wandered in the Wilderness, whose barren wastelands excluded a geographical "place" of operation. The Jew would, instead, "find his place" within the established confines of Torah, where G-dliness was firmly at the center.

The formation of the 12 Tribes of Israel was arranged such that 3 Tribes were represented on each of the 4 sides of the camp, each hoisting its respective banner.[41]

The Jew would, "find his place" within the established confines of Torah.

	NORTH Dan Asher Naftali	
WEST Ephraim Menashe Binyamin	MISHKAN (Sanctuary)	EAST Yehudah Yissachar Zevulun
	SOUTH Reuven Shimon Gad	

Every Tribe would find its approach in the service of G-d through its positioning in the camp.

Their encampment had at its center the *Mishkan*, Sanctuary, which housed the Tablets in the Holy Ark, where the *Shechinah*, Divine Presence, hovered.[42] At Sinai, G-d did not reveal Himself in 1 direction (that would have been too intense); He revealed Himself from 4 directions.[43] And He encircled with clouds the Jewish camp where they were positioned and divided into 4 camps.[44] Every Tribe would find its approach in the service of G-d through its respective positioning in the Jewish camp.[45] Later, the Jewish people would find their "place" in their national homeland in *Eretz Yisrael*, Land of Israel. Again, the settlement in the country had the *Beis HaMikdash*, Temple, at its center — that was called the *makom*, "the place that He will choose to rest His Name there."[46] Here the *korbonos*, sacrificial offerings, were brought.[47]

4: ORChARD OF TORAh

A Jew finds his "place" in Creation within the context of Torah.

In truth, a Jew finds his place in Creation within the context of Torah. The objective of the national creation of Israel at the Exodus through 4 stages was realized once Israel embraced the raison d'être of their existence at Sinai. G-d, the "One Who gives existence," defines "the place" in which Jewish living is to be enacted. Torah offers man the optimal place where he can actualize his potential.

Parallel to the universe revealed via the 4 spiritual worlds is Torah, similarly expressed through 4 layers of interpretation. Known by its acronym פַּרְדֵּס, *orchard*, Torah can be expounded in 4 distinct ways: (i) פְּשַׁט, *plain meaning*; (ii) רֶמֶז, *allusion*; (iii) דְּרַשׁ, *exposition*; (iv) סוֹד, *esoteric*.

Each layer penetrates more deeply into the Torah's infinite wisdom.[48] There is a 4-fold program stating how Torah is to be studied (4 groups of students,[49] 4 immediate times to review a topic,[50] 4 categories of those who go to study,[51] 4 types that sit before Torah sages[52]), where it is to be studied ("when you are at home, when you travel, when you go to sleep, when you arise"[53]) and its 4-pronged practical application: "to study, to teach, to observe, and to practice".[54]

A 4-fold program states how Torah is to be studied.

OUT OF PLACE

WE HAVE DISCUSSED THAT G-D ALLOCATES A PLACE TO A JEW TO fulfill his destiny by developing from potential to actual. His growth — like that of the nation — must be exclusively nurtured *inside* the designated space G-d gave him, and never *outside* of it.

Danger sets in where there is the rejection of the designated place in favor of "moving out." Exile denotes distance from G-d as the Source of Creation and distance from man shaping his destiny. Where man moves out of his place, he ideologically deserts his mission. His departure is measured by the number 4, that itself represents going away from the central point.

Exile denotes distance from G-d as the Source of Creation.

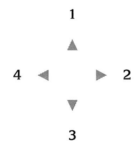

Here 4 comes to express groupings of negative forces.

4: ON THE OUTSIDE

G-d is the central Source of all existence. Idolatry is the worship of forces that are wrongfully deemed to be independent; forces that are "on the outside." The number that refers to external forces

G-d is the central Source of all existence.

The number
4 refers to
"external"
forces in
opposition to
that which is
"internal."

in opposition to that which is primary or "internal" is 4.[55] This is the reason that the sin of idolatry, in its inclusion in the Ten Commandments, encompasses a total of 4 prohibitions.[56]

In his inscrutable prophetic vision, Yechezkel beheld the likeness of 4 *Chayos*, angelic beings bearing the "Heavenly chariot," whose faces resembled 4 images: a lion, an ox, an eagle, and a man.[57] One of these 4 images — the ox — was utilized by the Jewish nation when they committed the sin of the *eigel hazahav*, Golden Calf (a calf being a young ox).[58]

4 RIVERS FROM EDEN

The descent from the higher realm of spirituality into our physical world is marked by the move from the singularity of 1 to the multiplicity of 4.[59] Perhaps the earliest precedent for this was symbolized in the water that emerged from *Gan Eden*, Garden of Eden. The Torah relates that this water divided and became 4 major rivers.[60]

Man did not
fulfill his
destiny and
consequently
forfeited his
optimal place.

This description would foreshadow Adam's subsequent exile from the original space within which G-d had placed him.[61] His primeval sin meant that man did not fulfill his destiny and consequently forfeited his optimal place. He would now be forced to wander in exile. Actually, this would be a precursor to the 4 instances of *galus*, exile, that the Jewish nation would historically experience.[62]

IN EXILE: 4 EMPIRES

Historically, the Jewish nation was exiled from *Eretz Yisrael*, Land of Israel, and placed under the authority of the *Arba Malchiyos*, 4 Empires or 4 Kingdoms. The Babylonian Empire (*Bavel*) led by Nebuchadnezzar destroyed the First Temple.[63] The Babylonian Empire was superseded by the kingdom of Persia-Media (*Paras U'Madai*). After the Jewish People returned to the Holy Land and the rebuilding of the Second Temple, there was the nefarious influence of the Syrian-Greeks (*Yavan*) and the partial victory in the miracle of the Chanukah story. Finally, the Roman Empire (*Edom*) destroyed the Second Temple at the onset of the two-millennia exile of the Jewish People that continues until today.

There are some fascinating historic allusions made to these exiles: the description of the emptiness before Creation,[64] the 4 kings that Avraham fought,[65] and the Covenant of the Parts G-d made with

Avraham.[66] Perhaps the most famous is the later prophetic vision of 4 beasts in the dreams of Daniel.[67]

Galus, exile, typifies departure from one's natural place.[68] The rise of 4 Empires symbolizes 4 outward forces attacking the inward singularity of Israel at the center of existence.[69] The 4 Empires took a symbolic stand against Israel, the "one unique nation" and ambassadors of the One G-d.[70] Their hostility led them to drive Israel out of their true geographical and spiritual place. The 4 Empires usurped the Kingdom rightly belonging to Israel by scattering the Jewish people to the 4 corners of the globe.[71]

4 NEGATIVE FORCES

Further expressions of the same negativity are found in the 4 non-kosher animals, the 4 primary categories of damaging forces, and the 4 judicial deaths.

NON-KOSHER ANIMALS

There are 4 nonkosher animals that the Torah identifies as having only one of the requisite two kosher signs. The *gamal*, camel; the *shafan*, the hyrax; the *arneves*, hare; and the *chazir*, pig[72] embody negative forces. These animals may not be consumed by Jews due to their spiritual defilement. The animals' impurity is accentuated because of the fear that these beasts could be construed as being half-kosher. They symbolically parallel the 4 Empires that exiled the Jewish nation.[73]

The nonkosher animals parallel the 4 Empires.

DAMAGING FORCES

The Mishnah enumerates 4 primary categories of *mazikim*, damaging forces. These refer to the damages caused by a *shor*, ox; *bor*, the pit; *mav'eh*, a reference to damages caused either by *adam*, man, or *shein*, tooth, as in the damage caused when an animal eats; and *aish*, fire. Here the owner is duty bound to prevent any damage by these 4 forces; failing which, he is obligated to pay for the losses incurred.[74]

The owner must prevent damage by these 4 forces.

JUDICIAL DEATHS

There were 4 forms of capital punishment imposed on a sinner by a Jewish court. These deaths were סְקִילָה, *stoning*; שְׂרֵיפָה, *burning*; הֶרֶג, *beheading*; and חֶנֶק, *strangulation*.[75] These deaths were adminis-

There were 4 forms of capital punishment imposed by a Jewish court.

tered when the sin was witnessed by at least a pair of witnesses[76] and the perpetrator was forewarned of the consequence of his actions.[77]

4 AMOS OF halachah

Remarkably, even in times of exile the Jewish people retain a "special place" where they can be forever connected to G-d. Despite being "out of place" geographically, the Jewish nation is still not lost. Their preservation throughout their long and bitter exile is attributed to the fact that, as a nation, they maintain fidelity to Torah within the strict confines G-d provides them within His Creation. Following the destruction of the Temple, the substitute "place" on Earth where G-d continues to reside, so to speak, is the ד׳ אַמּוֹת שֶׁל הֲלָכָה, *4 cubits of halachah.*[78]

The exalted stature of Torah, as expressed in practical conduct, occupies an autonomous, distinct place. Its beloved status means that its continuous existence is assured before G-d.[79] This is where a Jew frames his life: in the place where G-d and Torah reside. This is where he belongs. [80]

BACK INTO PLACE

DESPITE THE NEGATIVE CONNOTATIONS ASSOCIATED WITH THE number 4, symbolic of its departure from its true place, the 4 extremes will ultimately converge together as 1. They must transport their *4 cubits of halachah* to their homeland. Then the exile originally identified with the number 4 becomes the stepping stone toward redemption, as epitomized in the number 5.

FROM The 4 CORNERS OF The WORLD

The circumstance of *galus,* when Israel is exiled from their home, denotes an unnatural state of affairs.[81] It mirrors the situation in which the 4 directions of the physical world have diverged from its central spiritual point.

This unfortunate situation is not destined to last. Just as G-d redeemed the Children of Israel from the Egyptian exile, so too, will the Jewish people once again celebrate *geulah*, redemption. Though dispersed to the ends of the world, those at the 4 directions will converge back to their homeland: "And gather us from the 4 corners of the world [back to our Land]."[82]

Displacement will lead to *re-placement.* Israel will wholeheartedly return to G-d. In number terms, the directions epitomized by 4 then revert to its central 5th point that brings them together.[83]

In their redemption, the Jewish nation will finally be restored to its rightful place. The Jews will live in the Holy Land and merit to witness the rebuilding of the Temple. Here Israel will find themselves in their true placement in the symbolism of the number 4, as it epitomizes space used to convert potential to actual. Everything will expand to fulfill its Divine destiny within its designated place. In the Messianic Era, the 4 spiritual worlds will ultimately lead to the utopian place that is filled with the Glory of the Four-Letter Name of G-d.

Everything will expand to fulfill its Divine destiny within its designated place.

NOTES

1. See "3: Three-Dimensional."
2. See "2: Opposite and Equal."
3. *Maharal, Gevuros Hashem* 60. Mathematically, this is as graphically represented in the x and y axes. The expansion of this in 2 directions of 4 opens up further in the number 6 expanding into 3 dimensions. See "6: It's Only Natural."
4. The relationship between מָקוֹם and the Ineffable Name is depicted in terms of their numerical value. Squaring the numerical value of each letter of the Ineffable Name ($186 = 5^2 + 6^2 + 5^2 + 10^2 =$ יהוה) equals the numerical value of מָקוֹם (186) (*Bnei Yisaschar,* Nissan 7:1).
5. *Maharal, Ohr Chodesh, Esther* 4:14, p. 154a.
6. *Maharal, Netzach Yisrael* 24; *Nesiv HaAvodah* 4.
7. *Bereishis Rabbah* 68:9.
8. R' Chaim Volozhin, *Nefesh HaChaim* 3:1-2.
9. *Yeshayah* 6:3.
10. *Maharal, Chiddushei Aggados, Bava Metzia* 59b .
11. *Maharal, Gevuros Hashem* 3. Although it extends only to 4 sides, it lacks depth. The ultimate depiction, as in a solid body, is where it extend towards all 6 sides — up, down, plus the 4 directions. See "6: It's Only Natural."
12. *Bereishis* 28:14. A different wind blows from each of these 4 directions (*Gittin* 31b). The 4 directions are themselves identified with different forces of natural phenomena (see *Bamidbar Rabbah* 2:9 and *Pirkei DeRabbi Eliezer* 3).
13. *Yechezkel* 7:2.
14. "East" represents the direction toward which a person faces. "West" is that which he has turned his back on. "South," where a person facing "East" then turns to the right, refers to man's strengths that

must be actualized. And "North," where he veers to the left, refers to his weaknesses and failings. It is within the forum of the 4 directions that man has to function to actualize his potential.

15. *Pesachim* 93b. In modern measurements, 1 *mil* is equivalent to circa 0.6 – 0.7 miles. This means that a *parsah* is a distance of between 2.4 – 2.9 miles.

16. *Shulchan Aruch, Orach Chaim* 586:9 and *Mishnah Berurah* 54.

17. See *Eruvin* 48a, *Bava Metzia* 10a; *Shulchan Aruch, Orach Chaim* 349.

18. *Berachos* 25a; *Avodah Zarah* 17a; see *Shulchan Aruch, Orach Chaim* 79:1.

19. *Kiddushin* 33b; See *Rambam, Hilchos Talmud Torah* 6:6-7.

20. *Kiddushin* 31a; *Shulchan Aruch, Orach Chaim* 2:6. See also *Megillah* 28a, citing that Rav Zeira was lauded for not walking 4 cubits without reciting words of Torah and wearing *tefillin*.

21. *Succah* 3a-b.

22. *Mishnah Berurah, Orach Chaim* 184:2. When eating in an open area outdoors, if it is within 4 cubits, it is considered one place. However, inside a fenced area or home, it is all considered as if it is within 4 x 4 cubits (*Sha'ar HaTziyun* 5 ad loc). There are also other issues whereby the area within the same house is equated to being 4 *amos* (*Mishnah Berurah, Orach Chaim* 1:2).

23. *Succah* 3b, *Gittin* 77b; *Maharal, Chiddushei Aggados Gittin* 77b; see *Berachos* 18a, *Avodah Zarah* 50a.

24. See *Gittin* 78a for how this finds expression in the laws of acquisition.

25. *Pirkei Avos* 4:3.

26. See *Maharal, Netzach Yisrael* 1, for how G-d created a system wherein each nation is to be found in the place most suited to its specific nature.

27. *Maharal, Derech Chaim* 3:4.

28. For example, "The son fills the *makom*, 'place' of his father" (*Kesubos* 103b).

29. This concept finds greater expression in the number 40. See "40: True to Form."

30. R' Yehuda HaLevi, *Kuzari* 4:1. See "26: In the Name of G-d."

31. *Shulchan Aruch, Orach Chaim* 5:1 His preeminence is phrased in *Ein K'Elokeinu* using 4 descriptive terms: (a) "There is no one like our G-d; (b) there is no one like our Master; (c) there is no one like our King; (d) there is no one like our Savior" (*Rokeach, Devarim* 3:24, p. 169).

32. *Maharal, Gevuros Hashem* 60.

33. See *Yeshayah* 43:7 and R' Chaim Vital, *Shaarei Kedushah* 3:1. See *Ramchal, Derech Hashem* 4:6 for how the 4 universes parallel the 4 parts of the daily morning service.

34. See *Ramban, Bereishis* 1:1. Actually, this division is reflective of the innate forces within man's character. See R' Chaim Vital, *Shaarei Kedushah* 1:2.

35. See *Shelah HaKadosh, Perek V'Torah Ohr, Toras Kohanim*.

36. See "12: Tribes of Israel."

37. *Shemos* 6:6-7. See *Yerushalmi, Pesachim* 10:1. See "5: Give Me Five."

38. Even during the Temple era, there were 4 questions asked by the Seder, albeit with a variation in a question about the paschal offering. See *Pesachim* 116a.

39. *Bereishis* 15:16.

40. *Shemos* 6:3 and *Rashi* ad loc.

41. *Bamidbar* 2:1-31. In fact, the corresponding division into 4 is found in the heavenly realm with the 4 Archangels Gavriel, Raphael, Michoel, and Uriel (*Bamidbar Rabbah* 2:9) positioned in 4 directions around the Divine Chariot that itself had 4 feet (*Zohar* 1, 248b). The promise to Yaakov to spread out in 4 directions (*Bereishis* 14:15) is an allusion to 12 tribes arranged under 4 banners (*Sfas Emes, Vayeitzei* 5646).

42. See "22,000: The Divine Presence."

43. See *Rashi, Devarim* 32:11.

44. See ibid. v. 10.

45. The grouping of Israel into 4 divisions had its parallel in the appointment of 4 types of Jewish officials: officers of 10, 50, 100, and 1000 (*Devarim* 1:15 and *Baal HaTurim* ad loc.).

46. *Devarim* 14:23; see also ibid. 16:16, 23:17, 31:11.
47. See *Shelah HaKadosh, Perek v'Torah Ohr, Toras Kohanim.* The 4 sacrificial offerings incorporated all 4 categories: salt (inert matter), flour or wine (vegetation), cattle and birds (living creatures), man bringing the offering (speaker). There were 4 types of offerings: *olah,* elevation; *chatas,* sin-offering; *asham,* guilt-offering; and *shelamim,* peace-offering. Additionally, there are 4 essential procedures involving the blood of an animal offering: (1) *shechitah,* ritual slaughter of the animal; (2) *kabbalah,* receiving the blood, which is caught in a sacred vessel as it spurts from the animal's neck; (3) *holachah,* conveying the blood in the vessel to the Altar; and (4) *zerikah,* throwing or application of the blood to the appropriate part of the Altar.
48. Beginning with *peshat,* the most outward layer of meaning, Torah study is about progressively moving inward, until one ultimately studies *sod,* the innermost dimension (*Vilna Gaon, Mishlei* 1:20).
49. *Pirkei Avos* 5:15.
50. *Eruvin* 54b.
51. *Pirkei Avos* 5:17.
52. Ibid. 5:18.
53. *Devarim* 6:7.
54. *Pirkei Avos* 4:6 and blessing before Morning *Shema.* See *Rokeach, Devarim* 6:7.
55. *Maharal, Tiferes Yisrael* 38; see also *Maharal Gevuros Hashem* 6.
56. The 4 prohibitions are: "(1) You shall not have other gods before Me ... (2) You shall not make for yourself a carved image ... (3) You shall not bow down to them ... (4) [You shall not] worship them" (*Shemos* 20:3-5). See also *Rokeach, Shemos* 20:3-5 pp. 108,116.
57. *Yechezkel* 1:4-11. Additionally, each of the 4 *Chayos* had 4 faces and 4 wings.
58. See also *Maharal, Netzach Yisrael* 22.
59. *Maharal, Gevuros Hashem* 60. See also *Maharal, Ner Mitzvah.*
60. These rivers were Pishon, Gichon, Chidekel, and Peras (see *Bereishis* 2:10-14).
61. Ibid. 2:15.
62. *Bereishis Rabbah* 16:4. The 400 years of the Egyptian slavery is itself a manifestation of 4 as symbolic of exile (*Maharal, Gevuros Hashem* Ch. 26). See "400: Of All Places."
63. See "410: The First Temple."
64. The 4 exiles are hinted at in the respective phrases of *tohu,* chaos (Babylon); *vohu,* turmoil (Persia-Media); *choshech,* darkness (Greece); *al pnei sehom,* upon the face of the abyss (Rome) (*Bereishis Rabbah* 2:5 interpreting the phrases in *Bereishis* 1:2).
65. See *Bereishis Rabbah* 42:4.
66. G-d showed Avraham the 4 Empires at the Covenant of the Parts. This was symbolized by the choice of animals used. See *Pirkei DeRabbi Eliezer* 28 and *Yalkut Shimoni, Lech Lecha* 76.
67. *Daniel* 7:2-7, 7:17 See *Maharal, Ner Mitzvah.*
68. *Maharal, Netzach Yisrael* 1.
69. *Maharal, Ner Mitzvah;* and *Chiddushei Aggados, Menachos* 53b IV, 84.
70. *Maharal, Ner Mitzvah, Gevuros Hashem* 23, 26. See "1: The One and Only."
71. See *Zechariah* 2:10.
72. *Vayikra* 11:4-7 and *Devarim* 14:7-8.
73. *Vayikra Rabbah* 13:5; see also *Vilna Gaon, Peirush al Kamah Aggados.* See *Rokeach, Devarim* 28:22.
74. *Bava Kamma* 2a.
75. *Mishnah, Sanhedrin* 7:1; See *Rabbeinu Yonah, Shaarei Teshuvah* 3:126. These 4 deaths exactly parallel the 4 elements. Stoning uses *aphar,* earth, from the ground in the stones. Burning is the use of *eish,* fire. Beheading directly involves the spilling blood that flows to the ground like *mayim,* water. And strangulation kills by blocking up the *ruach,* wind, in the windpipe, through which one breathes.
76. *Devarim* 19:15.
77. *Sanhedrin* 8b.

78. *Berachos* 8a.
79. *Maharal, Tiferes Yisrael* 70. See also *Rambam, Introduction to Mishnah.*
80. See R' Tzadok HaKohen, *Kometz HaMinchah* p. 14.
81. *Maharal, Netzach Yisrael* 1.
82. *Shemoneh Esrei* weekday prayer.
83. See "5: Give Me Five."

5
GIVE ME
FIVE

5 is the inner, central point
that assembles 4 disparate parts
into a collective group.

It relates to the soul and to
the full expression of man's true being.

The doubling of 5 corresponding groups is
responsible for producing 10 that symbolizes
the full, complete picture.

THE INGATHERING

THE NUMBER 5, FOLLOWING THE NUMBER 4, RECONNECTS THE 4 directions of space, which would otherwise remain separate, through the central 5th point.

4, 5: GATHERING IN THE EXILES

The number 4 symbolizes "place." The world's creations find the essential space to operate within the 4 directions. But as it spreads outward, there is the danger of departing from its original point of reference. The chief examples of something "out of place" include the geographical dispersion of the Jewish People from their homeland to the 4 corners of the world and their historical subjugation in the 4 Exiles.[1]

In reassembling components, 5 becomes the formative number of a group.

The leap from 4 to 5 sees the 4 diverging directions converge around the earlier central position.[2] Here the 5th point gathers them back together to form one unifying collective entity. In successfully reassembling the disparate individual components, 5 becomes the formative number of a group.[3] While not reaching the completeness or wholeness of 10,[4] the number 5 nonetheless contains a unifying quality to complete a group or set; in Hebrew, this is denoted by the term אֲגוּדָה, *gathering*, as a unified bundle.[5]

5 is symbolic of גְּאוּלָה, redemption.

With 5 as the central point to which the 4 dispersed directions converge, we can clearly see why 5 is symbolic of גְּאוּלָה, *redemption*. This is the process that gathers in the 4 extremities of גָּלוּת, *exile*, so that they converge back to the inner, middle point that operates as the unifying 5th component. This new infrastructure returns objects to their true place of being.[6]

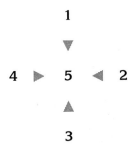

This transformation from 4 to 5, from *galus* to *geulah*, is brilliantly reflected in the Hebrew alphabet. The shape of the 4th letter, ד, contains 2 lines that extend to 4 directions on the horizontal and vertical axes. By contrast, the subsequent 5th letter, ה, incorporates the 4 directions within the letter ד but also includes a י that symbolizes the central 5th unifying point that joins the 4 directions together.[7]

$$ ה = ד \rightarrow י $$

The Exodus was the epitome of the redemption process. G-d's appointment of Moshe to redeem the Children of Israel came when Moshe took 5 paces to turn toward the 5-leaved burning bush,[8] whose location was actually at the site of Mount Sinai, which has a total of 5 different names.[9] Indeed, this set into motion the salvation of Israel in the merit of 5 people: Avraham, Yitzchak, Yaakov, Moshe, and Aharon.[10]

The Exodus was the epitome of the redemption process.

It is well known that the 4 Torah expressions of emancipation have their exact parallel in the 4 cups of wine drunk at Seder night.[11] Nevertheless, the climax in the ultimate level of *geulah* culminates in the final, 5th stage: וְהֵבֵאתִי אֶתְכֶם אֶל הָאָרֶץ, *I will bring you in onto the land [of Israel]*[12] — that has its parallel in the additional 5th cup. This 5th cup is referred to as *Kos Shel Eliyahu*, the Cup of Eliyahu. Eliyahu will be the harbinger for Mashiach.[13] In the Messianic Era, the Jewish People scattered into 4 directions will return to their rightful place in the Jewish national homeland, which symbolically serves as the unifying, central 5th point.

The Jewish People scattered into 4 directions will return to the Jewish national homeland, the unifying 5th point.

LIFE AND SOUL

WE HAVE SEEN THAT 5 IS THE NUMERIC EXPRESSION OF A GROUP, gathering its divergent parts into a complete unit. The number 5 is suitably associated with the soul as the unifying life-force within man.

5: WITH ALL YOUR SOUL

Sequentially, the soul centralizes the operations of the bodily forces in the 4 directions and unifies them in the service of G-d.

In the original formation of man, G-d first gathered the dust of the ground from all 4 directions of the world.[14] Into this lifeless earthly form, G-d blew into man's nostrils "the soul of life, and man became a living being."[15] Sequentially, then, the soul corresponds to the unifying 5th component that centralizes the operations of the bodily forces in the 4 directions and unifies them in the service of G-d.[16]

The Midrash describes the soul as being composed of 5 components. In ascending order of spirituality, they are known by the following names: (1) נֶפֶשׁ, (2) רוּחַ, (3) נְשָׁמָה, (4) חַיָּה, (5) יְחִידָה.[17] Furthermore, there are 5 primary powers invested into the soul: growth, feeling, imagination, desire, and reason.[18] On 5 occasions King David praised G-d using the expression "*Borchei Nafshei*, Bless G-d, O My soul," as a reference to the 5 phases he lived through.[19] These, in turn, were parallel to the 5 parts of the soul.[20] Similar to the phenomenon where the first 4 are bound together by the 5th, the highest component of the soul is the binding and unifying power that unifies them. This is implicit within its very name: *yechidah*, the singular one.[21]

YOM KIPPUR: 5 AFFLICTIONS

The expression of these 5 components of the soul comes to the fore on Yom Kippur, the Day of Atonement, when a Jew is spiritually cleansed from sin. This is accomplished through a withdrawal from the bodily urges that naturally lead to sin. The prohibition of the חֲמִשָּׁה עִנּוּיִים, *5 [bodily] afflictions*, refers to the abstinence from eating or drinking, washing the body, anointing the body, wearing leather shoes, and marital relations.[22] Symbolically, these 5 restrictions release the 5 components of man's soul from the shackles of his body. In touch with his true inner being, a Jew is elevated to the stature of an angel.[23]

These 5 restrictions release the 5 components of man's soul from the shackles of his body.

Additional incidences of 5 found in the context of this holy day include the 5 immersions of the High Priest during his special Temple sacrificial service[24] and his change of garments at 5 intervals.[25] The term *nefesh* (a general expression for the soul) is mentioned a total of 5 times in the Biblical passage regarding Yom Kippur.[26] And there are 5 prayers recited during the course of this day: Maariv, Shacharis, Mussaf, Minchah, and Ne'ilah.[27]

ALL WILL BE REVEALED

5

WE HAVE SEEN THAT THE UNIFYING 5TH COMPONENT OF THE SOUL centralizes the bodily forces that operate in the 4 directions by grouping them together in the service of G-d. Additionally, the soul is itself composed of 5 components. It therefore follows that the number 5 can be used as the *epitome of full expression* or of *a complete state of revelation*.

The number 5 can be used as the epitome of full expression or of a complete state of revelation.

Two important illustrations of this are how G-d originally reveals Himself through Creation and how G-d reveals Himself through His Torah. These respective forms of expression both make prominent use of the number 5 — in the 5th letter of the Hebrew alphabet that created This World and in the 5 Books of the Torah.

5: The World Revealed

G-d created *Olam Hazeh*, This World, with the 5th letter of the Hebrew alphabet: ה.[28] The purpose of the Creation was to enable G-d to be revealed. The medium through which He created This World was speech: "By the word of G-d the Heavens were made, and by the breath of His mouth all their hosts."[29] Actually, all speech begins with the 5th letter, *hei*, whose phonetic sound (*huh*) is associated with the exhalation of breath that precedes man's verbalizing any speech.[30]

Man reveals his innermost thoughts through his speech, articulating them to those outside of himself.

Man, like his Creator, is endowed with the faculty of speech — and, like his Creator, he reveals himself, his innermost thoughts, through his speech, articulating them to those who exist outside of himself.[31] It is in This World, created through the 5th letter of the Hebrew alphabet, that man can release his potential in the fulfillment of his Divine mission within Creation.[32]

Chumash: 5 Books of Torah

In addition to revealing Himself through Creation, G-d reveals His Will through Torah. Parallel to the "word of G-d" in the world's creation, which begins with the 5th letter, the Torah as the "word of G-d" similarly is connected to the number 5 in the חוּמָשׁ, *5 Books of Torah*.

G-d reveals His Will through Torah.

The 5 Books of Torah are בְּרֵאשִׁית, *Genesis*; שְׁמוֹת, *Exodus*; וַיִּקְרָא, *Leviticus*; בַּמִּדְבָּר, *Numbers*; and דְּבָרִים, *Deuteronomy*. There is a unique

A unique underlying common motif runs through each of these 5 Books.

The Chumash is the cornerstone of Jewish life and Torah study.

underlying common motif that runs through each of these 5 Books.[33] Together, they are inscribed onto a Torah Scroll. This serves as the basis for Jewish life and as the essential foundation of תּוֹרָה שֶׁבִּכְתָב, Written Torah.[34]

Everything is contained within the 5 books of the *Chumash*, which is the cornerstone of Jewish life and Torah study.[35] Indeed, a Jewish child traditionally starts studying the Written Torah from the age of 5.[36] Parallel to the Divine spark revealed through the 5 components in the human soul are the 5 Books of Torah,[37] which are the symbolic life force, or the soul of the universe.

The 5 Books of Torah were given over to the Jewish People. Of G-d's many creatures, man is the most beloved. Of all the nations in the world, the Jewish People is the most beloved.[38] The Midrash lists 5 Biblical expressions of love.[39] The title *Bnei Yisrael*, Children of Israel, is mentioned 5 times in the Torah in one verse.[40] This reflects their beloved status. While the highest of the 4 primary forms of creations is that of מְדַבֵּר, *articulate man*, there is an additional, more sublime 5th level: that of יִשְׂרָאֵל, *Yisrael*. In the spiritual hierarchy, the classification of "elite man" is reserved for the Chosen Nation entrusted with fulfillment of the 5 Books of Torah.[41]

5: SYMBOLS OF REVELATION

How G-d's reveals Himself in the Torah using the number 5 finds additional expression through various symbols used as vehicles of revelation. Three examples of this are *be'er*, wellspring; *kol*, voice; and *ohr*, light.

The water of the inner wellspring must be released from the depths so that it rises and emerges into the open.

WELLSPRING: The water of the inner wellspring hidden beneath the surface must be released from the depths so that it rises and emerges into the open. The 5 wells revealed by Yitzchak in the land of the Pelishtim correlate to the 5 Books of the Torah.[42]

In the giving of Torah, there was a 5-fold mention of the word קוֹל, *voice*.

VOICE: As mentioned earlier, a similar metaphor of revelation is found in speech, where man reveals his inner essence by outwardly verbalizing his innermost thoughts. In the giving of Torah at Sinai, there was a 5-fold mention of the word קוֹל, *voice*.[43] This finds broader expression in the record of how several Talmudic scholars (e.g., Rabbi Akiva,[44] Rabbi Yochanan ben Zakkai,[45] Rabbi Yehudah ben Bava[46]) each had 5 primary disciples. These students were active in the process of expounding the Torah teachings of their master — in other words, the revelation of Torah through speech.

LIGHT: An important metaphor of revelation is that of אוֹר, *light*.[47] The night darkens man's world. Shut off from the rest of the universe, blackness blinds man as it isolates him. There is no revelation — only concealment. Just as the internal soul must be revealed from within the external body that hides it, so too, must the light be drawn out of the darkness in order to witness its revelation. Often, the revelation of Torah is depicted in terms of *ohr*, light.[48] The word *ohr* is mentioned exactly 5 times on Day 1 of Creation,[49] which parallels the 5 Books of Torah.[50]

Often, the revelation of Torah is depicted in terms of ohr, light.

All this firmly establishes 5 and Torah as representative of how G-d's reveals His Will into the world.

HALF OF THE PICTURE

W E HAVE DISCUSSED HOW 5 GATHERS 4 DIVERGENT PARTS AND again binds them into one group — a task entrusted to the soul. This is what marks 5 as an appropriate medium to express a complete state of revelation. Nevertheless, the number 5 is often only "half of the picture."

5 doubles up on itself to form (2 x 5=) 10, which depicts a completely integrated whole.

A highly significant feature of 5 is that it doubles up on itself to form (2 x 5=) 10, which depicts a completely integrated whole.[51] Alternatively, 5 is the result when the complete set of 10 subdivides into 2 equal and opposite counterparts — lining up to make "2 halves of 1 whole." Illustrations of this find expression in man's hands and feet, each composed of 5 digits, the 10 Commandments engraved upon 2 Tablets of Stone, and the division of the 10 Plagues into 2 sets of 5.

5: ON THE ONE HAND

Each half of 10 represents an all-inclusive unit. The 5 fingers — as separate yet interconnected digits — complete a hand. Together, the coordination of the fingers on man's hand can effectively accomplish many activities. Yet they are only half of the complete set. Parallel to the 5 fingers of the right hand are the 5 fingers on the left. It is the interaction of the 10 fingers of both hands that enables man to carry out multiple functions. Similarly, the 5 toes on the right foot

Together, the fingers on man's hand can accomplish many activities. Yet they are only half of the complete set.

have their counterpart in the 5 toes on the left. It is through taking them together — using both his feet — that allows man to stand and function in a highly effective manner.

5: TABLET OF STONE

The 10 Commandments were engraved upon *Shnei Luchos Habris*, 2 Tablets of the Covenant. Significantly, they appeared upon 2 stones, not on 1. The division is evenly split into 5 commandments of מִצְוֹת שֶׁבֵּין אָדָם לַמָּקוֹם, *laws between man and G-d*, on the right Tablet and the 5 commandments of מִצְוֹת שֶׁבֵּין אָדָם לַחֲבֵרוֹ, *interpersonal laws*, on the left Tablet. Parallels abound illustrating how they precisely correlate to each other.[52]

The laws between man and G-d are considered more spiritually elevated vis-à-vis the interpersonal laws.

The laws between man and G-d are considered more spiritually elevated or "Heavenly" vis-à-vis the interpersonal laws. These, by contrast, are more "earthly," as they deal with issues that arise between people. This division into 5 "higher" commandments versus 5 "lower" commandments finds similar expression within the human anatomy: there are 5 essential organs (2 eyes, 2 ears, tongue) in the upper part of the body versus 5 organs (2 hands, 2 feet, male organ) in the lower part.[53]

5: HANDFUL OF PLAGUES

Each of the 10 Plagues that G-d brought upon the Egyptians was separately classified as the "finger of G-d."[54] By extension, the 10 Plagues can be divided into 2 sets: each group of 5 constitutes a "hand" composed of 5 digits.[55] There is an amazing correlation between the first 5 plagues and later 5 plagues. The blood of the river (plague 1), for example, corresponds to boils on the human body that afflicted the blood system (plague 6); the lice (plague 3) as insects on the ground parallel the locusts (plague 8) as insects from the sky, etc.

There is an amazing correlation between the first 5 plagues and later 5 plagues.

We earlier noted the division of the 10 Commandments and human anatomy into upper and lower components. This division of 10 into 2 sets of 5 is also found within the 10 Plagues. Here the first 5 plagues (Blood, Frogs, Lice, Wild Beasts, and Pestilence) affected the water, earth, and the animals roaming on Earth; namely, they were related to the lower realm. By contrast, the second 5 plagues (Boils, Hailstones, Locusts, Darkness, Death of the Firstborn) reflect the upper realm. Boils afflicted man, who belongs to the upper spiritual realm, and death of the firstborn removed the souls of human beings, who originate from the breath of G-d in the upper realm. Locusts were flying teeming creatures from the sky; darkness was the absence of sunlight, the sun belonging to the upper realm; and hailstones rained down from the sky.

Because the first 5 plagues relate to the lower realm, they were of a lower intensity. Here Pharaoh chose to harden his own heart. But he could not have naturally withstood the higher intensity of the latter 5 plagues, which related to the upper realm. Therefore, for the last 5 plagues, it was necessary for G-d to harden Pharaoh's heart.[56]

pARALLeL WORLĐS

We earlier noted that *Olam Hazeh*, This World, was created with the 5th letter of the Hebrew alphabet (*hei*). Just as 5 is only the halfway point to the completion within the number 10, This World is similarly only "half of the story." That is because man's existence cannot be narrowly restricted to the imperfect, temporary life of this natural world. There is the follow-up in the eternity of the hereafter. The world of *Olam Hazeh* finds its perfect parallel and its full completion in *Olam Haba*, World to Come, created with the 10th letter of the Hebrew alphabet (*yud*).[57] The World to Come is dependent upon what man accomplishes here in This World, which will determine the reward he is destined to inherit.[58]

So the 5th letter of This World is doubled up in the 10th letter of the World to Come. It is the future world that celebrates the full expression of man's true being in This World. And it lies within *Olam Haba* that the 5 parts of man's soul return home from their exile in the physical realm of *Olam Hazeh* to draw ever closer in the spiritual realm of G-d. Then, it will ultimately come to represent the full and complete picture.

Man's existence cannot be restricted to temporary life. There is the follow-up in the eternity of the hereafter.

NOTES

1. The number 4 represents an affront to G-d's Oneness and Singularity. See *Maharal: Gevuros Hashem* 60, *Ner Mitzvah*; see "4: Finding the Place."
2. *Maharal, Gevuros Hashem* 23; see also *Maharal, Chiddushei Aggados, Kesubos* 67b (Vol. 1, p. 155).

3. 5 is the smallest combination of the formative odd and even numbers (3+2=5) that join together to form a full group. 1 is not included as it is technically not a number (*Maharal, Derech Chaim* 3:6).

4. See "10: Top Ten."

5. This is adduced by the Mishnah from the verse, "He has established His bundle (*agudaso*) upon Earth" (*Amos* 9:6), with the resting of the *Shechinah* among a group of 5 (*Maharal, Derech Chaim* 3:6; see also *Maharal, Gevuros Hashem* 23 and 58.

6. *Maharal,* ibid. 23, *Chiddushei Aggados, Kesubos* 67b (Vol. 1, p. 155).

7. *Maharal, Derech Chaim* 5:1.

8. *Shemos Rabbah* 2:11.

9. The names were *Har HaElokim* (Mount of G-d), *Har Bashan* (Mount of Edible), *Har Gavnunim* (Mount of Unblemished Cheese), *Har Chorev* (Mount of Destruction), *Har Sinai* (Mount of Hatred). See *Shemos Rabbah* 2:4; see *Shabbos* 89a about the 5 names of the Wilderness in which the Children of Israel wandered.

10. *Maharal, Gevuros Hashem* 23. See *Yerushalmi, Taanis* 1:1; *Devarim Rabbah* 2:14.

11. See "4: Finding the Place."

12. *Shemos* 6:8.

13. *Mishnah Berurah* 480:10.

14. *Tanchuma, Pekudei* 3, as cited by *Rashi, Bereishis* 2:7; see *Sanhedrin* 38a-b.

15. *Bereishis* 2:8.

16. Significantly, the interrelationship between 4 and 5 on a 2-dimensional plane finds its fuller expression in the 3-dimensional world with the 6 directions similarly centralized around the 7th inner point as its spiritual center. See "6: It's Only Natural" and "7: A Holy Spark."

17. *Bereishis Rabbah* 14:9. See *Ramchal, Derech Hashem* 3:1:4. The lowest level of *nefesh*, for example, is associated with the blood system whose circulation enables all limbs to function (*Devarim* 12:23). Above this, there is the *ruach* that maps to man's emotional state and the faculty of speech (see *Targum, Bereishis* 2:7). A higher level is the *neshamah* that links to the mind and the thought process. Finally, the last two levels of *chayah* and *yechidah* are so lofty that they envelop man; they are considered to be too holy to be contained within his body. The life force related to 5 may be related to David giving Yoav 5 curses for his cold-blooded assassination of Avner by striking him in the 5th rib and causing the life force to leave his body (see *II Shmuel* 3:27-29, *Sanhedrin* 48b-49a. See also *Rokeach, Devarim* 19:7-8).

18. *Rambam, Shemonah Perakim* 1.

19. *Tehillim* 103-104. See *Berachos* 10a. These phrases about which he praised G-d, were (1) residing within his mother's womb, (2) his emergence from the womb to gaze upon the constellations, (3) being nursed by his mother, (4) the downfall of wicked, (5) regarding the day of death.

20. See *Pnei Yehoshua, Berachos* 10a; R' Tzadok HaKohen, *Sichos Malachei HaShareis* pp. 46-49.

21. See *Tehillim* 22:21, *Bamidbar Rabbah* 17:2. This refers to a kabbalistic level where everything is of an absolute Unity.

22. See *Mishnah, Yoma* 8:1 and *Rashi, Yoma* 73b

23. See *Maharal, Derashah l'Shabbos Shuvah* pp. 81-82, who connects the 5 afflictions of Yom Kippur with the 5 components of the human soul.

24. See *Mishnah, Yoma* 3:3.

25. See *Rashi, Vayikra* 16:4; *Yoma* 32a.

26. *Vayikra* 23:26-32.

27. See *Baal HaTurim, Vayikra* 23:27.

28. *Menachos* 29b. "When they were created" (בְּהִבָּרְאָם); this word is written in a manner that means "with [the letter] *hei*, they were created." Another association of the letter *hei* is related to the concept of "giving" (see *Bereishis* 47:23), with Creation as the giving of life being the ultimate level of giving.

29. *Tehillim* 33:6.

30. *Maharal, Gevuros Hashem* 61. Additionally, the 5th letter is used as the prefix -הַ (*ha-*) in the Hebrew language to depict *hei hayediah, the* definite article. It defines something by providing its definitive description. It is the precise act of specification that is accurately used to fully reveal its essence. The *hei hayediah* is then used to reveal what becomes the well-known example (see *Maharal, Ohr Chadash, Esther* 1:1, p. 72). This is why 5 is often identified as a number affiliated with *din*, judgment, that is similarly based upon definite boundaries of following the letter of the law within which one must operate. See *Maharal, Netzach Yisrael* 23.
31. There are 5 origins of speech in the phonetic families: (1) gutturals, (2) labials, (3) palatals, (4) linguals, and (5) dentals. See *Sefer Yetzirah* 2:3.
32. An alternative description of the act of Creation is the anthropomorphic use of G-d's "hand" as in the verse: "My hand has established the foundation of the Earth, and My right hand has spread out the Heavens" (*Yeshayah* 48:13). The human hand is composed of 5 fingers (see "500: Reach for the Sky") and is the physical, active instrument that man wields to reveal himself and implement his will in the world.
33. See *Ramban*, Opening Introductions to 5 Books of the *Chumash*, for how בְּרֵאשִׁית, *Genesis,* contains the Creation narrative and relates the lives of the Jewish forefathers in the creation of Israel. שְׁמוֹת, *Exodus*, records the redemption of the Jewish People from their exile in Egypt to receive the Torah at Sinai and the building of the Mishkan, Sanctuary, to house the *Shechinah*, Divine Presence, that would dwell in their midst. וַיִּקְרָא, *Leviticus*, focuses upon the laws of *Kohanim* and *Leviim* in the matters concerning sacrificial offerings and "guarding of the Sanctuary." בַּמִדְבָּר, *Numbers*, documents the travails in the Wilderness (and the relevant laws). דְּבָרִים, *Deuteronomy*, also termed *Mishneh Torah*, Repetition of Torah, was said by Moshe to the generation about to enter the Holy Land.
34. See *Ramban*, Introduction to *Sefer Bereishis.*
35. Moshe gave Israel 5 Books of Torah; David gave Israel 5 Books of *Tehillim* (*Midrash Socher Tov* 1:2).
36. *Pirkei Avos* 5:25.
37. *Maharal, Derech Chaim* 2:9.
38. *Pirkei Avos* 3:14. See also *Shir HaShirim Rabbah* 1:19.
39. *Bereishis Rabbah* 80:7 The 5 expressions of love correspond to the 5 components of the soul. See R' Yitzchak Isaac Chaver, *Yad Mitzrayim Haggadah.*
40. *Bamidbar* 8:18-19. See *Rashi* ad loc.
41. R' Yehudah Halevi, *Kuzari* 1:31-47 and 2:44.
42. *Bereishis Rabbah* 64:8. See "48: Stay Connected."
43. *Shemos* 19:16-19. There are 5 voices similarly mentioned in terms of marriage (*Yirmiyah* 33:11). See *Berachos* 6b, which explains that the reward for rejoicing before a bride and bridegroom is to merit Torah that was given with 5 "voices." See *Maharal, Tiferes Yisrael* 30 for how חֲמִשָּׁה, 5, has the same letters as שִׂמְחָה, happiness. It is through marriage that a bridegroom attains a "complete level of perfection."
44. *Yevamos* 62b
45. *Pirkei Avos* 2:8
46. *Sanhedrin* 13b-14a
47. Light is synonymous with existence and revelation, in contradistinction to darkness that is associated with nonexistence. See, for example, *Maharal, Tiferes Yisrael* 47, *Derech Chaim* 3:14.
48. See "36: See the Light."
49. *Bereishis* 1:3-5
50. *Bereishis Rabbah* 3:5. See *Maharal, Netzach Yisrael* 17 as to how *ohr*, light, is itself related to the number 5.
51. See "10: Top Ten."
52. *Mechilta, Bo* 8. See *Rashi, Shir HaShirim* 4:5.
53. *Maharal, Derech Chaim* 2:7. The basic distance between Heaven and Earth is symbolized in the num-

ber 10. It is the human being, himself composed of both Heavenly and earthly components, who has within him 10 corresponding components. Another representation is how the 5 digits of each hand find their parallel in the 5 digits of each foot.

54. See *Shemos* 8:15 concerning the Egyptian magicians' inability to duplicate the plague of lice.

55. "With a strong hand" (*Devarim* 26:8) refers to the [5th plague of] pestilence (*Haggadah shel Pesach*).

56. *Maharal, Gevuros Hashem* 31 and 56. See *Rambam, Shemonah Perakim* 8 for a discussion of the Divine retribution visited upon Pharaoh and his loss of free will.

57. *Menachos* 29b

58. See "310: Worlds Apart."

6
IT'S ONLY NATURAL

6 represents full physical expression in the natural world.

It denotes man's physical achievements in the 6 directions of the world, created in 6 days.

When used properly, it shows us the physical route to the spiritual destination.

THE NATURAL WORLD

Existence in the physical realm finds expression within the dimensions of time and space.

THE NUMBER 6 IS THE SYMBOL OF THE NATURAL WORLD.

Existence in the physical realm finds expression within the dimensions of time and space — both of which are closely connected with 6. This is seen in the units of time that unfolded in the 6 Days of Creation, and how space unfolds fully into the 6 directions.

6: DAYS OF CREATION

The Torah begins with a brief description of Creation. G-d created the natural world in 6 days. On the first day He created light and separated light from darkness, the second day saw the division of the Earth and Heaven, while the third day witnessed the emergence of plants and vegetation. The Heavenly luminaries were created on the fourth day, the fish and birds on the fifth day, and on the sixth day, the animal kingdom and then man. [1]

The weekly cycle follows this template: 6 days of the week culminating in the 7th day of rest.

Once it was all complete, the Torah records that G-d rested on the 7th day.[2] Into this time framework, He placed all of His creations. The weekly cycle continuously follows this template: 6 days of the week culminating in the 7th day of rest.

6: ACTIVITY AND LABOR

Like G-d's activity in the formation of existence, man similarly expresses himself through his activities throughout the week.

The 6 Days of Creation are the self-contained period of מְלָאכָה, *labor,* or of עֲבוֹדָה, *work.*[3] Like G-d's activity in the formation of existence, man similarly expresses himself through the activities he conducts throughout the days of the week. This serves as the preliminary passage of time necessary to approach Shabbos. This is why Shabbos is repeatedly described as the event that naturally follows the 6 days of labor that precede it.[4]

The weekdays, which are the שֵׁשֶׁת יְמֵי הַמַּעֲשֶׂה, *6 days of activity,*[5] are the framework of time in which man's deeds are meant to leave their mark. Typically, man creates a lasting impression in the universe by using his body, which can be subdivided into 6 major parts:

the eyes, ears, mouth, heart, legs, and hands.[6] In these 6 days, and with these 6 parts, man is obligated to complete all his work prior to reaching his point of rest — Shabbos, where the Jew finally arrives at his destination.

This is reflected also in the agricultural cycle of the Land of Israel. The Jewish farmer toils in his field or vineyard for 6 consecutive years. He exerts the greatest efforts to cultivate the soil in the Holy Land so that the ground will yield its produce. Then he ceases agricultural operations on *Shemittah*, the 7th Sabbatical year.[7]

This same structure finds expression in the laws of Jewish servitude. When sold into slavery as a bondsman, the Jewish servant must serve his master for a period of 6 years and is set free in the 7th year.[8] His servitude lasts for a total of 6 consecutive years — but not into the 7th year.

The Jewish servant must serve his master for a period of 6 years and is set free in the 7th year.

PHYSICAL COMPLETION

THE FULL PHYSICAL EXPRESSION OF THE NATURAL WORLD, CREATED IN 6 Days of Creation, is reflected in the number 6. It is the epitome of *gashmiyus*, corporeality, and symbol of *sheleimus*, completion, in terms of finding expression within the material environment.

The number 6 is the epitome of gashmiyus and symbol of sheleimus.

6 DIRECTIONS: physical world

Just as the material world was fashioned in 6 days of Creation, the physical environment finds its full extension in 6 directions.[9]

The number 4 defines a two-dimensional "place" in terms of length and width.[10] There are 4 directions toward which an object can expand upon a horizontal plane: forward, backward, left, and right. The number 6 defines three-dimensional "place" in terms of length, width, and depth. Here there are a total of 6 directions toward which an object can expand: forward, backward, left, right, up and down.[11]

There are a total of 6 directions toward which an object can expand

6 SIDES: CUBE

Every solid object in the three-dimensional physical world can be spatially referenced by means of the aforementioned 6 directions.[12] Graphically, this is best represented in the shape of a cube whose surface area comprises a total of 6 faces.

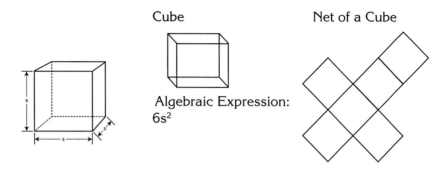

Cube

Algebraic Expression:
$6s^2$

Net of a Cube

6 reaches a state of completeness in its ability to fully represent the expression of reality within the natural world.

Due to the fact that there are 6 all-encompassing sides in the natural world, this number stands as the epitome of *gashmiyus*, corporeality.[13] That ability to incorporate all sides and directions on Earth means that 6 is the number used to denote the attainment of *sheleimus*, completion, in the physical realm. Here it reaches a state of completeness in its ability to fully represent the expression of reality within the natural world.[14]

6: EQUILIBRIUM

A central characteristic of the physical world is the characteristic of evenness or equilibrium. There is a delicate but harmonious balance within the 3-dimensions of Creation. Every one of the 6 directions is the balance of opposing counterparts — forward versus backward, left versus right, up versus down.[15]

The equilibrium of 6 finds memorable expression in its mathematical properties. The first three numbers, 1, 2, 3, are equal to 6 whether one adds or multiplies them.

$$1 + 2 + 3 = 6$$
$$1 \times 2 \times 3 = 6$$

Being equal to the sum of its factors, 6 is characterized as a "perfect number." Another interesting mathematical quality is that 6 is the total sum of its divisible components.

$6 \div 2 = 3,$
$6 \div 3 = 2,$
$6 \div 6 = 1; \qquad 3 + 2 + 1 = 6$

Such a phenomenon is not found with other divisible numbers such as 4 or 8.[16]

$4 \div 2 = 2,$
$4 \div 2 = 2,$
$4 \div 4 = 1; \qquad 2 + 2 + 1 = 5.$

$8 \div 2 = 4$
$8 \div 4 = 2$
$8 \div 8 = 1 \qquad 4 + 2 + 1 = 7$

The equilibrium of 6 — where the opposites of directions in the physical world consolidate and complete each other — is similarly evident in the 6 Days of Creation that can also be joined in pairs: the first 3 days correlate with the second 3 days. The light of Day 1 parallels the luminaries of Day 4, the water division of the Day 2 was occupied by fish and birds on Day 5 and the dry land and vegetation created on the Day 3 received its animal and human inhabitants on Day 6.[17] Additionally, the natural cycle divides into 6 seasons with the climates evenly balanced during the year (each season occupying 2 months): sowing and harvest, cold and heat, summer and winter.[18]

This balance of opposing forces is inwardly expressed within man — the climax of G-d's universe who was created on Day 6 of Creation. Man is a composite of body and soul. He stands perfectly poised. He was not fashioned to be naturally drawn more toward the pursuits of the body than to that of the soul. Had he been more inclined to either direction, it would unsettle or destabilize the purpose of his existence.[19] Because he is faced with two conflicting drives, he has the opportunity to exert his free will. He must live with his body within the physical world, but focus his efforts on spirituality in the service of G-d.

This balance of opposing forces is inwardly expressed within man. Faced with two conflicting drives, he has the opportunity to exert his free will.

SHEMA YISRAEL: 6 WORDS

In a 3-dimensional plane, a cube joins 6 sides of the same object into 1 entity. In truth, one looking at it from the outside cannot possibly see all of its 6 sides at once. Still, by observing it from all directions, he can rightly conclude that they are all part of the same single reality.

This, too, is true of the physical world. The different elements integrate to form one reality. Every side contributes and is combined into the equation. This concept is vividly brought out in the opening phrase of *Shema*: שְׁמַע יִשְׂרָאֵל ה׳ אֱלֹהֵינוּ ה׳ אֶחָד, *Hear O Israel, HASHEM is our G-d, HASHEM is the One and Only,*[20] This verse, specifically composed of 6 words, beautifully emphasizes how all of reality, like the 6 directions of the physical realm, is actually part of the same integrated reality — under the unified rule of G-d.[21] And this has a corresponding 6-word statement of בָּרוּךְ שֵׁם כְּבוֹד מַלְכוּתוֹ לְעוֹלָם וָעֶד, *Blessed be the Name of His glorious Kingdom forever and ever.*[22]

BIRTH OF ISRAEL: 6 CHILDREN IN ONE

The number 6, which expresses how the 6 directions form a singular reality under G-d's control, is mirrored in the nature of Israel. The Jewish People are also called "a unique nation on Earth"[23] and are the ones who proclaim G-d as the 1 G-d[24] through reciting the 6 words of *Shema*.

Israel's development to nationhood is intrinsically related to this number. The Torah describes how the more the Egyptians afflicted Israel, the more the Jewish people grew and multiplied.[25] The use of 6 words to recount that the Children of Israel multiplied teaches that each woman gave birth to 6 children at once. [26]

This represented the ideological bid by the Jewish mothers to attain national oneness and completion, as symbolized in the number 6. The inclusion of all sides in the number 6 implies a state of completeness. This led to the proliferation of Israel into a complete and self-contained nation composed of an expanded ultimate expression of 6: the 600,000 souls that left Egypt.[27]

6TH DAY: SHAVUOS

Only with the formation of man on Day 6 of Creation would the physical world finally be complete. Man was entrusted to operate within the natural order, to work the physical world, and in so doing to realize his perfection, and by extension, perfect the world. Still, the fate of the 6 Days of Creation was suspended pending the historic consequence of Shavuos more than two millennia in the future.

In the account of Creation, the emphasis using the definite article הַ, *the*, in the phrase יוֹם הַשִּׁשִּׁי, *the 6th day*,[28] hints to a future 6th day that would be of major significance. This is an implicit reference to Shavuos, whose date in the Jewish calendar is the 6th day in the month of Sivan. On that day the future of the universe tentatively hung in the balance. Had the Children of Israel not embraced the Torah, G-d would have invalidated the cosmos. Existence would have

This verse of 6 words emphasizes how all of reality, like the 6 directions of the physical realm, is part of the same integrated reality — under the unified rule of G-d.

The use of 6 words to recount that the Children of Israel multiplied teaches that each woman gave birth to 6 children at once.

Man was entrusted to operate within the natural order, to realize his perfection, and perfect the world.

returned to nonexistence. Consequently, the national acceptance of Torah on the 6th of Sivan finally gave completion to the physical realm originally formed during the 6 days of Creation.[29]

MISHNAH: 6 ORDERS

The Torah, which gives permanence to the world, is divided into *Torah Shebichsav*, Written Torah, and the *Torah Sheba'al Peh*, Oral Torah. The classic representation of these complementary parts lies in the numbers 5 and 6 respectively.

The most sacred text within the Written Torah is the *Chumash*, 5 Books [of Torah], that is the life and soul of Torah.[30] Still, it cannot be studied in isolation. It is impossible to deduce the practical application of Jewish law from the terse and sometimes opaque language of the Written Torah. It therefore demands the constant accompaniment of Oral Torah, which contains the traditional interpretations passed down through the generations that clarify, explain, and expound the laws, principles, and details.

The Oral Torah contains the traditional interpretations that clarify, explain, and expound the laws, principles, and details.

The primary text of the Oral Torah is שִׁשָּׁה סִדְרֵי מִשְׁנָה, *6 Orders of the Mishnah*. This was formulated by Rabbi Yehudah the Prince, who arranged its redaction. His decision to record in writing the entire corpus of the Oral Torah was in order that its transmission would not be forgotten. The Mishnah is arranged into 6 orders: (1) זְרָעִים, *Seeds* (agricultural laws); (2) מוֹעֵד, *Festivals* (laws of Shabbos and Festivals); (3) נָשִׁים, *Women*; (4) נְזִיקִין, *Damages*; (5) קָדָשִׁים, *Sanctities* (laws about Temple and sacrificial offerings); (6) טָהֳרוֹת, *Purities* (laws of ritual purity and impurity). This is based upon a corresponding 6 phrases found within a verse in *Yeshayah*.[31]

His decision to record the corpus of the Oral Torah was so that its transmission would not be forgotten.

The symbolism of 6 as the epitome of revelation in time and space finds exquisite expression in the exposition of the Torah laws to be enacted in the physical realm. And it taps into G-d exclusively entering a covenant with Israel — whose growth was through the number 6 — in the merit of *Torah Sheba'al Peh*[32] that is arranged in 6 orders.

AT 6S AND 7S

THE INTERRELATIONSHIP BETWEEN 6 AND 7 HAS GREAT IMPORTANCE. The accomplishments of 6 in the physical world must always be

The accomplishments of 6 chart the upward journey from chol to kodesh.

directed toward a spiritual end. This charts the upward journey from *chol*, mundane, to *kodesh*, holiness. Conversely, it is essential there should not be a downward regression in the opposite direction.

6 TO 7: PATH TO HOLINESS

The 6 units of activity are symbolic of direction. By contrast, the resting place of the 7th is indicative of the arrival. 6 can be likened to the חֹמֶר, *material*, that must find its צוּרָה, *form*, in the number 7 with its related holy connotations.[33]

The labor of the 6 days of the week are exclusively enacted in preparation for arriving at the final destination: Olam Haba.

The labor of the 6 days of the week symbolizes *Olam Hazeh*, This World. These activities are exclusively enacted in preparation for arriving at the final destination: namely, to enter *Olam Haba*, the World to Come, that is termed "the day that is completely Shabbos."[34]

Whereas This World of 6 directions is the arena for human activity, this is inconsequential unless and until it is directed toward a higher purpose. Once sanctioned by G-d, it now takes on a different form: it becomes the conduit for *kedushah*, holiness. Man readily admits he is not the master of the world — G-d is. Consequently, man willingly relinquishes ownership by ceasing from all work on the 7th. He rests on the 7th Day, Shabbos, and during the 7th Sabbatical year. In fact, his labor is dedicated toward spiritual pursuits.

Havdalah will assist 6 in its path to be the definitive direction en route to spirituality.

It is therefore imperative to clearly differentiate between 7 and 6. The end of the 7th day, Shabbos, necessitates *Havdalah*, separation. This ritual, performed on *Motza'ei Shabbos,* Saturday night, at the conclusion of Shabbos, is necessary to distinguish between "what is holy to what is mundane, light and darkness, Israel and the other nations, the 7th day to the 6 days of activity."[35] This reminder will assist 6 in its path to be the definitive direction en route to spirituality.

NOTES

1. *Bereishis* 1:1-31.
2. Ibid. 2:1-3.
3. See "39: Under Development."
4. *Shemos* 23:12, 35:2, *Vayikra* 23:3; *Devarim* 5:12-13.
5. See *Yechezkel* 46:1; *Havdalah*; see also *Shemos* 23:12.
6. *Maharal*, *Tiferes Yisrael* 55. See *Tanchuma*, *Toldos* 21 (Buber) who lists the same items while substitut-

ing the nose instead of the heart. The *Ramban* (*HaEmunah V'HaBitachon* 4) lists them as the head, 2 arms, 2 legs, and the male organ.

7. *Vayikra* 25:3-7.
8. *Shemos* 21:2, *Devarim* 15:12.
9. *Maharal, Gevuros Hashem* 46.
10. See "4: Finding the Place."
11. "Man was created on the 6th day because this is where he emerged to stand upright and move in all 6 directions" (*Rabbeinu Bachya, Bereishis* 1:31).
12. *Maharal, Gevuros Hashem* 3. It is noteworthy that the measuring yardstick in the physical world is an *amah*, cubit, that is usually made up of 6 *tefachim*, handbreadths.
13. *Maharal, Be'er HaGolah* 6[4], p. 112b.
14. *Maharal, Gevuros Hashem* 12. See *Esther Rabbah* 1:10 as to how there are 6 names used in reference to 6 realms of the land.
15. See "2: Opposite and Equal."
16. *Maharal, Derech Chaim* 2:14 quoting *Ibn Ezra, Shemos* 3:15. See also *Maharal, Chiddushei Aggados, Shabbos* 55a, p. 31.
17. *Bereishis Rabbah* 11:8 and 12:5. See *Maharal, Derashah L'Shabbos HaGadol* 198b.
18. *Bereishis* 8:22 and *Rashi* ad loc., citing *Bava Metzia* 106b.
19. *Maharal, Derech Chaim* 2:14.
20. *Devarim* 6:4. See "1: The One and Only."
21. *Maharal, Gevuros Hashem* 12.
22. See R' Chaim Volozhin, *Nefesh HaChaim* 3:6. See "24: The Division of Labor."
23. *II Shmuel* 7:23.
24. See "1: The One and Only."
25. *Shemos* 1:12.
26. Ibid. 1:7. *Maharal, Gevuros Hashem* 12. The *Maharal* also explains the symbolism of the other opinions, including 12, 60, or an unlimited number. He explains that this refers to the Jewish women's ability to bear these numbers of children.
27. "6 is the perfect number to symbolize the Jewish people who numbered 600,000" (*Maharal, Gevuros Hashem* 3, 12). See "600,000: The Jewish Nation."
28. *Bereishis* 1:31.
29. *Shabbos* 88a cited in *Rashi, Bereishis* 1:31.
30. See "5: Give Me Five."
31. "Your faithful times shall bring [you] strength, salvation, wisdom, and insight" (*Yeshayah* 33:6). "Faithful" — this is S*eder Zeraim*; "Times" — this is *Seder Moed*; "Strength" — this is *Seder Nashim*; "Salvation" — this is *Seder Nezikin*; "Wisdom" — this is *Seder Kodshim*; "Insight" — this is *Seder Tohoros* (*Shabbos* 31a).
32. *Gittin* 60b; See R' Yitzchak Hutner, *Pachad Yitzchak, Chanukah* 1.
33. See "39: Under Development" and "40: True to Form."
34. *Sanhedrin* 97a. See *Ramchal, Mesillas Yesharim* 1.
35. *Havdalah* prayer.

7
A holy spark

7 is the inner spiritual spark.

It infuses holiness into the natural
world of 6 directions that
bound the physical realm .

It is the all-encompassing number
that celebrates the sacred purpose
of a Jew to infuse holiness
into the whole of Creation.

THE BELOVED NUMBER

*The number
7 is infused
with the inner
7th point as
the spark of
holiness.*

OF ALL THE NUMBERS IN JUDAISM, 7 IS BY FAR THE MOST UBIQUITOUS. In the words of the Midrash, "All 7s are beloved."[1]

The number 7 contains two interrelated themes. It is the symbol of the natural world in its totality. And it is where the entire physical world of 6 directions is infused with the inner 7th point as the spark of holiness.

7: The NATURAL WORLD

*The completion
of the world
in 7 days
parallels the 7
primary Sefiros
to embrace the
natural realm.*

The standard means used to reference time is as a cycle of 7 units. This is typified in a week composed of 7 days. The Torah opens by relating the genesis of the universe. G-d "labored" during the first 6 Days of Creation and rested on the 7th: the Day of Shabbos.[2] These are termed the "7 pillars of Creation."[3] The completion of the world in 7 days parallels the 7 primary *Sefiros*, Divine Emanations (which are also called *middos*, Divine Attributes)[4] to embrace the whole natural realm.[5]

*The number 7
is the symbolic
"distance" of
the intervals
that typically
separate two
points.*

The natural world is identified with the number 7 both as the full scale of existence and as the all-embracing distance between extremities.[6] There are 7 notes in an octave as the full scale of musical expression. In rabbinic literature, the natural world is said to encompass 7 deserts, 7 lands,[7] 7 rivers, 7 seas,[8] and 7 mountains.[9] In the corresponding Heavenly realm, there are 7 Heavenly firmaments[10] and 7 primary stars[11] where the constellations are arranged in 7 formations.[12] Just as the full extent of a week stretches across 7 days, so too, is the number 7 the symbolic "distance" of the natural space or intervals that typically separate two points.[13]

7: IN FULL

In its physical composition, the natural realm is one of multiplicity. This explains why 7 is commonly used as the prototype of רִבּוּי, many (e.g., "A righteous person falls 7 times — only to rise again.”[14]).[15] Parallel to the Days of Creation, 7 relates to the whole spectrum within the universe where the natural world finally arrives at a state of completion. Here one sees the world “in full.”[16] This concept is reflected in the word שֶׁבַע, 7, which is cognate to שׂוֹבַע, *satisfaction*, to denote the situation where one has finally attained one’s fill.[17]

Hence 7 is the full range of the natural realm.[18] (This concept finds further expression in the number 49 [as the square of 7][19] and in the number 70.[20]) Traditionally, there are a total of 7 natural wisdoms within Creation, which are alluded to in the 7 branches of the Menorah.[21] The illumination of this knowledge, like the lights of the Menorah, is accessible to all of mankind.[22] It marks the fullest expression or extent of the natural realm.

7 natural wisdoms within Creation are alluded to in the 7 branches of the Menorah.

The word שְׁבוּעָה, *oath*, is etymologically related to שֶׁבַע, 7. The function of a vow is to impose or to reinforce a commitment. It creates a lasting and enduring set of circumstances. This is contained within 7 as the number used to establish something as rigid and permanent.[23] When Avraham and Avimelech struck a covenant after their dispute regarding the wells, 7 sheep were used to formalize their agreement and the location is named בְּאֵר שֶׁבַע (literally, *well of oath* or *well of seven [sheep]*.[24]

An additional application is how 7 represents man’s preservation of the natural order. The primeval man was originally instructed by G-d with 7 commandments.[25] Similarly, mankind was entrusted with the universally binding ז׳ מִצְוֹת בְּנֵי נֹחַ, *7 Noachide Laws*.[26] Their purpose was to create the necessary framework to preserve the natural order, to maintain human civilization, and to prevent it from deteriorating into anarchy by guaranteeing its continual existence.[27]

The universally binding Noachide Laws created the necessary framework to maintain human civilization.

7: THE COMPLETE SERIES

There are numerous examples scattered throughout Torah literature where 7 is used as the number symbolizing units that together form a complete series.

7 is the number symbolizing units that together form a complete series.

Here is a small sampling: 7 sons (Naomi considered Ruth better than 7 sons[28]), 7 daughters (Yisro[29]), 7 advisers (Achashverosh[30]), 7 relatives with whose corpse a *Kohen* is permitted to come into contact,[31] 7 maidservants (Queen Esther[32]), 7 sheep (in the covenant struck between Avimelech and Avraham in Be’er Sheva[33]), 7 names (for Yisro,[34] for the *Yetzer Hara*, Evil Inclination,[35]), and 7-fold punishments (to the killer of Kayin,[36]) stages of national tragedy,[37] mishaps to the world[38]). There are historical recorded periods of 7 days (G-d waited before the Great Flood,[39] after which Noach dispatched the dove to survey the landscape;[40] Moshe argued with G-d before being appointed Jewish leader;[41] the duration of each of the plagues in Egypt;[42] etc.), and the 7-year period (Yaakov worked for Lavan to marry Rachel and then again 7 years after being tricked by Lavan;[43] the years of plenty and famine in Egypt as Yosef interpreted Pharaoh's dream[44]).

IT'S HOLY

7 is the determining number to depict kedushah.

WE HAVE NOTED 7 AS THE ESSENTIAL PARTS THAT DESCRIBE THE world in its completed, finished state. In truth, the true picture is only finally attained where the outer physical world is continuously in synch with the unifying inner spiritual point within. This, too, is epitomized in 7 as the determining number to depict *kedushah*, "holiness."

Every area of Jewish living has to relate to the designated *kedushah* as fully embodied within the number 7.[45] (In the context of a communal whole, the *kedushah* is found in the number 10.[46]) Here the number *7 is part of the physical world as well as the sanctified component within it.*[47]

7: THE INNER CORE

Holiness requires taking the multiplicity of 7 and organizing it so that the 6 physical directions relate to the 7th spiritual spark.

The Jewish People are tasked with infusing the universe with holiness. What does this involve? It requires taking the full range or multiplicity of 7 within the natural world and organizing it so that the 6 physical directions relate inwardly to the 7th spiritual spark as the inner core or epicenter within.

Just as the 4 directions that branch out onto a 2-dimensional plane are centralized by the 5th central point,[48] so, too, are the 6 directions in the 3-dimensional plane the epitome of the physical world (body) that contains within it the spiritual Divine force (soul) as its inner root.[49] The Heavenly source of this inner G-dly, so to speak, component enters and animates the physical world. This can be graphically depicted by the inner point of a 6-faced cube.

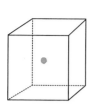
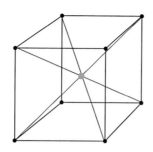
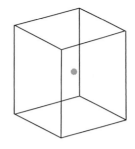

The image of 6 inward-facing points toward the 7th center is similarly found in the Menorah, candelabrum, made up of 6 branches emerging from the sides of a 7th center core.[50] Of the 7 lamps kindled on the Menorah,[51] the flames of the 6 branches miraculously turned inward to face the center branch.[52] In the Wilderness, 6 of the *Ananei HaKavod*, Clouds of Glory, enveloped the Children of Israel whose position took center stage as the 7th inner point.[53] The *Arba Minim*, 4 Species, taken on Succos, are waved in all 6 directions from the 7th central point, which is the person himself.[54] So 7 represents the spiritual locus.[55]

7 represents the spiritual locus.

A HOLY NATION

KEDUSHAH IS WHERE THE CHILDREN OF ISRAEL WHOLLY IDENTIFY themselves with G-d to live a sanctified state of existence. This preoccupation takes center stage in their lives. It separates and elevates them from the mundane. Both G-d and His Chosen Nation are termed *kadosh*, holy. The prophet declared, "There is none as holy as G-d."[56] And the Jewish People are sanctified by G-d and described as "the Holy People, the Redeemed of G-d."[57] Israel must be holy because their G-d is Holy.[58]

Both G-d and His Chosen Nation are termed kadosh, holy.

Holiness is the sacred heritage of the Jewish people. This is clearly manifest in their holy foundations and homeland, which, not surprisingly, are affiliated with the number 7.

7: holy foundations

The ancestors of the Children of Israel were the 3 Patriarchs (Avraham, Yitzchak, Yaakov) and 4 Matriarchs (Sarah, Rivkah, Rachel,

Leah). Together, they made up the 7 holy ancestors of Israel.[59] In addition, there were 7 generations from Avraham to Moshe until the giving of Torah to the entire Jewish nation.[60]

In terms of leadership, there were 7 holy "shepherds of Israel."[61] The Talmud numbers 7 prophetesses whose prophecies were recorded for the Jewish People for posterity.[62] There were 7 righteous individuals who were responsible for returning the *Shechinah*, Divine Presence.[63] There were 7 meritorious people who had their offering accepted.[64] There were 7 born circumcised.[65] There are 7 great personalities identified as the 7 *ushpizin*, guests, associated with the 7 days of Succos.[66] And the time continuum of This World spans 7 personalities beginning with Adam and culminating in Eliyahu, who will herald the Messianic Era.[67]

The time continuum spans 7 personalities beginning with Adam and culminating in Eliyahu.

7: HOLY LAND

Just as 7, the inner point, is surrounded by the 6 outer directions, Eretz Yisrael is the epicenter of holiness here on Earth.

The ideal habitat for the Holy Nation that was sanctified to G-d is the holiest country in the world: *Eretz Yisrael*, Land of Israel. Just as 7 is the inner point surrounded by the 6 outer directions, *Eretz Yisrael* is the epicenter of holiness here on Earth. This is where the Holy Nation is best situated to serve the Holy One.

The superiority of the Jewish homeland is such that even a lesser city (Chevron) was praised 7-fold relative to an Egyptian city (Tzoan).[68] It is celebrated by being blessed with the distinctive שִׁבְעַת הַמִּינִים, *7 species*, for which the Land of Israel is renowned: namely wheat, barley, grapes, figs, pomegranates, olives, and dates.[69] In its description, the word *eretz*, land, is mentioned 7 times.[70] The special 7 species are typically given precedence in the order of eating.[71]

A LIFE OF HOLINESS

7 is also the means to acquire that holiness.

JEWISH LIFE IS SUFFUSED WITH HOLINESS. NOT ONLY IS 7 THE SYMBOL of holiness; it is also the means of *how* to acquire that holiness.

Here 7 stands as the *essential number of parts, objects, times, or occasions necessary* to attain a special state of sanctity.[72] Indeed, the concept of holiness within the number 7 permeates the full length and breadth of Jewish life.

7: Shabbos and Cycles of Time

The 7 days of the week culminate in Shabbos, as Creation proudly proclaims the mastery of its Creator. Often characterized as *Shabbos Kodesh*, the holy Sabbath,[73] as a day "holy to G-d,"[74] man (together with all 7 parties of his household[75]) sets aside his work and weekly pursuits to spend the day sanctifying all his activities.[76] He consecrates this 7th day by reciting *Kiddush* (literally, sanctification, related to the word *kedushah*,) over a cup of wine. During Shabbos day, there are a minimum of 7 men called up to read the Torah portion.[77]

Shabbos functions as the "inner 7th point" that unifies the week into a complete unit and elevates the natural symbol of 6 by fully connecting to its inner spiritual dimension.[78] As the endpoint, Shabbos is a semblance of *Olam Haba*, the World to Come. This is the point of arrival — in the attainment of sanctity.

The Jewish Festivals are termed מִקְרָאֵי קֹדֶשׁ, *calling forth of holiness*.[79] Of the 3 Pilgrimage Festivals, both Pesach and Succos last for 7 days, with the Festivals' laws (not eating *chametz*, dwelling in a *succah*) observed during this period.[80] (Due to the original uncertainty in the Diaspora of the appearance of the new moon, an 8-day festival is observed outside of the Land of Israel until today). Though Shavuos does not last for 7 days, its name refers to the *shavuos*, weeks, in the cycle of 7 weeks of 7 days counted in the interval between Pesach and Shavuos.[81]

The holiness of Shabbos and the Jewish festivals is particularly evident in the formulation of the *Amidah* with its 7 blessings — with the central, inner blessing describing קְדֻשַּׁת הַיּוֹם, the *Day's Holiness*.[82] Additionally, the *mussaf*-offerings on the Festivals (except Succos)[83] were 7 lambs.[84] Tishrei, the 7th month of the Jewish year, hosts a disproportionate number of festivals compared to the other months: Rosh Hashanah, Yom Kippur, Succos, and Shemini Atzeres/Simchas Torah. There are the 7 circuits completed on Hashona Rabbah[85] (holding the 7 items comprising the *Arba Minim*, 4 Species [1 *lulav*, 1 *esrog*, 3 *hadassim* and 2 *aravos*][86]) and the 7 circuits embracing the Torah Scrolls on Simchas Torah.[87]

The Jewish calendar counts years, like days, in cycles of 7. It follows the pattern of week: 6 mundane units followed by 1 of holiness. *Shemittah*, 7th sabbatical year, is itself defined as "a Shabbos of rest for the land, a Shabbos to G-d."[88] Like the inactivity of physical, creative acts on the Shabbos, during the *Shemittah* year agricultural labor was forbidden, with the land lying uncultivated.[89] The 7th year, like the 7th day, is itself endowed with special sanctity. It maintained

The 7 days of the week culminate in Shabbos, as Creation proudly proclaims the mastery of its Creator.

The holiness of Shabbos and the Jewish festivals is particularly evident in the formulation of the Amidah with its 7 blessings.

The Jewish calendar counts years, like days, in cycles of 7.

a level of holiness — with no personal use or commercial gain to be garnered from *Shemittah* produce.[90]

7: CYCLES OF LIFE

The development of life is said to unfold in 7 distinct phases.

The motif of 7 in the attainment of holiness is likewise present within the personal passages of man's life. The development of life is said to unfold in 7 distinct phases.[91] There is an imperative that a Jew directs everything toward holy endeavors. Where this is not the case, everything in the natural world is labeled הֶבֶל, *vanity* or *futile* — a word King Shlomo uses 7 times in close succession.[92]

Matrimony is the key to holiness. Indeed, the term *kiddushin*, marriage, relates to the word *kedushah*, sanctity.[93] There is the widespread custom for the bride to encircle the groom with 7 circuits under *chupah*, the wedding canopy. There are שֶׁבַע בְּרָכוֹת, *7 blessings*, recited under the wedding canopy,[94] with the wedding celebrations for a maiden who has never been wed lasting 7 days.[95] Here both husband and wife assume their marital responsibility which, again, is comprised of 7 primary matters.[96]

The week-long mourning of a *shivah*, 7 [day term], as the initial bereavement period upon the passing of an immediate family member is the counterpart of the week-long celebration of *sheva berachos* in marriage.[97] The mourner traditionally recites the *Kaddish* prayer to sanctify the Name of G-d — a minimum of 7 times daily[98] — where the key phrase is a 7-word formula response by the congregation: יְהֵא שְׁמֵהּ רַבָּא מְבָרַךְ לְעָלַם וּלְעָלְמֵי עָלְמַיָּא, *May His Great Name be Blessed forever and ever."*[99]

After Tishah B'Av, the subsequent 7 weeks are termed "Seven [Weeks] of Consolation."

After the national mourning for the destruction of the Temple on Tishah B'Av, the subsequent 7 weeks are termed *Sheva d'Nechomoso*, Seven [Weeks] of Consolation.[100] The successive Shabbos *haftarah* readings are words of solace taken from 7 prophecies of Yeshayah.[101] This is an integral part of the rejuvenation process after death and destruction.

THE UNHOLY TO THE HOLY

IN ADDITION TO 7 AS THE MEANS OF ATTAINING A SPECIAL STATE OF sanctity, the number 7 is also used as a way of converting negative forces of impurity into positive forces of purity, to transfer them into a vehicle of holiness. As the extent of the natural world, 7 represents the full range that can be contaminated by sin. Conversely, it must be purified and filled, instead, with holiness. Examples include the purification process of the Holy Land and of a ritually impure person.

7: CONQUEST OVER THE CANAANITES

Prior to the Children of Israel entering the Promised Land, the country was occupied by the 7 immoral Canaanite nations.[102] Spiritually, they contaminated the innate holiness within the Holy Land by corrupting the 7 primary forces of good in Creation through their idolatrous occupation.[103]

The Jewish leader Yehoshua had to conquer and consecrate the land. The first phase of this campaign was the 7-year war to "besiege the land."[104] His first major offensive was the siege of Yericho, the town that was considered the symbolic "lock" of the Holy Land. The walls of Yericho sank into the ground following circuits around the town on 7 successive days culminating in 7 circuits by the Ark on the 7th day with 7 priests holding 7 rams' horns.[105] The second phase of occupation was the 7-year "consecration of the land." Here the 7 levels of defilement were purified and converted into a bastion of holiness to become the Jewish homeland.[106]

The 7 levels of defilement were purified and converted into a bastion of holiness to become the Jewish homeland.

7: PURIFICATION FROM IMPURITY

The concept of *tumah*, ritual impurity, is symbolically associated with death. Conversely, *taharah*, ritual purity, relates to life and holiness. Indeed, the period of 7 is the requisite passage in this transition. One who came into contact with a corpse was impure for 7 days.[107] This same period is found in other forms of ritual impurity (e.g., the *metzora*, leper,[108] and *yoledes*, woman who has given birth[109]).[110] While in a state of impurity, the person was symbolically distant from *kedushah* — and barred from entering the *Beis HaMikdash*, the Temple that was the "House of holiness."[111]

The ashes of the *parah adumah*, Red Cow, were used to purify a ritually impure person, who had come into contact with a corpse. In its preparation, its blood was sprinkled 7 times towards the *Ohel Moed*, Tent of Meeting.[112] Biblically, a woman who has become subject to the impurity of *zivus* must experience 7 clean days prior to

While in a state of impurity, the person was symbolically distant from kedushah.

7 weeks
between Pesach
and Shavuos
symbolize the
transition of
the Jewish
People from
their spiritual
contamination
to their ascent
to holiness.

immersion in a *mikveh*.[113] The 7 weeks between Pesach and Shavuos parallel the 7 clean days and symbolize the transition of the Jewish People from their spiritual contamination in Egypt to their ascent to holiness at Sinai.[114]

7: FOREVER HOLY

In summary, the ubiquitous nature of 7 is resounding testimony of how *kedushah* is the central and all-encompassing theme of Jewish life.

Kedushah is the
central and all-
encompassing
theme of Jewish
life.

It is essential for a Jew to elevate the full spectrum of the natural world — in all of its multiple components — toward this higher noble goal. All his endeavors are to be sanctified as the means to serve G-d. He must direct the 6-directional physical world to the spiritual, 7th point within. He must identify with his inner, spiritual core that is "a holy spark." This attitude must then come to penetrate into all areas of Judaism.

The Jew lives a
life of holiness
because he is
holy and his
G-d is Holy.

The Jew lives a life of holiness because he is holy and his G-d is Holy. Where he has sullied himself in sin, he has that amazing ability to purify himself and to return spiritually cleansed. In the end, the Jew is joyously destined to symbolically arrive at *Olam Haba*, the World to Come, that is equivalent to the 7th day, Shabbos[115] — when the world reached its ultimate endpoint.

NOTES

1. *Vayikra Rabbah* 29:11 and *Pirkei DeRabbi Eliezer* Ch. 18.
2. *Bereishis* 1:1-2:3. See "6: It's Only Natural."
3. *Sanhedrin* 38a, interpreting *Mishlei* 9:1. See also *Chagigah* 12b.
4. The mystical teachings note that the 7 *Sefiros*, as based upon the verses in *I Divrei HaYamim*, 29:11-12, are: (1) *Chesed*, Lovingkindness, (2) *Gevurah*, Strength, (3) *Tiferes*, Beauty/Harmony, (4) *Netzach*, Eternity, (5) *Hod*, Glory, (6) *Yesod*, Foundation, (7) *Malchus*, Royalty. See *Pri Tzaddik, Balak* 4, for how "Every instant of the number 7 alludes to 7 traits (emanations) and 7 days of Creation." There are in fact a total of 10 *Sefiros* (which include 3 more transcendental Emanations; see "10: Top Ten"). Every component of Creation is a reflection of these Divine Attributes, as they are manifest in our world. The "7 eyes of G-d to cover the entire world" (*Zechariah* 4:10) are seen as a reference to the Divine Providence that G-d uses (through the 7 *Sefiros*) to oversee the world.
5. R' Tzadok HaKohen, *Pri Tzaddik, Noach* 6.
6. Other examples where 7 relates to Creation include the 7 items created before world itself (*Pesachim*

54a), the 7 ascending levels of Creation (*Avos DeRebbi Noson* 37:1) and how G-d created the world with 7 matters (*Avos deRebbi Nassan* 37:6).

7. *Midrash Tehillim* 92:2; See *Avos deRebbi Nassan* 37:9 that there are 7 synonyms for the word *eretz*, land.

8. *Pirkei deRebbi Eliezer* 12. See *Rabbeinu Bachya, Bamidbar* 19:16 for how the term "water" is mentioned on 7 occasions within the Creation narrative. See also *Bava Basra* 74b about 7 bodies of water surrounding the Holy Land.

9. See ibid., *Zohar Chodosh, Bereishis* 241; *Pirkei deRebbi Eliezer* Ch.18.

10. *Chagigah* 12b.

11. *Sefer Yetzirah* 4; see also *Shabbos* 156a about the planetary influences.

12. *Zohar Chodosh, Bereishis* 241.

13. *Maharal, Chiddushei Aggados, Avodah Zarah* 11b (Vol. 4, p. 40). See also *Maharal, Nesiv Yiras Hashem* 3.

14. *Mishlei* 24:16. Other examples include "On 1 road they will go out toward you; on 7 roads they will flee from you" (*Devarim* 28:7) and "7 women will grasp 1 man on that day" (*Yeshayah* 4:1).

15. *Maharal, Netzach Yisrael* 5. See *Rashbam, Vayikra* 26:18; *Radak, I Shmuel*, 2:5; *Radak, Yirmiyah* 15:9; *Ralbag, Mishlei* 9:1; *Ibn Ezra, Vayikra* 26:18.

16. *Maharal, Netzach Yisrael* 7, *Derech Chaim* 5:21. See *Maharal*, ibid. 46 for how 7 represents a "completed number."

17. *Maharal, Ohr Chadash* 1:10. See also "8: Out of This World."

18. *Rabbeinu Bachya, Vayikra* 9:1. The number 7 as the completeness of the natural universe is similarly reflected in the 7-string harp used by both the Levites in the Temple (*Arachin* 13b, *Bamidbar Rabbah* 15:11) and by King David to sing praises to G-d in This World (*Bamidbar Rabbah* 15:11). See *Maharal, Netzach Yisrael* 32 for how this harp is destined to be replaced by 8-stringed instruments in the Messianic era (see "8: Over and Above") and a 10-stringed instrument in the World to Come (See "10: Top Ten").

19. See "49: The Full Measure."

20. See "70: The Sum of the Parts."

21. See *Malbim, Terumah, Rimzei HaMishkan, Menorah; Meiri, Mishlei* 9:1; *Rabbeinu Bachya, Avos*, end of Ch. 3, *Ibn Ezra, Yesod Morah* 1; and *Yaaros Devash* 2, p. 39.

22. Again, the wisdom of Torah as the exclusive rights of Israel belongs to a different category. The non-Jews are in possession of wisdom but have no connection to Torah (*Eichah Rabbah* 2:13).

23. *Sefer HaChinuch, Mitzvah* 330; *Ramban, Bamidbar* 30:3. The *Targum* rendering of the word *shavuah*, oath, is קְיָימָא, established. See *Targum, Bereishis* 26:3. See *Maharal, Gevuros Hashem* 9.

24. *Bereishis* 21:28-32 and *Targum Yonason* ad loc. Later on, corresponding to the 7 lambs Avraham gave Avimelech, the Pelishtim killed 7 righteous Jews and did not return the captured Ark for 7 months (*Bereishis Rabbah* 54:5).

25. *Sanhedrin* 56b; *Shir HaShirim Rabbah* 1:16. See *Maharal, Tiferes Yisrael* 7.

26. The laws are: (1) Not to worship idols, (2) Not to curse G-d, (3) Not to murder, (4) Not to be promiscuous, (5) Not to steal, (6) To establish courts of justice, (7) Not to eat flesh from a living animal (*Sanhedrin* 56b; see *Rambam, Hilchos Melachim* 9:1). See "613: At Your Command."

27. *Maharal, Gevuros Hashem* 66. See R' Yitzchak Hutner, *Pachad Yitzchak, Chanukah* 9 for the fundamental distinctions between the 7 Noachide Laws (preserving the natural universe) where there was no need for their prior acceptance by mankind and the 613 commandments of the Torah (entering a special covenant with G-d) as embraced by Israel at Sinai.

28. *Rus* 4:15.

29. *Shemos* 2:16. See *Maharal, Gevuros Hashem* 19, as to how this relates to "general" level and to the 7th being sanctified above the rest.

30. *Esther* 1:10. Interestingly, the leadership in ancient times was typically headed by the *sheva tuvei ha'ir*, seven elders of the city (see *Megillah* 26a).

31. See *Vayikra* 21:1-4 as to how a *Kohen* can come into contact with a corpse only for the funerals of 7 close relatives: father, mother, son, daughter, wife, (paternal) brother, and (unmarried) sister.
32. *Esther* 2:9.
33. See note 24.
34. *Rashi, Shemos* 18:1.
35. *Succah* 52a.
36. *Bereishis* 4:15, 4:24.
37. See "98: In Admonition."
38. *Pirkei Avos* 5:8.
39. *Bereishis* 7:10.
40. Ibid. 8:10, 8:12.
41. *Shemos* 4:10 and *Rashi* ad loc
42. Ibid. 7:25. Each of plagues lasted for 7 days; 7 days of blood was punishment for causing Israel 7 days of mourning (*Rokeach, Shemos* 7:25).
43. *Bereishis* 29:18, 20, 27-28.
44. Ibid. 41:26-37, 41:47-54.
45. *Maharal, Gevuros Hashem* 19, *Netzach Yisrael* 27, *Chiddushei Aggados, Sanhedrin* 97a (Vol. 3, p. 209)
46. See "10: Top Ten."
47. *Maharal, Derech Chaim* 5:15.
48. See "5: Give Me Five" and "4: Finding the Place."
49. *Maharal, Gevuros Hashem* 46.
50. *Shemos* 25:32-33.
51. Ibid. 25:37.
52. *Bamidbar* 8:2. See R' Tzadok HaKohen, *Pri Tzaddik, Beha'aloscha* 3 as to how the 7 branches of the Menorah parallel the 7 Days of the week with the middle branch symbolic of Shabbos. Though Shabbos is positioned at the end of the week, there are Shabbos laws that symbolically position Shabbos as the center between the week that has passed and the week that follows. One may not start to travel by boat in an ocean 3 days before Shabbos (*O.C.* 248:1-2). If one forgot to say *Havdalah*, he may do so until 3 days later. Thereafter, the next 3 days belong to the following week (*Pesachim* 106a, *Rashi* ad loc.; see *Shulchan Aruch, Orach Chaim* 299:6, *Mishnah Berurah* 16).
53. See *Tanchuma, Beshalach* 3, for how there were 7 Clouds of Glory. See *Rashi, Bamidbar* 10:34. See *Rokeach, Shemos* 13:21 p. 71.
54. *Shulchan Aruch, Orach Chaim* 651:9.
55. *Maharal, Gevuros Hashem* 69.
56. *I Shmuel* 2:2. See also "For Hashem our G-d is holy" (*Tehillim* 99:9) and "Holy, holy, holy is Hashem; the entire world is filled with His glory" (*Yeshayah* 6:3). There are 7 principal Holy Names of G-d that must be respected and cannot be erased. See *Rambam, Yesodei HaTorah* 6:2; *Shulchan Aruch, Yoreh Deah* 276:9.
57. *Yeshayah* 62:12. See also ibid. 29:23
58. See *Vayikra* 20:26, 20:8, 21:8; 11:45; *Bamidbar* 15:40; see also *Ramban Vayikra* 19:2.
59. *Pri Tzaddik, Eikev* 3. In total, the *Avos* were responsible for digging 7 wells (*Bereishis Rabbah* 64:7) and for building a total of 7 altars (see *Bamidbar* 23:4 and *Rashi* ad loc.; see also *Shem MiShmuel, Balak* 5675). See *Pirkei DeRabbi Eliezer* Ch. 18 for how G-d chose Israel out of 7 main nations.
60. *Yalkut Shimoni, Shemos* 19, 276. See also *Rokeach, Devarim* 34:7.
61. The 7 shepherds are identified as Adam, Sheis, Mesushelach, Avraham, Yaakov, Moshe, and David (*Succah* 52b) The 7 shepherds are the chariot for the 7 Divine Attributes (*Pri Tzaddik, Lech Lecha* 2, quoting *Zohar Chadash Toldos*).
62. The 7 prophetesses were Sarah, Miriam, Devorah, Chanah, Avigayil, Chulda, and Esther (*Megillah* 14a).

63. *Bamidbar Rabbah* 13:2. There are 7 groups that will merit receiving the *Shechinah* (*Vayikra Rabbah* 30:2).
64. *Bamidbar Rabbah* 20:18. Conversely, Bilaam built 7 altars upon which he sacrificed 7 oxen and 7 rams (*Bamidbar* 23:4, 29).
65. *Tanchuma, Noach* 5.
66. *Zohar* 3, 103b The 7 *ushpizin* are Avraham, Yitzchak, Yaakov, Moshe, Aharon, Yosef, and David. See also *Bava Basra* 17a, which states that the bodies of 7 people did not decompose after their deaths.
67. *Bava Basra* 121b. Additionally, there are 7 wedding canopies for the righteous in the World to Come (*Bava Basra* 75a). There are 7 groups of righteous in *Gan Eden* (*Sifrei, Devarim* 10).
68. *Bamidbar* 13:22. See *Bava Basra* 74b, which discusses how the Holy Land is encircled by 7 seas.
69. *Devarim* 8:8. See *Pesachim* 36a.
70. *Vilna Gaon, Aderes Eliyahu, Devarim* 1:7 as found in *Devarim* 8:7-10.
71. See *Shulchan Aruch, Orach Chaim* 211:1-2.
72. See Samson Raphael Hirsch, *Collected Writings*, Vol. 3, p. 97 .
73. See *Shemos* 20:8.
74. Ibid. 31:15.
75. The 7 parties are "you, your son, your daughter, your servant, your maidservant, your animal, and your convert" (*Shemos* 20:10). See *Rokeach, Shemos* 20:10.
76. *Shemos* 20:8-11, 31:12-17; *Devarim* 5:13-14, 15:1.
77. *Megillah* 21a.
78. *Maharal, Gevuros Hashem* 46.
79. *Shemos* 12:16.
80. Ibid. 12:15-16, 12:19, 13:6; *Devarim* 16:3, 16:15.
81. *Vayikra* 23:1-16; *Devarim* 16:9. In its relationship to Torah, Shavuos as the 50th day relates to the 8th dimension. See "50: All the Way."
82. *Yoma* 87b. The 7 blessings of the Shabbos *Amidah* correspond to 7 voices in *Tehillim* 29 (*Berachos* 29a).
83. See *Ohr HaChaim, Bamidbar* 28:26
84. See ibid. 28:9.
85. *Shulchan Aruch, Orach Chaim* 664:1.
86. Ibid. 651:1-2.
87. See *Zohar, Ki Seitzei* 283a, as to how this resembles the 7 times the Altar was encircled (see *Mishnah Berurah, Orach Chaim* 651:10) and the 7 circuits in besieging the town of Yericho (*Yehoshua* 6:4, 8).
88. *Shemos* 23:10-11; *Vayikra* 25:1-7. See also *Devarim* 31:10-13.
89. See *Ramban, Vayikra* 25:2.
90. *Avodah Zarah* 54b. There is a parallel cycle of 6 years of labor followed by a 7th year of rest regarding a Jewish servant. He is obligated to work for his master for a term of 6 years and is automatically released from bondage in the 7th year (*Shemos* 21:2; *Devarim* 15:12). See "6: It's Only Natural." Observance of the Sabbatical laws was the basis for Israel's continual residence in the Holy Land. In fact, the expulsion from the Land of Israel was attributed to the Jewish people not observing *Shemittah* (*Vayikra* 26:34).
91. The 7 phases unfold as follows: (1) a king (a newborn until 1-year-old, treated regally), (2) pig (2-year-old toddler rolling in dirt), (3) kid (5-year-old dancing before his mother), (4) horse (18-year-old youth proudly running in his vigor), (5) donkey (40-year-old heavily laden by the yoke of parenthood), (6) dog (imprudence without shame), and (7) monkey (old age). See *Tanchuma, Pekudei* 3.
92. *Koheles* 1:2. See *Bava Basra* 100b and *Koheles Rabbah* 1:2 — 1:3.
93. See *Kiddushin* 2b.
94. *Kesubos* 7b-8b. See also *Zohar, Va'eschanan* 266b.
95. See *Kesubos* 4a for how the first bridal week of 7 days has the status of a holiday. See *Rambam, Hilchos Ishus* 10:12.

96. There are 7 rabbinic obligations placed upon a husband (*Rambam, Hilchos Ishus* 12:2) and the wife also covenants to undertake 7 activities for her husband (*Kesubos* 59b; *Bereishis Rabbah* 52:12).

97. *Shulchan Aruch, Yoreh Deah* 375:1and 395:1. See *Bereishis* 50:10 detailing the mourning upon the death of Yaakov. See also *Moed Katan* 20a and *Tanchuma*, end of *Vayechi*.

98. See *Mishnah Berurah Orach Chaim* 55:5.

99. See *Rokeach, Devarim* 32:3 how this 7-word formula is parallel to the 7 words of the verse כִּי שֵׁם ה׳ אֶקְרָא הָבוּ גֹדֶל לֵאלֹקֵינוּ, *For I will proclaim the name of HASHEM; ascribe greatness unto our G-d* (*Devarim* 32:3). See also "28: In Season."

100. *Mishnah Berurah* 428:8.

101. *Shulchan Aruch, Orach Chaim* 428:8.

102. See *Bereishis* 15:19-21 and *Rashi* ad loc.; *Rashi, Shemos* 13:5, 33:2; 34:11; *Nechemiah* 9:8.

103. *Devarim* 7:1. The 7 Canaanite nations represent the 7 shells of impurity that stand against the 7 forces of holiness (*Arizal, Likkutei Torah, Lech Lecha*). The conquering of the 7 nations by Israel was through the force of Israel's 7 *middos* (*R' Tzadok, Kometz HaMinchah* 12a). The 7 nations were the basis for all the 70 nations of the world; every king who had not purchased a palace in the Land of Israel was not considered worthy of sovereignty (*Tanchuma, Mishpatim* 17). See also *Shem MiShmuel, Chanukah* 5676 1st Night, p. 213. It was decreed that Moshe would be prevented from entering the Holy Land ruled by 7 nations and would die on the 7th of Adar (*Sotah* 12b) (see *Rokeach, Shemos* 6:6).

104. The first consecration of the land achieved upon Yehoshua's conquest continued until the national expulsion from the land after the destruction of the First Temple. The second phase began with Ezra and the return to the Holy Land. See *Arachin* 32b regarding the halachic ramifications of the original and subsequent consecrations and the length of their effectiveness.

105. *Yehoshua* 6:4, 8. See also *Berachos* 54b.

106. *Zevachim* 118b.

107. *Bamidbar* 19:11, 14-16, 31:19.

108. *Vayikra* 14:9.

109. Ibid. 12:1-5.

110. The number 7 features in how food can become *machshirin lekabel tumah*, susceptible to ritual impurity. It first must come into contact with one of 7 specified liquids. The 7 liquids, best known by their acronym יַד שֶׁחָט דָּם, refer to *yayin*, wine; *devash*, date honey; *shemen*, olive oil; *chalav*, milk; *tal*, dew; *dam*, blood; and *mayim*, water (*Mishnah, Machshirin* 6:4).

111. See, e.g., *Vayikra* 12:4 for the woman who has given birth. The Torah juxtaposes the High Priest (whose work was exclusively in the Temple and who was forbidden both from contact with a corpse [even that of his father or his mother]) with not leaving the Sanctuary or desecrating it (*Vayikra* 21:11-12).

112. *Bamidbar* 19:4. Throughout history, there was a total of 7 Red Cows used in both Temples (see *Mishnah Parah* 3:5).

113. In a sense, this symbolizes her rebirth after a brush with death in shedding blood. There follows the weekly cycle as reminiscent of the 7 Days of Creation. See "40: True to Form." There are also a total of 7 cleansing agents that were to be applied to a garment stained with menstrual blood before its immersion in the *mikveh* so that it is no longer ritually impure (*Mishnah, Niddah* 9:6).

114. See "49: The Full Measure" and "50: All the Way."

115. *Mishnah, Tamid* 7:4.

8
OUT OF THIS WORLD

8 is the number of transcendence.
It is about going beyond
and above physical reality.

It relates to everything that is above nature
and to the incredible ability of a Jew
to rise "over and above" the limitations
of the physical realm.

AN OTHERWORLDLY EXISTENCE

The number 8 goes beyond — to reach a level that is higher than nature.

IN THE SEQUENCE OF NUMBERS, 8 FOLLOWS 7.

We have seen how the number 7 corresponds to the 7 days of Creation, and by extension, to the sanctification of the natural world.[1] Its successor, the number 8, goes one stage further. It goes beyond — to reach a level that is higher than nature.

The distinction between 7 and 8 is readily apparent in their respective names. שֶׁבַע, 7, is similar to שׂוֹבַע, *satisfaction* — the satisfaction one feels when he completes his worldly requirements.[2] But שְׁמוֹנָה, 8, relates to שׁוּמָן, *fat* — that is, having more than is necessary.[3]

8: OVER AND ABOVE

The number 8 denotes "transcendence."

The number 8 denotes "transcendence." It symbolizes that a Jew is not subject to the natural realm. He has the ability to break free from This World and its limitations. He rises לְמַעְלָה מִדֶּרֶךְ הַטֶּבַע, *above the natural order.*[4]

The Jew lives "over and above."

Jewish living cannot be described as ordinary; it is completely *extra*-ordinary. The Jew — both individually and nationally — does not make an attempt to conform to the rules of the natural order that regulate all other creatures in existence. He does not truly belong in This World. He is not subservient to its natural laws. He defies the laws of history. He flaunts all the rules in the book. He lives "over and above."

BRIS MILAH: 8TH DAY

This ceremony proudly proclaims his initiation into the Chosen Nation of G-d.

This supernatural state in the lifetime of a Jew begins almost immediately in the beginning stage of life through בְּרִית מִילָה, *covenant of circumcision.* On the 8th day after the birth of a Jewish boy he is circumcised.[5] This ceremony proudly proclaims his initiation into Israel, the Chosen Nation of G-d.[6] It is the physical sign that he is a servant of G-d, His Master.[7]

This *mitzvah* was first given to the Jewish forefather Avraham as the 8th of his 10 trials.[8] Actually, this was the 8th Divine instruction to mankind.[9] The earlier זֵ מִצְוֹת בְּנֵי נֹחַ, *7 Noachide Laws*, universally binding upon all of mankind, were given with regard to conserving a proper worldly order.[10] This covenant with Noach after the Flood was given to preserve the natural world of 7, as symbolized in the colors of the rainbow, which was used as a sign.[11] But the Divine covenant with Israel is concerned with the supernatural realm of 8.

In the natural world, man is uncircumcised. Through the ceremony on the 8th day, the circumcised Jew enters into a special בְּרִית, *covenant*, with G-d. This elevates him "over and above" the natural world.[12] Here he takes his place as a proud member of a people whose covenant declares that their life force exclusively exists for G-d. In turn, their survival through the millennia, against all the odds, is nothing short of miraculous. There can be no doubting that it clearly lies above nature.

The grand introduction to Jewish living through *bris milah* marks entry into a life deeply committed to Torah, whose otherworldly stature is similarly reflected in the number 8.

He takes his place as a proud member of a people whose covenant declares that their life force exclusively exists for G-d.

TORAH: 8TH DIMENSION

Different facets of Torah find expression in several different numbers.[13] Nevertheless, the dimension in which Torah specifically relates to the number 8 is to be found in terms of its lofty and supernatural stature.

Torah is not of this natural world. It originates from On High and essentially belongs to the Heavenly realm. This is why the angels forcefully resisted Moshe's efforts to present Torah to mankind on the Earth below.[14]

All the wisdom of the natural world connects to the number 7.[15] But the Divine Wisdom of Torah, which transcends everything else, has to do with the number 8. So while the first 7 verses of *Tehillim* 19 address the magnificence of the natural world, the 8th verse declares, "The Torah of G-d is perfect, restoring the soul."[16] Furthermore, *Tehillim* 119, which almost exclusively describes the preeminence of Torah, similarly follows an 8-verse alphabetical sequence.[17]

The Divine Wisdom of Torah, which transcends everything else, has to do with the number 8.

Like *milah*, Torah is itself termed a *bris*, referring to the otherworldly covenant as forged between G-d and Israel.[18] Torah is the exclusive possession of the Jewish people. It is only those circumcised on the 8th day who can relate to the supernatural Torah of 8 to shape their lives. It is the Torah, in turn, which permits the Jew to transcend the limitations of the natural world.

SPACE AND BEYOND

This dimension of transcendence is beautifully established inside the Mishkan.

WE HAVE NOTED THE TRANSCENDENCE OF THE NUMBER 8 AND ITS application in the special covenant the Jewish People have with G-d. Unlike the physical world, the Jewish People are not bound by the natural confines of space. This dimension of transcendence is beautifully established inside the *Mishkan*, Sanctuary, and specifically the *Kodesh HaKodashim*, Holy of Holies.

MISHKAN: 8

At the point where reality is transcended, one discovers the number 8.

In the House of G-d, the rules of space were miraculously suspended. Inside the *Kodesh HaKodashim*, "the place of the Ark and *cherubim* did not occupy any measured space."[19]

Here, again, at the point where reality is transcended, one discovers the number 8. The 8 blood sprinklings of Yom Kippur were performed by the High Priest on the curtain of the Holy of Holies.[20] The sprinkling of 1 above and 7 below[21] symbolizes how the 8th dimension goes "over and above" the 7 of the natural order.[22] Indeed, it was only the High Priest, himself elevated by his usual wearing of 8 special garments,[23] who was permitted entry into the *Kodesh HaKodashim* (though he was only permitted to enter that chamber clothed in 4 garments).[24]

The transcendence of the number 8 is specifically present in the Jewish festivals intrinsically related to the number 8.

Other appearances of 8 in the *Mishkan* include:[25] the inauguration of the Sanctuary transpired upon the 8th day;[26] its animals were suitable for sacrificial offerings from the 8th day onward;[27] there were 8 poles used to transport the main vessels;[28] and there were 8 types of spices: 4 for oil of anointment,[29] 4 for incense.[30]

The transcendence of the number 8 is specifically present in the Jewish festivals intrinsically related to the number 8: Shemini Atzeres, Atzeres (Shavuos), and Chanukah.

8TH FESTIVE DAY: SHEMINI ATZERES, ATZERES:

The Sinai experience on Shavuos occurred after 7 cycles of 7 days from the second day of Pesach.

The Torah was given at the beginning of the 8th week after Israel's deliverance from Egypt. The Sinai experience on Shavuos occurred after 7 cycles of 7 days from the second day of Pesach, as commemorated in the counting of the *Omer*.[31]

Shavuos can thus be viewed as the 8th day of the 7-day Pesach festival. It fulfills the objective of the Exodus: the liberation of the Jews from slavery in order for them for them to embrace the Torah. Its rabbinic name עֲצֶרֶת (*Atzeres*) [32] whose root means to "stop" or "halt," alludes to its parallel with Shemini Atzeres, the 8th day of Succos, as a separate and yet interconnected festival.[33] The acceptance of Torah on Shavuos has its amazing parallel in the rejoicing of the Torah in the festivities of Simchas Torah, which forms an integral part of Shemini Atzeres.[34]

CHANUKAH: 8 DAYS

Perhaps a more famous example of Israel not being bound by the natural limitations of time is manifest in the 8-day rabbinic festival of Chanukah.

Chanukah records the military and spiritual victory against the Syrian-Greeks in the capture and re-inauguration of the Second Temple. Here a small flask of pure, uncontaminated olive oil was used to kindle the Menorah, which miraculously burned for 8 days.[35]

The enemy forces that waged an ideological war against Israel are depicted as "darkness."[36] Despite making great strides in philosophy and the sciences, Greek culture centered upon the natural phenomena. They heaped scorn upon the existence of anything transcendental.[37] Their efforts to Hellenize Israel sought to seduce them to "forget their Torah."[38] One of their main decrees was to discontinue *bris milah*.[39]

One of the Syrian-Greeks' main decrees was to discontinue bris milah.

But they could not defile Israel's supernatural link to the number 8. In the Temple, the Greeks were able to desecrate only the *Heichal*, Holy, associated with the number 7, but not the otherworldly 8th dimension of the *Kodesh HaKodashim*.[40]

They could not defile Israel's supernatural link to the number 8.

In fact, this theme of 8 extends to the uncontaminated oil in a jar bearing a seal of the High Priest.[41] The similarity between שֶׁמֶן, oil, and שְׁמוֹנָה, 8, goes beyond their similar Hebrew words. Just as oil does not mix with another other liquid but rises to the top, so too, would Israel refuse to assimilate into the natural world but retain their transcendence.[42]

Just as oil rises to the top, so too, would Israel refuse to assimilate into the natural world but retain their transcendence.

The Chanukah lights on the 7-branched Menorah in the Temple banished the darkness of Greek culture by miraculously burning for 8 days.[43]

WHEN MASHIACH COMES

T HE OTHERWORLDLY STATURE OF 8 ALLUDES TO TRANSCENDENCE, not only of the laws of the physical world, but also of our own limitations and errors; it refers to freedom from defilement following cleansing through penitence.[44] When a Jew falls, he picks himself up. "The righteous may fall 7 times; he will arise."[45] It is upon the 8th occasion that he starts a new phase. The spiritual purification process for the ritually impure often requires a 7-day count. On the 8th the person can arrive at a purified state.[46]

The otherworldly stature of 8 refers to freedom from defilement following cleansing through penitence.

Historically, Israel has not always lived up to their otherworldly mission as embodied within the number 8. Still, their eternal covenant means that through repentance they can remove the defilement of sin and inaugurate a new phase of purity.

The ultimate rectification of the world will be realized in the Messianic era.

MAShIACh: 8Th ERA

The miraculous oil of Chanukah is a harbinger of the anointing oil used to inaugurate the coming of the Messianic era.[47] This process can be traced to King David, who was the 8th of Yishai's sons.[48] The very name of the king, מָשִׁיחַ, *Messiah*, refers to the anointing of the Davidic dynasty with oil.[49] The oil used in the Menorah is related to the Messianic king who will illuminate the world with his light.[50]

The widespread repentance of mankind will inaugurate a new world order in the knowledge of G-d.

The purpose of the Messianic era is to return the world to the level of Adam before his sin. The widespread repentance of mankind will inaugurate a new world order in the knowledge of G-d.[51] It will be the expansion of Israel's original mission: to live "over and above" the natural world in order to reveal the glory of G-d.[52]

The Messianic epoch is intrinsically related to the number 8: "In the year after the 7th, the son of David [Mashiach] will come."[53] The harp, belonging to the natural world, has 7 strings; the musical instrument in the era of Mashiach will be 8-stringed.[54] This symbolically mirrors the reaching of an exalted level over and above the physical realm.[55]

The Jewish people, as observers of the Heavenly Torah and bearers of His covenant, live this supernatural existence even now, in This World. In so doing, they prepare the universe to welcome the Mashiach, the anointed one, who will inaugurate an existence that transcends the natural world. The world will then sing out to G-d with the music produced by the 8-stringed harp, in a tune that will rise toward G-d.

That era promises to be something "out of this world."

The Jewish people prepare the universe to welcome the Mashiach who will inaugurate an existence that transcends the natural world.

NOTES

1. See "7: A Holy Spark."
2. *Maharal, Ohr Chadash* 1:10.
3. R. Yitzchak Hutner, *Pachak Yitzchak, Iggeres U'Kesuvim* 38.
4. *Maharal, Ner Mitzvah.*
5. The 8th day is the earliest occasion for circumcision. Where it cannot be performed on the 8th day, it can be done on any subsequent date.
6. *Bereishis* 17:12.
7. *Maharal, Derashah L'Shabbos Shuvah*, p. 68.
8. *Pirkei Avos* 5:3, according to *Rashi's* counting. See also *Pirkei DeRabbi Eliezer* 29.
9. *Rambam, Hilchos Melachim* 9:1-3.
10. The laws are: (1) Not to worship idols, (2) Not to curse G-d, (3) Not to murder, (4) Not to commit adultery or incest, (5) Not to steal, (6) To establish courts of justice, (7) Not to eat flesh from a living animal (*Sanhedrin* 56b; *Rambam, Hilchos Melachim* 9:1).
11. *Bereishis* 9:12-13.
12. The *orlah*, foreskin, symbolizes the spiritual blockage (*Rashi, Vayikra* 19:23) in the natural world separating man from G-d. The removal of the *orlah* is necessary to establish a covenant with Him.
13. See "1: The One and Only" and "3: Three Dimensional."
14. *Shabbos* 88b-89a.
15. This was symbolized in 7 lamps of the *Menorah*. See *Rabbeinu Bachya, Kad HaKemach, Ner Chanukah* and *Rabbeinu Bachya, Shemos* 25:31.
16. *Tehillim* 19:8. See *Maharal, Ner Mitzvah* and *Tiferes Yisrael* 2.
17. See *Malbim, Tehillim* 119.
18. See *Nedarim* 32a interpreting *Yirmiyah* 33:25. See also R' Chaim Volozhin, *Nefesh HaChaim* 4:11.
19. *Yoma* 21a; *Bava Basra* 99a. Inside the Temple, while the space seemed adequate for all the pilgrims to stand, when they prostrate themselves, astoundingly there was ample room (*Pirkei Avos* 5:7).

Furthermore, the Mishnah notes that no one ever remarked with regard to Jerusalem that space was confined.

20. *Yoma* 56b.
21. *Rashi, Vayikra* 16:14.
22. *Maharal, Derashah L'Shabbos Shuvah* p. 82b. The High Priest was secluded 7 days prior to that 1 unique day of Yom Kippur (*Yoma* 2b) ,which was equivalent to the 8th day.
23. The 8 articles of clothing were: *Choshen*, Breastplate; *Ephod*, Apron; *Me'il*, Robe; *Kesones*, Tunic; *Mitznefes*, Turban; *Avneit*, Belt; *Michnasayim*, Breeches; and *Tzitz*, Headplate (*Shemos* 28:4-36).
24. See *Mishnah, Yoma* 7:5. The exalted level of *Kodesh HaKodashim* relates to the number 8, in terms of its transcendence (*Maharal, Ner Mitzvah*. See also *Maharal, Derashah L'Shabbos Shuvah* pp. 82-83).
25. *Rabbeinu Bachya, Vayikra* 9:1.
26. *Vayikra* 9:1.
27. Ibid. 22:27.
28. *Shemos* 25.
29. Ibid. 30:23-24.
30. Ibid. v. 34. There are four mentioned explicitly in the verse, but there are a total of eleven spices that are exegetically derived from the verse (*Kereisos* 6a-b).
31. *Vayikra* 23:15.
32. See, e.g., Mishnah, *Rosh Hashanah* 1:2; *Bikkurim* 1:3.
33. *Vayikra* 23:36-39. The interim 7-week period between Pesach and Shavuos is equivalent to Chol HaMoed, the Interim days within the Festivals (*Ramban, Vayikra* 23:36). See *Sfas Emes, Shemini* 5661.
34. *Shemini* Atzeres is the Festival that celebrates the exclusive relationship between G-d and Israel (*Maharal, Netzach Yisrael* 32).
35. *Shabbos* 21b.
36. "… with darkness" (*Bereishis* 1:2); this refers to the wicked Greeks, who darkened the eyes of Israel with their decrees (*Bereishis Rabbah* 2:4).
37. See *Ramban, Vayikra* 16:8, who characterizes Aristotle and the Greeks as arrogantly denying anything that they could not see. Any concept that the human mind could not grasp was rejected as being false.
38. *Al HaNissim* prayer. See also *Rambam, Hilchos Chanukah* 3:1.
39. *Megillas Antiochus* 31 and Rav Saadiah Gaon, *Daniel* 7:3.
40. See "50: All the Way."
41. *Shabbos* 21b.
42. See *Shemos Rabbah* 36:1, for how oil is the famous metaphor for Israel.
43. *Maharal, Ner Mitzvah*.
44. *Sfas Emes, Shemini* 5657.
45. *Mishlei* 24:16.
46. *Vayikra* 14:9-10, 15:13-14, 15:28-29.
47. *Rabbeinu Bachya, Kad HaKemach, Ner Chanukah*. See also *Sfas Emes*, Chanukah 5648, who speaks about how the inauguration of Chanukah is a preparation for this future redemption.
48. *I Shmuel*, 17:12. See also ibid. 16:10, which states that Yishai had 7 sons excluding David. See *I Divrei Hayamim* 2:15, which counts 7 sons including David. See *Metzudas David, I Shmuel*, 16:10.
49. See *I Shmuel*, 16:13.
50. "In the merit of the eternal lights of the menorah you will merit greeting the lights of the Messianic king (*Vayikra Rabbah* 31:11) In itself, the symbolism of oil is strongly suggestive of the anointing oil used to consecrate the Davidic dynasty that culminates in Mashiach (which itself means "the anointed"). See R' Gedalyah Schorr, *Ohr Gedalyahu*, Chanukah 11.
51. *Yeshayah* 11:9.

52. The inauguration associated with Chanukah is where the world returns to its original purpose, which is to glorify G-d (*Shelah,* quoted by *Sfas Emes*, Chanukah 5648 p. 226).
53. *Sanhedrin* 97a.
54. *Arachin* 13b. Mashiach is hinted at in *Tehillim* that refers to *haSheminis*, the 8th (*Tehillim* 12:1).
55. *Maharal, Netzach Yisrael* 32. See also *Shem MiShmuel, Shemini* 5672 p. 162.

9
WHERE
TO TURN?

9 refers to the individual parts
that are turning toward the completion
of an integrated unit.

G-d gives man the time and space
within Creation to turn 9 toward 10
in a process where he can bring himself
and the world to its perfection.

THE NUMBER 9 RESTS IN THE SHADOWS OF 10, THE NUMBER THAT follows it.

The unity of 1 has its parallel in 10, where a set of individual parts combine to form an integrated unit.[1] Therefore the preceding number, 9, is the final stage *before* reaching this point — where the parts are still considered individual and separate.

The symbolism of 9 primarily relates to its journey "turning toward" the number 10.

The symbolism of 9 primarily relates to its journey "turning toward" the number 10. It is the conceptual space in which man must decide whether or not he will partner G-d in the perfection of the universe.

9: INDIVIDUAL PARTS

The integration of 10 sees individual components form a communal whole. Hence 9, the last of the single digits, is the highest sum of "individual parts." It is the number in which a person can best explore his individuality.

9, the last of the single digits, is the highest sum of "individual parts."

This individuality takes its form within the 3 dimensions of the physical world: length, width, and breadth. Each one of these 3 dimensions is, in turn, composed of the 3 essential parts of every process: beginning point, end point, and the distance between them.[2] Here 9, the square of 3 ($3^2 = 9$), depicts the interrelationship of these dimensions.[3] Thus, the number 9 represents bringing individual expression into the physical realm. This is where a person can have an impact in both the dimensions of time and space.

A single portion accomplished by personal input is more beloved than 9 times of the same portion received from a friend.

The total of 9 parts is the highest possible number attributable to individual parts and the "many" expressions of an individual. This individual expression is particularly dear to a person. In the words of a notable rabbinic statement, "Man prefers his [1] portion more than 9 portions of his friend."[4] A single portion accomplished by man's personal input, something which is uniquely his, is far more beloved in his eyes than 9 times of the same portion he may have received from a friend.

9/10: AN OVERWHELMING MAJORITY

Although a completed unit is only reached with the number 10, "9 out of 10" constitutes the overwhelming majority — even if it is not quite yet a full set. Several examples of the 9:1 ratio are discussed in the Talmud with "9 out of 10" measures of a particular quality allocated to a single party. Two examples: Out of 10 measures of wisdom given to the world, 9 were taken by the Land of Israel. Out of 10 measures of beauty, 9 went to the Holy City of Jerusalem.[5]

This formulation of the 9:1 ratio indicates how much the specific trait characterizes the one in possession of 9 measures: the Land of Israel gives wisdom; Jerusalem is beautiful. The remaining 1 measure denotes a mere remnant left over, so to speak, as tithes for the rest of the world. [6]

The 9:1 ratio indicates how much the specific trait characterizes the one in possession of 9 measures.

A TURN FOR THE BETTER

W E HAVE SEEN 9 AS THE HIGHEST POSSIBLE NUMBER OF INDIVIDUAL parts. It is something that is almost there — but not quite. It is en route to attaining the completion associated with the number 10. Here lies the central objective within the number 9: the act of "turning toward" to ensure that one finally arrives at the endpoint.

9: TIME TO TURN

Instead of the final stop, 9 is the penultimate stage in the process of "turning toward" something higher and greater. The word תֵּשַׁע, 9, is derived from the root שָׁעָה, meaning *turning* or *facing*. One famous example of this is the verse "G-d turned (וַיִּשַׁע) to Hevel and his offering. But to Kayin and his offering, [He] did not turn (שָׁעָה) ..."[7] (Another variation of this is the word הַט, *incline*, whose basic consonant letter is ט, the 9th letter of the alphabet.)

Perhaps the most famous application of this concept of turning is found in the promise of the saintly Baal Shem Tov, founder of Chasidism, "When 9 Jews are waiting to form a *minyan*, quorum [in prayer], a 10th man will soon appear."[8] Here, too, 9 is shown to be

9 is the penultimate stage in the process of "turning toward" something higher and greater.

in a constant state of flux, "to turn toward" the state of completion symbolized by the number 10.

9: IT'S YOUR TURN

G-d intended that man be entrusted with the task of perfecting the world.

When G-d created the world, He did not seek to create the universe in a perfected state. In fact, He intended the world to be created imperfect and that man be entrusted with the task of perfecting it.[9]

Man, endowed with free will, was given space in which to complete G-d's Creation. Virtually everything was set into place in the first 6 Days of Creation. G-d then invited man to become His partner. He asked man to apply the "finishing touches" to Creation. It is a call for man to perfect himself — and by extension the entire cosmos — by choosing to fulfill the Will of G-d as expressed in the Torah. In effect, G-d informs man, "Now it's your turn."

It is a call for man to perfect himself by choosing to fulfill the Will of G-d.

In numeric terms, 10 characterizes a state of completion. In This World, the overwhelming majority — similar to the "9 out of 10" measures — is of G-d's doing. But G-d purposefully leaves the last stage to man. Man plays an integral role; he taps into the symbolism of 9 to "turn" himself and the world around him to finally reach the completion of 10.

PREGNANCY: 9 MONTHS

Man's role in creation — to partner with G-d and perfect the world by turning from 9 to 10 — is vividly illustrated in the course of human conception. The full term of a fetus' development lasts for 9 months. Gestation is a period of expectation (as in the expression, "expecting a baby"). It is a developmental process — one, which like the number 9, involves turning toward delivery — a higher state of completion. This will ultimately be reached in the birth of the newborn.

Man must undergo the equivalent of a 9-month embryonic development inside This World.

The passage from life inside the womb to the outside has its natural parallel in the transfer from This World to the World to Come.[10] *Olam Haba*, the World to Come, was created with י, the 10th letter of the Hebrew alphabet,[11] as the mark of completion.[12] But in order to get there, man must first undergo the equivalent of a 9-month embryonic development inside This World. So 9 marks the space in which man operates his life mission: turning toward 10 in a state of completion to pass into a higher dimension.

9: TIME AND TIME AGAIN

In his endeavors to partner with G-d and turn 9 to 10, man must know how to relate to the dimension of time. G-d is not subject to the parameters of time; the world is. Time was an act of creation first introduced at the inception of the universe.[13]

There are two possible ways to relate to the time continuum that operates in This World. The nations of the world perceive the passage of time as an ongoing cycle of what had earlier transpired. This is best characterized by the term שָׁנָה, *cycle [of a year]*, depicting a natural sequence that repeats itself over and over again.[14] There is no newness, no direction or signposts — just the continuous reenactment of the past that extends first into the present, and then into the future. Time is understood as an extension of the past. It appears destined to continuously repeat itself in a never-ending circle — something mirrored in the mathematical properties of the number 9.

The number 9 relates to a circle that turns back on itself, completing revolutions around — but never outside of — its circumference, which can continue indefinitely.[15] The inability to *move on beyond* is seen in this number, where all multiples of 9 do not escape their connection with this number. Adding the digits of a multiple of 9, the resultant answer, reduced to a single digit, always remains 9. For example:

987 x 9 = 8883
    ➔ 8+8+8+3 = 27
27 ➔ 2+7=9
    ➔ 9

12345 x 9 = 111105
    ➔ 1+1+1+1+0+5=9
    ➔ 9

Here the cyclical view of time plays out time and time again because it is perceived as stuck in the past. This prevents 9 from going beyond itself and rising to 10.

There is, however, another viewpoint of time. The Jewish view regards time not as an extension of the past but as a preparation for the future. The focus is exclusively forward-looking; it is about "turning toward" a designated objective and goal. This is beautifully reflected in the Hebrew term זְמַן, *time*, that relates to the concept of הַזְמָנָה, *preparation*,[16] or זִימוּן, *invitation*.[17] In other words, *time is the means that comes to determine man's ultimate future*; it is the means for him to reach eternity. So rather than being "stuck" continuously repeating the cycle, there is the concept of חֹדֶשׁ, *month*, that relates to חִידוּשׁ, *newness* or *innovation*.

Time was an act of creation first introduced at the inception of the universe.

Time appears destined to continuously repeat itself in a never-ending circle.

The Jewish view regards time not as an "extension of the past" but as a "preparation for the future."

This perspective of time as the passage "turning toward" the future, one not locked into the endless repetition of the past, is hinted at in the word שָׁעָה, *moment of time*, that relates to תֵּשַׁע, *9*. In other words, every moment in time, like the number 9, is the invitation to turn toward 10 to reach a state of completion and a life of eternity.

ROSh hAShANAh: DAY OF CONCEPTION

Man's ability to turn from 9 to 10 features prominently in Rosh Hashanah, the New Year, that marks the yearly start of recording time in the Jewish calendar.

Rosh Hashanah is described in the liturgy as הַיּוֹם הֲרַת עוֹלָם, *Today, the world was conceived.*[18] The time framework characterized by the 9 months of gestation begins with conception and concludes with the birth of the newborn. It was on Rosh Hashanah that G-d answered the heartfelt prayers of women.[19] The Torah reading recounts that the aged and barren Sarah miraculously conceived Avraham's son and heir Yitzchak.[20] The *haftarah* selection relates that Chanah, whose prayers were also answered on Rosh Hashanah, conceived the prophet Shmuel.[21] The 9 times G-d's Name is mentioned in her prayers is mirrored in the structure of Rosh Hashanah's special Mussaf prayer that is composed of 9 blessings.[22] Parallel to the 9 months when the fetus develops, the conception of Rosh Hashanah on Day 1 of Tishrei turns toward Yom Kippur, the 10th of Tishrei, 9 days later, with the rebirth of the repentant man as a pure, innocent newborn.[23]

Rosh Hashanah is when the proposed partnership between man and G-d is evaluated. The wake-up call rousing man to repentance from his spiritual slumber is the *mitzvah* of תְּקִיעַת שׁוֹפָר, *sounding of the shofar.*[24] This, also, relates to the number 9 — as the minimum requirement is to hear 9 blasts of the shofar: 3 sets of 3 sounds — תְּקִיעָה-תְּרוּעָה-תְּקִיעָה.[25]

The new year marks the anniversary of man's formation on Day 6 of Creation. It is a *Yom HaDin*, Day of Judgment. Every man is accountable to determine whether or not he has used his free will to perfect creation, to turn 9 into 10, by crowning G-d as the King over the world.

A TURN FOR THE WORSE

THE "TURNING TOWARD" THAT CHARACTERIZES 9 SEES MAN USE HIS free will to partner with G-d in the perfection of the universe — to reach toward the completion of 10. A Jew does not view time as an ongoing cycle, an extension of the past, that would indicate the failure to "turn" and go beyond 9. Rather, man's development in life, similar to the 9 months of gestation, must be a preparation for the future in the attainment of eternity.

The "turning toward" that characterizes 9 sees man use his free will to reach toward the completion of 10.

There is, however, a danger symbolically associated with the number 9: once 10 and a state of completion have been reached where there is a reversal that takes a "turn for the worse" and reverts to the number 9. Here the earlier completion and integration within 10 relapses to the imperfect level of 9.

10, 9: The Breakdown of Tishah b'Av

The most tragic application in the reversal from 10 to 9 was witnessed on Tishah B'Av, 9th of Av. On this day there was the departure of the *Shechinah*, Divine Presence, from the Temple and the subsequent destruction of the Temple — which culminated in exile.

The most tragic reversal from 10 to 9 was witnessed on Tishah B'Av.

The *Shechinah* is characterized by the communal integration of 10. [26] The descent of the *Shechinah* from Above stays at a height of 10 handbreadths from the ground; it does not go below this point.[27] Thus, the regression from 10 down to 9 conveys the loss of the *Shechinah* that is not present in the first 9 handbreadths above the ground.

Tishah B'Av, the most tragic date in the year, symbolically epitomizes a "turning away" from the completion of 10. The Jewish People were led into exile by their conquerors (the Babylonians during the First Temple; the Romans during the Second Temple). Many historic calamities would befall on this day of infamy. The breakdown was both the fracturing of relationship within the nation and of their relationship with G-d.[28] For many communities, Tishah B'Av is the culmination of national mourning that extends through the first 9 days of the month of Av.[29] There was a breakdown in the communal whole unit, with the number 10 fragmented back into the former state of 9 that remains disunited and splintered into its individual parts.

Tishah B'Av symbolically epitomizes a "turning away" from the completion of 10.

9: DAMAGED RELATIONSHIPS

The loss of the Shechinah is marked by the tragic reversal in turning back from 10 to 9.

We have noted that the loss of the *Shechinah* is marked by the tragic reversal in turning back from 10 to 9. One further expression of this is the breakdown in the marital relationship between husband and wife. Where a couple lives in marital harmony, G-d resides with them as His *Shechinah* rests in their midst.[30]

Conversely, a breakdown in their intimate relationship marks a move away from 10, which also marks a state of holiness, to the תֵּשַׁע מִדּוֹת, *9 characteristics*, in a damaged relationship, with any resultant offspring bearing a spiritual blemish.[31] Consequently, the marital harmony is sullied, and the relationship between husband and wife disintegrates.

9, 10: TURN BACK

Where there is a symbolic breakdown of the wholeness of 10 that fragments into 9, the response must be to reverse it by turning it once again, toward 10. Man must again identify with the theme of "turning toward" that exists within the number 9, and must transfer individual, separate parts into the communal, integrated whole of 10. Marital disharmony characterized by the "9 characteristics" or the loss of *Shechinah* that is not present at 9 handbreadths from the ground must be elevated to the level of 10.

This is man's role in This World. His annual review of accountability is set for every Rosh Hashanah on the date of man's creation. Man must maintain his obligation to partner with G-d to "turn" Creation toward its perfection. This means man must reverse the damage in the Temple's destruction on Tishah B'Av and the loss of the *Shechinah*, which led to the numeric regression from 10 to 9. His agenda must be to view time, like the number 9, as the process of turning toward the glorious future. Symbolically, his life is similar to the 9 months of gestation: it is an embryonic development prior to entry into the eternity of *Olam Haba*.

Man is obligated to "re-turn" and "turn" the world from the number 9 until it reaches perfection in the number 10.

Life is in a constant state of flux. Man is therefore obligated to "re-turn" and "turn" the world from the number 9 until it reaches its final state of perfection that is realized in the number 10.

NOTES

1. See "10: Top Ten."
2. See "3: Three-Dimensional."
3. *Maharal, Derech Chaim* 3:13.
4. *Bava Metzia* 38a.
5. *Kiddushin* 49b. Other "9 out of 10" measures include wealth taken by Romans, poverty by Babylonians, arrogance by Eilam, might by Persians, lice by Media, witchcraft by Egypt, disease by pigs, promiscuity by Arabia, brazenness by Meishan, drunkenness by Ethiopians, and sleep by slaves.
6. See *Maharal, Chiddushei Aggados, Kiddushin* 49b (Vol. 2, p. 145).
7. *Bereishis* 4:4-5. *Rashi* ad loc. explains the word *sha'ah* as *panah*, turned.
8. See "10: Top Ten," about how the concept of a *minyan*, a quorum of 10 men, transforms them into a communal unit. See *Berachos* 47b
9. See *Ramchal, Daas Tevunos* 158, quoting *Shir HaShirim Rabbah* 5:2, and R' Chaim Volozhin, *Nefesh HaChaim* 2:10. See also *Ramchal, Daas Tevunos* 24-28, as to how G-d intentionally did not create the world in a perfected state, but limited it, for the needs of His creations who can achieve perfection through their connection to G-d. In His desire to give to His creations, He fashioned them deficient. This would enable them to perfect themselves, and their reward and benefit would be dependent on how they have perfected themselves.
10. R' Yechiel Michel Tucazinsky, *Gesher HaChaim* 3:1.
11. *Menachos* 29b.
12. See "10: Top Ten" and "310: Worlds Apart."
13. *Vilna Gaon, Aderes Eliyahu* and *Sforno, Bereishis* 1:1.
14. See "2: Opposites and Equal."
15. See *Maharal, Derech Chaim* 3:13, about how the mathematical ratio between a circle and square can be taken as 3:4 or as 9:12, and citing the *Ibn Ezra* about how to plot the numbers 1-9 within a circle.
16. See *Berachos* 23b.
17. See *Shabbos* 153a; *Moed Katan* 9a; see *Targum Onkelos, Shemos* 19:15.
18. See *Rosh Hashanah* 10b-11a about the debate regarding whether the world was created in the month of Tishrei or Nissan.
19. *Berachos* 29a
20. *Bereishis* 21:1.
21. *I Shmuel* 1:1-2:10.
22. *Berachos* 29a.
23. See R' Yitzchak Isaac Chaver, *Haggadah Yad Mitzrayim.*
24. *Rambam, Hilchos Teshuvah* 3:4.
25. *Rosh Hashanah* 33b. There is a debate whether the Biblical term *teruah* means: (a) a *shevarim* (3 blasts), (b) *teruah* (9 short staccato notes), (c) or *shevarim-teruah* (a combination of 3 blasts and 9 short staccato notes). See *Shulchan Aruch, Orach Chaim* 590:3.
26. This spiritual state is ideally represented by an assembly of 10 Jews. See *Pirkei Avos* 3:5; *Sanhedrin* 39a.
27. *Succah* 5a.
28. See "410: First Temple" and "420: Second Temple."

29. See *Taanis* 29b-30a for a discussion of whether the mourning period of Av initiates from the 1st of Av or only during the week during which Tishah B'Av falls.
30. *Sotah* 17a.
31. *Nedarim* 20b. This includes marital relationships that are conducted where either of the spouses, is, for whatever reason, not emotionally or psychologically focused upon the other (e.g., if one of the parties is drunk).

10

TOP TEN

10 relates to an integrated system.

Here a full set of individual parts combines to make up a communal whole.

This number typifies holiness and the resting place of the Shechinah.

It is the pathway to reach spiritual perfection and the World to Come.

COUNTING UP TO 10

10 is the basis of the Jewish number system.

THE NUMBER 10 IS THE BASIS OF THE JEWISH NUMBER SYSTEM. A number system can adopt any number as its base. But, in general, base-10 has now been almost universally adopted. Here numbers are grouped into units of 10. The count starts with 1 and ends with 10, whereupon this process is repeated again and again (20, 30, 40 ...). Here numbers are organized as multiples of 10 (where 20 = 2 units of 10, 30 = 3 units of 10).[1]

Base-10 is actually reflected in the Hebrew language.

The adopting of base-10 is actually reflected in the Hebrew language. Each of the first 10 digits is assigned a distinctive name. No new designation is provided for subsequent numbers following 10. The number 11, for example, is אַחַד־עָשָׂר, literally, *1 plus 10*. It has no independent name. Later groupings are modeled based upon their identity as multiples of 10: e.g. 30 (3 base-10) is called שְׁלֹשִׁים based upon the plural of שָׁלֹשׁ, *3*, 40 (4 base-10) is אַרְבָּעִים, the multiple form of אַרְבַּע, *4*. Only when reaching new denominations such as 100 and 1000 are different names introduced.

Furthermore, the base-10 count is applied to higher numbers. Multiples of 10 are used to form new, higher bases for the next series of numbers. This is seen in numbers such as מֵאָה (100), אֶלֶף (1000), and רִבּוֹא (10,000), whose distinct Hebrew names indicate their position as basic units.[2]

10 acts as a point of closure.

There is a simple explanation for why 10 is the endpoint or rounding up of a count: 10 acts as a point of closure. Like the full number of digits on man's hands and feet, all 10 different parts combine to reach an integrated entity — an all-encompassing complete set.

THE COMPLETE SET

THE WORD עֶשֶׂר, *10*, IS SYNONYMOUS WITH עֹשֶׁר, *WEALTH*, AS ALL THE physical needs of a wealthy man are provided for. In this respect, such a person can be considered to have reached a state of completion in the physical realm.[3]

The innate quality of 10 as a complete set finds ample expression through the Divine act of Creation, the unfolding of Jewish history from Adam to Avraham, and the miraculous wonders of the Exodus leading to the giving of the Torah at Sinai.

10: UTTERANCES OF CREATION

G-d used עֲשָׂרָה מַאֲמָרוֹת, *10 Utterances*, in the creation of the universe.[4] The cosmos was built using these Divine 10 Utterances.[5] In the mystical tradition, this parallels the whole of Creation being composed by the עֶשֶׂר סְפִירוֹת, *10 Divine Emanations*. (They are *Keser*, Crown; *Chachmah*, Wisdom; *Binah*, Understanding; *Chesed*, Lovingkindness; *Gevurah*, Might; *Tiferes*, Beauty; *Netzach*, Eternity; *Hod*, Splendor; *Yesod*, Foundation; *Malchus*, Kingdom.[6])

The first generations of mankind were themselves grouped into two sets of 10. There were 10 generations from Adam to Noach and 10 generations from Noach to Avraham.[7] None of them began to fulfill the purpose of Creation. Indeed, they left no lasting impression upon Creation. Only in the merit of Avraham was the whole of Creation established.[8]

10: TESTS OF AVRAHAM

In his lifetime, Avraham withstood 10 great trials that tested every aspect of his character and his devotion to G-d.[9] He faced every sort of test humanly possible; from hiding from Nimrod who threw him into the fiery furnace, to being ready to sacrifice his beloved son to attest to the degree of his love of G-d.[10]

It was these tests that molded him into the first forefather of the Jewish people, who set out to teach the world how to live in the service of its Creator.[11] He became the ancestor of the Children of Israel who would be enslaved in Egypt yet would depart as the newly formed Chosen Nation ready to accept the Torah.

The innate quality of 10 as a complete set finds ample expression through the Divine act of Creation.

G-d used 10 Utterances in the creation of the universe.

Avraham withstood 10 great trials that tested every aspect of his character and his devotion to G-d.

10 pLAGUES

The Egyptians oppressively enslaved the Children of Israel for 210 years.[12] Their cruel ruler Pharaoh proclaimed himself a deity and arrogantly refused to accept G-d's Mastery over the Creation that was created with 10 Utterances.

Pharaoh and his people were punished through the miraculous 10 Plagues. These plagues — Blood, Frogs, Lice, Wild Animals, Pestilence, Boils, Hailstones, Locusts, Darkness, Death of the Firstborn — educated the idolatrous Egyptians to accept G-d's Authority. This is why the 10 Plagues correspond, in an inverse order, to the 10 Utterances of Creation. (For example, the 1st Utterance, *bereishis* — in the beginning — corresponds to 10th plague, the Death of the Firstborn; the 2nd Utterance, the creation of light, corresponds to the 9th plague, Darkness).[13]

The 10 Plagues correspond to the 10 Utterances of Creation.

The liberation came through 10 miracles in Egypt and 10 miracles at the sea.

The liberation of Avraham's descendants from Egypt into the Wilderness (where the Children of Israel would themselves be subject to 10 trials[14]) came through G-d's execution of 10 miracles in Egypt and 10 miracles at the sea.[15] This was in order that they accept the Torah as given to them by G-d Himself in the עֲשֶׂרֶת הַדִּבְּרוֹת, *10 Commandments.*

10 COMMANDMENTS

The 10 Commandments are distinct from the remaining 603 Commandments. Their special quality is highlighted as these were the laws openly presented by G-d to Israel at Sinai,[16] engraved upon *Shnei Luchos HaBris*, 2 Tablets of the Covenant, that Moshe brought down to the Jewish People.[17]

The 10 Commandments can be viewed as the ideological basis for all the commandments.

The 10 Commandments can be viewed as the ideological basis for all the commandments, or as the categories under which all the other precepts are included.[18] It is in their capacity as the opening set of laws that these 10 are said to be more closely attributed to G-d compared to the ensuing 603 laws.[19] In the covenant forged between G-d the Giver of Torah and Israel as the Recipient, the 10 Commandments, which intrinsically include all the other commandments,[20] can be most closely related back to G-d. The remainder of the laws, by contrast, are more closely attributed to Israel as the Recipient of the Torah.[21]

The fulfillment of Torah, as encapsulated in the 10 Commandments, is the purpose of existence, created by the 10 Utterances.[22] In turn, this was the very reason why Israel was redeemed from Egypt through the 10 Plagues.[23]

OTHER SETS OF 10

Other examples of 10 as an entire, complete set or as the full range of experiences (both for the good and the bad[24]) include the 10 kings to have ruled over the known world;[25] the 10 non-Jewish nations that originally occupied the Holy Land;[26] the 10 sons of Haman;[27] the 10 levels of impurity;[28] the 10 Biblical famines;[29] the 10 measures of qualities such as wisdom, beauty, etc. that descended to the world.[30] There are 10 expressions for song,[31] 10 expressions for prayer,[32] 10 verses for each of the 3 special blessings on Rosh Hashanah Mussaf prayer,[33] 10 authors of *Tehillim*.[34]

In sum, 10 is the number through which a full range comes together as a collective whole unit. This represents the leap from private to public, from individual to communal.

10 is the number through which a full range comes together as a whole unit. This represents the leap from individual to communal.

COMMUNAL WHOLE

WHILE NUMBERS UP TO 10 ARE DEFICIENT AND LACKING, THE completed set of 10 integrates all the individual parts into a greater whole.[35] Here the individual components find their full realization within a wider public setting, as seen in formation of a *minyan* and the make-up of 1 unified community.

MINYAN: THE 10TH MAN

Perhaps the most famous example of 10 creating a communal unit is the formation of a מִנְיָן, *quorum,* of 10 Jewish male adults needed for communal prayer. The arrival of the 10th man transforms 10 independent personalities into 1 group. This dynamic new entity powerfully possesses a far greater impact than what could have been achieved through just their individual efforts.[36] This is primarily because this group embodies the earliest formation of a community. There is now the development of a public forum.

The arrival of the 10th man transforms 10 independent personalities into 1 group.

10: PUBLIC FORUM

Moshe's height of 10 cubits accentuates his persona as a public servant.

10 relates to the level of the *public* rather than of the *individual*.[37] The symbolism of Moshe's height of 10 cubits[38] accentuates his persona as a public servant. He was equal to and equated with the entire Jewish community.[39]

The essential number of individuals that constitute an עֵדָה, *community*, is 10. This is derived from the grouping of the 10 treacherous spies in the Wilderness.[40] The assembly of 10 Jews creates a unit called *Knesses Yisrael*, Congregation of Israel. Something is not halachically considered to be in the public eye when there are fewer than 10 people present.[41] The gathering of 10 members creates a *tzibbur*, a public entity, where individual pursuits are sublimated to the greater good for the broader public.

The gathering of 10 members creates a tzibbur, where individual pursuits are sublimated to the greater good for the broader public.

WHERE 10 BECOMES 1

Due to the ability of 10 to integrate all the parts to achieve completion, the full set of 10 can rightly be viewed as 1 entity. In truth, 10 relates both to attributes of multiplicity and of singularity, with each set of 10 unified into 1 unit (10, 20, 30 …), before repeating this count again. Whereas 1 is absolute unity, 10 is where the many merge into 1 whole.[42] This completed state of 10 — in Creation, the Commandments, etc. — attests to the Oneness of G-d. One primary expression of 10 as a reflection of 1 is how it typifies *kedushah*, holiness.[43]

The full set of 10 can rightly be viewed as 1 entity. This completed state attests to the Oneness of G-d.

GATEWAY TO HOLINESS

The holiness associated with the number 10 finds expression in the High Holy Day of Yom Kippur

THE HOLINESS ASSOCIATED WITH THE NUMBER 10 FINDS PROMINENT expression in the High Holy Day of Yom Kippur, in the 10 levels of holiness whose apex is the Holy of Holies, and in the presence of the *Shechinah*, Divine Presence.

yom kippur: 10th of tishrei

Yom Kippur, the 10th of Tishrei, is the final day of the *Aseres Yemei Teshuvah*, 10 Days of Repentance.[44] In the Jewish calendar this date is the holiest day of the year.[45] This was when the primary sacrificial service was carried out by the individual on the highest level of holiness: the *Kohen Gadol*, High Priest. On this day, he pronounced the Ineffable Four-Letter Divine Name 10 times,[46] and was given exclusive rights to enter the *Kodesh HaKodashim*, the Holy of Holies.

kedushah: 10 levels

Often the final, 10th component — that will make something whole — is holy to G-d. The foremost example of this is that every 10th animal of the farmer's flock that passes through the barn door is designated as *maaser beheimah*, tithes of animals.[47] Once the 10th is attained, this sanctifies all the parts. Accordingly, there is the principle, "A holy matter shall not be with fewer than 10 present."[48]

The Mishnah lists 10 ascending levels of holiness within the Holy Land. The 10th-highest degree of sanctity was the *Kodesh HaKodashim*.[49] The dimensions of this innermost sacred chamber were 10 cubits long by 10 cubits wide.[50] This chamber was the permanent dwelling place of the 10 Commandments, housed within or alongside the Ark,[51] which was 10 handbreadths high;[52] also the two *cherubim* rose to a height of 10 handbreadths.[53] This was the central location for the holiness of the *Shechinah*, Divine Presence, that had its resting place within the Temple.

> There is the principle, "A holy matter shall not be with fewer than 10 present."

> The Mishnah lists 10 ascending levels of holiness within the Holy Land.

10: shechinah

The creation of the world through 10 Utterances beautifully captures its holy stature and the necessity for the universe to reach a state of completion as signified by the number 10.[54] The formation of Israel — through the 10 trials of Avraham and the 10 Plagues of the Exodus — was the precursor to receiving the 10 Commandments of the Torah that would sanctify Israel and enable the *Shechinah* to descend into This World.

G-d fills all of Creation. The resting of the *Shechinah*, Divine Presence, refers to where a place or situation possesses an additional

> The creation of the world through 10 Utterances captures the necessity for the universe to reach completion signified by the number 10.

awareness of G-d. It is there that His Presence is then said to reside (the word *Shechinah* comes from the root *shochen*, to dwell). There is the greater ability within this situation to experience the Divine.[55]

The *Shechinah* — Whose affinity to a collective unit is associated with the number 10 — is said not to descend lower than 10 handbreadths.[56] The *Shechinah* rested upon Mount Sinai at the national giving of Torah. It then transferred to the *Mishkan*, Sanctuary, that was the locus of the Jewish camp.[57] Its prestigious inaugural date (1st Nissan) was honored by "10 crowns" — a reference to 10 commemorations of unique events that were begun that year.[58] It accompanied them during their journeys and the *Shechinah* subsequently took up permanent residence inside the Temple (which itself was host to experience 10 miracles[59]). Thus the world became a receptacle to host the dwelling place of G-d in This World.[60]

The prayers of Moshe that the *Shechinah* exclusively rest upon Israel were affirmed by G-d.[61] The *Shechinah* forever resides amid the Jewish congregation, especially in an assembly of 10 Jews.[62] The Jewish nation cannot lose its sacred nature. Consequently, the *Shechinah* is destined never to depart from Israel — even in later times in Jewish history when they have fallen in their spiritual level: "He dwells with them amid their contamination."[63] This includes their long sojourn in exile away from their Holy Land.[64] They retain their ability to experience the Divine whatever their situation is, or would be.

On some level, the *Shechinah* is also said to reside inside every individual Jewish home. The *mezuzah*, which signals that holiness fills a Jewish home, is placed on the doorpost at a minimum height of 10 handbreadths.[65] Inside the home, the husband remains duty-bound to honor the 10 marital obligations.[66] Where marital harmony reigns, the *Shechinah* is then said to rest along with husband and wife.[67]

SPIRITUAL PERFECTION

THE EVERLASTING LEVEL OF HOLINESS AND PERMANENT RESIDENCE of the *Shechinah* is reserved for the future, when the world reaches its ultimate completion: in *Olam Haba*, the World to Come. This will be where existence reaches closure upon finally attaining its spiritual perfection.

10: WORLD TO COME

Olam Haba was created with *yud*, the 10th letter of the Hebrew alphabet.[68] This epoch is where the righteous glow in the radiance of the *Shechinah*.[69]

This spiritual realm is permeated with holiness.[70] This forthcoming world — also alluded to in the letter *yud*, which in the Hebrew language transfers a verb to the future tense[71] — will be an everlasting state where the universal picture of all existence is revealed. Just as the number 10 represents the completed set, so too, in the World to Come all aspects of Creation successfully integrate into 1 grand tapestry that, in harmony, proclaims the eternal Glory of G-d.

This forthcoming world will be where the universal picture of all existence is revealed.

This state of spiritual perfection, which simultaneously completes and begins a whole new order, is synonymous with the number 10. Indeed, a new song to glorify G-d will be composed and will be played on a 10-stringed lyre — which, like the number 10, represents the attainment of a completed state.[72]

Here, the spiritual journey to perfection will be attained. The entirety of existence symbolized in the number 10 integrates into a whole with every sanctified Jew reunited with his Creator for all of eternity.

This state of spiritual perfection is synonymous with the number 10.

NOTES

1. The extension of the base-10 number system into fractional parts gives the decimal system. In Latin, the prefix *deca* means *ten*; a decade refers to 10 years, etc. The metric measurement uses units in multiples of 10.
2. *Ibn Ezra, Shemos* 3:15.
3. *Maharal, Derech Chaim* 5:8.
4. *Pirkei Avos* 5:1; see *Rosh Hashanah* 32a.
5. Similarly, 10 items were created on the first day (*Chagigah* 12a), and ten items were created in the twilight period before Shabbos (*Pirkei Avos* 5:8).
6. *Rama, Toras HaOlah* 3:4. The 10 Emanations permeate the 3 spiritual realms of עוֹלָם, space; שָׁנָה, time; נֶפֶשׁ, spirit (*Sefer Yetzirah* 3: 4-8; "3: Three Dimensional"). The sphere of space contains the 6 directions (north, south, east, west, up, down). The time continuum essentially revolves around the axis of 2 points: past and future (or beginning and end). The spirit within man as an agent of free will fluctuates between the 2 opposites: good and evil. (See "2: Opposite and Equal"). In summation, there are a total of 10 choices within Creation that should reflect the Will of G-d.
7. *Pirkei Avos* 5:2-3.
8. Avraham, "pillar of the world" (*Shemos Rabbah* 2:6), justified Creation itself. His new beginning meant

Creation was revitalized because of him. Thus, Avraham is named as the reason for creation; the letters of בְּהִבָּרְאָם, *when they were created* (*Bereishis* 2:4) rearrange to form the word בְּאַבְרָהָם, *[created] for the sake of Avraham* (*Bereishis Rabbah* 12:4). Indeed, Avraham really should have been created before Adam (*Bereishis Rabbah* 14:6). See *Ramchal, Derech Hashem* 2:4.

9. *Pirkei Avos* 5:4.
10. See *Pirkei Avos* 5:3 and commentaries of *Rashi, Bartenura,* and *Rambam* for different opinions of the different listing. See also *Pirkei DeRabbi Eliezer* Chs. 26-31.
11. See *Maharal, Derech Chaim* 5:3, for why it was specifically the forefather Avraham who faced these trials rather than Yitzchak or Yaakov.
12. See "210: The Iron Furnace."
13. *Maharal, Gevuros Hashem* 57.
14. *Bamidbar* 14:22 and *Pirkei Avos* 5:6.
15. *Pirkei Avos* 5:5.
16. See *Rashi, Shemos* 20:1.
17. *Shemos* 32:15-6; *Devarim* 4:13.
18. *Rashi, Shemos* 24:12.
19. *Maharal, Tiferes Yisrael* 35.
20. There are 620 letters in the Ten Commandments corresponding to the 613 mitzvos plus 7 rabbinic precepts (or the 7 Noachide rules) (*Bamidbar Rabbah* 13:15). See "620: Crowning Glory."
21. *Maharal, Tiferes Yisrael* 56.
22. The 10 Commandments parallel the 10 Utterances (*Rabbeinu Bachya, Kad HaKemach, Shavuos; Shelah, Shavuos, Torah Ohr* 79).
23. The parallels —10 Utterances; 10 Plagues, 10 Commandments — are often interconnected. See, for example, *Sfas Emes, Bo* 5639, *Ohr Gedalyhu, Moadim* p. 138.
24. See, e.g., R' Tzadok HaKohen, *Pri Tzaddik, Vayigash* 5.
25. *Pirkei DeRabbi Eliezer* 11. The 1st and 10th King of the world is G-d.
26. *Bereishis* 15:19-21.
27. *Esther* 9:10.
28. *Mishnah, Keilim* 1:5.
29. *Bereishis Rabbah* 25:3.
30. *Kiddushin* 49b. See also "9: Where to Turn?"
31. It also comprises 10 forms of song (*Midrash Shocher Tov* 1:6). There are 10 expressions of praise said by David in *Tehillim* (*Pesachim* 117a).
32. *Devarim Rabbah* 2:1.
33. *Rosh Hashanah* 32a
34. *Bava Basra* 14b and *Koheles Rabbah* 7:19.
35. See *Maharal, Derech Chaim* 3:6 for how the concepts of increase and of deficiency exist in all numbers until 10 is reached. See "9: Where to Turn?"
36. There must be a minimum of 10 men present for the public (*tzibbur*) reading of the Torah, where no fewer than 10 verses are read (*Rambam, Hilchos Tefillah* 12:3). The exception to the rule is on Purim, when we read *Shemos* 17:8-16.
37. The *Maharal* suggests that this is why the retribution on the Egyptian public was with 10 Plagues, as anything less could have been interpreted as individual punishment (*Gevuros Hashem* 34).
38. *Berachos* 54b.
39. By extension, Moshe rejected the notion to annihilate the Children of Israel (*Shemos* 32:10) and to establish a new nation from him.
40. *Megillah* 23b. The minimal quorum of Jewish leadership to the public was "leaders of 10s" (*Devarim* 1:15).
41. *Sanhedrin* 74b.

42. *Maharal, Derashah L'Shabbos HaGadol* p. 197-8; *Maharal, Nesiv HaTorah* 1.
43. The holiness of 10 is often the exact mirror of the original first — dedicating the opening number 1 to become sanctified, See "1: The One and Only." The other number used to express holiness is 7; see "7: A Holy Spark."
44. See *Sfas Emes, Rosh Hashanah* 5632, 5633, 5642, about how the 10 Days of Repentance correspond to 10 Utterances and 10 Commandments. See also *Shelah HaKadosh, Rosh Hashanah Torah Ohr* in name of *Ramak*.
45. *Vayikra* 23:27.
46. *Yoma* 39b.
47. *Vayikra* 27:32.
48. *Megillah* 23b. This is why the prayers that are associated with *kedushah* — such as *Kaddish, Kedushah,* and *Borchu* — all require the presence of 10 men (*Shulchan Aruch, Orach Chaim* 55:1). Boaz summoned 10 elders of the city for the 7 blessings (*Sheva Berachos*) of his marriage with Rus (*Rus* 4:2; *Kesubos* 7a).
49. *Mishnah, Keilim* 1:6-9. See also *Rambam, Hilchos Beis HaBechirah* 7:13.
50. *Rashi, Shemos* 26:32.
51. *Bava Basra* 14a-b
52. *Succah* 4b.
53. The height of the *Cherubim* in the Temple was 10 cubits standing on the ground. In the *Mishkan*, Tabernacle, they were 10 handbreadths high from the wings to the *Kapores* cover (*I Melachim* 6:26; *Succah* 5b; *Rashi, Shemos* 25:20.
54. *Maharal, Derech Chaim* 5:1. That the world was created with 10 Utterances, rather than 1, gives testimony to its importance and its holiness. 10 is a requisite for every matter of holiness. *Olam Haba*, created with the letter *yud*, is a higher, exalted realm.
55. See "22,000: The Divine Presence."
56. *Succah* 5a. See "9: Where to Turn?"
57. *Ramban, Shemos* 25:2.
58. *Shabbos* 87b; *Rashi, Vayikra* 9:1. See *Seder Olam* 7.
59. *Pirkei Avos* 5:5.
60. *Tanchuma, Nasso* 16.
61. *Berachos* 7a.
62. *Pirkei Avos* 3:5; *Sanhedrin* 39a. But the *Shechinah* in a wider national capacity is seen with the numbers 22,000 and 600,0000. See "22,000: The Divine Presence" and "600,000: The Jewish Nation."
63. *Vayikra* 16:16. See *Yoma* 56b; *Bamidbar Rabbah* 7:9.
64. *Megillah* 29a; *Shemos Rabbah* 23:6.
65. *Shulchan Aruch, Yoreh Deah* 287:2. This is also the minimum height of a *succah* (*Mishnah, Succah* 1:1).
66. *Rambam, Hilchos Ishus* 12:2. There are similarly 10 principles (on the Torah level) for dissolving a marriage (*Rambam, Hilchos Geirushin* 1:1).
67. *Sotah* 17a.
68. *Menachos* 29b.
69. *Berachos* 17a; *Rambam, Hilchos Teshuvah* 8:2.
70. *Maharal, Derech Chaim* 5:1.
71. See *Rashi, Shemos* 15:1; *Sanhedrin* 91b.
72. *Maharal, Netzech Yisrael* 32 discusses how the instrument of This World has 7 strings, that of Mashiach will have 8 strings, and that of the World to Come will have 10 strings. See also *Shem MiShmuel, Rosh Hashanah* 5672 about the 10-stringed harp where the Glory of G-d reaches its perfection.

11

THE OUTSIDER

11 lies outside the completed
spiritual set of 10.

An example of where "more is less,"
it represents the futile, endless search for more
worldly assets than a person truly needs.

This outlook places man "on the outside" so
that he must draw himself back in.

ON THE OUTSIDE

The number 11 begins another grouping that conceptually lies "on the outside" of 10.

I N CONTRAST TO ITS PREDECESSOR, THE NUMBER 11 MAKES RELATIVELY few appearances in Judaism.

We have seen that 10 is the number where individual units combine in creation to make an integrated, communal whole, which is then sanctified to G-d.[1] As the number that follows 10, 11 begins another grouping but one that conceptually lies "on the outside" of 10. This is reflected in 11, which is the first number that is *not* designated by a new, distinct Hebrew name: 11 is called אַחַד־עָשָׂר which literally means "10 (עָשָׂר) + 1 (אֶחָד)."[2]

11: EISAV

The classic personification of an "outsider" is Eisav. Just as 11 exists outside 10, the sinful twin of Yaakov removed himself from the spiritual set of rules that govern the universe. His refusal to subjugate himself to the Master of the Universe signaled his ill-fated decision to "step outside."

There is a close affinity between Eisav and the number 11.

There is a close affinity between Eisav and the number 11. Listing Eisav's descendants, the Torah enumerates 11 Edomite chieftains.[3] It was an 11-day journey from Chorev to Kadesh Barnea via Eisav's homeland of Mount Seir.[4]

This gap between Eisav and Yaakov is reflected in their respective calendars. The descendants of Eisav use the solar calendar of circa 365 days; the Jewish calendar principally follows the standard lunar year of 354 days. That means there is an 11-day difference between them (in a non-leap year).[5] Rosh Chodesh, the time frame of the lunar year that runs contrary to Eisav's solar year, was marked by 11 sacrifices: 2 young bulls, 1 ram, 7 lambs, and 1 goat.[6]

Eisav's nemesis was Yosef, the 11th son of Yaakov.

Eisav's nemesis was Yosef, the 11th son of Yaakov.[7] It was Yosef's prophetic dream of the 11 stars that depicted that his 11 brothers would later bow down to him.[8] In turn, the Tribes suspected Yosef of resembling Eisav in a plot to exclude them (as Eisav was excluded from Yitzchak's blessing) in the establishment of the Children of Israel. Earlier, on the night prior to the historic encounter with Eisav, the Torah relates that Yaakov escorted his 11 children across the Yabbok River. When he returned to recover forgotten items,[9] he was attacked by Eisav's ministering angel.[10]

TOO MUCH

WE HAVE NOTED THAT EISAV IS SYNONYMOUS WITH THE NUMBER 11 because he viewed himself as an independent force outside of G-d's Creation. He ideologically placed himself as an addition. His description at birth as clad in a "hairy mantle"[11] is itself representative of a useless addition. Hair is an extraneous, outside growth, an attached, though non-integral, component to the human body.[12]

Eisav is synonymous with the number 11 because he viewed himself as "outside" of G-d's Creation.

11: MORE THAN YOU NEED

The succession from 10 to 11 resembles the journey from "completion" to "unnecessary excess." These two numbers beautifully encapsulate the respective diverging worldviews of Yaakov and Eisav.

Yaakov declared, יֶשׁ לִי כֹל, *I have everything.*[13] His search for spirituality meant that he would wholeheartedly use all of his possessions in the service of G-d. Everything was essential; nothing was extraneous. This explains why Yaakov risked his life to retrieve several insignificant utensils.[14]

The bed of Yaakov is depicted as "complete"[15] in the sense that none of his seed went to waste. Consequently, all of his children were righteous.[16] Furthermore, he was described as arriving at a destination "whole, intact."[17] His perfection was in body, spirit, family, and possessions.[18] Thus, Yaakov reached the level of holiness and completion alluded to by the number 10.[19]

This sharply contrasts with Eisav's outlook. His determination to grab "more and more"[20] meant a never-ending accumulation of wealth, well beyond his essential physical needs.[21] His proud boast, יֶשׁ לִי רָב, *I have much,*[22] declared an obsession with more possessions than he would ever need. Indeed, his enduring legacy is alive and well in Western civilization (known as the exile of Edom that perpetuates the legacy of Eisav).[23]

All this excess is reflected in the spiritual emptiness of Eisav,

The succession from 10 to 11 resembles the journey from "completion" to "unnecessary excess."

Eisav's determination to grab "more and more" meant a never-ending accumulation of wealth.

whose existence was spiritually compromised.[24] His pursuit of addition indicates an ideological failing, one that would interfere with the pursuit of perfection.

11: WHERE MORE IS LESS

The phenomenon "where more is less" finds expression in the number 11.

The phenomenon "where more is less" finds expression in the number 11. Once the requisite 10 men are present to form a מִנְיָן, *a quorum*, there is no intrinsic value whatsoever in the additional presence of an 11th man.[25] In terms of his contribution to the *minyan*, the 11th man is, in effect, redundant. The unit is complete without him.

In Torah and spiritual matters, not only is the rule "the more, the better" wrong, but the opposite is true. *Adding is equivalent to subtracting.* Where something is whole, it requires nothing more and nothing less. Surplus, like deficiency, contradicts or compromises the perfection of the system. Torah is described as complete.[26] It therefore cannot be tampered with without compromising its perfect state. Accordingly, there is the commandment that a Jew is not permitted to add or to subtract from any *mitzvah*.[27]

There in an important principle, "Anyone who adds detracts."

There in an important principle, כָּל הַמּוֹסִיף גּוֹרֵעַ, *Anyone who adds detracts*.[28] This concept is derived from one of the coverings draped over the *Mishkan*, Sanctuary, that consisted of 11 curtains.[29] The Hebrew word used for 11 is עַשְׁתֵּי עֶשְׂרֵה. If not for the additional presence of the first letter (ע), this would read שְׁתֵּי עֶשְׂרֵה, meaning 12. Consequently, the addition (of 1 letter) ironically leads to a detraction (in meaning); from the number 12 it decreases to the number 11.[30] One halachic application of the maxim, "Anyone who adds detracts," is that an extra limb on an animal is considered as much a blemish for use as a sacrificial offering as does a missing limb.[31]

11 CURSES

The respective outlooks of Yaakov and Eisav accord with the contrary concepts of blessings and curses.

Their respective outlooks accord with the contrary concepts of blessings and curses.

בְּרָכָה, *blessing*, results from closeness to G-d attained through observing His laws.[32] When serving G-d faithfully, man is rewarded with an abundance of bounty where all his endeavors are blessed.[33] This channel of blessing was opened when Avraham became the personification of *berachah*.[34] It was transmitted to Yitzchak, who in turn bestowed his blessings upon Yaakov.[35]

But Eisav, who excluded himself from the 10 Utterances of Creation, allied himself with the opposite concept of קְלָלָה, *curse*. This can take the form either of a blockage of goodness, where Divine blessings do not freely flow down to man from on High, or of complete severance from G-d. This is why 11, the number connected so closely with Eisav, is also synonymous with *tumah*, impurity, which spiritually denotes distance from G-d.[36] Indeed, Rambam categorizes 11 types of spiritual defilement.[37]

When entering the Holy Land, the Jewish people encamped at Mount Gerizim and Mount Eval, where they recounted the blessings and curses that would fall upon them based upon their compliance with or rejection of Torah. In the latter category, the Torah enumerates 11 particular curses that would strike them.[38] This denotes their exclusion from the ideal blessed state where Israel is one with G-d.

11 is also synonymous with tumah, which spiritually denotes distance from G-d.

BACK INSIDE

WE HAVE SEEN THE NEGATIVITY ASSOCIATED WITH THE NUMBER 11 as an outsider and something superfluous that compromises a state of perfection. Despite this detachment from G-d, there is always the possibility for the accursed outsider to return to the innermost circles of holiness. One powerful example of this is found in the *ketores*, incense.

There is always the possibility for the accursed outsider to return to the innermost circles of holiness.

KETORES: 11 SPICES

As the most powerful offering to create an intractable bond (in Hebrew, קֶשֶׁר, whose Aramaic equivalent, קְטֹר, is the root of the word קְטֹרֶת)[39] between Israel and G-d, *ketores* was composed of 11 ingredients.[40] Of these, 10 were sweet-smelling spices.[41] However, the *ketores* was incomplete without the inclusion of the 11th spice. This spice was the חֶלְבְּנָה, which had a foul, repugnant odor. But mixed together, the combination of all 11 emitted the most marvelous aroma for which the *ketores* was renowned.[42]

Taken in isolation, the offensive *chelbenah* spice represents the wicked of Israel. Though they imitate Eisav by sinfully declaring themselves independent of G-d, they are not cursed and not

The combination of all 11 emitted the most marvelous aroma.

excluded forever. If they shake off their affinity to demand more than they need, the wicked, like the 11th ingredient in the *ketores*, can be reconnected to the 10 of completion. Then, they can be reintegrated into G-d's cosmos as created by His 10 Utterances. The Jewish sinner then identifies himself as an indispensable part of his nation, as symbolized by the communal number 10, and not as an excluded individual left on the outside.

The wicked, like the 11th ingredient in the ketores, can be reconnected to the 10 of completion.

The believing Jew shrinks from Eisav's self-description as the excluded 11th, the additional one who is forever the outsider. All Eisav's attempts to accrue more wealth than he could possibly need originate from his cursed fixation on the present physical world — one created out of wanton disregard for the blessed spiritual realm that completes it.[43]

Eisav's attempts to accrue more wealth originate from his cursed fixation on the present physical world.

A Jew realizes that nothing in Creation is unnecessary or superfluous. Everything he owns is blessed if it furthers his relationship with G-d. When there is the realization that "more" is really "less," man realizes the importance of returning to the symbolic communality and perfection of the number 10. He will then turn away from 11, rightly concluding that it is "one too much."

NOTES

1. See "10: Top Ten."
2. *Maharal, Derech Chaim* 3:13.
3. *Bereishis* 36:40-43. The negative force within the number 11 is also evident in the prominent descendants of Eisav's son Amalek: Haman and his 10 sons (a total of 11 villains) were killed in the Purim narrative (See *Maor VaShemesh, Purim*).
4. *Devarim* 1:2.
5. See *Koheles Rabbah* 1:35 about how the shrinking of the moon in size compared to the sun (see *Chullin* 60b) was also reflected in the length of their respective years. Originally, the solar year and lunar years were identical in length (365 days). But the shrinkage of the moon was reflected in the decrease of the length of a lunar year to be 11 days shorter than the solar year.
6. *Rokeach, Bamidbar* 28:14.
7. See *Rokeach, Devarim* 21:15. Yosef's birth was the catalyst that prompted Yaakov to return to Canaan, now unafraid to face his twin brother (*Bereishis* 30:25 and *Rashi* ad loc.). "Yaakov's house will be fire, Yosef's house a flame, and Eisav's house is of straw ... they will ignite them and devour them" (*Ovadiah* 1:18). See *Bereishis Rabbah* 84:5.
8. *Bereishis* 37:9.
9. *Rashi, ibid.* 32:25.
10. Ibid. 32:22. Dinah was not mentioned as she was hidden in a box (*Rashi* ad loc. v. 23). See *Maharal, Gur Aryeh, Bereishis* 32:22 [28].

11. *Bereishis* 25:25.
12. See *Maharal, Chiddushei Aggados, Sotah* 8b (Vol. 2, p. 38). According to the opinions who maintain that Eisav was uncircumcised (*Da'as Zekeinim, Bereishis* 25:25), he retained an affinity with the unwanted excess of the *orlah*, foreskin.
13. *Bereishis* 33:11.
14. Ibid. 32:25 and *Rashi* ad loc.
15. *Vayikra Rabbah* 36:5.
16. See *Yevamos* 76a.
17. *Bereishis* 33:18.
18. *Shabbos* 33b; *Bereishis Rabbah* 79:5.
19. See "10: Top Ten."
20. Seeing his parents' disapproval of his idol-worshiping Canaanite wives, Eisav did not divorce them. Instead, Eisav went on to marry an additional wife (*Bereishis* 28:8-9).
21. *Rabbeinu Yonah, Shaarei Teshuvah* 2:27, notes the vicious cycle in the relentless quest for material goods.
22. *Bereishis* 33:9.
23. In contemporary society, yesterday's luxuries are marketed as today's necessities. This plays on the notion that the consumer of today is somehow "deficient" if he is not in possession of the latest, cutting-edge technology. This creates an unending cycle where man is never destined to be happy with his lot (*Pirkei Avos* 4:1).
24. The Midrash notes that G-d decries Eisav as being the epitome of "the meaninglessness (or vanity) (*shov*) created in the world" (*Bereishis Rabbah* 63:8).
25. "One should always arise early to attend synagogue and acquire the merit of being included in the first 10 people for a *minyan*" (*Berachos* 47b).
26. *Tehillim* 19:8.
27. *Devarim* 13:1.
28. *Sanhedrin* 29a. Another expression of this principle is that of כָּל יָתֵר כְּנָטוּל דָּמִי, *Anything additional is as if it were subtracted* (Mishnah, *Bechoros* 6:7).
29. *Shemos* 26:7.
30. *Sanhedrin* 29a and *Rashi* ad loc.
31. Mishnah, *Bechoros* 6:7. In some cases it is nonkosher as well and may not be eaten, even when it is not an sacrificial offering (*Chullin* 58b; *Shulchan Aruch Yoreh Deah* 55:4.) This is consistent with the principle that תָּפַסְתָּ מְרוּבָּה לֹא תָּפַסְתָּ, *One who overreaches to seize a large amount risks ending up not having attained anything* (see *Rashi, Succah* 5a and *Chagigah* 17a).
32. See "2: Opposite and Equal."
33. See, for example, *Vayikra* 26:3-13; *Devarim* 11:13-15.
34. *Bereishis* 12:2.
35. Ibid. 28:4.
36. *Vilna Gaon, Aderes Eliyahu,Terumah* 25:8 and *Be'er Yitzchak* ad loc.
37. *Rambam*, Introduction, *Seder Tohoros*. A further manifestation of 11 as distance from G-d is apparent in the laws pertaining to the relationship between husband and wife that corresponds to that between G-d and Israel. The *zivus* interval is 11 days (*Niddah* 72b).
38. *Devarim* 27:15-25. The 11 curses parallel 11 tribes (*Rashi, Devarim* 27:24). See *Maharal Gur Aryeh, Devarim* 27:24, for how the number 11 conceptually attests to "being cursed by G-d." See *Maharal,* op. cit. 29:28 how the 11 dots above the words לָנוּ וּלְבָנֵינוּ עַד allude to the aforementioned 11 curses. The *Vilna Gaon* (*Esther* 4:1, *remez*) sees the parallel between 11 as the curses and Haman and his 10 sons. See *Maharal* (*Tiferes Yisrael* 54 and *Gur Aryeh Devarim* 27:24) who offers an alternative approach to where 11 can be the beginning of the sequence of numbers related to the higher realm.
39. See *Maharal, Derashah L'Shabbos Shuvah*, p. 81.

40. *Kereisos* 6a-b. Furthermore, *Rokeach* (*Shemos* 30:34) observes that one of the main verses discussing the *ketores* offering (*Shemos* 30:37) has a total of 11 words.

41. Indeed, in the inauguration of the Sanctuary the princes brought 1 spoon of *ketores* that is equivalent to 10 gold weights (*Bamidbar* 7:14).

42. *Kereisos* 6b.

43. Eisav's nemesis Yosef did not abuse the notion of addition. Yosef's name means *addition* (*Bereishis* 30:24) and he was Yaakov's favorite son, loved more than his brothers and given an additional coat! (*Bereishis* 37:3). Nevertheless, he dealt efficiently with addition, as we see that he competently handled the abundance of the years of plenty to be stored in preparation for the years of famine (*Bereishis* 41:49).

12
TRIBES OF ISRAEL

12 is the framework wherein the natural world of 6 dimensions operates in practice.

This number corresponds to the 12 Tribes of Israel. It offers distinct yet equally authentic pathways in the service of G-d.

A PHYSICAL STRUCTURE

The structure within which these components operate and interact finds expression via the number 12.

THE NUMBER 12 IS THE FRAMEWORK GIVEN TO THE NATURAL WORLD first defined by the number 6.

We have seen 6 as the expression of the physical in terms of both space (6 directions) and time (6 Days of Creation).[1] The structure within which these components are able to operate and interact — both through space and time — finds expression via the number 12.

12: EDGES OF A CUBE

The number 4 is the original set of dimensions used to define space in the physical realm found in the 4 directions of a compass (north-east-south-west).[2] It is possible to subdivide each of the 4 sides into the essential 3 parts of every process: beginning, middle, and end.[3] Together, this creates a total of 12 components (4 x 3 = 12).[4]

The connections of the 6 faces of the cube mean that the cube is bound by a total of 12 edges.

There are 12 diagonals that bind together the different parts of a 3-dimensional structure (length, width, depth) together. Moreover, the connections of the 6 faces of the cube mean that the cube is bound by a total of 12 edges.[5]

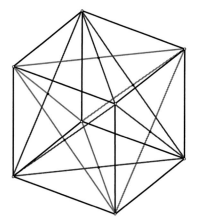
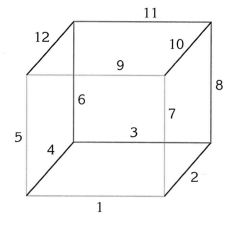

12: OF HOURS AND MONTHS

The physical world fashioned during the 6 Days of Creation finds its perfect structure in the subdivision of a day and of a year into units of 12.

Every day is measured as 12 hours of the daytime and 12 hours of night.[6] The 12 units of a day have their parallel in the 12 months of a standard year.[7]

Like a cube's 12 edges, time divided into 12 periods frame the life of Jew. This enables him to interact within the confines of the natural realm and to dedicate his energies to the service of G-d.

The time periods enable man to dedicate his energies to the service of G-d.

THE MAKINGS OF ISRAEL

EVERYTHING WITHIN EXISTENCE IN THE LOWER REALM REFLECTS A higher spiritual concept. There are 12 permutations of the Ineffable 4-Letter Name of G-d (יהו-ה), which represent the pathways of Divine influence in the universe.[8]

The foremost vehicle is through the *Shevatim*, 12 Tribes of Israel,[9] in whose merit the universe stands.[10] They are parallel to the "12 pillars that uphold the world."[11] Indeed, all of G-d's workings in This World (as overtly manifest in 12 hours and 12 months) correspond to the 12 Tribes[12] that are memorably referred to as the שָׁבְטֵי יָ-ה, *Tribes of G-d*.[13] Yaakov's 12 sons are responsible for giving the natural world a meaningful structure within which to interact.

12 Tribes of Israel are parallel to the "12 pillars that uphold the world."

BIRTH OF THE TRIBES

The Jewish nation has its origins in the 3 Avos, *Patriarchs*, and 4 *Imahos*, Matriarchs. The interrelationship between the numbers 3 and 4 — representative of the "process"[14] and "means of expression"[15] — led to the formation of the *Bnei Yisrael*, Children of Israel. Their interaction, reflected by the product of the numbers 3 and 4 (4 x 3 = 12), was ultimately realized in the birth of the 12 Tribes.

In actuality, the first human being, Adam, should have himself fathered 12 sons.[16] But his primeval sin meant the designation *Israel* in the mission to glorify G-d through 12 pathways in This World would

The interrelationship between the numbers 3 and 4 led to the formation of the Bnei Yisrael.

The mission
to glorify G-d
through 12
pathways in
This World
would not be
given to all of
mankind.

not be given to all of mankind. Instead, it would be reserved for the chosen descendants of Avraham.[17] This would also exclude several of Avraham's descendants. Most notably, Yishmael was excluded — even though he fathered 12 sons.[18] Rivkah was not granted the ability to herself beget 12 sons for Yitzchak, so there was the exclusion of the wicked Eisav and his descendants.[19]

Finally, it was left up to Yaakov. Of the 12 Tribes of Israel, Reuven, Shimon, Levi, Yehudah, Yissachar, and Zevulun were born to Leah; Yosef and Binyamin were born to Rachel; Dan and Naftali to Bilhah; and Gad and Asher to Zilpah.[20] (Yosef, the son who most resembled Yaakov, was himself meant to have 12 sons.[21])

ROSh ChODESh: 12 QUASI-FESTIVALS

We have noted that a cube extending in 3 directions (length, width, height) is bound by 12 boundaries. The mapping of 3 to 12 has its natural correlation in the relationship between the 3 *Avos* and 12 *Shevatim*. The holiness of the 3 forefathers flows through time to the 12 Tribes of Israel.[22] One manifestation of this is matched in the area of *Yom Tov*, the Jewish Festival.

The holiness of
the 3 forefathers
flows through
time to the 12
Tribes of Israel.

The 3 *Avos* correspond to the 3 Festivals: Pesach, Shavuos, and Succos.[23] By extension, the 12 Tribes parallel the 12 months and, in particular, the 12 times Rosh Chodesh, New Moon, occurs during a regular year.[24] In truth, the 12 occasions of Rosh Chodesh were intended to have also been festive days — were it not for the sin of the *Eigel*, Golden Calf. (It is for this reason that till this day Rosh Chodesh retains a quasi-festival aspect for Jewish women, since women did not participate in this sin).[25]

12: SIGNS OF ThE ZODIAC

The 12 Tribes
are the ones to
fill the universe
with G-dliness.

The objective of the natural world is entrusted to the 12 Tribes. They are the ones to fill the universe with G-dliness. The Divine influence descends from the higher realms to this lower world.

The channels through which this flows so that it operates within the natural world are the מַזָּלוֹת, zodiac.[26] This refers to the belt of constellations whose star formations are arranged as signs that are visible in the skies during the course of the year, dividing the ecliptic into 12 equal zones. In turn, these approximate the 12 lunar months of the year and are matched to the 12 Tribes.[27]

MONTH	MAZAL	SIGN	TRIBE [28]	TRIBE [29]
NISSAN	טָלֶה	The Ram (Aries)	Reuven	Yehudah
IYAR	שׁוֹר	The Bull (Taurus)	Shimon	Yissachar
SIVAN	תְּאוֹמִים	The Twins (Gemini)	Levi	Zevulun
TAMMUZ	סַרְטָן	The Crab (Cancer)	Yehudah	Reuven
AV	אַרְיֵה	The Lion (Leo)	Yissachar	Shimon
ELUL	בְּתוּלָה	The Maiden (Virgo)	Zevulun	Gad
TISHREI	מֹאזְנַיִם	The Scales (Libra)	Binyamin	Ephraim
CHESHVAN	עַקְרָב	The Scorpion (Scorpio)	Dan	Menashe
TEVES	קֶשֶׁת	The Archer (Sagittarius)	Naftali	Binyamin
KISLEV	גְּדִי	The Goat (Capricorn)	Gad	Dan
SHEVAT	דְּלִי	The Water Bearer (Aquarius)	Asher	Asher
ADAR	דָּגִים	The Fish (Pisces)	Yosef	Naftali

There are 12 Gateways to Heaven that, according to kabbalistic teachings, have their parallel in the 12 Tribes.

Related to the 12 signs of the zodiac and 12 different permutations of G-d's Name, there are 12 Gateways to Heaven that, according to kabbalistic teachings, have their parallel in the 12 Tribes.[30] These are the medium through which man can relate to G-d. The 12 gateways finds ideal expression in the forum of *tefillah*, prayer, for a synagogue is to be ideally constructed with 12 windows.[31]

12: pathways to G-d

Parallel to the 12 permutations of G-d's 4-Letter Name, each tribe chartered its unique, distinctive pathway.

Every one of Yaakov's 12 sons merited to be included in the composition of the Jewish nation. Parallel to the 12 permutations of G-d's 4-Letter Name, each tribe chartered its unique, distinctive pathway. Each was an equally legitimate avenue in terms of *avodas Hashem*, Divine service.

Yaakov's blessing of each son before his passing indicated that each tribe would be in possession of a key role in its individualistic pathway of holiness to connect to its G-dly Source.[32] In the inauguration of the *Mishkan*, each of the 12 princes brought his specific donation on 12 successive days. Though their offerings were identical, their repetition in the Torah attests to their precious nature — worthy of inclusion within Scripture.[33] Testimony to the uniqueness of each tribe was demonstrated by its unique banner and symbol.[34]

Just as every one of the 12 Jewish months has its significant noteworthy events, so too, do all the 12 Tribes exhibit their unique sets of characteristics.

I N ACCORDANCE WITH THE NUMBER OF TRIBES, 12 IS FOUND IN MANY objects and historic events throughout the ages — invariably arranged as 4 sets of 3 (4 x 3) or as 2 sets of 6 (2 x 6).

Importantly, there dare not be friction among them. Individual characteristics notwithstanding, all 12 Tribes must interconnect as essential components that unite to constitute *Klal Yisrael*, Congregation of Israel.

Individual characteristics notwithstanding, all 12 Tribes must interconnect as essential components that unite to constitute Klal Yisrael.

by The Dozen

Representation of the 12 Tribes finds numerous examples in Jewish history. Some examples of this include:

- ❖ The 12 stones Yaakov placed around his head en route to Lavan's house allude to the 12 Tribes that were destined to be born to him.[35]
- ❖ The Splitting of the Sea in the aftermath of the Exodus divided into 12 paths, one designated for each of the 12 Tribes.[36]
- ❖ Moshe built an altar at the foot of Mount Sinai using 12 pillars that would correspond to the 12 Tribes.[37]
- ❖ The 12 springs of water at Eilim hint at the 12 Tribes of Israel and their princes.[38]
- ❖ 12 rods were submitted by the tribal princes to affirm the role of Aharon as High Priest (whose staff blossomed) in the aftermath of Korach's rebellion.[39]
- ❖ 12 stones were extracted from the river bed by the Jewish nation when crossing the Jordan into the Holy Land, to be used as a remembrance.[40]
- ❖ In the tragic episode of the concubine of Giveh, the corpse of the assaulted woman was cut into 12 pieces and one piece was sent to each of the 12 Tribes of Israel.[41]
- ❖ The rending of the new garment by the prophet Achiah HaShiloni into 12 pieces.[42]
- ❖ Eliyahu's altar on Mount Carmel consisted of 12 stones to parallel the 12 Tribes.[43]

The grouping of 12 into 3 x 4 was seen in the arrangement of the Jewish camp in the Wilderness as 3 tribes were stationed on each of the 4 sides around the *Mishkan*, Sanctuary.[44] The walled Holy City of Jerusalem had 3 gates on each of the 4 sides.[45] The *Choshen*, Breastplate, worn by the *Kohen Gadol*, High Priest, had 4 rows of 3 gemstones, with the name of one of the Tribes engraved on each.[46] (In order to contain all 22 Hebrew letters, the words, *Avraham, Yitzchak, Yaakov, Shivtei Yeshurun*, were added such that each stone contained 6 letters).[47]

לוי רהם	שמעון ב	ראובן א
זבולון ח	יששכר צ	יהודה י
גד שבטי	נפתלי ב	דן ק יעק
בנימין	יוסף ון	אשר ישר

The grouping of 12 into 3 x 4 was seen in the arrangement of the Jewish camp in the Wilderness.

The alternative grouping of 12 into 2 x 6 is found in the 2 Shoulder Stones on the shoulder straps of the *Choshen* worn by the *Kohen Gadol*, with the names of 6 Tribes inscribed on each of them, and the 2 rows of 6 לֶחֶם הַפָּנִים, *showbread*, placed weekly on the *Shulchan*, Table.[48]

The alternative grouping of 12 into 2 x 6 is found in the 2 Shoulder Stones on the shoulder straps of the Choshen.

12: TRIBAL WARFARE

Historically, there was a schism in the harmonious coexistence between the 12 Tribes. The primary friction was originally played out between Yosef and his brothers, which tragically led to Yosef being sold into slavery and the eventual descent to Egypt.

The rupture later surfaced in the division of the Kingdom in the Holy Land between the Northern Kingdom of Israel (10 Tribes) and Southern Kingdom of Yehudah (Yehudah and Binyamin).[49] This included hostility and open warfare. The dissent among Israel was the primary catalyst for the baseless hatred that brought about the destruction of the Second Temple.[50] The wound of this schism will be healed and then the Jewish People will return as a single nation; and "they shall no longer be 2 nations, no longer will they be divided into 2 kingdoms."[51]

There was a schism in the harmonious coexistence between the 12 Tribes.

Dissent was the primary catalyst for the baseless hatred that brought about the destruction of the Second Temple.

12 TRIbes; 1 NATION

In the same way the 12 diagonals interrelate with one another, the Tribes of Israel interconnect with one another.

Each of the 12 Tribes was unique by being entrusted with its separate mission. But they were nevertheless united in their identity as a single unified nation. In the same way the 12 diagonals interrelate with one another, functioning within the same framework of the cube, the Tribes of Israel interconnect with one another. Indeed, the total length of the Jewish encampment in the Wilderness was 12 *mil*.[52] En route to Lavan, the 12 stones Yaakov placed around his head coalesced into 1. This signified that he would father the 12 Tribes of Israel who would unite as one.[53] They were inherently unified through Yaakov, who, as their locus, was likened to the 13th point at the center.[54]

Surrounding Yaakov on his deathbed, the 12 Tribes affirmed their loyalty to the G-d of their father Israel. They said שְׁמַע יִשְׂרָאֵל ה׳ אֱלֹהֵינוּ ה׳ אֶחָד, *Hear O Israel, HASHEM is our G-d, HASHEM is the One and Only.*[55] In response, Yaakov responded בָּרוּךְ שֵׁם כְּבוֹד מַלְכוּתוֹ לְעוֹלָם וָעֶד, *Blessed be the Name of His glorious Kingdom forever and ever.*[56] Indeed, these two verses have a total of 12 words, which parallel the 12 Tribes of Israel.[57]

It was essential for the Tribes to join together in the framework of the 12 Tribes forming Klal Yisrael.

Despite their differences, it was essential for the Tribes to join together in the framework of the 12 Tribes forming *Klal Yisrael*. The verse beginning, "You [Israel] are children to HASHEM your G-d" has 12 words that correspond to the 12 Tribes, who are called "children of G-d."[58] The unity of the Jewish people — using their respective pathways in the service of G-d — will merit the Final Redemption when all of Israel will function as an integrated nation.

NOTES

1. See "6: It's Only Natural."
2. See "4: Finding a Place."
3. See "3: Three-Dimensional."
4. *Maharal, Derech Chaim* 3:13.
5. *Sefer Yetzirah* 5:2.
6. See *Sanhedrin* 38b about the 12 hours of the 6th day of Creation. Similarly, the day of G-d is also divided into 12 hours arranged as 4 periods of 3 hours each (*Avodah Zarah* 3b). See *Rokeach, Devarim* 4:37, who speaks about the parallel between the 12 months of a year and the 12 hours in day/night. The division of a 24-hour day into 12 hours of day and 12 of night might be parallel to the 12 good forces in Creation vs. 12 forces of evil (*Yalkut Reuveni, Chayei Sarah*, p. 219).
7. The names of the 12 months of the lunar calendar are: Nissan, Iyar, Sivan, Tammuz, Av, Elul, Tishrei, Cheshvan, Kislev, Teves, Shevat, and Adar. A 13th month (Adar II) is added in a leap year so that the

lunar and solar calendars remain in sync. See also Mishnah, *Ediyos* 2:10 about the year-long punishment in *Gehinnom* that is said to last for a period of 12 months.

8. There are 24 *tzeirufim*, permutations, of the 4-Letter Name of G-d as it is pronounced in This World (אֲדֹנָי), but due to the double-letter ה in the 4-Letter Divine Name *Havayah* (יְהֹוָה), this limits the number of permutations to 12. See *Tikkunei Zohar* 9b; *Pri Etz Chaim, Rosh Chodesh* 3. See "24: Division of Labor."

9. The 12 Tribes correspond to 12 permutations of the Divine Name as demonstrated later in this chapter (*Megaleh Amukos* 138).

10. *Shemos Rabbah* 15:6; *Pesikta Rabbasi* 4.

11. *Chagigah* 12b; *Zohar Chodosh, Rus* 76a.

12. *Yalkut Shimoni, Vayeishev* 143. The mystical sources map the 12 respective lunar months with the parallel 12 Tribes.

13. See, e.g., *Tehillim* 122:4.

14. See "3: Three-Dimensional."

15. See "4: Finding a Place."

16. *Bereishis Rabbah* 24:6.

17. *Ramchal, Derech Hashem* 2:4.

18. *Bereishis* 17:20, 25:13-15.

19. See *Bereishis Rabbah* 63:6 as to how Rivkah was originally intended to bear 12 sons.

20. See *Bereishis* 29:32–30:24; 35:16-18. The interface between 3 and 4 in arriving at 12 relates to the known tradition that Yaakov was destined to have 12 children; his 4 wives anticipating they would each bear 3 sons. This is apparent in Leah's reasoning in naming her 3rd son Levi and the reason Leah praised G-d for the birth of Yehudah, her 4th son — where she received more than her due. See *Rashi, Bereishis* 29:34. See *Berachos* 60a with regard to Leah praying for her male fetus to be transformed to Dinah.

21. *Sotah* 36b. This was fulfilled through the 2 sons of Yosef and Binyamin's 10 sons, whose names were all allusions to Yosef.

22. *Sfas Emes, Vayeitzei* 5646; *Shaarei Orah* 5, 65a,

23. See "3: Three-Dimensional."

24. *Tur, Orach Chaim Hilchos Rosh Chodesh* 417. There are several versions of how the 12 Tribes exactly relate to the 12 months. See *The Wisdom in the Hebrew Months* (2009: Mesorah Publications). King Shlomo divided the nation into 12 parts — each obligated to provide the king with provisions for 1 month out of the year (*I Melachim*, 4:7; *Metzudos David* ad loc). See also *Sfas Emes, Noach* 5647, *Vayeitzei* 5646).

25. The 12 occurrences of Rosh Chodesh, which were quasi-festivals, refer to 12 small openings of Divine benevolence (*Sfas Emes, Noach* 5647, *Vayeitzei* 5646). 3 fathers — above the natural realm; 12 sons — within the natural realm. This is why the *Shevatim* are susceptible to sin (*Sfas Emes, Chanukah* 5639 and 5646). The 3 fathers are above This World, while the placement of the 12 tribes is where life spreads out into the boundaries of the natural realm that correspond to the 12 months. The 12 occasions of Rosh Chodesh should have been Festivals if not for the sin of the Golden Calf. Roshei Chodesh are closer to nature and thus the force of sin controls them (*Sfas Emes, Chanukah* 5642-5643).

26. *Ramban, Vayikra* 18:25, *Siach Yitzchak, Shabbos Zachor*. In *Kabbalah*, out of the 22 letters in the Hebrew alphabet, 12 elemental letters parallel the 12 *mazalos* (R' Yitzchak Isaac Chaver, *Haggadah* 12).

27. The 12 Tribes of Israel are parallel to the 12 *mazalos*. See *Tanchuma*, Buber ed., *Vayeishev* 8.

28. This order of the 12 Tribes of Israel is based upon *Shemos* 1:2-4.

29. This order of the 12 Tribes of Israel is based upon their encampment in the Wilderness.

30. *Magen Avraham, Orach Chaim* 68. (See also *Chasam Sofer, Orach Chaim* 16.)

31. *Shulchan Aruch, Orach Chaim* 90:4; see *Zohar* 2, 251a. The original composition of the daily week-

day *Amidah* prayer itself consisted of 12 central requests that man asked of G-d. See *Sfas Emes, Vayeishev* 5643.

32. See *Sfas Emes*, Chanukah 5642 *Ma Shetiknu* and *Sfas Emes, Vayechi* 5643.
33. *Bamidbar* 7:12-7:83.
34. *Bamidbar Rabbah* 2:6.
35. *Bereishis* 28:11; *Bereishis Rabbah* 68:11.
36. *Mechilta, Beshalach* 2:4; *Esther Rabbah* 7:11.
37. *Shemos* 24:4.
38. *Rashi, Shemos* 15:27. Each respective Tribe had its designated *nasi*, prince, who represented it (see, e.g., *Bamidbar* 7:84). The princes are mentioned in the offerings brought at the inaugural of the Sanctuary. There were 12 other princes who were delegates dispatched to spy out the Holy Land.
39. *Bamidbar* 17:17.
40. *Yehoshua* 4:3.
41. *Shoftim* 19:29.
42. *I Melachim* 11:30.
43. *Pesikta Rabosai* 3:14.
44. *Bamidbar* 2:1-31. Here Yosef was subdivided into 2 Tribes (Ephraim and Menashe) and Levi was encamped, separately, around the *Mishkan*.
45. *Yechezkel* 48:31-33. See R' Yitzchak Isaac Chaver, *Haggadah, Yad Chazakah*.
46. *Shemos* 28:15-21.
47. See *Rabbeinu Bachya, Shemos* 28:15.
48. *Vayikra* 24:5-6. The 12 Showbreads correspond to the 12 Tribes (*Sfas Emes, Vayeitzei* 5658).
49. *I Melachim*, 12.
50. *Yoma* 9b.
51. *Yechezkel* 37:22.
52. *Sotah* 13b.
53. *Bereishis Rabbah* 68:11.
54. See "13: Everlasting Love."
55. *Devarim* 6:4. See *Pesachim* 56a.
56. *Zohar, Terumah* 139b; see also *Tikkunei Zohar* 13. See "24: Division of Labor."
57. See *Tanchuma* Buber ed., *Vayeishev* 8 and *Rokeach, Devarim* 6:3-4.
58. *Devarim* 14:1 and *Baal HaTurim* ad loc.

13
AN EVERLASTING LOVE

13 refers to the loving relationship
between Israel and G-d.

This all-encompassing love is reflected
in each side's timeless commitment.

Every opportunity is used to showcase a selfless
dedication to one's beloved.

This creates an everlasting covenant
in a bond of love that will never be severed.

A DECLARATION OF LOVE

Man lives to bestow love onto others and, in turn, longs to be loved.

LOVE IS ONE OF THE MOST POWERFUL FORCES IN THE UNIVERSE. This most basic of human emotions fills life with meaning. Man lives to bestow love onto others and, in turn, longs to be loved.[1]

One who is lovesick is so infatuated with his beloved that he cannot think of anything else. In truth, real love is only realized where the parties fuse their identities as one, so that they come to *define* themselves in reference to their beloved. Here אַהֲבָה, *love,* results in אֶחָד, *oneness* — both words sharing the same numerical value of 13.

The eternal love between G-d and Israel is symbolized in the number 13.

These sentiments anchor the eternal love between G-d and Israel. The wide-ranging impact of this relationship is prominently symbolized in the number 13.

FOR THE LOVE OF G-D

HOW DOES ONE INITIATE AND SUSTAIN A LOVING RELATIONSHIP? There are several stages involved in this enterprise. It starts with a genuine commitment to enter into a lifelong covenant. There must be the fullest realization of what duties and responsibilities — both great and small — this relationship entails. It is essential that one gets to know the defining attributes of one's beloved. Once these elements are in place, they translate into a lifetime of expressing this love in practice. All these factors are present within Israel's loving relationship to G-d.

Creation was an altruistic act of love in G-d's desire to bestow good upon His creations.

Placing G-d at the center of the universe, the Jew is constantly aware of Him.[2] Despite the fact that G-d is unknowable, a Jew recognizes that Creation was an altruistic act of love in G-d's desire to bestow good upon His creations.[3] And G-d's love for His creation is magnified in His love for every Jew.

On his part, the Jewish soul is bound to the Master of the Universe. The Jew has the constant *mitzvah* to love G-d with every fiber of his being: ... *with your whole heart, your whole soul, and with all your resources.*[4] Any activity outside this objective is considered an unwelcome distraction. His life and outlook exist exclusively "for the love of G-d."

His lifelong commitment begins at two early but important milestones: *bris milah*, covenant of circumcision, and bar mitzvah.

MILAH: 13 COVENANTS

Of the 613 commandments, only *milah*, circumcision, is regularly characterized as a *bris*, covenant. This *mitzvah*, performed upon the 8th day after birth, is the indelible sign of the eternal treaty between Israel and G-d.[5] The Jewish nation has joyously performed this *mitzvah* throughout their turbulent history. It signifies the dedication that every Jew has to life in the service of his Maker.

Bris milah signifies the dedication that every Jew has to life in the service of his Maker.

Love and unity toward G-d suffuse this *mitzvah*. The word בְּרִית is featured 13 times in the Torah passage of this *mitzvah*.[6] Despite his advanced age, Avraham, the forefather whom G-d called *His loved one,*[7] circumcised himself along with every male in his household. In Avraham's house the only other individual mentioned by name is his 13-year-old son Yishmael.[8]

Milah classifies the descendants of the 13-letter names of the Patriarchs (Avraham, Yitzchak, and Yaakov) and 13-letter names of the Matriarchs (Sarah, Rivkah, Rachel, and Leah)[9] as the exclusive members of the Chosen Nation.[10]

אַבְרָהָם + יִצְחָק + יַעֲקֹב   = 5 + 4 + 4 = 13 letters

שָׂרָה + רִבְקָה + רָחֵל + לֵאָה   = 3 + 4 + 3 + 3 = 13 letters

Every male Jewish child, then, is subject to this "covenant of love." But, as he is still an infant, his intellectual immaturity means he does not yet have the ability to express this love. That must wait until he reaches adulthood.

The ability to express this love must wait until he reaches adulthood.

BAR MITZVAH: 13-YEAR-OLD

Bar mitzvah (which literally means *son of the commandment*)[11] marks the Jew's coming of age.[12] He enters adulthood at the age of 13 years and one day.[13] This special occasion is traditionally celebrated with a festive meal,[14] the recital of a blessing upon the Torah, and the donning of *tefillin* upon his arm and head.

Proudly taking his place as a full-fledged member of the Jewish community, the 13-year-old becomes personally responsible for his actions.[15] His true character surfaces with the emergence of the inner *Yetzer Tov*, Good Inclination.[16] His classification as a גָּדוֹל, *mature adult*, means that he is someone who is able to combine all his actions into one unified perspective (the root of *gadol* is the word a*gad,* meaning *to bind*).[17] That means he is now ready to begin conveying his love of G-d. How? By embracing *mitzvah* observance: *13-year-old to [observe] the mitzvos.*[18]

A 13-year-old is now ready to begin conveying his love of G-d.

Nevertheless, to correctly put this love into practice, it is necessary to know the basis for his love of G-d. This is contained within the elementary 13 tenets of his faith.

The basis for love of G-d is contained within the elementary 13 tenets of faith.

13 ARTICLES OF FAITH

The Rambam famously formulates the beliefs of Judaism into 13 articles of faith.[19]

These articles define what a Jew, as a Jew, must believe. This incorporates the nature of G-d (His existence, eternity, unity, and non-corporeality), the Divine authorship of the unchanging Torah (including the nature of prophecy), and the concept of reward and punishment (the coming of Mashiach and resurrection).[20] Their acceptance as the authoritative articles of Jewish faith[21] have seen them condensed in the 13 *Ani Maamin*, I believe, statements and the composition of liturgy such as the *Yigdal* prayer.

The 13 articles of faith are condensed in the 13 Ani Maamin, statements.

Why are these 13 fundamentals the cornerstone to loving G-d? The main reason is that someone who does not believe in G-d or does not know His ways cannot be said to truly love Him. Any false assumption — whether it relates to G-d, the Divine origins of Torah, or His Providence — nullifies *the existence of a relationship!* It is like entering a marriage under false pretenses, where one does not know the true identity of one's spouse. Obviously, love is not possible in such circumstances. Conversely, a Jew's authentic belief in and knowledge of G-d enable him to imbue his behavior with meaningful acts of love. This is primarily accomplished through his sincere commitment to Torah, which can be interpreted through 13 ways.

A Jew's authentic belief in and knowledge of G-d enable him to imbue his behavior with meaningful acts of love.

13 RULES OF TORAH INTERPRETATION

Torah study is the optimal means man has to connect to the Mind of G-d. It is, so to speak, how Israel is able to know their Beloved. As the sacred, loving covenant between Israel and G-d, Torah is appropriately revealed through the number 13 — both in its transmission and its exegesis.

On the last day of his life, Moshe wrote 13 Torah Scrolls for the Jewish people.[22] The Talmud refers to 13 different schools of interpretation.[23] Rabbi Yishmael listed the 13 hermeneutic principles of how Torah is to be expounded. These methods, using logical derivation and textual analysis, explain how the *Torah Sheba'al Peh*, the Oral Law, emerges from *Torah Shebichsav*, the Written Law.[24]

Israel's bond of love — personally established through *milah* and bar mitzvah — is nationally seen through their faith and affinity to Torah.[25]

A BELOVED PEOPLE

Israel's bond of love is seen through their faith and affinity to Torah.

MIRRORING ISRAEL'S DEVOTION TO HIM, G-D RECIPROCATES THIS love.

Shir HaShirim, Song of Songs, is the allegorical reference of G-d's unremitting love of Israel: *I am to My beloved and My beloved is to me.*[26] History showcases G-d's incontrovertible bond to Israel. His unconditional love of the Chosen Nation has truly withstood the test of time. *I loved you [Israel], says G-d.*[27] And Israel responds in turn, *With an abundance of love You have loved us.*[28]

History showcases G-d's incontrovertible bond to Israel.

13 ATTRIBUTES OF MERCY

The most powerful expression of His unswerving love came when G-d revealed the secret of the 13 Attributes of Mercy.

The sin of the Golden Calf was Israel's greatest national crime, when their fate hung in the balance. Guaranteeing forgiveness, G-d revealed to Moshe that He would always accept Israel's heartfelt recitation of the 13 יי׳׳ג מדות הרחמים, Attributes of Mercy.[29] G-d wrapped Himself [in a *tallis*] like a *Shaliach Tzibbur*, communal representative, to indicate to Moshe the order of this prayer. "Whenever Israel sins," G-d advised, 'Let them perform before Me this order [of prayer] and I will forgive them.'[30] This prayer, recited in a communal capacity, taps into the national identity of Israel. So even if members of the Jewish community have individually sinned, their communal identity is never suspended. It is this factor that is the guarantee to invoke

The most powerful expression of His love came when G-d revealed the secret of the 13 Attributes of Mercy.

Divine Mercy. In our *Selichos*, this formula is termed בְּרִית שְׁלֹשׁ עֶשְׂרֵה, *the covenant of 13.*[31]

The symbol of a *Shaliach Tzibbur* is perfect because this role provides a standard for how the people have to conduct themselves.[32] This image used by G-d to inspire Israel to emulate His 13 Attributes of Mercy represents a defining set of Divine Attributes that can serve as Israel's model in their bid to emulate the Creator.[33]

13: The Spiritual Core

G-d's love was manifest in the resting of His *Shechinah*, Divine Presence, in the midst of Israel; this center is symbolized by the number 13.

We have seen that the 6-sided cube interfaces 12 diagonals and has 12 edges.[34] The inner point of a cube is considered the 7th point of spirituality that comes to unify the 6 directions (north, east, south, west, up and down) which typify the physical world.[35] The relationship between the numbers 6 and 7 has its parallel in the relationship between 12 and 13, where the extremities of the 12 edges of a cube are brought together by the 13th that is similarly classified as the spiritual center.[36]

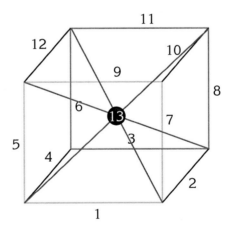

In the Wilderness, the *Shechinah* rested within the hallowed walls of the *Mishkan*, Sanctuary. This was the national locus where the 12 Tribes of Israel were encamped as one around this 13th spiritual center.[37] Naturally, the number 13 features in its construction. Its architect was the 13-year old Betzalel,[38] and it was constructed using 13 donated materials.[39]

	NORTH (10) Dan (11) Asher (12) Naftoli	
WEST (7) Ephraim (8) Menashe (9) Binyamin	MISHKAN (13)	EAST (1) Yehudah (2) Yissachar (3) Zevulun
	SOUTH (4) Reuven (5) Shimon (6) Gad	

The symbolism of Israel uniting their efforts around G-d, as they had done around Mount Sinai,[40] was reproduced in their encampment around the *Mishkan*. The *Mishkan* was testimony that God had forgiven the incident of the Golden Calf.[41] His *Shechinah* residing in their midst, as the 13th spiritual center, demonstrated to the world that G-d had not rejected His beloved people.

His Shechinah residing in their midst, as the 13th spiritual center, demonstrated to the world that G-d had not rejected His beloved people.

In the Holy Land, the *Beis HaMikdash*, Temple, became the permanent 13th spiritual religious center for the 12 Tribes of Israel who dwelled there. Again, the symbolism of 13 is prominent. Examples include the use of 13 boxes for half-*shekalim* donations,[42] 13 sieves used for sifting flour,[43] and, in the Second Temple, 13 places where the people bowed down to G-d.[44]

13-PETALED ROSE

The timeless metaphor used by G-d to describe his beloved people is a 13-petaled rose.

The universal symbol of love, the rose is exquisitely a delicate object of eye-catching beauty that is both distinct and untouchable. In the allegory of *Shir HaShirim*, G-d says about His beloved people, *Like a rose among thorns, so is My love among the daughters.*[45] Like the 13 petals of a rose, so is Israel safeguarded by G-d through His 13 Attributes of Mercy that surround her.[46]

Like the 13 petals of a rose, so is Israel safeguarded by G-d through His 13 Attributes of Mercy that surround her.

This is apparent from the Jewish people's remarkable survival.

The sins of Israel led to the destruction of the Temple, whose function had united the 12 Tribes of Israel by focusing their love toward G-d and where G-d reciprocated that love. Nevertheless, by invoking the 13 Attributes of Mercy, G-d's love for them lives on.[47] His *Shechinah* continues to rest in their defiled midst throughout their exile.[48] G-d has upheld His promise never to abandon them or to substitute them for another nation, and that He will bring a "redeemer … in His Name *with love.*"[49] On their part, Israel has not wavered in their tenacity by never surrendering their sacred Torah beliefs or their commitment to *mitzvah* observance.

G-d has upheld His promise never to abandon Israel and that He will bring a "redeemer … in His Name with love."

Their love for each other, as symbolized in the number 13, has not died; indeed, it has survived and intensified over the millennia.

Theirs is the greatest love story ever told.

NOTES

1. *Ibn Ezra, Devarim* 30:19.
2. *Rambam, Hilchos Teshuvah* 10:3.
3. *Tehillim* 89:3. The attainment of love of G-d is through contemplating the wondrous deeds and creations of G-d and of His incomparably great wisdom (*Rambam, Hilchos Yesodei HaTorah* 2:2).
4. *Devarim* 6:5. See also *Berachos* 61b as to how he is prepared to give up his life.
5. See "8: Out of This World."
6. *Bereishis* 17:1-22; Mishnah, *Nedarim* 3:11.
7. *Yeshayah* 41:8.
8. *Bereishis* 17:25-26. The merit of this circumcision as practiced by Yishmael's descendants has held the Arab nations in good stead within the Land of Israel (R' Chaim Vital, *Eitz HaDaas Tov V'Ra, Tehillim* 124).
9. The combined Hebrew letters of the names of the 3 Patriarchs total 13 letters (see *Ben Yehoyada, Bava Basra* 122a), as do the combined Hebrew letters of the names of the 4 Matriarchs.
10. The Jewish people are called בְּנֵי בְרִיתֶךָ, *children of Your covenant.* Conversely, at times a non-Jew is often called *areil*, uncircumcised.
11. The Aramaic word *bar* or Hebrew equivalent *ben* denotes inclusion into a specified group. A *ben Olam Haba*, member [literally, *son*] of the World to Come, refers to one whose focus and identity are tied up with the eternal life. "Bar mitzvah" connotes "an [agent] subject to Scriptural commands" (*Bava Metzia* 96a).
12. See Rashi, *Nazir* 29b based on *Bereishis* 34:25; see also *Tosefos Yom Tov Avos* 5:21; *Teshuvos HaRosh* 16:1.
13. *Niddah* 45b.
14. See *Shulchan Aruch, Orach Chaim* 225:2, *Magen Avraham* 4.
15. A child is not a *bar onshin*, son of punishment; his father is held culpable until the child's bar mitzvah, when the father relinquishes responsibility with a special blessing said as he is called to Torah. Yitzchak's twins followed diverse paths once they reached the age of 13 (*Bereishis Rabbah* 63:10-11).
16. See *Avos DeRabbi Nassan* 16:2, about how until bar mitzvah, the *Yetzer Hara*, Evil Inclination, holds

exclusive sway over the intellectually immature child. The vacuum formed by the lack of the *Yetzer Tov* creates a spiritual blockage that prevents the full luster of the soul to shine forth (*Zohar, Vayishlach*). A child is likened to the first 3-year *orlah* fruits whose soul is not yet ready to serve G-d (*Zohar Chadash, Bereishis* 14a). The *orlah* of the body is removed at *milah* on the 8th day but the *orlah* of the heart is uprooted only at 13 years of age. A child is exempt from *mitzvos* until then (*Ramchal, Derech Eitz HaChaim*).

17. Conversely, he is no longer a קָטָן, *minor*, whose inconsistent actions are disconnected; קָטָן relates to the word קְטָטָה, *cutting* or discord.

18. *Pirkei Avos* 5:21. See *Maharal, Derech Chaim* 5:21 about how a person cannot be obligated with *mitzvah* observance until he is classed a man. At bar mitzvah, the responsibility to make sure he is circumcised (formerly a duty upon his parents or Jewish court) devolves onto him (*Kiddushin* 29a). He can now be included as one of 10 men in a *minyan*. A minor may acquire property through an adult who sells, bequeaths, or gives it him, but cannot acquire an ownerless property [from *Hefker*] (*Shulchan Aruch, Choshen Mishpat* 270;1 and *Sma* there) and is not old enough to marry.

19. *Rambam*, Commentary to the Mishnah, *Sanhedrin* 10.

20. The *Sefer HaIkkarim* 1:4 divides the fundamental principles of faith into 3 rather than 13: existence of G-d, the Heavenly origins of Torah, and the concept of reward and punishment.

21. See, e.g., *Alshich, Devarim* 5:20-24.

22. *Devarim Rabbah* 9:9, as cited in *Rambam*, Introduction to the Mishnah.

23. Rav Pappa said about their generation that they studied the Tractate of *Uktzin* in 13 different versions — either 13 different approaches to learning this or taught in 13 different schools (*Berachos* 20a. See *Rashi* and *Tosafos* ad loc. and *Rashi, Taanis* 24b).

24. Introduction to *Sifra*.

25. See R' Yitzchak Aizik Chaver, *Ohr Torah* 16, annotations to *Maalos HaTorah* for how the numerical value of 13 as *echad*, oneness, and *ahavah*, love, corresponds to the 13 rules of Torah interpretation.

26. *Shir HaShirim* 6:3.

27. *Malachi* 1:2. See also *Yirmiyah* 31:2-3.

28. These are the opening words to the blessing recited before the morning *Shema*.

29. *Shemos* 34:6-7. There are several opinions as to how to divide the words in these verses into the 13 Attributes. See a corresponding enumeration of the 13 Attributes (mystically called "higher rungs of mercy") in *Michah* 7:18-20 and in Rav Moshe Cordovero's classic work *Tomer Devorah*, which elaborates upon these Attributes.

30. *Rosh Hashanah* 17b. See Rav Shlomo Wolbe, *Maamarei Yemei Ratzon,* pp. 103-105.

31. This is contained in the words, *Behold I am making a covenant* (*Shemos* 34:10).

32. The 13 Attributes are compared to the *Shemoneh Esrei* repeated by the *Shaliach Tzibbur* — which explains why they are preceded by *Ashrei* and followed by *Tachanun* and *Kaddish Shalem* (*Levush, Orach Chaim* 581;1).

33. See *Tomer Devorah* 1. See *Sotah* 14a as to how man has to imitate G-d's Attributes of Mercy.

34. There are 12 lines connecting one vertex to another. See "12: Tribes of Israel."

35. See "7: Spiritual Spark."

36. See "12: Tribes of Israel."

37. The historical precedent to this arrangement of 12 gathered around a 13th central point in the love of G-d occurred when the 12 sons of Yaakov gathered around their father Yaakov on his deathbed to recite the *Shema,* affirming that the love of G-d was central in their lives (*Pesachim* 56a). This was also evident in the 12 Tribes escorting Yaakov's coffin from Egypt to its final resting place. The Tribe of Levi was not included in the encampment of the 12 Tribes in the *Machaneh Yisrael,* Camp of Israel. They dwelled in the inner encampment of *Machaneh Levi'ya,* the Camp of Levi.

38. *Sanhedrin* 69b.

39. *Shir HaShirim Rabbah* 4:12:2 cited by *Rashi, Shemos* 25:2; see also *Rashi, Yechezkel* 16:13. When

departing from Egypt, G-d adorned Israel with 13 types of ornaments that served as an expression of His love for them. As the recipients of 13 favors at the Exodus, there was almost a moral obligation for Israel to donate 13 materials to the *Mishkan*. Nevertheless, in His love for them, G-d considered this to be a voluntary contribution, rewarding them with 13 signs of protective love in times of Mashiach (*Yeshayah* 4:5-6); *Tanchuma, Terumah* 5 and *Pesikta Rabbasi* 33; this is derived from the list enumerated in *Yechezkel* 16:9-14; see also *Yalkut Shimoni, Yechezkel* 355).

40. See *Ramban, Shemos* 25:1 for how the function of the *Mishkan* was to be an extension of the glory evident at Mount Sinai.
41. *Rashi, Shemos* 38:21.
42. Mishnah, *Shekalim* 6:1-6.
43. *Menachos* 76b.
44. The Sages state that the 13 prostrations were opposite the 13 places where the Greeks had breached the latticework perimeter of the Temple Mount, and which had been repaired by the Hasmoneans (*Yerushalmi, Shekalim* 6:2; *Middos* 2:3; see *Rambam, Pirush HaMishnayos Shekalim* 6:3, *Middos* 2:6).
45. *Shir HaShirim* 2:2.
46. *Zohar* I, Introduction 1.
47. See, for example, *Yechezkel* 20:2-20 and *Yirmiyah* 3:1, about how Israel wrongly presumed that they had been rejected by G-d.
48. *Vayikra* 16:16.
49. Closing words to the opening blessings of the *Amidah*.

15
Ups and Downs

15 are the steps that man
takes to rise or to fall.

Climbing these steps represents an
upward ascent toward G-d,
one where a Jew — both individually and
nationally — can reach
the greatest spiritual heights.

LIGHT AND DARKNESS

The cyclical up-and-down nature of Israel finds expression in the number 15.

THE CYCLICAL UP-AND-DOWN NATURE OF ISRAEL FINDS EXPRESSION IN the number 15.

The Jewish calendar is arranged in accordance with the movement of the moon, whose changing face and shape are the perfect symbol of this cycle.

15: FULL MOON

The period of a full lunar month is 30 days.[1] The changing appearance of the moon divides the month into 2 halves. Starting from a sliver of a crescent on the 1st day, it waxes, i.e., grows in size,

Just as the cyclical sequence of the moon incorporates periods of light and periods of darkness, so, too, does Jewish destiny.

until the 15th day, when the light of the full moon shines upon the Earth. During the second half of the month, however, this process is reversed: the moon wanes until it finally disappears from sight, 15 days later, at the month's end. This cycle then begins once again.

The relationship between Israel and the moon goes beyond Israel's calendar being measured in terms of the lunar months. On a profound level, just as the cyclical sequence of the moon incorporates periods of light and periods of darkness, so, too, does Jewish destiny.

Historically, the Jewish people are subject to a series of ups and downs. The fortunes of Israel vis-à-vis the gentile nations are subject to a reciprocal relationship. Like the affiliation between Yaakov and Eisav, "the rise of one marks the downfall of the other."[2] They can be compared to opposing weights on a measuring scale. The weight of Israel's sins leads them to sink down while enabling other nations to rise and gain ascendancy.[3]

Symbolically, the moon's fluctuations chart the two alternative pathways in Jewish history.

15: GENERATIONS

Symbolically, the moon's fluctuations chart the two alternative pathways in Jewish history.

When they are worthy, 15 generations can represent the climax in the Jewish People's nationhood. Starting from Avraham, the Children of Israel developed over the course of 15 generations. They reached their high point during the reign of King Shlomo — during the celebrated 15th generation. During this era, the Chosen Nation finally lived in peace and prosperity, having attained a preeminent spiritual stature. The *Shechinah,* Divine Presence, resided in the First Temple built by Shlomo. Likened to the moonlight on the 15th day of the month, the *Shechinah's* revelation shone brightly out into the world.[4]

Just as the moon wanes into blackness, so would Israel's fortunes tragically turn. The spiritual summit of Shlomo's era was not sustained; Israel did not follow Torah law. There was a shift in the opposite direction. Subsequent generations suffered a spiraling downfall. The Jewish kingdom was divided, and over the course of 15 generations, matters degenerated until the Jewish nation was exiled and the First Temple was destroyed.[5]

The spiritual summit of Shlomo's era was not sustained.

15 VS. 15: ÒARKNESS VS. LIGḟT

Man is a composite of soul and body. Within him there is a portion of light in his soul, described as the "light of G-d,"[6] but also an element of darkness, in terms of the material component of his body.[7] This means that man exercises *bechirah,* free will, with these two respective components in constant conflict.[8]

Man exercises free will, with these two respective components in constant conflict.

The physical body delights in the fleeting pleasures of This World. Typically this urge is strongest during the formative stages of human life, when the mind is not yet fully developed. Pursuits of the material tend to wane during the course of a lifetime. Bodily cravings decrease with age until their allure dissipates.

The opposite pull is that of the intellectual soul. This prods man to dedicate his life to spiritual pursuits, elevating him toward G-d. This matures and grows in intensity during the course of man's lifetime. Indeed, it is meant to become the dominant factor within him. The degree of wisdom within a Torah scholar increases with age. Those bereft of Torah knowledge, however, become more foolish with age.[9]

The pull of the intellectual soul prods man to dedicate his life to spiritual pursuits, elevating him toward G-d.

This inner struggle is symbolically played out in the cycles of the moon. The spherical face of the moon in space does not change during the course of the month; it is the degree of illumination of the moon reflecting the sun that waxes and wanes. When drawn after his body, the wicked man turns light into darkness.[10] Here the light of the soul is obscured by the darkness of bodily materialism. The objective is for

The highest
state is where
man is so
righteous that
the light of the
soul brightly
illuminates his
whole being.

the light within the individual to vanquish the darkness. The highest state is where man is so righteous that the light of the soul brightly illuminates his whole being. Similarly, the fullest lunar illumination possible occurs during the full moon on the 15th day of the month.[11]

STEP BY STEP

JUST AS THE MOON MUST DEVELOP DAILY OVER THE COURSE OF 15 days in order to reach a full moon, the passage toward the spiritual light necessitates a step-by-step process.[12] The program consists of 15 successive steps until a spiritual high point is reached. The number 15 represents the spiritual apex, as it is the numerical value of the Divine Name (י-ה) through which G-d created both This World and the World to Come.[13]

15 represents
the spiritual
apex, as it is
the numerical
value of the
Divine Name
through which
G-d created This
World and the
World to Come.

SEDER: 15 ORDERS

One example of a 15-step journey toward greatness was the Israelites' ascent to holiness at the Exodus. There was a 15-day period beginning with their first *mitzvah* relating to the 1st day of Nissan,[14] and continuing up until their liberation 15 days later.[15] The annual commemoration of this national experience on the night of 15th of Nissan is the Seder, whose proceedings are famously set forth in a 15-word formula.[16]

Israel's redemption set into motion a sequence of events in their national development. Each stage of redemption, when examined in isolation, would have itself been sufficient cause for gratitude to G-d. In total, 15 stages are enumerated at the Seder in the beautiful song, דַּיֵּינוּ, *it would suffice*. The stages begin with the Exodus and end with the Temple in the Holy Land.[17]

Israel's
redemption
set into motion
a sequence
of events in
their national
development.

15: SONGS OF ASCENTS

The model for upward, spiritual progression was the 15 steps within the Temple from the *Ezras Nashim*, Women's Courtyard, to the *Ezras Yisrael*, Israelites' Courtyard.[18] During the joyous Succos ceremony of שִׂמְחַת בֵּית הַשּׁוֹאֵבָה, *Rejoicing of the Water Drawing*, the Levites recited the 15 שִׁיר הַמַּעֲלוֹת, *Song of the Ascents psalms*, while standing on these 15 steps.[19]

Actually, the historic context of the water libation that was drawn from an underground spring similarly relates to the number 15. When David was digging the foundations of the Altar, the subterranean reservoirs threatened to flood the world. The king cast a shard with the Divine Name into the deep, but the waters receded too far. When David composed these 15 psalms, the waters rose 15,000 cubits to remain 1,000 cubits beneath the Earth's surface.[20] This refers to the ascents inherent within the name, *Shir HaMa'alos*.[21]

15: SONGS OF PRAISE

The 15 Songs of Ascents sung to G-d upon the 15 steps in the Temple are parallel to the many sequences of 15 expressions of praise or blessings within our daily prayers:

The 15 Songs of Ascents parallel many sequences of 15 expressions of praise or blessings within our daily prayers:

- ❖ The Morning Prayer begin with a sequence of 15 consecutive blessings conveying man's heartfelt gratitude to G-d for the succession of marvels within existence that each new day ushers in.[22]

- ❖ The פְּסוּקֵי דְזִמְרָה, *Verses of Song*, commence with הוֹדוּ, whose opening 15 verses were sung upon the return of the Ark.[23]

- ❖ The Divine Attributes in the verse לְךָ ה', *To You O G-d ...*,[24] are delineated using 15 words.[25]

- ❖ The *Pesukei d'Zimrah* section itself concludes with יִשְׁתַּבַּח, which is composed of 15 expressions of praise.[26]

- ❖ The first two paragraphs of the morning *Shema*[27] contain 15 verses. The *Shema* is followed by the prayer אֱמֶת וְיַצִּיב that begins by extolling G-d using 15 phrases, each prefaced by the letter *vav*.

- ❖ *Birchas Kohanim*, Priestly Blessings, the conduit for the Heavenly blessing to descend to the world, is composed of 15 words.[28]

These 15 stages are the full set of blessing and praises through which a person ascends toward G-d. The Jew rises step-by-step together with his prayers as he presents his petition before the Master of the Universe.

ON A HIGH

W̲E HAVE MENTIONED THAT SPIRITUAL ASCENT REACHES ITS PEAK with the number 15. Examples of this are evident in the monthly placement of the major festivals and the overlapping lives of the *Avos*.

ÒAY 15

It is no accident that the 15th is the chosen date for the celebration of national salvation, when many Jewish festivals begin.

The moon is at its brightest on the 15th day. The majesty of the Jewish nation, symbolized by the glow of the moon in its fullness, radiates outward to the whole world.[29] It is no accident that the 15th is the chosen date for the celebration of national salvation, when many Jewish Festivals begin.[30]

Consider the following dates in the Jewish calendar: Pesach begins on the 15th of Nissan; Tu B'Shevat, new year of the trees, is on the 15th of Shevat; Tu B'Av is the 15th of Av;[31] Succos begins on the 15th of Tishrei; and 15th of Adar is Shushan Purim.[32] (The Torah does not give a fixed date for the Festival of Shavuos which would take place 50 days after Pesach.[33])

15: MAKING OF ISRAEL

The formation of the Chosen Nation was specifically fashioned through the 3 outstanding forefathers and the righteous 12 Tribes of Israel.

The high point of what Israel could attain was established by their illustrious ancestors. The lifespan of the 3 *Avos* (Avraham, Yitzchak, and Yaakov) overlapped by 15 years. Thus Avraham died when Yaakov was age 15.[34] And G-d appeared to the forefathers on a total of 15 occasions.[35]

The formation of the Chosen Nation, one that would be able to reach the highest level, was specifically fashioned through the 3 outstanding forefathers and the righteous 12 Tribes of Israel — a total of (3 + 12 =) 15 personalities.[36]

Conversely, the rejected offshoots of the *Avos* began their downward slide into the spiritual wastelands from the age of 15. Yishmael was 15 years old when he bought an image from the market and began worshiping it. This led to his banishment from Avraham's house.[37] On the day that Avraham died, Yitzchak's older son Eisav was also 15 years old. He committed several grave sins that indicated his departure from the spiritual legacy of the *Avos* in the formation of Israel.[38]

15: DOWN BUT NOT OUT

Steps are not only used for going up; they are also used for going down. Throughout their turbulent history, the Jewish nation has been subject to many ups and downs. In truth, the movement of Israel should ideally chart an ongoing climb toward ever-increasing levels of spiritual greatness to ascend higher and higher. Indeed, holiness and spirituality are the means of exchanging the darkness of the body for the light of the soul and directing both toward G-d in Heaven.[39]

Alas, Israel has historically suffered many agonizing setbacks. The fullness of the moonlight on the 15th day ceded to the darkness of spiritual decline. Redemption gave way to exile. But their time-based link with the lunar cycle means that Israel is never down and out. The Jewish People take their cue from the moon. This satellite around Earth may diminish and seem to disappear from sight. But it does not disappear. In fact, darkness becomes the springboard to a rebirth in the illumination of the next month. Out of the gloom the brilliant radiance of the moon — and of Israel — will shine forth again in a state of renewal.

Paradoxically, the individual or national descent can often be channeled as the means of a later ascent.[40] Any fall can become an impetus for a reinvention. The verse "though I have fallen I shall arise"[41] indicates that it was *because* of my fall that I subsequently arose.[42] This leads to the acknowledgment: "I thank You [G-d] *because* You were angry with me."[43]

So the cyclical motion of the moon provides a comforting ray of light that banishes the darkness of night. Man is a creature whose spiritual level is in a constant state of flux. He is either on the ascent or on the descent — but never stationary.[44] The optimal way is to climb up to the spiritual peak like the moon on the 15th day. Nevertheless, there is the assurance that even if darkness puts out the light, there is the opportunity for renewal in the next month. The symbolism of a חֹדֶשׁ, *month*, links into the symbolism of חִדּוּשׁ, *change* and *renewal*.[45] So even if a Jew falls, he always has the ability to rejuvenate himself, to be reborn, and to rise again up through the 15 levels to reach up to the greatest heights.

Darkness becomes the springboard to a rebirth in the illumination of the next month.

The cyclical motion of the moon provides a comforting ray of light that banishes the darkness of night.

NOTES

1. See "30: It's About Time."
2. *Bereishis* 25:23 and *Rashi* ad loc.
3. See *Kli Yakar, Olelos Ephraim, Maamar* 49.
4. *Sanhedrin* 41b-42a; *Shemos Rabbah* 15:26 and *Pesikta Rabbasai* 15.
5. There were 30 generations from Avraham to Tzidkiyahu and the era of the first *Beis HaMikdash* (*Shemos Rabbah* 15:26). The royal line extends as far back as Avraham, who was treated regally by the non-Jews as a "prince of G-d in our midst" (*Bereishis* 23:6). See *Bereishis Rabbah* 38:16 for how 30 families emerged from Avraham's household — 16 children of Keturah, 12 children of Yishmael, and 2 children of Yitzchak.
6. *Mishlei* 20:27.
7. See *Kli Yakar*, op. cit., *Maamar* 52.
8. *Ramchal, Derech Hashem* 1:3.
9. *Shabbos* 152a.
10. See *Iyov* 18:5-6.
11. *Kli Yakar*, ad loc.
12. See *Maharal, Gur Aryeh, Vayikra* 2:13.
13. *Maharal, Gevuros Hashem* 59 based on the verse "Using the Name (יה) He created worlds" (*Yeshayah* 26:4).
14. *Shemos* 12:2.
15. *Bamidbar* 33:3.
16. These are: (1) *Kadesh*, Recite *Kiddush* (2) *Urchatz*, Wash Hands (3) *Karpas*, Eat Vegetable (4) *Yachatz*, Break the Matzah (5) *Maggid*, Recite the Pesach Story (6) *Rachtzah*, Wash Hands for Meal (7) *Motzi*, Blessing for Bread (8) *Matzah*, Blessing for Matzah (9) *Maror*, Eat Bitter Herbs (10) *Korech*, Eat Sandwich of *Marror* and Matzah (11) *Shulchan Orech*, Festive Meal, (12) *Tzafun*, Eat Afikoman (13) *Bareich*, Blessings After Meal (14) *Hallel*, Recite *Hallel,* and (15) *Nirtzah*, Concluding Prayers.
17. The 15 stages are (1) G-d brought us out of Egypt, (2) carried out judgments against them, (3) and against their idols, (4) killed their firstborn sons, (5) gave us their wealth, (6) split the sea, (7) took us through the sea on dry land, (8) drowned our oppressors in it, (9) supplied our needs in the Wilderness for 40 years, (10) fed us the manna, (11) gave us the Shabbos, (12) brought us before Mount Sinai, (13) gave us the Torah, (14) brought us into the Land of Israel, and (15) built for us the Chosen House (Temple) to atone for all our sins. Of course, the First Temple was constructed by Shlomo, in the 15th generation from Avraham.
18. Mishnah, *Middos* 2:5.
19. *Tehillim* 120-134. See Mishnah, *Succah* 4:9-5:4.
20. *Succah* 53a.
21. Interestingly, the number 15 also notably features in the worldwide Flood at the time of Noach. The waters of the depths that rose to flood the world reached a height of 15 cubits above the mountains (*Bereishis* 7:20; see also *Yoma* 76a). The waters prevailed on Earth for 150 days (*Bereishis* 7:24) — 10 units of 15 — and finally left as the waters receded after 150 days (ibid. 8:3). The area of each floor of the Ark was 300 cubits by 50 cubits (ibid. 6:15). This equals (300 x 50=) 15,000 square cubits of space.

22. *Berachos* 60b. See *Rambam, Hilchos Tefillah* 7:4; *Shulchan Aruch Orach Chaim* 46:6. [Nowadays, even Sephardim say the blessing of *Hanosan la'Ya'ef Ko'ach,* because they follow *Arizal* in these matters, even when it is against *Rambam* or *Beis Yosef*— see *Birkei Yosef* 46:11] .

23. *Tehillim* 105:1-15. See *Seder Olam.* See *Rashi, I Divrei HaYamim* 16:35; quoting *Bereishis Rabbah* 54:4.

24. *I Divrei HaYamim* 29:11

25. *Rokeach, Devarim* 26:17

26. The 15 expressions are (1) *shir* (2) *shevachah* (3) *hallel* (4) *zimrah* (5) *oz* (6) *memshalah* (7) *netzach* (8) *gedulah* (9) *gevurah* (10) *tehillah* (11) *tiferes* (12) *kedushah* (13) *malchus* (14) *berachos,* and (15) *hoda'os.*

27. *Devarim* 6:4-9; 11:13-21.

28. *Bamidbar* 6:24-26.

29. *Yeshayah* 49:6; *Maharal, Chiddushei Aggados, Chullin* 91b, p. 112. The monthly *mitzvah* of *Kiddush Levanah,* Blessing on the New Moon, is extant for as long as the light of the moon continues to increase (*Shulchan Aruch,Orach Chaim* 426:3, *Mishnah Berurah* ad loc.).

30. *Maharal, Gevuros Hashem* 59.

31. See *Taanis* 26b, 30b-31a for details about the joyous events of the 15th of Av.

32. *Esther* 9:18.

33. See "50: All the Way."

34. Avraham was 100 when Yitzchak was born (*Bereishis* 21:5). Avraham was 175 when he died (*Bereishis* 25:7). Yitzchak was 60 when Yaakov and Eisav were born (*Bereishis* 25:26). Thus, they were 15 when Avraham died.

35. *Rokeach, Bereishis* 35:10.

36. See *Sfas Emes, Pinchas* 5645, for how this relates to the 15 levels of *Dayeinu,* which correspond to 15 types of pathways to attach oneself to the Source.

37. *Shemos Rabbah* 1:1.

38. *Bava Basra* 16b.

39. Immigration to the Holy Land is called *aliyah,* ascending. See *Kiddushin* 69a where the Land of Israel is described as "more elevated that all other lands"; it alludes to the fact that it is the highest from a spiritual perspective (*Sfas Emes Ha'azinu* 5657). And the highest point within Israel is Jerusalem, and within it, the Temple. Pilgrimage to Jerusalem was called *oleh regel,* ascending by foot, up the Temple Mount. See *Maharal, Gur Aryeh, Devarim* 1: 25. The stress was on the ascending to reach a higher spiritual plateau. There is the maxim מַעֲלִין בַּקּוֹדֶשׁ וְאֵין מוֹרִידִין, *in matters of sanctity there can only be an upward rather than downward movement* (*Berachos* 28a).

40. There is a phenomenon where a *yeridah,* descent, is considered a necessary prelude to an *aliyah,* ascent (See *Makkos* 7b). A similar concept is that a fall provides a springboard to rise (*Midrash Tehillim* 22; see *also Rabbeinu Yonah, Shaarei Teshuvah* 2:5).

41. *Michah* 7:8.

42. See *R' Yitzchak Hutner, Pachad Yitzchak,* Iggeres p. 217.

43. *Yeshayah* 12:1.

44. *Vilna Gaon, Mishlei* 15:24.

45. See *Rashi, Sanhedrin* 13b.

18
THE LIFELINE

18 relates to man's lifeline
that is based upon his connection
to G-d as the Source of all Life.

The perfect medium where this was
realized was in the Temple,
the "House of Living."

Nowadays, this force can be accessed
through the medium of prayer.

THE KEY TO LIFE

The number
18 has the
well-known
numerical value
of חַי, life.

THE NUMBER 18 HAS THE WELL-KNOWN NUMERICAL VALUE OF חַי, *LIFE*. Life is the most prized asset that man possesses. The life force makes everything possible. With it, he can accomplish extraordinary feats. Without it, his existence in This World abruptly ends.

Despite being his most precious possession, the life force within man is ironically not really his. Human existence relies upon the soul as the inner life force animating his body. The Divine spark draws man toward spirituality, enabling him to enter into and develop a relationship with G-d.

The key to
eternal life is
inextricably
linked to the
concept of
tefillah, prayer.

The fulcrum of existence that holds the key to eternal life is the Jew's reverent relationship with G-d. This is inextricably linked to the concept of *tefillah*, prayer.

TEFILLAH: LIFELINE

Tefillah is the language of the human soul, as man — who is himself referred to as *maveh*, a being that prays [1] — masters the art of how to speak to G-d.

Prayer is
the foremost
expression of
the service and
worship of G-d.
What then is
the purpose of
prayer?

Prayer is the foremost expression of עֲבוֹדַת ה׳, *the service and worship of G-d.*[2] It is submission to the Master of the Universe. But the very concept of prayer poses many theological difficulties. Is prayer for G-d or for man? How is it meant to operate? The fact that G-d is All-Knowing means that He is cognizant of man's needs without him having to verbalize them. G-d also knows whether or not it is truly in man's best interests to receive that for which he petitions. Does G-d really need man to spell it out for Him? Can man's prayer apply "pressure" to change G-d's Mind? And if not, what then is the purpose of prayer?

Tefillah is for
the benefit of
man, not G-d.

Tefillah is for the benefit of man, not G-d.

In a universe where man's actions have a cosmic impact upon the higher realms, prayer is the process through which Divine benevolence descends into This World.[3] The religious expression of *tefillah* is the means for man to create a meaningful relationship with G-d through the object he desires — even if it is not ultimately granted to him. Here a person contemplates the grandeur of the Master of the Universe. He raises himself above the physical realm to establish a connection with G-d. He humbly stands before his Creator and pours out his soul. His soul is nourished by prayer, like food nourishes the body.[4] He verbalizes his thanks for all the good that he receives. He uses this opportunity to petition G-d in times of need. He cries out in a time of distress. He opens up. He airs his deepest thoughts and feelings before his Heavenly Father.

The more that man expresses his dependency upon G-d, the more he undergoes a process of judgment (the root of תְּפִילָה is related to פָּלַל meaning *to judge*)[5] and introspection. Through this he deepens and strengthens this relationship. *It is not G-d Who changes with each successive prayer; it is the person himself.* In other words, the person ascends to a higher spiritual level, which means that he is now no longer the same person he was before. Consequently, he may now be better suited to have his petition granted by becoming a more worthy recipient of G-d's providence and benevolence.[6] And even if his requests are not granted, man uses prayer as the means to draw closer to G-d.

It is not G-d Who changes with each successive prayer; it is the person himself.

18: house of the Living

The chosen place to relate to G-d was the portable *Mishkan*, Sanctuary, in the Wilderness and its permanent successor, the *Beis HaMikdash*, Temple, in Jerusalem.[7] This sacred site was most conducive to connecting to G-d. Indeed, the *korbanos*, sacrificial offerings, and other dedications (such as *bikkurim*, first fruits, in the Holy Land) would be presented at this setting.

The life-affirming qualities of the House of G-d were already apparent in the *Mishkan*. The construction of the *Mishkan* came as atonement for the sin of the Golden Calf after the decree for the eradication of the Jewish nation was rescinded.[8] In relating the construction of the *Mishkan* in *Parashas Pekudei*, the Torah uses the phrase כַּאֲשֶׁר צִוָּה ה' אֶת מֹשֶׁה, *... as G-d commanded Moshe,* a total of 18 times.[9] Like the numerical value of the word חַי, the *Mishkan* would proclaim Israel's continuous relationship to G-d.

The Temple is termed בֵּית תְּפִלָּתִי, *My House of Prayer,*[10] and בֵּית חַיֵּינוּ, *House of Our Life.*[11] All prayers in the world ascend on high through the Temple.[12] Just as life is the union of body and soul, the life of the universe is similarly reliant upon the connection between Earth and Heaven as realized in the Temple.[13] In the same way that

The Mishkan would proclaim their continuity and their spiritual relationship to G-d.

the human body requires food to survive, so too, were the sacrificial offerings equated to the foodstuff that sustain life.[14] In its capacity as the House of Living, the Temple was where a person would connect to G-d, either through offerings or prayer, in the knowledge that life itself is dependent upon man being bound to Him.

The Temple was where a person would connect to G-d in the knowledge that life itself is dependent upon man being bound to Him.

STANDING IN PRAYER

WE HAVE SEEN THAT PRAYER AND THE TEMPLE RELATE TO THE number 18 and to man's lifeline. The celebrated centerpiece of post-Temple *tefillah* is the *Amidah*, Standing Prayer. This prayer was instituted by the 120 elders of the *Anshei Knesses HaGedolah*, Men of the Great Assembly.[15] They formulated the structure of the *Amidah*, generally known by the original number of weekday blessings: שְׁמוֹנֶה עֶשְׂרֵה, 18.[16]

The centerpiece of post-Temple tefillah is the Amidah.

18: Shemoneh Esrei

The structure of prayer is closely modeled upon the *avodah*, sacrificial order, of the Divine service enacted in the Temple. The daily prayers were instituted to correspond to the תָּמִיד, *communal* (literally, continual) *offerings*.[17] In lieu of animal offerings, man's prayers substitute in accordance with the saying, "Let our lips substitute for bulls."[18]

The order and arrangement of the *tefillos* mirrors the Temple architecture. There is an inward progression through the various chambers until the arrival at the innermost sanctum, which corresponds to the point in prayer when one recites *Shemoneh Esrei*.[19] This is where the individual now stands ready to enter the King's most intimate chamber. *Shemoneh Esrei* is therefore the pinnacle of *tefillah* where the individual is granted a rare, private audience. Here he stands, "face to face," before G-d.

The individual now stands ready to enter the King's most intimate chamber.

The 18 blessings begin with 3 preparatory blessings of בִּרְכַת הַשֶּׁבַח, *blessings of praise*, and end with 3 final blessings of בִּרְכוֹת הוֹדָאָה, *blessings of thanks*.[20] The central 12 blessings are בַּקָשׁוֹת, *requests*, for wisdom, good health, sustenance, ingathering of Israel from the Diaspora, the rebuilding of Jerusalem, and so on. (On Shabbos and

196 / Jewish Wisdom in the Numbers

Yom Tov, the requests of the central 12 blessings are replaced with a single blessing about the sanctification of the day — to make a total of 7 blessings).

Parallel to the *Shemoneh Esrei* are the 18 occasions in the Torah that all the 3 Jewish Patriarchs (Avraham, Yitzchak, Yaakov) are grouped and mentioned together in the same verse.[21] Indeed, the 3 daily prayers, whose centerpiece is the *Amidah*, were respectively instituted by our 3 Jewish Forefathers.[22] The Torah itself recounts 18 occasions where a person recited a *tefillah* to G-d.[23]

18: DIVINE NAMES

The template of 18 blessings in *Shemoneh Esrei* is also alluded to in the 18 Divine Names found in *Tehillim* 29.[24] This well-known psalm defines the glorified, elevated loftiness of G-d and His Greatness, repeatedly using the 4-Letter Name of G-d that is characteristic of *Rachamim*, Mercy.[25] Its words are strongly reminiscent of David's song when escorting the *Aron* (Ark) to its permanent home in Jerusalem.[26]

The template of 18 blessings in Shemoneh Esrei is also alluded to in the 18 Divine Names found in Tehillim 29.

The 3 paragraphs of *Shema* are similarly composed of a total of 18 Divine Names.[27] One of the central themes of *Shema* revolves around the relationship between man and G-d, resembling that of "a subject and his Sovereign." Here the Jew accepts the rule of G-d In his capacity as the King's loyal citizen, he looks to his King, Who carries the obligation to sustain the needs of His people. The Jew does this by petitioning Him through the 18 blessings of *Shemoneh Esrei*.[28]

The Jew accepts the rule of G-d. As the King's loyal citizen, he looks to his King.

18 VERTEBRAE: MAN'S PHYSICAL FRAME

A further parallel the Talmud makes to the 18 blessings of *Shemoneh Esrei* is the 18 main vertebrae of the spinal column. Together, these parts are responsible for supporting the human body's frame.[29]

Here the relationship between the Jew and G-d takes on a different face: it is comparable to that of a "servant before his Master." This calls for an act of submission on man's part. This is physically evoked in the human posture where man, a creature who walks upright rather than on all fours, willingly bends all 18 of these joints in an act of submission before G-d.[30]

Man willingly bends all 18 of these joints in an act of submission before G-d.

Bowing and prostrating are acts of subservience. The servant humbly bends his body in willing negation before his master. In this guise, the servant hopes that he will be found deserving to have his requests granted.[31] The bending of the 18 vertebrae is thus the appropriate position that a Jew adopts within his prayers.

18: STANDING IN AWE

The Jew must approach G-d in a state of reverence.

Whether adopting the template of a servant before his master or a subject before his king, the praying Jew must approach G-d in a state of יִרְאָה, *awe, veneration,* or *reverence.* There were strict laws of conduct for attendees in the Temple to ensure their reverent conduct in the worship of G-d.[32] There was no excuse for frivolity or lightheadedness. Indeed, the inauguration of the *Mishkan,* predecessor to the *Beis HaMikdash,* was marred by the transgression of Aharon's sons Nadav and Avihu, whose tragic deaths resulted from their failure to act with due reverence, as evidenced by their unsolicited fire-offering.[33]

Tefillah is itself synonymous with "serving G-d with fear."

Tefillah is itself synonymous with "serving G-d with fear."[34] Therefore it is appropriate that the usage of יִרְאָה, *fear,* in context with G-d, is mentioned 18 times in the *Chumash,*[35] 18 times in *Tehillim,*[36] and 18 times in *Mishlei.*[37] Like the laws regarding one's entry into the Temple or Sanctuary, there are practical applications that extend to the laws of prayer to ensure that it is conducted in an appropriate setting, in suitable attire, the right code of conduct, and the right frame of mind.[38]

The relationship to G-d defines the lifeline of a Jew.

The number 18 is found in many areas of the life of King David, who said about himself וַאֲנִי תְפִלָּה, *I am the embodiment of prayer.*[39] Most of the verses within prayer are extracted from David's compositions in *Tehillim.* And this King of Israel married 18 wives[40] and fought a total of 18 battles.[41]

The relationship to G-d defines the lifeline of a Jew. He is alive when he reverently relates to G-d through *tefillah* in humble subservience.

NOTES

1. *Bava Kamma* 3b.
2. *Midrash Tehillim* 66:1; *Zohar* 1, 59b; *Zohar* 2, 115b; *Zohar* 3, 111b, 223a. There is a dispute among rabbinic authorities whether prayer is one of the 613 commandments. The *Rambam* (*Sefer HaMitzvos* 5; *Hilchos Tefillah* 1:1) holds that the essence of prayer is a *mitzvah.* Others (including the *Ramban*

in his *Commentary on Sefer HaMitzvos L'Rambam* 5) maintain that it is only rabbinic in nature. See *Berachos* 21a and *Sefer HaChinuch* 433.

3. R' Chaim Volozhin, *Nefesh HaChaim* 2:4.
4. R' Yehuda HaLevi, *Kuzari* 3:5.
5. R'Samson Raphael Hirsch, based upon *I Shmuel*, 2:25.
6. *Sefer HaChinuch* Mitzvah 433.
7. See "410: The First Temple."
8. *Shemos Rabbah* 51:8
9. *Yerushalmi, Taanis* 2:2; *Vayikra Rabbah* 1:8; *Yerushalmi, Berachos* 4:3.
10. *Yeshayah* 56:7.
11. Blessings of the *Haftorah*.
12. See *Bereishis* 28:17, where Yaakov refers to the Temple Mount, saying, "... This is the gate of the Heavens."
13. See "410: First Temple."
14. See R' Chaim Volozhin, *Nefesh HaChaim* 2:14. Consequently, the tragedy in the destruction of the Temple is compared to mourning for the dead. See "410: The First Temple."
15. *Megillah* 17b.
16. The 18 original blessings of the *Amidah* are as follows: (1) *Avos*, Fathers (2) *Gevuros*, [G-d's] Might (3) *Kedushas Hashem*, Holiness of G-d's Name (4) *Binah*, Insight (5) *Teshuvah*, Repentance (6) *Selichah*, Forgiveness (7) *Geulah*, Redemption (8) *Refuah*, Healing (9) *Bircas HaShanim*, Year of Prosperity (10) *Kibbutz Galuyos*, Ingathering of Exiles (11) *Din*, Restoration of Justice (12) *Tzaddikim*, Righteous (13) *Yerushayalim*, Rebuilding of Jerusalem (14) *Malchus beis David*, Davidic royal dynasty (15) *Kabbalas Tefillah*, Acceptance of Prayer (16) *Avodah*, Temple Service (17) *Modim*, Thanksgiving, and (18) *Shalom*, Peace. An additional 19th blessing, *Bircas HaMinim*, Against Heretics, was added at a later date. See *Berachos* 28b and *Megillah* 17b.
17. *Berachos* 26b.
18. *Hoshea* 14:3.
19. See Mishnah, *Berachos* 9:5.
20. *Kol Bo* 11. If one interrupted in the opening 3 blessings of the *Amidah*, he must return to the beginning (*Shulchan Aruch, Orach Chaim* 104:5).
21. *Yerushalmi, Berachos* 4:3. See the commentaries ad loc. about a number of other verses not included in the count of 18.
22. *Berachos* 26b.
23. R' Saadiah Gaon, *Siddur.*
24. *Berachos* 28b; *Tanchuma, Vayeira* 1.
25. See *Maharal, Nesiv HaAvodah* 9.
26. *I Divrei HaYamim* 16:28-29.
27. *Berachos* 28b; The total of 18 is inclusive of both the 4-Letter Name of G-d and the Name *Elokim*.
28. *Maharal, Nesiv HaAvodah* 9.
29. *Berachos* 28b. See *Mishnah, Oholos* 1:8.
30. *Tanchuma, Vayeira* 1.
31. *Maharal, Nesiv HaAvodah* 9.
32. See Mishnah, *Berachos* 9:5.
33. *Vayikra* 10:1-3.
34. *Berachos* 30b based upon *Tehillim* 2:11.
35. *Rokeach, Shemos* 40:33. This count excludes one additional special mention (*Devarim* 28:58). The 18 occasions are said to parallel the 18 blessings of *Shemoneh Esrei* (*Rokeach, Devarim* 10:13).
36. *Rokeach, Devarim* 10:13. This is said to be parallel to the 18 blessings.
37. *Rokeach, Shemos* 40:33.

38. *Shulchan Aruch, Orach Chaim* 89-99.
39. *Tehillim* 109:4.
40. Mishnah, *Sanhedrin* 2:4. A king is permitted to have a maximum of 18 wives. See *Sanhedrin* 22a, which discusses the fact that David had 18 wives, and did not want to exceed this number, and therefore did not marry Avishag. Even when ill, David fulfilled marital duties to 18 wives (*Sanhedrin* 107a).
41. *Vayikra Rabbah* 1:4.

20
MANHOOD

20 is the age when man reaches intellectual and spiritual maturity.

Now he takes full responsibility for his actions.

MAKINGS OF A MAN

THE NUMBER 20 MARKS THE ATTAINMENT, IN YEARS, OF FULL MANHOOD. The transition from child to adult occurs at the age of bar *mitzvah* (13 years old for a boy) or bas *mitzvah* (12 years old for a girl). It is at this age that they enter a life of *mitzvah* observance.[1] Nevertheless, the jump to becoming a full member of the Jewish community is marked at a later stage: the age of 20.

Becoming a full member of the Jewish community is marked at the age of 20.

The title אִישׁ applies to a person from the age of 13, but the word גֶּבֶר is reserved for a man above the age of 20.[2] The end of adolescence is attained at the physical maturity that comes at the age of 20.[3] This is significant, as the celebration of physical maturity has its parallel in a corresponding intellectual maturity.

The 20-year-old is assumed to be able to evaluate what choices to make, to be responsible and accountable for his conduct.

The 20-year-old's spiritual and intellectual capacities are developed enough that he is capable of dealing with weighty life issues. He is trusted to effectively run his own affairs and look after his business interests, such as managing the estate left to him as an inheritance.[4] He is assumed to be able to evaluate what choices to make, to be responsible and accountable for his conduct.[5]

20: A CALL TO ACCOUNT

Every individual who has reached intellectual maturity is expected to live a life of accountability. While a person is liable to punishment in a Jewish court from the earlier age of 12 or 13, in the eyes of the Heavenly Tribunal, he or she is punished for any sinful conduct only from the later age of 20.[6] Here there is the realization that man's decisions carry cosmic significance — be it for the good or for the bad. Standing before his Creator, man is held accountable for his speech and his actions.[7] The outlook of a mature individual assuming full responsibility for his conduct readily translates into every aspect of man's life. Despite the instinctive tendency to avoid the consequences of one's actions, a cornerstone of Judaism is the concept of reward and punishment.[8] Man must constantly consider, *before Whom will you [man] have to give justification and reckoning?*[9]

A cornerstone of Judaism is the concept of reward and punishment.

G-d did not originally create Man and Woman as newborn children; He formed them as fully mature 20-year-old adults.[10] Significantly, it was at this age that Adam and Chavah sinned by eating from the Tree of Knowledge, on the very same day as their creation.[11] In the aftermath of their sin, they were judged by G-d and punished for their transgression.

Another illustration that shows 20 as the time of Heavenly punishment can be seen from the depiction, after her death, of the greatness of the matriarch Sarah.[12] Her 127 years are divided into hundreds, tens and single units.[13] The objective of this exercise is to stress that each stage of her life was righteous. In the words of the Sages, "When 100 years old, Sarah was equivalent to a 20-year-old, who is free of sin in the eyes of Heaven."[14]

20: IN FOR THE COUNT

In the laws of consecrating *Arachin*, Valuations [of people to the Sanctuary/Temple], the classification of a male adult is from the age of 20 years.[15] This same age of 20 was the inclusion point in the Jewish national census in the Wilderness[16] and of each tribe individually.[17] Indeed, the very act of counting signals the importance attached to each individual included in the census. Each Jew was counted individually, indicating that each was an indispensable, precious, and full member of G-d's Chosen Nation.

Due to the sin of the Spies, however, the Israelites who left Egypt were subject to the Heavenly punishment that they die out in the Wilderness. This decree was passed only upon those members of the generation from 20 to 60 years old; they were the people who died and did not enter the Holy Land.[18]

The very act of counting signals the importance attached to each individual included in the census.

HE'S YOUR MAN

THE DEVELOPMENT OF A TEENAGE ADOLESCENT INTO AN ADULT IS achieved when the person is able to navigate his path through the difficult choices of life, secure in the knowledge that he alone bears responsibility for his decisions.

An adult bears the responsibility for his decisions.

shekel: 20 gerah

A person must weigh options prior to making a decision.

The basic unit of currency used by the Torah was the שֶׁקֶל (plural: שְׁקָלִים).[19] The Torah notes that 1 *shekel* was itself made up of 20 גֵּרָה.[20] The word *shekel* itself connotes *weight*[21] or *balance*.[22] It is the accepted unit used in the measure of value. Thus, in decision-making, a person must engage in the process of שִׁקּוּל הַדַּעַת, *weighing the options*, prior to making a decision. This necessitates man's intellectual maturity to contemplate and ascertain what is the right or wrong course of action before pursuing it. Just as a *shekel* is composed of 20 *gerah*, the man who has reached the age of 20 is now well-suited to examine and evaluate all of his actions and is accountable to Heaven.

This skill is a key element in the making of a man. Prominent examples of how and where this finds expression include a person assuming responsibility for others, the commitment of marriage, the pursuit of a livelihood, and engaging in warfare.

20: age of responsibility

Moshe was 20 years old when he lovingly shouldered the burden of the Jewish people.

The association between 20 years of age and the motif of responsibility is beautifully illuminated in the development of Moshe Rabbeinu. The Midrash notes that Moshe was 20 years old when he left the comfort of Pharaoh's palace and went out to witness firsthand the plight of his brothers.[23] Immediately, he lovingly shouldered the burden of the Jewish people who were being bitterly oppressed by the cruel Egyptian taskmasters.[24]

Moshe's care and concern for the Children of Israel — beginning at this point — led to G-d confirming the eminent suitability of Moshe to be appointed to assume the mantle of leadership.

20: best-by marriage date

His arrival to manhood obligates him to marry.

The attainment of manhood requires that man be in a married state. In the words of the Talmud, "One aged 20 and unmarried [is doomed to] spend all his days in sinful thought."[25] His arrival to manhood obligates him to marry, a state in which husband and wife complement and complete each other.

The physical bodily (*chomer*) development of man is completed at 18: *the 18-year-old for the chupah*.[26] However, his spiritual form (*tzurah*) reaches completion at the slightly later age of 20. These two successive dates are highly appropriate for the institution of marriage, which itself contains the symbolic combination of material (*chomer*) and form (*tzurah*) that come together in the union of husband and wife.[27]

20: HARD AT WORK

This newly acquired status of being fully responsible for his actions also marks man's desire to be victorious and to have dominion over others.[28] The Mishnah notes, בֶּן עֶשְׂרִים לִרְדוֹף, *20-year-old in pursuit.*[29] This pursuit primarily refers to earning a living. One of the central obligations of marriage is for a husband to support his wife. In the words of the *kesubah*, wedding contract, "I will work for, esteem, feed, and support you as is the custom of Jewish men who work for, esteem, feed, and support their wives faithfully." Here the bridegroom promises to labor for his bride, who is to become one of his dependents.

After Adam and Chavah's sin at the age of 20, the punishment given to man was that now he would have to pursue a livelihood — "*by the sweat of the face shall you eat bread*"[30] — and in terms of their marital status, the woman would be subservient to the man — "*your desire shall be for your husband and he shall rule over you.*"[31]

The newly acquired status of being fully responsible for his actions also marks man's desire to be victorious and to have dominion over others.

20: A CALL TO ARMS

It was at 20 years old that Jewish men would be enlisted to fight as soldiers in the army.[32] This is when a man bravely places his life on the line for the sake of his beloved nation. This endeavor involved deadly confrontations in the bid to emerge victorious in battle. Delegation of such responsibility could only be entrusted to one in possession of that hallmark of accountability duly accorded to a mature man.

Whether in the struggle for bread or the conflict on the battlefield (note the similarities between לֶחֶם, *bread*, and מִלְחָמָה, *battle*; זָן, *food*, and זַיִן, *weapon*),[33] his manhood is reached and he is now intellectually mature enough to note the impact of his actions and to understand his accountability.

In summary, the activities that devolve upon a 20-year-old are those that provide the essential hallmark of Jewish maturity. Here he bears responsibility and accountability — qualities that are mainstays of one living his life as a Jew.

He is now intellectually mature enough to note the impact of his actions and to understand his accountability, mainstays of one living his life as a Jew.

NOTES

1. See "13: An Everlasting Love."
2. See *Maharal, Gur Aryeh, Shemos* 12:37.
3. Ramban, *Bamidbar* 1:3. The higher *neshamah* component of the soul is said to enter man when he reaches the age of 20 years (*Zohar, Mishpatim* 98a).
4. See *Bava Basra* 156a, which discusses how from the age of 20 an orphan can sell the real estate of his father that was left to him as an inheritance. Earlier, he lacks the legal capacity and is not considered to have the requisite business acumen.
5. See *Ohr HaChaim, Shemos* 30:14.
6. *Shabbos* 89b and *Rashi* ad loc.
7. R' Chaim Volozhin, *Nefesh HaChaim* 1:4.
8. See *Rambam's* 11th Principle of Faith.
9. *Pirkei Avos* 3:1.
10. *Bereishis Rabbah* 14:7.
11. *Sanhedrin* 38b.
12. See *Rashi, Shabbos* 89b that it is derived from the ones who died in the Wilderness.
13. See "127: Wake Up Call."
14. *Rashi, Bereishis* 23:1.
15. *Vayikra* 27:3-5.
16. *Bamidbar* 1:3, 1:45.
17. *Bamidbar* 1:20-42. This was with the notable exclusion of the Levites, whose count was separate (*Bamidbar* 1:47), and whose age parameters differed (*Bamidbar* 3:22).
18. *Bamidbar* 32:11. See *Rashi, Shabbos* 89b.
19. See *Vayikra* 5:15.
20. See *Shemos* 30:13, *Bamidbar* 3:47.
21. See *Bereishis* 24:22; *Vayikra* 19:35.
22. See, for example, *Rashi, Shemos* 6:26 as to how Moshe and Aharon were *equal* and *balanced*.
23. *Shemos Rabbah* 1:27.
24. *Shemos* 2:11.
25. When he reaches 20 and has not married, G-d says, "Let his bones swell" (*Kiddushin* 29b). See also *Rambam, Hilchos Ishus* 15:2.
26. *Pirkei Avos* 5:21.
27. *Maharal, Derech Chaim* 5:21.
28. Ibid.
29. *Pirkei Avos* 5:21.
30. *Bereishis* 3:19.
31. Ibid. 3:16.
32. *Bamidbar* 1:3.
33. R' Samson Raphael Hirsch, *Bereishis* 14:2.

22
THE SACRED LETTERS

22 relates to the sacred letters
of the Hebrew alphabet.

It is symbolic of the building blocks
of creation that establish
the ideal sequence that constitutes order.

THE NUMBER 22 IS DEEPLY ASSOCIATED WITH THE LETTERS OF THE holy Hebrew alphabet.

22: LETTERS OF CREATION

There is an essential distinction between all world languages and *Lashon HaKodesh*, the Holy Language of Biblical Hebrew. The number of letters/characters within man-made languages (e.g., English or Russian) is arbitrary. It holds no significance whatsoever. It is simply based upon convention and is naturally subject to evolutionary development.

The uniqueness of Hebrew is that it originates from the Divine.

In contrast, the uniqueness of Hebrew is that it originates from the Divine. It objectively describes spiritual reality as contained within the Torah.

As the raw material of creation, the Hebrew letters are the elementary 22 building blocks of existence. Nothing exists that is not represented by these letters.[1] They join and combine through the construction of words by which man expresses himself and communicates with others.

The countless combinations of the letters and their orders reflect cosmic spiritual forces.

Anything G-d wants to say in *Lashon HaKodesh* would be channeled through the sacred 22 letters.[2] And *everything* that is possible to say, in the formation of words, must be said using the 22 characters in the Hebrew alphabet. The countless combinations of the letters and their orders reflect cosmic spiritual forces.

Lashon HaKodesh, unlike other languages, says it *as it is*. G-d used these letters to create the universe: *He spoke and it came to be.*[3] Furthermore, He used them to orally give over and to write the Torah. In other words, these letters describe Torah on their own objective terms — undiluted, untarnished, and unfettered by any subjective translation or interpretation. In this respect, the Hebrew alphabet is likened to the DNA of existence.[4] Everything that G-d determined had to be said was inscribed in the Torah to function as the blueprint of creation.[5] G-d used the combination of the 22 letters in the formation of words that were used to translate His Will into reality. Like 22

Everything was inscribed in the Torah to function as the blueprint of creation.

channels of spirituality,[6] the letters are used to form words of Torah, which is itself wholly composed of Divine Names.[7]

Clothing is the means used by the wearer to project himself to others. So too, the 22 letters of Torah are likened to the "clothing of G-d," the medium He uses, so to speak, to present Himself to the world.[8] Indeed, the honor of Torah is embodied within these letters. In spite of his evil conduct, Achav reigned for 22 years as King of Israel as reward for honoring the Torah given with 22 letters.[9]

The 22 letters of the Hebrew alphabet are the essential properties to teach man the ways in the service of G-d. Through this he will become an embodiment of a Torah Scroll.[10] Conversely, sinful behavior is comparable to ruining or tearing the Torah Scroll.[11]

22: ALL PRESENT AND CORRECT

The full range of letters means that all the essential components are factored into the equation.

Torah is the be-all and end-all of Creation. This makes the 22 letters of Torah the natural device to portray the all-encompassing nature of something. Typically, the full range of letters means that all the essential components are factored into the equation.

Traditionally, 26 verses in *Tanach* contain all 22 Hebrew letters.[12] One famous expression of this phenomenon is the presence of all 22 letters within the Ten Commandments, which encapsulate the giving of the Torah that is composed through these letters.[13] By extension, the appearance of the 22 letters but with some exceptions is also noteworthy.[14]

22: THE ALPHABETIC SEQUENCE

This magnificent construction by the Divine Architect is brilliantly revealed through the orderliness that pervades existence and that facilitates all life forms on this planet.

The "whole picture" that we see in the complete set of the Hebrew alphabet receives additional significance when not only are they all present, but when the 22 letters are also arranged according to their alphabetic sequence, starting from א-ב-ג-ד ... and finishing with the letter ת.

This presents a clearly defined, sequential structure programmed into Creation. Its magnificent construction by the Divine Architect is brilliantly revealed through the orderliness that pervades existence and that facilitates all life forms on this planet.

The source for the order and sequence within the building blocks of existence is the arrangement of the א–ב. This is the reason that an increasing numeric value (*gematria*) is attributed to the Hebrew letters that reflects their respective sequential order (2 = ב, 1 = א). But the optimal combination in the ordering of these letters lies in the Torah.

There are many instances of prayers, liturgy, and hymns in which the full range of 22 letters appears in an alphabetic acrostic.

Typically, an arrangement made in accordance with the א–ב denotes that everything is in order; everything is carefully positioned according to its designated order. Consequently, there are many instances of prayers, liturgy, and hymns in which the full range of 22 letters appears in an alphabetic acrostic. This occurs in a sequence of words (e.g., אֵ-ל בָּרוּךְ גְּדוֹל in the weekday morning blessings of *Shema*[15]), a sequence of phrases (e.g., *Tehillim* 112[16]), or as a sequence of verses (e.g., *Eishes Chayil*[17]).

The numerous examples of this phenomenon in Jewish liturgy include *Selichos*, *piyutim*, and the additional prayers (*Yotzros*) recited on Rosh Hashanah, Yom Kippur, and other festivals. Here the 22 letters are used to denote the comprehensive glorification of G-d. In the *Hoshanos* recited during Succos and on Hoshana Rabbah, the 22 letters encompass *all* manner of Divine salvation.

OUT OF ORDER

The slightest deviation from the alphabetical sequence means something is amiss.

WHILE THE PRESENCE OF 22 LETTERS SIGNIFIES THE TOTALITY OF Creation, it can simultaneously be used to depict the breakdown of a structured existence. The slightest deviation from the alphabetical sequence automatically means something is amiss and signifies that matters are "out of order."

22: DISORDERLY LETTERS

In all but the concluding chapter, the verses within *Megillas Eichah*, the Book of *Lamentations,* are arranged according to the Hebrew alphabet. Due to Israel violating the Torah composed of 22 letters, their due retribution of destruction and exile was recorded using all 22 letters of the Hebrew alphabet.[18]

The use of the א–ב indicates that the original order of Torah belonging to Israel was displaced in favor of an alternative order — a substitute state of reality within which they would have no true existence. The disorder is reflected in the alphabetic sequence, which after the first chapter of *Megillas Eichah* is disarranged and characterized by switching the order of the letters such that the פ precedes the ע.[19]

BEIN HAMITZORIM: 22 DAYS

The tragedy of this disorderly sequence finds its annual expression in the 22-day period of *Bein HaMitzorim* (literally, *between the straits*), also known as the Three Weeks.[20] This refers to the 22 days in the Jewish calendar beginning with 17 Tammuz and lasting through and including Tishah B'Av (9 Av).[21] The period between the fast days is characterized by days of disaster — from the worship of the Golden Calf and the breach of the stronghold of Jerusalem on 17 Tammuz, to the destruction of the Temple and the many national calamities on Tishah B'Av, this is a time of devastation and mourning.[22]

During this epoch, many national calamities historically befell the Jewish people. The 22 letters as the building blocks of Creation and order were reversed. Hence this period came to denote 22 days of total destruction.[23] It was as if Creation — symbolized by the number 22 — were being undone. Consequently, during this period the Jewish nation faced the severe consequences of its sins.

Conversely, there is a corresponding period to make amends for the 22 days of destruction during *Bein HaMitzorim*. There are 22 days beginning with Rosh Hashanah (1 Tishrei) and culminating on Shemini Atzeres (22 Tishrei). This symbolizes the time of "re-creation" that taps into the 22 Hebrew letters as the building blocks of creation.

The tragedy of this disorderly sequence finds its annual expression in the 22-day period of Bein HaMitzorim, Three Weeks.

22 days from Rosh Hashanah on Shemini Atzeres symbolize the time of "re-creation" that taps into the 22 Hebrew letters as the building blocks of creation.

ABSENT AND MISSING: 22 YEARS

Other examples of 22 that reflect a disorderly state of banishment, distress, or rejection can be found in the time span of 22 years.

Yaakov was forced into exile. Fleeing his homeland, he took refuge for 22 years with Lavan before finally returning home. Due to his absence, the patriarch was unable to fulfill the *mitzvah* of honoring his parents for those 22 years. Accordingly, Yaakov's own son Yosef was separated from him for that same length of time.[24] During those 22 years that the grieving father mourned for his lost son, the *Shechinah* departed from Yaakov.[25]

Another instance of the *Shechinah* departing for 22 years occurred in the aftermath of the episode of Bathsheba.[26] Distraught at the painful absence of the *Shechinah*, David spent those 22 years in mourning, crying bitter tears, and eating bread with dust.[27]

ORDER RESTORED

The order of Creation as exemplified in the 22 letters of the alphabet will be reestablished.

Nevertheless, all these examples of disorder will disappear when order will ultimately be restored. The order of Creation as exemplified in the 22 letters of the alphabet will be reestablished. In the *Viduy* confession, for example, the arrangement according to the alphabetic sequence signifies the penitent's *complete* regret for every type of iniquity.[28] The sacred 22 letters of the Hebrew alphabet — which may have been misused in sin — must be returned to their rightful position.[29]

Not simply "order for the sake of order," the 22 letters set in place a comprehensive, unified system in which every component is essential, interdependent, and reliant upon all the others for its completion.[30]

All the building blocks will unite to reveal the magnificent order in G-d's Creation.

This is true with Torah and Creation which must work with one another in harmony. Then, all the building blocks will unite to reveal the magnificent order in G-d's Creation.

NOTES

1. See *Rabbeinu Bachya*, *Shemos* 16:16.
2. The kabbalistic work *Sefer HaYetzirah* describes the sacred letters as the agency of Creation.
3. *Tehillim* 33:9. See *Bereishis Rabbah* 18:4 (cited in *Rashi*, *Bereishis* 2:23) as to how the Hebrew language was used to create the universe. Everything in the universe was created through combinations of spiritual forces depicted by 22 letters (*Rabbeinu Bachya*, *Shemos* 16:16). See *Pirkei Avos* 5:1 as to how the world was created with 10 Utterances and *Berachos* 55a regarding how Betzalel knew how to combine the letters with which Heaven and Earth were created.
4. See *Maharal*, *Tiferes Yisrael* 34, who analyzes the Midrash (*Osiyos DeRabbi Akiva*) about all the letters of the Hebrew alphabet vying for the opportunity to lead as the first letter in the Torah.
5. *Bereishis Rabbah* 1:1; see *Maharal*, *Nesiv HaTorah* 1.
6. See *Megaleh Amukos*, *Va'eschanan* 171.
7. *Zohar* 3, 13b. See *Ramban*, Introduction to Torah Commentary.
8. *Zohar* 3, 152a. Here, from man's perspective, the letters are also the means by which he can relate to G-d.
9. *Sanhedrin* 102b.
10. See *Moed Katan* 25a; one who sees a person expiring is obligated to rend his garment as if he witnessed a Torah Scroll burning.

11. R' Chaim Volozhin, quoted by *Michtav MeiEliyahu* 4, p. 91.
12. The 26 verses are (1) *Shemos* 16:16. (2) *Devarim* 4:34. (3) *Yehoshua* 4:34. (4) *II Melachim* 4:39. (5) Ibid. 6:32. (6) Ibid. 7:8. (7) *Yeshayah* 5:25. (8) Ibid. 66:17. (9) *Yirmiyah* 22:3. (10) Ibid. 32:29. (11) *Yechezkel* 17:9. (12) Ibid. 38:12. (13) *Hoshea* 10:8. (14) Ibid. 13:2. (15) *Amos* 9:13. (16) *Tzefaniah* 3:8. (17) *Zechariah* 6:11. (18) *Koheles* 4:8. (19) *Esther* 3:13. (20) *Daniel* 2:15. (21) Ibid. 2:43. (22) Ibid. 4:20. (23) Ibid. 7:19. (24) *Ezra* 7:28. (25) *Nechemiah* 3:7. (26) *II Divrei HaYamim* 26:11. (It is noteworthy that in *Tzefaniah* 3:8, all five end letters appear as well.)
13. *Rabbeinu Bachya, Devarim* 4:34 in reference to the Ten Commandments mentioned in *Devarim* 5:6-18.
14. See *Rabbeinu Bachya* on *Bereishis* 47:28, where he discusses how all 22 letters are found within the 12 Tribes, with several exceptions; ibid. 49:12, where he discusses how all 22 letters are found in the blessing of Yehudah, bar 1. See also *Rabbeinu Bachya, Shemos* 25:10.
15. See also *Zohar* 2, 205b.
16. *Tehillim* 112:1-10.
17. *Mishlei* 31:10-31.
18. *Sanhedrin* 104a.
19. Based on the meaning of these letters, this reflects how the spies dispatched by Moshe foolishly put their פ, *mouth*, before their ע, *eye*.
20. This is based on *Eichah* 1:3; see also *Eichah Rabbah* 1:29 and *Yalkut Shimoni, Devarim* 9:45.
21. In other sources, the Three Weeks are depicted as being 21 days. See *Rashi, Yirmiyah* 1:12, and *Maharal, Netzach Yisrael* 5.
22. See *Taanis* 26a-b, which lists the 5 tragedies of 17 Tammuz and corresponding 5 tragedies of Tishah B'Av.
23. Conversely, there are a parallel 22 days from Rosh Hashanah ending on Shemini Atzeres (22 Tishrei) that culminates in the greatest joy.
24. *Megillah* 17a.
25. *Rashi* and *Chizkuni, Bereishis* 45:27.
26. *Yalkut Shimoni, Shmuel* 165.
27. *Tanna DeVei Eliyahu Rabbah* 2.
28. See R' Chaim Volozhin, *Nefesh HaChaim* 4:32, who explains that the 22 letters of the Torah in *Viduy* are intended to arouse the Heavenly root of the soul that is tied up and dependent upon Torah, in order to cleanse and sanctify the soul.
29. R' Eliyahu Dessler, *Michtav MeiEliyahu* 4, p. 91.
30. Ibid. 1, pp. 92-93.

24
THE DIVISION
OF LABOR

24 refers to the loving relationship
between Israel and G-d.

This all-encompassing love is reflected
in each side's timeless commitment.

Every opportunity is used to showcase a selfless
dedication to one's beloved.

This creates an everlasting covenant
in a bond of love that will never be severed.

THE DIVISION

The optimal way for man to relate to a complex structure is to break down that information into its major headings.

DIVISION OF A WHOLE ENTITY INTO ITS COMPONENT PARTS IS OFTEN represented by the number 24.

The optimal way for man to relate to a complex structure that contains masses of data is to break down that information into its major headings. Individual parts are organized according to their appropriate category. Once sorted into clearly defined groupings, the structure can now systematically be reconstructed in the context of the whole.[1]

The number 24 relates to the 24 tzirufim, permutations, of the 4-Letter Name of G-d.

The choice number of division is 24. In kabbalistic sources, this relates to the 24 *tzirufim*, permutations, of the 4-Letter Name of G-d as it is pronounced in This World (אֲ־דֹ־נָ־י), which represent 24 pathways of Divine influence in our world.[2] The mathematical explanation for the choice of this particular number has to do with the divisibility of 24 into several smaller whole numbers (1, 2, 3, 4, 6, 8, and 12).

$$24 \div 24 = 1 \qquad 24 \div 4 = 6$$
$$24 \div 12 = 2 \qquad 24 \div 3 = 8$$
$$24 \div 8 = 3 \qquad 24 \div 2 = 12$$
$$24 \div 6 = 4 \qquad 24 \div 1 = 24$$

Some of the most familiar applications of the use of 24 are found in the standard division of a day, the books of *Tanach*, and the head or tip of 24 limbs in the human body.[3]

ᗞAY: 24 ᕼOᑌᖇS

In many ancient civilizations, the day was divided into 24 hours. In Judaism, a full 24-hour period is technically termed מֵעֵת לְעֵת, *from time to time.*[4] Here the day is divided into 24 שָׁעוֹת זְמַנִיּוֹת, *Halachic hours*, where both daytime and nighttime hours respectively subdivide into 12 equal periods. The length of a Halachic hour during the daytime fluctuates between the winter months (less daylight) and

216 / Jewish Wisdom in the Numbers

the summer months (more daylight). Together, they constitute a day whose total duration is 24 hours.[5]

In practice, the prospect of assessing a day as one indivisible unit is simply not feasible. How would a person be able to apportion varying lengths of time (e.g., ½ hour, 2 hours, etc.) to be assigned toward his many daily activities? The process of breaking up a day into 24 hour-long intervals allows man to individuate his actions. Out of his whole day, man can now allocate his time effectively by organizing his affairs into his daily timetable.

TANACh: 24 bookS

תנ״ך contains all the tomes of תּוֹרָה שֶׁבְּכְתָב, *Written Torah*. The mechanism for how a Jew can study this magnificent work necessitates splitting this document into 24 distinct volumes. These are the חוּמָשׁ, *5 Books of Torah* (*Bereishis, Shemos, Vayikra, Bamidbar,* and *Devarim*); 8 Books of נְבִיאִים, *Prophets* (*Yehoshua, Shoftim, Shmuel, Melachim, Yeshayah, Yirmiyah, Yechezkel, Trei Aser*); and 11 Books of כְּתוּבִים, *Writings* (*Tehillim, Mishlei, Iyov, 5 Megillos, Daniel, Ezra-Nechemiah, Divrei HaYamim*).[6] Each of the 3 sections of *Tanach* has its distinctive characteristic; similarly, each of the 24 individual books has its unique character and content.

Each of the 3 sections of Tanach has its distinctive characteristic; similarly, each of the 24 individual books has its unique character and content.

This subdivision transforms *Tanach* into a usable and coherent body. A Torah scholar is duty-bound to learn and master all 24 books.[7] The works of *Tanach* are adornments for a Jew; they are classified as 24 bridal ornaments.[8] So too, is the systematic knowledge of all areas of *Torah She'bichsav* an essential feature in the life of a Jew. Indeed, the number 24 was employed by the Sages to teach the importance of systematizing all one's studies. The Talmud records how a scholar repeated his studies 24 times, to parallel the 24 Books of *Tanach*.[9]

The number 24 was employed by the Sages to teach the importance of systematizing all one's studies.

bODy: 24 MAJOR LIMbS

The male body has 24 רָאשֵׁי הָאֵבָרִים, *tips of limbs*. These are the 10 digits of the hands, 10 digits of the feet, 2 ears, nose, and the male organ. Damage to any one of these 24 bodily parts finds its application in the laws of a non-Jewish slave.[10] If a master injures only the tip of one of these limbs, the law is that the slave is automatically freed from servitude to compensate for this bodily damage.[11]

THE FULL SET OR GROUP IS OFTEN THE COMBINATION OF ALL 24 individuated parts. The division into 24 essential components is found in particular reference to the description of the Holy City and in the groupings in the Divine worship in the Temple.

24: The holy city

The division of the Holy City is depicted using this number. "There were 24 open places in Jerusalem; each open place had 24 alleys; each alley had 24 marketplaces; each marketplace had 24 streets; each street had 24 courtyards; each courtyard had 24 houses."[12] Furthermore, the weekly blessing in the *Amidah* that petitions G-d to rebuild the Holy City is comprised of exactly 24 words.[13]

24: ALTAR AND priestly gifts

The Mishnah associates כְּהֻנָּה, *Priesthood*, with 24, the number of מַתְּנוֹת כְּהֻנָּה, *Priestly Gifts*.[14] The מִזְבֵּחַ, *Altar*, one of the components in the main chamber of the *Mishkan*, Sanctuary, exemplified the crown and symbol of *Kehunah*.[15]

In the sacrificial offerings brought in the dedication of the *Mishkan*, a total of 24 bulls for the feast peace-offerings were placed on the *Mizbei'ach*.[16] The measurements of the מִזְבַּח הַקְּטֹרֶת, *Altar of the Incense Offering*, were 1 cubit (6 handbreadths) by 1 cubit (6 handbreadths). If one were to encircle the perimeter of the *Mizbei'ach* with a thread, to symbolize grasping its essence, this measurement would total 24 handbreadths (6 + 6 + 6 + 6).[17]

The perimeter of the Mizbei'ach would total 24 handbreadths.

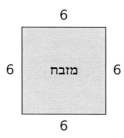

6

6   מזבח   6

6

Furthermore, there were 24 rings to the north of the *Mizbei'ach* employed in the slaughter of the sacrificial animals and 8 pillars, each with 3 iron hooks (8 x 3 = 24), used to hang and flay the slaughtered animals.[18]

24: ON THE WATCH

The number 24 is also linked to members of the Tribe of Levi. There are 24 times that the *Kohanim* are called *Levi'im*.[19] Parallel to the priests, the *Levi'im* were similarly divided into, כ"ד מִשְׁמָרוֹת *24 watches*, that would to serve in the Temple following an orderly rotation.[20] Every week a different watch ascended to serve in the Temple.[21] The *Kohanim's* watch was inside and the *Levi'im's* was on the outside — stationed in a total of 24 places.[22] These 24 groups from the Tribe of Levi were to stand guard over the Temple to protect its sanctity.

In the division of labor, there were a corresponding כ"ד מַעֲמָדוֹת, *24 representatives*, to the 24 *mishmaros*. Each represented his geographic area of residence, with the Holy Land divided into 24 districts. They were the righteous representatives of the Israelites and represented the people at the Temple Service.[23] When the time came for one watch to ascend, the representatives stationed in Jerusalem served as witnesses to the daily sacrificial rite. They were the representatives of their groups and of the entire Jewish congregation.[24]

24/7

24 groups from the Tribe of Levi were to stand guard over the Temple to protect its sanctity.

The representatives stationed in Jerusalem served as witnesses to the daily sacrificial rite.

W E HAVE NOTED THAT 24 IS A CLASSIC SUBDIVISION OF PARTS IN A group that make a whole. It finds expression in the divisions of the Holy Land and in the group of Levites involved in the service of G-d. Indeed, the ideal worship of G-d is for a Jew to be constantly serving G-d every moment of his life: 24/7 — namely 24 hours every day, 7 days in a week. In so doing, his life mission is dedicated to proclaiming the Kingdom of G-d.

The ideal worship of G-d is for a Jew to be constantly serving G-d every moment of his life: 24/7.

24: Baruch Shem

There are 24 letters in the well-known phrase בָּרוּךְ שֵׁם כְּבוֹד מַלְכוּתוֹ לְעוֹלָם וָעֶד, *Blessed be the Name of His glorious Kingdom forever and ever.*[25]

Particular concentration is necessary when mentioning the Divine Name in the first verse of Shema.

This statement is recited daily immediately upon pronouncing the first verse of *Shema*, when a Jew declares his allegiance to the One G-d.[26] Particular concentration is necessary when mentioning the Divine Name in the first verse of *Shema*.[27] Indeed, the appropriate response to a misuse of the Divine Name is to recite the statement *Baruch Shem*.[28] *Baruch Shem* relates to a Jew's acceptance of the yoke of the Heavenly Kingdom.[29] Symbolically, its juxtaposition to *Shema* takes the frequent division of components into 24 and combines them to declare the Unity of G-d.[30]

DIVIDED

I N ITS DIVIDED STATE, THE SPLITTING OF A WHOLE INTO 24 COMPONENTS cannot proclaim the Heavenly Kingship because it then contradicts the unity of G-d. Where it does not come together to be united as one, this same number stands apart and remains divided.

24: Of Tragedy and Woe

Perhaps the most horrific national sin perpetrated by the Jewish People at the foot of Sinai was the sin of the Golden Calf. It occurred after their earlier acceptance of the Heavenly Kingship, having embraced G-d's Torah. The sinners committed idolatry, a crime that is an affront to proclaiming the unity of G-d. Consequently, G-d threatened to eradicate His chosen nation, but was dissuaded by Moshe.

Due retribution was exacted on the Jewish people only after 24 generations.

Due retribution was exacted on the Jewish people only after 24 generations. No future historical mishap was visited upon Israel that did not contain within it a 24th part of a *litra* (i.e., a small measure) as punishment due to the great sin of the Golden Calf.[31]

Historically, 24 sins were committed within the city of Jerusalem prior to the destruction of the First Temple.[32] These sins have their parallel in the 24 curses mentioned by the Psalmist.[33] Indeed, the word אוֹי, *woe*, which connotes tragedy, occurs 24 times throughout *Tanach*.[34] Here the use of 24 operates as the diametric opposite to the Divine service that must permeate all parts of man's being.

The misapplication of the division of the whole into 24 that diverges from unity finds its parallel in the 24 situations that prevent man from engaging in *teshuvah*, repentance.[35] Conversely, the pathway to once again returning to G-d demands that one do whatever is necessary to attain כַּפָּרָה, *atonement*. The concept of *kapparah* is actually found in 24 occasions within the *Chumash*.[36] This puts man back on track to use all his faculties in the service of G-d.

The concept of kapparah is found in 24 occasions within the Chumash.

BACK IN ONE PEACE

W E HAVE SEEN HOW THE DANGER OF DIVISION OF A WHOLE INTO 24 may be wrongfully used to tragically depart from proclaiming the Unity and Kingship of G-d. The opposite of this fragmentation is the attainment of harmony and peace into one cohesive whole.

The opposite of this fragmentation is the attainment of harmony and peace into one cohesive whole.

24: peace

The word שָׁלוֹם, *peace*, is found a total of 24 times in the *Chumash*.[37] Conflict is synonymous with divisiveness, where 2 or more parties are in dispute.[38] By contrast, peace is conceptually synonymous with unity. It is when all the individuated parts are integrated back into one whole. Significantly, the individual functions within all the diverse parts then systematically combine.

Every one of the 24 hours in a day must be dedicated in the service of G-d. This commitment is absolute and all-inclusive. Like a servant obligated to dedicate his 24 (tips of) limbs to his master, every Jew systematically uses all 24 individuated parts of a full set or group (such as 24 watches or 24 Books of *Tanach*, etc.) toward one end: proclaiming the Unity and Kingship of G-d.

The Talmud relates that on his deathbed, Yaakov was concerned that the departure of the *Shechinah* indicated a blemish in one of his children. To allay these fears, the 12 Tribes of Israel unanimously recited, שְׁמַע יִשְׂרָאֵל ה׳ אֱלֹהֵינוּ ה׳ אֶחָד, *Hear, Yisrael [our Father], HASHEM*

Every Jew systematically uses all 24 individuated parts toward one end: proclaiming the Unity and Kingship of G-d.

is our G-d, we affirm that HASHEM is the One and Only. In response, Yaakov responded with the phrase, בָּרוּךְ שֵׁם כְּבוֹד מַלְכוּתוֹ לְעוֹלָם וָעֶד, *Blessed be the Name of His glorious Kingdom forever and ever,*[39] which, as mentioned, contains 24 letters.

This pronouncement encapsulates man's mission of creation. He may divide the universe into 24 parts to arrange his actions, but these actions are all meant to unite to give glory to the One G-d.

NOTES

1. See the *Rambam's Sefer HaMitzvos*, where he sets out the essential principles for the division of Torah into the 613 *mitzvos*.
2. "4 stones build 24 houses" (*Sefer Yetzirah* 4:12), meaning that 4 letters can make 24 different combinations (*Vilna Gaon* ad loc.). Due to the double letter ה in the 4-Letter Divine Name *Havayah* (יה-ו-ה), the number of permutations is limited to 12, which parallels the 12 months. See "12: Tribes of Israel."
3. *Mishnah, Negaim* 6:7.
4. See *Niddah* 2a.
5. See *Avodah Zarah* 3b, which discusses that G-d's day and night are both divided into 12 hours — 4 periods of 3 hours each. See *Yerushalmi, Berachos* 1:1, as to how divisions of time are of 24 parts.
6. *Bava Basra* 14b-15a; *Koheles Rabbah* 12:12.
7. *Shemos Rabbah* 41:5.
8. Ibid; *Rashi, Shemos* 31:18. See also *Shabbos* 59b.
9. *Taanis* 8a.
10. See *Rashi, Shemos* 21:7.
11. *Rashi, Shemos* 21:26. See *Ran, Kiddushin* 24b.
12. *Eichah Rabbah* 1:2.
13. *Tur, Orach Chaim* 118.
14. *Pirkei Avos* 6:5. There were 24 gifts reserved exclusively for the priests (*Rambam, Hilchos Bikkurim* 1:1-8). See *Chullin* 133b and *Bava Kamma* 110b; see also *Bamidbar Rabbah* 5:1.
15. *Pirkei Avos* 4:12 and *Rashi* ad loc.
16. *Bamidbar* 7:88. There were 12 more for the elevation offerings. See *Bamidbar* 7:87.
17. *Maharal, Derech Chaim* 6:7.
18. Mishnah, *Middos* 3:5.
19. *Chullin* 24b.
20. *Taanis* 26a, 27a. This division was introduced by David, who increased the number of groups from those established by his predecessors, Shmuel and Moshe. While half were serving in the Temple, the other half journeyed to Yericho to secure food and water for their brethren.
21. *Rambam, Hilchos Klei Mikdash* 3:9, 4:3.
22. *Rambam, Hilchos Beis HaBechirah* 8:4. The *Leviim* were also responsible for the singing and playing of the musical instruments. See *Arachin* 11a-b; *Rambam, Hilchos Temidin U'Musafim* 6:5.
23. *Rambam, Hilchos Klei HaMikdash* 6:1. See also *Ritva, Taanis* 26a and *R' Ovadiah Bertinoro, Bikkurim* 3:2.

24. *Taanis* 26a.
25. *Zohar, Terumah* 139b; see also *Tikkunei Zohar* 13.
26. This phrase was recited in the Temple in response to hearing the pronouncement of the 4-Letter Name; see Mishnah, *Yoma* 3:8; *Rashi, Devarim* 32:3. See also *Nechemiah* 9:5 and *Berachos* 63a.
27. *Shulchan Aruch, Orach Chaim* 60:5, 63:4.
28. *Yerushalmi, Berachos* 6:1; *Shulchan Aruch, Orach Chaim* 206:6.
29. See *Biur Halachah* 61:13.
30. This angelic prayer was heard by Moshe when he ascended to Heaven (*Devarim Rabbah* 2:36). This is said aloud only on Yom Kippur, when man stands on same lofty pedestal as the angels.
31. *Sanhedrin* 102a. See "13: An Everlasting Love."
32. This is according to *Rokeach, Vayikra* 27:34, as derived from *Yechezkel* 16. See *Rokeach*, ad loc. for other sins that are found in 24 categories.
33. *Tehillim* 109. See *Rokeach, Vayikra* 27:34.
34. *Rokeach, Vayikra* 27:34.
35. *Rambam, Hilchos Teshuvah* 4:1-6; See also *Rabbeinu Yonah, Shaarei Teshuvah,* end of *Shaar* 1.
36. This is according to *Rokeach, Vayikra* 27:34.
37. *Rokeach, Vayikra* 27:34. This enumeration includes the words *shalom, b'shalom, l'shalom,* and *ha'shalom.*
38. See "2: Opposite and Equal."
39. *Pesachim* 56a; see also *Zohar* 2, 139b. See "6: It's Only Natural."

26
IN THE NAME OF G-D

26 is synonymous with
the unique 4-Letter Divine Name

The ultimate level of creation is
where the entire cosmos comes
to recognize the Glory of G-d.

Then, the Name of G-d will be One.

ALL IN A NAME

THE *SHEM HAMEFORASH*, EXPLICIT [DIVINE] NAME (י־ה־ו־ה), IS OFTEN associated with 26, the sum of its numerical value.

THe NAMe OF G-d

This Holy Name relates to G-d as the Source of Existence.

This Ineffable 4-Letter Name of G-d (*Tetragrammaton*, from the Latin meaning "4 Letters," sometimes referred to as שֵׁם הֲוָיָה, *Name of Being*), is considered to be His definitive Name.[1] It relates to G-d as the eternal Master of the universe, *the One Who is, Who was, and Who will be*.[2] This Holy Name relates to G-d as the Source of Existence.[3] It relates to His Essence, so to speak, unlike the many other Divine Names, which refer to how man views or perceives G-d in the world through His Divine Attributes.[4]

None of the Divine Names may be recited unnecessarily. The Torah exhorts us, *Revere this glorious, awesome Name of HASHEM Your G-d*.[5] It explicitly warns against blaspheming or saying the Name of G-d in vain.[6] The sacred nature of the 4-Letter Name of G-d means that it was almost never pronounced as it appears in written form — whether in prayer or in the reading of a Torah Scroll. The only circumstance in which it was permissible to articulate this Name was within the Temple.[7] In all other instances, the Name אֲ־דֹ־נָ־י, meaning *My Master*, is used in its place. Colloquially, to avoid any misuse, the non-sacred appellation הַשֵׁם, *HASHEM*, meaning "The Name," is generally used. (This is often simplified when writing, using the abbreviated form, ה׳.)

UNKNOWN BY NAMe

The natural realm appears to function mechanically. It conceals G-d as the Creator and Mover.

In This World, the Glory of G-d is obscured by nature. The natural realm appears to function mechanically. It conceals G-d as the Creator and Mover. So the 4-Letter Name is similarly hidden in *Olam Hazeh*, This World, in the sense that it is not commonly uttered as it is written.[8] The ultimate revelation of the *Shem HaMeforash* is postponed pending the vanquishing of evil.

The non-revelation of G-d's Name is ideologically depicted in Israel's timeless struggle against Amalek. The Jewish People are instructed not to forget the unforgivable attack Amalek launched in the aftermath of their miraculous departure from Egypt.[9] The unprovoked attack in Refidim was intended to "cool down" the invincibility of G-d and His Chosen Nation.[10] This was an affront to G-d Himself — an attack that targeted Israel as His ambassadors on Earth.[11]

The Jewish People call out "in the Name of G-d." In the words of the verse, *When I call out the Name of HASHEM, ascribe greatness to our G-d.*[12] Every moment in life is the opportunity to reveal G-d.

The Jewish People call out "in the Name of G-d."

Amalek was the chief proponent of "coincidence" and "happenstance," as though G-d did not figure. The continuous existence of Amalek — and its ideology — perforce oppose the Name of G-d. Consequently, the Name of G-d is incomplete with Amalek's continual presence. The 4-Letter Name (יהׄוׄהׄ) was truncated (appearing as the Divine Name יׄהׄ) in the aftermath of their encounter.[13] It denotes their spiritual blockage against revealing the Glory of G-d through His 4-Letter Name.[14] Consequently, the very existence of Amalek is antagonistic to the sacred mission of Israel. Amalek and Israel cannot coexist. Not until the Messianic Era and the World to Come will mankind universally proclaim G-d: *It will be on that day, that G-d will be One and His Name will be One.*[15] Then the Glory of G-d will be unveiled, with permission to pronounce the 4-Letter Name as it is written.[16]

Not until the Messianic Era and the World to Come will mankind universally proclaim G-d.

26: IN THe IMAGE OF G-D

The ultimate goal is for the entire universe to unanimously declare the glory of G-d.

Man was created *in the image of G-d.*[17] He is the preeminent creature armed with free will and intelligence to reveal G-d in This World. His life must therefore be a constant model of *Kiddush HASHEM*, sanctifying the Name of G-d. The ultimate goal is for the entire universe to unanimously declare the glory of G-d.

Just as G-d is the King of the Heavenly realm, man is crowned king of the lower realm.[18] He must mirror his Creator by emulating His characteristics. The Torah describes man's formation, beginning from the 26th verse of the *Chumash*.[19] Nevertheless, the fulfillment of man's purpose in life — to reveal G-dliness — would have to wait 26 generations until the giving of the Torah at Sinai.

The fulfillment of man's purpose in life would have to wait 26 generations until the giving of the Torah at Sinai.

26: GENERATIONS

The creation of the universe was exclusively for the sake of Torah. In truth, it was only fitting for the word of G-d to have been given after 1000 generations.[20] G-d arranged that the 974 generations originally decreed to be created were transplanted into later periods.[21] Thus, it would only be 26 generations (974 + 26 = 1000) until the Torah would be given at Sinai. Subsequently, the world would be sustained only through continuous Torah study. Should this stop for one moment, the universe would immediately return to its original state of nonexistence.[22]

The Psalmist extols the kindness of G-d in the phenomena of the natural world and in the supernatural acts throughout Jewish history.

But for the first 26 generations of mankind, in the absence of Torah, G-d sustained the world exclusively through His great kindness. This is reflected in the psalm (*Tehillim* 118) known as *Hallel HaGadol*, The Great *Hallel*. Here the Psalmist extols the kindness of G-d in the phenomena of the natural world and in the supernatural acts throughout Jewish history. Its 26 verses all conclude with the refrain כִּי לְעוֹלָם חַסְדּוֹ ... , *for His kindness endures forever.*[23] Here these 26 statements parallel the 26 generations that existed in the world prior to G-d giving Torah to mankind.[24]

There were 10 generations from Adam to Noach, and another 10 generations till Avraham.[25] There were 6 more generations, including Moshe (Yitzchak, Yaakov, Levi, Kehas, Amram, and Moshe), making Moshe the 26th generation from Creation. This is also alluded to in the 26 letters of the renowned phrase, תּוֹרָה צִוָּה לָנוּ מֹשֶׁה מוֹרָשָׁה קְהִלַּת

The preeminence of Moshe as the greatest prophet is alluded to in the 26-word blessing recited before the reading of the Haftorah.

יַעֲקֹב, *The Torah that Moshe commanded us is the heritage of the Congregation of Yaakov.*[26] Torah was given through Moshe, who was of the 26th generation of mankind. The preeminence of Moshe as the greatest prophet is alluded to in the 26-word blessing recited before the reading of the *Haftorah.*[27]

26: FOR THE SAKE OF HIS NAME

The most altruistic area of serving G-d is to do every action לִשְׁמָהּ, *for [the sake of] His Name.* In other words, the objective is to learn Torah and perform the 613 Commandments, not because of the reward promised, but as a goal in itself,[28] executed out of man's love for G-d.[29] *The very act of serving G-d is the vehicle to reveal G-d.*

This underlines a Jew's mission in This World. His existence is not for his personal self-glorification; it is exclusively for the glorification of G-d. It is focused upon the revelation of His Name. The Jewish People exists to generate *Kiddush HASHEM*. When they live according to the Torah ideals, the words of the following verse will be fulfilled: *Then all the peoples of the Earth will see that the Name of G-d is proclaimed over you, and they will revere you.*[30]

The Jewish People embody the mission of the first human being, whose formation is recorded in the 26th verse of the Torah. They were the ones who lovingly embraced Torah in the 26th generation of mankind. They live for the day when evil, as embodied in Amalek, will finally be wiped off the face of the Earth. The world will embrace the Kingship of G-d as the *Shem HaMeforash*, with its numerical value of 26, that will, at long last, be fully revealed to the universe.

The world will embrace the Kingship of G-d as the Shem HaMeforash, with its numerical value of 26, that will be fully revealed.

NOTES

1. R' Yehudah HaLevi, *Kuzari* 4:1; R' Chaim Volozhin, *Nefesh HaChaim* 3:11.
2. *Shulchan Aruch, Orach Chaim* 5:1. See also R' Chaim Volozhin, *Nefesh HaChaim* 2:2.
3. R' Chaim Volozhin, *Nefesh HaChaim* 3:9.
4. R' Yehudah HaLevi, *Kuzari* 4:1.
5. *Devarim* 28:58.
6. *Shemos* 20:7; *Devarim* 5:11.
7. *Sotah* 38a. See *Devarim* 12:5, 11, 21 as to how the Holy Name was associated with the Temple. See Mishnah, *Yoma* 3:8 about its pronouncement on Yom Kippur, and Mishnah; see *Sotah* 7:6 about the priestly blessings.
8. *Pesachim* 50a.
9. *Devarim* 25:17-19.
10. *Rashi, Devarim* 25:18, citing *Tanchuma, Ki Seitzei* 9.
11. "Whoever stands in opposition to Israel, it is as if he stands against G-d" (*Mechilta, Beshalach* 6). "One who hates Israel, hates G-d" (*Sifri, Beha'aloscha* 84).
12. *Devarim* 32:3.
13. *Shemos* 17:16.
14. *Rashi, Shemos* 17:16, citing *Tanchuma, Ki Seitzei* 11.
15. *Zechariah* 14:9.
16. *Pesachim* 50a.
17. *Bereishis* 1:26.
18. See *Maharal, Derech Chaim* 3:14.

19. *Bereishis* 1:26.
20. *Tehillim* 105:8.
21. *Chagigah* 13b-14a. See "974: The Lost Generations."
22. R' Chaim Volozhin, op. cit. 4:25.
23. *Tehillim* 118:1-26.
24. *Pesachim* 118a. See also R' Yitzchak Hutner, *Pachad Yitzchak, Rosh Hashanah* 4 and *Shavuos* 8.
25. *Pirkei Avos* 5:2-3.
26. *Devarim* 33:4 and *Rokeach*, ad loc. Additionally, the 7 words allude to the inclusive generations from Avraham up to and including Moshe.
27. *Rokeach, Devarim* 32:3.
28. See *Rambam, Perush HaMishnayos, Sanhedrin* 10:1
29. *Pirkei Avos* 1:3. See R' Chaim Volozhin, op. cit. 4:1-3 for a discussion about learning Torah *lishmah.*
30. *Devarim* 28:10.

28
IN SEASON

There are a total of 28 seasonal divisions within creation.

Each seasonal division has its unique time and place, playing an essential role in the overriding objective: to give honor to G-d by glorifying His Holy Name.

IN EVERY SEASON

Belief in a Divinely designed universe demands that man realize the brilliant workings of G-d that permeate Creation.

THE NUMBER 28 IS SYNONYMOUS WITH THE SEASONS OF CREATION. Everything G-d made was in order to give honor to His Holy Name.[1] Belief in a Divinely designed universe demands that man realize the brilliant workings of G-d that permeate Creation. It is here that every object finds its designated place and purpose: As the verse states, *There is nothing [in existence] that does not have its [rightful] place.*[2] The entire spectrum of Creation can be organized into 28 seasons.

28: A TIME FOR . . .

King Shlomo says, "There is a time for everything; a season to every purpose under the Heaven."

King Shlomo says, *There is a time for everything; a season to every purpose under the Heaven.*[3] He then proceeds to enumerate 28 periods or seasonal divisions,[4] which are organized as 14 couplets, with each pair composed of opposites.[5]

These pairs are a combination of phases of life (e.g., "A time to be born, and a time to die"), emotional responses ("A time to weep, and a time to laugh"; "A time to love, and a time to hate") or modes of behavior that are appropriate for different occasions ("A time to mourn, and a time to dance"). Each season has its optimal time or place, depending upon the circumstances.

28: THE ORIGINS OF CREATION

The opening sentence of the Torah contains the blueprint for all that would later emerge.

The source for the concept of the universe arranged around the 28 seasons can be traced back to the opening sentence of the Torah: בְּרֵאשִׁית בָּרָא אֱלֹקִים אֵת הַשָּׁמַיִם וְאֵת הָאָרֶץ, *In the beginning of G-d's creating the Heavens and the Earth.*[6] This first verse contains the blueprint for all that would later emerge, both in Creation and in the Torah itself.[7]

This formative verse is composed of 7 words and 28 letters. This beautifully alludes to the fact that the universe would unfold over 7 days and would be organized into 28 seasons. This division also finds expression in the course of a week. Each day can be split into 4: before noon, after noon, before midnight, and after midnight. It is therefore possible to subdivide a week of 7 days into (7 x 4 =) 28 periods.[8]

There is a close mathematical relationship between 7 and 28. The number 28 is a multiple of 7. It is a "perfect number" that is the sum of its positive divisors. And it is also the sum of all the integers from 1 to 7 inclusive.

Multiple:	7 x 4 = 28
Perfect Number:	1 + 2 + 4 + 7 + 14 = 28
Sum of integers:	1 + 2 + 3 + 4 + 5 + 6 + 7 = 28

The universe was created with 10 Utterances.[9] This has its parallel in the human being — who is himself classified as a world in miniature[10] — and the 10 digits on the two hands.[11] There are 14 joints in each of man's hands (2 joints in the thumb and 3 joints in the other fingers), which match the 14 pairs of seasons in *Koheles*, to make a grand total of 28.[12]

28: THE ORIGINS OF TORAH

The opening word of the Torah, *bereishis*, in the beginning,[13] refers to the Torah and to Israel, the Jewish people, which are both called *reishis*, "first" or "beginning."[14] The ultimate purpose of the universe was Israel's acceptance of the Torah at Sinai, when they dedicated their lives to glorifying the Name of G-d.

There are many parallels between the world's creation and the acceptance of Torah. The very formation of Creation was contingent upon Israel receiving the Torah; without this the world would have lost its raison d'être.[15] The correlation between the 10 Commandments to the 10 Utterances of Creation is exact — the former represents the observance of Torah, which establishes the world that G-d fashioned with the latter.[16] Just as the opening verse of the Torah is composed of 7 words and 28 letters, the introductory verse preceding the 10 Commandments (וַיְדַבֵּר אֱלֹקִים אֵת כָּל הַדְּבָרִים הָאֵלֶּה לֵאמֹר, *And G-d spoke all these words saying*)[17] similarly consists of 7 words and 28 letters.[18]

The correlation between the 10 Commandments to the 10 Utterances of Creation is exact.

IN ITS FULL GLORY

ALL OF NATURE COMES TO PROCLAIM G-D'S EXISTENCE AND GLORY. In the words of the Psalmist, כֹּחַ מַעֲשָׂיו הִגִּיד לְעַמּוֹ, *The Power of*

His works He declares to His nation.[19] It is the obligation of man, the premier creature within Creation, to see the Glory of G-d within the 7-day week and the 28 seasons; thus the word כֹּחַ, *power*, has the numerical value of 28.[20]

PRIMORDIAL DAY: 28 HOURS

Sin emerges where there is a conflict between the will of man and the Will of his Creator.

Sin emerges where there is a conflict between the will of man and the Will of his Creator — when man's objective becomes proclaiming his personal glory rather than revealing the glory of G-d. It is only through repentance that man can make amends and realize that the natural cycles of 28 rightfully proclaim G-d.

Day 6 of Creation was when Adam disobeyed the command of G-d by eating from the Tree of Knowledge. The model relationship between man and G-d should have been similar to that of the moon and the sun. The moon, like man, has no independent light. It is supposed to faithfully reflect the illumination of the sun.[21]

G-d gave man the 7th day, Shabbos, as the opportunity to return to Him.

When Adam's repentance was accepted, he sang, מִזְמוֹר שִׁיר לְיוֹם הַשַּׁבָּת, *A song composed for the Day of Shabbos.*[22] G-d gave man the 7th day, Shabbos, as the opportunity for man, and by extension the whole of Creation, to return to Him (שַׁבָּת has the same letters as the central root letters of the word תָּשׁוּב, *return*).[23] Rather than the primordial week being 6 days of 28 hours each (28 x 6 = 168 hours), in His kindness, G-d rearranged the week to consist of 7 days of 24 hours each (24 x 7 = 168 hours).[24] On this seventh day man refrains from engaging in the forbidden labors that epitomize human creativity, thus declaring the primacy of G-d's Will.

SUNLIGHT: 28 YEARS

Man must affirm the remarkable, Divine workings of the sun within the natural world.

There is a special blessing called *Bircas HaChamah,* Blessing of the Sun, recited when the sun completes its 28-year great cycle. At this point, the sun returns to its position at the moment of its creation.[25] It usually occurs in the month of Nissan and is recited on Wednesday — the sun having been fashioned on Day 4 of Creation.[26]

Just as man must see the glory of G-d in all 28 seasons, he must similarly affirm the remarkable, Divine workings of the sun within the natural world. The formulation of the blessing on the sun, ... *Who makes the work of Creation,* is the same as that which is recited on other natural phenomena (e.g., lightning or exceptional geographical phenomena such as lofty mountains, comets, etc.).[27] This is where man acknowledges the glory of G-d.

MOONLIGHT: 28 DAYS

The full lunar month stretches up to 30 days.[28] Discounting the first and last days of the month, where the moon's light is primarily shrouded, there are 28 full days of moonlight.[29] The moon does not have any light of its own. Moonlight is a reflection of the sun's illumination. Similar to the moon, which reflects the illumination of the sun and brilliantly lights up the night, so within the 28 periods of creation must man act as a faithful reflection of G-d's Will in the world.

KADDISH: 28 LETTERS

The central sentence in the response to the recitation of the *Kaddish* prayer is the phrase: יְהֵא שְׁמֵהּ רַבָּא מְבָרַךְ לְעָלַם וּלְעָלְמֵי עָלְמַיָּא, *May His Great Name be blessed forever eternally.*[30] This statement, recited with deep feeling and total concentration, is powerful enough to nullify the most severe of evil edicts.[31]

Like the opening statement of creation and the giving of Torah, the primary response in *Kaddish* is similarly made up of 7 words and 28 letters.[32] This encapsulates the theme of the number 28. Although each season has its unique time and place, it is the life goal of the Jew — voiced with intense vigor — to use each and every season to glorify the Name of G-d throughout the universe.

The Kaddish, recited with deep feeling and total concentration, is powerful enough to nullify the most severe of evil edicts.

NOTES

1. *Pirkei Avos* 6:10.
2. Ibid. 4:3. See "4: Finding the Place."
3. *Koheles* 3:1.
4. (1) A time to be born and (2) a time to die; (3) a time to plant and (4) a time to uproot the planted; (5) a time to kill and (6) a time to heal; (7) a time to break down and (8) a time to build up. (9) A time to weep and (10) a time to laugh; (11) a time to mourn and a (12) time to dance. (13) A time to scatter stones and (14) a time to gather stones; (15) a time to embrace and (16) a time to refrain from embracing. (17) A time to seek and (18) a time to lose; (19) a time to keep and (20) a time to cast away. (21) A time to rend and (22) a time to sew; (23) a time to keep silence and (24) a time to speak. (25) A time to love, and (26) a time to hate; (27) a time for war and (28) a time for peace (*Koheles* 3:2-8).
5. See *Sfas Emes, Mikeitz* 5652, for how the division of 28 seasons in *Koheles* into 14 positives versus 14

negatives is an allusion to Pharaoh's dreams of 7 fat cows and 7 fat stalks (total of 14 good) versus 7 thin cows and 7 thin stalks (total of 14 bad).

6. *Bereishis* 1:1.
7. See, for example, *Vilna Gaon, Aderes Eliyahu, Bereishis* 1:5.
8. *Baal HaTurim, Bereishis* 1:1; *Megaleh Amukos* 212; See also *Kav HaYashar* 80.
9. *Pirkei Avos* 5:1.
10. See *Avos DeRabbi Nassan* 31:3; *Moreh Nevuchim* 1:72; *Nefesh HaChaim* 1.
11. See "10: Top Ten."
12. R' Yitzchak Isaac Chaver, *Ohr Torah* 34, annotations to *Maalos HaTorah.*
13. *Bereishis* 1:1.
14. *Rashi, Bereishis* 1:1. See "1: The One and Only."
15. See *Shabbos* 88a.
16. See "10: Top Ten."
17. *Shemos* 20:1.
18. R' Yitzchak Isaac Chaver, op. cit. 10, annotations to *Maalos HaTorah.*
19. *Tehillim* 111:6.
20. *Megalah Amukos* 212; See also *Kav HaYashar* 80.
21. See "30: It's About Time."
22. *Tehillim* 92:1-16.
23. *Bereishis Rabbah* 22:28.
24. *Gevul Binyamin* 2:5, citing the *Ramak*; also quoted in *Siddur Ohr Zoruah.*
25. *Berachos* 59b.
26. *Bereishis* 1:14-19.
27. *Shulchan Aruch, Orach Chaim* 227:1, 228:1, 229:2.
28. See "30: It's About Time."
29. See *Megaleh Amukos* 212, who mentions the "28 periods of the moon."
30. In fact, the phrase *Yehai shmai rabbah m'vorach, l'olam u'olmai olmayah* is a close Aramaic translation of the oft-recited Hebrew verse *Baruch shem kevod malchuso le'olam va'ed* recited in *Shema.*
31. *Shabbos* 119b and *Rashi* ad loc.
32. *Ba'al HaTurim, Bereishis* 1:1.

30
IT'S ABOUT TIME

30 is a complete period of time.

As determined by the monthly cycle
of the moon, the passage of
this time period represents
the life cycle in miniature.

THE DIVISION OF TIME IN THE JEWISH CALENDAR CENTERS AROUND the number 30.

Days are determined by the natural daily cycle of sunrise and sunset. The Jewish calendar establishes the days in terms of the monthly cycle of the moon. The duration of a full lunar month is 30 calendar days. In this context, the number 30 is used as the definitive "period of time."[1]

The number 30 is used as the definitive "period of time."

30: period of time

The classic time period of 30 days finds many applications in Jewish life.

The classic time period of 30 days finds many applications in Jewish life.

- ❖ The minimum duration of a Nazirite period (where a person vows to become a *Nazir*, such that he will not drink or eat wine or grape products, will not come into contact with a corpse, and will not cut his hair) is a 30-day period, unless otherwise stated.[2]

- ❖ The customary period given by a court to execute its orders is 30 days.[3] The length of *nidui*, banishment, was 30 days.[4]

- ❖ This is similarly the time frame for a brother-in-law to consummate his relationship with his recently-widowed sister-in-law following a levirate marriage,[5] and, according to one opinion, the length of time for a bridegroom to accuse his bride of prior infidelity.[6]

- ❖ Should a husband vow that his wife may not derive any benefit from his house for 30 days, he becomes obligated to divorce her.[7]

- ❖ A wholesaler was obligated to clean his liquid-measuring utensils every 30 days to ensure that the measurements retained their accuracy.[8]

- ❖ Often, an *indefinite length of term* is taken to mean 30 days. One example of this is that a loan of unspecified duration is deemed to extend for 30 days.[9]

PREPARATION: 30 DAYS

The impact of an event in the Jewish calendar can be felt 30 days before its arrival.

Like the remoteness of a far-off location, a distance of more than 30 days is treated as being in a different time zone. It, so to speak, resides outside man's consciousness and does not feature in his life. Within the 30-day period before an impending Festival, its proximity begins to register and become relevant. Perhaps the most well-known illustration is that 30 days prior to the arrival of a Festival, a Jew becomes obligated to begin learning the relevant laws.[10]

30 days prior to a Festival, a Jew must begin learning the relevant laws.

More than 30 days before Pesach, one need not be concerned about the upcoming prohibition of eating or possessing *chametz,* leavened foodstuffs. This is why if a Jew is leaving his home for Pesach within 30 days before the Festival, he is obligated to search for *chametz;* if he leaves more than 30 days before, there is no such obligation.[11] According to one opinion in the Mishnah, only a *succah* made within 30 days of the holiday of Succos is valid.[12]

CYCLES OF LIFE

30 is not just a complete unit of time; it depicts a life cycle in miniature.

THE SOURCE FOR 30 DAYS AS THE MODEL TIME PERIOD IS OBVIOUSLY derived from the monthly lunar cycle. But 30 is not just a complete unit of time; by undergoing a continual state of renewal, it depicts a life cycle in miniature.

30: A JEWISH MONTH

The first mitzvah given on the eve of the Exodus was the sanctification of the months.

Jewish time is defined by the cycles of the moon. The first *mitzvah* given on the eve of the Exodus was the sanctification of the Jewish months.[13] In ancient times the new month was determined by a reported sighting by 2 valid witnesses, of the moon's visible crescent.[14] The length of a Jewish month incorporates the waxing and waning of the moon's shape as viewed from Earth. From the 1st day, the crescent waxes until the 15th day, when there is a full moon.[15] Thereafter the moon wanes until it disappears completely from view, only for it to reemerge as a new month is "born" and the monthly period repeats itself. In general, the full lunar cycle (called *chodesh molei*, a full month) lasts for 30 days.[16]

In fact, the monthly cycle is a microcosm for the cycle of life. The new month comes into being: a state of birth. This is followed by its ongoing growth and development until it reaches its fullness — a reference to man at the peak of his powers. The waning denotes the gradual diminishment in man's prowess as he ages, which eventually culminates in man's death. But just like death does not mean the end, so too does the conclusion of one period give way to a rebirth in a new phase. This reflects the Jewish belief in *techiyas ha'meisim*, revivification of the dead, when the dead are destined to return to life.[17]

The monthly cycle is a microcosm for the cycle of life.

NIÐÐAh: MONThLY CYCLE

A natural parallel to the "life in miniature" within the monthly lunar period is the reflection in a woman's cycle.

A natural parallel to the "life in miniature" within the monthly lunar period is the reflection in a woman's cycle and its application in the laws of *taharas hamishpachah*, family purity.[18] A woman's biological clock is naturally programmed to a monthly basis — although, the exact length between each cycle varies from woman to woman and is often subject to irregular patterns.

Once a woman experiences the onset of a uterine discharge of blood, she is ritually impure and classified as a *niddah*. The parallel between the cycle of life and death is mirrored in menstruation, when the unfertilized egg is expelled. Symbolically, the lost potential for life is a woman's brush with death. Her purification is achieved through her immersion in the *mikveh*, gathering of water for ritual immersion, which is symbolic of new life.[19]

Halachically, when a Jewish woman is calculating the probable date of her next cycle, one computation takes account of the *onah beinonis,* median period, that is defined as a period of exactly 30 days.[20] Notwithstanding obvious variations, this has a clear parallel to the symbol of the lunar month, whose fullness is expressed in 30 days.[21]

NEWBORN: 30-ÐAY-OLÐ

The presumption that a newborn baby is a viable entity takes effect 30 days after birth.

In Jewish law, the presumption that a newborn baby is a viable entity takes effect 30 days after birth.[22] Before this period elapses, the infant is classified a נֵפֶל, *nonviable infant* (literally, *fallen*), due to the concern that it might not survive. Prior to 30 days, the infant has not symbolically lived through a full life cycle. Consequently, it cannot really be considered to have lived. With the passing of 30 days, however, the child's existence and viability are firmly established.

The *mitzvah* of *pidyon haben*, redemption of the [firstborn] son, is relevant to a firstborn Jewish boy who is born via a natural birth (i.e., where there were no previous miscarriages, no Caesarean section, etc.) and neither of his parents is a *Kohen* or Levi. The firstborn is considered holy and there is an obligation to redeem him from a Kohen with 5 silver coins.[23] The earliest occasion that this ceremony can be performed is 30 days after birth, once the newborn baby boy can be presumed to be a viable, living entity.[24]

sheloshim: in mourning

We have noted that a 30-day period can be viewed as symbolic of the cycle of life, death, and renewal. One clear example of this can be seen in the laws of mourning upon the death of a close family member.

The initial time frame of the bereavement process is *shivah*, 7 [-day period], which begins immediately after the burial.[25] The ensuing stage runs to the end of the *sheloshim*, 30 [-day period], (including the 7 days of *shivah*) following the burial.[26] There were 30 days of crying following the death of Yaakov.[27] Similarly, the Torah recounts that the national mourning period upon the deaths of Moshe and Aharon lasted for 30 days.[28]

During the *sheloshim*, the strict *shivah*-period restrictions (e.g., mourners forbidden to go to work) are lifted, while other practices (e.g., hair-cutting, social engagements, etc.) remain in effect. With the notable exception for the extended one-year mourning for the loss of a parent, the *sheloshim* marks the official conclusion of the mourning process.

One reason for this is because the close family relatives remain under the influence of the deceased even after his death. This influence is continually felt until 30 days have passed, and then it dissipates. Like the cyclical process of the moon, the 30-day mourning process of *sheloshim* echoes the emotional journey from darkness to light, and from despair to hope.

shehechiyanu: 30 days

The first time a person sees a friend after a 30-day period, he recites the *Shehechiyanu* blessing: "… Who has granted us life, sus-

A 30-day period symbolic of the cycle of life, death, and renewal can be seen in the laws of mourning the death of a close family member.

The 30-day mourning process of sheloshim echoes the emotional journey from darkness to light, and from despair to hope.

tained us and enabled us to reach this occasion."[29] (Elsewhere, this *berachah* celebrates other moments of renewal or rejuvenation. It is recited on the first occasion that one eats a seasonal fruit, on the initial annual performance of a seasonal *mitzvah*,[30] or upon the acquisition of a new house or the purchase of new, costly clothes.[31]) Its recital after 30 days have elapsed is because the effect or impression that was earlier made has faded. Now, the cycle starts anew.

The Jew must make use of time as the preparatory passage into the timeless realm of eternity in the World to Come.

In summary, the life of a Jew is set against the backdrop of the lunar calendar. He lives through the cycles of life every 30 days. Like the moon, every month the Jew has the ability to rejuvenate himself. He must make use of time — the most precious commodity in This World — as the preparatory passage to pass through into the timeless realm of eternity in the World to Come, his ultimate destination.[32]

NOTES

1. See *Rosh Hashanah* 10b for the time period of 30 days that can be considered equivalent to 1 year, the next unit and grouping of time.
2. The minimum period for a term of being a *Nazir* is 30 days (Mishnah, *Nazir* 1:3).
3. *Bava Metzia* 118a and *Tosafos*, ad loc.
4. *Moed Katan* 16a and *Rashi*, ad loc.
5. This must take place within 30 days of the brother-in-law performing the levirate marriage (*yibum*) with his widowed sister-in-law, who is childless from her marriage to his recently deceased brother (see *Shulchan Aruch, Even HaEzer* 167:6).
6. *Yevamos* 111b; according to R' Meir only, but not halachically, see *Shulchan Aruch, Even HaEzer* 68:10.
7. *Kesubos* 70a.
8. *Bava Basra* 88a.
9. *Makkos* 3b.
10. *Pesachim* 6a regarding Pesach (the source for the halachah is from Pesach Sheni [*Pesachim* 6b]). See *Sanhedrin* 12b, which discusses that there are 30 days from Purim to Pesach in the juxtaposition of Festivals of redemptions. In a leap year, Purim is always fixed in the second Adar to connect it to Pesach (*Megillah* 6b).
11. *Pesachim* 6a; *Shulchan Aruch, Orach Chaim* 436:1-3.
12. Mishnah, *Succah* 1:1. See *Shulchan Aruch, Yoreh Deah* 347:1, which states the custom not to eulogize those who had died prior to 30 days before the Festival, within 30 days of the Festival.
13. *Shemos* 12:2.
14. Mishnah, *Rosh Hashanah* Chapters 1- 3.
15. See "15: Ups and Downs."
16. The mean of a lunar month is approximately 29.53 days, which can be rounded up to 30 days.
17. See *Rambam, Mishnah Commentary*, Introduction to 10th chapter of *Sanhedrin*, 13th principle.
18. *Vayikra* 15:19, 18:19.
19. *Sefer HaChinuch* 173; *Shem MiShmuel, Shabbos Shuvah* 5674. See "40: True to Form."
20. *Niddah* 9b.

21. See R' Yonasan Eibeshutz, *Kreisi U'Pleisi, Yoreh De'ah* 184:4.

22. See *Rambam, Hilchos Milah* 1:13. While murder is punishable by capital punishment, one who kills an *infant* within 30 days of birth is not subject to the death penalty (*Rambam, Hilchos Rotze'ach* 2:6).

23. *Bamidbar* 18:15-16; see also *Sefer HaChinuch, Mitzvah* 392.

24. *Bechoros* 49a. See *Shulchan Aruch, Yoreh Deah* 305:11. See also opinion of *Shach, Yoreh Deah* 305:12 that the *pidyon* may be after 29½ days.

25. *Shulchan Aruch, Yoreh Deah* 375:1, 395:1. See also "7: A Holy Spark."

26. *Shulchan Aruch*, ibid. 391-392.

27. *Rashi, Bereishis* 50:3.

28. *Devarim* 34:8; *Bamidbar* 20:29.

29. *Berachos* 58b; see also *Shulchan Aruch, Orach Chaim* 225:1. One who sees the Atlantic Ocean once in 30 days makes a special blessing (*Berachos* 59b; see *Mishnah Berurah* 228:2).

30. For example, lighting Chanukah candles on the first night or taking the Four Species on first day of Succos.

31. *Berachos* 54a. The law of other blessings (and not only *Shehecheyanu*) recited upon natural phenomena is also upon seeing them for the first time after 30 days. See *Shulchan Aruch, Orach Chaim* 228:1 and *Mishnah Berurah* 2 and 225:2. The blessing recited upon visiting a cemetery (… *asher yatzar eschem ba'din*) is said only once within any 30-day period (*Shulchan Aruch Orach Chaim* 224:13, *Mishnah Berurah* 17 there).

32. See "9: Where to Turn?" Events in time, such as Festivals, are called *moed,* a word that denotes "meeting place" or "true destination."

31
There's
Nothing to It

31 hints at how nonexistence
gives way to existence.

It is essential that life be a constant
process of turning "nothing" into "something."

A Jew has the ability to elevate
his existence to inherit eternity
in the World to Come.

OUT OF NOTHING

The number 31
relates to a state
of nonexistence
that precedes
and is then
replaced by
the subsequent
introduction
of a state of
existence.

THE NUMBER 31 RELATES TO A STATE OF NONEXISTENCE THAT precedes and is then replaced by the subsequent introduction of a state of existence.

The word אַל, *[there is] not*, which has a numerical value of 31, depicts a state of nonexistence.[1] Its diametric opposite, contained within the word יֵשׁ, *there is*, which has a numerical value of 310, depicts a state of existence.

31: NONEXISTENT

Nothing — with
the exception of
G-d — existed
before He
brought the
Torah and then
the world into
being.

G-d used two distinct phases in the creation of the universe. The first was the original act of Creation *ex nihilo*. In rabbinic literature, this is commonly referred to as יֵשׁ מֵאַיִן, *existence from nonexistence*, or *something from nothing*.[2] Nothing — with the exception of G-d — existed before He brought the Torah and then the world into being. Creation ex nihilo changed everything. It was then followed by the next phase: taking the created matter and fashioning it to give it form. This phase is termed יֵשׁ מִיֵּשׁ, *existence from existence*, or *something from something*.[3] The original stage lasted a moment; the arrangement of matter to take form would unfold during the 6 Days of Creation.

The new
existence can
only come into
being through
a nullification of
the old one.

Actually, the principle of יֵשׁ מֵאַיִן finds ample expression in the spiritual battle waged between the forces of good and evil in the world. It was not just that a new form takes over that which preceded it; *the new existence can only come into being through a nullification of the old one.* So, for example, the arrival of day necessitates a new period because it has ended the night. The kindling of a light banishes and supplants the former state of darkness. Truth is fully revealed by the rejection of falsehood. And the ultimate level of good can only appear with the destruction of evil. These are all illustrations of *yeish m'ayin* — where the newly introduced state of existence now turns whatever preceded it into a state of nonexistence.

31: KINGS OF CANAAN

The principle that the way to reveal יֵשׁ as a new state of existence necessitates the destruction of everything earlier, to render it into אַל, nonexistence, is highlighted in the conquest of the Holy Land. Yehoshua bin Nun led the Jewish People in many great battles against the original inhabitants, successfully defeating the 31 kings of Canaan.[4]

G-d waged war on behalf of the Children of Israel. The Promised Land was a Divine gift to His Chosen Nation. So it was appropriately named after them: *Eretz Yisrael*, Land of Israel. Originally, it was occupied by the 7 Canaanite nations who spiritually defiled the Holy Land through their sinful conduct.[5] Their destruction was therefore essential to make way for the יֵשׁ, *existence*, of Israel, to emerge anew to sanctify the Land. The 31 kings, alluded to in the numerical value of אַל (31), were rendered nonexistent. In works of kabbalah, they were equivalent to the outer husk that must be discarded in order to get to the luscious fruit within.[6]

The 31 kings were equivalent to the husk that must be discarded to get to the luscious fruit within.

TO BECOME SOMETHING

WE HAVE NOTED ONE APPLICATION OF THE PRINCIPLE OF *YEISH m'ayin* in the need to negate the 31 of אַל, like the 31 kings of Canaan, in order to reveal יֵשׁ — the settlement of Israel in the Holy Land. Importantly, this marks the emergence of something from nothing, a new state of reality that negates anything before it. This dramatic reversal is apparent in the relationship between 31 and 310 as related to the Holy Land and the World to Come.

The settlement of Israel in the Holy Land marks the emergence of something from nothing.

31 OR 310: OUR INHERITANCE

The inheritance of *Eretz Yisrael* through the process of *yeish m'ayin* has its parallels to the eternal inheritance of *Olam Haba*, the World to Come. The Jewish People wandered through the Wilderness until they came into their own homeland. So, too, is the passage in This World the means to inherit the hereafter, where the righteous

The inheritance of Eretz Yisrael has its parallels to the eternal inheritance of Olam Haba.

are destined to inherit 310 worlds — the numerical value of the word *yeish*.[7]

The inheritance of *Eretz Yisrael* involved defeating 7 nations of Canaan and vanquishing their 31 kings. In the eternal inheritance of *Olam Haba*, this will increase tenfold.[8] All 70 gentile nations (7 x 10 = 70) will be subservient to Israel, who will then take control over 310 portions (31 x 10 = 310) — alluding to the righteous inheriting 310 spiritual worlds.[9]

The passage from Olam HaZeh to Olam Haba follows the yeish m'ayin template.

The passage from *Olam HaZeh* to *Olam Haba*, from This World to the World to Come, similarly follows the *yeish m'ayin* template: the temporary world is ultimately rendered nonexistent in relation to the ensuing state of existence in *Olam Haba*.[10]

31 OR 310: YISRAEL

The Jewish People were nationally destined to receive a portion in the Holy Land. Similarly, every Jew is individually guaranteed a portion in *Olam Haba*.[11]

A Jew can rise by transforming himself into something truly significant.

Man, created in the image of G-d, is empowered to similarly be a creator.[12] In his limited capacity, man is supposed to reenact the principle of *yeish m'ayin*. Yisrael, the Jewish People, are expected to emulate and embody this ideal.

More than any other nation, the Jewish People have the amazing propensity to vacillate between two extremes. A Jew can rise from a state of lowliness and nothingness by transforming himself into something truly significant. He can soar to reach the stars. Conversely, he can plummet from the heights of nobility and sink to the lowly depths of the Earth.[13] When *Bnei Yisrael* preserve the Torah, no nation can dominate them. When they fall, they are humiliated and can be ruled over by the most inferior nation.[14]

This capacity lies within the name *Yisrael*, whose central letter, *reish* (ר), is enclosed by the word אַל, *[there is] not*, to the left and יֵשׁ, *there is*, to the right.

The middle of the name Yisrael consists of the letter reish (ר), which has two diametrically opposite connotations.

יֵשׁ - ר - אַל

The middle of the name *Yisrael* consists of the letter *reish* (ר), which has two diametrically opposite connotations. The words רֵאשׁ or רָשׁ are used in *Tanach* to refer to poverty,[15] or as an epithet meaning "one who has nothing."[16] Alternatively, רָשׁ implies *to inherit*,[17] which indicates "one who has many possessions."

The precise placement of the words within the name *Yisrael* is also highly significant: to the left, which symbolizes the *Yetzer Hara*, Evil Inclination,[18] is אַל. By following his Evil Inclination, man is and has nothing. But if he identifies with יֵשׁ, on the right, which represents the *Yetzer You*, Good Inclination, then he is "head of everything" and will rightly inherit eternity.[19]

3I OR 3I0: DO I EXIST?

We have noted that a Jew must emulate G-d by the creative process of *yeish m'ayin*: to transfer a state of nothing into something that will earn him eternity to inherit the World to Come.

Nevertheless, in terms of man's relationship to G-d, the converse is true. Whereas G-d creates יֵשׁ מֵאַיִן, *something from nothing*, a Jew must return everything to G-d through the creation of אַיִן מִיֵּשׁ, *something into nothing*. The Jew turns his present existence of יֵשׁ into a state of אַיִן, *nonexistence*. He surrenders his יֵשׁ, *existence*, by readily nullifying himself into insignificance before his Creator. In so doing, he reverts to the stage before Creation when only G-d existed and our universe was אַיִן.[20]

Paradoxically man exists — but only to the extent that he yields his own existence to G-d. His life is characterized as one that seeks to transfer the nonexistence of אַל, with its numerical value of 31 within This World, into the spiritual realm of יֵשׁ, in the 310 worlds in *Olam Haba*.

Man exists only to the extent that he yields his own existence before G-d.

NOTES

1. It is interesting that the word לֹא, *no* or *not*, contains the same letters as אַל and also implies nonexistence.
2. See *Ramban* and *Ibn Ezra, Bereishis* 1:1; *Shaarei Teshuvah* 1:12; *Sefer Halkkarim* 1:1-2.
3. *Pardes Rimonim* 16:1.
4. *Yehoshua* 12:9-24. See *Megillah* 16b about how the kings of Canaan were listed in a Torah Scroll in two narrow columns (half-brick above a half-brick and whole brick above a whole brick) like the 10 sons of Haman, to symbolize that once they fell, they would be unable to recover and rise again. See *Bamidbar Rabbah* 23:7 about how later in history during the period of the Judges, the king of Canaan launched a counter-offensive, headed by his general, Sisera (*Shoftim* 4:2 – 5:31) to reconquer the Holy Land seized by Yehoshua. Appropriately, Sisera was escorted in battle by 31 kings to parallel the original 31 kings who had been defeated by Yehoshua.

5. *Vayikra* 18:25, 27-28.

6. *Shelah HaKadosh, Mesechta Pesachim, Matzah Ashirah*, 2nd *Derashah*, 8.

7. *Mishnah, Uktzin* 3:12. See "310: Worlds Apart."

8. The Holy Land, which is holier than all other lands, is subject to 10 ascending spiritual levels of holiness (*Mishnah, Keilim* 1:6). See *Shelah HaKadosh, Mesechta Pesachim, Matzah Ashirah*, 2nd *Derashah*, 8, as to how the conquest over the 31, which is 1 tenth of 310, represents *maaser*, tithes, where the tenth is holy for G-d (*Vayikra* 27:32).

9. *Tosafos Yom Tov, Uktzin* 3:12.

10. *Shelah HaKadosh*, loc. cit.

11. *Sanhedrin* 90a. There are many parallels between inheritance of *Eretz Yisrael* and inheritance of *Olam Haba,* in both of which a Jew is guaranteed a portion. One who walks 4 cubits in the Land of Israel is assured a portion in the World to Come (*Kesubos* 111a). G-d gave Israel 3 precious gifts ... Torah, *Eretz Yisrael*, and *Olam Haba* (*Berachos* 5a).

12. See *Kiddushin* 30b about how a father and mother partner G-d as "creators" in the creation of man.

13. *Rashi, Esther* 6:13.

14. *Kesubos* 66b.

15. *Mishlei* 30:8.

16. *II Shmuel*, 12:3.

17. *Devarim* 1:21.

18. *The heart of the wise is to the right* (*Koheles* 10:2) — this refers to the *Yetzer Tov; The heart of the fool is to the left* (ibid.) — this refers to the *Yetzer Hara* (see *Bamidbar Rabbah* 22:9).

19. *Rama MiPano, Yonas Eilem* 1. There is one division of the Hebrew alphabet into the *al-bam* (א״ל ב״ם) letter transformation. Here the 22 letters are divided into 2 equal groups of 11 letters, which are then paired; the word *al-bam* is a reference to the first two sets of these transformation pairs: *aleph-lamed* and *beis-mem*. Two of the pairings are the words *al* and *yeish*.

כ	י	ט	ח	ז	ו	ה	ד	ג	ב	א
ת	ש	ר	ק	צ	פ	ע	ס	נ	מ	ל

20. *Degel Machaneh Ephraim, Vezos HaBerachah; Sfas Emes; Behar* 5645, *Pinchas* 5643, *Rosh Hashanah* 5642, and *Pinchas* 5643.

32
YOUR HONOR

32 relates to glory or honor,
as the inner self is
revealed in the world.

IN ALL ITS GLORY

THE NUMBER 32 RELATES TO THE GLORY THAT IS CONFERRED ONTO G-d and man.

The universe is the place where both G-d and man reveal themselves to This World. Here the outer expression makes known the inner self. This, in turn, elicits appreciation and admiration from others.

The concept of כָּבוֹד, *honor* or *glory*, whose *gematria*, numerical value, is 32, is the central expression of one's essential identity or existence. Here the inner essence is outwardly projected and elegantly revealed in all its glory.

32: DIVINE GLORY

The design of the universe proclaims G-d's Glory. The handiwork of His Creation majestically attests to the greatness of its Creator. It evokes a sense of love and awe in the eyes of the beholder when he contemplates its splendor and workings.[1]

The Mishnah asserts, *Everything G-d created in This World, He only created for His Glory.*[2] In our daily prayers, we *bless our G-d Who created us for His Glory.*[3] The entire existence is established to be a projection of His Will. Conversely, "whoever pays no heed for the glory of his Creator, it would have been better had he never come into the world."[4]

Mankind, as the pinnacle of creation, must glorify G-d by obeying His Will. Through this, he fulfills the raison d'être of existence. Man must proclaim, *The whole world is filled with His Glory.*[5] Indeed, the number 32 features prominently in the Creation of the universe that would proceed to give glory to G-d.

32: PATHWAYS OF WISDOM

A primary function of clothing is as a medium of revelation. Clothes are the outer layer of the person wearing them; often, they confer honor and prestige.[6] This is how the individual appears and presents himself before others. So, too, the natural world is considered to be the Divine garb that G-d "dons" in order to reveal Himself within creation.[7]

Creation, which proclaims the glory of its Creator, was formed by the word of G-d.[8] The universe was fashioned through the 10 Divine Utterances[9] making use of the 22 letters of the Hebrew alphabet.[10] Together, they combines to make a total of (10 + 22 =) 32 components.[11] The Torah relates the Creation narrative in which the Divine Name אֱלֹקִים is used on exactly 32 occasions.[12] Every Divine Name comes to express a particular Divine Attribute through which G-d reveals Himself. *Elokim* expresses G-d as "the Master of all powers" within the cosmos.[13] G-d's mastery is brilliantly revealed within creation through the Divine workings of הַטֶּבַע, *the natural [world]*, which, like *Elokim*, has the numerical value of 86.[14]

The combination of 10 Divine Utterances and 22 Hebrew letters, and the 32 times *Elokim* appears in the creation narrative indicates that G-d fashioned the world with ל"ב נְתִיבוֹת הַחָכְמָה, *32 pathways of wisdom*.[15] This reflects the Divine ingenuity within Creation: *You have fashioned them all with chochmah!*[16]

The quality of *chochmah*, wisdom, often refers to the first source in terms of the process of revelation — the source from which everything else unfolds.[17] These 32 pathways of wisdom used in Creation are the means that will ultimately lead to the revelation of G-d's *kavod*, glory. Man glorifies G-d on Earth by seeing His Will being projected through the realm of nature, so that ultimately he comes to coronate Him as the מֶלֶךְ הַכָּבוֹד, *the King of Glory*.[18]

These 32 pathways of wisdom are the means that will ultimately lead to the revelation of G-d's kavod.

TZITZIS: 32 STRINGS

The *mitzvah* of *tzitzis* relates to the concept of glorifying G-d. The 8 strings attached to the edges of a 4-cornered garment consisted of a combination of threads of *lavan*, white, and *techeiles*, blue. Viewing the *tzitzis* on his garment, a Jew must see beyond the natural world; his vision must penetrate up to the Heavens. The blue color resembles the sea, which reflects the Heavens, which, in turn, remind him of the כִּסֵּא הַכָּבוֹד, *[G-d's] Throne of Glory*.[19]

Viewing the tzitzis on his garment, a Jew must see beyond the natural world; his vision must penetrate up to the Heavens.

Tzitzis contain a famous allusion to the 613 *mitzvos* of the Torah: the numerical value of *tzitzis* is 600; adding the 8 strings and 5 knots on each edge brings the total to (600 + 8 + 5 =) 613.[20] Seeing the *tzitzis* on the corner of his garment exhorts the Jew to remember all of G-d's *mitzvos* and to perform them.[21]

Interestingly, the theme of *kavod*, glory, inundates this *mitzvah*. Man takes clothing, usually a tool to reveal his inner self, and uses it instead to reveal the glory of G-d. The 32 strings of *tzitzis* (8 strings on each of its 4 corners; 8 x 4 = 32) allude to the numerical value of the word *kavod*. Here man realizes that the fabric of creation — the 32 strings that correlate to the 32 pathways of wisdom[22] and the 32 times *Elokim* is mentioned in Creation[23] — comes to reveal the glory of G-d, with man's gaze piercing the cosmos to arrive at G-d's Throne of Glory.

The fabric of creation comes to reveal the Glory of G-d, with man's gaze piercing the cosmos to arrive at G-d's Throne of Glory.

A MATTER OF HONOR

WE HAVE NOTED THAT THE 32 PATHWAYS OF WISDOM UTILIZED IN Creation outwardly reveal the glory of its Creator. The concept of honor is similarly manifest when man reveals himself in the world. Nevertheless, the epitome of Jewish honor is where man's revelation of self serves as a reflection of the Will of G-d. Man's crowning glory, in truth, is where he does not take glory for himself but redirects the glory onto his Creator.

32: A MAN OF HONOR

The term כָּבוֹד *is actually a synonym for man's unique identity and deep sense of self.*

Like his Maker, man similarly projects his unique self by outwardly revealing himself in This World. The term כָּבוֹד, *glory* or *honor*, with a numerical value of 32, is actually a synonym for man's unique identity and deep sense of self.

Man's sense of self-esteem emanates from his central being.

Honor is conferred onto an object that has value or upon a person of importance. This sees the inner worth within being recognized from without. Honor is therefore the essence of man's psyche. His sense of self-esteem emanates from his central being. Take away any semblance of importance from man, and you succeed in morally dehumanizing him. Strip him of all sense of worth and you have effectively killed him.[24] (On the other end of the spectrum, the proactive and relentless pursuit of *kavod* by a person leads to his undoing. Craving honor from others is self-destructive and drives man from This World.[25])

Man's soul is characterized by the name *kavod*, as in the phrase, *So that my kavod* (read: *soul*) *may sing*.[26] In turn, man's inner soul projects itself such that it finds outward expression through the body. *Here the human body is equated with clothing that paradoxically envelops but also reveals the soul.* Clothing is likewise associated with the concept of *kavod* insofar as a garment confers glory upon its wearer. The magnificent garments of the *Kohen Gadol*, High Priest, for example, were expressly fashioned to evoke *honor and splendor.*[27]

32: RUN FOR YOUR LIFE

The magnificent garments of the Kohen Gadol, High Priest, were expressly fashioned to evoke honor and splendor.

    The centrality of man's honor as the essence of his psyche sheds some light on the abstruse laws of the *goel hadam*, avenger of blood. One who accidentally kills must seek sanctuary by fleeing to one of the 48 *Arei Miklat*, Cities of Refuge.[28] Interestingly, the roads leading to these cities were 32 cubits wide.[29] The killer had to run for his life from a blood relative who was out to avenge the death.[30] (This protection remained in place as long as the killer stayed within one of the cities, where he was to remain until the demise of the *Kohen Gadol*.[31])

    Notwithstanding the inadvertent nature of the killing, the *goel hadam* nevertheless can come to redeem the harm inflicted upon man's innermost being: his *kavod*. Obviously, the deepest harm imaginable is that of killing another (even if unintentionally), which removes man's soul, also called *kavod*, from within a person. Consequently, it is on the roads leading to the *Arei Miklat*, with their width of 32 cubits, that the fleeing killer is vulnerable to the blood relative avenging the *kavod*, with its numerical value of 32, of the victim. Nevertheless, the killer can travel upon these roads and ultimately take refuge from the pursuing *goel hadam* in the safe haven of one of the *Arei Miklat*.[32]

32: TAKE HEART

The heart serves as a metaphor for man's inner core, which is, in turn, associated with his kavod.

    We have already noted that *kavod* relates to man's essential inner being: his soul. It is highly significant that *kavod* shares the same numerical value (32) as לֵב, *heart*. The heart, which is located at the center of the human body, serves as a metaphor for man's inner core, which is, in turn, associated with his *kavod*.

    Within the body, the heart is often described as the source of life.[33] Biologically, this organ is responsible for circulating the blood throughout the body, giving life to all limbs. Both in terms of its centrality and its functionality, this is symbolically identical to the con-

Parallel to the
32 pathways
of wisdom that
fill the entire
Creation, the
heart within
man likewise
animates the
whole body.

cept of *kavod* as an expression of man's essential existence, which is then projected outward. Parallel to the 32 pathways of wisdom that fill the entire Creation, the heart within man likewise animates the whole body, so that through the use of his body his inner essence can be brought into the open.[34]

32: GLORIOUS

We noted that the universe was created through the 32 pathways of wisdom. Creation must reveal the glory of G-d. This is the central, unifying strand that joins together every component within existence: *Everything G-d created in This World, He only created for His Glory.*[35] This effort is spearheaded by man. This lies at the heart or center point of man's *kavod*. His essential identity is where his true glory is revealed by giving glory to His Creator — like the 32 strings of *tzitzis* that point to the Divine Throne of Glory.

When man
gives glory to
G-d, the world
is on track to
reach its final
glorious goal.

When man gives glory to G-d, the world is on track to reach its final glorious goal, when all the components of the universe will reveal the glory of G-d.[36] This will be the fulfillment of the words of *Tehillim, May the glory of G-d last forever; let G-d rejoice in His works!*[37]

NOTES

1. See *Rambam, Hilchos Yesodei HaTorah* 2:2.
2. *Pirkei Avos* 6:11. See *Yalkut Reuveni, Bereishis,* citing *Koheles Rabbah,* which discusses how everything during the 6 Days of Creation came to give honor to G-d.
3. *U'Va LeTzion* prayer.
4. Mishnah, *Chagigah* 2:1.
5. *Yeshayah* 6:3.
6. *Bava Kamma* 91b.
7. G-d Himself is said to figuratively don garments of majesty and splendor in terms of the Creation of the universe (*Tehillim* 104:1-2).
8. One can paraphrase this in the oft-repeated blessing, "… *shehakol niheyeh b'dvaro,* … everything was created with His word."
9. *Pirkei Avos* 5:1. This is the number of times the statement, "G-d said," appears in the creation narrative. See "10: Top Ten."
10. See "22: The Sacred Letters."
11. See R' Yehudah HaLevi, *Kuzari* 4:25. In the mystical tradition, the 10 points of the *Sefiros* (Emanations) are linked by 22 lines (3 horizontal, 7 vertical, 12 diagonal). A variation of this is the way the number 32 denotes the totality of the Hebrew language. It is the combination of 22 letters and 10

Hebrew vowels used to enunciate the words. See *Tikkunei Zohar* 70, 126a; *Pardes Rimonim* 19:4, 32:2. See *Tikkunei Zohar* 129a as to how the 10 vowels parallel the 10 *Sefiros*. Indeed, the teeth in the mouth, whose lips part in order for man to speak, also number 32. See *Sfas Emes Mattos* 5646, and *Megaleh Amukos* 164.

12. *Bereishis* 1:1-31. See *Rokeach, Bereishis* 2:1.

13. *Shulchan Aruch, Orach Chaim* 5.

14. *Shelah HaKadosh, Shevuos* 42. See also *Pardes Rimonim Shaar* 17, Ch. 4.

15. *Sefer Yetzirah* 1:1. See also *Zohar* 3, 81b; *Tikkunei Zohar*, Introduction 13a. For the parallels of 32 pathways of wisdom to 32 mentions of *Elokim* (22 letters + 10 *Utterances*), see *Raavad* and Vilna Gaon, *Sefer Yetzirah* 1:1; *Megaleh Amukos* 164; see *Shelah, Shaar HaOsiyos, Shin Shetikah* 4. See also *Sfas Emes, Mattos* 5646.

16. *Tehillim* 104:24.

17. Take, for example, the verse: *The beginning of wisdom is fear of G-d* (*Tehillim* 111:10). In kabbalah, *Chochmah* is the first of the 10 *Sefiros* while *kavod*, a synonym of *Malchus*, kingship, is the final *sefirah*.

18. *Tehillim* 24:7-10.

19. *Menachos* 43b and *Rashi*, ad loc.

20. *Bamidbar Rabbah* 18:21, cited in *Rashi, Bamidbar* 15:39.

21. *Bamidbar* 15:39.

22. *Rabbeinu Bachya, Bereishis* 1:1 and *Bamidbar* 15:38. See also *Sfas Emes, Shelach* 5650 and 5657.

23. See *Sfas Emes, Korach* 5656.

24. This is why embarrassing another is equated to murder (*Bava Metzia* 58b).

25. *Pirkei Avos* 4:28.

26. *Tehillim* 30:13; see also ibid. 16:9. See *Ibn Ezra, Bereishis* 49:6.

27. *Shemos* 28:2.

28. *Bamidbar* 35:9-34; *Shemos* 21:13; *Devarim* 19:1-10. See also "48: Stay Connected."

29. *Bava Basra* 100b.

30. Mishnah, *Makkos* 2:7. The relative was not allowed to kill him on the way to the City of Refuge. According to some opinions, he was permitted — though it was not a *mitzvah* or obligation to do so. If the person who killed left the City of Refuge, there is a dispute whether he may be killed or whether it is a *mitzvah*. Rambam maintains that even then it is only permissible; not that it was a *mitzvah* or obligation. See *Makkos* 10b and *Rashi* ad loc.; *Rambam, Hilchos Rotze'ach* 5:9-10.

31. *Bamidbar* 35:25.

32. This explanation was suggested by Rabbi Yehoshua Pfeffer.

33. See *Maharal, Derech Chaim* 2:9.

34. Note the frequent association made between the words לֵב and חָכָם. (See *Shemos* 31:6, 35:10, 36:1, 2, 8; *Mishlei* 10:8, 16:21, 23; *Koheles* 7:4, 10:2; *Iyov* 37:24). The phrase, *the wise of heart seize good deeds* (*Mishlei* 10:8) is applied to someone like Moshe. In the rush to leave Egypt, the Israelites were occupied with borrowing riches from the Egyptians. Meanwhile, Moshe was involved in the *mitzvah* of locating and taking along Yosef's remains (*Shemos Rabbah* 20:19).

35. *Pirkei Avos* 6:11.

36. *Ramchal, Daas Tevunos* 58, 128.

37. *Tehillim* 104:31.

36
see The Light

36 is synonymous with light.

It is the symbol of illumination
and Divine revelation that reveals
the inner light of Torah hidden within.

LET THERE BE LIGHT

Light reveals the inner quality or the hidden essence lying within existence.

THE MAIN THEME WITHIN THE NUMBER 36 IS THAT OF *OHR*, LIGHT.
In Jewish thought, light is the symbol of revelation. It reveals the inner quality or the hidden essence lying within existence. The number 36 is found both in the introduction of light on Day 1 of Creation and in the symbolism of Torah illumination.

36: PRIMORDIAL LIGHT

The sources of natural light illuminating life on Earth are the Heavenly luminaries. But the light of the sun, moon, and stars was fashioned only on Day 4 of Creation.[1] So what was the nature of the light created on Day 1, when *G-d said "Let there be light" and there was light*[2]?

The primordial light created on the first day refers to the spiritual essence embedded within existence.

In truth, the primordial light created on the first day refers to *the spiritual essence embedded within existence*. It is about *how* G-d is manifest within Creation and the way that the universe relates to Him.

The ability to tap into this primordial light would have enabled man to see the "whole picture." Through this light it was possible to see "from one side of the world to the other." However, this brilliant revelation would not be accessible to one and all. Due to the unworthiness of the wicked, G-d decided to hide this primordial light, which was then set aside for the use of the righteous in the future.[3]

Prior to Adam's expulsion from the Garden of Eden, he was given use of this primordial light for a 36-hour period.[4] This revolved around Shabbos: the 12 hours preceding Shabbos, followed by the 24 hours of Shabbos itself (12 + 24 = 36).[5]

Mankind had, at its inception, experienced this sublime dimension.

That Adam was exposed to this light meant that mankind *had*, at its inception, experienced this sublime dimension. This exposure opened a portal through which man would be able, at a later stage, to at least partially tap into the spiritual purpose of existence. It would be possible for him to perceive this as G-d had originally intended. So while the primordial light was hidden, it is up to man to take whatever steps are necessary to reveal this light once again in the universe.

36: LIGHT OF TORAH

The access to the 36 hours of primordial light in the future will be reserved for the righteous who are exclusively engaged in Torah study. Due to the spiritual decline of man, G-d concealed the primordial light for Torah scholars to perceive the hidden meanings of the Torah that would otherwise be hidden from all other creatures.[6]

The hidden light reserved for the righteous relates to the radiance contained within the deep meaning of the Torah. Indeed, Torah is itself synonymous with light: כִּי נֵר מִצְוָה וְתוֹרָה אוֹר, *A mitzvah is a lamp and the Torah is light.*[7] Like the primordial light, Torah teachings illuminate the life of a Jew — even in This World. Torah enables a Jew to navigate This World, which is compared to darkness,[8] as it enlightens his pathway so that he may fulfill the spiritual purpose of life.

Light neatly ties in with the number 36, as there are a total of 36 expressions of light found within the Torah.[9] One of the foremost symbols of Torah were the *Luchos*, Tablets, given by G-d to Moshe, upon which the 10 Commandments were engraved. Its dimensions were 6 handbreadths by 6 handbreadths, namely, 36 square handbreadths.[10] And in the period leading up to his passing, Moshe's final teaching of Torah in *Mishneh Torah* (Book of *Devarim*) began on 1 Shevat and continued for 36 days, up until his death on 7th Adar.[11]

There are a total of 36 expressions of light found within the Torah.

HIDE AND SEEK

D ARKNESS IS THE NECESSARY BACKDROP TO THE EMERGENCE OF light. It is from out of the shadows, where man finds himself in the dark, that light shines forth.[12] Indeed, the ordering of the Days of Creation is described sequentially: *There was evening and there was morning*[13] — with darkness a prelude to light. The enlightenment of an answer similarly dispels an earlier state of darkness posed by a question.[14] Likewise, certainty causes all element of doubt to effectively dissipate.

Perhaps the most prominent expression of this phenomenon of "hide and seek" in the revelation of hidden light relates to the number 36 during the festival of Chanukah.

Darkness is the necessary backdrop to the emergence of light.

CHANUKAH: 36 LIGHTS

These lights correspond to the 36 hours of the primordial light that is now concealed.

The prevalent custom is to light 1 candle on the 1st night of Chanukah, 2 candles on the 2nd night, etc.[15] During the 8 days, a total of 36 lights are kindled. In the works of kabbalah, these lights correspond to the 36 hours of the primordial light that is now concealed.[16]

Hellenistic culture glorified the natural order, which obscures the Divine Hand in creation and the *ohr haganuz*, the hidden light.[17] Due to their opposition to G-dliness and their worship of nature, the Syrian-Greeks, as the epitome of *choshech*, darkness,[18] defiled the *Beis HaMikdash*, Temple, which is termed *orah shel olam*, light of the world.[19]

On Chanukah, Israel's victory over its adversaries was marked by the discovery of a hidden jar of uncontaminated oil. The light of this oil miraculously burned for 8 days.[20] Symbolically, the spiritual illumination of Chanukah, as a symbol of the primordial light, vanquished the Syrian-Greek darkness.[21]

The privilege of expounding Torah was entrusted into the hands of man, personified by the Sages.

The illumination of the 36 lights of Chanukah was to draw out and tap into the *ohr haganuz* hidden in the natural world. This was specifically accomplished through the light of *Torah She'be'al Peh*, Oral Law. In contrast to *Torah Shebichsav*, Written Law, received prophetically beyond man, the nature of *Torah She'ba'al Peh* lies deeply buried inside man's soul. The privilege of expounding Torah, with the hidden lights shining forth from within, was entrusted into the hands of man, personified by the Sages.

36 HIDDEN RIGHTEOUS

In every generation there are said to exist ל"ו צַדִּיקִים, *36 righteous people.*[22] Traditionally, these pious individuals are said to be hidden from the public eye. Still, they continue to exist through the annals of time in each generation. Their presence continues even after the Temple's destruction and the discernable absence of the *Shechinah*.

This group of 36 tzadddikim corresponds to the 36 lights related to the ohr haganuz.

It follows that this group of 36 *tzadddikim* corresponds to the 36 lights related to the *ohr haganuz*. Their shared characteristics include an unswerving dedication to the Torah as the mainstay of existence and the preservation of its inner light. It is up to these concealed 36 righteous people to draw the light out of the darkness and reveal it to the world, in still another exercise of hide-and-seek.

One historical affiliation between 36 and the righteous is evident in the 36 casualties suffered by the Israelites at the battle of Ai in their conquest of the Holy Land.[23] According to one opinion, the loss of 36 refers to the single death of Yair ben Menashe.[24] He was as great as 36 judges, which constitutes the number majority of the 70-member court of the Sanhedrin.[25] (It is noteworthy that the meaning of his name, Yair, *He will illuminate*, also relates to the symbolism of *ohr*, light).

Light up the world

Just as the soul is hidden within the body, so is the hand of G-d concealed within the natural world. The Jew's mission is to reveal both his own soul and G-d's hand by projecting out the light. In effect, this means tapping into *the spiritual essence embedded within existence and within his very being.* One must identify and be in touch with the all-important inner dimension hidden by the natural realm. That means that he is to release into the universe the connecting "lights" of his soul, of G-dliness, and of the Torah.

He is to release into the universe the connecting "lights" of his soul, of G-dliness, and of the Torah.

The Children of Israel light up the world by dispelling the darkness that covers the Land.[26] In their capacity as *a light unto the nations*,[27] the Jewish nation paves the way for the glorious future era. Then the hidden light of Creation will be restored. The world will once again be filled with the illumination of G-d: *A new light will shine on Tzion. May we all speedily merit to benefit from this light.*[28]

NOTES

1. *Bereishis* 1:14-19.
2. Ibid. 1:3.
3. *Chagigah* 12a; *Shemos Rabbah* 35:1.
4. *Pesikta Rabbasai* 2:2 and *Yerushalmi, Berachos* 8:5.
5. *Pesikta Rabbasai* 20:6.
6. See R' Chaim Volozhin, *Nefesh HaChaim* 4:21.
7. *Mishlei* 6:23.
8. *Pesachim* 2b; *Bava Metzia* 83b.
9. *Rokeach, Hilchos Chanukah Siman* 225, as cited by *Bnei Yissoschor*, Kislev-Teves 2:8. The 36 times is inclusive of all expressions of light, including *ner, meoros,* and *ohr.*
10. *Nedarim* 38a and *Bava Basra* 14a.
11. *Seder Olam Rabbah* 10.
12. "There is no light but that which emerges out of darkness" (*Zohar, Tetzaveh* 183b).
13. *Bereishis* 1:5, 8, 13, 19, 23, 31.

14. A similar concept to this is that a fall provides a springboard from which to rise (*Midrash Tehillim* 22). See also *Rabbeinu Yonah, Shaarei Teshuvah* 2:5.

15. *Shabbos* 21b; *Shulchan Aruch, Orach Chaim* 671:2.

16. *Rokeach, Hilchos Chanukah* 225.

17. See *Bereishis Rabbah* 11:2, 12:6; *Pesikta Rabbasai* 46.

18. *Bereishis Rabbah* 2:4.

19. *Bava Basra* 4a. This title was retained despite the *Shechinah*, Divine Presence, being hidden during the Second Temple era. Interestingly, the 5 missing components that had been present in the First Temple but not in the Second all somehow relate to light (*Maharal, Gur Aryeh, Bamidbar* 4:9).

20. *Shabbos* 21b; *Sfas Emes, Chanukah* 5661.

21. Despite their persecution and exile, G-d had not forsaken Israel. This reaffirmed that there was a hidden light in the darkest night waiting to be revealed and to radiate outward.

22. *Succah* 45b.

23. *Yehoshua* 7:5.

24. He was the one who captured Chavos Yair; the conquered villages were named after him to memorialize his name, as he had no sons (*Rashi, Bamidbar* 32:41). He also came from tribe of Yehudah (*Ramban*, ad loc., based upon *I Divrei HaYamim* 2:21-22).

25. *Bava Basra* 121b; see also *Vayikra Rabbah* 11:7.

26. *Yeshayah* 60:1-3.

27. Ibid. 42:6, 49:6.

28. Blessing before morning *Shema*; see also *Yaavetz's* commentary.

39
UNDER DEVELOPMENT

39 relates to matter that is unfinished because it is lacking a definitive form.

It symbolizes those activities of the physical world that are still missing a spiritual direction.

MATTER WITHOUT FORM

I N THE SAME WAY THAT 9 TURNS TOWARD 10,[1] SO TOO, THE NUMBER 39 is the final stop before reaching 40.

The relationship between 39 and 40 sheds light on the interrelationship of 2 categories within creation: חוֹמֶר, *matter*, and צוּרָה, *form*.

The stamp of tzurah is impressed upon the chomer to give it its direction and goal.

One way to conceptualize this would be through the following analogy: a piece of wood is the material (*chomer*) ready to be designated for a definitive purpose (*tzurah*) that occurs at the endpoint — once it is fashioned into a chair. The stamp of *tzurah* is, so to speak, impressed upon the *chomer* to give it direction and meaning.[2]

Whereas *chomer* relates to the physical and to the non-holy, *tzurah* is identified with the spiritual and sanctified.

WOMB: THE FIRST 39 DAYS

In the development process, 39 symbolizes the point at which the *chomer* component is finished. Nevertheless, the object is still missing the finishing touches of the *tzurah*, which relates to the number 40, to give it form, so that it will assume an identity and a defined objective.[3]

The final spiritual imprint, its form, which will definitely establish its identity, is imprinted on the 40th day.

The classic example of the progression from the 39 of *chomer* to the 40 of *tzurah* lies in the formation of a fetus. The material development of its *chomer* component is fashioned in the womb during the first 39 days from conception. Nevertheless the final spiritual imprint, its *tzurah,* form, is imprinted on the 40th day.[4] Now, the embryo has reached a vital stage in its development such that it is now halachically classified as a child.[5]

SHABBOS: 39 MELACHOS

Perhaps the most striking symbolism of 39 as matter lacking a definitive form to imbue it with meaning is found in the laws of Shabbos observance. The Mishnah lists ל"ט מְלָאכוֹת, *39 activities*, forbidden on the holy day of Shabbos.[6] Additionally, the word מְלָאכָה, [forbidden] activity is found a total of 39 times in the Torah.[7]

The universe contains both elements of *chol*, mundane matter, and elements of *kedushah*, holiness. A balance of these opposites is essential in order for man to exercise his free will. There is, however, the danger where the physical world is not directed toward spiritual endeavors and perhaps man will be overwhelmed by the pull of what is *chol*. What can neutralize this risk?

Man is caught up in the physical world from which he cannot totally escape. G-d therefore arranged that a Jew would be enveloped in special days of additional *kedushah* with the weekly arrival of *Shabbos Kodesh*, the holy Sabbath day.[8]

It is on Shabbos that a Jew attains a sanctified state through his non-performance of the 39 *melachos*. These 39 refer to the routine activities that encompass man's extensive involvement in the mundane world. But on Shabbos, a Jew disengages — and these now become 39 forbidden activities.[9] Furthermore, to disconnect, a Jew similarly abstains from the pursuit of typical weekday mode of business affairs and commonplace conversations.[10]

Shabbos is when the *chomer*, the physical realm, is given its *tzurah* by being consecrated to the service of G-d. As the grand finale of the mundane weekdays, Shabbos gives the entire week its spiritual form. Our daily actions, in and of themselves, lack form and purpose if not directed toward holy endeavors.

A Jew would be enveloped in special days of additional kedushah with the weekly arrival of the holy Sabbath.

Shabbos gives the entire week its spiritual form.

39: Tbe Misbkan's Construction

The 39 *melachos* are based on the *Mishkan's* construction in the Wilderness. Included are the production of the coverings (in the growing of herbs for use as dyes, the manufacture of the wool threads, the use of a fire to produce dyes, the capture of animals and the processing of animal hides), the construction of the wall beams (including building), completing of an object, and the transportation of the beams and vessels.

Shabbos regulations are intrinsically related to the *Mishkan*. Their juxtaposition in the Torah passages teach that building the *Mishkan*, important as it may be, could still not override this holy day.[11] Following its construction in the 2nd year after the Exodus, the *Mishkan* functioned in the desert for a total of 39 years.[12]

Just as the *chomer*, the materials of the *Mishkan*, were sanctified to become the *tzurah* of a building used to house the *Shechinah*, so

Building the Mishkan could not override this holy day.

too would the consecration of Shabbos give a spiritual direction to the *chomer* nature of the week.

SIN AND ITS AFTERMATH

WE HAVE SEEN THAT 39 RELATES TO MATTER THAT STILL LACKS THE form that would otherwise give it purpose. The 39 *melachos*, derived from the construction of the *Mishkan*, run counter to the motif of Shabbos that provides the form and true sense of purpose to the world and to the Jew.

The *Mishkan's* construction came as atonement for the sin of the Golden Calf.[13] This sin occurred because of the Children of Israel's miscalculation in computing the 40 full days of Moshe's ascent to Heaven to receive the Torah. It was on one day earlier — the 39th day — that the nation came to Aharon with a request that they find a substitute for their absent leader Moshe.[14]

The *Mishkan*, as a microcosm of the world,[15] was the creation of a new world — one that was untarnished by sin. G-d wanted man to partner Him in creation and bring the world to its perfection. But this lofty goal was frustrated because man sought to pursue his own agenda in the pursuit of sin. Invariably, sin is associated with the number 39.

39: CURSES OF SIN

The number 39, with its symbolic absence of the tzurah, means that man is subject to his base physical nature.

The ideal set of circumstances occurs when the determination of the Divine Will (read: *tzurah*) is loyally executed by man's bodily faculties (read: *chomer*) so that man conducts himself exactly as G-d wants. Then man's soul (*tzurah*) leads and is not led by the body (*chomer*); his intellect (*tzurah*) leads and is not led by his imagination (*chomer*).[16] The number 39, with its symbolic absence of the *tzurah*, means that man is subject to his base physical nature. Alone, the dominance of *chomer* leads to sin.

Man's primeval sin resulted in 39 curses being cast upon the perpetrators of this crime: Adam, Chavah, the snake, and the land.[17] Had he not sinned, Adam would have sanctified the universe by giving the *chomer* of the world its *tzurah* in Divine service by welcoming in the

Shabbos day. The blessing of Shabbos (the opposite of the curses of sin) would successfully have "completed" Creation,[18] impressing upon it a *tzurah* identity.

Instead, the resultant sin witnessed the world's descent into materialism. Conceptually, the 39 curses are the byproduct of the 39 *melachos* of weekly activities, when not brought back to G-dliness.

MALKUS: 39 Lashes

One who contaminates his soul in sin is deserving of the retribution of מַלְקוּת, *lashes*, (also called *makkos*, smiting) that was administered 39 times. The punishment of lashes was given for transgressing certain negative commandments,[19] and was administered using a quadrupled calfskin scourge.[20] The maximum number of lashes was 39.[21] In some respects, *malkus* constitutes a substitute for the death sentence.[22]

Despite the Torah explicitly stating that the sinner be subjected to 40 lashes,[23] the rabbis legislated that the total number was to be 39.[24] If the Torah explicitly states 40, why would the actual number administered be a total of only 39? And if 39 was the suitable number, why did the Torah state 40?

Symbolically, the 40 lashes were intended to punish the sinner.[25] Still, the component responsible for sin was man's *chomer* nature — corresponding to the first 39 days of man's conception. In truth, though he truly deserves 40 lashes, G-d has mercy upon the sinner — only 39 lashes are necessary to atone for the evil perpetrated by his materialistic nature. He does not receive the 40th additional lash that corresponds to the pristine, spiritual *tzurah* part of man, unsullied by sin, which relates to man's conception on the 40th day.[26]

In truth, the means by which a Jew can rise above the mundane, *chomer*-driven level of 39 requires that he be in tune with his innermost, sanctified, *tzurah* component of 40. He must inject his physical activities with a spiritual direction. Once his focus is firmly fixed upon the spiritual dimension, a person can readily progress from being in a stage of matter still "under development" to being of perfect form.

Though he deserves 40 lashes, G-d has mercy upon the sinner — only 39 lashes are necessary to atone.

He must inject his physical activities with a spiritual direction.

NOTES

1. See "9: Where to Turn?"
2. The interface between the two respective categories of *chomer* and *tzurah* denotes, among other examples, the relationship between woman and man, non-Jew and Jew, body and soul, etc. See *Maharal, Gevuros Hashem* 29, *Netzach Yisrael* 31. See also *Ramban, Bereishis* 1:2, for an explanation of how *chomer* and *tzurah* relate to the words *tohu* and *vohu*.
3. See "40: True to Form."
4. *Tanchuma Yashan, Bamidbar* 28. See *Maharal, Be'er HaGolah* 1:7; *Gur Aryeh, Devarim* 25:2.
5. *Niddah* 30a, *Berachos* 21a-b; *Rabbeinu Bachya, Vayikra* 12:4. See "40: True to Form."
6. *Mishnah, Shabbos* 7:2.
7. *Shabbos* 49b and *Yerushalmi, Shabbos* 7:2. See *Tosafos Yom Tov, Shabbos* 7:2; Vilna Gaon, *Shabbos* 7:2; *Rabbeinu Chananel, Shabbos* 49b, and other commentators for explanations of which specific instances to enumerate to make up the 39.
8. See "7: A Holy Spark."
9. *Ramchal, Derech Hashem* 4:7.
10. *Yeshayah* 58:13; see *Shabbos* 150a, *Shulchan Aruch, Orach Chaim* 306:1
11. *Shemos* 31:1-17 and 35:2, and *Rashi* ad. loc.
12. *Zevachim* 118b. See *Baal HaTurim, Shemos* 35:2 for further allusions to the number 39.
13. See *Rashi, Shemos* 38:21.
14. See *Ben Yehoyada,* end of *Makkos,* who relates this 39th-day mistake to the calfskin used for the 39 lashes. One should note, however, that there are different opinions as to when Moshe ascended the mountain, depending on which date in Sivan the Torah was given.
15. The *Mishkan* was built by Betzalel (*Shemos* 35:31), who was fully versed in the esoteric secrets of the universe, including the letters used by G-d to create the universe (*Berachos* 55a). See also *Malbim, Shemos* 25:8 and R' Chaim Volozhin, *Nefesh HaChaim* 1:4, 17.
16. One parallel between the relationship of matter and form is that of imagination and the intellect. R' Yisrael Salanter (*Iggeres HaMussar*) writes about the importance of the firm intellect imprinting its command over the wild imagination rather than vice-versa.
17. *Shelah HaKadosh, Shabbos, Ner Mitzvah* 68. See *Pri Tzaddik, Korach* 17; *Reishis Chochmah, Shaar HaKedushah* 2. However, see *Pirkei DeRabbi Eliezer* 14 and *Bamidbar Rabbah* 5:4, which mention that there were 40 rather than 39 curses.
18. *Bereishis* 2:2 and *Rashi* ad. loc.
19. *Malkus* was imposed for negative commandments except those that did not involve action, which are stated in general terms and serve as a warning for a death penalty, or which are rectifiable by fulfilling an accompanying positive commandment or by monetary compensation (See *Rambam, Hilchos Sanhedrin* 18:1-2).
20. Mishnah, *Makkos* 3:12.
21. This was administered and supervised by the courts, who ensured that no life was endangered. This meant that they sometimes estimated that sinners in a weakened condition would receive fewer than the requisite 39 lashes (Mishnah, *Makkos* 3:10-11).
22. *Sanhedrin* 10a and *Rashi,* ad. loc.
23. *Devarim* 25:3.

24. *Makkos* 22a.

25. See "40: True to Form."

26. *Maharal, Be'er HaGolah* 1:7; *Gur Aryeh, Devarim* 25:2; see also *Shem MiShmuel, Noach* 5675.

40
TRUE TO FORM

40 relates to the completed
process of development. It is here that
matter finally takes on its
definitive form.

This marks the symbolic
transfer of potential to actual,
in the celebration of a process realized.

4 signals the transformation from potential to actual in the physical world.

THE NUMBER 40 MAKES FREQUENT APPEARANCE IN TORAH AND Rabbinic literature.

We have seen that 4 signals the transformation from potential to actual in the physical world, one that finds expression in the 4 horizontal directions as the dimension of place.[1] This concept is more fully developed through 40, a prominent multiple of 4, which specifically relates to the essential process necessary to reach this goal.

40: OF BEAUTIFUL FORM

The original material was poised to be fashioned into a specific structure.

In a sense, the number 40 is where raw *matter* takes on a *form*. The original material was without a specific shape or function. It was poised to be fashioned into a specific structure. Only once it is directed toward a designated purpose does it take on a prescribed definitive form. This is the transformation from חוֹמֶר, *matter*, to צוּרָה, *form*, and its corresponding evolution from *potential* to *actual* once he realizes his objective.[2]

He completed His master creation by investing the soul of life into man.

One example of this was the creation of man. G-d first fashioned a humanoid shape as earth from the ground (*chomer*). Then He completed His master creation by investing the soul of life into man. This transformed man into a living being who now assumed a definitive form (*tzurah*).[3]

Three famous examples of the development process within the number 40 can be found in the formation of human life, the giving of Torah, and the establishment of Jewish leadership.

CONCEPTION: 40 DAYS

The formation of a human fetus occurs exactly 40 days into a woman's pregnancy after its original conception. Parents are able to petition G-d to change the designated gender of their baby up to the 40th day — but not later.[4] The reason for this is that a fetus does not take on a definitive form until this point. Prayer is efficacious for as long as no exact form has been determined.[5] Consequently, the Talmud notes that life is formed in the fetus — giving it is unique nature and identity — on the 40th day after conception.[6]

So it is only on its 40th day that the embryo has reached a sufficient stage in its development such that it is now halachically classified as a child.[7] In certain respects, it has now assumed its autonomous identity, distinct from its mother.

ACCEPTANCE OF TORAH:
40 DAYS; 40 NIGHTS

Parallel to the formation of a child (which learns the entire Torah as a fetus in the mother's womb[8]) is the national giving of Torah at Sinai. Throughout 40 days and 40 nights, Moshe studied the Torah.[9] During this time, he mastered the Torah in its entirety and then proceeded to transmit the Divine Law to the Children of Israel. The soul implanted into a baby after 40 days corresponds to the spirituality of Torah given after 40 days.[10]

The soul implanted into a baby after 40 days corresponds to the spirituality of Torah given after 40 days.

The form of Torah related to the number 40 is highlighted through the following examples:

❖ The *Luchos*, Tablets, weighed 40 *se'ah*,[11] as did the stone monument (taken from the River Jordan) upon which Torah was inscribed.[12]

❖ Talmudic scholars are wont to review their Torah studies 40 times.[13]

After 40 years of Torah study, a student is finally able to fully fathom the depths of his teacher's teachings.

❖ The age of 40 years is when man attains *binah*, understanding.[14] This marks the time span, after 40 years of Torah study with a teacher, that a student is finally able to fully fathom the depths of his teacher's teachings.[15]

❖ The blessings of *Bircas haTorah*, recited before and after a public Torah reading, are composed of exactly 40 words.[16]

❖ The transmission of Torah from Moshe to Rav Ashi (who redacted the Talmud) spanned 40 generations.[17]

The relationship between Torah and 40 is associated with man realizing his true form through Torah study.

In general, the relationship between Torah and 40 is associated with man realizing his true form through Torah study. In this endeavor, he taps into his soul and into the Divine Word that gives his life its true meaning.

LEADERSHIP: 40 YEARS

The most frequent tenure of Jewish leadership lasted 40 years.

Parallel to 40 as the requisite period necessary to develop a form, 40 is found in the typical length of Jewish leadership experienced by many outstanding Torah personalities. The most frequent tenure of Jewish leadership — whether for kings,[18] prophets,[19] or judges[20] — lasted 40 years.[21] Perhaps the most famous example was Moshe leading the Children of Israel for 40 years in the Wilderness.[22]

Moshe was the embodiment of *Torah She'bichsav*, Written Torah. His counterpart was the Talmudic scholar Rabbi Akiva, who personified *Torah Sheba'al Peh*, Oral Law. Interestingly, both their lives and their achievements were subdivided into 40-year periods: Moshe lived 40 years in the Egyptian palace; 40 years in Midian; and 40 years as leader of the Jews. Rabbi Akiva was an unlearned shepherd for 40 years; he studied Torah for 40 years; and was a leader for 40 years. [23] In conjunction with the number 40, their Torah lives developed so that they reached their objectives.

NEW FORM

The procedure toward attaining a new form often necessitates the prior shedding of an earlier form or identity.

WE HAVE OBSERVED THAT IN THE FORMATION OF LIFE AND OF Torah, the number 40 marks the passage that transforms *matter* into *form*. But what about where something already has some form? Here, the procedure toward attaining a *new* form often necessitates the prior shedding of an earlier form or identity.

Where something is irreparably damaged, then the original state must first be dissolved or abandoned prior to ushering in a new form. This is typified in the rainfall of the Great Flood and the process of repentance. In turn, this serves as the precursor to the attainment of purification.

FLOOD: 40 DAYS; 40 NIGHTS

The wickedness of civilization at the time of Noach was so horrific that G-d decreed He would blot out mankind by bringing the *Mabul*, Flood. With the notable exception of the remaining creatures inside the Ark necessary to repopulate the world, all life on the Earth's surface was destroyed. The rain fell upon the Earth for 40 days and 40 nights.[24] And 40 days after the mountain tops were seen, Noach opened the window of the Ark.[25]

In its 40 days, the waters of the Flood nullified all forms of earlier existence. Symbolically, they washed away sin from the face of the planet. Destroying the form of the universe set the stage for the introduction of a new era to begin immediately in its aftermath.[26]

Teshuvah: 40 days

The symbolism of 40 being necessary to destroy an earlier form so that a new one can be created taps into the essence of *teshuvah*, repentance. Here the penitent seeks the process of atonement. He does this by uprooting his sinful past to assume a new identity. (The spiritual remedy of the punitive 40 מַלְקוּת, *lashes*, serves as atonement for the sinner, to cleanse him of all vestige of evil.[27])

The symbolism of 40 taps into the essence of teshuvah.

Every year the appropriate period for *teshuvah* begins from the onset of the month of Elul and lasts for 40 days, up until Yom Kippur.[28]

Historically, when Israel's national existence was threatened in the aftermath of the episode of the Golden Calf, Moshe spent 40 days beseeching G-d to revoke the edict calling for Israel's destruction.[29] During the 40 days, Moshe again ascended to Heaven, the Jewish people were engaged in penitence and fasting.[30] (Many generations later, in the time of Yonah, a period of 40 days was allocated to the citizens of Nineveh to repent from their sinful conduct.[31]). A parallel of 40 in terms of years was seen in the 40 years of exile in the Wilderness experienced by the Children of Israel as atonement for the sin of the spies in their 40-day expedition in the Holy Land.[32]

Moshe spent 40 days beseeching G-d to revoke the edict for Israel's destruction.

Mikveh: 40 se'ah

The formula to emerging as a new form lies within the purification process. This also relates to the number 40, in the prominent symbolism of a מִקְוֶה, *gathering of ritual water*. The immersion of an object or subject in the natural waters of the *mikveh* eradicates all traces of any earlier existence.

The formula to emerging as a new form lies within the purification process.

A valid *mikveh* has a minimum volume of 40 *se'ah*.[33] In rapport with the theme of repentance, these waters wash away all impurity. The rainfall of 40 days and 40 nights during the Great Flood functioned like the volume of a *mikveh* to similarly purify the Earth from its sinful form.[34] The *mikveh* waters induce a pristine identity that emerges as a new, unsullied life form.[35] The final state of a woman's purification[36] and the closing stage of conversion to Judaism are likened to a "newborn emerging from the mother's womb."[37]

The *mikveh* acts as a preparatory phase of holiness. It serves as the stepping stone in the Jew's enthusiastic readiness to perform a *mitzvah*. Similarly, it is also about wanting to embrace a higher or more exalted state. Here, too, a person sheds his earlier state in order to take on a new form.[38]

40: shape of things to come

Once the number 40 has enabled the nullification of an earlier form, it is the harbinger of the new form about to arrive. The classic examples of this concept include the future spouse of a child, the destruction of the First Temple, and the coming of Mashiach.

One illustration of 40 as a portent of the form of things to come, on a personal level, is the famous rabbinic statement that 40 days before the birth of a child a Heavenly call rings out and proclaims: "The daughter of so-and-so will marry so-and-so."[39]

Another example in reference to national events is that the Temple's destruction was hinted at in the series of events that occurred 40 years earlier. It was then, 40 years before the destruction, that the earlier miracles present in the House of G-d and the spiritual status quo began their decline.[40] This indicated the imminent fall of this form. Nevertheless, at this time, the seeds for the continuity of Israel were sown. It was 40 years before the national exile that palm trees were planted in Bavel — serving as a symbol for the preservation of Torah.[41]

One final example using 40 relates to the Messianic Epoch. The kingdom of Mashiach, according to one opinion, is destined to last for 40 years.[42] Mashiach will lead the world to be reborn in a brand-new form. The universal call for mankind to repent will be heeded. G-d's Word will be heard and observed. All previous spiritual defilement in the world will be rectified in the purification of the universe to take on a sinless form.

So 40 will, once again, symbolize that the potential of the world will be realized. Here the process of Creation will attain its true form, to be finally complete.

NOTES

1. See "4: Finding the Place."
2. See "39: Under Development."
3. *Bereishis* 2:7.
4. *Tosafos, Sanhedrin* 22a.
5. *Berachos* 60a; *Shulchan Aruch, Orach Chaim* 230:1. In itself, the typical length of gestation is 40 weeks after conception.
6. *Menachos* 99b. See *Sanhedrin* 91b, stating that the soul is implanted much earlier.
7. *Niddah* 30a, *Berachos* 21a, *Bechoros* 21b; *Rabbeinu Bachya, Vayikra* 12:4.
8. *Niddah* 30b.
9. *Shemos* 24:18. During this time, Moshe neither ate nor drank (*Devarim* 9:9).
10. *Menachos* 99b. The Talmud concludes noting that the soul of one who safeguards Torah is reciprocated by also being safeguarded.
11. *Yerushalmi, Taanis* 4:5. See *Tanchuma, Va'eira* 9, which related that Moshe's staff, which he used to perform the supernatural miracles, was also made of sapphire and weighed 40 *se'ah*.
12. *Sotah* 34a.
13. One who reviews Torah 40 times is guaranteed it will be rooted in his memory (*Pesachim* 72a). See *Taanis* 8a about how Reish Lakish would repeat his Torah studies 40 times. See *Rosh Hashanah* 18a about how because of Rabbah's study of Torah, he lived for 40 years. See *Bava Metzia* 85a about Rav Yosef undertaking a series of 40 fast days so as not to forget the Torah.
14. *Pirkei Avos* 5:21. According to some opinions, it is from this point on that a Torah scholar is permitted to delve into the mystical literature (*Shulchan Aruch, Yoreh Deah* 246:4, *Shach* ad loc.).
15. *Avodah Zarah* 5b. See *Tosafos, Sotah* 22b. This explains why 40 is the choice age for a person to take on the authority to render judgments.
16. *Rokeach, Shemos* 24:18.
17. *Rambam*, Introduction to *Mishneh Torah*.
18. David (*II Shmuel* 5:4) and Shlomo (*I Melachim* 11:42), the two formative kings of Israel from the Tribe of Yehudah, each reigned for 40 years.
19. For example, Yirmiyahu was a prophet for 40 years (*Eichah Rabbah* 4:25).
20. The tenure of judges such as Osniel (*Shoftim* 3:11), Devorah (ibid. 5:31), Gidon (ibid. 9:28), and Eli the *Kohen* each led the Jewish people for 40 years (*I Shmuel* 4:18). (Osniel, Devorah, and Gidon each ruled less than 40 years. Their "40 years" was inclusive of earlier years of bondage as well before they ruled. See *Metzudot David* and other commentaries there.)
21. Conversely, it was 40 years after the Jewish people requested that they have a king that Avshalom launched his rebellion to become king (*II Shmuel* 15:7). (See *Temurah* 14b.)
22. *Devarim* 29:4.
23. *Bereishis Rabbah* 100:10.
24. *Bereishis* 7:4, 7:12.
25. Ibid. 8:6 and *Rashi* ad loc.
26. See *Rokeach, Bereishis* 7:4, who notes that the sins of the Era of the *Mabul* are mentioned in *Iyov* 24.
27. *Devarim* 25:3. See "39: Under Development," for the relationship between 39 and 40.
28. See *Shulchan Aruch, Orach Chaim* 581:1.
29. *Devarim* 9:18, 25, 10:10; see ibid. 9:11, *Shemos* 34:2-9, *Rashi, Devarim* 9:18.

30. *Yalkut Shimoni, Ki Sisa* 391.
31. *Yonah* 3:4. See also *Pirkei DeRabbi Eliezer* 42.
32. *Bamidbar* 13:25, 14:34; *Devarim* 29:3-4. That whole generation had to die out in its entirety before the next generation could enter *Eretz Yisrael* (*For 40 years I quarreled with a generation ...* (*Tehillim* 95:10; see *Maharal, Netzach Yisrael* 46).
33. Mishnah, *Mikvaos* 1:7. The cubic volume of 40 *se'ah* in *mikveh* measures 1 cubit long by 1 cubit wide by 3 cubits deep (*Eruvin* 14b).
34. See *Rekunti, Parshas Noach* 6:26.
35. *Sefer HaChinuch*, Mitzvah 175, and *Shem MiShmuel, Shabbos Shuvah* 5674. There is the universal custom of immersing in a *mikveh* before Yom Kippur (*Mishnah Berurah*, 606:21).
36. In the purification process for the mother of a baby boy, she is impure for 7 days and then waits 33 days, for a total of (33 + 7 =) 40 days (this period is doubled after the birth of a girl) (*Vayikra* 12:2-5).
37. The convert ascends from the *mikveh* spiritually reborn as a full-fledged Jew. His halachic classification is indistinguishable from that of a newborn child (*Yevamos* 22a; *Bechoros* 47a). The symbolism is particularly potent as the fetus is similarly surrounded by water until its birth.
38. Many pious individuals immerse regularly in a *mikveh* to continuously revitalize their spiritual entity.
39. *Sotah* 2a.
40. See, e.g., *Yoma* 39b, *Shabbos* 15a.
41. *Yerushalmi, Taanis* 4:5.
42. *Sanhedrin* 99a.

42
THE INCREDIBLE JOURNEY

42 relates to the number
of journeys taken by man to
reach the ultimate destination.

In the process, it is the means by which
man reveals his true self.

ON THE ROAD

A journey is not simply about arriving at a final geographical location; just as important are the steps taken along the road toward the final destination.

THE NUMBER 42 OFTEN DENOTES THE STAGES OF REVELATION OR journeys undertaken to arrive at a given endpoint.

A journey is not simply about arriving at a final geographical location; just as important are the steps taken along the road toward the final destination. Every stage is intrinsically significant.[1] This principle applies to an individual's journey through life, as mirrored in the national journeys of the Children of Israel through the Wilderness.

The Journey of Becoming

Man should not view his existence as a *fait accompli*. It is a mistake to think that prior to his birth, man did not yet exist; now after his birth, he does. This outlook is erroneous. No living person exists in This World in a *finished* state of being. Every moment in This World, man is *coming into a new state of existence*.

Every moment on This World, man is coming into a new state of existence.

Life is a *continuous state of becoming* — every additional second, minute, hour, day, month, or year provides an additional opportunity for spiritual growth, progress, and development. His true identity is revealed only after life in This World is ended. *Death marks his fully formed state of existence.* This final state will exist for all eternity in *Olam Haba*, the World to Come.[2]

The rabbinic term מְצִיאוּת, *existence*, is derived from the root word יְצִיאָה, *coming out*, hinting at the continuous transformation in life from potential to actual; where a state that was earlier concealed is now revealed.[3] The journey of life, which involves journeying from one place to another, from one situation to the next, is about living life in a continuous state of revelation.

The journey of life is about living life in a continuous state of revelation.

42: Journeys in The Wilderness

This philosophy of life as revelation finds national expression in the journeys of the Children of Israel after their Exodus. The Torah records the travels the Jewish People took during their 40-year trek through the Wilderness to the Promised Land. All the stages of their sojourning add up to a total of 42 journeys.[4]

The nascent nation's journey of self-revelation is specifically described using the term מוֹצָאֵיהֶם, *goings forth*,[5] a variation of the term *yetziah*, coming out. This process immediately began after *yetzias Mitzraim*, going out of Egypt. It was ultimately completed following a total of 42 journeys upon their entry to the Holy Land.

Nothing is recorded in Torah merely as historical facts. All Biblical events provide a precedent or a template for eternity. Just as the wandering Children of Israel undertook journeys in the wilderness until they reached their homeland, so the Jewish People were also historically destined to undertake numerous journeys in the "wilderness of the nations" following their later states of exile, until their final return to their homeland.

42: JOURNEYS OF A LIFETIME

Actually, the Jewish People's journey to their homeland acts as an important metaphor for the passage from the barren wastelands of *Olam Hazeh*, This World, en route to the spiritual plateau of *Olam Haba*, the World to Come. The ascent toward the lofty spiritual heights of the Holy Land is a symbol the journey of life.[6] Man's accomplishments on the Earth below earn him eternal life in the spiritual world above. The end of life sees his arrival to the Heavenly land and *Yerushalayim shel Maalah*, Jerusalem's Heavenly counterpart above.[7]

Likewise, the 42 national journeys in the Wilderness find their parallel in the 42 journeys of the individual that begin from birth (the Exodus is symbolic of the birth of the Jewish Nation) and continue until his arrival to his final destination and eternal inheritance (entry into the Holy Land).[8] The passage through human life is itself a journey of revelation. Each leg of the journey serves as another step toward the attainment of his goal. Together, his activities and pursuits in *Olam Hazeh* serve as the essential means of revealing his spiritual, eternal existence in *Olam Haba* — his ultimate destination.

The ascent toward the lofty spiritual heights of the Holy Land is a symbol of the journey of life in the World to Come.

His activities and pursuits in Olam Hazeh serve as the essential means of revealing his spiritual, eternal existence in Olam Haba.

REVEALED: A HIGHER STATE

THE 42-STAGE PROCESS OF REVELATION REFLECTS THE MYSTICAL 42-Letter Name of G-d connected with Creation, which is an expression of G-d's Oneness. Here we see creation as the medium through which man readies himself for the revelation of something greater.

42-LETTER NAME OF G-D

One of the Holy Names of G-d is שֵׁם מ״ב, *the Name of 42*, as it is composed of 42 Hebrew letters.[9] This Divine Name is derived from the 42-letter sequence between the first letter of the Torah (*beis of Bereishis*) to the *beis* of the word *tohu u'vohu*, without form and void.[10]

The genesis of the universe unfolded during the 6 Days of Creation, climaxing with its grand conclusion on the 7th Day, Shabbos. We have noted that the numbers 6 and 7 are symbolic of the completed physical realm of 6 that is, in turn, directed toward the holiness of 7 in the full service of G-d.[11] Their interplay links to the full revelation of 42 as hinted at in the product of these two numbers (6 x 7= 42). Together, the elements in the universe join the process to reveal the Oneness of G-d.[12]

The 6 Days of Creation as the weekly journey toward reaching the 7th Day, Shabbos, corresponds to the 6 millennia of existence in This World as the antechamber leading to the World to Come, which is equivalent to the Day of Shabbos.[13] Both the week and the world are the requisite preparations to reaching a higher, spiritual realm.

42 WORDS: ANA B'KOACH

The 42-letter Divine Name relates to the 42-word prayer of אָנָא בְּכֹחַ, *Please, with the power*, a heartfelt plea composed by Rabbi Nechuniah ben HaKoneh asking G-d to accept man's prayers.[14]

Its structure is organized as 7 verses each composed of 6 words. This prayer carries the motif of transformation from a lower mode of existence to a higher level. One well-known example of this can be seen in the Friday night service. It opens with the saying of 6 psalms[15] before reciting *Ana B'Koach*, which serves as a prelude to the poetic composition *Lecha Dodi*. This 42-word prayer marks the transformation from the mundane 6 weekdays to the 7th Day of Shabbos. Standing at the threshold, it attaches the secular to the holy to mark a new form of existence.

42 WORDS: SHEMA

The revelation of Creation as a journey toward a higher ideal finds its expression within the 42-word formulation of *Shema*. The proclamation of G-d's Oneness is contained within the opening 6-word formula: שְׁמַע יִשְׂרָאֵל ה׳ אֱלֹקֵינוּ ה׳ אֶחָד, *Hear O Israel, HASHEM is our G-d, HASHEM is One.*[16]

The Oneness of G-d's Holy Name must spread out to permeate all of Creation, which is linked to the 42-Letter Name of G-d. So the ensuing first paragraph of *Shema* following the first verse contains an additional 42 words.[17] Reciting this passage, a Jew lovingly accepts upon himself the Oneness and Heavenly Kingship of G-d.[18] With these words he pledges to devote his 42-leg journey in the physical world to the service of G-d. Every ensuing step in his journey through life is to reveal yet another dimension, going higher and higher.

A Jew lovingly accepts upon himself the Oneness and Heavenly Kingship of G-d.

42: JOURNEY OF ASCENTS

Existence — both in its genesis and in its ongoing development — is a double process of revelation. There is the revelation of G-d in the universe through the 42-Letter Divine Name. Every stage of the journey serves to spread the unity of G-d throughout Creation. There is also the revelation of man as manifest through his 42 stages of life, represented by the national journey from Egypt through the Wilderness into the Holy Land[19] and the passage from This World to the World to Come.

Actually, these revelations are interrelated. The true revelation of "who man is" works in concert with the revelation of "Who G-d is." Man was created to use his free will to reveal G-d. And by revealing G-d, man is simultaneously revealing the true essence of his being — namely the G-dliness of his Divine soul.

The true revelation of "who man is" works in concert with the revelation of "Who G-d is."

Jewish life is an eye-opening journey of discovery. Each stage constitutes another step in the revelation of man's true self. Every step of the way is a transformation in what is a continuous ascent

Every step of the journey contains the possibility for man to transfer himself into a higher state of existence

to a higher level. The 42 journeys join together to provide a unified picture of the full person. Often, the journey contains many unexpected twists and turns along the way. But these should not cause man to stop in his tracks. They are simply another opportunity for man to actualize his potential. Every step of the journey contains the possibility for man to transfer himself into a higher state of existence — and he can then make the jump by taking the temporary physical realm of 6 and directing it to the spiritual world of 7.

NOTES

1. See "An Overview: Judaism by the Numbers" and "50: All the Way."
2. See "310: Worlds Apart."
3. R' Shlomo Eliashiv, *Leshem Sh'vo V'Achlamah, Hakdamos U'She'arim, Shaar* 1, *Perek* 2.
4. *Bamidbar* 33:1-49.
5. Ibid. 33:2.
6. See "310: Worlds Apart."
7. *Rama MiPano, Asarah Maamaros, Chikur HaDin* 3:22.
8. *Dagel Machaneh Ephraim, Maasei*, based on teachings of the Baal Shem Tov.
9. *Kiddushin* 71a. See *Rashi* ad loc.
10. *Tosafos, Chagigah* 11b; *Rabbeinu Bachya, Bereishis* 1:1.
11. See "6: It's Only Natural" and "7: A Holy Spark."
12. See *Meshech Chochmah, Shemos* 3:14, who explains that the Ineffable 4-Letter Name of G-d is inscribed inside the *tefillin* a total of 42 times.
13. *Mishnah Tamid* 7:4, *Rus Rabbah* 3:3, *Osiyos DeRabbi Akiva* 4.
14. See *Tikkunei Zohar* 21, p. 47b.
15. *Tehillim* 95-99 and 29.
16. *Devarim* 6:4. See "1: The One and Only" and "6: It's Only Natural."
17. See *Shem MiShmuel, Maasei* 5675, in the name of the *Arizal*. See "48: Stay Connected."
18. See Mishnah, *Berachos* 2:1. See *Shulchan Aruch, Orach Chaim* 61:14, 63:6.
19. The 42 journeys in the Wilderness parallel the 42-Letter Divine Name and the ascent from level to level in the preparation from the 6 days of the week to the 7th Day, Shabbos (R' Tzadok HaKohen, *Pri Tzaddik, Beha'aloscha* 1 and *Maasei* 1; see also *Malbim, Bamidbar* 33:5). Each journey corresponds to another letter of the 42-Letter Name. The goal is to elevate and attach ourselves to the spiritual energy of that specific letter.

48
STAY CONNECTED

48 reflects the human ability
to attach or to reattach oneself
to the inner force of life.

This demands tapping into a constantly
renewable source — like a wellspring deep beneath the earth — that grants
freshness and vitality.

*The number
48 is about
maintaining
a constant
connection to
a vibrant life
source.*

THE NUMBER 48 IS ABOUT MAINTAINING A CONSTANT CONNECTION TO a vibrant life source — one that is unending and always able to replenish itself.

We have repeatedly noted that the soul is the life force within the body. It is this which gives man his existence. Life revolves around developing a relationship with the Living G-d.[1] This determines whether a Jew is "spiritually alive" or "spiritually dead"; whether he is spiritually connected or spiritually disconnected.[2] The closer one is to G-d, the more alive one is; the more one is in touch with the eternity of life. Not so the wicked. Even when technically alive, in spiritual terms they are classified as dead.[3]

*Man has the
innate ability
to connect or
reconnect to the
source of his
spiritual center
at any time.*

The existence of the soul means that man has the innate ability to connect or reconnect to the source of his spiritual center at any time. This connection to a life-source finds expression both in Torah — where man attaches himself to G-d — and in the symbol of a well-spring — where man attaches himself to his own soul.

48: WELLSPRINGS OF THE SOUL

Much of Earth is covered by water. But in addition to the readily available "revealed" sources of water, such as rainfall, the rivers, and the seas, there are also "concealed" sources of water. The בְּאֵר, *well-spring* or *spring water*, lies hidden from view, beneath the surface. In order to draw forth these waters from their subterranean depth, great efforts must be expended to displace the earth lying above them. This water must be drawn from its underground source all the way to the surface.

*A wellspring
can be
compared
to the soul
lying beneath
the material
earth, which is
likened to the
body.*

Symbolically, a wellspring can be compared to the soul. It is found beneath the material earth which is likened to the body. G-d first fashioned the body of Adam from the dust of the earth, before breathing into him the soul of life.[4] One must be in touch with the spiritual dimension that is the inner point within man.

The wellspring of the soul is the inner source of life buried deep beneath the physical surface. Its living waters continuously replenish themselves. They act as a constant source of inspiration from which man can draw. But this demands that he acquire this inspiration by tapping into this life source. Digging away dirt to reach the subterranean wellspring calls for a mindset to symbolically displaces the surface presence of the earth's physical composition in favor of uncovering the wondrous undercurrent of spirituality lying beneath.

This perspective is evident in the lives of the Jewish forefathers as they dug deep to uncover the wellspring, the *be'er*. As he embarked upon his iconoclastic mission of disseminating spirituality in the world, Avraham dug wells.[5] Opposing him were the Pelishtim, who repeatedly blocked them up with earth.[6] Avraham's son and successor Yitzchak took upon himself to reopen these wellsprings.[7] He, too, faced antagonism from the Pelishtim.[8] Yaakov removed the stone from the mouth of the well in order to draw water for Rachel's flocks.[9]

Water is a recurrent metaphor for Torah.[10] In reference to the phrase בְּאֵר מַיִם חַיִּים, *a well of living waters*,[11] the Midrash notes that these words appear a total of 48 times in the Torah.[12] So the *wellspring* relates to mastery of Torah in terms of the 48 acquisitions of Torah.[13]

Water is a recurrent metaphor for Torah.

48: TORAh MASTERY

The letters of the word בְּאֵר, *well*, can be read בָּאֵר, *explain*, used in the context of Torah exposition.[14] The surest way for a human being to be connected to G-d is to grasp the Holy Torah. As the word of the Living G-d, Torah is synonymous with חַיּוּת, *life itself* — both the temporary life in This World and the eternal life in the World to Come."[15] Consequently, the study and acquisition of Torah — the means to relate to the word of the Living G-d — is the surest way for man to come close to G-d. Despite the unknowable nature of G-d, man has access to the Divine instructions found within the Torah.[16]

The surest way for a human being to be connected to G-d is to grasp the Holy Torah.

The attachment of man to G-d through Torah mirrors man's attachment to the wellspring of his soul. The Jew's relationship to Torah deeply relates to his spiritual life force and essential identity. It is Torah that defines the life and purpose of a Jew demanding that he tap into the inner recesses of his soul.

The word מוֹרָשָׁה, *inheritance*,[17] used in connection with the legacy of Torah can be rendered מְאֹרָסָה, *betrothed*.[18] The Jew's sacrosanct relationship to Torah echoes the intimate holiness within marriage. On his part, the Jew must approach Torah as something that he must take steps to acquire — similar to Jewish marriage that is achieved

The Jew's sacrosanct relationship to Torah echoes the intimate holiness within marriage.

through a formal act of *kinyan*, acquisition. The Mishnah relates that Torah is grasped through a total of 48 *kinyanin*, acts of acquisition. These qualities are essential features and techniques of how to acquire a strong grip over Torah.[19]

One powerful symbol of Torah is the אָרוֹן, *Ark*, that housed the *luchos*, Tablets, upon which were engraved the Ten Commandments. The dimensions of this vessel contain a beautiful allusion to the 48 attributes of Torah. Its length was 2½ cubits long and its width 1½ cubits.[20] As 1 cubit is equivalent to 6 handbreadths, the total distance of a thread that could encircle the *Aron* would be the length of the perimeter, which was [(2½ x 6) + (1½ x 6) + (2½ x 6) + (1½ x 6) =] 48 handbreadths.[21] The complete measurement surrounding all 4 sides signifies the ability to firmly hold onto it.

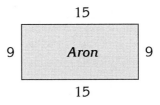

The obligation to master Torah devolves upon every Jew.

The obligation to master Torah devolves upon every Jew, irrespective of his lineage;[22] it is something he must "grasp onto." He must relentlessly pursue Torah and procure it for himself — whatever the cost or effort involved. He must connect to the wellsprings of his soul, and by extension, connect to the life force of Torah. He has to exert the requisite effort to draw out these "living waters" by attaining a grasp of the material and the concepts within. Through Torah study, the Jew is given the wondrous opportunity to connect to G-d by studying the word of G-d and, in turn, fulfilling His Will.

48: COVENANTS

The lifetime of commitment to Torah is founded upon the covenant, forged between Israel and G-d.

The lifetime of commitment to Torah extends from its theoretical study to its practical application. Importantly, it is founded upon the בְּרִית, *covenant*, forged between Israel and G-d. The concept of a *bris* relates to the word בְּרִיאָה, *creation*.[23] This highlights the fact that the *bris* reconnects the Jewish People to the Source of existence. Keeping the original purpose of Creation in sight is the guaranteed means to be constantly connected. It is often an assurance of our loyally staying attached and prevents any deviation.

It is not only the Torah that is synonymous with *bris*.[24] Every *mitzvah* given by G-d to the Jewish People was actually established by means of 48 covenants — formalized on 3 separate occasions in the Wilderness: Sinai, *Ohel Moed* (Tent of Meeting)" and on the plains of Moav.[25]

HOW TO RECONNECT

NOT ONLY THE SYMBOL OF INITIAL CONNECTION TO G-D BY MEANS of Torah and the soul, the number 48 also shows us how to reconnect once those bonds have been loosened. A sinner may have been lured by the material nature of his physical body, whose fate is to ultimately decompose in the grave. Nevertheless, he can still dig deeply and tap into the wellspring of his eternal soul, which lives on beyond death. He has the ability to draw forth inspiration and to replenish himself in order to reconnect himself to his life force.

Number 48 also shows us how to reconnect once those bonds have been loosened.

Perhaps the two most prominent examples of the ability of a Jew to reconnect to G-d can be found in the 48 prophets charged with exhorting Israel to repentance and the method of rehabilitation for the accidental murderer who flees to the 48 cities of the Levites.

48: Jewish prophets

Prophecy flourished until the destruction of the first Temple.[26] Many men and women within the Holy Land reached an exalted spiritual level to experience G-d "speaking" to them. There were a total of 48 men whose prophecies are recorded for posterity within the 24 Books of Tanach.[27] (This number does not include the separately enumerated 7 prophetesses.[28])

Every prophetic revelation was a continuation of Torah as the word of G-d.

Every prophetic revelation was a continuation of Torah as the word of G-d.[29] The words of the prophets — and the authority vested in them — were an extension of Torah itself and therefore transcribed into Scripture. The primary function of a נָבִיא, *prophet*, was to serve as the spokesperson of G-d.[30] This title, derived from the phrase נִיב שְׂפָתַיִם, *fruits of the lips*,[31] depicted a prophet as the mouthpiece publicly broadcasting the word of G-d.[32]

One of the main tasks entrusted to the 48 prophets was issuing admonitions to inspire the wicked to repent.

One of the main tasks entrusted to the 48 prophets was issuing admonitions to inspire the wicked to repent. Their mission was to exhort sinners to reconnect and return to G-d.[33] In the Purim narrative, the threat of annihilation resulting from the removal of King Achashveirosh's ring was the catalyst for a surge in national repentance. This is considered to have been equivalent to the rebuke of the 48 Jewish prophets.[34]

48: CITIES OF REFUGE

The Levites were allocated 48 cities — 6 refuge cities and 42 other towns.

There is a parallel between the 48 Jewish prophets and the 48 עָרֵי מִקְלָט, *Cities of Refuge*.[35] The Levites did not receive a regional portion in the Holy Land. Instead, they were allocated 48 cities — 6 refuge cities and 42 other towns.[36]

The 6 cities had Levite residents but also played an additional role. They were the cities to which the inadvertent killer could flee in the bid to seek refuge from the vengeful relative of the victim. The killer was required to dwell within the strict borders of the city for an indefinite time. Only upon the death of the High Priest was he free to leave.[37]

By causing another to lose his life, the killer had similarly 'forfeited' his own life. He had, in effect, lost his right to a connection to his life force. This was the reason why the victim's relative was permitted to kill him if he left the refuge city.[38] His only option was to remain in "one of the Cities of Refuge and live."[39] The emphasis "*and live*" indicates that this offers the refugee his solitary chance to reattach himself to an alternative life force. He must connect to the life force of the Levites living within these 48 cities. He must tap into their source of life in lieu of his own. He resides among the spiritually exalted Levites, who are set apart from mundane world to devote their lives to serve G-d and to teach and study Torah.[40]

The spiritually exalted Levites are set apart from mundane world.

48: SHEMA YISRAEL

The connection man has with G-d has its allusion in the words of the first paragraph of Shema.

Finally, the everlasting connection man has with G-d as his eternal life force has its allusion in the words of the first paragraph of *Shema*. The well-known opening verse is composed of 6 words.[41] The rest of this paragraph consists of an additional 42 words.[42] In total, this comprises 48 words.[43]

The Jew expresses his overwhelming love for G-d with every fiber of his being.

Through the acceptance of G-d's Sovereignty, the Jew expresses his overwhelming love for G-d with every fiber of his being. He maintains contact with the wellspring of his soul. It is his source of inspiration — his unbreakable connection to his eternal being. Even when he appears to be disconnected, the Jew can move to uncover his spiritual essence and reconnect.

NOTES

1. See, for example, *I Shmuel* 17:26.
2. "Every one of you who cleaved unto HASHEM your G-d — you are all alive on this day" (*Devarim* 4:4).
3. *Berachos* 18a-b. See *Maharal, Gur Aryeh, Bereishis* 11:32 and *Chiddushei Aggados, Rosh Hashanah* 16b (Vol. 1, pp. 109-110).
4. *Bereishis* 2:7.
5. Ibid. 21:25, 30-31.
6. Ibid. 26:15.
7. Ibid. v. 18.
8. Ibid. vv. 19-22, 32-33.
9. Ibid. 29:10.
10. See *Bava Kamma* 17a.
11. *Shir HaShirim* 4:15.
12. *Yalkut Shimoni, Shir HaShirim* 988. See *Sfas Emes, Toldos* 5647, and *Sfas Emes, Chukas* 5652.
13. Ibid.
14. See, e.g., *Devarim* 1:5; 27:8.
15. "Great is Torah, for it gives life to its practitioners, both in This World and in the World to Come" (*Pirkei Avos* 6:7).
16. *Maharal, Nesiv HaTorah* 4 and *Derech Chaim* 6:8.
17. *Devarim* 33:4.
18. Ibid. 22:23. *Berachos* 57a. See *Shemos Rabbah* 33:7.
19. *Pirkei Avos* 6:6.
20. *Shemos* 25:10.
21. *Maharal, Derech Chaim* 6:7.
22. This is in contrast to the aforementioned levels of *Kehunah*, priesthood, (which has 24 distinctions) and *malchus*, kingship, (which has 30) mentioned in *Pirkei Avos* (6:6), that are determined by paternal descent.
23. See *Rabbeinu Bachya, Bereishis* 1:2, how the word *bereishis*, creation, is made up of the words *aish*, fire, and *bris*, covenant.
24. See, for example, *Shemos* 24:7 and 34:28.
25. *Sotah* 37b. See also *Baal HaTurim, Devarim* 1:1.
26. *Bava Basra* 12a. Prophecy is endemic to holiness and is most specifically related to the holiness of the Jewish People as an inheritance from the forefathers (R' Yehudah HaLevi, *Kuzari* 1:100-103) and of the innate sanctity of the Holy Land (*Moed Katan* 25a; *Zohar* 1, 187; *Midrash Tanchuma Bo* 5).
27. *Megillah* 14a.
28. Ibid. 14a. See also "7: A Holy Spark."
29. In fact, the source of all prophecy relates back to Sinai (see *Devarim* 18:16-18, *Berachos* 5a, and *Shemos Rabbah* 28:6). All prophets have an element of Moshe's level of prophecy, as G-d said to Moshe: "I will establish a prophet … like you" (*Devarim* 18:18). The 12 permutations of the 4-Letter

Name of G-d — totalling 48 letters — parallel the 48 prophets who disseminated His word (*Zohar, Chayei Sarah* 125).

30. See *Shemos* 7:1-2, where Aharon is termed a *navi* as the spokesperson of Moshe to relay his message to Pharaoh.
31. *Yeshayah* 57:19; see *Rashi, Shemos* 7:1.
32. *Devarim* 18:18.
33. See *Rambam, Hilchos Teshuvah* 4:2. A significant function of *Nach* is as rebuke to Israel for their sins that have angered G-d (*Ran, Nedarim* 22a). See *Berachos* 34b, which discusses that one of the main themes of the prophecies is repentance and the rewards for penitents. See also *Reishis Chochmah, Shaar HaTeshuvah* 1:42.
34. *Megillah* 14a.
35. *Tanna DeVei Eliyahu Rabbah* 16; see also *Rokeach, Devarim* 19:7.
36. *Bamidbar* 35:7; *Yehoshua* 21:39.
37. *Bamidbar* 35:28.
38. The Torah characterizes him as someone who "has no blood" (*Bamidbar* 35:27); he has already forfeited his life force and he is technically a dead man.
39. *Devarim* 19:5.
40. See *Rambam, Hilchos Shemittah V'Yovel* 13:12-13.
41. *Devarim* 6:4. See "6: It's Only Natural."
42. *Devarim* 6:5-9. See "42: An Incredible Journey."
43. See *Shem MiShmuel, Masei* 5675 who offers an explanation of the parallels between the 48 cites of refuge and the 48 words of the *Shema*.

49
THE FULL MEASURE

49 relates to the fulfillment
of the natural cycle.

It is the standard of the full measure —
both of good and of bad.

It is the journey where man fulfills his maximum
to reach the extent of his capabilities.

THE FULL CYCLE

The number 49 symbolizes the natural end of a cycle or the attainment of one's full quota.

THE NUMBER 49 IS BOTH THE SQUARE OF 7 AND THE NUMBER THAT precedes 50.

49 symbolizes where one has either come to the natural end of a cycle or where one has successfully attained one's full quota.

49: 7 X 7

This depicts the totality that can be reached within the confines of the natural world.

The most prominent mathematical property of 49 is as the square of 7 (7^2 = 49). We have observed the recurrent use of 7 as completion of the natural world.[1] This concept is amplified in 7 squared.[2] This depicts, in a fuller measure, the totality that can be reached within the confines of the natural world.

Two of the most well-known examples of this are the 49-day cycle in the count up to Shavuos and the 49-year cycle in the count up to *Yovel*.

49: cycles up to shavuos

In the Jewish calendar, the period leading up to Shavuos is marked by the counting of 49 days. Starting from the second day of Pesach, with the bringing of the *Omer* offering, the full term of סְפִירַת הָעֹמֶר, *count of the Omer* (often called the *Sefirah*, count), is described by the Torah as *7 complete weeks until the morrow after the 7th week.*[3]

This frames the count in the context of attaining the complete term of 7 weeks composed of 7 days.

This is not a simple count from 1 to 49 where only the number of the specific days is declared. The actual count is phrased in cyclical terms: mention is made of both the number of weeks and number of days that have elapsed. For example: "Today is 22 days that total 3 weeks and 1 day of the *Omer*." This frames the count in the context of attaining the complete term of 7 weeks composed of 7 days. Together, the 49 days join together in the completion of the full cycle. This is capped by the 50th day, which is the festival of Shavuos, marking the Jewish national acceptance of Torah at Sinai.

49: CYCLES UP TO YOVEL

The Jewish cycle of days in a week has its parallel in terms of years: 6 units of activity followed by the 7th period of inactivity. The "Shabbos of the week" (the 7th day) has its parallel in the "Shabbos of the years" (*Shemittah*, the 7th, Sabbatical, year).

There is the close resemblance between the units of 49 as both the cycle of days and the cycle of years. The time frame of 49 days (= 7 weeks of 7 days) in the lead-up to Shavuos exactly corresponds to the sequence of 49 years (=7 cycles of 7 years) in the lead-up to the 50th year, the *Yovel*, Jubilee Year. The Torah states: *You shall count for yourself 7 Sabbatical years, 7 years 7 times; and there shall be for you, the days of 7 Sabbatical years, 49 years.*[4] Together, the 49 years join in the completion of the full cycle. This is capped by the 50th year, *Yovel*.[5]

Whether this is framed in terms of days or years, the passing through 49 units signals the natural conclusion in the measure of these cycles of time.

Together, the 49 years join in the completion of the full cycle.

FOR GOOD MEASURE

It is the epitome of a מִדָּה, measure, also used to describe a trait or characteristic.

TYPICALLY, 49 IS THE NUMBER USED TO DENOTE THE NATURAL parameters in This World of what is quantifiable. It is the epitome of a מִדָּה, *measure*, whose numerical value is itself 49.[6] The term *middah* is also used to describe a trait or characteristic. This hints at the fact that every human personality trait (e.g., kindness, strictness, jealousy, etc.) can be quantified by levels or degrees. It requires the awareness to know when and where every quality should be employed and in what measure.

49: GATES OF UNDERSTANDING

The number 49 is used to depict the full measure of something in the world.

The number 49 is the standard that is used to depict the full measure of something in the world. The classic example is the מ״ט שַׁעֲרֵי בִּינָה, *49 Gates of Understanding*. Of the 50 Gates of Understanding through which G-d created the world, a maximum of 49 gates were made accessible to mankind. Moshe, whose level surpassed that of all other men, was worthy enough to attain all 49 levels.[7]

Moshe's perception of the universe and of G-d was as complete as was humanly possible.

Moshe's perception of the universe and of G-d was as complete as was humanly possible. It reached the full measure associated with the number 49. Nevertheless, the 50th Gate eluded him because this extra level relates to understanding G-d's Essence. It is impossible for man to tap into this unknowable dimension while still a part of This World where he is not yet one with G-d, as he will be in the World to Come.[8]

49: PURITY VS. IMPURITY

49 as the maximum quota man can symbolically attain finds further expression in the opposite measures used for interpreting Torah.

49 as the maximum quota man can symbolically attain finds further expression in the opposite measures used for interpreting Torah. There are 49 sides (faces) to prove something is pure and a corresponding 49 sides (faces) to prove something is impure.[9] One of the Sages declared: "I can purify a [dead] insect in a total of 49 ways."[10]

This was not a boast about the use of logic or the manipulation of exegesis to vindicate something that the Torah explicitly forbids. Rather, this was a self-professed testimony by a Talmud scholar about his all-encompassing grasp of the topic. He had mastered the full measure of 49 dimensions to discern the breadth of factors involved in a Torah ruling. Here the topic was viewed and understood from all possible angles.

A holistic view incorporates all the opinions involved in a dispute.

The quality of truth in Torah is even present in reasoning or arguments that are ultimately rejected in the final ruling. A holistic view incorporates all the opinions involved in a dispute; each opinion is factored into the equation.[11] This is why conflicting opinions in rabbinic literature are an integral part of Torah: "These and these are the words of the living G-d."[12] Hence the final ruling would be bequeathed to the sages of each generation to determine.

MEASURE FOR MEASURE

WE HAVE SEEN THAT 49 IS THE FULL MEASURE. IN THE WORLD OF counterbalancing opposites,[13] the number 49 can either characterize measures used for the good or those used for the bad.

Here there is the imperative for man to trade "measure for measure." This involves reversing the 49 measures of bad into the 49 measures of good. This was the secret of Israel's transformation at the Exodus, which revolves around the number 49.

49: GATES OF IMPURITY

The number 49 as the full measure of evil is epitomized in the depths to which the Jewish nation sank in the Egyptian exile. They reached the spiritual nadir of מ״ט שַׁעֲרֵי טוּמְאָה, *the 49th level of impurity*.[14] There was the real danger that had they remained in Egypt any longer, their assimilation within the host nation would have been permanent. Israel would then have irretrievably lost its spiritual identity. Consequently, the Exodus was more than the release from physical captivity; it was the emancipation of the spirit. The task now entrusted to the newly liberated Children of Israel was to take the necessary steps in their bid to transfer these 49 levels "measure for measure," from the bad to the good.

The journey en route to Sinai required that the previous 49 levels of impurity of Egypt to be converted into 49 levels of purity. This spiritual purification would be accomplished during the 49-day period of the *Omer* — the designated period linking the Festivals of Pesach and Shavuos. Every day called for another step in turning impurity into purity, negative into positive, sin into righteousness, and distance from G-d into closeness. These 49 steps toward purity reflected this number as the highest measure of expression in any human endeavor.

The journey en route to Sinai required that the previous 49 levels of impurity of Egypt to be converted into 49 levels of purity.

49: CURSES OF ADMONITION

Prior to the Festival of Shavuos, we follow an ancient Jewish custom established by Ezra to read the passage of the *Tochachah*, Admonition, as enumerated at the end of *Vayikra*.[15] These passages are composed of a total of 49 curses. A similar phenomenon is evident before Rosh Hashanah as we read the *Tochachah* enumerated in *Devarim*, which contains a double number of curses: (i.e., 49 x 2 =) 98.[16] The intent is that the curses may end along with the year.[17]

The 49 reprimands reflect 7 curses for each of Israel's grievous 7 sins, which have severely impaired its relationship with G-d.[18] The exhortation of the 49 curses demands that man repair the damaged

The 49 reprimands reflect 7 curses for each of Israel's grievous 7 sins.

relationship with G-d. The 49 days of the *Omer* were the obligatory preparation for man to elevate himself to reconnect with G-d. The 49 curses or rebukes were directed at the Children of Israel if they strayed from the commandments, reminding them of their responsibilities as a holy nation.

The 49 curses or rebukes were reminding them of their responsibilities as a holy nation.

TO ITS (SUPER)NATURAL CONCLUSION

SOMETHING HAS REACHED ITS NATURAL CONCLUSION AT THE 49TH level. This marks where man has naturally achieved all that can be expected of him.

Nevertheless, this is not the end of the line. There remains one final stage in the Jew's journey — one where he touches a dimension that lies beyond 49, beyond man's natural effort: the transcendental, Divine level of 50.

He touches a dimension that lies beyond 49: the transcendental, Divine level of 50.

49 TO 50: FROM WORK TO GIFT

Once man has invested his maximum input to naturally progress and complete the cycle from 1 to 49, he has, by all accounts, attained the pinnacle of human achievement. Thereafter, G-d takes over. The Master of the Universe rewards man with the gift of actually attaining a higher spiritual level. This stage is far beyond that which he could achieve on his own initiative.[19] This last stage is the leap from 49 to 50, which means entering a supernatural state.

He is now transported onto a higher pedestal — to a level above the natural order. He attains a higher, transcendental level. The 50th follows — but is not counted along with the 49th.[20] And it is the level of Torah given on the 50th day, Shavuos. It is the level of spiritual freedom in the 50th year, *Yovel*.[21] Both lie outside the natural confines; they relate to the number 8 (the stage after 7) and to the dimension that transcends that which can be measured or counted.[22]

Man's primary objective is to progress through the natural cycle of 49.

Nevertheless, the 50th can come only after 49. Man's primary objective is to progress through the natural cycle of 49, to maximize his efforts to attain the full measure humanly available, and from his perspective, to reach the highpoint in terms of human achievement — whether in terms of self-purification (49 days of the *Omer* up to

Shavuos), yearly count (49 years up to *Yovel*), or Gates of Understanding (49 levels attained by Moshe).

NOTES

1. See "7: A Holy Spark."
2. The unique quality of a "square number" is *that every part of the structure is individually mapped to every other part of the whole*. Here all dimensions of expression are revealed in their entirety.
3. *Vayikra* 23:15-16.
4. Ibid. 25:8.
5. Ibid. 25:10-11.
6. See *Arizal, Likkutei Torah, Yeshayah; Megaleh Amukos* 48.
7. *Rosh Hashanah* 21b; *Nedarim* 38a.
8. See "50: All the Way."
9. *Yerushalmi, Sanhedrin* 4:2; *Shir HaShirim Rabbah* 2:4:1; *Koheles Rabbah* 8:3; *Tanchuma, Bamidbar* 10 and *Chukas* 4; *Masechtos Soferim* 16:6.
10. *Yalkut Shimoni Tehillim* 658.
11. This is why certain laws that are usually prohibitive can be seen to have a permissible counterpart. A classic example of this is the prohibition for a man to marry his brother's widow. However, should his brother have died without issue, he is permitted to perform *yibum*, levirate marriage (*Devarim* 25:5-6). See *Yerushalmi, Shevuos* 3:8. See also *Yotzros Parashas Parah*, s.v. *Ain L'Soche'ach*.
12. *Eruvin* 13b. See also *Rashi, Kesubos* 57a.
13. See "2: Opposite and Equal."
14. *Zohar Chadash, Yisro* 31a.
15. *Megillah* 31b.
16. See "98: The Admonition."
17. *Megillah* 31b.
18. *Rashi, Vayikra* 26:18.
19. *Ramchal, Mesillas Yesharim* 26.
20. See *Maharal, Nesiv HaTorah,* who explains that in the *Omer* count the 50th day is not counted because it represents the ethereal elevated world that is not subordinate to time.
21. See "50: All the Way."
22. See "8: Out of This World."

50
ALL THE WAY

50 is the transcendental point of arrival in the final step of man's journey.

Passing through all 50 stages indicates traveling the full distance in order to reach the designated endpoint.

GOING BEYOND

The ultimate level transcends everything that came before it.

THE NUMBER 50 IS THE DISTINGUISHED NUMBER OF TRANSCENDENCE. The milestone of the 50th is reached after passing through all the necessary stages. Here the cumulative levels combine to arrive at the ultimate level — one that transcends everything that came before it.

$$7, 8 = 49, 50$$

The count up to 50 is composed of two essential and distinct stages.

The first phase is the step-by-step progression rising from 1 up to 49. As the square of 7 (7^2=49), 49 denotes the complete cycle within the physical universe.[1] This is a natural development, one that reaches the extremities of the outer boundaries. This may be the furthest limit as far as nature is concerned — but it is not the endpoint. But the ultimate destination of a Jew is his arrival at the second phase — one where he somehow manages the supernatural leap from 49 to arrive at the transcendental quality of 50.

A Jew manages the supernatural leap from 49 to arrive at the transcendental quality of 50.

The progression from 49 to 50 has, as its precedent, the stepping stone from 7 to 8. The soul is likened to the 7th center of holiness within the body that sanctifies the 6 directions of the physical world toward spiritual pursuits.[2] Through this process, the soul is able to elevate itself, and the body with it, toward perfection.[3] In number terms, the 7 is elevated beyond to reach 8, which is synonymous with entry onto the higher transcendental plane.[4] And the arrival at 50 similarly marks the entry into this exalted state.

The arrival at 50 marks the entry into this exalted state.

A PASSAGE TO SINAI

PERHAPS THE COUNT TOWARD THE NUMBER 50 FINDS ITS MOST WELL-known historic expression in the Exodus and its aftermath.

EXODUS: 50

The momentous event that commemorates the birth of the Children of Israel as a nation was יְצִיאַת מִצְרַיִם, *departure from Egypt*. Not only is there a twice-daily remembrance of this milestone,[5] but much of *mitzvah* observance is marked by repeated references to the Exodus. Its central importance is due to this event celebrating the Jewish People's brand-new *state of existence*.

Their deliverance was not only from physical slavery but also from the Egyptian worldview. The Exodus released them from an outlook constrained by the natural realm.[6] The redemption catapulted Israel into an alternate state of reality. They exchanged the restricted for the unrestricted, the natural for the supernatural, and the ordinary for the extraordinary. It was *the* seminal event that would define what Israel had now become: G-d's Chosen People. Their transcendental quality was now evident in the aftermath of their trailblazing liberation.

The redemption catapulted Israel into an alternate state of reality.

The historic event of the Exodus is mentioned in the *Chumash* a total of 50 times.[7] And the redemption process which started on the first day of Pesach finally reached its completion stage 50 days later at Sinai. Indeed, G-d freed the Children of Israel *in order* that they accept the Torah. The Divine instruction given to Moshe at the burning bush was to lead Israel out of Egypt and bring the nation to serve G-d at that mountain.[8]

SHAVUOS: DAY 50

The 50 stages of redemption required a minimum 49-day interval for their national metamorphosis. Prior to their liberation, the Children of Israel had sunk to the nadir of spiritual impurity: מ״ט שַׁעֲרֵי טֻמְאָה, *the 49th level of impurity*. The Exodus introduced a spiritual cleansing process. Israel embarked upon a gradual path of ascension, one level after another. Theirs was a phenomenal rise from their degraded position on the 49th gate of impurity up to the 49th gate of purity.[9] Finally, they arrived at the highest spiritual pinnacle on the 50th day.[10]

The Exodus introduced a spiritual cleansing process.

This period bridges the Festivals of Pesach and Shavuos. The journey is alluded to in the *mitzvah* that famously links this time frame: the 50-day סְפִירַת הָעוֹמֶר, *Omer count*, from date of the cutting of an *Omer* measure of the new crop of barley, which was brought up as an offering on the second day of Pesach: *You shall count for your-*

The journey from one Festival to another is alluded to in the 50-day count of סְפִירַת הָעוֹמֶר.

self ... 7 weeks that shall be complete until the morrow after the 7th week — it shall be 50 days ...."[11]

TORAh: 50

Shavuos is the only Festival not referenced by a specific date in the Jewish lunar calendar. Its classification as זְמַן מַתַּן תּוֹרָה, *time of the giving of Torah*, is recorded as Day 50 after the Exodus. This firmly establishes Shavuos as *the* climax of the Exodus. In the relationship between G-d and Israel, the giving of Torah at Sinai is termed *on your wedding day*.[12]

Marriage celebrates the total commitment of two parties to each other. The obligations of a Jewish marriage arrangement are recorded in the כְּתוּבָּה, *document*. The set monetary settlement allocated to a maiden was 50 silver *shekels* (equivalent to 200 *zuz*/dinars in Mishnaic currency).[13] This sum finds its perfect parallel in the giving of the Torah, where the contractual duties of Israel's wedding day came into effect on the 50th day after the Exodus.

The contractual duties of Israel came into effect on the 50th day after their Exodus.

Here G-d showered His beloved nation with the best wedding gift of them all: the gift of Torah. The metaphysical quality of Torah often sees its depiction as שֵׂכְלִי, *qualities of the Divine intellect*. Its transcendental nature is over and above the physical existence of This World. Appropriately, Torah was given at the beginning of the 8th week after the Exodus. It taps into the symbolism of 8 transcending the natural realm epitomized by the number 7. In this respect, 50, which follows the cycle of 7 weeks each consisting of 7 days, shares the "out of this world" quality of the number 8.[14]

As the 50th day after Egyptian deliverance, in the 8th week, Shavuos relates to the transcendental nature of Torah.[15] In the singular form, the word *Torah* is said to occur 50 times in the *Chumash*.[16]

The 50th level relates to that which is "out of this world."

Parallel to the number 8, the 50th level relates to that which is "out of this world."[17] The *Mishkan*, Sanctuary, and subsequently the *Beis HaMikdash*, Temple, revolved around Torah as represented by the *Luchos*, Tablets, housed in the *Kodesh HaKodashim*, Holy of Holies. (In itself, the construction of a House of G-d served to immortalize the giving of Torah at Sinai.[18]) The purchase of the Temple site took effect through the 50 *shekels* of silver paid by each tribe.[19] The maximum age for a Levi to serve in the Temple was 50 years old.[20] In particular, the innermost chamber, the *Kodesh HaKodashim* relates to this 50th transcendental level.[21] And there were 50 golden hooks upon the roof spread directly above the curtain cover at the entrance of the *Kodesh HaKodashim*.[22]

ABOVE NATURE

5O

WE HAVE NOTED THAT 50 REPRESENTS THE FULL JOURNEY TOWARD acceptance of Torah in the 50 days bridging Pesach and Shavuos. The passage through life calls for the Jew to emulate the national passage to Sinai. He must proceed until the natural end — and then go beyond it. He must transcend the finite and touch the sublime 50th gate that belongs *over and above* the natural rules of This World.[23]

5O: AT A DISTANCE

The number 50 is used as the measure that places something at a distance. The Talmud notes the use of a rope measuring 50 cubits for matters such as measuring the 2,000-cubit distance of *techum Shabbos,* the distance beyond the city one may travel on Shabbos.[24] Because of the negative impact of a granary, leather tannery, and cemetery, these were not halachically permitted to be located within 50 cubits of the city.[25] Of course, the 50-day journey from Egypt to Sinai ensured that Israel was no longer under the sinful influence of their idolatrous past.

No less than 50 stages of redemption — parallel to the 50 times the Exodus is recorded in the Torah — were required to achieve a clean break from the past. Now, on the 50th day, Shavuos, the shackles of bondage were finally broken. This is recorded in the mention of the Exodus in the opening verse of the 10 Commandments: *I am HASHEM your G-d Who took you out of the land of Egypt from the house of slavery.*[26]

5O: GATES OF UNDERSTANDING

The creation of Israel in the 50 days between Pesach and Shavuos ties into another aspect of symbolism found in this number. G-d created the universe with נ' שַׁעֲרֵי בִינָה, *50 Gates of Understanding.*[27] The 50 Gates relate to the ascending spiritual levels within the world through which man must pass in order to uncover the inner secrets of creation and in order to comprehend the powers, capabilities, and life forces within.[28]

The Jew must touch the 50th gate that belongs over and above the natural rules of This World.

The number 50 is used as the measure that places something at a distance.

No less than 50 stages of redemption were required to achieve a clean break from the past.

The 50 Gates relate to the ascending spiritual levels through which man must pass.

In a sense, the 50 *Sha'arei Binah* signify the distance of how far removed man is from G-d's wisdom. It is incumbent upon man to pass through these Gates of Understanding in a journey to uncover the Divine wisdom hidden in the words of Torah. This often involves the deductive reasoning of בִּינָה, *understanding*, to derive "one thing from something else."[29] בִּינָה is cognate to בֵּין, *between*,[30] which indicates the gap that man must bridge in order to approaches his Creator.

The count of the Omer is the process of building from the lowly level of an animal to the spiritual heights of a G-dly being.

The 50 days of the *Omer* parallel the 50 *Shaarei Binah*.[31] The word *binah* further relates to בִּנְיָן, *building*.[32] The count of the *Omer* toward Shavuos is the process of building where the Jew builds himself up from the lowly level of an animal up to the spiritual heights of a G-dly being.[33] It is his bid to traverse the 50 gateways of Divine wisdom. He endeavors to transcend the natural and to touch the supernatural realm where he will gain a clearer perception of G-d.

The highest level humanly possible is 49 gates; it is G-d Who enables a person to make the final leap from 49 to 50. The human being who passed through the full 49 gates was Moshe.[34] However, the final 50th gate still lay beyond his grasp. The secret of this ultimate step would lie within the secret nature of *Yovel*.[35]

YOVEL: YEAR 50

Yovel marked the cumulative conclusion of an epoch.

The 7 weekly cycles of 7 days lasting until the 50th day, Shavuos, has its obvious parallel to the 7 *Shemittah,* Sabbatical cycles of 7 years that culminate in the 50th year, *Yovel,* Jubilee Year.[36] *Yovel* marked the cumulative conclusion of an epoch. Everything that had occurred previously — even something termed as lasting *l'olam*, forever[37] — comes to an end. The slate is wiped clean. It returns to its original pristine state to enable the process to begin anew.

Shemittah is classified both as holy and as Shabbos.

Shemittah is classified both as קֹדֶשׁ, *holy*, and as שַׁבָּת, *Shabbos*; *Yovel* is קֹדֶשׁ קָדָשִׁים, *Holy of Holies,* and שַׁבָּת שַׁבָּתוֹן, *Shabbos of Shabbosos*.[38] Actually, *Yovel's* description as שַׁבָּת שַׁבָּתוֹן is shared by the festival of Yom Kippur, *Day of Atonement*.[39] On this date, the Jewish nation was forgiven for the sin of the Golden Calf that had undermined the Torah given on Day 50. A new era began as Israel was given the second set of Tablets, delivered by Moshe on Yom Kippur.[40] This signaled that G-d had forgiven Israel, affirming that He would not destroy them.

The process of *teshuvah*, repentance — itself related to *binah*[41] — is such that sin is eradicated. What happens? A person relates to his transcendental roots, returns to G-d, and emerges as a new creation.[42] Interestingly, there is a total of 50 days of *teshuvah* from Rosh Chodesh Elul (29 days) until the end of Hoshana Rabbah (21 Tishrei).[43]

The word *yovel* also refers to the *shofar*-horn of a ram.[44] Indeed, the 50th year assumed the status of the Jubilee year only once the *shofar* was sounded.[45] The *yovel/shofar* was blown on Yom Kippur[46] of the 50th year. It would herald that people and objects would revert to their original position. Sold fields returned to their original owners. Jewish slaves were released from their captivity.[47] Here they freely return to their true identity.

Yovel replicates the impact of the *shofar* to awaken man toward repentance.[48] The freedom of *Yovel* was unhindered by any constraints. It denotes the transcendental point that stretches above any prior attachment to what came before.

Yovel replicates the impact of the shofar to awaken man toward repentance.

50: ALL-IN-1

In This World, there can be no independent human expression on the 50th level. It remains the ultimate, yet unknowable G-dly dimension. It can be characterized as נִבְדָּל, *elevated* or *apart*, from everything that precedes it. It transcends the natural world and human experience.[49]

In one respect, the 50th is the *uncountable number*. The *Omer* period lasts for 50 days — yet only 49 are to be counted. The counting of 49 *automatically* leads to the arrival of the 50th. This *nivdal* state was reached at Sinai. It truly surpassed everything that came before it.[50] It was on the 50th day, Shavuos, that the union between Israel and G-d, like a marriage, was solemnized.[51]

With this act the Jewish nation supernaturally transcended worldly existence to become one with G-d.[52] Israel achieved this unity when they arrived at Sinai to encamp in a unified state: כְּאִישׁ אֶחָד בְּלֵב אֶחָד, *like a single person with a single heart*.[53] The names of the 12 Tribes of Israel, which were engraved upon the Stones worn by the *Kohen Gadol,* have a total of 50 letters,[54] merged as one entity with their Creator.

Thus, the 50th is the point of arrival. This is where man has come "all the way." This is the ultimate level; man has successfully completed the requisite stages of the natural passage and progressed to transcend up to the G-dly level of eternity. This is the dimension of Torah, of Divine understanding, of true freedom. It is where Israel transcends to truly become one with G-d.

The 50th level remains the ultimate, yet unknowable G-dly dimension.

Israel achieved unity with G-d when they arrived at Sinai to encamp in a unified state.

Man has successfully progressed to transcend up to the G-dly level of eternity.

NOTES

1. See "49: Full Measure."
2. See "7: A Holy Spark."
3. *Ramchal, Derech Hashem* 1:3. The reentry of the soul into the body after revivification is destined to propel man to a higher spiritual level than he could attain in life.
4. See "8: Out of the World."
5. *Berachos* 12b.
6. The root of the word מִצְרַיִם is related to the word מֵיצַר, *straits*, as in the verse, *all her pursuers overtook her within the straits* (בֵּין הַמְּצָרִים) (*Eichah* 1:3).
7. *Zohar* 2, 85b; 3, 262a. See *Sfas Emes, Shabbos HaGadol* 5634, for how the 50 references to the Exodus correspond to the 50 weeks and 50 Shabbosos in every year. See also *Vilna Gaon, Tikkunei Zohar,* p. 84.
8. *Shemos* 3:12.
9. See "49: The Full Measure."
10. Their development is beautifully symbolized in the 50-day ripening period of an apple — an allusion to receiving of Torah. The Midrash notes that the apple takes 50 days to ripen and this occurs in Sivan (*Shir HaShirim Rabbah* 2:2). This is a reference to the 50-day period between Pesach and Shavuos, when the Jewish nation embraced the Torah. (The apple symbolically relates to the declaration *Na'aseh v'nishma*, "We will do and we will hear" — *Shabbos* 88a. See *Tosafos*, ad loc. for how the apple refers to the *esrog*.)
11. *Vayikra* 23:15-16.
12. *Shir HaShirim* 3:11 and *Rashi* ad loc.
13. Mishnah, *Kesubos* 1:2. A divorced or widowed woman who remarries is entitled to half this sum: namely 100 *zuz*. The basic amount of 50 silver *shekels* for a maiden is derived from the laws of the penalty payable by a man who violates or seduces a maiden (*Devarim* 22:29; *Kesubos* 10a).
14. *Maharal, Tiferes Yisrael* 25.
15. *Maharal* ibid. Though the *Omer* count is stated to be for 50 days, only 49 are counted. One does not — indeed, cannot — count the 50th. It is not simply another day in succession to the 49 before it. It is separate and apart; it goes beyond the possible, beyond the countable.
16. *Rokeach, Devarim* 6:7.
17. See *Tanchuma, Pinchas* 15, about how Shemini Atzeres, the 8th day after the onset of Succos, should have ideally been positioned 50 days after Succos in the same way that Shavuos was placed 50 days after Pesach. See "8: Out of This World."
18. *Ramban, Shemos* 25:1 (Introduction to *Terumah*). See "410: First Temple."
19. *Zevachim* 116b. See also *Succah* 53a and *Sifri, Nasso* 42 for how David purchased the site of the altar for 50 *shekalim*.
20. See *Bamidbar* 4:3, 23, 30, 35, 39, 43, 47.
21. *Maharal, Chiddushei Aggados, Rosh Hashanah* 21b. See "8: Out of This World."
22. *Shemos* 26:6. See *Rokeach, Shemos* 26:6, p.141, for how the 50 golden hooks attaching the curtains parallel the 50 times the word *Torah* is mentioned in the singular in *Chumash*.
23. See *Maharal, Nesivos Olam, Nesiv HaTorah* 1 for how the 50th is uncountable, as it belongs to the ethereal, elevated world that is not subordinate to time.
24. *Eruvin* 57b.

25. *Bava Basra* 24b-25a. See *Rambam, Hilchos Beis HaBechirah* 7:13.

26. *Shemos* 20:2.

27. *Rosh Hashanah* 21b; *Nedarim* 38a. "The 50 occasions Exodus is mentioned in the Torah correspond to the 50 Gates of Understanding" (*Vilna Gaon, Aderes Eliyahu, Balak*).

28. *Ramban,* Introduction to *Sefer Bereishis.* See also Vilna Gaon, *Safra D'Tzniusa* 1.

29. See *Rashi, Shemos* 31:3.

30. *Ibn Ezra, Shemos* 31:3; R' S.R. Hirsch, *Bereishis* 41:33.

31. *Vilna Gaon, Aderes Eliyahu, Balak.*

32. See *Niddah* 45b.

33. The *Omer* brought on Pesach was an offering of barley, a grain that is used for animal feed. By contrast, the 2 Breads of Shavuos were made of wheat, a human food. This symbolizes the spiritual transformation from a non-spiritual beast to a spiritual human. See *Sotah* 15b; *Maharal, Tiferes Yisrael* 25.

34. *Rosh Hashanah* 21b. See "49: The Full Measure." Parallel to Moshe's inability to attain all 50 Gates of Understanding, he was unable to pass over the River Jordan, whose width is said to be 50 cubits (*Tosafos, Sotah* 34b) and pass onto even 1 cubit of the ground of the Holy Land (see *Baal HaTurim, Devarim* 3:25 and *Rokeach* ad loc.).

35. *Ramban,* Introduction to *Sefer Bereishis.*

36. *Vayikra* 25:8-13.

37. *Shemos* 21:6; *Kiddushin* 21b. This refers to a Jewish servant who rejected going free after his original 6 years of enslavement.

38. *Maharal, Chiddushei Aggados, Rosh Hashanah* 21b.

39. *Vayikra* 23:32.

40. See *Taanis* 26b expounding the verse, *the day of His wedding* (*Shir HaShirim* 3:11). See *Rashi* ad loc.

41. In the *Amidah,* the blessing of *teshuvah* is juxtaposed to *binah* (*Megillah* 17b). See *Shelah HaKadosh, Chullin, Torah Ohr* 63, *Shelah Toldos HaAdam, Beis Chochmah* (2nd) 24. See R' Tzadok HaKohen, *Pri Tzaddik, Tu B'Av,* 6, as to how the level of 50 Gates of Understanding is the level of knowledge given to a penitent.

42. See R' Yitzchak Hutner, *Pachad Yitzchak, Yom HaKippurim* 1. See *Shelah Toldos HaAdam, Beis Chochmah* (2nd) 24, as to how Yom Kippur is a source of *binah,* returning the past year back to its roots and source.

43. See *Panim Yafos, Vayikra* 16:30.

44. *Rosh Hashanah* 26a and *Rashi, Shemos* 19:13. In the acceptance of Torah at Sinai, an extended blast from the *yovel* (*shofar*) indicated that the *Shechinah* had departed and the people could now ascend the mountain (*Shemos* 19:13). This, too, relates to the cessation of a phase.

45. *Rosh Hashanah* 9b.

46. See *Minchas Chinuch, Mitzvah* 335.

47. *Vayikra* 25:10-13. See also "9: Where to Turn?"

48. On Yom Kippur the 50th and most profound of all gates is opened, the closest level to gain insight into the ways of G-d (*Sfas Emes, Yom Kippur* 5653).

49. Incidentally, we can explain with this the reason that, in the Purim narrative, Haman constructed a gallows that was specifically 50 cubits high (*Esther* 5:14). Symbolically, the wicked Haman presented himself as a deity who "supposedly" was not subject to the natural law of the land — namely, that he was on the transcendental 50th level (*Maharal, Ohr Chodosh, Esther* 5:14). See also *Maharal, Ohr Chodosh,* p.175 and *Be'er Hagolah* 4:14 for the symbolism of this 50-cubit gallows being constructed from the wood of Noach's Ark (*Yalkut Shimoni,* 1056). See also R' Tzadok HaKohen, *Pri Tzaddik, Purim,* 2, for how Haman's gallows of 50 cubits corresponds to the 50 Gates of Understanding.

50. *Maharal, Rosh Hashanah* 21b, *Chiddushei Aggados.*

51. One who assaults a maiden must give her 50 coins of silver to marry her (*Devarim* 22:29). This is

parallel to Israel receiving Torah on Shavuos, the 50th day after leaving Egypt (*Rokeach, Bereishis* 32:11).

52. See *Tikkunei Zohar*, end of *Tikkun* 22.
53. *Shemos* 19:2 and *Rashi* ad loc.
54. The 12 Tribes of Israel were represented on the *Avnei Shoam*, the stones affixed to the shoulders of the High Priest's Apron. There were 6 names, consisting of 25 letters, on each of the 2 stones, a total of 50 letters (*Sotah* 36a-b).

60 IN PRINCIPLE

60 typifies the klal, general principle or congregation.

It is the generalization that is responsible for shaping identity and concern for the national interest.

FROM SIX TO SIXTY

The natural world that opens up into 6 directions conceptually expands to reach a state of wholeness within each direction.

THE NUMBER 60 RELATES TO THE SYMBOLISM OF THE NUMBER 6.

We have noted that 6 is associated with the complete physical expression in the natural world.[1] This state of completion is more fully represented in the number 60. Here the natural world that opens up into 6 directions (denoted by the number 6) conceptually expands to reach a state of wholeness (symbolized by the number 10) within each direction (60 = 6 x 10).[2]

The fullness of 60 as the expansion of 6 is meaningfully reflected in one of its mathematical properties: 60 is the first number that is a factor of all numbers from 1 to 6 (1, 2, 3, 4, 5, 6).

$$1 \times 60 = 60 \qquad 4 \times 15 = 60$$
$$2 \times 30 = 60 \qquad 5 \times 12 = 60$$
$$3 \times 20 = 60 \qquad 6 \times 10 = 60$$

60: AGE OF SENIORITY

The Jewish census in the Wilderness only counted individuals who could serve in the army: every man between 20 and 60.

The Jewish census in the Wilderness only counted those individuals who could be enlisted to serve in the army: every man between the ages of 20 and 60.[3] Here the upper end of the count was 60 years old. This identical age bracket was also used in the laws of consecrating *Arachin*, Valuations, when someone pledged the "monetary value" [of a particular person] as a gift to the Temple. The Torah specifies fixed monetary amounts based on gender and age; one bracket designated for a person between the ages of 20 and 60.[4]

Just as 6 signifies the extent of man's productivity in his labors during the 6 days of the week, 60 is similarly the "age limit" of man's productivity in terms of years in the physical world. Indeed, the Mishnah characterizes 60 as the age of זִקְנָה, *seniority*.[5]

Surviving past 60 indicates that one has not warranted a premature death.

Surviving past 60 is considered a milestone in human life. It indicates that a person has not warranted the Heavenly punishment of a premature death.[6] The word זָקֵן is a contraction of the words זֶה שֶׁקָנָה (חָכְמָה), *the one who has acquired (wisdom)*.[7] The weakening of the body means that the intellectual faculties of man can now take over and gain ascendancy.[8]

60: TRACTATES

The expansion of 6 into 60 is similarly apparent in the acquisition of Torah wisdom in the Oral Torah. The שִׁשָׁה סִדְרֵי מִשְׁנָה, *6 Orders of the Mishnah*, that were formulated by Rabbi Yehudah the Prince[9] are subdivided and arranged as a total of 60 מַסֶּכְתּוֹת, *tractates*.[10] This, too, serves as an extension of the Torah laws that are then to be enacted in the physical realm. The 60 tractates are the completed works of the 6 Orders of the Mishnah.

IN GENERAL

T HE COMPLETE EXPRESSION INTO THE NATURAL WORLD WITHIN THE number 6 extends to 60. Whereas 6 is completion on an individual scale, 60 is a synonym for the complete כְּלָל in its dual meaning of *general principle* or *communal*.[11] As such, it is the fitting number used to categorize the Jewish nation.

60 is a synonym for the complete כְּלָל in its dual meaning of "general principle" or "communal."

60 MYRIADS: KLAL YISRAEL

The number 60 relates to the full expression of כְּלַל יִשְׂרָאֵל, *the Jewish congregation*. The count of Israelites assembled at Sinai — as numbered in the category of men between the ages of 20 and 60 — was 600,000 strong, often termed שִׁשִּׁים רִבּוֹא, *60 myriads*.[12] The symbol of the "collective general roots of Israel," the number *60 myriads* was the hallmark of G-d's Chosen Nation.

The number "60 myriads" was the hallmark of G-d's Chosen Nation.

Significantly, this number is said to constitute *the perfect, unified national identity of Israel*.[13] The Torah was not given to the *Avos*; spiritual greatness notwithstanding, they did not constitute a nation. The Divine Revelation was exclusive to the Jewish People only after Israel came into existence as a *klal*. This was realized once they had reached a complete form as symbolized by their number of 60 myriads.[14] Here their national identity was established.

Israel came into existence as a klal, symbolized by their number of 60 myriads.

60: PRIESTLY BLESSINGS

The Priestly Blessings are composed of 3 verses, comprising a total of 60 letters.

Another example of 60 applying to a communal setting is found in the blessings bestowed by Aharon and the priests on the Jewish nation. בִּרְכַּת כֹּהֲנִים, *Priestly Blessings*, are composed of 3 verses, comprising a total of 60 letters.[15]

The blessings of Yaakov and Moshe were customized to each individual tribe and highlighted each tribe's particular strengths and specific areas of development. By contrast, the blessings within *Birchas Kohanim* form a generic, "one-size-fits-all" blessing. This would empower Israel as a whole community by identifying the criteria necessary to fulfill their potential.[16]

A QUESTION OF IDENTITY

The standing of an individual within the wider setting is often characterized by the relationship between the numbers 1 and 60.

WE HAVE OBSERVED THAT 60 RELATES TO THE COLLECTIVE communal identity of the Jewish nation. The standing of an individual within the wider setting is often characterized by the relationship between the numbers 1 and 60. They respectively denote the interface between the individual and the community.

LOSS OF IDENTITY: 60 TO 1

The importance of the group calls for the individuality of each particular component to be subsumed in the face of the communal setting. Generally, the public concern identified with the number 60 is powerful enough to render the impact or presence of a פְּרָט, *individual component*, impotent until it no longer counts.

This principle is beautifully found in halachah in the laws of בִּיטֵל, *nullification*. Here the greater quantity is the factor that determines the entire status of a mixture of forbidden and permitted foods. The

The measure by which a prohibited food is nullified is בָּטֵל בְּשִׁשִּׁים.

measure by which a prohibited food is nullified is בָּטֵל בְּשִׁשִּׁים, *a ratio of 60 to 1 negates*.[17]

For example, if a piece of nonkosher meat accidentally falls into a pot of kosher meat that contains 60 times the volume of this non-kosher meat, then the food is deemed kosher and a Jew may eat from the mixture.[18] Halachically, the identity of the individual forbidden food no longer exists; it has become subsumed into the greater amount of 60 that comes to determine the collective status.[19]

1/60: BORDERLINE OF EXISTENCE

The ratio of 60:1 sweeps away the identity of the opposing minority. Something that is no greater than $^1/_{60}$ of something else symbolically means that it exists as part of something greater — but only just.

The Talmud lists many fascinating examples of matters that tangentially relate to each other. Egypt is $^1/_{60}$ of Cush; Cush is $^1/_{60}$ of the world; the world is $^1/_{60}$ of Gan; Gan is $^1/_{60}$ of Eden; and Eden is $^1/_{60}$ of *Gehinnom*, Purgatory.[20] Other illustrations include the idea that dreams are $^1/_{60}$ of prophecy, sleep is $^1/_{60}$ of death, the weekly Shabbos is $^1/_{60}$ of *Olam Haba*, fire is $^1/_{60}$ of *Gehinnom*, and the sweetness of honey is $^1/_{60}$ of *mahn*, manna.[21]

Just as 60 is the age at which one reaches the upper limit of the Jewish census, $^1/_{60}$ stands at the threshold of existence. The proportion of $^1/_{60}$ represents the lowest denomination that *still* retains a resemblance to and the slightest of connections with the entity to which it is compared. Here the individual component (1) still belongs to and reflects the group (60). Anything less than $^1/_{60}$ would mean a loss of identity.

The proportion $^1/_{60}$ represents the lowest denomination that still retains a resemblance to and connection with the entity to which it is compared.

60: OF PUBLIC INTEREST

Parallel to the principle of בָּטֵל בְּשִׁשִּׁים, where the individual sheds his identity before the whole, the individual Jew should similarly be willing to negate his personal interests and desires. Of course, the primary concern of any individual is his spiritual development. In the words of the Mishnah: *If I am not [concerned] for myself, who will be [concerned] for me?*[22] Nevertheless, he must be willing to selflessly nullify his personal preference before the public need of the congregation — the 60 myriads.

Dedication to communal needs and the betterment of *Klal Yisrael* must be a constant concern for every Jew who identifies with the Jewish congregation. That means not seeing himself exclusively as an individual but to proudly identify himself as a member of the collective whole grouping of *Klal Yisrael*.

Dedication to communal needs and the betterment of Klal Yisrael must be a constant concern for every Jew who identifies with the Jewish congregation.

NOTES

1. See "6: It's Only Natural."
2. *Maharal, Gevuros Hashem* 12.
3. *Bamidbar* 1:3. See *Bava Basra* 121b and "20: Manhood."
4. *Vayikra* 27:3.
5. *Pirkei Avos* 5:21.
6. *Moed Katan* 28a.
7. *Kiddushin* 32b and *Rashi* ad loc.
8. *Maharal, Derech Chaim* 5:21.
9. See "6: It's Only Natural."
10. The verse, *60 queens, 80 concubines, and innumerable maidens* (*Shir HaShirim* 6:8) refers to the 60 tractates of the Mishnah, 80 chapters of *Toras Kohanim* (which was divided in the past into 80 chapters; see *Torah Temimah Shir HaShirim* 6:8.), and unlimited *Toseftas* (*Torah Temimah* ibid) (*Shir HaShirim Rabbah* 6:9). In the division within our text, there are actually different ways of grouping the tractates to yield 60, 61, or 63. See *Meiri*, Introduction to *Avos*, who states that the honorific גָּאוֹן (*Gaon*) was bestowed on someone who had mastered all 60 tractates (numerical value of גָּאוֹן).
11. See *Maharal, Tiferes Yisrael* 4, 18, *Be'er Hagolah* 5 (125) (p. 89 in London edition).
12. See "600,000: The Jewish Nation."
13. *Maharal, Gevuros Hashem* 3 and 12.
14. *Maharal, Tiferes Yisrael* 17. See "600,000: The Jewish Nation."
15. *Bamidbar* 6:24-26.
16. The 60 letters of *Bircas Kohanim* are alluded to in the verse, *Behold the bed of the King of Peace, 60 of Israel's mightiest warriors surround it* (*Shir HaShirim* 3:7); (see *Shir HaShirim Rabbah* 3:11 and *Tanchuma, Nasso* 16).
17. *Chullin* 98a.
18. *Rambam, Hilchos Ma'acholos Assuros* 15:17.
19. See *Maharal, Chiddushei Aggados, Bava Basra* 73b (Vol. 3, pp. 88-89).
20. *Pesachim* 94a.
21. *Berachos* 57b.
22. *Pirkei Avos* 1:14.

70
THE SUM OF THE PARTS

70 is the sum of all the constituent parts.

When broken down, the whole is apportioned into individual pieces.

It is then up to Israel, the "singular nation," to unite the 70 disparate components in the world, in the service of G-d.

PARTS OF A WHOLE

70 contains within it the full range of components.

THE NUMBER 70 RELATES TO THE PARTICULARS THAT MAKE UP A whole.

70 is a multiple of 7 which we have noted are the number of parts necessary to attain a specific purpose.[1] In magnifying this concept, 70 similarly contains within it the full range of components.[2]

There are several well-known illustrations of this, most notably within man's life and in the Torah that governs and defines that life.

70: A LIFETIME

The conventional measure given for a generation is a period of 70 years.

The average human lifespan is associated with this number. In the words of the Psalmist, *The days of our years are 70 years.*[3] The conventional measure given for a generation is a period of 70 years.[4] The chief proponent of this concept was King David who lived for exactly 70 years.[5] The whole of man's life — namely all 70-years — must be dedicated to holiness.[6] By extension, reaching the age of 70 years is now considered the point in life at which a person can be said to have attained *the fullness of age.*[7]

70: FORCES WITHIN MAN

A lifetime of 70 years used to serve G-d has its parallel in the 70 forces within man. There are said to be 70 distinctive כוחות, *qualities*, within a human being.[8] Each one of these characteristics must be developed independently. The combination of all 70 traits enables man to fully reveal all facets of his personality.

Man embarks upon the course to fulfill his Jewish identity all 70 years of his life.

The wholeness of man is realized in the parallel these 70 forces have to the 70 "forces of illumination" within the *neshamah*, soul. After the birth of a boy, this light is unveiled following the removal of the foreskin at *bris milah*, circumcision.[9] It is from this point that man embarks upon the course to fulfill his Jewish identity all 70 years of his life.

TORAH: 70 FACES

Torah study is the engine that powers the 70 forces within man during his 70 years. The many dimensions of Divine Revelation within the infinite word of G-d are expressed as the שִׁבְעִים פָּנִים לַתּוֹרָה, *70 faces of Torah*.[10] There are multifaceted layers of depth within every letter and word of Torah. Studying Torah is the most direct way to access the Word of G-d. These 70 dimentions of Torah must be put into practical determining in deciding Torah law.

SANHEDRIN: 70 ELDERS

The highest judicial authority in the Land was the Sanhedrin, *Great Court*. This court was an assembly of 70 elders.[11] The precedent for the Sanhedrin was set in the Wilderness where Moshe assembled together 70 זְקֵנִים, *elders*.[12] (One allusion to these elders was the 70 date palms of Eilim found in the Children of Israel's sojourn in the Wilderness.[13])

The 70 elders in the Sanhedrin — who have their parallel in the Heavenly Court[14] — were to guarantee that every possible opinion, without exception, was taken into the equation. All viewpoints were considered within their deliberations to determine the Torah law.[15]

The 70 elders in the Sanhedrin were to guarantee that every possible opinion was taken into the equation.

DISPERSION

WE HAVE SEEN HOW 70 RELATES TO THE PARTS OF THE WHOLE. But these 70 constituent parts of the whole do not remain in a constant state. There is the danger that these 70 components, though originally 1 entity, may splinter to form disparate parts. Often this divergence leads to unmitigated disaster.

Primary examples of this phenomenon include the *Dor HaPhlagah*, Era of Dispersion, and the first *galus*, exile, from the Holy Land.

There is the danger that these 70 components, may splinter to form disparate parts.

70 NATIONS; 70 LANGUAGES

The generation into which Avraham was born was unified, as the whole of human civilization were one people speaking a common tongue. But rather than use this unity as the tool to serve the One G-d, this idolatrous generation constructed the Tower of Bavel to wage an ideological battle against the Holy One.

G-d frustrated their plans by dispersing them across the world.[16] They were divided into 70 nations who would speak 70 distinct languages.[17] Each nation's unique identity and distinguishing features have their parallel in their corresponding 70 administering angels in the spiritual realm.[18]

Each nation's unique identity and distinguishing features were their parallel in their corresponding 70 administering angels in the spiritual realm.

The dispersion from Bavel led to a state of *confusion* and of *mixture* — which are the actual meanings of the word *Bavel*.[19] This divergence away from G-d, to worship many idols and forces of nature, led to the nations' expulsion from one central habitat into many directions.

BAbyLONIAN EXILE: 70 yEARS

The dispersion from one central point also had a later historical application in the first Jewish exile from the Holy Land. Nebuchadnezzar, the Babylonian king, swept Israel into exile and ordered the destruction of the First Temple. In the fulfilment of Yirmiyah's prophecy, the length of the Babylonian exile would last for 70 years.[20]

The Exile resulted from Israel's failure to use the 70 forces within their psyche to access the 70 faces of Torah and observe its law.

Due to the non-observance of the 70 *Shemittah* cycles during their occupation of the Holy Land, the Jewish people were sentenced to a 70-year exile during which the land would remain fallow and in a state of desolation.[21] The Exile resulted from Israel's abject failure to use the 70 forces within their psyche to access the 70 faces of Torah and observe its law as determined by the 70 elders of the Sanhedrin throughout the 70 years of their lives.

70 VS. 1

All the many forces whose single Source was G-d must be unified to once again reflect His Oneness.

THE OBJECTIVES OF CREATION IS יְחוּד ה', *MAKING MANIFEST THE Oneness of G-d*.[22] But dispersion and exile, as reflected in the division into 70 parts, actually contradict this ultimate goal.

What is the solution? All the many forces whose single Source was G-d must be unified to once again reflect His Oneness. However, in order to reach the state of perfection and completion, the multiple parts of 70, like 7 before it, must all be present and proper and unified as 1.

This, in fact, goes to the heart of the conflict between the 70 world nations and the Jewish people, which will determine the world's destiny.

70 wolves vs. 1 sheep

The dispersion of human civilization into 70 nations did not affect Avraham, forefather of the Jewish people. Single-handedly teaching monotheism to the idolatrous 70 nations in the Generation of the Dispersion, Avraham was himself suitably identified with the number 1.[23]

Whereas the other 70 nations converse in their respective 70 languages, the language of Avraham's descendants was *Lashon HaKodesh*, the unique Holy Language, through which G-d spoke.[24] In turn, the existence of Israel, "the singular nation in the world,"[25] is linked to revealing the One G-d in the universe.

Throughout history, the 70 nations have opposed *the nation that dwells alone.*[26] Israel's precarious existence among her enemies is likened to the miraculous survival of 1 lone sheep surrounded by 70 ravenous wolves.[27] In general spiritual terms, the 70 nations correspond to 70 impure forces[28] that ideologically oppose the idea of unifying the 70 individual traits within man in the service of G-d.[29]

Avraham was himself identified with the number 1.

Throughout history, the 70 nations have opposed the nation that dwells alone.

70 OXEN VS. 1 OX

The journey to return the 70 to 1 whole is spearheaded by the Jewish nation it is richly alluded to in the sacrificial offerings of Succos. During this 7-day Festival, a total of 70 oxen were offered on the Altar.[30] But on the 8th day, the Festival of Shemini Atzeres, only 1 ox was brought.[31] This portrays the transition toward the Messianic era — the end of Exile — as the 70 nations of the world, represented by the 70 oxen, recognize the truth of the world view of the Jewish nation — represented by the lone ox of the 8th day.[32]

Israel is perfectly suited to take the sum of 70 parts and make it into one whole they carry this inner ability within their national makeup. This began with Yaakov's family migrating to Egypt. The Torah describes the 70 souls in the singular form (נֶפֶשׁ, soul, rather than נְפָשׁוֹת, souls) to express that they were essentially one unit.[33]

The journey to return the 70 to 1 whole is richly alluded to in the sacrificial offerings of Succos.

Israel is responsible for uniting the dispersed components of the world.

Like the 70 elders overseen by Moshe and the 70 sages of the Sanhedrin who also had a leader presiding over them,[34] so too, is Israel responsible for uniting the dispersed components of the world.[35] They are charged with leading mankind toward the universal acceptance of G-d.

The Jewish nation will educate the 70 nations to find their spiritual fulfillment on Succos, also called *Chag HaAsif*, Festival of Ingathering,[36] whose forces are likewise "gathered." This Festival culminates in the single day of Shemini Atzeres whose messianic overtones depict the Oneness of G-d.[37]

WHERE 70 BECOMES 1

The final endpoint of Creation is where Israel, observing the Torah, returns to Jerusalem, the city of holiness, in the worship of G-d. Appropriately, there are 70 Names of G-d, 70 names of Israel, 70 names of Torah, and 70 names of Jerusalem.[38] Nevertheless, all these parts come together in a whole, unified state.

The Jewish people exist to integrate all the forces in the universe toward the One G-d.

The Jewish people exist to integrate all the many forces in the universe toward the One G-d. In man's inner world, all his 70 forces and all the years of his life must be directed toward the single goal: *You shall love HASHEM, your G-d, with **all** your heart, with **all** your soul, and with **all** your resources.*[39] In the outside world, Israel will reunite the dispersed 70 nations to fulfill the 70 facets of Torah[40] and proclaim the Oneness of G-d in the Messianic Era: ... *on that day, G-d will be One and His Name will be One.*[41]

Then, as the saying goes, the whole will be greater than the sum of the parts.

NOTES

1. See, e.g., *On one road they will go out toward you; on 7 roads they will flee from you* (*Devarim* 28:7). See "7: A Holy Spark."
2. See *Maharal, Tiferes Yisrael* 31, who differentiates between 7 as a "specific" form compared to 70 (the multiple of 7 according to units of 10) that is a more "general" form. He describes 70 as "multiplicity that converges into 1 point."
3. *Tehillim* 90:10.
4. *Maharal, Netzach Yisrael* 17. Other examples include: Choni HaMaagel waking up after 70 years to find his entire generation deceased (*Taanis* 23a); a star that misguides sailors once every 70

years (*Horayos* 10a); once in 70 years, the incidence of execution by the *Sanhedrin* (*Makkos* 7a); and a 70-year Roman circus performance (*Avodah Zarah* 11b).

5. See *I Divrei HaYamim* 29:28. All his years were actually a gift from Adam, who lived 930 years; namely 70 years shy of 1,000 years (*Bamidbar Rabbah* 14:24; *Zohar* 1, 91b).

6. In fact, the 70 years correspond to 70 days in every year that are imbued with extra holiness, namely, 52 weekly days of Shabbos and 18 Festivals (in the Holy Land this comprises 7 days of Pesach, 1 day of Shavuos, 1 day of Rosh Hashanah (the 2 days are considered one long day; see *Tur, Orach Chaim* 600; *Shulchan Aruch, Orach Chaim* 393:1), 1 day of Yom Kippur, 7 days of Succos, and 1 day of Shimini Atzeres (*Bamidbar* Rabbah 14:24).

7. *Pirkei Avos* 5:24.

8. See *Vilna Gaon, Yeshayah* 11:1.

9. *Zohar* 1, 80b. The 318 forces accompanying Avraham in battle (*Bereishis* 14:14) metaphorically refer to the 248 bodily limbs and 70 illuminations of the soul (*Sfas Emes, Lech Lecha* 5661).

10. *Bamidbar Rabbah* 13:15. See also *Zohar* 1, *Bereishis* 47b, which states that there are 70 facets of Torah. The concept of "face" denotes revelation of Divine Providence. Conversely, the conceal-ment of the Divine Hand is depicted as *I will surely hide My Face* (*Devarim* 31:18).

11. Mishnah, *Sanhedrin* 1:6.

12. *Bamidbar* 11:24 and *Shemos* 24:1, 9.

13. Ibid. 15:27 and *Rashi* ad loc., quoting the *Mechilta*.

14. *Sifri, Beha'aloscha* 92. See also *Sfas Emes, Shemini* 5651.

15. *Ramban, Bamidbar* 11:16.

16. *Bereishis* 11:1-9.

17. See ibid. 10, where all 70 descendants of Noach are enumerated.

18. *Ramban, Bamidbar* 11:16; see also *Pirkei DeRabbi Eliezer* Ch. 24.

19. *Bereishis* 11:9.

20. *Yirmiyahu* 29:10; *Daniel* 9:2; *II Divrei HaYamim* 36:21.

21. *Vayikra* 26:33. See *Rashi*, ibid. 25:18.

22. See *Ramchal, Daas Tevunos.* 42, 124, 166.

23. *Yechzekel* 33:24. See "1: The One and Only." Interestingly, Avraham emerged out of the 70 nations dispersed into the world and was born to his idol-worshipping father Terach when Terach was 70 years old (*Bereishis* 11:26; *Bamidbar Rabbah* 14:24).

24. *Lashon HaKodesh* is not just another language. It is the Divine language of Creation and the Torah and thus relates to objective reality. All other languages are subjective, namely from the perspec-tive of man. See also *Binyan Yehoshua, Avos D'Rabbi Nassan* 37:2.

25. Shabbos Minchah *Amidah.*

26. *Bamidbar* 23:9.

27. *Esther Rabbah* 10:11; *Tanchuma, Toldos* 5.

28. *Sfas Emes, Devarim* 5631.

29. *Michtav MeiEliyahu* 3, pp. 212-213. The 70-member Sanhedrin, who were required to be conver-sant in all 70 languages (*Megillah* 13b; *Menachos* 65a), were to negate the evil schemes devised by the 70 nations (*Midrash HaGadol, Bamidbar* 11:16).

30. There were 13 animals offered on the first day, with 1 fewer offered on each successive day (*Bamidbar* 29:12-32).

31. Ibid. 29:35-6.

32. See *Succah* 55b.

33. *Bereishis* 46:15-27; *Shemos* 1:5; *Devarim* 10:22. The 70 migrants correspond to the 70 nations and languages (*Rashi, Devarim* 32:8) and to the 70 angels ruling over the Jewish nation in exile (*Yalkut Reuveni, Bamidbar* 75). Note that the Egyptians mourned Yaakov's death for 70 days (*Bereishis* 50:3).

34. See Mishnah, *Sanhedrin* 1:6 about the court comprising a total of 71 members.
35. *Rabbeinu Bachya, Bereishis* 46:27. See *Ramchal, Maamar HaChochmah* for how the future Divine Revelation is contingent upon the victory of good over evil and of Israel being dominant over the 70 non-Jewish nations.
36. *Shemos* 23:16.
37. See "8: Out of This World."
38. *Bamidbar Rabbah* 14:24. See also *Midrash Osiyos DeRabbi Akiva* for a detailed list of matters related to the number 70.
39. *Devarim* 6:5.
40. Every commandment subdivided, like a hammer smashing a rock, into 70 languages (*Shabbos* 88b). The Divine word at Sinai split into 70 languages and was heard throughout the world (*Maharal, Tiferes Yisrael* 31). Later, when crossing the Jordan into Holy Land, the Torah laws were inscribed in 70 languages onto stone monuments in order to be accessible to members of every nation (*Sotah* 32a, based on *Devarim* 27:8).
41. *Zechariah* 14:9.

80

WITH ALL YOUR MIGHT

80 is identified with might.

It denotes man's ability to extend himself
and overpower the opposition.

As an extension of the number 8,
80 relates to reaching beyond the
limitations of the natural.

THE MIGHTY

The number 80 is the number associated with *gevurah*, might.

80: OVERPOWERING

Might refers to a situation in which one party proves to be more powerful than something else.

The quality associated with man reaching the age of 80 years is that of power or might.[1] Simply put, this refers to the ability of man to overcome any obstacle that stands in the way. In dealing with an enemy, for example, *gevurah* enables a man to overpower his opponent. The power that he wields over an antagonist indicates great strength. *Might* refers to a situation in which one party proves to be more powerful and the ability to gain the upper hand.

The ultimate gevurah applies only to G-d.

Obviously, the ultimate *gevurah* is wielded only by G-d, Who, in rabbinic literature, is described with the phrase מִפְּי הַגְּבוּרָה, *from the Almighty*.[2] In other words, G-d is the One with Absolute Might. He called Creation into existence and can easily overpower any force at will by negating its existence or by other Divine means.

Where this phrase is used to describe man as the "mighty one," it need not be exclusively identified with the powerful soldier who uses his physical strength to defeat his external foe. It is equally applicable to an internal show of strength exercised by one who upholds the Word of G-d to overpower his Evil Inclination by not sinning: *Who is the* גִּבּוֹר *[mighty one]? One who overpowers his inclination.*[3]

80: MAGICAL POWERS

One negative application of gevurah can be found in the Torah prohibition regarding the use of black magic.

One negative application of *gevurah* can be found in the Torah prohibition regarding the use of magic and the black arts.[4] The Hebrew term כְּשׁוּף, *magic*, is a contraction of the phrase שֶׁמַּכְחִישִׁין פַּמַלְיָא שֶׁל מַעְלָה, *they coerce the Heavenly spiritual agents.*[5]

Black magic employs the trait of *gevurah* to manipulate forces in the spiritual realm so that they do man's bidding. It is the imposition of unnatural authority over these forces. The Talmud relates the story of the great scholar Shimon ben Shetach, who captured and hanged

80 witches on one day.[6] Here the number 80 is found in the context of *gevurah* as it relates to overcoming magic.

The country that was best known as the hotbed of witchcraft was Egypt.[7] The Egyptians made use of magical forces to overpower others with magicians as the king's special advisers. Egypt imposed its authority over other civilizations to become the superpower of the ancient world. They enslaved the Children of Israel for 210 years.[8] They used using magical, supernatural might to prevent any slave from escaping.[9]

Ironically, the magical application of *gevurah* used by the Egyptians was undermined by the G-dly nation of Israel. The Jewish People were able to survive and thrive; they were not beholden to this magic. Yaakov's favorite son, Yosef, established the precedent for the Jewish nation to later survive the Egyptian exile. Though sold into slavery, Yosef became viceroy at the age of 30 and held that position until his death at the age of 110. He ruled for a total of 80 years.[10]

Yosef became viceroy at the age of 30 and ruled for a total of 80 years.

Moreover, the Exodus began when Moshe was appointed leader to execute the 10 Plagues leading to the release of Israel. Pharaoh was initially unimpressed by the miracles, summoning his magicians to perform similar feats. The Plagues that would overpower the earlier might of Egyptian magic arose from Moshe's leadership which began when he was exactly 80 years old.[11]

Moshe's leadership began when he was exactly 80 years old.

SURPASSING ALL EXPECTATIONS

Gevurah refers to the circumstances in which man goes beyond his natural boundaries.

WE HAVE SEEN THAT THE NUMBER 80 REFERS TO THE MIGHT associated with overpowering another force. By extension, *gevurah* specifically relates to the circumstances where man goes beyond his natural boundaries and where he extends himself by asserting his control over others. This taps into the symbolism of 80 that overreaches and surpasses 70.

70 AND 80; 7 AND 8

The Psalmist associates 70 and 80 in the context of the age of man: *The days of our years are 70 years, or if through gevurah, 80 years.*[12] The natural span of human life is set at 70 years.[13] Con-

One whose age
extends beyond
70 up to 80 is
given special
strength and
vigor by G-d.

sequently, one whose age extends beyond 70 up to 80 — the next number in a series of 10s — is given special strength and vigor by G-d. It means that man's existence transcends the ordinary allotted lifespan. In this respect, he has the fortitude to overpower the confines of nature with the strength to stretch beyond.

The development from 70 to 80 mirrors the conceptual transition from 7 to 8 — namely, extending from the fullness of the natural realm[14] (7) to that which goes beyond the confines of nature (8).

80: priesthood

The Kohen
Gadol, who
wore a total
of 8 garments
epitomizes
the level of
transcendence
within the
Temple.

The number 8 is the symbol of transcendence in a general sense. This finds more particular expression in the number 80.[15]

One famous example is the *Kohen Gadol*, High Priest, who wore a total of 8 garments. He epitomizes the level of transcendence within the Temple — most specifically, his entry into the *Kodesh HaKodashim*, Holy of Holies.[16] By extension, there are many rabbinic statements linking *Kehunah*, Priesthood, in general, and in particular, the *Kohen Gadol*, to the number 80 and higher multiples of 80, as a reflection of the transcendental number 8.

❖ During the Second Temple, Yochanan Kohen Gadol served as the High Priest for 80 years before he became a Sadducee.[17]

❖ 80 pairs of brothers who were *Kohanim* married 80 pairs of sisters who were the daughters of *Kohanim*.[18]

❖ The righteous gentile Dama ben Nesina refused to wake his father to access a precious stone needed for the *Choshen*, Breastplate, one of the 8 garments of the High Priest, despite being offered an exorbitant sum of 800,000 dinars.[19]

❖ 8,000 young *Kohanim* were slaughtered upon the seething blood of the prophet Zechariah.[20]

80: to excel

The force of
might within
the number 80
is not exclusive
to the Jewish
priesthood.

The force of might within the number 80 is not exclusive to the Jewish priesthood. The penchant to excel is an inbuilt drive — one that is deeply and often unconsciously buried deep within the Jewish psyche. Throughout history, in every endeavor in which they have dabbled, Jews have excelled like no other people.

Jews have always been at the forefront in attempts to bravely push the boundaries — even when dealing with secular, academic, or scientific disciplines. Historians have marveled at their accomplishments that are truly disproportionate to their miniscule size. Again and again, the Jewish nation refuse to conform to natural rules. They regularly confound all expectations placed upon them.

Their capacity to mightily overpower opposition is best employed in religious matters. This sees a Jew conquering his Evil Inclination, triumphing over personal adversity, and living a supernatural existence by observing the exalted level of Torah.

The capacity to mightily overpower opposition is best employed in religious matters.

NOTES

1. *Pirkei Avos* 5:25.
2. See, e.g., *Megillah* 31b.
3. *Pirkei Avos* 4:1.
4. *Shemos* 22:17, *Vayikra* 20:27, *Devarim* 18:9-13.
5. *Sanhedrin* 67b.
6. Ibid. 45b and *Yerushalmi, Chagigah* 2:2.
7. *Shabbos* 104b.
8. See "210: The Iron Furnace."
9. R' Tzadok HaKohen, *Pri Tzaddik, Parashas Shekalim* 1.
10. See *Bereishis* 41:46, 50:22.
11. *Shemos* 7:7.
12. *Tehillim* 90:10.
13. See "70: The Sum of the Parts."
14. See "7: A Holy Spark."
15. *Maharal, Netzach Yisrael* 7.
16. See "8: Out of This World."
17. *Berachos* 29a.
18. Ibid. 44a.
19. *Kiddushin* 31a. Another opinion cited in the Talmud states that the profit would have been 600,000 golden *dinars*.
20. *Eichah Rabbasi* 2:4.

98
The
ADMONITION

98 are the number of curses
in the Admonition of
Mishneh Torah
(Book of Devarim).

THE CURSES

THE NUMBER 98 IS THE NUMBER OF CURSES MENTIONED IN THE second Admonition of the Torah.

98: DOUBLE DOSE

There are two instances of *Tochachah*, Admonition, in the *Chumash*. (*Tochachah* is derived from the word *toi'cheach*, rebuke[1]) The Jewish People were warned of the Divine retribution that would be meted out to them should they violate the word of G-d. Instead of being the beneficiaries of untold blessing and goodness, their failure to live according to the ways of Torah would lead to relentless suffering.

The First Admonition is found in *Parashas Bechukosai* at the end of *Toras Kohanim* (Book of *Vayikra*).[2] Here the punishments include being struck down by enemies, the fertile land drying up, the plague of pestilence, rampant abject poverty, the desolation of cities and sanctuaries, and the Jewish People being exiled among the nations of the world. The Admonition contains 7 series of afflictions and a total of 49 curses.[3] Nevertheless, this Torah passage concludes with an optimistic message. Despite their suffering, the Jewish People will not be rejected or obliterated, as G-d will recall His *bris*, His covenant.

The Second Admonition is recorded in *Parashas Ki Savo* within *Mishneh Torah* (Book of *Devarim*).[4] This is comprised of a double dose of curses, (49 x 2 =) 98, that contain all manner of suffering and atrocities.[5] These are powerfully delivered in vivid and shocking detail. Striking images include the Jewish nation being struck down with madness, Jewish carcasses becoming food for birds and beasts, the confiscation of a Jew's family (wife, sons, daughters) and possessions (ox, donkey, field). In contrast to the First Admonition, here there are no comforting words of solace.

FIRST CURSE VS. SECOND CURSE

There are several key distinctions between the two sets of Admonitions. The First Admonition (in *Toras Kohanim*) was transmitted

directly from G-d through Moshe. By comparison, the Second Admonition (in *Mishneh Torah*) was said by Moshe himself (through *Ruach HaKodesh*, Divine Inspiration).[6]

These two passages refer to the two exiles following the destruction of the Temples. The First Admonition refers specifically to the years leading to the destruction of the First Temple and the Babylonian exile. Thus, the Torah records that the Jews would ultimately not comply with the laws of *Shemittah*, the Sabbatical year, and how the land would finally have its rest — by lying fallow as its inhabitants were driven into exile. The upbeat ending possibly alludes to the reprieve as a portion of the Jewish People would return after 7 decades (70 years) of exile.[7] By contrast, the Second Admonition refers to the fading years of the Second Temple and the protracted impact of the Roman exile, which has stretched out almost two millennia.[8] This exile cruelly appears to go on with no end in sight.[9]

The Second Admonition is a reference to the waning years of the Second Temple and the protracted impact of the Roman exile.

There is another important distinction. The formulation of the First Admonition is in the plural (*lashon rabbim*). Here G-d addresses the Jewish People *as many different and unique individuals.* By contrast, the Second Admonition is phrased in the singular (*lashon yachid*). In so doing, G-d addressed the totality of the Congregation of Israel, not as an amalgamation of many individuals, but as a *unified, national entity.*[10] This all-inclusive message applies to the Jewish People in all future generations.[11]

YEAR'S END

Ezra the Scribe, who lived at the beginning of the Second Temple period, instituted the public Torah reading of the curses in *Toras Kohanim* before Shavuos and ruled that the curses of *Mishneh Torah* be read before Rosh Hashanah. The basis for this practice was to let "the past year end along with all its curses" and to usher in a year of blessing. (In this context, Shavuos is categorized as a new year, as the day the world is judged for "the fruit of the trees"[12]).[13]

What is the underlying theme to the reading of these admonitions before the "year's end"? During the Second Temple period, the *Shechinah*, Divine Presence, was no longer present.[14] Nevertheless, the covenant with Israel was not irrevocably broken.

The Shechinah was no longer present. Nevertheless, the covenant was not irrevocably broken.

The concept of a *bris*, covenant, is central to "creation."[15] There are two ways in which man can accept this covenant in order to uphold the purpose of Creation. The primary, preferred option is where man faithfully follows the word of G-d. In doing so, he sets himself up to become the deserving recipient of a world replete with *berachah*, blessing. The other alternative is the instance where man transgresses the word of G-d. He must now accept the negative consequences of his behavior, leaving him exposed to the full range of curses as Divine retribution. Whichever of the two he chooses — faithfulness or transgression, blessing or retribution — the *bris* has been upheld.

Every year is the start of a new cycle that extends from "the beginning of the year until the year's end."[16] Consequently, every year requires the reenactment of this *bris*. Reading the Admonitions before the "new year" indicates a Jew's acceptance of this covenant. Even the 98 curses of the Admonitions, in turn, allow him to become a worthy beneficiary of G-d's blessings in the upcoming year. It was specifically in the seeming absence of blessing after the First Temple's destruction that Ezra instituted the yearly affirmation of the *bris* prior to the year's end.

Every year requires the reenactment of this bris. Reading the Admonitions before the "new year" indicates a Jew's acceptance of this covenant.

Jewish Survival

The Jewish people's negative reaction to hearing the 98 curses was to become despondent. How could they possibly survive such a dreadful sentence? Moshe mollified them by pointing out that "You are all standing today before Hashem Your G-d."[17] Despite the many sins the Jewish people committed in the Wilderness, the Jewish nation had survived. So too are they guaranteed deliverance from future atrocities. While the gentile nations were destroyed for their sins, the Jewish nation was not. Instead of rebelling because of their afflictions, the reaction of Israel is to humbly negate themselves before G-d in prayer.[18]

Instead of rebelling because of their afflictions, the reaction of Israel is to humbly negate themselves before G-d in prayer.

The covenant the Congregation of Israel, as a unified entity, has with G-d is eternal. The Jewish People defy the natural laws of history by their supernatural tenacity and determination to survive no matter what the circumstances. In spite of their continual anguish after the destruction of the Second Temple, through the acceptance of curses in the Second Admonition, the Jew affirms that, despite all the suffering, "we have not forgotten You, and have not been false to Your *bris*, Your covenant."[19]

NOTES

1. See *Vayikra* 19:17.
2. Ibid 26:14- 46.
3. See "49: The Full Measure."
4. *Devarim* 28:15-69.
5. *Tanchuma, Nitzavim* 1. See *Kli Yakar, Devarim* 29:11, who enumerates a total of 100 curses but explains that 2 are different from all the others.
6. *Megillah* 31b; See *Tosafos* ad loc. Today, it is customary for there to be no breaks in reading either of the Admonitions from a Torah Scroll (*Shulchan Aruch, Orach Chaim* 428:6.). However, originally, breaks were not possible in the First Admonition but were in the Second Admonition.
7. See "70: The Sum of the Parts."
8. *Ramban, Vayikra* 26:46.
9. See *Mishnah Berurah* 428:18, stating that the First Admonition is harsher than the Second Admonition. However, see *Bava Basra* 88b, which states that the Second Admonition was greater in terms of the number of curses, and is therefore considered more difficult.
10. *Vilna Gaon, Aderes Eliyahu, Devarim* 29:18. See R' Yitzchak Hutner, *Pachad Yitzchak, Chanukah* 10.
11. *Devarim* 29:13 and *Rashi* ad loc. This point is highlighted in the later Torah passage that follows the Second Admonition. Anyone who excludes himself from the national entity will suffer the fate of ultimately being cut off and swiftly destroyed (*Devarim* 29:17-20; see also *Tosafos, Megillah* 31b).
12. *Rosh Hashanah* 16a.
13. *Megillah* 31b. See *Tosafos* ad loc., who note that the custom today is to read the curses 2 weeks before Rosh Hashanah rather than immediately before.
14. A nominal presence of the *Shechinah* was reserved for great leaders such as Ezra and Shimon Ha-Tzaddik.
15. See *Rabbeinu Bachya, Bereishis* 1:2 for how the word *bereishis*, creation, is a combination of the words *aish*, fire, and *bris*, covenant.
16. *Devarim* 11:12.
17. Ibid. 29:9.
18. *Tanchuma, Nitzavim* 1.
19. *Tehillim* 44:18.

100
COUNT YOUR BLESSINGS

100 is the number that often includes everything within it.

Over 100 refers to access to the Heavenly realm. 100 is the total number of daily blessings that successfully open the Heavenly Gates of Blessings upon Earth.

100 PERCENT

T HE NUMBER 100 TAKES THE COMPLETION OF 10 TO A HIGHER LEVEL. We have noted that the integration of individual components occurs in the complete set of 10.[1] The wholeness of 10 now expands to reach a fuller representation in 100 as the square of 10 ($10^2 = 100$). As such, 100 readily lends itself as the symbol of something that is all-encompassing and as the optimal numeric benchmark for comparative purposes.

100 is the symbol of something that is all-encompassing

100: EVERYTHING INCLUDED

The number 100 marks an important milestone in the counting process. It is the endpoint of one numeric classification and the forerunner of another. Just as the number 10 closes and completes the single-digit numbers preceding it (1-9),[2] 100 replicates this with the double-digit numbers (1-99). One further extension of this will be manifest in 1000, which comes to group three-digit numbers (1-999).[3]

All those from 1 to 100 can be grouped together in the same context.

All those from 1 to 100 can be grouped together in the same context.[4] The Talmud notes that the same lamp illuminates for "1 as it does for 100."[5] It is commonplace to evaluate all sorts of matters by marking them out of a base-100. The highest level is 100 percent ("percent" from the Latin root meaning "out of 100") that is considered to be the sum total of "everything."

The selection of 100 as man's "all-encompassing number" reflects the unique mathematical properties of 100. The number 10 is the standard base for an integrated whole — a base that transforms this wholeness further in its square of 100. In the selection of a number with base-10, the square root of 100 produces a whole number ($\sqrt{100} = 10$), in contrast to 10 ($\sqrt{10} = 3.162$) and 1,000 ($\sqrt{1000} = 31.62$).[6] This level of wholeness establishes it as the ideal number to be widely used as the quintessential standard measure.[7]

This level of wholeness establishes it as the ideal standard measure.

hundreds of times

As an adjunct to this number being used to denote everything, 100 is frequently used to portray *continuous repetition*. Typically, it will come to depict an activity performed incessantly — one that extends up to "100 times."

One prominent example of this repeat performance is the description, "a sinner perpetrates evil 100 times."[8] Conversely, there is the obligation to continuously revisit a *mitzvah* again and again. Illustrations of this are the sending away of the mother bird up to 100 times,[9] the requirement to rebuke one's friend up to 100 times when necessary,[10] and the attempt to return a lost article to its rightful owner as many as 100 times.[11]

100: The upper Limit

The universe can be divided into 3: the lower, middle, and upper realms. These levels have their respective correspondence in the division of numbers into units, into tens, and into hundreds.[12] Here 100 is the symbolic transition across the boundary line separating the physical and spiritual realms, the worldly and the otherworldly. Therefore this number is synonymous with the higher realm of שָׁמַיִם, Heaven,[13] that is beyond man,[14] and as the point where the Heavenly takes over.[15]

100 is the symbolic transition across the boundary separating the physical and spiritual realms.

100: cut down to size

Before the primeval sin, Adam was of such an outstanding spiritual stature that his remarkable inclusive standing was termed as "from the Earth up to the Heaven."[16] He was designated to live up to the highest numeric denomination in the Torah: 1000 years.[17] That drastically changed, however, because of his primeval sin of eating from the Tree of Knowledge. One of the significant repercussions of disobeying G-d was that the stature of Adam was greatly diminished. According to one opinion, he was drastically reduced to a size of only 100 cubits.[18]

One of the repercussions of disobeying G-d was that the stature of Adam was diminished to only 100 cubits.

Symbolically, this meant that the level of Adam shrank to now occupy the strict *confines of the physical world*. Despite his lofty original state, Adam now lost most of his spiritual qualities. His spiritual level plummeted. He was now condemned to live a more earthly existence: his height was curtailed to 100 cubits.

G-d did not allow Adam to degenerate to the point that he would totally lose his spiritual "Divine image."

Nevertheless, the fact that Adam was reduced to this level — not lower — signifies a measure of Divine kindness. In other words, G-d did not allow Adam to degenerate to the point that he would totally lose his spiritual "Divine image" with its associated Heavenly dimension. That his stature remained at the level of 100 meant that his ability to emulate G-d by living a spiritual "Heaven-like" existence was still possible.[19]

BE BLESSED

Reciting a blessing means man is forever connected to the Heavenly realm of 100.

THE POSITION OF 100 AS THE PLACE WHERE THE HEAVENLY TAKES over in the realm of the spirit is meaningfully expressed via the concept of בְּרָכָה, *blessing*. Reciting a blessing means man is forever connected to the Heavenly realm of 100. He sees beyond the demarcation of the physical by attributing all blessings on Earth to G-d in Heaven. In turn, this results in his actions increasing an awareness of G-d by the world's inhabitants here on Earth.[20]

100: DAILY BLESSINGS

One of the most famous associations of the number 100 is the rabbinic institution that obligates a Jew to recite 100 blessings every day.

One of the most famous associations of the number 100 is the rabbinic institution that obligates a Jew to recite 100 blessings every day. This is based on the verse "What does HASHEM your G-d ask of you?"[21] and a reading of the word מַה, *what?*, as מֵאָה, *100*.[22] Even the letters within this verse allude to the number 100.[23]

The Talmud resolves the apparent contradiction between the verse, "The Earth and its fullness are G-d's,"[24] and the verse "He has given the Earth to the children of man."[25] Does the Earth belong to man or to G-d? Prior to reciting a blessing, every object in the world rightly belongs to G-d. But once man has recognized the Divine Source, this item now transfers into man's jurisdiction.[26]

Historically, the decree of structuring the 100 blessings to revolve around the "order of the day" was introduced by David. Every stage of man's day — starting from opening his eyes, putting his feet on the floor, getting dressed, etc.[27] — would find exquisite expression in one of the 100 blessings. It was meant to combat the phenomenon of 100 Jewish lads dying each day. The daily 100 blessings offer protection against the 98 specific curses mentioned in the second Torah Admonition to Israel,[28] plus the 2 generalized categories of "all ailments and afflictions" (98+2=100).[29] By ensuring that man constantly recognizes and thanks his Creator in Heaven, the recitation of the 100 blessings offset the curses that distance man from G-d.[30]

MEAh ShEARIM: 100 GATES

The 100 daily blessings correspond to the 100 Gates in the higher world. Each of these Gates represents the fount through which blessing would be channeled.[31] Hence the 100 Gates of Blessing are opened specifically through the recitation of 100 blessings.

The Torah relates that Yitzchak, born to his father Avraham at the age of 100 years,[32] was most successful in the Land of Pelishtim. He reaped 100-fold of crops, described in the verse as מֵאָה שְׁעָרִים, 100 Gates.[33] Here all the 100 Heavenly Gates were opened and were assumed by Yitzchak, who benefited from this blessing on Earth.[34]

100 SILVER SOCKETS

There were 100 אֲדָנִים, [silver] sockets, in the Mishkan as the base to support the wall beams.[35] Just as the Divine Presence on Earth housed within the Sanctuary would be "supported" by the man-made sockets, so too, would the proclamation of G-d's Mastery be conferred by the daily recitation of 100 blessings. As such, each of the silver sockets represented a receptacle to receive and hold the Heavenly blessing.[36]

The silver sockets represented a receptacle to receive and hold the Heavenly blessing.

hEIChAL: 100 CUBITS

The interconnection between Earth and Heaven, where the otherworldly spiritual realm of the Heavens descends to the Earth, is the Temple. The blessing flowed down into the "House of G-d" from on high, and from there, spread outward to the whole world.

Significantly, the dimensions of the Heichal, the main anterior chamber of the Temple, measured 100 cubits long by 100 cubits

The interconnection between Earth and Heaven is the Temple.

wide and 100 cubits high.[37] Like the silver sockets in the Sanctuary, this holy chamber was the forum in which mankind was the fortunate beneficiary of G-d's constant goodness.

100: GO THE DISTANCE

100 is the start of a new category in the grouping of numbers within the counting process.

Crossing the border between realms, 100 is the start of a new category in the grouping of numbers within the counting process. It is placed on a higher pedestal than what came before. Its elevation means this number can be used to denote something that is detached from others or placed "at a distance."[38]

But as far as the Jew is concerned, this is not a barrier that stands in his way. On the contrary, he is fully expected to "go the distance." In other words, he must be fully prepared to repeatedly perform a *mitzvah* 100 times if necessary. Moreover, he refuses to be constrained by the physical world that conceptually stops at the number 100. Even after Adam's sin, the diminishment of the first man to 100 cubits indicates that he still retains a link to the Heavenly realm; thus, the Jew must continually identify with his "Divine image."

It is up to mankind to break through the "upper limit" to comfortably connect to the Heavenly.

It is up to mankind to break through the "upper limit" to comfortably connect to the Heavenly. Declaring that the Creator is not only G-d of Heaven but also of the Earth, the representation in the 100 daily blessings will facilitate the flow of Divine benevolence through the 100 Heavenly Gates and down into This World. In this way, we will be able to truly "count our blessings."

NOTES

1. See "10: Top Ten."
2. See ibid.
3. See "1000: A Thousand to One."
4. See Mishnah, *Parah* 12:2, where the sprinkling of the ashes on ritually impure people in need of purification need not be performed individually but collectively, "even if there are 100." See also ibid 12:6-8.
5. *Shabbos* 122a.
6. The number 10,000 does not really denote a new category of number even though it has a separate name. See "10,000: A Great Many."
7. *Maharal, Gur Aryeh, Devarim* 4:32 and *Chiddushei Aggados, Bava Basra* 75a (Vol 3, p. 112).
8. *Koheles* 8:12.

9. *Chullin* 141a.
10. "Rebuke frightens an understanding person more than smiting a fool 100 times" (*Mishlei* 17:10-11).
11. *Bava Metzia* 31a.
12. *Maharal, Ohr Chodosh* p. 74.
13. *Maharal, Nesiv HaAvodah* 14; *Chiddushei Aggados, Menachos* 43b (Vol. 4, pp. 78-79).
14. "The Heavens [belong] to G-d, but the Earth was given to man" (*Tehillim* 115:16).
15. See *Rokeach, Devarim* 10:12.
16. *Chagigah* 12a.
17. See "1000: A Thousand to One."
18. See *Sanhedrin* 38b and *Maharal, Gur Aryeh, Devarim* 4:32, saying that there was a different version in the Talmud text, which we do not have, that stated that Adam was reduced to 100 cubits.
19. *Maharal, Gur Aryeh, Devarim* 4:32.
20. See R' Chaim Volozhin, *Nefesh HaChaim* 2:4, which discusses how each *berachah* increases blessing in the upper worlds through the flow and holiness achieved via the interconnection between the higher and lower worlds.
21. *Devarim* 10:12.
22. *Menachos* 43b, *Rashi* ad loc.
23. There are 99 letters in the relevant verse (*Devarim* 10:12), which, when rounded out by the number 1, equal 100 (*Rokeach, Devarim* 10:12). See also *Tosafos, Menachos* 43b.
24. *Tehillim* 24:1.
25. Ibid. 115:16.
26. *Berachos* 35a-b.
27. See *Rambam, Hilchos Tefillah* 7.
28. *Bamidbar Rabbah* 18:21. See *Tur, Orach Chaim* 46. See *Rashi, Devarim* 29:12, *Baal HaTurim Devarim* 6:7.
29. *Rokeach, Devarim* 10:12 p. 200; *Devarim* 27:61. See "98: The Admonition."
30. *Maharal, Nesiv HaAvodah* 14.
31. *Recanati,* cited by *Shelah HaKadosh, Parashas Toldos, Torah Ohr.*
32. *Bereishis* 21:5.
33. Ibid. 26:12.
34. *Shelah HaKadosh, Parashas Toldos, Torah Ohr.*
35. *Shemos* 38:27.
36. *Shelah HaKadosh, Parshas Toldos, Torah Ohr.*
37. Mishnah, *Middos* 4:6.
38. See *Maharal, Chiddushei Aggados, Bava Metzia* 59b (Vol. 3, p. 27).

101
REPEAT YOURSELF

101 is the epitome of love for Torah.

It goes beyond the requirement for repetition necessary in order for man to master the material.

It is also the guaranteed means to ensure that it is never forgotten.

GOING ONE BETTER

THE NUMBER 101 IS THE OPTIMAL NUMBER OF TIMES FOR LEARNING Torah.

101 is the introduction to a new level.

We have observed that 100 is an extended grouping of 10 that includes everything within it.[1] So whereas 100 can be said to mark the conclusion of one numeric categorization, 101 is the introduction to a new level — one that goes beyond what was there before.

101 REVIEWS

The prominent example that indicates the distinction between 100 and 101 lies in the comparison of the number of times a person reviews his studies.

The prophet states, "You will return and see the difference between … one who serves G-d and one who does not serve Him."[2] The example of this distinction, as expounded by the Talmud, is the startling contrast made in the number of times that Torah is to be reviewed: "One who repeats what he has learned 100 times cannot be compared to one who repeats it 101 times."[3]

There is a world of difference between the 100th and 101st review.

The Talmud poses the obvious question: Why should the individual who reviewed it 100 times be characterised as "one who does not serve Him"? Is the absence of 1 extra review a real impediment to becoming "one who serves G-d"? Somehow, there is a world of difference between the 100th and 101st review. What is it?

101 is the point at which one enters onto a new level. Here he is catapulted up into a higher "spiritual milieu." This can be understood through an analogy given by the Talmud, where the rates for hiring a donkey-driver for travelling a set distance of 10 *parsaos* is 1 coin. For going any distance further, even to travel just 11 *parsaos*, the rate increases up to the higher tariff of 2 coins.[4]

101: GOING THE EXTRA MILE

The description, "servant of G-d," is reserved for the one willing to go the extra mile. This is characterised by one who does not stop at the natural endpoint of 100, but moves up to 101.

In this model, the first 100 times represent the standard requirement. It is equivalent to going through the motions. It is up to here that man expends his efforts — but no further.[5] Consequently, up until this point, this is self-serving. He can therefore be characterized as "serving himself" and as "one who does not serve Him."

By contrast, the 101st occasion represents the admission to a new level. Studying it on that 1 extra occasion serves as a clear demonstration that this endeavor represents total devotion to G-d. It symbolizes the state of a servant whose sole desire is to lovingly embrace the will of his master — no matter the frequency of the request. Reviewing Torah that one extra 101st time demonstrates that this review emanates out of pure love for the service of G-d. It is in that merit that it remains with him forever.

Reviewing Torah that one extra 101st time demonstrates that it emanates out of pure love in the service of G-d.

101: MOSHE, "SERVANT OF G-D"

The conduct of a Jew must always be in a spirit of subservience to G-d. The paragon "servant of G-d" — as he is described by the Torah — was Moshe.[6] The life of the greatest Jewish leader was dedicated to executing the Will of G-d. He exemplified what it meant for man to subordinate his will to the Will of G-d — from the moment he reluctantly accepted the position of leadership. Moshe's redemption of the Jewish People from Egypt and guidance through the Wilderness was a thankless task — but one that he dutifully fulfilled nonetheless. G-d attests to this in the statement about his servant Moshe: "In My entire house he is the trusted one."[7]

As the "servant of G-d," Moshe was eminently suitable to lead the Jewish People. He was always prepared to go until the natural extent — and beyond. His ascension to a level that would transcend everything that came before is perfectly underscored by Moshe's prophetic spirit, which transcended that of all other prophets.[8] Fitting the bill as "the one who serves Him," Moshe relates to the number 101. One allusion can be found in the hidden letters contained within the full spelling of the Hebrew letters in Moshe's name (הא + שין + מם) whose numerical value equals (40 +10 + 50 + 1=) 101.[9]

As the "servant of G-d," Moshe was eminently suitable to lead the Jewish People.

Moshe relates to the number 101.

101: FORGET-ME-NOT

Man's Torah studies must be an integral component of living as a Jew

There is an absolute imperative for a Jew not to forget his Torah learning.[10] He is no different from a servant who is obligated to be knowledgeable in all the dictates his master has established. He endeavors to learn the requisite ways and takes particular care to constantly review them. So too, man's Torah studies must be an integral component of living as a Jew — both to study and to follow the Torah laws.

Once he has learned it that 101st time, it now takes permanent root.

There is a tradition that despite having reviewed something 100 times, man is still susceptible to forgetfulness. But once he has learned it that additional occasion, the 101st time, the Talmud implies that it now takes permanent root. It cannot be dislodged.[11] The importance of reviewing something no less than 101 times is beautifully hinted at in the numeric difference between the Hebrew words זָכַר, *remember*, (227) and שָׁכַח, *forget*, (328) that is exactly (328 – 227 =) 101. When we deduct 101 from the word that means "forgetting" (*shocho'ach*), we remain with the word that means "remembrances" (*zecher*) — obliging man to remember and retain what he has learned.[12]

The teachings of Moshe were supposed to leave an indelible impression upon the Jewish People. If those teachings had permanently taken root in their psyche, they would not have been able to forget them. But that was not to be. The tragic episode of the Golden Calf led to the shattering of the first set of *Luchos*, Tablets. There was an interruption from the ideal. Its repercussions meant that forgetfulness became a reality.[13]

Subsequently, in the aftermath of Moshe's death, many Torah laws were forgotten from Israel.[14] But even though Moshe died before entering the Holy Land, his legacy lives on. Moreover, his spirit is said to illuminate the souls of Torah scholars in ensuing generations who continue transmitting Torah to the next generation. This has specific application to the one reviewing his Torah learning 101 times, as he now merits experiencing an illumination from Moshe. This is hinted at in *Parashas Tetzaveh*, the Torah portion in the Biblical narrative in

The Torah portion in which mention of Moshe's name is glaringly absent is composed of precisely 101 verses.

which the name "Moshe" is glaringly absent. Moshe had demanded that his name be erased from the Torah, G-d's Book, if the Creator would follow through on His threat to eradicate Israel after the sin of the Golden Calf. Of course, G-d relented and forgave the Jews, but as a result of Moshe's words his name was erased from one *parashah*. Interestingly enough, this Torah portion, in which mention of Moshe's name is glaringly absent — despite his actual presence — is composed of precisely 101 verses.[15]

In turn, every Jew who wants to emulate the characterization of Moshe as "the servant of G-d" must tap into the symbolism of 101. That means exhibiting a passionate yearning to retain one's Torah learning; to do whatever is necessary not to forget his learning.

His repetitious review is a loving expression of his deep-rooted love for G-d and His instructions. The Jew places Torah learning and practice as the leading interest in his mind. Hence, there cannot here be forgetfulness. The principle of forgetfulness is only possible where something is not continuously foremost within man's mind. But where something stands before him at every moment of his life, when he constantly reviews it, it is omnipresent. This is the value of Torah that is successfully transmitted from Moshe down the generations to you and me.

His review is a loving expression of his love for G-d and His instructions.

NOTES

1. See "100: Count Your Blessings."
2. *Malachi* 3:18.
3. *Chagigah* 9b.
4. Ibid. 9b.
5. See *Baal HaTanya, Tanya, Likkutei Amarim* Ch. 15, for how it was customary in the days before the Talmud was transcribed for all the students to review it 100 times.
6. *Devarim* 34:5; *Yehoshua* 1:1.
7. *Bamidbar* 12:7.
8. *Rambam*, Commentary to the Mishnah, *Sanhedrin* 10, 7th principle.
9. R' Yitzchak Isaac Chaver, *Ohr Torah*, annotations of *Maalos HaTorah* (end) pp. 290-292.
10. *Pirkei Avos* 3:10; see *Menachos* 99b.
11. R' Yitzchak Isaac Chaver, loc. cit.
12. *Kli Yakar, Devarim* 4:9.
13. *Eruvin* 54a.
14. *Temurah* 16a.
15. R' Yitzchak Isaac Chaver, loc. cit.

120
TO LAST A LIFETIME

120 is the number of years
that denote the totality of the
life experience. This is best personified
in the life of Moshe.

THAT'S LIFE

The optimal length of life extends to 120 years.

THE NUMBER 120 MARKS A FULL LIFETIME.

We have noted that the average human lifespan (and standard measure of a generation) is associated with 70: "The days of our years are 70 years."[1] Nevertheless, the optimal length of life, as echoed in the conventional blessing given for long life ("You should live until 120!") extends to 120 years. This epitomizes the sum of years in which man is to live out his life.

The most famous individual whose 120-year lifespan is explicitly recorded in the Torah was the greatest Jewish leader of them all: Moshe Rabbeinu.

Rabbinic literature records several scholars within the historic period of the Mishnah who lived for 120 years.[2] But the most famous individual whose 120-year lifespan is explicitly recorded in the Torah was the greatest Jewish leader of them all: Moshe Rabbeinu.

120 YEARS: LIFE OF MOSHE

The life of Moshe began with his secret birth against the backdrop of the Egyptian edict to kill all the newly born Jewish boys. He was rescued from the River Nile by Pharaoh's daughter, who drew him from the water.[3] Growing up in the royal palace, he shouldered the burden of his oppressed brethren who were brutally forced into backbreaking labor.[4] After Moshe fled Egypt, G-d chose him at the burning bush to become the redeemer of Israel.[5] Moshe was 80 years old when he stood before Pharaoh demanding that he let the Jewish People go.[6] Moshe's 40-year leadership spanned the decades from the Exodus through the years in the Wilderness, until just prior to their entry into the Holy Land.[7]

Moshe died on the same date as his birthday, his life in This World spanning exactly 120 years.

The Torah stresses that Moshe's physical and mental prowess did not diminish nor wane in old age.[8] Prior to his demise, Moshe gave testimony that all his faculties were fully functional and completely intact. His inability to enter the Holy Land was due only to G-d having decreed it. In line with the righteous, whose years are complete,[9] Moshe died on the same date as his birthday,[10] his life in This World spanning exactly 120 years.[11]

The defining feature of Moshe's life was the Torah. His role in redeeming the Children of Israel from Egypt was solely so that they would receive G-d's Torah at Sinai, with Moshe playing an essential role in its transmission to the Jewish People.[12] Indeed, there is a parallel between days and years in terms of the process of Moshe's receiving the Torah. In ascending the mountain to receive the Torah, there were three 40-day periods, namely (40 x 3 =) 120 days in total.[13] This contains in microcosm the 120-year life of Moshe, which was dedicated to teaching Torah to the Jewish People.[14]

120: ABOVE WATER

The Jewish baby was named "Moshe" by Pharaoh's daughter because she saved him when he was an infant in a casket floating on the River Nile: כִּי מִן הַמַּיִם מְשִׁיתִהוּ, *for I drew him from the water*.[15] This reflects the unique spiritual nature of Moshe in his affinity to *tzurah*, form, which is taken out and raised above the level of *chomer*, matter. *Chomer* is exemplified by water, whose liquid state has no definite form.[16]

The Talmud sees a cryptic allusion to Moshe in the episode recounting the corruption in the world before the Flood. "G-d said: 'My spirit shall not abide in man forever, insofar as he is also flesh; therefore his days shall be 120 years.'"[17] The term בְּשַׁגַּם, *insofar as he is also*, has the same numerical value (345) as the name מֹשֶׁה.[18] Furthermore, the 120-year period in the verse is a clear reference to the years of Moshe's life.[19]

The 120-year period in the verse is a clear reference to the years of Moshe's life.

There are several striking correspondences between the period of the Flood and the life of Moshe. Interestingly, the theme of succumbing or rising above water features strongly in both.

Just as Moshe survived by being "drawn from the water," so was mankind temporarily spared the waters of the Flood in the merit of Moshe, and also for the equivalent time frame of 120 years.[20] During these 120 years, G-d restrained His anger. He did not immediately punish the wicked; He afforded them the opportunity to repent.[21] The Divine instruction given to Noach about publicly constructing the *teivah*, Ark,[22] was the means of warning mankind that G-d was ready to bring about the destructive Flood.[23]

During these 120 years, G-d restrained His anger to afford them the opportunity to repent.

The newborn Jewish boys in the Egyptian exile were condemned to drown in the water,[24] with only Moshe surviving by being contained within a *teivah*. This has its parallel in the times of the Flood, where all of civilization was similarly drowned in the waters, with the notable exception of Noach and the remnants of civilization, who were preserved by being housed within a *teivah*.[25]

The teivah
was the
environment
in which the
last remnants
of civilization
would live and
survive.

The *teivah* built by Noach over the course of 120 years symbolized a "lifetime." It was the environment in which the last remnants of civilization would live and survive until after the Flood. In its aftermath, they would reestablish themselves on the land.

120: LIFE IN JUBILEE CYCLES

In the same way the *teivah* was used to reestablish life on Earth after the Flood, Moshe was responsible for the acceptance of Torah, which would give the world its endurance. Indeed, even the world's creation has a connection to Moshe — the opening word of the Torah, *bereishis*, "in the beginning of …" contains an allusion to Moshe, who is also described with the term *reishis*, first.[26]

By extension, Moshe's 120-year lifespan relates to the full time continuum.[27] The maximum length destined for the physical universe is 6 millennia: "The world will exist for 6000 years."[28] Time is arranged in concentric units. Hours are turned into days, days into months, months into years, years into Sabbatical cycles, and finally, Sabbatical cycles into cycles of *Yovel*, 50th-year Jubilee. This is the ultimate cycle — as the reaching of *Yovel* symbolically marks the point that a cycle is complete. It now is primed to start anew.[29]

Reaching
of Yovel
symbolically
marks the point
that a cycle is
complete.

If one divides the 6000 years of world existence into these 50 Jubilee cycles, one would then produce a total of 120. In the same fashion that a period of 50 years is classified as an "epoch," so too, the expanded expression of the universe's lifetime (6000) is manifest in the combination of *Yovel* (50) and a human lifetime (120), taken together (50 x 120 = 6000).

The expanded
expression of
the universe's
lifetime is
manifest in the
combination
of Yovel and a
human lifetime.

120: TERUMAH OF TIME

Not only is the life of Moshe that which gave the universe — and the time continuum — its raison d'être, he is also the one who established its sanctified status.

The primary tithing that a Jewish farmer separated from his produce (applicable once it was made [or gathered] into a pile of grain) was *terumah*.[30] This sanctified portion was given to the *Kohen*.[31] No fixed amount is prescribed by the Torah; one kernel out of a pile of grain is biblically adequate.[32] Nevertheless, the rabbis gave 3 measures depending on one's level of generosity. The average amount is 1/50th — the name תְּרוּמָה can be interpreted as a contraction of the words תְּרֵי מִמֵּאָה, *2 out of 100*, namely, 1/50th.[33]

תְּרוּמָה can be
interpreted as
a contraction of
the words תְּרֵי
מִמֵּאָה, 2 out of
100, namely,
1/50th.

Terumah is "designated" for holiness. It is exalted (תְּרוּמָה can also relate to the root רָם, exalted [or lifted]). The taking of terumah renders the rest of the produce chullin, non-designated or mundane. The sanctified portion sets the precedent. It establishes the nature and character of the remainder — with holiness as its focus.[34]

The life of Moshe was equivalent to the sanctified portion of a terumah for the world. The world is meant to survive a maximum of 6000 years.[35] Applying the average proportion of terumah of 1/50th to the 6000 years yields a sum of (1/50 x 6000 =) 120 years. So the lifetime of Moshe, the pillar of Torah, was equivalent to the sanctified portion of terumah that elevates everything else.[36]

120: FROM MOSHE TO MEN OF THE GREAT ASSEMBLY

The outstanding legacy of Moshe's 120-year life would be successfully transmitted through the generations. The first historical chain of Torah transmission, documented by the opening Mishnah to Pirkei Avos, began with Moshe and stretched down to the Anshei Knesses HaGedolah, Men of the Great Assembly, who lived at the beginning of the Second Temple period.[37]

The life of Moshe was equivalent to the sanctified portion of a terumah for the world.

This lineage represents the transition from the prophetic revelation of the Written Torah (Moshe) to the grasp of the Oral Torah (Anshei Knesses HaGedolah). This assembly included the surviving prophets of the First Temple era. Its members included Mordechai, Ezra, and Nechemiah. They introduced many edicts to reflect the change in circumstances (e.g., the standard textual formulation of the Amidah prayers).

Functioning in the capacity of a Great Sanhedrin, entrusted with the preservation of Jewish life in a new epoch of Jewish history, the total composition of the Anshei Knesses HaGedolah was of 120 members.[38] Interestingly, the size of a Jewish community that necessitates a Sanhedrin is one that serves a congregation of no fewer than 120 people.[39]

Entrusted with the preservation of Jewish life in a new epoch of Jewish history, the total composition of the Anshei Knesses HaGedolah was of 120 members.

120: FROM MOSHE UNTIL TODAY

In truth, the mark of Moshe's life continues to reverberate in all later generations — down to this day. That Moshe died on his 120th birthday symbolizes that there is a never-ending cycle. This was Haman's fatal mistake: to think that the month of Adar — during which Moshe died — was a tragic date in Jewish history. The fact that this was on his birthday means that Moshe symbolically lives on — not through himself but through his successors. Rather than his passing creating a void, it denotes a constantly renewable state through later Torah scholars.[40]

The sacred task of consecrating a life of Torah observancec is what human life is all about.

The persona of Moshe is said to be reincarnated into the Jewish leaders of each era. They continue the sacred task of consecrating a life of Torah observance that animates existence and life. It is what human life is all about — a life that hopefully extends to the same length as that of Moshe — 120 years.

NOTES

1. *Tehillim* 90:10. See "70: The Sum of the Parts."
2. See *Bereishis Rabbah* 100:10 about Rabbi Akiva, Rabbi Yochanan ben Zakkai, et al. See also *Rosh Hashanah* 31b.
3. *Shemos* 2:5-6, 10.
4. Ibid. 2:11-13.
5. Ibid. 3:1-10.
6. Ibid. 7:7. See "80: With Great Might."
7. See "40: True to Form."
8. *Devarim* 31:2 and *Rashi* ad loc. 34:7.
9. See *Tosafos, Chagigah* 17a citing *Yerushalmi, Chagigah* 2:3 stating that David died on Shavuos. See *Kiddushin* 38a and *Sotah* 13b about the righteous dying on their birthdays.
10. *Sotah* 12b.
11. *Devarim* 31:2, 34:7.
12. *Pirkei Avos* 1:1.
13. See *Rashi, Shemos* 32:1 and 33:11.
14. *Rokeach, Devarim* 34:7.
15. *Shemos* 2:10.
16. *Maharal, Gevuros Hashem* 14. See "39: Under Development" and "40: True to Form."
17. *Bereishis* 6:3.
18. *Chullin* 139b.
19. See *Rashi, Chullin* 139b.
20. *Maharal, Chiddushei Aggados, Chullin* 139b (Vol. 4, pp.115-116).
21. *Rashi, Bereishis* 6:3.
22. *Bereishis* 6:13-16.
23. *Rashi,* ibid. 6:14.
24. *Shemos* 1:22.
25. Note the similar description of both the *teivah* of Noach and the *teivah* of Moshe being smeared with pitch (*Bereishis* 6:14 and *Shemos* 2:3; see *Rashi, Bereishis* 6:14).

26. *Bereishis Rabbah* 1:4.
27. Both Adam and Noach lived almost 1000 years — 930 and 950 years respectively. The combination of their deficient years to reach 1000 (70 for Adam and 50 for Noach) equals 120 years — the lifetime of Moshe. See *Chida, Devash L'Fi, Erech Moshe.*
28. *Rosh Hashanah* 31a; *Avodah Zarah* 9a. See "6000: The End of the World."
29. See "50: All the Way."
30. See *Rambam, Hilchos Terumah* 5:5 and *Kesef Mishnah* ad loc.
31. *Devarim* 18:4.
32. *Chullin* 137b.
33. Mishnah, *Terumos* 4:3 and *Rambam*, commentary ad loc.
34. See "1: The One and Only."
35. See "6000: The End of the World."
36. *Vilna Gaon, Aderes Eliyahu, Devarim* 34:7.
37. *Pirkei Avos* 1:1.
38. *Megillah* 17b.
39. *Sanhedrin* 2b and 17b; see *Rambam, Hilchos Sanhedrin* 1:10.
40. See *Tanchuma, Ki Sisa* 3, mentioned in the context of *Parashas Shekalim.*

127
wake-up call

127 is the lifespan of Sarah,
whose royal bearing and spiritual legacy
merited that her descendant
Esther rule over 127 provinces.

It is meant to stir man from his slumber
and awaken him to glorify G-d even in
the trying times of exile.

TWO ILLUSTRIOUS WOMEN

THE NUMBER 127 IS USED IN RELATION TO TWO BIBLICAL WOMEN. Sarah, wife of Avraham and mother of Yitzchak, lived for 127 years. 127 was also the number of provinces that were ruled by King Achashveirosh and his Jewish wife, Queen Esther of the Purim narrative.

127: LIFETIME OF SARAH

Of the 4 *Imahos*, Jewish Matriarchs, only the lifespan of Sarah is explicitly recorded in the Torah. "Sarah's lifetime was 100 years, 20 years, and 7 years; the years of Sarah's life."[1] The strange formulation is grouped into 3 distinct periods: 100 years, 20 years, and 7 years. Insights into the greatness of Sarah are derived by comparing and contrasting these terms. Even at the advanced age of 100 years, she was comparable to a woman of 20 years old in that she was free from sin.[2] In addition, when Sarah was 20 years old, she was as naturally beautiful as a 7-year-old.[3]

127: PROVINCES

The other seemingly unrelated occurrence of the number 127 is found in the opening verse of *Megillas Esther*. It begins by recording the extent of Achashveirosh's power and sovereignty. "It came to pass in the days of Achashveirosh — he was Achashveirosh who ruled from Hodu to Cush over 127 provinces."[4]

Setting the scene for the unfolding of the Purim story, Achashveirosh made a grand banquet. In his drunken stupor, he had his queen, Vashti, executed, setting into motion events that led to Esther being crowned as his new queen. Through her forced marriage to Achashverosh, Esther became queen over 127 provinces.

127: ESTHER, DAUGHTER OF SARAH

The Midrash records a fascinating narrative that links these 2 seemingly unrelated occurrences of the number 127. Rabbi Akiva was giving a lecture and his students were slumbering. He aroused his audience with a startling statement: "Why did Esther merit to rule over 127 provinces? G-d said, 'Let Esther, daughter of Sarah who lived for 127 years, come to rule over 127 provinces.'"[5]

Rabbi Akiva's declaration was not a random, irrelevant, but curious statement designed to jolt his students; it was a pedagogical response to their slumbering — one whose message sought to establish the deeper connection between Esther and Sarah.

There are striking parallels between the lives of Sarah and Esther.[6] They were both paragons of modesty,[7] prominent Jewish leaders and prophetesses.[8] They were similarly described as being exceptionally beautiful in their appearance.[9] Their royal bearing resulted in being forcefully seized by guards and presented as a bride fit for the king.[10] Indeed, the name Sarah denotes her status of being a "princess" (sar is a "prince") to the entire world.[11] Esther, who succeeded Vashti as queen, was herself born of royal blood from the family of King Shaul.[12]

Both Sarah and Esther were able to nullify the will of their captors to their own.

Despite being aliens in foreign countries, both Sarah and Esther were able to nullify the will of their captors to their own. In Sarah's case, Pharaoh released her with many gifts and riches. Avimelech also sought to make Sarah his wife and ultimately released her. Sarah was a full partner in Avraham's efforts to turn the masses from their idol-worship to believing in G-d.[13] Once Esther revealed her heritage, she succeeded to convince Achashveirosh to kill Haman, and subsequently brought about the salvation of the Jewish People living in his kingdom.

127: SOVEREIGNTY

Sarah displayed מַלְכוּת, *sovereignty*— not over an Earthly kingdom but over her life on Earth.

Sarah exercised complete control over her allocated 127 years in this temporary world.

Sarah exercised complete control over her allocated 127 years in this temporary world. She complemented her husband Avraham who achieved mastery over all 248 limbs of his body.[14] Sinless at 100 years old, Sarah ruled over her *Yetzer Hara*, Evil Inclination, which is termed a king,[15] just as she asserted control over Pharaoh and Avimelech.[16] In this regard, she typified a Jewish sovereign whose task is to redirect his kingship over human subjects into submission to the sovereignty of G-d: the King of all kings.

Esther's subsequent dominion over the 127 provinces could find its basis in the 127 years of Sarah's life. Esther personifies the state of *hester panim*, concealment of [G-d's] Face[17] — the word *esther* is cognate to *hester*, concealment.[18] She lived at a time when G-d was hidden: the Jewish People's exile after the destruction of the First Temple. The continuity of the Jewish People — which began with Avraham and Sarah — hung in the balance.

Esther's dominion over the 127 provinces could find its basis in the 127 years of Sarah's life.

Along came "Esther, daughter of Sarah." As an extension of the principle, מַעֲשֵׂה אָבוֹת סִימָן לְבָנִים, *the events of the Patriarchs are portents for [what would happen to] the children*,[19] the spiritual strengths of the ancestors were genetically imprinted into their descendants.[20]

Esther "donned royalty" to appear before the king in her royal apparel.[21] Despite her dire predicament, Esther saw beyond the darkness and recognized that G-d was hiding Himself. She used her circumstances — her placement in the royal palace — to passionately plead on behalf of her people. She used her influence to bring about a turnaround for the Jewish People living throughout the 127 provinces under threat from Haman's edict.

Esther saw beyond the darkness and recognized that G-d was hiding Himself.

127: WAKE UP!

In his derogatory reference to the Jewish People, Haman began by using the phrase יֶשְׁנוֹ עַם אֶחָד, *there is a certain nation*.[22] The word *yeshno*, there is, can be rendered *yashnu*, they have slept — a reference to their lackadaisical *mitzvah* observance. The charge leveled against the Jewish People was that they had sinned and G-d would therefore allow them to be punished.[23]

Sleep occurs when man, who is exhausted, enters into a state of inactivity. Sleep contains a semblance of death.[24] Consequently, it contradicts the purpose of life, which is geared toward activity and continuous growth. In exile, the sinful condition of the Jewish People is encapsulated by the phrase, "I am asleep but my heart is awake."[25] In the darkness of exile, G-d is hidden from view. Enthusiasm and alacrity to serve G-d are missing. Obstacles and the *Yetzer Hara*'s schemes hinder a Jew from following through on his heart's true desire to serve G-d. When man is in this state, he must stir himself from his slumber.[26] The "wake-up call" must reinvigorate his life, allowing him to serve G-d even in trying circumstances.[27]

The "wake-up call" must reinvigorate his life, allowing him to serve G-d even in trying circumstances.

Rabbi Akiva lived through the Roman persecutions following the destruction of the Second Temple. He witnessed the plague that claimed the lives of his 24,000 pupils.[28] He witnessed the failed uprising of Bar Kochba against the Roman occupiers. He lost his life for teaching Torah[29] — imprisoned and tortured, his skin flayed by iron combs, and dying with the words of *Shema* on his lips.[30]

And yet, whatever the terrible circumstances that engulfed him or the Jewish People, Rabbi Akiva consistently refused to surrender to despair. His reaction to tragic events around him was with laughter[31] — indicating his ability to see beyond the present disaster.

Rabbi Akiva highlighted the spiritual strengths imbued within every Jew by virtue of his ancestry and spiritual connection to the Jewish Patriarchs and Matriarchs. He was teaching his disciples in exile to similarly stir themselves from their slumber. By referring to Sarah and Esther, he was teaching them to use every moment in life productively to reveal *Malchus Shamayim*, the Kingship of G-d, over the whole universe.[32] The model example of this was how Esther derived her strength from Sarah — as we see from their shared affinity to the number 127 — to use sovereignty as the means to reverse the "sleepiness" of exile.

Rabbi Akiva was teaching his disciples to similarly stir themselves from their slumber in exile.

NOTES

1. *Bereishis* 23:1.
2. A person younger than the age of 20 years is not subject to Heavenly punishment (*Shabbos* 89b, *Rash* ad loc.). See "20: Manhood."
3. *Rashi, Bereishis* 23:1 citing *Bereishis Rabbah* 58:1.
4. *Esther* 1:1, 8:9.
5. *Esther Rabbah* 1:8; *Bereishis Rabbah* 58:3.
6. *Maharal, Ohr Chodosh* 1:1 pp. 74-75. See *Maharal* (ad loc.) for an explanation of the significance of how 127 refers to the universe composed of 3 realms: the lower world, the middle world, and the upper world.
7. See *Rashi, Bereishis* 18:9 and *Bava Metzia* 87a; see *Esther* 2:10 and *Megillah* 13b.
8. *Megillah* 14a.
9. *Bereishis* 12:11 and *Esther* 2:7. See *Megillah* 15a, which discusses how Sarah and Esther were included in the count of the 4 most beautiful women to have lived.
10. Sarah was captured by Pharaoh in Egypt (*Bereishis* 12:15) and by Avimelech in Gerar (ibid. 20:2). Esther was similarly forcefully taken to the king's harem (*Esther* 2:8).
11. *Berachos* 13a. See *Bereishis* 17:15 and *Rashi* ad loc. She was a parallel to Avraham who was a prince and father over the nations of the world (*Bereishis* 17:5).
12. See *Megillah* 13b, which compares the modesty of King Shaul and Esther.
13. *Rashi, Bereishis* 12:5.
14. See "248: In Action."

15. *Nedarim* 32b, interpreting *Koheles* 9:14.
16. See, e.g., *Rashi, Bereishis* 12:17.
17. *Devarim* 31:17-18.
18. *Chullin* 139b.
19. *Midrash Tanchuma, Lech Lecha* 9.
20. See R' Chaim Volozhin, *Ruach Chaim* 5:3.
21. *Esther* 5:1.
22. Ibid. 3:8.
23. *Megillah* 13b.
24. *Berachos* 57b.
25. *Shir HaShirim* 5:2.
26. The *Rambam* (*Hilchos Teshuvah* 3:4) sees the blowing of the shofar on Rosh Hashanah as symbolic of the need to arouse the sinner. "Arise, O sleepers, from your sleep! Arise, O slumberers, from your slumber!"
27. The Psalmist projects this onto G-d by questioning, "Awaken, why do You seem to sleep, O G-d? Arouse Yourself, forsake not us forever" (*Tehillim* 44:24).
28. See "24,000: The Fallen Ones."
29. *Berachos* 61b.
30. See ibid.; *Yerushalmi, Berachos* 9:5, the death of the Ten Martyrs described in the *kinnah* of Tishah B'Av of *Arzei HaLevanon* and the *piyut* of *Eileh Ezkerah* of Yom Kippur *Mussaf*.
31. See *Makkos* 24a-b.
32. R' Gedalyah Schorr, *Ohr Gedalyhu, Chayei Sarah* pp. 78-79. See also R' Tzadok HaKohen, *Pri Tzaddik, Chayei Sarah* 11, which explains how every Jew can reach the highest level (and even understand the deepest secrets of Torah taught by Rabbi Akiva). The reason he can do this is because he is able to look up to and emulate the Patriarchs and Matriarchs.

130
A FIRM FOUNDATION

130 is the epoch where sin
seems to be given a life form of its own.
It is where what is "unreal" takes on
the appearance of "reality."

Alternatively, 130 can be rightly
directed to building a firm,
spiritual, and G-dly existence.

FOUNDED OR UNFOUNDED

The first appearance of the number 130 in world history is seen in the aftermath of the primeval sin that threatened the very foundation of existence.

THE FIRST APPEARANCE OF THE NUMBER 130 IN WORLD HISTORY IS seen in the aftermath of the primeval sin that threatened the very foundation of existence.

130: YEARS OF SEPARATION

By violating the word of G-d, Adam introduced death into the world. His mortality — and that of the whole human race — was irrecoverably sealed on the day he ate from the Tree of Knowledge of Good and Evil. G-d had promised, "on the day you eat from it you will surely die."[1]

In response to the central role that Chavah played in leading her husband to sin, Adam ceased marital intimacy for a period of 130 years. During that time, he did not father any human children. Instead, the Talmud notes that Adam created a number of impure entities.[2]

This continued for over a century. Only when Adam was asked to arbitrate between Lemech and his wives (who sought to divorce Lemech after he inadvertently killed Kayin) did Adam resume marital relations with Chavah.[3] Sheis was born following this 130-year period.[4] While Adam's descendants from Kayin and Hevel were wiped out in the Great Flood, human civilization was permanently established through Noach and his family, the descendants of Sheis — whose name (שֵׁת) innately relates to שְׁתִיָה, *foundation.*[5]

130: IT'S UNREAL

The period of 130 years can be understood in terms of the spiritual impact wrought by the primeval sin.

The period of 130 years can be understood in terms of the spiritual impact wrought by the primeval sin and by Adam's inability to father human children during this time.

What Adam's sin did was *to give existence to that which was unreal.* The pleasure of sin belongs to the realm of fantasy. It is a figment of man's imagination that falsely tempts man by presenting itself as something real.[6] Consequently, when man perpetrates evil, it is he — and not G-d — who grants it existence. The sinner gives "life" to that which is "dead." In his subjective viewpoint, it takes on a semblance of reality. But in objective terms, according to G-d's perspective, it contains no element of truth whatsoever.

Where man sins, he attaches himself to an unreal, illusionary world. In this artificially constructed world, he creates, or "gives birth," to entities that then take on a life of their own. This is the explanation for why Adam's sin was responsible for giving existence to the negative forces of impurity. In other words, his evil created an *alternate reality* wherein evil becomes an integral component of life.

This phase finally ended after 130 years. Having repented, Adam turned his back upon a sinful life of make-believe. It brought to an end that time when he had given existence to what was nonexistent. Consequently, his reunion with Chavah and the birth of Sheis were the symbolic construction of a new world order based on reality in the service of G-d.

130: Yaakov's Life before Egypt

When Yaakov migrated to Egypt and stood before Pharaoh, he was asked his age. The Jewish Patriarch responded that his age was 130 years — describing his years until then as having been "few and evil."[7]

The "evil" calamities that befell Yaakov in the first 130 years of his life find their parallel in the "evil" 130 years of Adam's separation.[8] The lives of Adam and Yaakov were closely related. One example of many is the saying "The beauty of Yaakov resembled the beauty of Adam."[9]

In Yaakov's life, he hardly had any respite from all the ills that struck him — many of them related to the birth and raising of his children.[10] He had to deal with his scheming father-in-law Lavan who swapped Leah for Rachel on Yaakov's wedding day, the assault on Dinah, the sale of Yosef to Egypt, the transportation of Binyamin to secure food, etc.

During the last 17 years of Yaakov's life, however, his fortunes changed and he experienced goodness and peace.[11] Yaakov lived out his last years in peace and harmony. This has its parallel in the newly conditioned life of Adam that came about after 130 years, starting from the birth of Sheis.

Yaakov lived out his last years in peace and harmony. This has its parallel in the newly conditioned life of Adam that came about after 130 years.

130: LIFE IN EGYPT BEFORE MOSHE

Another correspondence to the 130 years of negativity in Adam's life are the first 130 years of the Egyptian exile. The Divine decree that the Jewish People were to be exiled to a foreign land resulted in Yaakov and his household descending to Egypt. In fact, the 70th member of Yaakov's household was Levi's daughter Yocheved, who was born just as they entered Egypt.[12] In the Egyptian exile, the Children of Israel proliferated but were negatively influenced by the idolatrous culture and the spiritual impurity.

Yocheved was 130 years old when she gave birth to Moshe.

Parallel to Adam's separation from Chavah before reuniting, which resulted in the birth of another child (Sheis), Yocheved and her husband Amram separated because of the Egyptian edict to kill all newborn Jewish boys; they later remarried and subsequently became parents to Moshe. In fact, Yocheved was 130 years old when she gave birth to Moshe, who would redeem the Jewish People in the Exodus when he was 80 years old[13] after a total of (80 + 130 =) 210 years of Egyptian exile.[14]

The birth of Moshe, 130 years after the migration to Egypt, was highly significant, similar to the birth of Sheis. This was because Moshe's birth firmly established the necessary foundations to support a new world order. In effect, it drew a line under the sinful events that had hitherto occurred. It signified an end to the earlier forces of negativity that had turned nonexistence into existence. And it introduced a new state of true reality.

The Exodus served as a springboard for the newly redeemed Jewish People to ascend to spiritual heights.

As the Jewish redeemer, Moshe demonstrated the futility of the Egyptian magic so prevalent in that society. Thereafter, Moshe extricated the Children of Israel from the contamination of Egypt. Here the Exodus served as a springboard for the newly redeemed Jewish People to ascend to spiritual heights.

NOTES

1. *Bereishis* 2:17.
2. *Eruvin* 18b. The statement that Adam fathered Sheis, "a son in his likeness and his image" (*Bereishis* 5:3), carries the implication that, until then, he fathered spirits that were unlike his form.
3. *Rashi, Bereishis* 4:25; *Midrash Aggadah Bereishis* 4.
4. *Bereishis* 5:3.
5. See *Rashi, Bamidbar* 7:19, for how the silver dish that weighed 130 shekels used in the offerings of the

nesiim, princes, of each Tribe (see *Bamidbar* 7:13) alludes to the age of Adam when he established offspring through Sheis that led to the perpetuation of the world.

6. See the opening remarks of R' Yisrael Salanter in his *Iggeres HaMussar*, where the *Yetzer Hara* subverts man through the power of imagination: "Man is free in his imagination and bound by his intellect. His unrestrained imagination draws him mischievously in the way of his heart's desires ...."

7. *Bereishis* 47:8-9.

8. *Yalkut Reuveni, Vayigash* citing the *Arizal*. See also *Megaleh Amukos, Vayigash*. The waste of seed is described as "evil" (*Bereishis* 38:7 and *Rashi* ad loc.; see *Rashi, Bereishis* 6:11-13, about immorality at time of Flood; see also *Zohar Chadash, Midrash Rus,* in reference to *Yeshayah* 3:11).

9. *Bava Basra* 58a.

10. See *Rashi, Bereishis* 43:14.

11. *Midrash HaGadol, Bereishis* 47:28.

12. *Bava Basra* 123a-b; see *Rashi, Bereishis* 46:15. See *Maharal Hilchos Yayin Nesech V'Issuro*, end of *Gevuros Hashem* as to how Yocheved's birth celebrates the formation of the Jewish nation upon their arrival in Egypt.

13. *Shemos* 7:7.

14. *Yalkut Reuveni, Vayigash*, citing the *Arizal*. See also *Shelah HaKadosh, Vayeishev-Miketz-Vayechi, Torah Ohr* for additional parallels, brought in mystical sources, which link Moshe as a reincarnation of Sheis.

210
THE IRON FURNACE

The length of the Egyptian exile
was 210 years.

During this period Israel was conceived,
ultimately becoming G-d's Chosen Nation
upon their Exodus.

THE JEWISH PEOPLE WERE IN EGYPT FOR A TOTAL OF 210 YEARS.[1]
The national experiences of their exile in this period and the subsequent Exodus are indelibly impressed upon the Jewish psyche.

210: JUST IN TIME

Avraham's prophetic vision at the *Bris bein HaBesarim*, Covenant between the Parts, was that his descendants would be exiled, incarcerated, and oppressed in a foreign land for a period of 400 years.[2] Every aspect of this prophecy came to pass — except for the length of the exile. In fact, the Exodus came about after only 210 years in Egypt rather than continuing to last for a full period of 400 years.[3]

The Exodus came about after only 210 years in Egypt rather than continuing to last for a full period of 400 years.

The Jewish People were on the lowest level imaginable. They were downtrodden slaves. The Egyptians exercised control over their bodies with backbreaking labor and by murdering their children with impunity. In addition to the physical bondage, there was the spiritual enslavement. The Children of Israel were entrenched in the idolatrous culture of Egypt, whose spiritual contamination gave them a license to commit all forms of sin. The allure was so strong that four-fifths of the Jewish population in Egypt did not want to leave.[4]

G-d's supernatural rescue of Israel was critical. G-d knew that were the Children of Israel to remain in Egypt any longer, there was a danger they would spiritually slip down to the 50th level of impurity. At that point, they would be totally integrated into the Egyptian culture, never to be extricated.[5]

Rather than leave them in such a perilous predicament, the calculation of the 400 years as wandering, displaced strangers would be measured from the birth of Yitzchak.[6] In addition, the reduction of the exile from 400 years could also be explained by the severity of the servitude. In other words, there were "400 years' worth" of slavery and hardship suffered by the Israelites compressed into 210 years.

The reduction of the exile from 400 years could also be explained by the severity of the servitude.

210: EGYPTIAN SLAVERY

Several of Avraham's minor "misdeeds" are cited to explain the harshness of this exile.[7] Nevertheless, the underlying reason for the Egyptian exile was because it was Divinely preordained. It was a historic event that G-d determined had to unfold in the creation of the Chosen Nation.[8] In the end, the Egyptian exile lasted a total of 210 years. This epoch began when Yaakov's household of 70 members migrated to Egypt.[9] The three mentions of the 70 migrants in the *Chumash*[10] alludes to the 210 years (3 x 7 = 210) that the Children of Israel were in exile.[11]

During the brief span of two centuries, the Jewish People proliferated greatly.[12] The Children of Israel were subject to torturous physical labor and horrific suffering at the hands of their Egyptian taskmasters. In the Torah, the exile and redemption are recounted in *Sefer Shemos*, Book of *Exodus*. Here the 210 years of exile are actually hinted at in the opening paragraph of this Book,[13] which is comprised of precisely 210 letters.[14]

210 years of exile are hinted at in the opening paragraph of Shemos, which is comprised of 210 letters.

210: THE GESTATION PERIOD

This historic period of exile was necessary for the emergence of the Children of Israel. The metaphor of birth is used to describe the process: "G-d took a nation from within another nation."[15] While the birth of Israel took place on the festival of Pesach, with their departure from Egypt, the 210 years prior to that was their "gestation."

The Israelites were formed like a fetus, attached and enveloped within their host country. They had no independent existence to call their own. Their redemption ultimately came once the Shepherd (G-d) stretched out His hand to remove the unborn infant (Israel) from the mother sheep (Egypt).[16] Alternatively, the extraction of the Jewish nation is likened to a goldsmith stretching his hand into a fiery crucible ("G-d took Israel out of the iron furnace"[17]) to remove molten gold. The Egyptian nation exercised control over Israel, overpowering them like fire melts gold in a furnace.[18] Just as the iron furnace refines a metal from all impurities, so was the corporeal side of the Jewish people refined through the affliction of Egypt[19] — a process that continued until they were pure.[20]

The historic event of the Exodus as the "birth of Israel" after 210 years is therefore accorded a preeminent position in Judaism — one

Just as the iron furnace refines a metal from all impurities, so the corporeal side of the Jewish people refined through the affliction of Egypt.

that is immortalized by the many laws of the Torah and is a fundamental of Jewish faith.[21]

210: BECOMING A SERVANT

The Jewish liberation from Egypt resulted in the birth of the Children of Israel as a nation.

The 210 years of Egyptian exile were the prelude to *yetzias Mitzrayim*, departure from Egypt. The obligatory twice-daily remembrance of this milestone[22] emphasizes the importance of the Exodus. The Jewish liberation from Egypt resulted in the birth of the Children of Israel as a nation. Here began the history of the world where G-d, so to speak, enters the picture to enact His "Providence" through the Jewish people. His miraculous Divine Intervention set into motion all subsequent events that would revolve around the destiny of Israel.

There was the transformation of Israel from "slaves to Pharaoh" into "slaves to G-d." The *Shechinah*, Divine Presence, would rest upon Israel. The very harsh conditions Israel endured during the 210 difficult years of servitude facilitated their transition to readily accept upon themselves the servitude to G-d.[23]

The Divine Revelation of the Master obligates their subjugation to Him.

The objective of the redemption was not liberty or freedom per se; it was in order that Israel would come to know their Redeemer.[24] The purpose of their passage from Egypt was for them to reach Sinai, where they would embrace and fulfill the Torah.[25] Indeed, the Divine Revelation of the Master obligates their subjugation to Him — something that was encapsulated in the opening sentence of the Ten Commandments: "I am HASHEM your G-d Who has taken you out of the land of Egypt, from the house of slavery."[26] G-d said "The [salvation of the] Exodus is reason enough for you [Israel] to serve Me"; it obligated the acceptance of the Heavenly yoke.[27]

The Torah is synonymous with cheirus, freedom — denoting man's emancipation from forces of evil.

The Torah is synonymous with *cheirus*, freedom — denoting man's emancipation from forces of evil, thus freeing him to engage in his spiritual destiny through the pursuit of a lifetime devoted to Torah.[28] Even though the Jewish people would later revert to a state of exile, the Exodus is a cause for celebration as it brought Israel to a state of *cheirus olam*, eternal spiritual freedom, in the embrace of Torah.[29]

Importantly, the Jewish people did not lose their identity in Egypt — as characterized by retaining their names and language, not speaking *lashon hara,* and not being promiscuous.[30] Breaking free at the Exodus, the Jewish nation was no longer subservient to contamination and evil. That the stronghold of impurity within them had been repelled meant that Israel could now make the transition from contamination to purity. Following 210 years of Egyptian exile, Israel as a nation finally entered the world of holiness. They broke out of the confines of Egypt to embrace the transcendental level of Torah. Ultimately, this redemption was complete upon the festival of Shavuos 50 days later, with the acceptance of Torah.

Following 210 years of Egyptian exile, Israel entered the world of holiness.

NOTES

1. *Nedarim 32a, Shemos Rabbah* 1:23 and *Bamidbar Rabbah* 13:19.
2. *Bereishis* 15:13.
3. See "400: Of All Places," about the significance of this 400-year exile.
4. *Tanchuma, Beshalach* 1. See *Rashi, Shemos* 13:18.
5. *Shelah HaKadosh, Pesachim, Torah Ohr* 10. See also *Yaros Devash* 8 and *Chemdas HaYamin* 6. See "49: The Full Measure" and "50: All the Way."
6. See *Maharal, Gevuros Hashem* 10 for how the first of the stages of exile began with Yitzchak.
7. See *Nedarim 32a*.
8. *Maharal, Gevuros Hashem* 9.
9. *Bereishis* 46:5-27.
10. Ibid. 46:27, *Shemos* 1:5, *Devarim* 10:22.
11. *Rokeach, Shemos* 1:5.
12. *Shemos* 1:7.
13. The opening paragraph of *Sefer Shemos* comprises the first 7 sentences (ibid.).
14. *Rokeach, op. cit.* 1:7.
15. *Devarim* 4:34.
16. *Maharal, Gevuros Hashem* 3.
17. *Devarim* 4:20 and *Maharal, Gur Aryeh* ad loc. See also *Derashos HaRan* 3.
18. *Maharal, Gevuros Hashem* 3.
19. Through the oppression in Egypt, Israel became fit to receive the Torah: one of the gifts G-d conferred upon Israel with their affliction (*Berachos* 5a).
20. See *Kli Yakar, Devarim* 4:20.
21. See *Maharal, Gevuros Hashem* 3, for how the Exodus is considered more significant and is equal to all other supernatural miracles.
22. *Berachos* 12b. See *Maharal, Gevuros Hashem* 66, as to how the significance of actions is a good indication of its purpose. Something as momentous as the supernatural miracles of the Exodus must have been for an awesome reason.
23. *Shelah HaKadosh, Torah Ohr, Parashas Lech Lecha.*
24. See *Iyov* 19:25.
25. *Sefer HaChinuch* 306.
26. *Shemos* 20:2. See also *Devarim* 16:12 and *Rashi* ad loc.
27. *Rashi, Shemos* 20:2; see also *Ramban* ad loc. The liberation of Israel after 210 years was actually in the merit of Torah that they would embrace (*Shemos Rabbah* 3:12).
28. *Pirkei Avos* 6:2.
29. *Maharal, Gevuros Hashem* 61.
30. *Vayikra Rabbah* 32:5.

248
IN ACTION

248 is the number of bodily limbs that correspond to the number of Positive Commandments in the Torah.

This parallel symbolizes that man must actively use his body to faithfully perform the Divine Will.

There are 248 Positive Commandments in the Torah.

THERE ARE 248 POSITIVE COMMANDMENTS IN THE TORAH.

There are a total of תַּרְיַ״ג מִצְוֹת, *613 commandments*, which subdivide into 2 categories.[1] The first is the רְמַ״ח מִצְוֹת עֲשֵׂה, *248 Positive Commandments*, and the second is the שְׁסָ״ה מִצְוֹת לֹא תַעֲשֶׂה, *365 Prohibitive Commandments*.[2]

The common denominator to the 248 Positive Commandments is how they relate to the performance of positive actions. These actions are responsible for building up the relationship between man and G-d.

248: A CALL FOR ACTION

It is through performance of the 248 Positive Commandments that man effectively "constructs" his intimate relationship with G-d.

It is within the physical environment that man was created to serve the Master of the Universe. The 248 Positive Commandments are the essential means to empower a Jew to create a bond with his Creator. It is through performance of the 248 Positive Commandments that man effectively "constructs" his intimate relationship with G-d.[3] Every *mitzvah* within this category is therefore a call for action. It clearly determines exactly what he must do.

This contrasts starkly with the primary role of the 365 Prohibitive Commandments. Their intent is not the positive act of building, but rather a preventive measure against anything that will have a "deconstructive" effect upon his relationship with G-d.

The 248 Positive Commandments are on a higher level compared to the 365 Prohibitive Commandments.

This is why the 248 Positive Commandments are placed on a higher level compared to the 365 Prohibitive Commandments. This finds expression in the halachic principle of עֲשֵׂה דּוֹחֶה לֹא תַעֲשֶׂה, *[performance of] a Positive Commandment pushes aside [the noncompliance of] a Prohibitive Commandment*.[4] Take the following example. There is a Prohibitive Commandment to wear *shaatnez*, a mixture of wool and linen. And there is a Positive Commandment to wear *tzitzis* at the corners of a 4-cornered garment. The juxtaposition of these two commandments in the Torah[5] teaches that the positive fulfillment of the *mitzvah* of *tzitzis* could even include a *shaatnez* mix whose prohibition would be pushed aside.[6]

248: LOVE OF THE MITZVAH

The relationship between the 248 Positive Commandments and the 365 Prohibitive Commandments respectively parallels the concepts of אַהֲבָה, *love*, versus יִרְאָה, *awe*.

Man observes the 248 Positive Commandments in his loving worship of G-d. This is founded upon the feelings of *ahavah*; love has an "expansive" effect. It powerfully motivates man to act in order to honor G-d. The force that emanates from the soul propels man in the direction of "positive" action.

Meanwhile, abstaining from the 365 Prohibitive Commandments is a demonstration of the opposite force of *yirah*.[7] Awe causes a "contraction" effect. It advances the honor of Heaven through the avoidance of sin by turning inward through inactivity to not commit a negative sin.[8]

The force that emanates from the soul propels man in the direction of "positive" action.

THE BODY OF WORK

WE HAVE NOTED THAT THE 248 POSITIVE COMMANDMENTS RELATE to the positive acts that are responsible for building up man's relationship with G-d. The perfect vehicle to accomplish this is through the human body with its 248 bodily limbs.

248: BODILY LIMBS

Man is created בְּצֶלֶם אֱ-לֹהִים, *in the image of G-d.*[9] His spiritual form is mirrored, in some sense, by his physical body.[10] The Mishnah divides the human anatomy into רְמַ"ח אֵבָרִים, *248 limbs.*[11] There is an exact correlation between the 248 Positive Commandments and *ramach eivarim.*[12]

The Torah laws that obligate man relate to his biological make-up. Every part of the body corresponds to a specific Divine command. The 248 bodily limbs are said to "yearn" to perform the 248 Positive Commandments — which is precisely what they were created to do. Man's body was designed to fulfill the Divine Will. This is the purpose of his "machine" and what it was built to do. Accordingly, the 248

The 248 bodily limbs are said to "yearn" to perform the 248 Positive Commandments.

limbs cry out to man daily, "Make sure you use us and live in our merit to prolong your days."[13] Here each limb will testify that it was used as a tool to perform the Divine Will. When a Jew, created in the image of G-d, fulfills the 248 commandments using the correspond-ing 248 limbs, he successfully transfers his potential into actual. His conduct enables him to strive to reach a state of perfection.

248: OF bOΘY ANΘ SOUL

The 248 Positive Commandments direct the limbs along the path of righteousness. They purify and sanctify man as body and soul work in partnership.

The commandments come to refine and sanctify the body.[14] This is true of every *mitzvah* whose effect is the same: to refine man's soul; "Torah was given לְצָרֵף הַבְּרִיּוֹת, *to purify creatures.*"[15] How does this purification process operate? The refinement occurs when the soul in the body is not drawn down into the physical world, but is spiritually drawn upward. The exalted qualities within every *mitzvah* exhort man to attain spiritual perfection.[16] He is not an animal formed of 248 limbs who is driven by his base instincts. His body is a vehicle that responds to a higher calling: a machine whose components can be used to observe all 248 Positive Commandments.

We will later see that the 365 Prohibitive Commandments cor-respond to the 365 days within the solar calendar that is symbolic of the protection within the natural order.[17] But the focus of the 248 Positive Commandments is about man perfecting his physical frame so that it mirrors his G-dly mission. This is the forum where man can actualize his potential and, through his attachment to G-d, attain some measure of perfection.[18] Every *mitzvah* has an impact to build his relationship with G-d. By not being drawn down into the coarse-ness of physicality and nature, the 248 Positive Commandments empower him to tap into the dimension of the spiritual.

248: AVRAhAM

When man masters his body, he dedicates it toward the fulfillment of all 248 Positive Commandments. The exemplar of this was Avra-ham, the first Jewish Patriarch.

Avraham originally had near control over all his bodily compo-nents with the exception of a handful.[19] After his circumcision, which is the indelible bodily sign of a servant of G-d,[20] he now gained control over all 248 limbs. This coincided with the name change from Avram to Avraham — the latter name having the numerical value of 248.[21]

Avraham pioneered a life that reflected the ultimate level of refinement that observing *mitzvos* can accomplish. Avraham taught the world that access to the Divine did not require separation from the body. By personal example, Avraham demonstrated that the opposite was true: the way to G-d necessitated that man perfect all 248 parts of the body which would result in their elevation.[22] All 248 bodily limbs were כֵּלִים, *vessels*, to receive holy influence from the soul.[23] The obligation rests upon Avraham's descendants, the Jewish nation, to emulate their forefather through their commitment to observe the 248 Positive Commandments.

248: SHEMA

Finally, the complete acceptance of G-d's Kingship requires that man observe all 248 Positive Commandments, which correspond to man's 248 limbs. It is impossible for man to observe every commandment every day. Nevertheless, the daily recital of the Torah passages of the *Shema*, which has a total of 248 words (245 words plus 3 opening or closing words),[24] is the way for the Jew to declare his absolute acceptance of G-d's Kingship, which, in turn, guarantees him Divine protection.[25] Here every part of man's being (the 248 parts of the body parallel to 248 words of *Shema*) is rectified by the illumination of G-d's Oneness that he accepts upon himself.[26]

The Jew whose 248 bodily limbs dwell in This World must ensure that he lovingly dedicates each and every part of his being toward *mitzvah* performance. In so doing, he willingly accepts the Heavenly Kingship of G-d and takes positive and active steps to develop a relationship to the Master of the Universe through a lifetime of worship — a relationship that builds him his eternal world.

The complete acceptance of G-d's Kingship requires that man observe all 248 Positive Commandments.

The Jew must ensure that he lovingly dedicates each and every part of his being toward mitzvah performance.

NOTES

1. See "613: At Your Command."
2. See "365: For Your Protection."
3. The verse, "Its ways are ways of pleasantness" (*Mishlei* 3:17), corresponds to the 248 Positive Commandments that actively bring man toward perfection (*Maharal, Tiferes Yisrael* 7).

4. *Maharal, Chiddushei Aggados, Makkos* 23b (Vol. 4, p. 7).
5. *Devarim* 22:11-12.
6. *Yevamos* 3b-4a.
7. *Ramban, Shemos* 20:8.
8. R' Yitzchak Hutner, *Pachad Yitzchak, Shabbos* 2.
9. *Bereishis* 1:27.
10. *Maharal, Chiddushei Aggados,* op. cit. (Vol. 4, p. 6-7).
11. See Mishnah, *Oholos* 1:8, for the computation of the 248 limbs.
12. *Makkos* 23b.
13. *Tanchuma, Ki Seitzei* 2.
14. *Ramban, Shir HaShirim* 4:11.
15. *Bereishis Rabbah* 44:1.
16. *Maharal,Tiferes Yisrael* 7.
17. See "365: For Your Protection."
18. *Maharal,* op. cit. 4, 7. See "613: At Your Command."
19. The 5 organs were his 2 eyes, his 2 ears, and his male organ.
20. *Maharal, Gevuros Hashem* 35.
21. *Nedarim* 32b; *Tanchuma Korach* 12.
22. *Maharal, Derech Chaim* 5:3.
23. *Sfas Emes, Vayishlach* 5658.
24. *Shulchan Aruch, Orach Chaim* 61:3.
25. *Maharal, Nesiv HaTorah* 16; see also *Nesiv HaAvodah* 9.
26. *Ramchal, Derech Hashem* 4:4.

250
KORACH'S REBELS

There were 250 men in
Korach's assembly
that challenged Moshe
in the Wilderness.

THE REBELLION

THE JEWISH DIGNITARIES WHO SUPPORTED KORACH NUMBERED 250.

Korach spearheaded the infamous, ill-fated rebellion against Moshe in the Wilderness. Joining him in this challenge to Moshe's authority were the brothers Dasan and Aviram, as well as Ohn ben Peles (who withdrew due to his wife's influence).[1]

In addition to the primary antagonists, there was also a group of 250 men who are described by the Torah as the *adas Korach*, congregation of Korach.[2]

The group of 250 antagonists are described by the Torah as the "adas Korach, congregation of Korach."

250: heads of the sanhedrin

Significantly, the 250 men were not a rabble of troublesome no-good-doers from among the community. They were in a different league from the renowned troublemakers Dasan and Aviram. Rather than ordinary individuals, they actually represented some of the most prominent communal leaders.

Significantly, the 250 men were not a rabble of troublesome no-good-doers from among the community.

The 250 men were heads of the Sanhedrin, the Great Court of judges; the majority of them were from the Tribe of Reuven.[3] Indeed, the Torah confirms their elevated nature by classifying them as "princes of the congregation, elected men of the assembly, men of renown."[4]

250: blue garments

Korach's rabble sought to ridicule the integrity of Moshe and the Torah laws.

In their dispute, Korach's rabble sought to ridicule the integrity of Moshe and the Torah laws. There is a *mitzvah* that a 4-cornered garment requires that *tzitzis* strings be attached to them.[5] Whilst most of the *tzitzis* strings were white, there was the inclusion of a *techeiles* string, dyed sky-blue, a color that alluded to the sea, the Heavens, and G-d's Throne of Glory.[6] The requirement that one of the strings be *techeiles* was irrespective of the color of the garment.

The Midrash relates that the 250 men each donned a *tallis* dyed with *techeiles*, sky-blue coloring, and came before Moshe with the following halachic inquiry. "Is this garment obligated with *tzitzis* and the *techeiles* string or not?" they asked. "Yes" replied Moshe. They ridiculed this ruling as being illogical. "How could this possibly be a requirement? Is not the whole garment itself of this same color? Why, then, is there even the need for this *techeiles* string?"[7]

250: high priesthood

That the insurgence led by Korach was made up of different parties that came with different agendas is evident from their respective complaints, their actions, and their dissimilar fates.

The main attack voiced by Korach was leveled against Moshe's leadership. Korach was jealous that he had not been appointed the prince of Levi — a title that went to his cousin. Dasan and Aviram — continuing their past history of troublemaking — brazenly sought to stir up more mischief by engaging in argument through their opposition to Moshe.[8]

But the grievances of the 250 men did not propose to challenge Moshe's preeminent prophetic excellence or to oppose his supreme Torah authority. Instead, their protestations were directed against the exclusivity of Aharon with the rights and entitlements of the High Priesthood.

There were some noble intentions within the position taken by the 250 men. Implicit in the 250 blue garments they donned was their declaration that, in fact, "the entire congregation is holy and amongst them dwells G-d."[9] In the symbolic terms of their analogy, a single *techeiles* thread should not be any holier than a garment that is fully blue. No Jew deserves a higher level of holiness. Did not every Jew behold the Divine Revelation in the giving of Torah at Sinai? They deemed that the very position of High Priesthood itself was unnecessary.[10]

The grievances of the 250 men were directed against the exclusivity of Aharon with the rights and entitlements of the High Priesthood.

250: fire-pans

Their position carried many of the hallmarks of the sin of Nadav and Avihu, Aharon's sons who died for bringing a "strange fire." Like Nadav and Avihu, the 250 men who followed Korach craved to elevate their spiritual station by drawing close to G-d to reach the apex

Their position carried many of the hallmarks of the sin of Nadav and Avihu, Aharon's sons who died for bringing a "strange fire."

of holiness.[11] They pined for the privileges of the High Priesthood. One of the most prominent sacrificial offerings associated with this position was the קְטֹרֶת, *incense*, that epitomizes closeness to the Holy One (קְטֹרֶת is derived from the word קֶשֶׁר and its Aramaic equivalent קַטַר, which denotes "connection").[12] The contest in which the 250 men were challenged was for each to bring a *ketores*-offering on the morrow of the rebellion, outside the *Ohel Moed*, Tent of Meeting.[13]

Despite their noble motivations, the 250 men suffered the same fate as Aharon's sons, Nadav and Avihu.[14] A Divine fire issued from the innermost chamber to consume them.[15] Whereas Korach, Dasan, and Aviram were swallowed by the ground along with all of their possessions, the fire pans of the 250 men were actually consecrated. They were collected and used for services of holiness befitting the sanctified intent of their owners.[16]

Despite their noble motivations, the 250 men suffered the same fate as Aharon's sons.

250: FIRE OF THE SOUL

The theme of fire is hinted at in the Hebrew word נֵר, candle, whose numerical value is 250

The theme of fire — the fire-pans of incense, the fire that consumed the men — is hinted at in the Hebrew word נֵר, *candle*, whose numerical value is 250 — the number of rebels in Korach's assembly.

The life force of the *neshamah*, soul, is described as a *ner* in the sense that "The candle of G-d is the soul of man."[17] The flame of a candle resembles man's soul as it craves to rise upward and draw close to its Creator. Conversely, man's body pulls him down into the physical environment of This World.

The function of the Positive Commandments is to direct man's actions to serving G-d.[18] Here the physical body joins together with the spiritual soul in the ideal partnership. There are the 248 Positive Commandments. In addition, there are the 2 different attitudes in the general approach to *mitzvah* observance: אַהֲבַת ה׳, *love of G-d*, and יִרְאַת ה׳, *fear of G-d*. These combine (248 + 2) totaling 250.[19] This is the ideal *ner* — a soul aflame in its burning desire to worship G-d.

This is the ideal ner — a soul aflame in its burning desire to worship G-d.

The soul of the Jew burns brightly to serve G-d. This yearning was epitomized in the 250 members of Korach's assembly. Regrettably, noble intentions notwithstanding, they sought to do something that G-d had not commanded. A Jew should similarly be content to operate within the context of his personal circumstances and where he finds himself. This is where he has to do his best. He must therefore not covet another's position; he should focus instead on pursuing and fulfilling his designated mission.

388 / Jewish Wisdom in the Numbers

NOTES

1. *Sanhedrin* 109b-110a.
2. *Bamidbar* 16:1-35.
3. See *Rashi, Bamidbar* 16:1.
4. *Bamidbar* 16:2. See *Sanhedrin* 110a and *Midrash HaGadol, Korach.*
5. *Bamidbar* 15:37-41.
6. See "32: Your Honor."
7. *Yerushalmi Sanhedrin* 10:1, *Tanchuma Yashan, Korach* 5.
8. See *Maharal, Chiddushei Aggados Sanhedrin* 109b (Vol. 3, p 265), who explains that Dasan and Aviram were not interested in procuring the priesthood.
9. *Bamidbar* 16:3.
10. *Maharal, Gur Aryeh, Bamidbar* 16:1 [10].
11. *Shelah HaKadosh, Parashas Korach, Torah Ohr* 5; p.54-58. They mistook the exalted connection of Moshe's closest relatives to spiritual positions of grandeur as attributed to Moshe praying on their behalf rather than this being a Divine decree.
12. R' Menachem Recanati, *Tetzaveh.* See *Maharal, Derashah L'Shabbos Shuvah* p. 81. See also "11: The Outsider."
13. *Bamidbar* 16:16-18.
14. Ibid. 26:10.
15. Ibid. 16:35.
16. Ibid. 17:2-4.
17. *Mishlei* 20:27; see *Shabbos* 30b.
18. See "248: In Action."
19. *Zohar* 2, 166b.

300
THE WAY OF LIFE

300 relates to the strength
or vibrancy of life.

Like the number 3, this number calls for
not deviating to the 2 extremities
but to follow the straight middle pathway of life.

It is the wisdom of loyally walking in the
path of G-d through the Jewish nation's
unswerving dedication to halachah.

A POSITION OF STRENGTH

3 enables the establishment of something strong and enduring.

THE NUMBER 300 RELATES TO THE THEMES WITHIN 3.

We have noted that 3 enables the establishment of something strong and enduring.[1] This is contained within the statement that a "3-ply cord is not speedily cut."[2] Once there are 3 pillars in place, there is the strength of a permanent state.

The position of strength first exhibited within 3 finds greater expression in 300.

The position of strength first exhibited within 3 finds greater expression in 300. Aside from containing the numeric symbolism of 3, the number 300 extends it to encompass 3 consecutive numeric denominations: single units (1 x 3 = 3), tens (10 x 3 = 30) and hundreds (100 x 3 = 300). Consequently, 300 stands as an exceptional display of strength with the power to conquer or vanquish others.[3]

Prominent examples of 300 as the symbol of strength are found within the 300 soldiers of Gidon's army and other armies, in the context of the strength of military warriors.

300: GIDON'S ARMY

During the era of the *Shoftim*, Judges, there was a call to arms to fight the Midianites. Out of an assembled army of 32,000 Jewish soldiers, Gidon sent away 22,000. But this did not conclude the selection process. Of those remaining, a further test was arranged to excise the idolaters from the Jewish army. In the end, Gidon was left with only 300 righteous men — a miniscule fraction of the original number.[4]

Gidon was left with only 300 righteous men — and they were able to miraculously secure a great victory against their enemy.

Gidon and his 300 men entered the enemy camp at the dead of night. They created pandemonium and, despite being outnumbered, were able to miraculously secure a great victory against their enemy.

300: WARRIORS

The strength of David's mighty warriors is similarly associated with the number 300. The prophet records that the warrior Avishai wielded a spear over 300 corpses.[5] An identical show of strength is mentioned when Yashvam slew 300 with a spear.[6] In an earlier era, Shimshon wrought havoc with the Pelishtim using 300 foxes. He tied the foxes' tails into pairs and placed a burning torch between them. He then released the 300 foxes into the countryside, where they set his enemies' fields ablaze.[7]

Many generations later, in the campaign to conquer Jerusalem, Nebuchadnezzar sent his general Nevuzaradan 300 mules laden with iron hammers with which to break the walls of Jerusalem.[8] This was the Babylonian tyrant's assertion of strength in an offensive against the Holy City, which resulted in the destruction of the First Temple.[9]

Other examples of 300 used in the context of a powerful army include: the 300,000 men from Israel who comprised King Shaul's army in Bezek[10]; the 300,000 troops from the tribe of Yehudah led by King Asa[11]; and an army of 300,000 Roman troops with drawn swords that conquered Tur Malka.[12]

300: BLOODBATH

One infamous use of 300 occurred during the Egyptian exile. Because Pharaoh suffered from leprosy, his ministers instructed that he daily bathe in the blood of 300 Jewish infants.[13] Mercilessly, Pharaoh had children slaughtered every day to meet this quota.

Blood denotes the life force within the human body: "for the blood, it is the spirit."[14] As long as blood flows through man's veins, he is alive and vibrant. Conversely, the ending of life is associated with the spilling of blood. Like blood, the number 3, and by extension the number 300, symbolize life-affirming qualities. The ends of 2 extremities have their parallel in death by placing definite limits upon man's lifespan: the point when man is born and the point when he dies. (Contrast this to what is said concerning the 3rd Jewish Patriarch: "Yaakov our father did not die."[15]) But the number 3, which conceptually lies at the midpoint between the two ends, relates to the vibrancy of life itself. Consequently, the daily spilling of the blood of 300 Jewish infants was symbolically intended to give Pharaoh the qualities of life and strength by taking it away from the Jewish infants by spilling their blood — their life force.[16]

Number 3, which conceptually lies at the midpoint between the two ends, relates to the vibrancy of life itself.

THE WAY TO GO

THE STRENGTH OF 3, WHICH FORMS THE REQUISITE PARTS OF A PROCESS (beginning, middle, and end), introduces a state of equilibrium.[17] Two contradictory opposites deviate away from each other. In a negative sense, 2 relates to the dichotomy of sin[18] and the extremities that turn toward death.[19] But the positioning of a 3rd point assumes the "middle ground" — one that veers neither toward the left nor toward the right — and that therefore creates a peaceful state of harmony.[20] 300, like the number 3, also represents the pathway of life — the path which man should ideally select in his journey through life.

300 represents the pathway of life — the path which man should ideally select in his journey through life.

300: ThE hALAChIC pATh

Man can adhere to the "straight and narrow" by adopting a 3rd option: the "golden mean."

When facing forward, there are 3 available options that unfold before man: he can (1) turn to the right, (2) turn to the left, or (3) adhere to the "straight and narrow." Symbolically the 3rd option represents the "golden mean"[21] or "middle road." This calls for resilience; man doggedly refuses to be blown off course even where confronting the ideological winds of change. He will not break with tradition.

This concept finds expression in fidelity to Torah law, which clearly defines Jewish observance — one that is appropriately termed הֲלָכָה, literally, *the way*.[22] Here the Jew loyally walks in the pathway of G-d — no matter what life throws at him — and will not depart from it. Halachah, as associated with 3 as the "middle road," finds its greater expression through 300 as found in terms of the number of "300 laws."[23]

Halachah finds its greater expression through 300 as found in terms of the number of "300 laws."

There were 300 laws that were forgotten upon the death of Moshe, until they were later reinstated for the Jewish People by Osniel ben Kenas.[24] There were 300 laws regarding a leprous spot.[25] There are 300 laws derived from a verse that on the surface deals solely with genealogy.[26] And there are 300 passages used in interpreting the laws regarding a sorceress.[27]

300: A TOWER FLOATING IN ThE AIR

Doeg and Achitophel were two major Jewish antagonists of King David. Both were outstanding Torah scholars who raised 300 halachic inquiries concerning "a tower floating in the air."[28] Nevertheless, they tragically lost their portion in the World to Come.[29]

Several interpretations are given to explain the "tower floating in the air."[30] The image is graphically represented by the Hebrew letter *lamed* (ל), whose upper part protrudes above the rest of the letter and which stands higher than all other letters of the Hebrew Alphabet. It is therefore symbolic of *seichel*, intellectual qualities, within man, in reference to the ability to connect to G-d and the spiritual worlds. Like a tower, this is neither fully integrated nor absolutely grounded within the physical realm. It floats in the air in the sense that it gravitates upward due to its G-dly origins.[31]

Once the time the Torah was given at Sinai, its home rests among the Torah scholars on Earth without interference from Heaven.[32] Nevertheless, it is based upon a Divinely given Torah. A tradition of a certain halachah being faithfully transmitted down the generations triumphs — even in the face of any rational arguments or exegetical proofs to the contrary.

A tradition of a certain halachah being faithfully transmitted down through the generations triumphs.

Perhaps the most famous historical example of this was the Torah law excluding a Moabite man from marrying into the Jewish congregation. The question is: What is the law concerning a Moabite woman? This issue became relevant upon investigating the status of Ruth the Moabite, a proselyte who became David's great-grandmother.

Here the great Torah scholar Doeg irrefutably proved that Ruth should not be included in the Jewish congregation. He marshaled an impressive array of logical arguments and exegetical proofs in support of this position. Doeg questioned the validity of David. He claimed that David was a Moabite male due his paternal ancestry through Yishai, the grandson of Ruth, and thus halachically prohibited from marrying a Jewess.[33] Furthermore, Doeg also called into question David's anointment as a viable king fit to rule over Israel.[34]

But the halachic ruling is that a Moabite woman is permitted even though a Moabite man is not.

But the halachic ruling is otherwise. The Torah scholarship of Doeg and Achitophel was tainted by their personal animosity. Notwithstanding their proficiency in Torah, their rulings were contrary to the transmitted tradition that a Moabite woman *is* permitted even though a Moabite man is not. This was a fine example of "a tower floating in the air" — a ruling determined by accepted tradition despite human logic.

300: NOT OF THIS WORLD

The affinity of the number 300 to halachah taps into its frequent usage as the "numeric extremity." In an abstruse aggadic passage, a description of waves rising up to a height of 300 *parsaos* in the ocean is used to denote that "which is raised from the depths." Similar to the "tower floating in the air," 300 indicates that which is elevated over the land.[35] Indeed, 300 symbolizes something that is not upon the ground but that which rises above it.[36]

This is an accurate description of halachah: the Torah laws may be *for* This World, but they are not *of* This World. They fully relate to how to live within the physical world. Nevertheless, they are not grounded in it because their origins emanate from Above.

300: The halachic process

Halachah calls for a Jew to walk in the "ways of G-d." He must willingly nullify human wisdom to the Divine wisdom. 300, as a symbol of halachah in reference to the laws of a tower floating in the air — like something that is not grounded on Earth but rather is in the Heavens — which comes to defy the logic of the Earthly realm.

Halachah is the unswerving fidelity of the Jewish People, throughout their history, to continually walk in pathways of G-d. Torah is lovingly transmitted from parent to child, from teacher to pupil, down the generations.[37] Indeed, an integral component in the nature of halachah is for later generations to readily apply the principles and rulings of earlier halachic codifiers to contemporary circumstances.

Just as 3 denotes a continuous chain, the 300 of halachah also epitomizes the ongoing, unbroken transmission of Torah. Indeed, the Talmud records that Rabbi Yehudah ben Bava defied the Roman decree and continued to confer the unbroken chain of *semichah*, rabbinic ordination — even at a cost of his life — as soldiers pierced his body with 300 iron spears.[38]

Thus we see that 300 marks the Jewish People's fierce loyalty to fulfill the Torah's dictates throughout the centuries. Their dedication is extant even where the law does not conform to their logic.

NOTES

1. See "3: Three Dimensional."

2. *Koheles* 4:12.

3. *Maharal, Chiddushei Aggados, Sanhedrin* 96a (Vol. 3, p. 202).

4. *Shoftim* 7:3-8.
5. *II Shmuel* 23:18; *I Divrei HaYamim* 11:20.
6. Ibid. 11:11.
7. *Shoftim* 15:4-5.
8. *Sanhedrin* 96b. After triumphing over Chizkiyahu king of Yehudah, Sancheirev king of Assyria required from him a tribute that included 300 talents of silver (*II Melachim* 18:14).
9. *Maharal*, loc. cit.
10. *I Shmuel* 11:8.
11. *II Divrei HaYamim* 14:7. See also ibid. 17:14.
12. *Gittin* 57a. See *Maharal, Netzach Yisrael* 6.
13. *Shemos Rabbah* 1:34.
14. *Vayikra* 17:11,14, *Devarim* 12:23.
15. *Taanis* 5b.
16. *Maharal, Gevuros Hashem* 54.
17. See "3: Three-Dimensional."
18. See "2: Opposite and Equal."
19. *Maharal*, loc. cit.
20. See "3: Three-Dimensional."
21. See *Rambam, Hilchos Deios* 1:1-7, and *Shemoneh Perakim* about the ideal of the "golden mean."
22. "'The ways of the world are His' (*Chabakkuk* 3:6); do not read *halichos*, 'ways,' but *halachos*, 'laws'" (*Megillah* 28b).
23. *Maharal, Chiddushei Aggados, Sanhedrin* 106b (Vol. 3, p. 250).
24. *Temurah* 16a.
25. *Sanhedrin* 68a, based upon *Vayikra* 13:1-28. See also *Maharal, Chiddushei Aggados, Sanhedrin* 68a (Vol. 3, p. 167).
26. *Zohar* 1, 145b. The verse in question is *Bereishis* 36:39.
27. *Yerushalmi, Sanhedrin* 7:13; see *Chagigah* 13a where 300 barrels of oil in an attic were used to reconcile the words in the book of *Yechezkel* in line with Torah.
28. *Sanhedrin* 106b; *Chagigah* 15b.
29. *Sanhedrin* 90a.
30. See *Rashi* to ibid. 106b and to *Chagigah* 15b.
31. *Maharal, Chiddushei Aggados, Sanhedrin* 106b (Vol. 3, p. 250).
32. *Bava Metzia* 59b, 86a; See *Derashos HaRan* 5.
33. David's Jewish identity was never under dispute as his mother was Jewish. But Doeg claimed David was a Moabite male. The halachah is that although a Moabite male can marry a convert or one born from most illicit relationships, he is nevertheless prohibited to enter the "Jewish congregation," namely, to marry a Jewish woman. See *Rambam, Hilchos Issurei Biah* 12:17-18.
34. *Yevamos* 76b. See *Rus Rabbah* 4:9.
35. *Maharal, Chiddushei Aggados, Bava Basra* 73a (Vol. 3, p. 86).
36. Ibid., 74a (Vol. 3, p. 102).
37. The Torah that Moshe commanded us is the heritage of the Congregation of Yaakov (*Devarim* 33:4). See *Rambam, Introduction to Mishnah,* who lists the historic personalities in the transmission of Torah from Moshe until the codification of the Talmud.
38. See *Sanhedrin* 13b-14a.

310
WORLDS APART

A righteous person is set to inherit
a total of 310 spiritual worlds
in the World to Come.

BEST OF BOTH WORLDS

The number
310 represents
the number of
worlds reserved
for the righteous
in the hereafter.

THE NUMBER 310 REPRESENTS THE NUMBER OF WORLDS RESERVED
for the righteous in the hereafter.

Jewish tradition teaches that life exists on two interrelated realms:
עוֹלָם הַזֶּה, *This World*, and עוֹלָם הַבָּא, *the World to Come*. Of key significance are the contrast and interrelationship between these worlds.

THIS WORLD; THE WORLD TO COME

*Eisav staked
a claim over
the ephemeral
physical arena
of Olam Hazeh
Yaakov chose
the spiritual
inheritance of
the future in the
eternity of Olam
Haba.*

Yitzchak's twin sons apportioned these worlds between them. Eisav
staked a claim over the ephemeral physical arena of *Olam Hazeh* that
he would lord over.[1] Yaakov chose the spiritual inheritance of the future
in the eternity of *Olam Haba*.[2] Consequently, Yaakov's descendants
would never truly belong to the present world. No matter how hard
they would try to integrate, the Jewish People would always remain
outcasts. They were foreigners who would never really fit in.[3] For them,
"home" territory was not in *Olam Hazeh*; it was reserved for *Olam Haba*.

Belief in the existence of *Olam Haba* is a fundamental of Jewish
faith.[4] What are the unique features of *Olam Hazeh* and *Olam Haba*?
Are these worlds independent or interrelated? What is the relationship between them? Is it possible to have "the best of both worlds"?

*Olam Hazeh
is a temporary
mode of
existence. And
it is the process
of "becoming."*

Olam Hazeh is a temporary mode of existence. It is the fleeting
life of the physical world — a short time period that does not continue
indefinitely. Both on an individual and on a national level, *Olam Hazeh*
is the realm of preparation in the Earthly hallway that leads to the
celestial palace.[5] It is the time of hard work. It is the place of growth
and movement. It is the means to an end.[6] And it is the process of
"becoming." Like the transient state of a fetus carried by its mother
prior to its emergence as an infant at birth, the world of *Olam Hazeh*
is the necessary passageway to the ultimate "birth" in the reality of
Olam Haba.[7] This is why *Olam Hazeh* is characterized as "today" in the
here-and-now vis-à-vis the hereafter of the "tomorrow" of *Olam Haba*.[8]

*Olam Haba
celebrates
man's arrival
at his ultimate
destination.*

Olam Haba celebrates man's having reached his ultimate destination. It is the process of "being." Here man earns spiritual reward
for his work in *Olam Hazeh*. All the pleasures of *Olam Hazeh* can-

not compare to one moment of spiritual ecstasy in *Olam Haba*.[9] The world of reward is created as a direct result of the life choices made by man in *Olam Hazeh*.[10] Every *mitzvah* that a man performs in *Olam Hazeh* gives him merit in *Olam Haba*.[11] It is not the means to an end; it is the end itself.

There are many misconceptions about the nature of *Olam Haba*. Some mistakenly portray *Olam Haba* as the continuous *on-going life* of *Olam Hazeh*, albeit in a utopian state. They wrongly assume that there are essentially no real differences between the respective worlds.[12] Others view *Olam Haba* as the introduction of an entirely new existence; something completely unrelated to man's Earthly existence. This presupposes that the worlds are unconnected — something contradicted by the name *Olam Haba*, which indicates that it is the future world that naturally follows This World (הַבָּא, *next*), coming about as a direct result of man's life in *Olam Hazeh*.[13] While the world of *Olam Haba* is different from *Olam Hazeh*, the two are nevertheless inextricably linked.

In truth, the nature of *Olam Haba* as the world of reward lies far beyond man's comprehension.[14] Perhaps the most significant difference between the two worlds is that *Olam Haba* will be where man experiences a *timeless state of existence*! This does not mean "living on and on ad infinitum"; it means living an existence that is not restricted by the time continuum that operates in *Olam Hazeh*.[15] In the eternal world, man lives within those worlds that are the natural outgrowth of his deeds created during his lifetime in *Olam Hazeh*. This reward is defined in terms of man's connection and level of relationship to G-d. It is this that determines man's true state of existence. This relates to the number 310, the worlds the righteous will inherit.

The reward of Olam Haba is defined in terms of man's connection and level of relationship to G-d.

310: EXISTENCE

Every Jew is designated a portion in the spiritual realm of *Olam Haba*.[16] This general entitlement relates to his *identity as a member of the Jewish People*. Nevertheless, his specific portion is individually determined depending upon how he lived his life in *Olam Hazeh*. It is shaped to the degree that the individual develops a relationship with G-d through his Torah study and *mitzvah* performance. The phrase, "For man goes to his everlasting home,"[17] which uses the singular expression ("his ... home"), clearly denotes that a person is individually responsible for creating the spiritual realm that he can then call his own.[18] Likewise, G-d will construct 7 *chuppos,* canopies, for each

Every Jew is designated a portion in the spiritual realm of Olam Haba.

The Mishnah
teaches that
G-d is destined
to give the
righteous
individual a
total of 310
worlds in Olam
Haba.

righteous person, depending on his level.[19] This mirrors his individual efforts, his personal circumstances, and his life's tribulations.[20]

The Mishnah teaches that G-d is destined to give the righteous individual a total of 310 worlds in Olam Haba. This is derived from the verse "... those who love Me to inherit יֵשׁ, and I will fill their storehouses"[21]; the numerical value of yeish is 310.[22] It is up to man to create his "worlds of existence" by using his Yetzer Tov, Good Inclination, to serve G-d and defeat his Yetzer Hara, Evil Inclination.[23]

The meaning of yeish is existence, being, or reality. In spiritual terms, the true designation of the term "existence" is not the short-lived, illusory nature of Olam Hazeh that falsely purports to be "the real thing." Reality is reserved for the spiritual world that epitomizes the true state of existence as something very real and everlasting.[24] Here the superficial darkness of Olam Hazeh will be dispelled by the brilliantly illuminating revelation of G-d's Glory. Here man will take eternal delight in his everlasting attachment to G-d as the One Who defines Existence and Reality.[25]

Reality is
reserved for the
spiritual world
that epitomizes
the true state
of existence
as something
very real and
everlasting.

310: JEWISH INHERITANCE

In addition to the meaning of the word yeish as "existence," yeish also describes that which has "substance." Man exists to direct all his energies and possessions so that they turn into matters of substance. This substance is directed toward a designated purpose, in an act where everything in existence has meaning. Then it becomes his sacred נַחֲלָה, inheritance.

The fruit of
man's labors
exerted in Olam
Hazeh earns an
eternal portion
in Olam Haba.

Typically, an inheritance taps into the motif of continuity. In the context of the two worlds, inheritance is where existence extends from one world to the next. Here the fruit of man's labors exerted in This World of Olam Hazeh earns a Jew an eternal portion in the Next World, Olam Haba.

The correlation between man's efforts in Olam Hazeh earning him a "portion" in Olam Haba has its precedent in history when the Children of Israel inherited their individual portion in Eretz Yisrael, Land of Israel. The Holy Land serves as a potent prototype that captures the essential spiritual nature of Olam Haba. Just as every Jew had a portion in the Land of Israel, so too would every Jew be designated a portion in Olam Haba.[26] More than in all other countries, the existence of Israel in the Holy Land revolved around the principle of reward and punishment that is similar to that which governs the nature of Olam Haba.[27]

The reward of the 310 worlds for the righteous in *Olam Haba* is earned when the Jew dedicates his life in *Olam Hazeh* to spiritual, enduring pursuits. This is a sacred inheritance that is destined to exist for all eternity. The nature of *Olam Haba* depends entirely upon the life choices that an individual makes in *Olam Hazeh*.

The reward of the 310 worlds f is earned when the Jew dedicates his life in Olam Hazeh to spiritual, enduring pursuits.

NOTES

1. See "11: The Outsider."
2. See *Rashi, Bereishis* 25:22; see *Yalkut Shimoni Bereishis* 110 and *Tanna deVei Eliyahu Zuta* 19.
3. *Maharal, Netzach Yisrael* 15.
4. See *Rambam's Commentary to the Mishnah*, Introduction to *Sanhedrin*, Ch. 10.
5. *Pirkei Avos* 4:17.
6. Ibid. 4:18; *Maharsha, Avodah Zarah* 10b.
7. R' Yechiel Michel Tucazinsky, *Gesher HaChaim* 3:1. See "9: Where to Turn?"
8. *Eruvin* 22a.
9. *Pirkei Avos* 4:18; R' Dessler, *Michtav MeiEliyahu* 1, pp. 4-5.
10. See Midrash, *Mishlei* 11:21 that G-d made 2 worlds: one where man is to do good deeds, the other world in which he is to be rewarded. See *Kiddushin* 39b, which explains why This World is not the appropriate arena for reward.
11. *Avodah Zarah* 4b.
12. See *Pesachim* 50a about the distinction between *Olam Hazeh* and *Olam Haba* in the different blessings recited and how to pronounce the Name of G-d.
13. Otherwise, the opposite of עוֹלָם הַזֶּה, *This* World, should really have been עוֹלָם הַהוּא, *That* World.

14. See *Maharal, Tiferes Yisrael* 57-60 for several reasons why *Olam Haba* is not explicitly mentioned in the Written Torah.
15. R' Dessler, *Michtav MeiEliyahu*, 2, pp. 150-154.
16. *Sanhedrin* 90a.
17. *Koheles* 12:5.
18. *Koheles Rabbah* 12. See *Maharal, Derashah L'Shabbos Shuvah*, p. 70.
19. *Bava Basra* 75a, *Maharsha, Avodah Zarah* 10b.
20. The reward for the same *mitzvah* will vary according to the person performing it. This is the concept behind the principle, "According to the pain is the reward" (*Pirkei Avos* 5:27).
21. *Mishlei* 8:21.
22. Mishnah, *Uktzin* 3:12; *Midrash Tehillim* 31:6; *Sanhedrin* 100a. See "620: Crowing Glory," for the significance of the relationship between the numbers 310 and 620.
23. See *Vilna Gaon, Aderes Eliyahu, Bereishis* 2:7 for how man will inherit the 310 worlds through the manipulation of both inclinations. He earns 300 worlds by overpowering his *Yetzer Hara* (300 = יֵצֶר) that stands on his left. The final 10 are acquired by heeding the words of his *Yetzer Tov*, that stands on his right. This is beautifully alluded to by the letters of the word שֵׂי that are an acronym for יָמִין, *right*, and שׂמאל, *left*.
24. See "42: The Incredible Journey."
25. See also *Rambam, Mishnah Commentary, Uktzin* 3:12. See "31: There's Nothing to It!"
26. See *Kesubos* 111a for how one who walks 4 *amos* in the Holy Land is guaranteed to be one who belongs in *Olam Haba*. See, for example, *Shelah HaKadosh, Parashas Va'eschanan, Torah Ohr*, where the phrase טוב, *good*, is used for both the Holy Land and *Olam Haba*.
27. The inheritance of 310 worlds in *Olam Haba* is linked to the conquest of the Land of Israel and the defeat of her 31 kings. See *Tosafos Yom Tov*, end of *Uktzin* and "31: There's Nothing to It!"

318
The Loyal Servant

318 relates to the life and legacy of
Eliezer, the faithful servant
of the Patriarch Avraham.

TO SERVE

Ⓐ VRAHAM HAD A FORCE OF 318 MEN THAT HE LED INTO BATTLE against the 4 Kings.

318: AVRAHAM'S ARMY

The world war that erupted in the time of Avraham enveloped all of human civilization.

The world war that erupted in the time of Avraham enveloped all of human civilization. In the battle of the 4 Kings against the 5 Kings, Avraham's nephew Lot was taken prisoner. Actually, his capture was strategically orchestrated in a bid to lure Avraham into the fray.[1] News of Lot's imprisonment was relayed to Avraham by a fugitive from the battlefield.[2]

Risking his life for his errant nephew, who had earlier elected to leave the company of his righteous uncle, Avraham led 318 soldiers into battle. The Torah tells us that Avraham led "forth his trained men, those born in his house." Lot was freed from captivity. Avraham was victorious as he pursued the losing side a great distance, until he reached the region of Dan.[3]

318: WEAPONS IN BATTLE

The 318 men whom Avraham brought with him from his household in battle symbolically parallel the spiritual weapons in man's arsenal that he can use in his Divine service.

The 4 kings that Avraham fought symbolize the negative spiritual forces that oppose Israel.[4] Thus, the 318 men whom Avraham brought from his household symbolically parallel the spiritual weapons in man's arsenal that he can use in his Divine service. Here Avraham's perfection in both body and soul came to combat the forces of negativity.

In the verse, כִּי נֵר מִצְוָה וְתוֹרָה אוֹר, for *mitzvah* is a lamp and Torah is light,[5] the "*mitzvah* lamp" refers to *mitzvah* observance as performed through the 248 limbs of the human body,[6] while the phrase "Torah is light" refers to the Divine secret of the Jewish soul, said to be kabbalistically illuminated by 70 lights (following circumcision). Avraham's army of 318 alludes to the combination of 248 revealed limbs of the body together with 70 concealed parts of the soul (248 + 70 = 318).[7] This proves to be the ammunition necessary to overcome all types of hostilities that stand in opposition to Avraham and his spiritual legacy.

318: ELIEZER

The Talmud interprets the 318 men as a reference to Avraham's renowned servant, Eliezer.[8] In truth, the company of 318 men that escorted Avraham into battle was not necessary to guarantee that Avraham would emerge triumphant. What purpose, then, did they serve? The 318 men came to provide some opposition, according to the laws of nature, to counter the mighty kings. This was in order to conceal the extent of Avraham's miraculous victory, earned against an army that was superior both in military prowess and in number.

This concept is highlighted by Avraham's choice of exactly 318 men. The number was not arbitrary. It actually serves as an allusion to Eliezer, whose name has a numerical value of 318. It symbolizes that the victory against the kings could, in truth, be wholly attributed to Avraham, operating in partnership with his faithful servant, Eliezer.[9]

318 symbolizes that the victory be wholly attributed to Avraham, in partnership with his faithful servant, Eliezer.

318: MASTER AND SERVANT

What was the nature of the relationship between Avraham and Eliezer?

Man can be compared to the "master" who is in control over all his faculties, which are his "servants." Avraham was truly a master who exhibited control over all 248 of his limbs, which functioned as his servants, gainfully employed in his worship of G-d.[10] It was most befitting for a spiritual personality like Avraham to own a servant like Eliezer, who subjugated himself completely before his great master.

Avraham was no ordinary master. And Eliezer was no ordinary servant.

Their relationship saw the righteousness of Avraham projected through Eliezer. In turn, Eliezer was a reflection of Avraham, embodying his master's unique qualities.[11] Like his master Avraham, Eliezer also ruled over his passions.[12] Despite Eliezer's accursed background as a descendant of Canaan and Cham,[13] he was reared in *mitzvah* performance and would emulate the righteous ways of Avraham.[14]

Like his master Avraham, Eliezer also ruled over his passions.

In all Eliezer's actions and speech, he functioned in lieu of his great master. The Torah records Eliezer's travels and interactions at great length, illustrating the axiom, "The conversation of the Jewish Forefathers' servants is preferable to the teachings of the children."[15] As a servant, he was a natural, direct continuation of his master — something that was most immediately revealed through his dialogue. The root of the Hebrew word for *conversation* is שִׂיחַ, whose numerical value of 318 is the same as that of the name אֱלִיעֶזֶר, *Eliezer*.[16]

He was the loyal servant Avraham personally entrusted to find a bride for Yitzchak.[17] Pushing away all personal prejudice,[18] Eliezer operated as a virtual substitute for his master. He humbly introduced himself to Rivkah's family using the self-effacing words "I am the servant of Avraham."[19] This meant that, in essence, *Eliezer had no identity to call his own but that of his master.* The rabbinic comment that Eliezer bore a facial resemblance to Avraham conceptually symbolizes his absolute subjugation: he would perfectly reflect the will of his master.[20]

In essence, Eliezer had no identity to call his own but that of his master.

318: The INTERMEDIARY

Eliezer was the "one who drew up and gave others to drink from the Torah of his master."

Apart from his role as faithful servant of his master, Eliezer played a pivotal role as the intermediary between his master Avraham and the masses.

In history, Avraham marks the beginning of the 2,000 years of Torah.[21] In conveying the word of G-d to creation, Eliezer was a disseminator second only to Avraham himself. He was Avraham's protégé — the phrase דַּמֶּשֶׂק אֱלִיעֶזֶר is interpreted to reference Eliezer as the "one who drew up and gave others to drink from the Torah of his master."[22]

Eliezer was the intermediary to elevate Rivkah from the depths of impurity.

It was Eliezer who brought the elevated Torah of his master Avraham down to the level of the general populace. In this respect, his role was identical to the use of the bucket in a well, which serves as the essential medium to draw water from the pit. So, too, was Eliezer selected by Avraham as the intermediary responsible to elevate Rivkah from the depths of impurity (raised in the house of Besuel and Lavan) so that she would merit to become attached to the household of Avraham.[23]

318: FROM CURSED TO BLESSED

His greatness and achievements meant Eliezer was a serious contender to become his master's spiritual successor. But G-d said to Avraham that the accursed nature of Eliezer meant he was unsuitable.[24] Nevertheless in reward for Eliezer faithfully serving his master, he merited being able to transcend his station. He left the category of "accursed" and entered the category of "blessed."[25] In this respect, he would personify the Divine promise to Avraham, "You shall be a blessing."[26]

So while he would not usurp the position of Avraham's biological child and heir, Yitzchak, miraculously born to Avraham's wife, Sarah, Eliezer played a pivotal role in the emergence of the Jewish People through his selection of Rivkah as a partner to Yitzchak.

in reward for Eliezer faithfully serving his master, he merited being able to transcend his station.

NOTES

1. *Pirkei DeRabbi Eliezer* 27.
2. *Bereishis* 14:12-13.
3. Ibid. 14:14.
4. See "4: Finding the Place."
5. *Mishlei* 6:23.
6. See "248: In Action."
7. *Zohar* 1, 80b. *Bris milah*, covenant of circumcision, joins the soul and body in the removal of foreskin to reveal 70 lights (*Sfas Emes, Lech Lecha* 5661).
8. *Nedarim* 32a. See *Rabbeinu Bachya* (ad loc.) that the 318 members of Avraham's household returned home, leaving only Eliezer. See also *Daas Zekeinim Baalei Tosafos;* since Eliezer had chosen to stay, G-d gave him the strength of all 318 men.
9. *Maharal, Gur Aryeh, Bereishis* 14:14.
10. *Nedarim* 32b. See "248: In Action."
11. *Maharal, Chiddushei Aggados, Bava Basra* 58a (Vol. 3, p. 82).
12. *Bereishis Rabbah* 59:8.
13. Ibid. 59:9 and *Ayin Yosef* 12 ad loc.
14. *Rashi, Bereishis* 14:14.
15. *Bereishis Rabbah* 60:8.

16. Heard from Rav Moshe Shapiro, *shlita*.
17. *Bereishis* 24:1-8.
18. See *Rashi*, *Bereishis* 24:39, citing *Bereishis Rabbah* 59:9, for how Eliezer sought that his own daughter be considered as a suitable marriage partner for Yitzchak.
19. *Bereishis* 24:34.
20. *Bereishis Rabbah* 59:8 and *Maharzu* ad loc.
21. See "2000: The Borderline" and "6000: The End of the World."
22. *Yoma* 28b; see *Rashi*, *Bereishis* 15:2.
23. *Shem MiShmuel, Chayei Sarah* 5676. The *kifitzas haderech*, which can be understood to mean "jump up in space," that Eliezer experienced en route to Charan symbolizes an elevation for the inhabitants of Charan to miraculously become suitable to enter Avraham's household.
24. *Bereishis* 15:4.
25. *Bereishis Rabbah* 60:7.
26. *Bereishis* 12:2.

365
FOR YOUR
PROTECTION

365 are the number of sinews
in the human body, which correspond
to the Prohibitive Commandments.

Its central theme is to obligate
the Jew not to deviate from
his set boundaries.

THE PROHIBITIONS

HERE ARE 365 PROHIBITIVE COMMANDMENTS IN THE TORAH.
There are a total of תַּרְיַג מִצְוֹת, *613 commandments*, that subdivide into 2 categories.[1] The first is the רְמַ"ח מִצְוֹת עֲשֵׂה, *248 Positive
Commandments*, and the second is the שָׂסָ"ה מִצְוֹת לֹא תַעֲשֶׂה, *365 Prohibitive Commandments*.[2]

The common denominator within the 365 Prohibitive Commandments is that they relate to the nonperformance of certain actions.
These commandments are responsible for not permitting man's relationship with G-d to be torn asunder.

365: A CALL FOR INACTION

We have seen that the central focus of the רְמַ"ח מִצְוֹת עֲשֵׂה, *248
Positive Commandments*, is a call for action in the performance of
good deeds that positively contribute to man building his eternal relationship with G-d.[3]

The 365 Prohibitive Commandments have a different objective. In
terms of the relationship between man and G-d, they can be characterized as the "call for inaction." What is important here is not "what
you do," but rather "what you don't do." The 365 Prohibitive Commandments do not in themselves build up a relationship; rather, they
prevent the existing relationship from breaking down. In essence,
these 365 Prohibitive Commandments come to safeguard and maintain the existing status quo. They serve as essential deterrents so that
man does not sin, for this may jeopardize his relationship with G-d.
Breaking any one of the 365 Prohibitive Commandments constitutes
a violation that fractures this connection.

365: ON TRACK

The Jew must exclusively operate within the Torah framework
for living. The observance of the 365 Prohibitive Commandments

relates to this important principle. It means that he pledges to remain "inside" his set boundaries and vows not to throw off the yoke of Heavenly Kingship by heading "outside."[4]

Perhaps a simple analogy would be that of a train that passes from one place to another by traveling within the rail lines. The train driver must constantly operate by remaining on the tracks. So, too, must a Jew similarly operate exclusively within the set confines designated by G-d.

The Torah's dictates are not meant to be inhibitive; they are the essential safeguards to keep a Jew on the right path — on the straight and narrow.[5] He may not deviate even momentarily. Otherwise, he runs the risk of veering off course — something that could lead to fatal consequences.

The self-restraint a Jew displays by observing the 365 Prohibitive Commandments in order not to sin indicates the trait of *yirah*, awe or reverence.[6] His abstinence from sin is the means of advancing the honor of Heaven.[7] Throughout, he remains a loyal servant of G-d, heeding his Master's bidding and harnessing all the human faculties placed at his disposal in the worship of G-d.

The Torah's dictates are the essential safeguards to keep a Jew on the right path.

365: SINEWS

The human body is the Divinely designed machine with which to execute the Will of G-d. This is clearly seen in the close correlation between the 248 Positive Commandments and 248 bodily limbs.[8] This relationship extends to the 365 Prohibitive Commandments that find their parallel in the שְׁסָ"ה גִּידִים, *365 sinews/ligaments,* in the human body.[9]

The distinction between the types of commandments is similarly reflected in the different categories of bodily parts. Whereas the 248 Positive Commandments are deeds executed by the 248 limbs that are responsible for action, the 365 sinews are ligaments or tissues that are responsible for maintaining the body parts in their proper position.

This is symbolic of the 365 Prohibitive Commandments, whose role is to provide a rigid framework of law that holds man back from doing anything negative. It gives him the means to remain within the boundaries of Torah.[10] Alternatively, the 365 Prohibitive Commandments deter the bodily sinews from permitting a Jew to pursue an evil path. This development ensures that the body and soul of a Jew are journeying in the same direction.[11]

The 365 Prohibitive Commandments provide a rigid framework of law that holds man back from doing anything negative.

The concept of 365 maintaining firm boundaries finds expression in the solar year.

WE HAVE NOTED HOW THE 365 PROHIBITIVE COMMANDMENTS ARE the essential safeguards to prevent man from anything that could ruin his relationship with G-d. This has its parallel in the 365 sinews/ligaments that hold the limbs in place. The concept of 365 maintaining firm boundaries finds expression in the solar year.

365: SOLAR YEAR

There is a striking parallel between the 365 Prohibitive Commandments and the 365 full days of the solar calendar.

There is a striking parallel between the 365 Prohibitive Commandments and the 365 full days of the solar calendar.[12] The sun's movement, as viewed by man on Earth, operates exactly according to its fixed orbit: it rises in the morning, passes across the skies during the day, and sets in the evening.[13] It is a picture of consistency, never deviating from its path or from its natural course.[14]

The sun's impact upon our world cannot be overstated. Nature operates under its aegis. It is one of the primary forces responsible for the preservation of existence, which could not exist without it. The sun is understandably compared to the king of the natural world. Its dominion spans all 365 days of the solar year. Like the sun, man is also considered a king in the lower world. Consequently, not transgressing the 365 Prohibitive Commandments guarantees that man will not do anything to alter his existence or the existence of the world.[15]

A Jew must operate within the framework of the 365 days in a solar year so that he does not transgress any one of the sins from within the 365 Prohibitive Commandments.

This symbolism accords with the central theme of the 365 Prohibitive Commandments: to preserve the relationship with G-d. The Midrash relates that there were 365 cults in Damascus. Each was accorded 1 day of the year assigned to its worship. Tragically, the Jews adopted all 365 foreign gods. Pitifully, they were unable to find a single day upon which to worship G-d.[16] It is incumbent upon a Jew to operate within the established framework of the 365 days in a solar year so that he does not transgress on any one of these days any one of the sins from within the 365 Prohibitive Commandments.[17]

365: UNDER THE SUN

There is a major difference in the respective calendars computed by the non-Jewish world and the Jewish people. While the non-Jews in the Western world exclusively base their calendar on the solar year, the Jewish nation primarily bases its calendar on the moon and its monthly cycles.[18]

In truth, the Jewish People do not really belong in the natural world whose operations are conducted "under the sun"; that is, subject to its dominion. The physical realm boasts consistency and repetition but it has no affinity to the concept of newness: "There is nothing new under the sun."[19] This absence of freshness, however, has a negative dimension insofar as it can lead to staleness, lethargy, or rote.

DAY 365: YOM KIPPUR

Like the sun, the Evil Inclination, also called שָׂטָן, *Satan*,[20] is described as a great king.[21] The Satan's main objective is hindrance (*l'satein* means "to hinder"), to prevent man from worshiping G-d. But even if evil rules over man throughout the year, it cannot fully control him. On all 365 days of the solar year except for 1, the Satan is first given power to seduce the Jewish people into sin and is then given permission to stand before G-d and indict the sinners for their evil actions. This is hinted in the numerical value of the word *HaSatan,* the Satan, that equals 364. But on Yom Kippur, Day 365, there is no jurisdiction granted to the Accuser.[22] The atonement of this day means that the Children of Israel return to their purified, uncontaminated state.

On Yom Kippur, Day 365, there is no jurisdiction granted to the Accuser.

In a sense, the day of Yom Kippur affords a Jew the ultimate protection. It releases man from his affinity to sin. It frees him from a sinful existence. And it redirects him onto the path of Torah, where he reaffirms his commitment to journey within the framework symbolized by the 365 Prohibitive Commandments.

In summary, the 365 Prohibitive Commandments prevent the Jew from engaging in any activity that might come to jeopardize man's relationship to G-d. This category complements the 248 Positive Commandments that are responsible for building that relationship. Together, through the fulfillment of the 613 Commandments, a Jew creates and maintains an eternal relationship with his Creator.

The 365 Prohibitive Commandments prevent the Jew from engaging in any activity that might jeopardize his relationship to G-d.

NOTES

1. See "613: At Your Command."
2. See "365: For Your Protection."
3. See "248: In Action."
4. See also "11: The Outsider."
5. *Maharal, Tiferes Yisrael* 4, 7. See *Sfas Emes, Vayishlach* 5658, who characterizes the 248 limbs as the vessels able to receive holy influence from the soul while the 365 are safeguards for this light not to be dispersed elsewhere.
6. *Ramban, Shemos* 20:8.
7. R' Yitzchak Hutner, *Pachad Yitzchak, Shabbos* 2.
8. *Makkos* 23b. See "248: In Action."
9. *Zohar* I, 170b.
10. *Maharal,* op. cit. 7. He notes that the 248 limbs that actively bring man to his perfection correspond to first part of the verse, "Its ways are ways of pleasantness" (*Mishlei* 3:17), while the 365 sinews that ensure man stays within his boundaries correspond to the second part of the verse. "... all its pathways are of peace."
11. *Ramban, Shir HaShirim* 4:11. The Positive Commandments direct the limbs in the path of righteousness and goodness. They purify and sanctify him to emulate his Master.
12. *Makkos* 23b. The 365 days are not mathematically exact. The true length of the solar year is 365.25 days. This is consistent with the principle that Torah and halachah typically deal with "whole units" rather than parts. The Torah is therefore content with the use of an estimation rather than exactitude and precision. See *Chazon Ish, Orach Chaim* 138:4. This is the same reason that the irrational number π (*pi*) is also taken in Torah literature to be the whole figure of 3 rather than the more precise 3.14159 ... (*Eruvin* 13b; *Succah* 7b).
13. See *Koheles* 1:5.
14. See *Sanhedrin* 42a.
15. *Maharal,* op. cit. 4, 7. See also *Maharal, Chiddushei Aggados, Makkos* 23b (Vol. 4 pp. 6-7).
16. *Pesikta d'Eichah Rabbah* 10; *Shir HaShirim Rabbah* 1:6
17. The sun's symbolic exhortation to man is: "Make sure you do not transgress today [namely any one of the 365 days in the solar calendar] the equivalent transgression [of the 365] that might unsettle the balance of the universe by turning it into demerits" (*Tanchuma, Ki Seitzei* 2; *Rashi, Makkos* 23b).
18. *Succah* 29a. See "30: It's About Time."
19. *Koheles* 1:9.
20. See *Bava Basra* 16a.
21. *Koheles* 9:14, *Nedarim* 32b.
22. See *Yoma* 20a.

400
OF ALL PLACES

The number 400, as an extension of 4, deals with the correct use of space as the perfect forum for existence and achievement.

Just as 4 opposes the unity of 1, 400 also denotes opposing forces, such as exile or idolatrous intent, that lead to the displacement from one's true place

WHERE TO PLACE IT

T HE NUMBER 400 IS AN EXPANSION OF THE NUMBER 4 AND ITS symbolism.

The number 400 denotes where something is either "in place" or "out of place."

We have noted that 4 is the original number that conveys the concept of space and where something is either "in place" or "out of place."[1] 4 transposes into 400 and gives expression to this concept in terms of dimensions and distance.[2] The most prominent example of this is seen in the dimensions given to the Holy Land.

400 SQUARE AMOS: LAND OF ISRAEL

Eretz Yisrael, Land of Israel, is the homeland of the Jewish People. G-d gave the Holy Land to His Chosen Nation as the optimal place within which to worship G-d, to dutifully perform His commandments, and to forge a relationship in which man draws close to Him.[3] This country merits a unique level of Divine Providence. It is the place where "the Eyes of G-d are always upon it, from the beginning of the year until its end."[4] Living within its borders is the optimal environment in which to experience the Oneness of G-d. Conversely, one who dwells outside of it is as if he lives "without a G-d."[5]

The symbolic dimension given for the "national" space in Eretz Yisrael is the area of 400 square parsah.

Parallel to the "individual" space of man being 4 square *amos*,[6] the symbolic dimension given for the "national" space in *Eretz Yisrael* is the area of 400 square *parsah*.[7] (The computation of a *parsah* is a distance that is composed of 4 *mil*.[8]) In a symbolic act of acquisition, Avraham was instructed to walk the length and breadth of the land.[9] This would indicate that this land would later belong to his descendants. The number 400 features in the context of the occupation of holy space. It is within the sanctity of this appropriate "place" that the Jew can best worship G-d.

It is within the sanctity of this appropriate "place" that the Jew can best worship G-d.

BURIAL PLOT: 400 SHEKALIM

The first transaction Avraham made in *Eretz Yisrael* was the purchase of a burial plot for his beloved wife Sarah. The Jewish forefather identified *Me'aras HaMachpailah*, Double Cave, at the edge of a field as an appropriate plot. This was located in Kiryas Arba, literally "City of 4," prophetically named because of the 4 celebrated couples who were to be buried there: Adam and Chavah, Avraham and Sarah, Yitzchak and Rivkah, Yaakov and Leah.[10] Avraham paid the princely sum of 400 *shekalim* to the greedy owner, Ephron.[11]

In a spiritual sense, this real estate in Kiryas Arba was a microcosm of *Eretz Yisrael*.[12] The "City of 4" was a replica of the Holy Land in its dimensions of 400 square *parsah*. It epitomized the sanctification of the homeland chosen for the Jewish nation, the descendants of their saintly ancestors who were interred in this burial plot.

DISPLACEMENT

N OT ONLY DOES 4 DETERMINE "THE PLACE," IT ALSO STANDS FOR something that diverges "out of place." We noted that this is comparable to the 4 directions on a 2-dimensional horizontal plane that moves away from a 1 central unified point.[13]

Thus, the number 400 is also synonymous with idol worship, which diverges from the Singular, the Unity of G-d. 400 also reflects the state of national exile when the Jewish nation, as a united entity, is displaced from its rightful location.

400: TRACTATES OF IDOL WORSHIP

The number 4 represents idol worship in the multiplicity of negative forces that are an affront to the Oneness of G-d.[14] This theme is carried through to the number 400.

The first Patriarch, Avraham, single-handedly taught the world monotheism. He took an iconoclastic stand against the paganism of his era by devoting his full energies to call out in the Name of the One G-d.[15] There were a total of 400 chapter divisions in Avraham's comprehensive "Talmudic" tractate, his expert analysis of the laws of idolatry.[16]

The life of Avraham was directed toward proclaiming the Oneness of G-d. His purchase of a burial plot — representing a microcosm of *Eretz Yisrael* — paying 400 *shekalim* symbolically enabled

This real estate in Kiryas Arba epitomized the sanctification of the homeland of the Jewish nation.

The number 400 is also synonymous with idol worship, which diverges from the Singular.

The number 4 represents idol worship in the multiplicity of negative forces that are an affront to the Oneness of G-d.

Avraham was effectively able to nullify the 400 "chapter divisions" in his comprehensive tractate of the laws of idolatry to negate the abundance of idols that filled the Holy Land.

The 4 Empires would impinge upon Israel's autonomous existence within the Holy Land.

The elected "place" of exile chosen for Israel to be "out of place" was a country that substituted those same boundaries for their true home.

him to take possession of the entire Land. Avraham was effectively able to nullify the 400 "chapter divisions" in his tractate of the laws of idolatry to negate the idols that filled the Holy Land.[17] Indeed, the sanctity of *Eretz Yisrael* cannot tolerate the defilement of idolatry.[18]

Avraham was forced to confront those negative spiritual forces that would make themselves known through the numbers 4 and 400. Perhaps the most prominent example of the number 400 would unfold during the Egyptian Exile.[19]

400 Years: Egyptian Exile

Following their entry into the Holy Land, the Jewish People would be subject to 4 periods of exile. The 4 Empires, Babylon, Persia-Media, Greece, and Rome, would undermine Israel's autonomous existence within the Holy Land. Israel would be "displaced" by these antagonistic enemy nations. Ideologically, the hostile adversaries opposed Israel's national mission to glorify the Oneness of G-d.[20]

The forerunner to this was the original exile that took place at the infancy of Jewish nationhood: 400 years of the Egyptian Exile.

Avraham was foretold at the בְּרִית בֵּין הַבְּתָרִים, *Covenant of the [Animal] Parts*, that his descendants would be "… aliens in a land not their own — and they will serve them, and they will afflict them — 400 years."[21] They would be displaced and placed into an alien environment. G-d computed the onset of the 400 years of exile from the birth of Yitzchak.[22] The majority of the 400-year exile (a total of 210 years[23]) was the Jewish nation's persecution within *Mitzrayim*, Egypt — a land known for its idolatry.[24] The two main prominent figures in Egyptian life — Pharaoh and the River Nile — were both worshiped as gods.[25]

The exile from the 400 square *parsah* of *Eretz Yisrael* was to *Mitzrayim*, which itself possesses the exact same dimensions of 400 square *parsah*.[26] Here the elected "place" of exile chosen for Israel to be "out of place" was a country that substituted those same boundaries for their true home.

400: Eisav's Men

The Jewish forefather Yaakov experienced exile firsthand when he was forced to flee *Eretz Yisrael* to escape the wrath of Eisav for having deceived their father, Yitzchak, to obtain the blessings. Upon his return from Charan to enter the Holy Land, Yaakov was met by his angry twin Eisav, accompanied by "400 men."[27] Moreover, each of these 400 men was, in turn, a leader over 400 soldiers.[28]

Eisav, an idolater who had turned his back on the monotheistic pathway forged by his grandfather Avraham,[29] intended to oppose Yaakov's return to settle *Eretz Yisrael.* Eisav's anger was subdued and a battle between the two brothers was averted. In the end, the G-d-fearing Yaakov settled in the Holy Land while Eisav and his family departed to Mount Seir.[30]

The homecoming

The historic subjugation of the 4 Empires that has dispersed the singular nation of Israel into exile is not permanent and will not last.[31] The opposition of the 400 negative forces of Eisav will not defeat Yaakov.

Like the Exodus from Egypt after 400 years, the Jewish people will once again return from exile. They will come back to their homeland of 400 *parsah* by 400 *parsah.* Just as Avraham purified the land from the defilement of its idols, so will the Jewish nation, his descendants, cleanse it from impurity. They will then merit to return to their unified designated "place" to reveal the Oneness of G-d.

Like the Exodus from Egypt after 400 years, the Jewish people will once again return from exile.

NOTES

1. See "4: Finding the Place."
2. See *Sanhedrin* 64a and *Bava Metzia* 59b for 2 episodes in which a distance of 400 is employed to denote a distance. See *Maharal, Chiddushei Aggados* ad loc.
3. See *Ramban, Vayikra* 18:25 quoting *Sifri, Eikev* 43, for how true fulfillment of the commandments is reserved for their performance within *Eretz Yisrael.*
4. *Devarim* 11:12.
5. *Kesubos* 110b.
6. See "4: Finding the Place."
7. *Megillah* 3a; *Bava Kamma* 82b. See *Maharal, op. cit., Rosh Hashanah* 23b (Vol. 1, pp.125-126). See *Tanchuma, Shelach* 8, for how G-d hastened the spies' journey across the 400 square *parsah* of the Holy Land in order not to prolong the ensuing punishment of exile of 1 year for each of the 40 days of their trip (*Bamidbar* 14:34).
8. *Pesachim* 93b, *Rashi* ad loc.
9. *Bereishis* 13:17. See *Bereishis Rabbah* 41:10 about walking the length and breadth of the field as an act that signifies acquisition.

10. *Eruvin* 53a.
11. *Bereishis* 23:16.
12. *Zohar* 1, 128b.
13. The deviation of 4 forces away from the original central position place represents a departure from G-d as the Singular Source of existence (*Maharal, Tiferes Yisrael* 38 and *Gevuros Hashem* 6). See also "4: Finding the Place."
14. This is represented in the 4 prohibitions of idolatry included in the Ten Commandments: (1) You shall have no other gods before Me; (2) You shall not make for yourself a carved image; (3) You shall not bow down to them; (4) [You shall not] worship them" (*Shemos* 20:3-5). See also *Rokeach, Shemos* 20:3-5.
15. *Bereishis* 12:8.
16. *Avodah Zarah* 14b. Other symbolic references to 400 in terms of idolatry include the 400 idolaters of Asheirah fed at the royal table of the idolatrous Queen Izevel (*I Melachim* 18:19) and before entering into battle against Aram, Achav consulted 400 idolatrous prophets (ibid. 22:6; see also *II Divrei HaYamim* 18:5).
17. *Rokeach, Bereishis* 23:15.
18. *Vayikra* 18:25-29.
19. *Maharal, Gevuros Hashem* 10.
20. See "4: Finding the Place."
21. *Bereishis* 15:13.
22. *Rashi*, ibid.
23. See "210: The Iron Furnace."
24. See, e.g., *Toras Kohanim* on *Vayikra* 18:3.
25. See *Yechezkel* 29:3.
26. *Pesachim* 94a.
27. *Bereishis* 32:7, 33:1.
28. *Bereishis Rabbah* 75:12. The symbolism of an army with 400 soldiers marching upon a destructive path is also seen with King David (See *I Shmuel* 22:2, 25:13, 30:10). It is known that there were many resemblances between David and Eisav. David's depiction as having a "ruddy complexion" (*I Shmuel* 16:12) is reminiscent of the murderous Eisav who is similarly described (*Bereishis* 25:25). But David also had "beautiful eyes," an allusion to the fact that David would kill only when he had the sanction of the Sanhedrin, whose elders are described as "eyes of the nation" (*Bereishis Rabbah* 63:8; R' Tzadok HaKohen, *Poked Akarim,* p. 33).
29. The incense of the idolatrous offerings of Eisav's wives was responsible for blinding Yitzchak (see *Rashi, Bereishis* 27:1, citing *Tanchuma, Toldos* 8).
30. *Bereishis* 36:6-8.
31. *Maharal, Netzach Yisrael* 1.

410
THE FIRST TEMPLE

410 is the total number
of years that the
First Temple stood in Jerusalem.

THE HOUSE THAT SHLOMO BUILT

The First Beis HaMikdash stood for 410 years.

T
HE FIRST *BEIS HAMIKDASH*, TEMPLE, STOOD FOR 410 YEARS.[1]

The *Beis HaMikdash*, literally, Consecrated House, was the magnificent "House of G-d"[2] upon which G-d would place His Holy Name.[3]

BUILDING THE MIKDASH

The "House of G-d" came to replicate the dwelling place of the Shechinah that had earlier rested upon Mount Sinai at the giving of the Torah.

One of the 3 main commandments given to the Jewish People upon entering the Holy Land was to build the *Beis HaMikdash*.[4] In the Wilderness, the *Shechinah*, G-d's Presence, rested inside the *Mishkan*, Sanctuary.[5] With their return to the Holy Land, the "House of G-d" came to replicate the dwelling place of the *Shechinah* that had earlier rested upon Mount Sinai at the giving of the Torah.[6]

It would be over four centuries before this *mitzvah* of building the Temple would be realized. Its construction had to wait until the Jewish nation was ruled by kings. In spite of King David's deep yearning to be the one to build the Temple, G-d did not sanction it. The Davidic royal line had not yet been firmly established; the construction would not begin until the reign of Davd's heir, his son Shlomo.[7] Additionally, because King David had spilled blood in battle he was not a fitting candidate to construct the life-affirming Temple.[8]

The actual construction began in the fourth year of the reign of David's son and successor, King Shlomo.

Nevertheless, David was responsible for supervising all the groundwork: the capture of Jerusalem, the purchase of the Temple Mount plot, the transportation of the Ark, and the laying of the Temple's foundations.[9] The actual construction began in the fourth year of the reign of David's son and successor, King Shlomo. He used a large crew and also asked Chiram king of Tzor for craftsmen. The construction took 7 years.[10] The inauguration of the Temple — whose induction is attributed to David[11] — led to celebrations lasting for 14 days.[12]

TEMPLE: CENTER OF THE WORLD

Jewish tradition sees the Temple Mount as the point from which the universe unfolded.[13] The location of the Temple, which is said to be higher than all other places,[14] is considered to be the main object of beauty in This World.[15] It is described as "fairest of sites, joy of all the Earth is Mount Zion."[16] The Temple was constructed in Jerusalem straddling the tribal portions of Yehudah and Binyamin. This edifice would serve as the focus of Jewish life. Here the nation would converge to bring their sacrificial offerings and first fruits and make their visitations on the *Shalosh Regalim*, Three Pilgrimage Festivals. The sacred nature of the Temple necessitated strict laws to maintain an awesome state within its hallowed walls.[17]

The Temple was the spiritual epicenter of the universe.[18] The concept "central" is indicative of the most important component; everything else revolves around that pivotal point.[19] The Temple unites the Jewish People as the G-dly Nation that are unified in their worship of G-d. The Temple on Earth is mirrored by a corresponding Temple in Heaven.[20]

The Temple on Earth is mirrored by a corresponding Temple in Heaven.

Additionally, the Temple is the "gateway to Heaven."[21] Symbolically, it is like the ladder in Yaakov's dream joining the lower and higher worlds.[22] As the interface between Heaven and Earth, it is like the union of body and soul that animates and sustains life. Thus, the Temple is befittingly termed *House of Our Life*.[23] All life and blessing comes to the world by virtue of the Temple as the channel through which they descend from On High.[24] It is similarly the conduit through which all prayer passes. Ironically, had the non-Jews known how beneficial the Temple was for them, they would have readily surrounded it and protected it like a fortress.[25]

410: ÐIVINE pRESENCE

The instruction to build a Temple is found in the verse, וְעָשׂוּ לִי מִקְדָּשׁ וְשָׁכַנְתִּי בְּתוֹכָם, *They shall make a Temple for Me — so that I may dwell among them.*[26] One allusion to the duration of the First Temple is found in a rearrangement of the letters וְשָׁכַנְתִּי to וְשָׁכַן תי"י, *and dwell 410 [years].*[27] During the 410 years of the First Temple period, prophecy flourished. The Jewish nation was imbued with sanctity to the highest degree. This was mirrored in the First Temple era that was on a far higher level of spirituality than the epoch of the Second Temple. Indeed, the First Temple was established in the merit of the 3 Jewish Forefathers whose level was most exalted.[28]

During the 410 years of the First Temple period, prophecy flourished.

The *Shechinah* resided inside the First Temple. This was obvious and apparent to every observer.[29] Non-Jewish nations converged upon Jerusalem to offer their prayers to G-d — as per Shlomo's

The Shechinah resided inside the First Temple.

prayers.[30] The Mishnah vividly records the phenomenal miracles ever-present within the House of G-d. The 10 recorded supernatural wonders included the smoke stretching from the Altar that did not disperse in the wind and how the sacrificial meat did not become putrid to attract flies hovering over it.[31] The First Temple was fully operational in every respect with all the requisite vessels (including the *Aron*, Ark) present and fully functional.

ÐESTRUCTION ANÐ EXILE

There is a striking correlation between the Divine glory in the Sanctuary of G-d and the glory of the soul within the sanctuary of the human body.

There is a striking correlation between the Divine glory in the Sanctuary of G-d and the glory of the soul residing within the sanctuary of the human body. By extension, the defilement of man mirrors the defilement of the Temple.

During the First Temple, the Jewish People were guilty of the 3 cardinal sins: idolatry, murder, and promiscuity.[32] These sins respectively correspond to the 3 faculties within the person: (a) כֹּחַ הַשִּׂכְלִי, *intellectual faculty*, (b) כֹּחַ הַנַּפְשִׁי, *spiritual faculty*, (c) כֹּחַ הַגּוּף , *physical faculty*. Idolatry is transgressed by a mental action through denying the belief in G-d. Murder corresponds to the spirit by spilling the blood of the human spirit and life. And promiscuity is a sin that contaminates a person's body through adultery.[33]

Once the faculties of the spirit within Israel were contaminated, the Temple, as man's parallel, was also deserving of destruction.

The 3 cardinal sins present in the First Temple era left a negative impact on the spiritual stature of Israel as the embodiment of a man. Once the faculties of the spirit within Israel were contaminated, the Temple, as man's parallel, was also deserving of destruction. The *Shechinah* could no longer dwell within it. The departure of the Presence of G-d left the Temple an empty physical shell that would now be ruined.[34]

The demolition of the Temple on Earth was preceded by the demolition of the Temple in Heaven.[35] The Babylonian king responsible for the physical demolition was the wicked despot Nebuchadnezzar. And the tragic date of its destruction began on Tishah B'Av, 9th of Av, which would be stamped as the date of national mourning.[36]

Due to the sundering of the Israel's symbolic lifeline to G-d provided by the Temple, the departure of the *Shechinah* was equivalent to the soul's departure from the body. The theme of death is a prominent one in the Tishah B'Av mourning, where a Jew behaves as if there is a corpse lying before him.[37]

Just as the Jewish people's sins were known and revealed, by extension, the End [of their exile] was similarly revealed. The exile would only last for 70 years before they would return to the Holy Land to build the Temple anew.[38]

NOTES

1. *Yoma* 9a.
2. See *Megillah* 26a.
3. *Devarim* 12:5, *I Melachim* 8:43, *II Divrei HaYamim* 20:8-9. As we say in *Bircas HaMazon* "… and on the Great House and *Mikdash* upon which He placed His Name." See also *Maharal, Netzach Yisrael* 5.
4. *Sanhedrin* 20b.
5. "They shall make a Temple for Me — so that I may dwell among them" (*Shemos* 25:8).
6. *Ramban, Shemos* 25:1 (Introduction to *Parashas Terumah*).
7. *II Shmuel* 7:2-3 and 7:12-13.
8. *I Divrei HaYamim* 22:8. The motif of the Temple was that of peace, the opposite of military warfare. The Altar of stone could not be hewn from iron tools that are typically used to shorten life; in contrast the Altar, with repentance, prolongs it (*Rashi, Shemos* 20:22). See *Midrash Shocher Tov* 62, which discusses that if David had built the Temple, it would have lasted forever.
9. *Bamidbar Rabbah* 13:14.
10. See *I Melachim* 6:38 and *Yalkut Shimoni, I Melachim* 184. See also *Moed Katan* 9a.
11. *Tehillim* 30:1. So that the *Aron* could be brought into the Holy of Holies, the Temple gates opened for Shlomo in the merit of David (*Shabbos* 30a and *Shemos Rabbah* 8:1). See also *Mechilta, Beshalach* 15.
12. *I Melachim* 8:65
13. *Yoma* 54b. It was the cornerstone of Creation; from this point the universe expanded.
14. *Sanhedrin* 87a; *Rashi, Devarim* 1:25, 17:8, and 32:13. See also *Maharal, Be'er HaGolah* 6. See also *Kiddushin* 69a, which explains how the Temple was the high point of the Holy Land and how the Holy Land is the high point over and above all other lands.
15. *Maharal, Netzach Yisrael* 26.
16. *Tehillim* 48:3.
17. The laws of conduct within the Temple Mount prohibited anyone entering with a walking stick, shoes, or bundle (*Yevamos* 6b; *Tanchuma, Vayikra* 6). Yaakov was upset and fearful for having slept in this locality: "How awesome is this place?" (*Bereishis* 28:17).
18. *Tanchuma, Kedoshim* 10. The Temple is the essence and primary level of the world (*Maharal,* op. cit. 23).
19. *Maharal,* op. cit. 4. See "7: A Holy Spark" and "13: An Everlasting Love," where 7 is the central point of 6 sides of a cube and 13 is the central point of 12 corners of a cube.
20. *Yerushalmi, Berachos* 4:5.
21. *Bereishis* 28:17.
22. *Maharal, Nesiv HaAvodah* 18.

23. Blessings of the *Haftarah*. See "18: The Lifeline."

24. *Sotah* 48a. See *Maharal, Nesiv HaAvodah* 11.

25. *Bamidbar Rabbah* 1:3. See also *Maharal, Netzach Yisrael* 5.

26. *Shemos* 25:8.

27. *Baal HaTurim, Shemos* 25:8. Additionally, it contains an allusion to the Second Temple. See "420: Second Temple"

28. *Maharal, Netzach Yisrael* 4.

29. Ibid. See "420: Second Temple."

30. *I Melachim* 8:41-3.

31. *Pirkei Avos* 5:7.

32. *Yoma* 9b.

33. *Devarim* 12:23.

34. *Maharal, Netzach Yisrael* 4.

35. See R' Chaim Volozhin, *Nefesh HaChaim* 1:4.

36. See "9: Where to Turn?" It was on Tishah B'Av, when the Jewish people in the Wilderness wept unnecessarily after hearing the spies' report (*Bamidbar* 14:1), that G-d decreed that this date would be fixed as a day for weeping throughout the ages (*Taanis* 29a).

37. Ibid. 30b. Many of the day's laws reflect the conduct and restrictions placed upon a mourner. This is prominently evident in the mourners' meal eaten before the fast (see *Shulchan Aruch Orach Chaim* 552-3). The recitation of *Eichah (Lamentations)* and *Kinnos* on Tishah B'Av night while sitting on the floor are according to the customs of a mourner bereaving a deceased relative. See *Shulchan Aruch, Orach Chaim* 559:3 and *Mishnah Berurah* 11.

38. *Yoma* 9b. See *Maharal, Netzach Yisrael* 4 and "420: The Second Temple."

420
THE SECOND TEMPLE

420 is the total number
of years that the
Second Temple stood in Jerusalem.

THE SECOND HOUSE

The sanctity of the Second House of G-d was not on the same spiritual level.

THE SECOND *BEIS HAMIKDASH*, TEMPLE, STOOD FOR 420 YEARS.[1]

This was a turbulent time in Jewish history. Even though the Second Temple existed for one decade longer than the First Temple, the sanctity of the House of G-d was not on the same spiritual level.

The Rebuilding of the Mikdash

The Jewish community replanted in Bavel would be subject to a relatively brief exile whose duration would be only 70 years.

We have seen that the First Temple built by King Shlomo lasted for 410 years before being destroyed by the Babylonians.[2] With its destruction, the majority of the Jewish population was banished by the tyrannical King Nebuchadnezzar. The Holy Land was left desolate and in ruins. The Jewish community — starting from the first wave of refugees who had been exiled several years before the First Temple's destruction — was replanted in Bavel against the backdrop of Yirmiyahu's well-publicized prophecy that Israel would be subject to a relatively brief exile whose duration would be only 70 years.[3]

Only a tiny minority of the Jewish survivors returned to the Holy Land several decades after the exile. The Land of Israel was in ruins. It was a vassal state of the Persian Empire. Permission to return to their homeland and rebuild the Temple was granted by the Persian king Cyrus, but there was a hiatus during the reign of Achashverosh. In the second year of King Darius's rule, however, the rebuilding resumed.

The great leaders Ezra and Nechemiah, took the necessary steps to raise the glory of the Jewish people.

The construction took 4 years to complete. The heads of the small Jewish community in Jerusalem, the great leaders Ezra and Nechemiah, took the necessary steps to strengthen religious observance, rebuild the walls of the Holy City, and raise the glory of the Jewish people.[4]

420: Reduced Splendor of the Mikdash

The instruction to build a Temple is found in the verse, וְעָשׂוּ לִי מִקְדָּשׁ וְשָׁכַנְתִּי בְּתוֹכָם, *They shall make a Temple for Me — so that I may dwell among them.*[5] In addition to containing an allusion to the First Temple,[6] there is also a hint to the Second Temple, with the letters וְשָׁכַנְתִּי rear-ranged to form the phrase וְשֵׁנִי תי״ך, *and Second [Temple] 420 [years]*.[7] The edifice that was the Second Temple (especially in its renovated condition) was truly a wondrous object to behold. In the words of the Sages, "One who did not see the Temple when it stood [intact] had not seen a beautiful building."[8] However, despite the exceptional joy of the rebuilding of the Temple, this new House of G-d could not recapture the spiritual glory of its predecessor. Starting with the destruction of the First Temple, the world had entered into a degenerative state, with each day more accursed than the day that preceded it.[9]

Perhaps the most fundamental difference was the absence of the *Shechinah*, Divine Presence, within the Second Temple compared to the degree experienced in the First Temple.[10] Tragically, there were little supernatural phenomena to discern in the Second Temple.[11]

The centerpiece of the Temple — the *Aron*, Ark, together with its *Keruvim*, angelic figures — was missing.[12] In lieu of the *Aron*, within the innermost chamber lay the Foundation Stone from which the world was founded. In the Second Temple there was no longer the *Urim v'Tumim*, the Divine Name placed in the fold of the *Choshen*, Breast-plate, worn by the High Priest. The Heavenly fire did not descend to consume the offerings; the *Kohanim* themselves kindled the Altar fire. Another omission in this era was *Ruach HaKodesh*, Divine Inspiration.[13] Interestingly, all these matters relate to the symbolism of *ohr*, light. This conveyed the clear message that the spiritual illumination of the First Temple was glaringly absent in the Second Temple.[14]

The spiritual illumination of the First Temple was glaringly absent in the Second Temple.

This epoch was a tumultuous time in Jewish history. The Jew-ish People struggled with bitter enemies from both within and with-out. Within their ranks, the workings within the Second Temple were undermined or interfered with by the Sadducees or Hellenists. The High Priesthood was auctioned to the highest bidder or its position appointed by the ruling power. It was during this period that the mir-acle of Chanukah occurred. Here the greatly outnumbered *Chash-monaim*, Hasmoneans, revolted against the Syrian-Greek oppres-sors. Once victorious in battle, the *Chashmonaim* reinaugurated the Temple by lighting the Menorah with uncontaminated oil that miracu-lously burned for 8 days.[15]

The Jewish People struggled with bitter enemies from both within and without.

420: THE DESTRUCTION

Despite the diminished stature of the Second Temple, the presence of the Temple was an essential feature that assumed center stage. The

First Temple was established in the merit of the 3 Jewish forefathers; the Second Temple stood in the national merit of Israel. Consequently, the spiritual downfall occurred once this national unity was sadly lost.[16] This was primarily expressed through the sin of *sinas chinam*, baseless hatred, concealed within their hearts, which led to division and strife.[17]

The tragic destruction of the Second Temple by the Romans in the first century of the Common Era was truly a calamity of epic proportions. On the 17th of Tammuz, Titus' army breached the last wall of the Holy City. Three weeks later, on Tishah B'Av, the Temple was set ablaze. The wealth of the Temple treasury was plundered. The beautiful city of Jerusalem was decimated. Hundreds of thousands were killed or sold into slavery. Titus celebrated his victory with a coin minted with the words *Judea Capta* (Judea Captured) and a stone carving on the Arch of Titus in Rome. All that was left standing of the Second Temple was one outer wall of the courtyard: the *Kosel HaMa'aravi*, Western Wall, as the sole remnant.

The Third Temple

This tragedy led to a long, bitter exile spanning close to two thousand years. Moreover, the continuous absence of the Second Temple is something that weighs heavily over the national consciousness. Our Sages comment that each generation is obligated to act in a manner that will merit the rebuilding of the Temple. Conversely, "Anyone who does not see the Temple rebuilt in their days, it is considered as if he destroyed it."[18]

Nevertheless, all is not lost. There is a Divine promise that, in the end, the Jewish People will be gathered en masse from the 4 corners of the world to return, once again, to their homeland. This will be in the coming of the Messianic Era that will result in the rebuilding of the House of G-d for the third and final time. The *Shechinah* will rest upon it again. The Temple will truly be restored to its true splendor — with none of the features missing. May we merit seeing it speedily in our days.

The Second Temple stood in the national merit of Israel.

The tragic destruction of the Second Temple was truly a calamity of epic proportions.

There is a Divine promise that, in the end, the Jewish People will be gathered en masse from the 4 corners of the world to return, once again, to their homeland.

NOTES

1. *Yoma* 9a.
2. See "410: The First Temple."

3. *Yirmiyahu* 29:10; *Daniel* 9:2; *II Divrei HaYamim* 36:21. See "70: The Sum of the Parts."

4. See *Ezra* 1:10 and *Nechemiah* 1:13.

5. *Shemos* 25:8.

6. See "410: The First Temple."

7. *Baal HaTurim, Shemos* 25:8.

8. *Succah* 51b.

9. *Sotah* 49a; *Tanchuma, Tetzaveh* 13.

10. *Maharal, Netzach Yisrael* 4.

11. See *Bamidbar Rabbah* 15:10, that the original golden Menorah was absent during the Second Temple. See also *Rambam, Hilchos Beis HaBechirah* 3:4.

12. See *Yirmiyah* 3:16 as to how in the future the *Aron* will not be necessary for the resting of the *Shechinah,* as It will be carried by the people themselves. See *Rashi* ad loc.

13. *Yoma* 21b.

14. *Maharal, Gur Aryeh, Bamidbar* 4:13. In another parallel between the Temples, the First Temple draws a parallel to Avraham, while the Second Temple, which was lacking all areas synonymous with light, is parallel to Yitzchak, who was blind (*Bereishis* 27:1). By extension, the future Third Temple is parallel to Yaakov.

15. *Shabbos* 21b.

16. *Maharal, Netzach Yisrael* 4.

17. *Yoma* 9b; *Yerushalmi, Yoma* 1:1.

18. Ibid.; *Midrash Shocher Tov* 137.

500
REACH FOR THE SKY

500 symbolically relates to
the distance between worlds —
like the years separating
Earth and Heaven.

It is up to man to reach up
and bridge the gap.

The number 500 epitomizes the "great divide" that separates man on Earth from G-d in Heaven.

THE NUMBER 500 REPRESENTS THE SYMBOLIC DISTANCE IN MAN'S journey to reach up to the spiritual realm.

The number 500 epitomizes the "great divide" that separates man on Earth from G-d in Heaven: "The Heaven — the Heavens belong to G-d — but the Earth was given to man."[1] The spirituality associated with the Heavenly realm is not the natural habitat of man, who lives within the physical setting of This World. Still, it is possible, and in fact necessary, to break through the barrier to forge a meaningful connection between them.

1:500

Man must realize the enormity of the gap: "Like the Heavens are higher than the Earth, so are My ways higher than your ways, and My thoughts than your thoughts."[2]

One fine example that highlights this divide is the ratio used to contrast the punishment of a sinful man, which extends to the 4th generation, with the reward given to man for goodness, which stretches up to 1000 generations.[3] Here the ratio of "Divine goodness" compared to "punishment for human evil" is 1:500.[4] G-d's goodness is 500-fold over and above the punishment or affliction reserved for man.[5] This distinction is because G-d has no comparison. In the words of the Psalmist, "As the Heaven is high above the Earth, so great is His mercy toward those who fear Him."[6] This, in turn, relates to the 500-year distance that, so to speak, separates G-d in Heaven from man on Earth.

Here the ratio of "Divine goodness" compared to "punishment for human evil" is 1:500.

500: FROM bEAVEN TO EARTb

The Torah begins with *Genesis*, when G-d created "the Heaven and the Earth."[7] Perhaps the most famous use of the number 500 is as the years needed to travel between the Earth and Heaven. King

Nebuchadnezzar, the despot Babylonian leader, is ridiculed by the Talmud for arrogantly trying to rebel against G-d. The typical lifespan of man is 70 to 80 years. But "the Earth until the first Heaven is a 500-year journey. And the thickness of the Heaven is a 500-year journey. So, too, is there the same 500-year distance between each of the [7] Heavens."[8]

It is, of course, impossible to apply quantifiable measurements for something non-physical such as the Heavens. A metaphorical understanding of the "500-year journey" relates to the Torah's use of anthropomorphic terms: G-d created the universe with His "Hand," as it states "My Hand has established the foundation of the Earth, and My right Hand has spread out the Heavens."[9] The human hand is composed of 5 fingers, which, when expressed in terms of hundreds, equal 500. The expanse of the universe — from Earth to Heaven — was Divinely fashioned and remains constantly under His aegis.[10]

So the number 500 symbolizes the vast chasm between Earth and Heaven, between man and G-d. Man must therefore expend supreme effort to successfully bridge this gap — something that is said to equate to an equivalent 500-year journey of continuous spiritual growth.[11]

The number 500 symbolizes the vast chasm between Earth and Heaven, between man and G-d.

500: The ends of the world

The original, all-encompassing figure of Adam was simultaneously described as reaching "from the Earth to the Heaven" and of stretching "from one end of the world to the other." The 500-year distance between "the Earth and the Heaven" is equal to the distance between "one end of the world to the other."[12] What does this mean? It symbolically denotes that all of existence, from up above to down below, from one side of the world to the other, and indeed the course of world history was wholly dependent upon Adam realizing the purpose of existence.

All of existence was wholly dependent upon Adam realizing the purpose of existence.

Man was tasked with "making the connection" between Creation and Creator. Despite the earthly composition of man's physical body, he must elevate his existence to be drawn after his soul, to gravitate upward and return to its Heavenly source. And Adam could have accomplished this by originally fulfilling the word of G-d. This would have bridged that 500-year distance between Earth and Heaven to create an eternal connection. It would have also perfected the whole of Creation.

Adam could have accomplished this by originally fulfilling the word of G-d.

500: The Tree of Life

Before his downfall, Adam was granted the ability to eat from almost all the trees in *Gan Eden*, Garden of Eden. The 2 trees at the center[13] of the garden were the עֵץ הַדַּעַת טוֹב וָרָע, *Tree of Knowledge of Good and Evil* and the עֵץ הַחַיִּים, *Tree of Life*.[14] Adam was instructed not to eat from the Tree of Knowledge. The term *da'as*, knowledge, connotes the "power of connectivity." For example, the description of the marital union between Adam and Chavah utilizes the term *da'as*.[15] Fatally, Adam did not use this connectivity to join Heaven and Earth through the submission of the human will to the Will of G-d. He did not dedicate his *chaim*, life, to be a mirror of G-d — the *Mekor HaChaim*, Source of all life.[16] Indeed, Adam could have achieved this by partaking of the *Eitz HaChaim*, Tree of Life. Interestingly, the far-reaching influence of the *Eitz HaChaim* extends to a distance of 500 years.[17] The *Eitz HaChaim* was the means for man to ascend in his spiritual endeavors in order to lovingly connect with the Source of all life.[18]

> The Eitz HaChaim was the means for man to ascend in his spiritual endeavors.

Defying G-d, Adam improperly used the power of connection. His sinful connectivity was to the *Eitz Hadaas Tov V'Ra* — partaking of the tree (*eitz*) in the joining together (read: *da'as*) of good and evil (*tov v'ra*).[19] Instead of bridging the 500-year distance, the primeval sin sustained the gulf between man and G-d, between Earth and Heaven. Adam would die; a direct consequence of disobeying the Divine command was the diminishment of Adam's greatness and cosmic influence.[20] Expulsion from the Garden prevented him from now eating of the *Eitz HaChaim* that relates to the opposite themes of life and immortality.[21]

> The primeval sin sustained the gulf between man and G-d

BACK UP

The 500-year distance between Heaven and Earth must be bridged by man. Following Adam, his descendants' universal task was to climb back "up" and reconnect Heaven and Earth. Man's objective to "reach for the sky" would resume in earnest with the *Avos*, Jewish Patriarchs, starting with the emergence of Avraham.[22]

> Man's objective to "reach for the sky" would resume with the Avos.

500: LIVES OF THE AVOS

Nimrod, the spiritual forerunner of Nebuchadnezzar,[23] rebelled against G-d.[24] He was the instigator behind the building of *Migdal Bavel*, Tower of Babel: "Come, let us build for ourselves a city and a tower with its top in the Heaven."[25] These idolaters had no intention to rectify Adam's sin by bridging Heaven and Earth through their connection to G-d. Paradoxically, this was used as a vehicle to wage war against G-d in Heaven. Their cry was "We will go up to the firmament and battle with Him."[26]

Nimrod's lone challenger was Avraham, whose life was dedicated to convincing mankind to connect with G-d. Through Avraham, G-d would now be crowned by mankind as both "G-d of the Heavens and G-d of the Earth."[27] The lives of the 3 *Avos* would start to reverse the negative impacts of the primeval sin.

Together, the inspiring lives of the *Avos* combine to make a total of 500 years. There were the 173 years of Avraham's life in Divine service (excluding his first 2 years, as Avraham only attained knowledge of G-d in his 3rd year),[28] the 180 years of Yitzchak,[29] and the 147 years of Yaakov's life[30] (173 + 180 + 147 = 500).[31] Together, the 3 *Avos* were responsible for the birth of the Jewish People.[32] Their 500-year lifespan would draw spiritual inspiration from the influence of the *Eitz HaChaim,* which symbolizes the return of mankind's true connectivity to the Living G-d in a life that connects Heaven and Earth.[33] This splendid legacy was passed onto the Chosen Nation in their spiritual journey toward Heaven.

TEMPLE MOUNT: 500 X 500

The undisputed place which best exemplified the attainment of connectivity between Heaven and Earth was the *Beis HaMikdash,* Temple. The Temple was the spiritual and national epicenter of the Jewish homeland that was promised to the *Avos'* descendants. It served as the finest interface between Earth and Heaven. This was where the Temple sacrificial service celebrated man's worship of G-d. And it was where the *Shechinah,* Divine Presence, dwelled.

The Temple was the famous place of connection between Heaven and Earth. Historically, this space was where Yaakov dreamt about the ladder with its feet set on Earth and its top reaching up to Heaven.[34] This dream highlights that this location joins the lower and higher

The Temple was the epicenter of the Jewish homeland promised to the Avos' descendants.

The Temple was the famous place of connection between Heaven and Earth.

worlds.[35] Even after the destruction of the Second Temple, this location remains the "gateway to Heaven" and an auspicious place for man's prayer to ascend upward.[36]

The dimensions of the Temple Mount were 500 square cubits.[37] This number beautifully ties in with the Temple as the platform for man to begin his ascent in the bid to bridge the 500-year distance between Heaven and Earth. Jewish tradition sees this place as the inception of Earth's formation.[38] The means for mankind to maintain its continual existence in its attachment to Heaven would be affected in the Temple. The building's description as the Jewish People's בֵּית חַיֵּינוּ, *House of Our Life*,[39] echoes the 500-year influence of the *Eitz HaChaim*, Tree of Life, located at the center of the Garden of Eden.

The interface between Heaven and Earth finds its parallels within man and woman. Heaven is symbolic of the masculine prototype of *mashpia*, giver, compared to Earth, whose feminine counterpart stands as the *mekabel*, recipient.[40] There are 248 limbs in man's body but 252 in a woman. Together, the combined bodily parts of man and woman total 500 bodily parts.[41] This corresponds to the 500-year journey to bridge Heaven and Earth through their connectivity, as accomplished by the Temple occupying a space of 500 square cubits.

INNER SPACE

THE 500-YEAR DISTANCE BETWEEN HEAVEN AND EARTH IS NOT reserved for the realm that exists outside man; its parallels are similarly expressed within man himself. The connectivity exemplified by the Temple must be replicated within man's being.

500: TAKING IT TO THE HEART

Man is an all-encompassing microcosm of the universe. There is a deep correlation between his outer world and his inner world. The corresponding counterparts of Heaven and Earth within man are that of *mind* and *heart*. Just as man must connect the upper and lower realms, he must similarly bridge the chasm between thought and action. These parallels are found in the Torah exhortation, "You shall *know* today, and place it upon your heart, that HASHEM, He is your G-d in the Heavens above and upon the Earth below; there is no other."[42]

Knowing the truth is not enough; one must act upon this information. Knowledge of G-d in Heaven must be internalized within man's heart so that it finds practical application here on Earth. This calls for the intellectual pursuit of Torah to find its full expression in *mitzvah* performance. Judaism is not based upon theological beliefs that are detached from human conduct. Torah is a way of living that readily permeates every aspect of human life — without any exception.

The crossover between mind and heart, thought and practice, is not an easy one. Man may know what he must do — but fail to do it nonetheless. Man may concede that he is destined to be judged by the Heavenly Tribunal after his brief sojourn on Earth — yet still sinfully act as if there is no tomorrow. Consequently, the distance between *knowing* and *doing* is similarly set at an equivalent symbolic measurement of 500-years between Heaven and Earth.[43] It requires man's absolute *avodah*, [Divine] service, to attain the connection originally manifest in the dimensions of 500 square cubits within the Temple.[44]

500: GOING UP ONE LEVEL

The 500-year distance between Heaven and Earth depicts an ascent to a higher world. In turn, this 500-years is the same symbolic distance that respectively separates each of the 7 Heavens in the celestial realm.[45] In terms of man's inner world, there is the necessity to undertake a program of continuous climbing from a lower spiritual realm up to a higher dimension.

Life demands growth, where man strives to ascend higher and higher.[46] He cannot become complacent and to never progress beyond his present spiritual station. In a bid to "reach the sky," man must repeatedly work to go up one level, then another, and another, toward his Creator.[47] Despite the greatly diminished stature of man and the vast distances involved, man can elevate himself above his physical environs on Earth by associating himself with the flame of his soul that constantly flickers upward, yearning to return to the Heavenly realm.[48]

In truth, the impact of man's behavior reverberates through the cosmos.[49] Descended from the *Avos* who lived for 500 years, the Jewish People were the ones to worship G-d in the 500 square cubits

The 500-year distance between Heaven and Earth depicts an ascent to a higher world.

Man can elevate himself above his physical environs on Earth by associating himself with the flame of his soul that constantly flickers upward.

Through a lifetime of work, man is able to bridge the 500-year distance and reach the spiritual realm of Heaven.

of the Temple. They would be instrumental in arranging the connectivity between Heaven and Earth in the outside world and between mind and heart in their inner worlds. Through a lifetime of work on Earth, man is able to bridge the 500-year distance and ultimately reach the spiritual realm of Heaven. Then, he will reveal the truth about HASHEM: "He is your G-d in the Heavens above and upon the Earth below; there is no other."[50]

NOTES

1. *Tehillim* 115:16.
2. *Yeshayah* 55:9; see also *Tehillim* 103:11.
3. *Shemos* 20:5-6; see also ibid 34:7.
4. *Rashi, Shemos* 20:5-6 and 34:7; see also *Tosefta, Sotah* 4:1.
5. *Maharal, Gur Aryeh, Shemos* 20:5-6 [12]. See also ibid. 34:7 [6]. See also "2000: The Borderline."
6. *Tehillim* 103:11.
7. *Bereishis* 1:1.
8. *Chagigah* 13a; *Pesachim* 94b.
9. *Yeshayah* 48:13; see also ibid. 51:13 and 51:16. See *Rambam, Hilchos Yesodei Hatorah* 1:7.
10. *Maharal's Hesped,* published in Prague 5358 (printed at end of *Gur Aryeh, Bamidbar*, p. 191).
11. *Maharal, Be'er HaGolah* 6 [5], p. 115.
12. *Chagigah* 12a.
13. *Midrash Zuta, Shir Hashirim* 1:4.
14. *Bereishis* 2:9.
15. Ibid. 4:1.
16. "For with You is the source of life — by Your light we shall see light" (*Tehillim* 36:10).
17. *Bereishis Rabbah* 15:6; *Tanna deVei Eliyahu Rabbah* 2:11.
18. *Ramchal, Daas Tevunos* 126.
19. R' Chaim Volozhin, *Nefesh HaChaim* 1:6, gloss.
20. See "100: Count Your Blessings."
21. *Bereishis* 3:22.
22. *Ramchal, Derech Hashem* 2:4.
23. *Chagigah* 13a.
24. See *Pirkei DeRabbi Eliezer* 24. The name "Nimrod" conveys that he rebelled (*morad*) against G-d (*Rashi, Bereishis* 10:9).
25. *Bereishis* 11:4; *Chullin* 89a.
26. See *Rashi, Bereishis* 11:1. See also *Sanhedrin* 109a.
27. *Bereishis* 24:3. See *Rashi, Bereishis* 24:7, citing *Bereishis Rabbah* 59:8.
28. *Rokeach, Devarim* 11:21. This differs, however, from the computation given in *Nedarim* 32a, that reckons Avraham's life after he discovered G-d to have been (175 – 3=) 172 years. The Torah records that Avraham died at the age of 175 years (*Bereishis* 25:7).
29. *Bereishis* 35:28.
30. Ibid. 47:28.
31. *Rokeach,* loc. cit.

32. See "3: Three-Dimensional."
33. *Sfas Emes, Chayei Sarah* 5650.
34. *Bereishis* 28:12.
35. *Maharal, Nesiv HaAvodah* 18. Like the union of body and soul that sustains life, the Temple is befittingly termed *Beis Chayeinu*, House of Our Life. See "410: The First Temple."
36. *Bereishis* 28:17. See *Sifri Devarim* 354; *Shir HaShirim Rabbah* 2:2.
37. *Mishnah, Middos* 2:1; *Sifri Beha'aloscha.* See also *Shemos Rabbah* 15:8 as to how Avraham said to G-d, "If You do not give me a Temple resting on 500 square cubits, it is as if You have not given me anything." Parallel to this area was a sanctified area of 500 square cubits in Yericho designated to be allotted to the tribe within whose portion the *Beis HaMikdash* would eventually be built (*Rashi, Bamidbar* 10:31-32).
38. *Yoma* 54b; *Tanchuma, Kedoshim* 10; *Zohar* 1, 231.
39. See "18: The Lifeline."
40. *Maharal, Nesiv HaEmunah* 1.
41. *Bechoros* 45a. See "248: In Action."
42. *Devarim* 4:39. See also *Yehoshua* 2:11 for how the Canaanites took to heart the reports of the miraculous victories of the Children of Israel over their enemies. They internalized this knowledge and thereupon proclaimed, "G-d in Heaven above and on the Earth below."
43. See R' Gedalya Schorr, *Ohr Gedalyhu, Korach,* p. 131, citing the Rebbe of Kotzk. R' Moshe Shapiro relates that once he asked Rav Dessler for an explanation of the 500-year distance between Heaven and Earth, whereupon Rav Dessler pointed to the distance between his head and his heart.
44. There are many parallels between man and the Temple. The Temple is intrinsically related to the motif of *daas,* connectivity. The Talmud notes, "One who has the quality of *daas,* it is as if the Temple is being built in his days" (*Berachos* 33). This relates to the Temple that "connects Heaven and Earth." See R' Chaim Volozhin, *Nefesh HaChaim* 1:4, gloss, how the Temple finds parallels within man.
45. *Chagigah* 13a.
46. See "15: Ups and Downs."
47. See *Michtav MeiEliyahu* 3, p.113-114.
48. *Sefer HaYashar* 1. "The souls of the righteous are stored under the Heavenly Throne of Glory" (*Shabbos* 152b).
49. R' Chaim Volozhin, op. cit., 1:4.
50. *Devarim* 4:39.

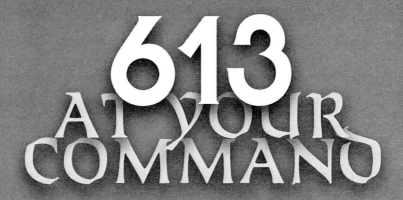

613 AT YOUR COMMAND

613 is the total number of commandments in the Written Torah.

The fulfillment of G-d's dictates creates a unique relationship between man and G-d.

Man is fashioned according to his actions, which relate to the G-dliness invested in the precepts. This completes and refines man's inner world and, in turn, the world outside of him.

YOUR WISH IS MY COMMAND

T HERE ARE תַּרְיַ"ג מִצְווֹת, *613 COMMANDMENTS*, IN THE WRITTEN TORAH.[1]
Jewish living demands allegiance to Torah as the comprehensive manual of Divine instructions given by G-d to the Children of Israel at Sinai. The 613 Commandments are the Jewish People's immutable "living law." Their objective is to observe the 613 Commandments as the Will of G-d whether or not it conforms to societal norms, whether or not the laws are readily understood, and whether or not their performance is easy or difficult.

The 613 Commandments are the Jewish People's immutable "living law."

TORAh AND MITZVOS

Learning Torah is insufficient if it does not naturally result in mitzvah observance.

Torah is the blueprint of Creation.[2] It is the "plan of action" conveyed as the word of G-d. The 613 Commandments are how the Torah finds expression in the practical realm — they are the action or inaction itself that must be observed by man.

The 613 Commandments have their source in the infinite dimension of Torah. Because every *mitzvah* has its foundation within Torah, there is nothing that is equal in importance to Torah study.[3] Nevertheless, learning Torah is insufficient if it does not naturally result in *mitzvah* observance. Studying Torah must therefore see the transfer from theory into practice.[4] This means that Torah, in addition to its own merit, carries within it the merit of the *mitzvah* observance that it helps bring about.[5]

A mitzvah is specific and often time-bound; Torah is a single general unified whole.

Every *mitzvah* is likened to an individual lamp that emerges from the unified light of Torah. A *mitzvah* is specific and often time-bound; Torah is a single general unified whole.[6] Consequently, the protection afforded by a *mitzvah* lamp is temporary compared to the continuous protection offered by Torah.[7]

613: BY ROYAL APPOINTMENT

At the core of every *mitzvah* is the meaningful relationship that it creates between man and G-d. This element is borne out by the word מִצְוָה, *commandment*, associated with the Aramaic word צַוְותָא,

meaning *connection* or *togetherness*.[8] Man as the *metzuveh*, one who is commanded, becomes one with G-d, his *Metzaveh*, Commander. Where man submits his will to the Will of G-d, he is now able to go beyond himself and become part of something infinitely greater: he now experiences togetherness with G-d.[9]

The basis of the 613 Commandments is that they must be faithfully executed as גְּזֵירַת הַמֶּלֶךְ, *decrees of the King*. This means that a Jew lovingly accepts the Sovereignty of G-d upon himself; he yields himself as a loyal subject.[10] He obeys the royal edict because *this is what G-d wants*. The Jew confirms to G-d: "Your command is my wish." This stands as the exclusive reason of *why I want to do it*. There is no other intention or ulterior motive attached whereby man questions, "What is in it for me?"[11]

This does not imply that a Jew does not benefit from *mitzvah* observance — he does. But he sees the resultant good as incidental; it should not feature as his original objective.[12] This acceptance of G-d's Kingship means that a Jew is prepared to fulfill not just 612, but all 613 Commandments in their entirety.[13]

The acceptance of G-d's Kingship means that a Jew is prepared to fulfill all 613 Commandments.

613: The Living Law

The Divine decrees of the 613 Commandments encompass every area of a Jew's life. They pertain to every situation in which man may find himself. They have universal application: from arising in the morning to retiring at night, from a Jew's birth until his dying breath, from the lowly servant to the powerful king. Every sphere of human activity — without exception — comes under the umbrella of Torah.

The 613 Commandments encompass every area of a Jew's life.

In the end, the one who benefits most from *mitzvah* practice is *man himself*. It would be a travesty for a Jew to view the 613 Commandments as painful, restrictive impositions that impede man's enjoyment of life. Nothing could be further from the truth.

The one who benefits most from mitzvah practice is man himself.

Actually, the 613 Commandments are not dissimilar to the definitive set of instructions issued by the manufacturer of an appliance for the benefit of the recent purchaser to get the most out of the product. So, too, did G-d give the 613 Commandments as the complete manual of living to teach a Jew how he can effectively get the most out of his life, draw close to G-d, and earn eternity in *Olam Haba*, the World to Come. This is why the 613 Commandments are also termed "613 pieces of advice."[14] They are the best directives for how to effectively live a fulfilled, meaningful life. A life of Torah is perfectly suited to the identity of a Jew.[15]

The 613 Commandments are the best directives for how to effectively live a fulfilled, meaningful life.

613: GETTING CLOSE

Every mitzvah is a glorious opportunity to connect to G-d.

Every *mitzvah* is a glorious opportunity to connect to G-d. Due to Israel's higher spiritual level, they are given hundreds more commandments than the non-Jews.[16] Even in the most desperate set of circumstances when all seems lost, the Jew will discover some *mitzvah* opportunity that will throw him a lifeline. Imagine someone falling overboard from a ship into the churning, chopping seas; he will desperately cling for dear life to a rope connected to the vessel.[17] The 613 Commandments are the rope that lifts man from the depths of the physical world and elevates him to the higher world to return him to G-d.[18]

Every single *mitzvah* — without exception — is empowered to create an inner relationship with G-d. The ability to achieve דְּבֵיקוּת, *cleaving [to G-d]*, is exclusively achieved through loyally fulfilling His Torah and 613 Commandments.[19] A Jew is more in touch with the spiritual, Divine intellect association within every *mitzvah*, which marks him as a worthy receptacle to receive Torah.[20] Together, the 613 Commandments are characterized as 613 pathways of the Torah.[21] The relationship with G-d formed by the *mitzvos* comes to define the life of a Jew.

Through fulfilling the Divine Will, man actively builds up his relationship and draws close to his Creator.

In every relationship, there are rules that define what to do and what not to do. First, there must be an area in which to establish the bond between the parties through deeds. Every act positively solidifies the relationship. This is manifest in the רְמַ״ח מִצְוֹת עֲשֵׂה, *248 Positive Commandments*. Through fulfilling the Divine Will, man actively builds up his relationship and draws close to his Creator. These Positive Commandments provide man with the medium to go from potential to actual and attain a measure of perfection.[22] Second, there is the imperative to prevent any deviation that may negatively fracture the relationship. This is manifest in the שְׁסָ״ה מִצְוֹת לֹא תַעֲשֶׂה, *365 Prohibitive Commandments*. Their purpose is to ensure that man does not depart from the right pathway.[23]

IN PRACTICE

WE HAVE SEEN THAT THE 613 COMMANDMENTS OF THE TORAH ARE G-d's all-encompassing instructions for living. They are the royal edicts that man, as G-d's subject, dutifully performs, which draw him closer to the Master of the universe. The way that man can observe the 613 Commandments is through the human body.

613: The human body

Man is categorized as an עוֹלָם קָטָן, *world in microcosm.*[24] Everything G-d wishes to reveal in the universe can be viewed in miniature within man. Man was not created complete; he was created to complete himself. There is the famous principle, אָדָם נִפְעָל כְּפִי פְּעֻלּוֹתָיו, *man is formed according to his actions.*[25] Just as creation finds expression through the physical world, so too, man's potential is realized in the actual through the practical enactment of the 613 Commandments. The commandments, which relate to the Divine intellect of Torah, enable man to connect with his spiritual self. He is then not pulled down by his coarse physical composition.[26]

Strikingly, the 248 Positive Commandments have their parallel in רְמַ"ח אֵבָרִים, *248 limbs,*[27] while the 365 Prohibitive Commandments match up with the שַׁסָ"ה גִּידִים, *365 ligaments/sinews.*[28] Together, they parallel the 613 Commandments such that every *mitzvah* has its living expression via its corresponding physical component.

The human body is the tailored garment of the soul. Because there are 613 spiritual components of the soul, it is appropriately clad in the 613 parts of the body. The essence of man, his soul, operates by means of his limbs and ligaments, which find expression through the 613 components of the body. Parallel to the food needed by the physical body to sustain itself, the 613 Commandments are the spiritual sustenance of the soul.[29]

Every single *mitzvah*, like its physical equivalent, is unique. No two are precisely the same. A Jew must relate to G-d using every facet of his biological anatomy. Here the resounding message is that the physical makeup of man's body is purposely designed to fulfill the Divine Will.

It is the G-dliness within the 613 Commandments that refines man's soul from his coarse physical side: "G-d wanted to purify Israel — which is why He gave them Torah and commandments in abundance."[30] They sanctify the 613 parts of the human body to truly become a vehicle for spirituality in achieving *d'veikus*, closeness to G-d.[31]

Man's potential is realized in the actual through the practical enactment of the 613 Commandments.

The essence of man, his soul, operates by means of his limbs and ligaments.

"G-d wanted to purify Israel — which is why He gave them Torah and commandments in abundance."

613: FRUITS OF ONE'S ACTIONS

Man's physical actions have a cosmic impact — one that stretches all the way up and that leaves a deep influence upon the Heavenly realm.[32] Apart from his compliance with the command of G-d, the individual's action regarding any of the 613 Commandments contains the awesome power to either sustain or destroy the universe. In truth, the world's fate is said to lie in his hands. He must view it as if the world's continuity hangs in the balance pending his choice.[33]

The 613 Commandments themselves are that very factor that is responsible for completing man.

Knowing the strength latent within every *mitzvah*, it is essential that *mitzvos* be performed in the most perfect possible way — with intention, with zeal, and with joy. It is fitting that they be brought to completion, especially as the 613 Commandments themselves are the very factor that is responsible for completing man.[34]

The 613 Commandments are like the multiple fruits that a tree bears following the successful implanting.

Man thus earns eternal reward by the fruit of his actions here in This World. The soul implanted in man's body is comparable to the seed implanted in the ground. By enacting the 613 Commandments, the inner force of the soul, or seed, breaks through the body, or ground. It takes root and gradually sprouts into a tree that will grow tall and strong. This tree has the ability to produce delicious fruits year after year. Similarly, the 613 Commandments are like the multiple fruits that a tree bears following the successful implanting of the seed (read: soul) into the ground (read: body). These fruits are equivalent to the reward reserved for man in the hereafter.[35]

In summary, the Jew is the one who benefits from *mitzvah* observance. He uses the 613 physical components in the execution of the 613 Commandments. This is responsible for forging a relationship between him and his Creator that will earn him eternal reward. A Jew must conduct all his affairs before G-d in the fulfillment of as G-d's dictates.

NOTES

1. *Makkos* 23b. Some of the greatest Torah scholars through the ages (including *Rav Saadiah Gaon* in *Sefer HaMitzvos, Sefer HaMitzvos HaGadol, Sefer HaMitzvos HaKatan, Sefer Yere'im*) have fiercely debated which laws are to be included in the 613 Commandments. Perhaps the most famous listing is the *Rambam's Sefer HaMitzvos,* which the author of the *Sefer HaChinuch* used in his codification of the 613 Commandments arranged according to the weekly portion in which they appear. (The *Rambam* uses 14 rules to determine the criteria necessary for a *mitzvah*'s inclusion as one of the 613 Commandments. See *Rambam's Introduction to Sefer HaMitzvos*).

2. *Zohar, Terumah* 161b.

3. *Mishnah, Pe'ah* 1:1.

4. R' Chaim Volozhin, *Nefesh HaChaim* 4:29-30.

5. *Maharal, Nesiv HaTorah* 1. Torah study conveys merit. The absence of merit from Torah study is not as great as the deficiency caused by neglecting to fulfill a *mitzvah* obligation. It is for this reason that where a *mitzvah* cannot be performed by others, it takes precedence over Torah study. See ibid. for how, because a man learning Torah uses his intellect to study the word of G-d, his study is on a far more superior level than *mitzvah* performance enacted through the lower medium of the physical body.

6. *Vilna Gaon, Mishlei* 1:9, 4:2.

7. *Sotah* 21a.

8. *Shelah HaKadosh, Yoma, Derech Chaim Tochachas Mussar* (16).

9. This casts light on the axiom, "Greater is the one who is commanded and acts than the one who is not commanded but acts" (*Kiddushin* 31a). The sincere self-expression of man is admirable, but it is never more than his will. However, where man submits himself to the Divine Will, he proceeds to touch and link with infinity.

10. See *Mechilta, Shemos* 20:3.

11. *Maharal, Tiferes Yisrael* 6.

12. The intrinsic nature of the 613 *mitzvos* as "Divine decrees" leads them, in turn, to provide many benefits. This is how the saying, "G-d wanted to merit/purify Israel — which is why He gave them Torah and *mitzvos* in abundance" (*Makkos* 23b), should be interpreted according to the *Maharal* (op. cit. 6).

13. See *Rabbeinu Yonah, Sha'arei Teshuvah* 1:6, for the ruling that a servant is obliged to accept all his master's instructions — without exception. Should he accept only 612 rules but not the 613rd, he is not a true servant. He continues to be the arbiter of what he does and what he does not accept.

14. *Zohar* 2, 82b.

15. See *Maharal, Tiferes Yisrael* 1, 5, 56.

16. Ibid.

17. *Bamidbar Rabbah* 17:6; *Tanchuma, Shelach* 15.

18. *Maharal*, op. cit. 4.

19. Ibid. 9.

20. Ibid. 1.

21. *Zohar* 3, 136a.

22. *Maharal, Tiferes Yisrael* 4, 7. See "248: In Action."

23. *Maharal*, ibid. See "365: For Your Protection". See *Sfas Emes, Vayishlach* 5658, who characterizes the 248 as the limbs that are vessels to receive holy influence from the soul while the 365 are safeguards for this light not to dissipate elsewhere.

24. *Tanchuma, Pekudei* 3; see also *Rabbeinu Bachya, Bereishis* 1:27; *Rambam, Moreh Nevuchim* 1:72; *Malbim*, Introduction to "Allusions of the *Mishkan*."

25. *Sefer HaChinuch, Mitzvah* 16.

26. *Maharal, Tiferes Yisrael* 2-4.

27. See *Mishnah, Oholos* 1:8, for the computation of the 248 limbs. See also *Makkos* 23b and "248: In Action."

28. *Zohar* 1, 170b.

29. R' Chaim Vital, *Shaar Kedushah* 1:1.

30. *Makkos* 23b. See *Maharal*, op. cit. 5, for how just as a loving father will coerce his son to do something that will eventually be to his benefit, G-d compels Israel to perform the Commandments that will ultimately be for their benefit.

31. *Maharal*, op. cit. 7.

32. R' Chaim Volozhin, *Nefesh HaChaim* 1:12.

33. *Kiddushin* 40b.

34. *Maharal, Nesiv HaTorah* 18.

35. *Maharal, Tiferes Yisrael* 7.

620 CROWNING GLORY

620 is the total number of Commandments in both the Written Torah and Oral Torah.

Torah is the crowning glory of Israel's role as the ones to crown their G-d as King of all kings.

ON YOUR HEAD

The number
620 includes
both the 613
Commandments
of the Written
Torah and the
7 Rabbinic
Commandments
of the Oral
Torah.

THE NUMBER 620 IS THE NUMBER THAT INCLUDES BOTH THE 613 Commandments of the Written Torah and the 7 Rabbinic Commandments of the Oral Torah.

It refers to how royalty — both that of G-d and that of man — relate to the concept of כֶּתֶר תּוֹרָה, *crown of Torah.*

613 + 7 = 620 COMMANDMENTS

We have seen 613 as the number of תַּרְיַ"ג מִצְוֹת מִן הַתּוֹרָה, *613 Commandments of the [Written] Torah.*[1] Taken together with the שֶׁבַע מִצְוֹת דְּרַבָּנָן, *7 Rabbinic Commandments [of the Oral Torah],*[2] this brings the tally to a total of (613 + 7 =) 620.[3]

G-d spoke to the Jewish People gathered around Sinai. He instructed them in the 10 Commandments that would later be inscribed onto the Two Tablets, which are the embodiment of Torah in its totality.[4] This finds its allusion in the 10 Commandments which is composed of 620 letters — a reference to the 613 Commandments in the Written Torah plus 7 Rabbinic Commandments [of the Oral Torah].[5] There are 620 pillars of light reserved for one who attaches himself to these 620 Commandments.[6]

These 10 Commandments are the embodiment of the Torah in its totality.

620: THE ROYAL CORONATION

The number 620 also relates to Torah as the numerical value of the word כֶּתֶר, *crown.*

The number 620 also relates to Torah as the numerical value of the word כֶּתֶר, *crown.*

What is the symbolism of a crown? Majestically placed on top of the wearer's head, a crown is placed at the highest point. This indicates how it is derived from and connected to a Higher Source that transcends the one who wears it. But it is nevertheless set upon the head, which confers the object with importance.[7] This demonstrates the twin roles of a crown: conceptually it relates to what is *above* the wearer, but which physically comes into contact (even if only just!) with the wearer *below.*

The classic application is the royal crown worn by a king. The crown is placed upon his head above the highest part of his physical frame.[8] But its status as the emblem of kingship originates from above him — from G-d as the King of all kings.[9] The crown retains a degree of separateness. It does not fully envelop the person in the same manner that a garment is worn on the body. Yet, the resting of the crown upon the monarch's head indicates the veneration that is due him by his subjects. So, too, is the ruler elevated above his citizens through his royal coronation.[10] He stands aloof, No one can lord over him.[11]

620: CROWNS AT SINAI

The regal symbol of a crown is synonymous with Torah. The Jewish People's eagerness to accept the Divine decrees of the Torah was immortalized in their unanimous declaration נַעֲשֶׂה וְנִשְׁמָע, *We will do and we will hear.*[12] As a reaction to the national submission to G-d, myriads of Heavenly hosts descended and conferred 2 crowns on every individual (to parallel the 2 words in their statement).[13]

The crowns placed above the head of every Jew indicate the Jewish outlook: to see himself rooted in a higher, spiritual dimension that transcends his body.

What was the significance of this event? In line with its symbolism, the crowns placed above the head of every Jew indicate the Jewish outlook: to see himself rooted in a higher, spiritual dimension that transcends his body. The readiness to embrace the 620 Commandments indicated an attachment to G-d and to the spiritual worlds above. The Jew adorned with the *keser*, with its numerical value of 620, comese to coronate G-d as the מֶלֶךְ הָעוֹלָם, *King of the universe.* In turn, the Jew himself assumes the mantle of kingship in This World.

620: THE TORAH CROWN

The Torah received at Sinai is related to the attainment of royalty whose adherents are similarly part of the "royal family."

The Torah itself is called the כֶּתֶר תּוֹרָה, crown of Torah.

G-d said about the Jewish People: "You shall be for Me a *kingdom of priests and a holy nation.*"[14] The Torah itself is called the כֶּתֶר תּוֹרָה, *crown of Torah.*[15] Torah is a crown in the sense that it originates from, and attests to, a higher, exalted level that transcends man — one to which he can attach himself even while living in the physical realm.[16]

Some of the Hebrew letters written in a Torah Scroll are adorned with crowns. When Moshe ascended to the Heavenly realm, he found G-d attaching crowns to the letters of Torah — crowns from which later Rabbi Akiva would later in history derive numerous laws.[17]

The crown of
Torah is freely
available to
anyone who
chooses to
crown himself
with it.
Torah is indeed the sacred inheritance of every Jew. In contrast to the crowns of כְּהֻנָּה, *priesthood*, and מַלְכוּת, *kingship*, the crown of Torah is freely available to anyone who chooses to crown himself with it.[18] Membership of a *kingdom of priests*, sees the Torah convert a Jew into a king. Interpreting the verse "Through me [i.e., the Torah], kings will reign,"[19] we see that righteous Torah scholars are themselves described as kings.[20] Their crowns are a reference to the Torah knowledge they amass.[21]

The Torah-
scholar king
readily taps
into the Will of
the King of the
Universe.
By studying the word of G-d and enacting His Torah, the Torah scholar king readily taps into the Will of the King of the Universe.

THE ROYAL TREATMENT

The true king
and owner of
the crown is
G-d Who is
beyond This
World.
WE HAVE SEEN THAT 620 REFERS TO THE TOTALITY OF Commandments (biblical and rabbinic) and to the symbolism of a *keser*, crown, that reflects the royalty of Torah. Of course, the true king and owner of the crown is G-d Who is beyond This World.

620: The Divine Crown

The crown lies over and above the subject; in contact but at the same time separate. This sheds light on the cryptic statement: "In the future, the Holy One, Blessed be He, will be a crown on the head of every righteous individual."[22]

The righteous person must relate to G-d using a crown as an analogy. The crown, exalted as it is, is placed upon the righteous person to glorify him. So too, is G-d the Crown, so to speak, above the head of the righteous — connected, but at the same time, beyond the person.[23]

So too, is G-d
the Crown
above the head
of the righteous.
In truth, the very idea of human kingship is a reflection of G-d as the King of all kings. "The kingdom on Earth is a semblance of the Kingdom of Heaven."[24] Submitting himself to Torah, man will coronate G-d through his declaration of קַבָּלַת עוֹל מַלְכוּת שָׁמַיִם, *acceptance of the Heavenly kingship.*

"The kingdom
on Earth is a
semblance of
the Kingdom of
Heaven."
There is never any question about G-d's sovereignty in the celestial realm. Angels sing His Glory. His Oneness and Kingship are self-evident. But it is up to man to declare the Kingship of G-d within the

physical milieu of *this* world. Man must translate the Will of G-d in the higher realm so G-d is crowned King down here on Earth by His subjects. It is because man straddles the two worlds that he can jointly relate to both the Heavenly realm and Earthly terrain.

620: BY HALF

In truth, there are 2 counterparts to man's soul. The Heavenly source of man's soul, which originates in the high celestial realm, is clothed in the physical body. Part of the soul is transplanted down below into This World. That means that a human being is half in the physical world below and half in the spiritual world above.[25]

This conceptually mirrors the twin roles of a crown. Half of it relates to what is *above* the subject — to the higher spiritual worlds. The other half interfaces with the physical world down *below*. It is similar to the soul. The Heavenly half above gives existence to the half that is found on Earth below.

This concept is beautifully alluded to in the numerical value of כֶּתֶר, *620*, which divides equally into 2 halves of (620 ÷ 2 =) 310, the numerical value of the word יֵשׁ, *existence*. This denotes the 310 spiritual worlds designated for a righteous individual.[26]

Whatever man achieves in This World, with the half of his soul enveloped within the body, will determine his existence in order to merit the 310 worlds in the World to Come.[27] Here man's existence sees him inheriting the Hereafter — an eternal bliss where "the righteous sit with crowns upon their heads."[28] This is where the Holy One, Blessed be He, is the Crown that gloriously rests upon the head of the righteous individual.[29]

620: CUT-OFF POINT

Finally, the opposite to the ultimate attachment symbolized by כֶּתֶר is the ultimate detachment from G-d seen in the punitive form of כָּרֵת, *excision*[30] — the two words כֶּתֶר and כָּרֵת sharing the same letters.[31]

Kares is a spiritual form of death; it connotes that the existence of a soul is, in some manner, "cut off" from its Source.[32] There are different levels of *kares*,[33] the most severe of which sees the person spiritually "cut off" both in This World and in the World to Come.[34] His soul is disassociated from his national identity[35] and he cuts himself off from his G-d.

It is because man straddles the two worlds that he jointly relates to both the Heavenly realm and Earthly terrain.

The numerical value of the word יֵשׁ, existence, denotes the 310 spiritual worlds destined for a righteous individual.

The Holy One, Blessed be He, is the Crown that gloriously rests upon the head of the righteous individual.

His soul is disassociated from his national identity and he cuts himself off from his G-d.

This is the antithesis to the 620 Commandments through which man attaches himself to G-d and the identity of the Jewish People. It is likewise the antithesis to the symbolism of the crown that come with obedience to the 620 Commandments.

When a Jew is connected to G-d and to His Torah, this guarantees him eternal existence.

The true mark of kingship is when a Jew is connected to G-d and to His Torah, which is the crown above him. This guarantees him eternal existence. His affinity to the half of his soul clothed within his body joins up with the half of his soul in the Heavenly realm. This is his crowning glory.

NOTES

1. *Makkos* 23b. See "613: At Your Command."
2. There are differing opinions of exactly which rabbinic ordinances are included within the *sheva mitzvos de'Rabbanan. Mitzvos Hashem* enumerates them as follows: (1) to recite a *berachah*, blessing, before deriving any pleasure from This World (*Berachos* 35a); (2) to wash one's hands before partaking of bread (*Chullin* 105a); (3) to publicly read the Scroll of *Esther* on Purim, the 14th day of Adar (*Megillah* 2a); (4) to light candles on the 8 nights of Chanukah (*Shabbos* 21b); (5) to light candles in honor of the Shabbos every Friday before sunset (*Shabbos* 25b); (6) to recite the *Hallel* (*Tehillim* 113-118) on the festive days (*Pesachim* 117a); and (7) to establish an *eruv* (*Eruvin* 21b.)
3. See *Shelah HaKadosh, Parashas Yisro* and *Shaar HaOsiyos, Beis, Berios* 1; *Toras HaOlah* 3, 38; R' David Vital, *Keser Torah* and *Megalah Amukos, Parashas Va'eschanan* 197.
4. *Rashi, Shemos* 24:12; *Rashi, Shabbos* 87a.
5. *Shelah HaKadosh, Parashas Yisro* and *Shaar HaOsiyos, Beis, Berios* 1. Other commentators substitute the "additional 7" to refer to the שֶׁבַע מִצְוֹת בְּנֵי נֹחַ, *7 Noachide Commandments* (*Baal HaTurim, Shemos* 20:13-14). See *Bamidbar Rabbah* 13:15 stating that the 7 days of creation are added to the 613. The 10 Commandments as they appear in *Shemos* 20:2–14 have a total of 620 letters.
6. R' Yitzchak Isaac Chaver, *Ohr HaTorah* 43.
7. The crown symbolizes the true level and purpose of the subject being crowned (*Maharal, Derech Chaim* 4:14, p. 186).
8. In the English language, the word "crown" is itself a synonym for "the top of the head."
9. *Berachos* 58a.
10. See *Esther* 2:17 for King Achashverosh placing the כֶּתֶר מַלְכוּת, *crown of kingship*, upon Esther to replace Vashti as his queen.
11. *Maharal, Derech Chaim* 3:16, p. 152.
12. *Shemos* 24:7. See also *Ramchal, Daas Tevunos* 158.
13. *Shabbos* 88a. The crowns were forfeited when the Jews transgressed at the sin of the *Eigel*, Golden Calf. This indicated that they lost their mark of kingship as they had now sinned through yielding to the materialism of their *Yetzer Hara*, Evil Inclination, meaning they had lost their elevated regal stature. See *Maharal, Tiferes Yisrael* 29.
14. *Shemos* 19:6.
15. *Pirkei Avos* 4:14
16. *Maharal, Derech Chaim* 4:15, p. 192.

17. *Menachos* 29b.

18. *Yoma* 72b, *Rashi* ad loc.

19. *Mishlei* 8:15.

20. *Gittin* 62a.

21. See *Rambam, Hilchos Teshuvah* 8:2.

22. *Megillah* 15b; *Sanhedrin* 111a.

23. *Maharal, Chiddushei Aggados, Sanhedrin* 100a (Vol. 3, p. 231).

24. *Berachos* 58a

25. R' Yitzchak Isaac Chaver, *Ohr Torah* 43. This is the Kabbalistic reason for why we find the righteous called in the Torah by the double mention of their names "Avraham, Avraham" (*Bereishis* 22:11), "Moshe, Moshe" (*Shemos* 3:4); it was a reference addressing both their spiritual components — in Heaven and on Earth.

26. *Maharal, Chiddushei Aggados*, loc. cit. See "310: Worlds Apart."

27. R. Yitzchak Isaac Chaver, loc. cit.

28. *Berachos* 17a; see *Rambam, Hilchos Teshuvah* 8:2. See *Maharal, Chiddushei Aggados, Gittin* 7a (Vol. 2 p. 94).

29. *Megillah* 15b; *Sanhedrin* 111a.

30. See *Shemos* 12:15, *Vayikra* 17:4, *Bamidbar* 15:31.

31. *Arvei Nachal, Toldos.* There are 36 mentions of *kares* in the Torah in commandments that are punishable by excision (*Mishnah, Kereisos* 1:1). Corresponding to this, we find that 36 crowns were suspended from the coffin of Yaakov (*Sotah* 13a).

32. See *Zohar* 1, 236b and R' Chaim Volozhin, *Nefesh HaChaim* 1:18.

33. *Ramban, Vayikra* 18:29 (end of *Acharei Mos*).

34. *Sanhedrin* 90b and *Rambam, Hilchos Teshuvah* 8:1.

35. "... that soul shall be cut off from its people" (*Vayikra* 7:21, *Bamidbar* 9:13).

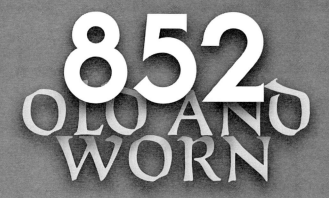

852 is the number of years
the Jewish People were destined
to live in their homeland
before being driven into exile.

This period ended with the destruction
of the First Temple.

TOO LONG

THE NUMBER 852 REPRESENTS THE LENGTH OF TIME THE JEWISH people were to settle in the Holy Land before being ejected.

852: IN THE PROMISED LAND

G-d promised the forefathers that their children would inherit the Promised Land. But there was no guarantee that their residence within *Eretz Yisrael*, the Land of Israel, would be a permanent one. Living within its borders would be conditional upon the Children of Israel not violating their sacred covenant with G-d. Even before crossing the River Jordan, Moshe warned Israel what would be their fate were they to sin and so "overstay their welcome." The inevitable outcome would be their banishment from the Holy Land.

Moshe warned Israel what would be their fate were they to sin and so "overstay their welcome."

The Torah reading for Tishah B'Av contains Moshe's prophetic vision of what was destined to befall the Jewish nation in the Holy Land. They would slide into corruption and engage in idol worship. Angering G-d, they would be earmarked to suffer their utter destruction. The Jewish People would be scattered among the nations of the world. Only in exile would they begin their search to repent and return to their Creator.[1]

The opening description of this passage traces the root problem of Israel's deteriorating condition: וְנוֹשַׁנְתֶּם בָּאָרֶץ, *you will have been long in the land.*[2] The word וְנוֹשַׁנְתֶּם carries an allusion to the Jewish People's future exile. Its numerical value, 852, indicates that the Chosen Nation would face exile from the Holy Land at the end of 852 years. Nevertheless, G-d mercifully advanced the date by 2 years. He did this so that the ensuing statement, "they [Israel] will be utterly destroyed," would not be fulfilled. Despite Israel's wayward ways, G-d did not desire the annihilation of His beloved nation. In His Divine Benevolence, G-d hastened their exile so that they would not degenerate to the point of no return.[3]

Despite Israel's wayward ways, G-d did not desire the annihilation of His beloved nation.

The computation of the 850 years is calculated as follows. The First Temple was built 480 years after the Exodus.[4] Following the 40 years of wandering in the Wilderness, this was (480 – 40 =) 440 years after they entered the Land. The First Temple stood for 410 years,[5] to make a grand total of (440 + 410 =) 850 years.[6]

852: GROWING OLD

The word וְנוֹשַׁנְתֶּם is derived from the word יָשָׁן, *old*. It indicates how Israel "will have grown old." Having become accustomed to living in the land, they would now take their circumstances for granted. This meant that they would not recall their humble origins. They would disregard their Divine mandate. And they would degenerate to the point that they would perform evil in the eyes of G-d.

The longer the Jewish People lived in the Holy Land, the more distant they found themselves from their past. They became estranged from G-d and from their eternal covenant that was originally struck when they accepted the Torah. The monumental events at their national birth (Egyptian slavery, the miraculous Exodus, the journey through the Wilderness, the Divine Revelation at Sinai) were largely forgotten. These were relegated to ancient history, and were not considered relevant to those generations living many centuries later. After more than eight centuries within their homeland, they had grown old and complacent. Israel had disassociated themselves from their origins — from their Creator and from the Torah.[7]

The older a person, the more he is distanced from his youth. Memories of the past rapidly fade away. They become remote, obscure, and musty. They are dismissed as a distant shadow or echo that is firmly entrenched in the historic past, but which has no bearing upon the present or future.

In a homiletic reading of the verse, "You shall bring forth the old from before the new,"[8] one sees the importance conferred upon the "newest" product (be it ideology, taste in fashion, or technological appliances), which invariably relegates its "old" predecessors to the dust heap. They are no longer considered significant or worthy of attention. The Jewish People's exile from their homeland at a designated time of 852 years was because of their mistaken outlook that Torah belonged to the ancient past rather than the present.[9]

The Jewish People's exile at a designated time of 852 years was because of their outlook that Torah belonged to the ancient past.

852: INDESTRUCTIBLE

Despite the decree that they be exiled from the Holy Land, G-d did not want Israel to fall to the place of "no return." If G-d had waited

*G-d mercifully
accelerated the
beginning of
the exile by 2
years.*

the full period of 852 years, the numerical value of word וְנוֹשַׁנְתֶּם, He would have been obliged to fulfill the continuation of the Torah verse: "I will utterly wipe them out quickly."[10] G-d mercifully accelerated the beginning of the exile by 2 years — after only 850 years — to avert the threat of complete destruction.

The concept of G-d not waiting for the complete unfolding of time but rather hastening a process for the ultimate benefit of Israel, finds its precedent in the Exodus. The original decree was for the Jewish People to be persecuted in a foreign land for 400 years.[11] But G-d did not want Israel to fall below the 49th level of spiritual impurity. So He redeemed them after only 210 years.[12]

Notwithstanding the acceleration of exile from their homeland, this would ultimately be of benefit for the Jewish People because it guaranteed their indestructibility. G-d exacted His wrath upon the Temple, destroying a structure of wood and stone, while at the same time taking care to preserve His beloved people.[13] They would be scattered to the 4 corners of the world. Despite all the odds, they would survive in exile. They would ultimately reconnect to their heritage. The remedy to having grown old is to reinvigorate Torah and *mitzvah* observance with freshness and passion. The approach to Torah must be as something new. It is timeless and unchanging;[14] its dictates are not "out-of-date." It is forever relevant to the present, as it was to the past and as it will be to the future.

NOTES

1. *Devarim* 4:25-40.
2. Ibid. 4:25.
3. *Sanhedrin* 38a; *Gittin* 88a.
4. *I Melachim* 6:1.
5. *Yoma* 9a. See "410: The First Temple."
6. *Rashi, Daniel* 9:14.
7. See R' Shimshon Raphael Hirsch, *Devarim* 4:25 and *Collected Writings, The Jewish Year*, Av, pp. 374-375.
8. *Vayikra* 26:10.
9. The plain meaning of the verse "You shall bring forth the old from before the new" refers to economic prosperity such that when new produce comes onto the market, there remains a surplus of the old crop that is still available on the market. Consequently, people will store the new produce [so that it will dry and not rot], and place the old fruits elsewhere (*Bava Basra* 91b; see also *Torah Temimah, Vayikra* 26:10 [23]).
10. *Devarim* 4:26.

11. *Bereishis* 15:13. See "400: Of All Places."
12. See "210: The Iron Furnace."
13. *Eichah Rabbah* 4:14.
14. See *Rambam*, Commentary to Mishnah, *Sanhedrin* 10, 9th Principle of Faith

974
THE LOST GENERATIONS

974 is the number of generations
that were originally
to precede Creation.

THE NUMBER 974 IS FOUND IN THE CONTEXT OF THE GENERATIONS that were said to exist before the Creation of our world.

Ideologically opposed to Torah ideals, their destructive influence would reverberate through world history.

974: PRE-CREATION GENERATIONS

The Talmud interprets the verse, "Those who were cut off before their time,"[1] as a reference to the 974 generations of souls that preceded the creation of our world.[2] (The term "preceding" should not be mistakenly understood chronologically in terms of "time," but rather in terms of the "sequence" within the spiritual worlds.) Prior to the creation of our universe, G-d would "build worlds and destroy them."[3] The 974 generations belong to the category of those elements that existed, so to speak, in G-d's mind, but were not physically created in terms of the perspective of This World.

Prior to the creation of our universe, G-d would "build worlds and destroy them."

Nevertheless, these 974 generations would still find some form of expression.

The historic transmission of the Torah to mankind was supposed to wait until after 1000 generations had elapsed.[4] In reality, the Jewish People experienced the Divine Revelation at Sinai many generations earlier. G-d transmitted the Torah through Moshe, the 26th generation from Adam after the Creation of the universe.[5] Taking these 26 generations together with the 974 pre-Creation generations adds up to a total of (974 + 26 =) 1000 generations. Post-Creation, the world could not have waited an additional 974 generations without Torah. So G-d dispersed the generations throughout the course of world history.[6]

G-d dispersed the generations throughout the course of world history.

974: THE ARROGANT

The universe is governed by the principle of reward and punishment. However in G-d's mind, so to speak, the world should have operated according to the strict quality of *din*, judgment. This state leaves no room for error. But G-d knew a world operating according to the strict letter of the law was simply not sustainable.

Consequently, G-d incorporated the quality of *rachamim*, mercy, into Creation. This means that a sinner is not immediately punished. The wicked appear to thrive and prosper in This World. Justice is temporarily suspended in the hope that a sinner will realize the error of his ways and return to the right path.[7]

Preceding the physical world of Creation, the 974 generations hark back to the world of pure *din*, judgment, that belongs to G-d's original plan of existence. In the same way that the world order could not endure exclusively based upon *din*, so too, the preexistent generations of 974 generations similarly could not endure.

A particular hallmark of the 974 generations was their עַזּוּת, *arrogance*. When dispersed throughout history, they are called the "brazen-faced people within each generation."[8] Actually, this has to do with their negative association within the trait of *din* where man conceitedly judges his existence to be something that is absolutely essential.

A particular hallmark of the 974 generations was their arrogance.

This association with *din* is ironically the same quality that undermines the arrogant 974 generations. The arrogant ones are not who they make out to be. Not being prepared to submit themselves before G-d, they automatically sever their attachment from the Ultimate Source of all Reality.[9] They do not really belong to the world of existence. They therefore have no justification to continue to exist.

They sever their attachment from the Ultimate Source.

974: ANTI-TORAh

All existence is founded for the purpose of Torah and because G-d wills it. That means man cannot arrogantly consider his existence to be obligatory. He exists not for himself but in order to serve his Creator through Torah study and *mitzvah* performance.

Without Torah, the world has no reason to exist.

Torah gives meaning and existence to the universe. The world hung in the balance for 26 generations until Israel came to accept the Torah at Sinai.[10] Without Torah, the world has no reason to exist. Conversely, the 974 generations may be symbolically categorized as being "anti-Torah" in the sense that they relate to a period prior to the revelation of Torah at Sinai, which would give Creation its purpose.

Opposing the arrogance of the 974 generations is the arrogance of Israel.

Opposing the arrogance of the 974 generations is the arrogance of Israel; the Jewish People are considered the most brazen of the nations. Their *azzus*, arrogance, can only be neutralized by an acceptance of Torah,[11] which is affiliated with the opposite trait of *anivus*, humility. Water, which is the symbol of Torah,[12] does not remain on an upper level; it descends to a lower plane.[13]

Therefore, the 974 generations are anti-Torah and anti-existence.

974: The EIREV RAV

The evil spiritual roots of these 974 generations were incarnated in the eirev rav, mixed multitudes.

G-d implanted the 974 generations into world history. The evil spiritual roots of these 974 generations were incarnated in the *eirev rav*, mixed multitudes.[14] This primarily refers to the mixed multitudes who accompanied the Jewish nation out of Egypt.[15] These were the non-Jews who converted and escorted the Children of Israel during the Exodus.[16] Moshe was insistent that they be permitted to accompany the Jewish People — despite G-d's expressed reservations.[17]

No good came from their attachment to Israel. Ideologically, the *eirev rav* had not severed their ties with the idolatrous Egyptian culture. Their association with the nascent Jewish People frustrated the Jews' desire to single themselves out as G-d's Chosen Nation — unaffiliated with other nations — to receive the Torah.

The eirev rav's anti-Torah beliefs represented an assault on the sacred nature of Jewish life.

The infiltration of the *eirev rav*'s anti-Torah beliefs represented an assault on the sacred nature of Jewish life. Their ways were diametrically opposed to Torah. The *eirev rav* were not included with the Jewish People in the giving of the Torah.[18] So the acceptance of Torah was outside their experience. Denying the revelation and the transmission of Torah at Sinai would be reason enough to classify a person as ideologically belonging to the *eirev rav*.[19] The *eirev rav* were the instigators of many of the spiritual misfortunes that befell the Children of Israel in the Wilderness, most notably the event that was an affront to the giving of Torah at the foot of Mount Sinai: the Golden Calf.[20]

Conceptually, the mixed multitudes of the *eirev rav* connote the mixture of good and evil — one that is highly evocative of the primeval sin when Adam ate from the *Eitz HaDaas Tov V'Ra*, Tree of Knowledge of Good and Evil.[21] There is the intermingling of good and evil — that is the opposite of the rectification of Creation achieved by fidelity to Torah that separates the two, allowing the follower of Torah to extract the good and discard the bad.[22]

974: The ADMONITION

The philosophy of the *eirev rav* did not die out in the Wilderness;

just as the persistent presence of the 974 generations spread out throughout history, it remains extant. Throughout the generations, foreign, anti-Torah influences would undermine belief or observance to frustrate the emergence of true Torah goals.[23]

The national admonition documents the Divine retribution that would be meted out onto the Jewish People were they to violate the word of G-d. The Second *Tochachah*, Admonition, recorded in *Parashas Ki Savo* within *Mishneh Torah* (another name for the Book of *Devarim*) includes curses, personal suffering, and national atrocities.[24] The primary reason given is because the Jewish nation had not listened to the voice of G-d and not served Him through rejoicing and gladness of heart.[25]

This phenomenon can be attributed to the influence of those 974 generations that personify feelings of apathy or hostility to fulfilling the Will of G-d. It is no coincidence that there are a total of 974 words in the Torah passage that records this admonition.[26]

Those 974 generations personify feelings of apathy or hostility to fulfilling the Will of G-d.

974: IN THE FOOTSTEPS OF MASHIACH

The Talmud presages that the era before the arrival of Mashiach will witness the intensification of insolence.[27] Such a wave of arrogance is highly reminiscent of the impact of the *eirev rav* and 974 pre-existent generations bent upon undermining authentic Torah behavior. Their influence will even plague the leadership of the Jewish community.[28] Opposition toward Torah will be waged both from within and without.

The era before the arrival of Mashiach will witness the intensification of insolence.

Mashiach will bring the world back to its utopian state. It is in the lead-up to this period that the negative forces face their demise. Consequently, they channel all their energies in a final last stand. Their spiritual battle is their opposition to a time when the world will find its ultimate rectification, as evil is separated from good forever, to be vanquished once and for all.

Mashiach will bring the world back to its utopian state.

Suppressing their innate national trait of arrogance through the acceptance of Torah, the Jewish People attach themselves to G-d. They do not consider their existence to be obligatory; instead, they use their existence to humbly submit themselves to G-d. Their take on Creation opposes the ideological position of the 974 generations or *eirev rav,* whose arrogance is their undoing. It leads to their non-existence: the brazen-faced are doomed to go to *Gehinnom.*[29]

Suppressing their innate arrogance through the acceptance of Torah, the Jewish People attach themselves to G-d.

NOTES

1. *Iyov* 22:16.
2. *Chagigah* 13b-14a; *Avos DeRabbi Nassan* 31:3; see also *Bereishis Rabbah* 28:4.
3. *Bereishis Rabbah* 3:7.
4. *Tehillim* 105:8. See "1000: A Thousand to One."
5. See "26: In the Name of G-d."
6. *Chagigah* 14a; *Avos deRabbi Nassan* 31:3; see also *Bereishis Rabbah* 28:4.
7. Ibid. 12:15, 14:1; see *Rashi, Bereishis* 1:1.
8. *Chagigah* 14a; see also *Bereishis Rabbah* 28:4.
9. See *Rambam, Hilchos Yesodei HaTorah* 1:1.
10. *Shabbos* 88a.
11. *Beitzah* 25b.
12. *Bava Kamma* 17a.
13. *Taanis* 7a.
14. See *Vilna Gaon, Sifra DiTzniusa*, 1. See also R' Shlomo Elyashiv, *Leshem She'vo V'Achlamah, Sefer Klalim* 18, 8, 9.
15. *Shemos* 12:38 .
16. The number of the *eirev rav* that left with Israel was twice that of the Jewish people (*Mechilta, Bo* on *Shemos* 12:38).
17. See *Rashi, Shemos* 32:7 for how when speaking to Moshe, G-d referred to the *eirev rav* as "your people," insofar as it was Moshe's idea to accept these converts without consulting G-d and now they have corrupted themselves and others as well. See also *Ohr HaChaim, Shemos* 13:17, for how Pharaoh relied upon the *eirev rav* to sow seeds of dissension among the ranks of the Children of Israel. See *Zohar* 1, 121 as to how Moshe sought to bring them under the wings of the *Shechinah*.
18. *Ramban, Shemos* 19:2.
19. *Rambam, Iggeres Teiman*.
20. *Yalkut Shimoni, Eikev*, 852. See *Rashi, Shemos* 32:7.
21. See *Zohar* 1, 284.
22. The numerical value of *eirev rav* is equivalent to *daas*, knowledge, (474), used in terms of connectivity. See *Arizal, Shaar HaPessukim* and *Likkutim, Parashas Shemos*.
23. See *Beitzah* 32b, where the Sages characterized the distinctly un-Jewish behavior of a group of individuals as originating from the *eirev rav*.
24. *Devarim* 28:15-69. See "98: The Admonition."
25. *Devarim* 28:45, 47.
26. *Rokeach, Devarim* 28:69.
27. *Sotah* 49b.
28. *Vilna Gaon, Sifra DiTzniusa*, 1. See *Tikkunei Zohar* 144a, as to the role of the *eirev rav* as an integral part of the final Redemption.
29. *Pirkei Avos* 5:20.

1000
A THOUSAND TO ONE

As the Torah's largest number denomination, 1000 is the ultimate standard of measurement.

Something exceptional is framed against a backdrop of 1000 that usually negates everything else before it.

The Jew's task is to ensure that 1000 — as the maximum within a possible range — comes to mirror 1 as a reflection of its One Source.

1 IN A 1000

I N THE TORAH, 1000 IS THE LARGEST OF THE NUMBER DENOMINATIONS.[1]
The series of number groupings in the decimal system naturally follow successive base-10 multiples. These are arranged in units

*1000 is
noteworthy as
the ultimate
standard of
measurement.*

(1 digit), tens (2 digits), hundreds (3 digits), and thousands (4 digits). No subsequent mathematical classification exists in the Torah.[2]
Hence, 1000 is noteworthy as the ultimate standard of measurement.

1000: OUTSTANDING

1000 represents the paramount level — that which distinguishes
itself over everything that preceded it. Its outstanding properties
allow this number to form a new and distinct grouping.

Its exalted greatness is alluded to in the similarity between

*The princes or
heads of the
Tribes were
themselves
referred to as
the heads of
thousands of
Israel.*

אֶלֶף, *1000*, and אַלוּף, *prince* or *chief*, used to refer to an official
whose stature is eminently raised above others.[3] Consequently, the
highest-ranking officers in either judicial or leadership positions within
the Jewish camp were given communal jurisdiction over groups of
1000.[4] The princes or heads of the Tribes were themselves referred
to as the רָאשֵׁי אַלְפֵי יִשְׂרָאֵל, *heads of thousands of Israel.*[5]

TORAH: 1000Th GENERATION

The preeminence of 1000 is illustrated in the Divine Revelation at
Sinai. The Torah is described as the "[Divine] word He commanded to
1000 generations."[6] Its outstanding quality is also conveyed by how

*The greatest
Jewish leader
was Moshe,
symbolically
positioned as
the planned
1000th
generation.*

it was originally designated 1000 generations before Sinai: 974 generations originally planned to precede the giving of the Torah were
dispersed in the future generations,[7] plus the 26 generations spanning from Adam to Moshe.[8] This lies behind the meaning of the verse
"G-d keeps his covenant for 1000 generations."[9] The most outstanding prophet and greatest Jewish leader was Moshe, who was symbolically positioned as the planned 1000th generation.

1000: CUT-OFF POINT

By virtue of 1000 being the highest numeric denomination in the Torah, this number conveys the optimal point of increase. The prophet notes the future destiny of Israel will be where "the smallest shall increase a 1000-fold, and the least into a mighty nation."[10] Furthermore, Moshe's personal blessing to Israel before his death was a blessing of 1000-fold: *May HASHEM, the G-d of your forefathers, make you 1000 times as many as you are, and Bless you as He has promised you.*[11]

Alternatively, 1000 can also denote the maximum number within a possible range.[12] Examples of 1000 as the greatest classification include money spent in pursuit of a *mitzvah* (Rabban Gamliel purchasing an *esrog* for 1000 golden coins[13]), or the volume of inherited assets (denomination of 1000 used in terms of land, cities, and ships[14]).

1000: OVERWHELMING

Where 1000 is used as the maximum number within a range, it is to be expected that everything else pales into insignificance. The large quantity and comprehensive nature of 1000 powerfully cancel out a single dissenting factor. Anything smaller does not stand a chance, leading it to be readily nullified before 1000.

This phenomenon has halachic implications. All items are deemed בָּטֵל, *annulled*, before 1000 except for something that possesses a distinctive quality that counters any attempt to negate it (e.g., an item permissible at a later date,[15] or a live creature or object that is important enough to be counted individually.[16])

The correspondence or ratio of 1000 to 1 has many applications. There is a phrase used in Iyov to denote the phenomenon of אֶחָד מִנִּי אָלֶף, *1 out of 1000*.[17] There are very rare instances in which 1 proves itself to be exceptional enough that it "stands out" and is placed on par with 1000. Where man is not worthy, G-d said, "1 will pursue 1000";[18] *Koheles* declares "1 man in 1000 I have found";[19] and in Torah scholarship "1 out of 1000 entering the study hall is destined to emerge as a great Torah authority."[20]

There are very rare instances in which 1 proves itself to be exceptional enough that it "stands out" and is placed on par with 1000.

1000 TO 1

A vital aspect of 1000 is that it is meant to map all the way back to 1. There is a correspondence between the "first number" and the "largest number." Indeed, the two numbers share many of the same characteristics.

The number denominations correspond to the 4 spiritual worlds

In the works of kabbalah, the number denominations correspond to the 4 spiritual worlds: 1000 relates to the lowest world of עֲשִׂיָּה, *Completion*; 100 to the world of יְצִירָה, *Formation*; 10 to the world of בְּרִיאָה, *Creation*; and 1 to the highest world of אֲצִילוּת, *Emanation*.[21]

WORLD	NUMBER
עֲשִׂיָּה *Completion*	1000
יְצִירָה *Formation*	100
בְּרִיאָה *Creation*	10
אֲצִילוּת *Emanation*	1

The greatest revelation of 1000 within the lowest of the worlds, עֲשִׂיָּה, must be traced back to the highest world, אֲצִילוּת, with its affinity to the number 1 in the Absolute Unity of G-d. This is brilliantly alluded to with אֶלֶף, *1000*, having the identical spelling as אָלֶף, the 1st letter of the Hebrew alphabet.[22] In fact, G-d is Himself called using the related term אַלּוּף, *Chief*, as in the verse, "You are the *Chief* of my youth,"[23] that relates to the number 1000. 1 as the beginning and 1000 as the end converge with G-d Who transcends all demarcations. It reverts to 1.

1 as the beginning and 1000 as the end converge with G-d.

1000: ONE DAY IN YOUR EYES

One famous correlation between 1000 and 1 is epitomized in the passage of time. In the words of the Psalmist, "1000 years in Your [G-d's] Eyes is like yesterday that has passed."[24] Though a millennium may elapse in human years, in fact, this is only equivalent to 1 day before G-d.[25] One famous illustration of this is G-d's vow to Adam that on the day he ate from the Tree of Knowledge, man would die.[26] Rather than dying immediately after the primeval sin, however, Adam lived nearly 1000 years — namely, equal to a day, based on G-d's reckoning.[27]

The first 6 Days parallel 6,000 years of human civilization.

The Days of Creation, as the microcosm of existence, contain within them the unfolding kaleidoscope of the entire Jewish history. Each day is equivalent to 1000 years of history and, in fact, reflects many aspects and characteristics of this day.[28] So the first 6 Days parallel 6,000 years of human civilization,[29] while the 7th Day, Shabbos hints to the 7th millennia of the World to Come.[30]

1000: KING SHLOMO

Remarkably, the number 1000 finds frequent expression in the life of King Shlomo. This great Jewish king was considered equivalent to 1000 people[31] and married 1000 wives.[32] After building the Temple, Shlomo sacrificed 1000 *olah* (burnt) offerings upon the Altar.[33] He refined 1000 times the gold used for the 10 Menorahs he made.[34] 1000 musical instruments were brought into his chamber when he married Pharaoh's daughter.[35] In the Temple there was a a musical instrument called a *magreifah* that was able to produce 1000 songs.[36] Even though G-d gave over His vineyard (a synonym for Israel) to the other nations, G-d affirmed that He retained ownership over them — with the gentile nations agreeing to pay Shlomo 1000 silver pieces.[37]

Like 1000, the life of Shlomo was outstanding, extended up to the maximum constraints of This World. His outlook toward worldly desires, pleasure, and wisdom incorporating non-Torah "foreign" wisdom all had to be framed and dedicated toward a holy cause.[38] His legendary throne was itself a parallel to G-d's Heavenly Throne.[39] Shlomo's conduct underlined the mission of taking 1000 within the all-encompassing nature of the physical world and mapping it back to mirror G-d's Unity within the number 1.

The important lesson is to ensure that 1000 reflects back to G-d in His Absolute Oneness.

The important lesson derived from the number 1000 is to similarly take the all-inclusive nature of the lowly world, to extend it to its natural extremities up to the number 1000, but to always ensure that this spiritually reflects back to 1, to G-d in His Absolute Oneness.

NOTES

1. *Maharal, Chiddushei Aggados, Bava Basra* 73a (Vol. 3, p. 86); *R' Tzadok HaKohen, Yisrael Kedoshim* 12b.
2. See "10,000: A Great Many" and *Ezra* 2:64 about the term רבוא, *10,000*.
3. See *Bereishis* 36, *Shemos* 15:15. This is also mirrored in colloquial English where the number 1000 is interestingly referred to by the slang term, " one grand."
4. *Shemos* 18:21, 25; *Devarim* 1:15.
5. *Bamidbar* 1:16, 31:5, *Yehoshua* 22:14.
6. *Tehillim* 105:8.
7. The 974 generations were scattered through time and are the brazen in every generation (*Chagigah* 13b). See "974: The Lost Generations."
8. See "26: In the Name of G-d." Despite the longevity of the earliest generations, it is noteworthy that none of the Biblical personalities lived to the age of 1000 years.

9. *Devarim* 7:9.
10. *Yeshayah* 60:22.
11. *Devarim* 1:11 and *Rashi* ad loc. In contrast to the blessing of the Divine that is not subject to limitation, the greatest quantity incorporated into his blessing was 1000-fold. This represented the definitive level of blessing (see *Zohar* I, 161a for how a Divine *berachah*, blessing, is at least 1000 of the same item).
12. "The liability of a slave is "... whether or not his actual monetary value was 1 *dinar* or 1000 *zuz*" (*Rashi*, *Shemos* 21:32).
13. *Succah* 41b.
14. *Eruvin* 86a, *Yoma* 35b.
15. *Beitzah* 3b.
16. *Zevachim* 72a-73a. See also *Chullin* Ch. 10 and *Yoreh Deah* 100-101.
17. *Iyov* 9:3, 33:23.
18. *Devarim* 32:30.
19. *Koheles* 7:28. The Midrash lists some references to outstanding individuals who were the 1 out of 1000. This is a reference to Avraham, Amram, or Moshe (*Koheles Rabbah* 7:28).
20. *Vayikra Rabbah* 2:1. See ibid. and Midrash on *Koheles* 7:28 for how the way of the world is that 100 out of 1000 emerge in knowledge of *Mikra* (Scripture), 10 with knowledge of *Mishnah*, and only 1 out of 1000 with knowledge of Talmud.
21. R' Tzadok HaKohen, *Takanas HaSharim* 6 p. 34; *Pri Tzaddik*, *Nasso* 17 See "4: Finding a Place."
22. *Maharal*, *Ohr Chodosh*, p. 139; *Maharal*, *Chiddushei Aggados Gittin* 56b (Vol. 2, p. 113). See also *Shem MiShmuel*, *Devarim* 5676 pp. 21-22; R' *Tzadok HaKohen*, *Dover Tzedek* 8a.
23. *Chagigah* 16a based on *Yirmiyah* 3:4. See also *Mishlei* 16:28.
24. *Tehillim* 90:4; see *Bereishis Rabbah* 19:8.
25. "There is no day before G-d that is less than 1000 years" (*Tanchuma*, *Vayeilech* 2).
26. *Bereishis* 2:17.
27. Though supposed to live for 1000 years, Adam died at the age of 930 (*Bereishis* 5:5) and donated his last 70 years (930+70=1000) as a gift to David. See *Zohar* 1, 91b; *Yalkut Shimoni*, *Bereishis* 41. See also *Pri Tzaddik*, *Noach* 6.
28. *Rosh Hashanah* 31a.
29. See "6000: The End of the World."
30. See *Ramban*, *Bereishis* 2:3; *Rabbeinu Bachya*, *Bereishis* 2:3. See also *Maharal*, *Chiddushei Aggados*, *Sanhedrin* 97a (Vol. 3, pp. 208-209).
31. See *Shemos Rabbah* 6:1: G-d said "Let Shlomo and 1000 others like him be eliminated, but I will not eliminate even the little point of the smallest letter *yud* from the Torah!"
32. *Bava Metzia* 86b.
33. *I Melachim* 3:4; see *Shabbos* 30a and *Makkos* 10a about G-d considering 1 day of David learning Torah as more precious than 1,000 offerings by Shlomo in the Temple.
34. *Menachos* 29a.
35. *Shabbos* 56b.
36. *Arachin* 10b-11a.
37. *Shir HaShirim* 8:11-12 and *Rashi* ad loc.
38. R' *Tzadok HaKohen*, *Dover Tzedek*, *Achrei-Mos* 4(5).
39. For a detailed description of Shlomo's legendary and symbolic throne (*I Melachim* 10:18-20) and its parallel to the Heavenly Throne, see *Targum Sheni* and *Bamidbar Rabbah* 12: 21. Shlomo is said to have sat on the "Throne of G-d" (*I Divrei HaYamim* 29:23. See *Zohar I*, 243a and *Rabbeinu Bachya*, Introduction to *Bereishis*).

2000

THE BORDERLINE

2000 is the number that depicts
the outer boundaries
of everything that belongs
within the same zone.
This is the borderline or outer limit.

THE LIMITS

The outer boundaries of a zone are often measured up to the number 2000.

THE OUTER BOUNDARIES OF A ZONE ARE OFTEN MEASURED UP TO the number 2000.

Perhaps the most famous applications of this can be found in the demarcation of time and space.

2000: TIME ZONES

The epochs of world history can be arranged into periods of 2000 years each. Torah, the blueprint of Creation, preceded the formation of the universe by 2000 years.[1] The 6000 years allocated for the existence of human civilization readily divide into 3 equal sections, with each unit lasting two millennia.[2]

The first era in the formative generations of mankind was characterized as 2000 years of *tohu*, emptiness. Starting from Adam and his primeval sin, mankind suffered a spiritual degeneration. The second segment, commencing from the appearance of Avraham who revolutionized the world, heralded 2000 years of Torah. Finally, the last era is composed of 2000 years in the epoch as the lead-up to Mashiach.[3] Each of these 2000-year periods marks a clear, distinctive phase in world history.

Each of these 2000-year periods marks a clear, distinctive phase in world history.

2000: GENERATIONS

No matter how long man lives, what possessions he accumulates, or the number of children he fathers, it is impossible for him to attain true happiness in This World — because his existence is destined to end in death. In the words of *Koheles*, "Even if he were to live 1000 years twice over [i.e., 1000 x 2 = 2000] but not find contentment — do not all go to the same place?"[4] His longevity notwithstanding, his existence must be in pursuit of spiritual endeavors that earn him eternity in the World to Come.

Man's existence must be in pursuit of spiritual endeavors that earn him eternity in the World to Come.

The reward of man's actions stretches far beyond his temporary lifetime. G-d vows to preserve the kindness that man performs before

Him for 2000 generations.[5] While an action that man performs out of *yirah*, fear [of G-d], extends up to 1000 generations, an action performed out of *ahavah*, love [of G-d], goes double the distance: it extends up until 2000 generations.[6] The latter level is far more exalted than the former, as it denotes the ideal situation. This is where man lovingly serves G-d and views this worship as an honored privilege.

WITHIN REACH

B EYOND MAN'S IMMEDIATE SPACE — AS DEFINED BY HIS PERSONAL place of 4 *amos*, cubits[7] — is the distance of 2000 *amos*. This measurement equals 1 *mil* (between 0.96 — 1.152 kilometers or 0.6-0.7 miles, an average walking distance of between 18–24 minutes).

Everything within these borderlines is halachically classified as belonging to the *same* zone or settlement. It all lies "within reach."[8] Conversely, anything positioned outside the 2000-*amos* boundary lies on the outside. This concept is principally found in the distance of the Ark from the Jewish people, in the green belt that surrounds a city, and in the restriction of leaving one's place on Shabbos.

2000 AMOS: AT A DISTANCE

Beyond the immediate distance of 2000 *amos* is the creation of a different zone, one that lies "out of bounds" of the original placement.

In the traveling formation in the desert, the Ark was carried 2000 cubits at a distance from the people, following the banners of Yehudah and Reuven.[9] When the nation crossed the River Jordan at the end of 40 years, G-d instructed the priests to carry the Ark ahead of the nation, maintaining a distance of 2000 *amos* between them and the rest of the Jewish People. The waters miraculously parted to enable the nation to safely pass through and enter into the Promised Land.[10]

The placement of the Ark in a different zone from the Israelites points at how it rightfully occupies a separate, distinctive realm. This is the distance that clearly differentiates "where one place ends and another one begins."

The *Shechinah* resided among the Jewish People in the *Mishkan*, Sanctuary, that would house the Ark. The *Mishkan* served as atone-

The placement of the Ark in a different zone from the Israelites points at how it rightfully occupies a separate, distinctive realm.

ment for the sin of the Golden Calf. In the aftermath of this national sin, Moshe pitched his tent at a distance of 2000 *amos* from the Jewish camp. Anyone who sought G-d had to go outside of his immediate vicinity and move to the temporary placement of Moshe's dwelling, which in turn became a yeshivah[11] and was referred to at the time as *Ohel Moed*, Tent of Meeting.[12] Only once the Jewish people were forgiven did the *Shechinah* return, with the *Mishkan* residing within their midst.

2000 AMOS: GREEN BELT

Surrounding the cities allocated to the Levites in the Holy Land were clearly designated open spaces.[13] The width of this green-belt perimeter was 2000 *amos* in all 4 directions around the city.[14] Though technically outside the city walls, this surrounding space was included as an extension of the city.

This ruling has its application in the laws of the accidental killer who was granted refuge when escaping the blood avenger by fleeing to the Levite cities (that doubled as Cities of Refuge). Here the 2000 *amos* outside the city walls were included as part of the city, and afforded him protection if he was inside it.[15]

2000 AMOS: TECHUM SHABBOS

The Torah instructs, "No man may leave his place on the 7th day."[16] The Biblical prohibition is for a Jew to walk farther than 12 *mil* from his originally designated Shabbos place of residence at the onset of that day.[17] The rabbinical decree imposes the *Techum Shabbos*, Shabbos boundary limit, which allows him to walk up to a distance of 2000 *amos* outside his station. In this regard, a city is considered to be one unified area. Hence, the 2000 *amos* are calculated starting from outside the city limits.[18]

Nevertheless, there is an ingenious rabbinic device for the construction of an *eiruv techumim*, an *eiruv* of borders. Here a Jew may set up a temporary home (by placing sufficient food for 2 meals as an *eiruv* before Shabbos) and position it at a distance of no farther than 2000 *amos* from the city. He is now able to begin his calculation of the requisite 2000 *amos* of his Shabbos boundary limit from this temporary home.[19]

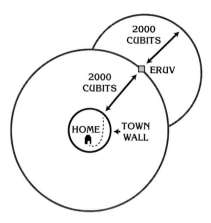

The rabbinic device of *Techum Shabbos* istraced back to the conduct of the Jewish forefathers. Avraham is said to have kept the entire Torah — even the rules of establishing *eiruvim* (plural of *eiruv*).[20] Moreover, the Torah relates that Yaakov purchased a field in the area of Shechem upon which to pitch his tent.[21] The Midrash sees this as an allusion of Yaakov taking the necessary steps to establish a *Techum Shabbos*.[22]

The holiness of Shabbos in time extends its influence to consecrate the realm of place. The principle of sanctified space is seen in the laws of transportation of objects on Shabbos. The place that is sanctified is the רְשׁוּת הַיָּחִיד, *private domain*, while the רְשׁוּת הָרַבִּים, *public domain*, is unsanctified space. Transportation into and out of, or even within, the unsanctified *reshus harabbim* is prohibited on Shabbos. The restriction of not going into non-consecrated space extends to not going outside 2000 *amos*, namely the natural boundaries of man's settlement.

The limits placed upon a Jew walking outside of his place — both the biblical and the rabbinic distance — relate to sanctification of space. The 12-*mil* distance corresponds to the consecration of space in the total expanse of the Jewish encampment in the Wilderness.[23]

The symbolism within the rabbinic distance of 2000 *amos* relates back to the basic defining measure of place: namely, 4 *amos*.[24] The inclusion of Shabbos, as an analogy of the World to Come within This World, symbolically hints at man's ability to sanctify his existing space and, additionally, how to push the boundaries. The Jew has the ability to sanctify space, and in turn, redefine the parameters. There is a principle that something that has a positive impact is 500-fold greater than something that has a negative impact.[25] So the standard individual place of 4 *amos* that may not be intrinsically holy can be

The limits placed upon walking outside one's place relate to sanctification of space.

The Jew has the ability to sanctify space, and in turn, redefine the parameters.

sanctified and elevated by use of the *Techum Shabbos,* into a place of holiness spanning a distance of (4 x 500 =) 2000 *amos.*[26]

Every Jew can create holiness in his immediate personal space (4 amos).

Actually, this capacity to broaden one's horizons to make the *unholy* into *holy* is the legacy transmitted by the Jewish Forefathers.[27] Every Jew can replicate this to create holiness in his immediate personal space (4 *amos*), within the 2000 *amos* that lie within the same zone, and to extend this further, like the 2000 *amos* of the *Eiruv Techumin* of Shabbos.

A Jew must not lose sight of the magnificence of Shabbos as a semblance of the World to Come.

But at the same time, the *Techum Shabbos* of 2000 *amos* taps into the function of barriers to protect and preserve the holiness of Shabbos within. That means a Jew must not lose sight of the magnificence of Shabbos as a semblance of the World to Come. Here it serves as a deterrent to sin, where man departs from his true position and calling.[28]

So the symbolism of 2000 defines the borderlines as the demarcation of everything that belongs within the same zone.

NOTES

1. *Bereishis Rabbah* 8:2.
2. See "6000: The End of the World."
3. *Sanhedrin* 97a.
4. *Koheles* 6:6 and *Rashi* ad loc. Other commentators (*Ibn Ezra*) understand this to mean 1000 squared: namely, $1000^2 = 1,000,000$.
5. *Shemos* 34:7 and *Rashi* ad loc.
6. *Sotah* 31b.
7. See "4: Finding the Place."
8. The telescope of Rabban Gamliel could view up to 2000 *amos* on dry land and 2000 *amos* at sea (*Eruvin* 43b).
9. *Bamidbar* 2:17; see *Bamidbar Rabbah* 2:9.
10. *Yehoshua* 3:4, 15-17.
11. *Targum Onkelos, Shemos* 33:7
12. *Rashi,* ibid. This should not be confused with the *Mishkan,* which was only built months later and would also be called by the name *Ohel Moed.* See *Rashi, Shemos* 33:11.
13. *Bamidbar* 35:3-5.
14. *Rashi,* ibid. 35:4. See also *Sotah* 27b. See *Rambam, Hilchos Shemittah VeYovel* 13:2, whose opinion is that there was a total of 3000 *amos,* with the outer 2000 used for agriculture.
15. *Eruvin* 51a; *Rambam, Hilchos Rotzeach* 8:11. Nevertheless, the accidental killer had to reside within the city and not within the 2000 cubit green belt.
16. *Shemos* 16:29. See *Maharal, Gur Aryeh, Shemos* 16:29 [29] for an allusion to the 2000 cubits derived from the words אַל יֵצֵא, *Do not leave* ….
17. See *Shabbos* 69a, *Sotah* 27b; *Yerushalmi, Eruvin* 3:4. See *Mishnah Berurah* 497:1, that there are

dissenting opinions who maintain that the verse of "Do not leave" teaches only the law against transporting from one domain to another, but that the laws of *techumin*, even for 12 mil, is not Biblically forbidden.

18. *Sotah* 27b, *Eruvin* 51a, see *Rashi* ad loc. The inference of a distance of 2000 cubits is actually derived from the laws of a city of refuge, the place to which an accidental murderer fled in order to escape the blood avenger. See *Shulchan Aruch, Orach Chaim* 397:1.

19. See *Mishnah, Eruvin* 4-5. See also *Shulchan Aruch, Orach Chaim* 408:1.

20. According to *Teshuvos HaRashba* 1:94, when the Gemara (*Yoma* 28b) states that Avraham kept the entire Torah, it says: *Even eruvei techumin* (based on *Bereishis* 26:5).

21. *Bereishis* 33:18-19.

22. *Bereishis Rabbah* 11:7.

23. *Sotah* 13b. See "12: Tribes of Israel."

24. See "4: Finding the Place."

25. See *Rashi, Shemos* 34:7.

26. R' Tzadok HaKohen, *Pri Tzaddik, Bereishis* 1 and *Vayishlach* 8, based upon *Zohar* 2, 63b.

27. The expansion of Shabbos into all man's dwellings (*Vayikra* 23:3) refers to Yaakov's ability to sanctify areas outside of the Holy Land, imbuing them with holiness. See *Pri Tzaddik, Vayishlach* 8 and *Sfas Emes, Vayishlach* 5632.

28. R' Tzadok HaKohen, *Kometz HaMinchah*, p. 15.

6000
THE END OF THE WORLD

The world is destined to last
for 6000 years.

This relates back to
the 6 Days of Creation.

THE WORLD AS WE KNOW IT

These 6 millennia have their source in the 6 Days of Creation.

THE NUMBER 6000 REPRESENTS THE MAXIMUM YEARS OF HUMAN existence in the universe. These 6 millennia have their source in the 6 Days of Creation.

FROM 6 TO 6000

We have noted that 6 is the primary symbol of the natural world. Its expression in the dimension of place unfolds into the 6 directions of the physical realm, while in the dimension of time, it opened out into the 6 Days of Creation.[1]

The Torah tells us that G-d created the world in 6 days and rested on the 7th Day, Shabbos.[2] This template is continuously played out on a weekly basis: 6 days of creative activity is then followed by the 7th day of rest and inactivity.[3] King Shlomo proclaimed "There is nothing new under the sun."[4] G-d implanted into those 6 Days of Creation everything that was later destined to emerge.[5] This was also true in terms of time.

The 6 Days of Creation contain the kaleidoscope of the entire Jewish history.

As the microcosm of existence, the 6 Days of Creation therefore contain the kaleidoscope of the entire Jewish history. In G-d's calculation, 1 day is equivalent to 1000 years: "1000 years in Your [G-d's] eyes are like yesterday which has passed."[6] Each Day of Creation is parallel to a 1000-year period of world history. Consequently, the 6 Days of Creation map the world's destiny for 6000 years.

There are striking similarities between the momentous events of each of the 6 Days of Creation and the events of its corresponding millennium.

There are striking similarities between the momentous events that happened on each of the 6 Days of Creation and the events of its corresponding millennium. The light of Day 1 of Creation, for example, has its parallel in Adam, the first human being, who lived during the 1st millennium and who illuminated the world by recognizing his Creator. The division of waters on Day 2 of Creation alludes to the 2nd millennium and the separation between Noach and his generation in the Waters of the Flood.[7]

These parallels highlight the underlying principle of G-d's *Hashgachah*, Divine Providence. This began with His role as Creator in the 6 Days of Creation, and it continues in His role as Director of the 6

Millennia of History. Everything that transpires in the world — including all historic events — occurs for a reason. Nothing is random. Everything operates under the constant supervision of G-d Who is fully aware of whatever happens.[8]

6000: 3 epochs

The Talmud divides the 6 millennia of world history into 3 distinct epochs: "The world will exist for 6000 years: 2000 years of chaos (*tohu*); 2000 years of Torah; and finally 2000 years [in the coming] of Mashiach."[9]

The first 2000 years of chaos extended from Adam to Avraham, until he reached the age that he would teach people to believe in G-d.[10] The second phase includes the time of the Jewish forefathers and acceptance of Torah at Sinai (in the year 2448 from Creation). This lasted until after the compiling of the Mishnah. The final third 2000 years set in motion the final phase of world history. This will culminate in the ingathering of dispersed Jews from around the globe, returning to the Holy Land during the arrival of the Messianic Era.

6000: 2 epochs

Alternatively, the panorama of 6000 years of world history can be divided into 2 opposite halves. The former has its focus on the world's origins; the latter is about the world heading toward its endpoint.

The first part is the influence upon mankind that originates from Creation. Here the universe is seen as the continuation of the beginning. The starting point of this epoch relates back to Adam *HaRishon*, the *first* man.

The starting point of this epoch relates back to Adam HaRishon, the first man.

The second part is the influence upon mankind associated with the journey as man travels toward the endpoint. This period began with David, whose life just preceded the halfway mark of 3000 years from the Creation of the world.[11] Indeed, David would be the ancestor of the future Mashiach (often called Mashiach ben David, *Messiah the son of David*) who is destined to bring the world to realize its objective.[12] In comparison to the first phase, this second phase relates to the ultimate human persona: Adam *HaAcharon*, the *last* man. This marks the point when mankind finally reaches the supreme, refined level of perfection.[13]

This second phase relates to the ultimate human persona: Adam HaAcharon, the last man.

6000: THE COMPLETE PICTURE

The development of mankind is an ongoing spiritual process.

Parallel to the directions of the natural world, 6 is the epitome of *gashmiyus*, corporeality.[14] It is the mark of *sheleimus*, completion, in the physical realm.[15] While the physical creation of the world was completed at the end of Day 6 of Creation, the unique spiritual development of mankind is destined to continue until the end of the world at the close of the 6th millennium.

Mashiach will herald in an era in which the world and mankind will, at long last, behave as they should.

Belief in the Messianic Epoch is a fundamental of Jewish faith.[16] This is because world history, along to its current course, has not followed the Will of G-d — not even for 1 day in all of human civilization! It was on Day 6 of Creation, the day Adam was created, that he sinned by eating from the Tree of Knowledge.[17]

Mashiach comes to rectify this. He will herald in an era where the world and mankind will, at long last, behave as they should. Drawing the 6th millennium to a close means that the universe will revert to the way G-d originally intended it to be. The times of Mashiach are when mankind returns to the level of Adam before his sin to finally recapture the task that man should have achieved on Day 6 of Creation. This leads to the 7th period: the 7th millennium — *Olam Haba*, the World to Come, that mirrors the 7th day, Shabbos.

The 6000 years of This World are the means to reach Olam Haba.

Parallel to the 6 days of the week as the requisite period of preparation to arrival at the 7th Day, Shabbos, the 6000 years of This World are the means to reach *Olam Haba*, the World to Come, that is contained in miniature in the 7th Day, Shabbos.[18]

And on that long-awaited day, the "complete picture" of G-d's Divine historic master plan for the universe will be revealed and understood in all its extraordinary detail.

NOTES

1. See "6: It's Only Natural."
2. *Bereishis* 1:1-31; 2:1-3.
3. See "7: A Holy Spark."
4. *Koheles* 1:9.
5. Perhaps the best analogy of this is the seed within a fruit that contains within it the genetic material of a tree and of its fruit, which, in turn, will contain further seeds for future trees and plants ad infinitum. See R' Yitzchak Isaac Chaver, *Ohr Torah* 3 commentary to *Maalos HaTorah*.
6. *Tehillim* 90:4. See "1000: A Thousand to One."

7. *Ramban, Bereishis* 2:3. See R' Elyah Weintraub's *B'Sod Yesharim,* who elaborates upon traditions from the *Vilna Gaon* that pertain to contemporary events and the last 250 years.

8. See *Ramban, Shemos* 13:16 end of *Parashas Bo.*

9. *Rosh Hashanah* 31a; *Avodah Zarah* 9a.

10. See *Avodah Zarah* 9a, *Rashi* ad loc., that this first epoch of Avraham being involved with converts (*Bereishis* 12:5) occurred when Avraham was 52 years old. See also *Maharal, Gevuros Hashem* 5.

11. See *Maharal, Gur Aryeh, Bereishis* 14:13 [21].

12. *Maharal, Derashah L'Shabbos Shuvah.* See *Yevamos* 64b for how the human life span began to shorten from the time of David. Adam was diminished in his stature to 100 *amos.* He is therefore associated with 100 compared to David, whose life span was only 70 years. See "70: The Sum of the Parts" and "100: Count Your Blessings."

13. This explanation was heard from R' Moshe Shapiro.

14. *Maharal, Be'er HaGolah* 6[4] p. 112b.

15. See *Esther Rabbah* 1:10, for 6 names used in reference to 6 realms of the land.

16. *Rambam,* Commentary to Mishnah, *Sanhedrin* 10, 12th Principle of Faith.

17. *Sanhedrin* 38b.

18. See *Ramban, Bereishis* 2:3; *Rabbeinu Bachya,* ibid.. See also *Maharal, Chiddushei Aggados, Sanhedrin* 97a (Vol. 3, pp. 208-209).

10,000
A GREAT MANY

10,000 is the symbol of a higher state of things, especially when compared to 1,000.

It is a concept denoting the eternity of Olam Haba.

TOO NUMEROUS TO MENTION

Base-10 multiples take on new Hebrew names in their respective classifications.

IN THE HEBREW LANGUAGE, THERE IS NO ACTUAL NUMERIC DENOM-ination of 10,000.

We have seen that successive base-10 multiples (10, 100, 1000) take on new Hebrew names in their respective classifications. This pattern is discontinued for groupings of ever-increasing higher numbers. (This is the reason that Modern Hebrew borrows terms for *millions* and *billions* from other languages).

The Hebrew term רִבּוֹא or רְבָבָה, *myriads*, is used to indicate 10,000. Nevertheless, 10,000 is not, strictly speaking, an exact description of a number. Nor is it technically a new numeric denomination. Instead, *myriads* offers a generic, non-precise term that reflects an exceptionally large sum. The implication is that 10,000 is a quantity that is "too numerous to mention." It is not an exact numeric figure within the context of This World. רְבָבָה is itself derived from its word root רַב, *multiple*, and the related word רִבּוּי, *many*.[1]

The fulfillment or widest expansion in This World stretches from 1 to 1000. This is seen in the relationship between *aleph*, the first letter as referenced in the number 1 and *eleph*, 1000 such that 1000 reverts to 1.[2] Subsequent numbers will be grouped into sets of thousands. Thus, 10,000 is classified as "10 thousands" (10 x 1000) rather than "100 hundreds" (100 x 100).

10,000 is the symbol of multitudes in a completed state.

Actually, 10,000 is the symbol of multitudes in a completed state. This is because it combines 10 as the all-encompassing number of completion[3] with 1000 as the last numeric denomination (10 x 1000 = 10,000).[4]

10,000: NO OFFICIALS

Different levels of administrators were entrusted with jurisdiction over groups within the Jewish People.

There were different levels of administrators who were officially entrusted with legal jurisdiction over groups within the Jewish People. The Torah notes that there were appointed officers for groups of 10s, 50s and 100s, with the highest position reserved for שָׂרֵי אֲלָפִים, *officers of 1000s.*[5]

In concert with 1000 representing the final numeric denomination according to Torah, the highest position of authority was delegated to rule over 1000s. There was no higher position than this. No authority was entrusted by the king to his officers or ministers for control over and above groups of 1000s. Any grouping over and above this figure, namely from 10,000 upward, went beyond the jurisdiction of any officials. Instead, it was directly under the official authority of the king.

THOUSANDS VS. TENS OF THOUSANDS

THE NUMBERS 1000 AND 10,000 ARE FREQUENTLY COMPARED AND contrasted. In so doing, they come to conceptually characterize opposite concepts.

Perhaps the most prominent examples of this include the transience of *Olam Hazeh*, This World, versus the eternity of *Olam Haba*, the World to Come; the opposing twin brothers, Eisav versus Yaakov; the left versus the right; Yosef's sons Menashe and Ephraim; and the Jewish kings Shaul and David.

1000 VS. 10,000: EISAV AND YAAKOV

Two phrases were used in the blessing given to Rivkah by her relatives before departing with Avraham's servant to marry Yitzchak: אֲחֹתֵנוּ אַתְּ הֲיִי לְאַלְפֵי רְבָבָה, *Our sister, may you become thousands of myriads.*[6] This blessing refers to the two children she was to bear: Eisav and Yaakov. The phrase אַלְפֵי, *1000s,* relates to Eisav, whose point of reference is *Olam Hazeh,* whereas רְבָבָה, *10,000,* refers to Yaakov, who identifies with *Olam Haba.*[7]

The responsibility of appointed legal officials up to the 1000s is indicative of the fleetingness of this physical world. Their authority was for a short term which the king was able to rescind it at any time. The title given to the early rulers of Eisav's descendants was אַלּוּף, *chief,*[8] that is cognate to the word אֶלֶף, *1000.*

By contrast, Yaakov embodied the trait of *emes,* truth, which is permanent and everlasting.[9] While Eisav took possession of this transient world, which ends after the 1000s, Yaakov staked a claim to the

The responsibility of appointed legal officials up to the 1000s is indicative of the fleetingness of this physical world.

spiritual World to Come that stretches from the uncountable level of 10,000 all the way to eternity.[10]

The position of Yaakov vis-à-vis Eisav was similar to that of a king compared to his officials. The authority of the king continues indefinitely, establishing a royal dynasty, in contrast to the officials whose position is always under review.[11] The long-term nature of 10,000 is similarly associated with the spiritual realm of the angels that are arranged in groups of 10,000,[12] or in the *holy myriads* that accompanied G-d when He descended to Earth to give the Torah.[13]

The long-term nature of 10,000 is similarly associated with the spiritual realm of the angels.

1000 VS. 10,000:
TO THE LEFT AND TO THE RIGHT

The comparative distinction between 1000 and 10,000 is respectively related to the left and the right. The Psalmist writes, "1000 shall fall at your side and 10,000 at your right hand."[14] Here the quantitative distinction between left and right similarly reflects a qualitative difference. The right, which always represents the stronger side, is considered primary. The weaker left is classified as secondary.[15]

The transitional world of Olam Hazeh aligns with the less-important left. Eternal existence is reserved for Olam Haba, aligned with the right.

The left is associated with "riches and honor" compared to the right that relates to "length of days."[16] These, in turn, align themselves with Eisav and Yaakov's division of the 2 worlds.[17] The transitional world of *Olam Hazeh* — with its emphasis on material gain such as "riches" — aligns with the less-important left.[18] Eternal existence — length of days — is reserved for *Olam Haba,* which is aligned with the right.[19]

1000 VS. 10,000:
MENASHE AND EPHRAIM

The two sons born to Yosef in Egypt were Menashe and Ephraim.[20] When Yaakov was on his deathbed, Yosef ushered in his sons so that they would receive blessings from their grandfather.[21] Yaakov placed Menashe and Ephraim on par with Reuven and Shimon, to be classified as two independent Tribes of Israel.[22]

Yaakov placed Menashe and Ephraim on par with Reuven and Shimon.

Presenting his sons before Yaakov, Yosef positioned his older son Menashe to the right of Yaakov and his younger son Ephraim to Yaakov's left. However, when Yaakov placed his hands on the heads of his grandchildren, ignoring Yosef's protestations, he placed his right hand upon Ephraim and his left hand upon Menashe.[23] Yaakov's reasoning was that the Tribe of Ephraim (whose descendants would include the Jewish leader Yehoshua bin Nun) would become greater than the Tribe of Menashe. It was therefore fitting for his primary, stronger right hand to be placed upon Ephraim, while placing his weaker, secondary left hand upon Menashe.[24]

In Moshe's parting blessings to the descendants of Yosef, the distinction between the two sons was accentuated by the words, "They are the 10,000s of Ephraim, and they are the 1000s of Menashe."[25] The "1000s of Menashe" parallels his secondary position to the left vis-à-vis the "10,000s of Ephraim" that relate to his primary position to the right.

1000S VS. 10,000S: SHAUL AND DAVID

The respective positions of 1000 and 10,000 find further contrast in the disntinction made between King Shaul and King David. In comparing their victories on the battlefield, the Jewish women chanted the refrain, "Shaul has killed his 1000s and David his 10,000s." This popular song aroused Shaul's anger as he questioned these numbers, adding, "all he [David] is missing is the kingdom."[26]

The reign of Shaul was a brief and temporal one. This was accurately reflected in his name: it was *shaul*, borrowed.[27] Though he was the first Jewish king, he tragically forfeited the throne by not eradicating the nation Amalek, born to the grandson of Eisav.[28] His kingship would not establish an enduring royal dynasty. So his praise only extended up to 1000s. By contrast, the rule of David would be an everlasting one. He established the Davidic dynasty that was destined to continue until the emergence of the Messianic king. In the words of the liturgy of *Kiddush Levanah*, Blessings of the New Moon, we proclaim "David, king of Israel, is alive and enduring."[29] Thus, the praising of David was with 10,000s to reflect its permanent nature.[30]

The rule of David would be everlasting.

IN PURSUIT OF 10,000

The ideal level of victory by Israel over their enemies, in the blessings they will receive by fulfilling the commandments, is described as their supernatural ability to pursue 10,000: "100 of you shall chase 10,000; your enemies shall fall before you by the sword."[31] Conversely, when G-d delivers Israel into their enemies because of their sins, He miraculously arranges it such that against the odds, "2 will pursue 10,000."[32]

The realm of 10,000 enables the Children of Israel to perpetually focus upon what is eternal.

The Jewish nation that descended from Yaakov is connected to the symbolism of 10,000s, which denotes that which is primary, permanent, and reflective of a distinctive higher realm — one that is not bound by a numeric denomination. It is the existence of the realm of 10,000 — a number that is "too numerous to mention" — which enables the Children of Israel to perpetually focus upon what is eternal.

NOTES

1. *Maharal Chiddushei Aggados, Sanhedrin* 95b (Vol. 3, p. 197), *Gevuros Hashem 3*. See *Shem Mi-Shmuel, Mishpatim* 5680 and *Devarim* 5676; also see R' Tzadok HaKohen, *Yisrael Kedoshim* 12b and *Dover Tzedek* 8a.
2. See "1000: A Thousand to One."
3. See "10: Top Ten."
4. R' Tzadok HaKohen, *Kometz HaMinchah* 58 (pp. 52-53).
5. *Shemos* 18:21, 25.
6. *Bereishis* 24:60.
7. See *Bereishis Rabbah* 60:13.
8. See *Bereishis* 36:15-43.
9. See *Shabbos* 104a for how the letters of the word אֱמֶת stretch from the beginning (א), through the middle (מ), and to the end (ת) of the Hebrew alphabet. Additionally, the structure of the letters are all firmly rooted and balanced. Conversely, שֶׁקֶר has three letters toward the end of the Hebrew alphabet. Moreover, the three letters stand on one leg (ש in the Torah Scroll script is pointy at the bottom). Thus, truth prevails, while falsehood is transient.
10. The 10,000s mentioned in *Yechezkel* 16:7 are a reference to Yaakov. See *Bereishis Rabbah* 60:13.
11. R' Tzadok HaKohen, loc. cit.
12. *Shir HaShirim* 5:10.
13. *Devarim* 33:2.
14. *Tehillim* 91:7.
15. The performance of all *mitzvos* is to be enacted with the right hand or with preference placed on the right side. See, for example, *Zevachim* 24a, *Shulchan Aruch, Orach Chaim* 2:4, *Mishnah Berurah* 5 ad loc.
16. *Mishlei* 3:16.
17. See *Rashi, Bereishis* 25:22, citing *Yalkut Shimoni* 110.
18. *Pirkei Avos* 4:21.
19. *Rabbeinu Bachya* and *Metzudos Dovid, Mishlei* 3:16.
20. *Bereishis* 46:20.
21. Ibid. 48:1.
22. Ibid. v. 5.
23. Ibid. vv. 13-14.
24. Ibid. v. 19 and *Rashi* ad loc.

25. *Devarim* 33:17.
26. *I Shmuel* 18:7-8.
27. *Bereishis Rabbah* 98:15; see also *Rama MiPano, Maamar Choker HaDin* 4:16.
28. See *I Shmuel* 15:1-35.
29. The phrase "David, king of Israel, is alive and enduring" was the secret code used in Roman times to depict the sanctification of the moon (*Rosh Hashanah* 25a). See also *Zohar* 1, 192b.
30. R' Tzadok HaKohen, loc. cit.
31. *Vayikra* 26:7-8.
32. *Devarim* 32:30.

22,000 IN THE DIVINE PRESENCE

22,000 relates to the resting of the
Shechinah, Divine Presence,
within the world.

This phenomenon is exclusively reserved
for Israel in the Sanctuary,
based upon their relationship to Torah
as the center of national life.

A RESTING PLACE

The central
concept is for
the glory of
G-d to descend
into the lower
world, residing
among man.

T HE NUMBER 22,000 IS CONNECTED TO THE *SHECHINAH,* DIVINE
Presence, that rests upon the Jewish people.

The central concept behind the *Shechinah* is for the glory of G-d
that fills the Higher Worlds to descend into the lower world, residing (*Shechinah* from the root *sh'chan,* reside) among man. The first
national appearance was at the giving of the Torah at Sinai. The construction of the *Mishkan,* Sanctuary, was an attempt to permanently
keep the *Shechinah* in their midst: "Make for Me a Sanctuary and that
I [G-d] may dwell amongst them."[1] Later, the Presence of the *Shechinah* would transfer to and dwell within its permanent edifice inside the
Beis HaMikdash, Holy Temple, in Jerusalem.

22,000: ḥEAVENLY ḥOSTS

The Shechinah
would
exclusively
dwell among
the Jewish
People.

The *Shechinah* would exclusively dwell among the Jewish People, and not any of the other nations.[2] The sanctified nation of Israel
accepted upon themselves the Torah, vowing to dedicate their lives
to glorify G-d and His Holy Name in the world below.

22,000
Heavenly hosts
accompanied
the Shechinah
as It descended
onto the
mountain.

The initial appearance of the *Shechinah* to the entire nation was at
the momentous event of the Divine Revelation at *kabbalas HaTorah,*
acceptance of the Torah. The Heavenly clouds descended upon the
mountain.[3] Smoke enveloped Mount Sinai, which was surrounded by
smoke and fire.[4] When they stood around Sinai to receive the Torah,
the eyes of the Jewish People beheld the 22,000 Heavenly hosts that
accompanied the *Shechinah* as It descended onto the mountain.[5]
This is derived from the verse "The chariot of G-d is myriads and
thousands upon thousands; the Master is among them in holiness as
in Sinai."[6] How is this exact number of 22,000 calculated? There is a
known principle that an unspecified plural form connotes the smallest plural form, which is the number 2.[7] The plural term "myriads"
indicates (2 x 10,000 =) 20,000 and the plural "thousands" suggests
another (2 x 1,000 =) 2,000. Together, this creates a total of (20,000
+ 2,000 =) 22,000 Heavenly hosts that accompanied the *Shechinah*
resting upon Sinai.[8]

22,000: ISRAELITES

Seeing the Heavenly hosts divided into camps and carrying flags led the Children of Israel to greatly yearn to resemble this through their formation and encampment in the desert.[9] Analogous to the 22,000 Heavenly hosts that escorted the *Shechinah* to Sinai, the *Shechinah* would only rest upon a group of no fewer than 22,000 members of the Jewish People.[10]

This concept is derived from the verse that describes the journey and resting of the *Aron*, Ark, in the Wilderness. When it rested, Moshe said, "שׁוּבָה ה׳ רִבְבוֹת אַלְפֵי יִשְׂרָאֵל, *Return O G-d, unto the myriads and thousands of Israel.*"[11] The plural forms, "myriads" and "thousands," refers to the combination of their minimum form, namely ([2 x 10,000] + [2 x 1,000] =) 22,000.[12]

22,000: LEVITES

The continuous presence of the *Shechinah* in the *Mishkan* relates to the total number of Levites. In the Wilderness census, there were 22,000 men counted from *Shevet Levi*, the Tribe of Levi.[13] Loyal to G-d by not participating in the sin of the Golden Calf,[14] they became the tribe stationed around the *Mishkan*. Their role, as the replacement of the firstborns, was to assist the *Kohanim*, priests, safeguarding the *Mishkan*.[15]

Like the 22,000 Heavenly hosts that were a befitting escort to the *Shechinah*, there was a parallel number of 22,000 Levites actively standing on duty to service the needs of the Holy Sanctum in which the *Shechinah* would dwell.[16]

A TORAH PRESENCE

T HE DWELLING OF THE *SHECHINAH* IN THE *MISHKAN*, MODELED UPON the national experience at Sinai, was firmly based upon placing the presence of G-d's Holy Torah at the epicenter.

The dwelling of the Shechinah was firmly based upon placing the presence of G-d's Holy Torah at the epicenter.

22,000 VS. 22:
LETTERS OF THE TORAH

Torah is the beginning and basis of Creation. Everything is founded upon it. The building blocks of Torah are the sacred 22 letters of the Hebrew alphabet. The letters that made up the Hebrew language say it *as it is*. They objectively describe spiritual reality from G-d's vantage point rather than using subjective human descriptions.[17]

G-d is the Source of everything and particularly close to whatever is similarly associated with the point of origin. Consequently, when the Jewish People are found in a group of 22,000, whose symbolism is highly evocative of the 22 letters of Torah, G-d then rests His *Shechinah* among them. Due to the fact that the *Shechinah* resides upon a completed community, rather than upon individuals, it therefore requires 22,000 — where 1000 relates back to the number 1[18] — rather than only 22 people.[19]

The Shechinah resides upon a completed community.

The paradigm of the *Shechinah's* Presence in the world began at Sinai with the giving of Torah, which is itself composed of the 22 letters of the Hebrew alphabet. Torah was the blueprint of Creation. All of existence was contingent upon the Jewish nation accepting the Torah at Sinai after their Exodus. By extension, Torah was the locus of both the *Mishkan* and the *Beis HaMikdash*, wherein the *Shechinah* would dwell.

The centerpiece inside the House of G-d was the *Aron*, Holy Ark, onto which the *Luchos*, Tablets, the foremost symbol of Torah, were placed. Additionally, a Torah Scroll was placed either inside or alongside the Ark within the Temple.[20]

The glory of the Shechinah that was manifest in the First Temple departed upon its destruction. When this prayer is answered, the Shechinah will finally return.

The glory of the *Shechinah* that was manifest in the First Temple departed upon its destruction. It did not feature during the Second Temple, which lacked the *Aron*. Nevertheless, the rebuilding of the Temple is included in the prayer asking that the Children of Israel be granted a share in Torah, composed of the 22 letters: "May it be Your Will before You ... that the holy Temple be speedily rebuilt in our days and grant us our share in Your Torah."[21] When this prayer is answered, the *Shechinah*, which required the congregational presence of 22,000 members of the Jewish People, will finally return: "Blessed are You G-d Who restores His *Shechinah* to *Tzion*."[22]

NOTES

1. *Shemos* 25:8. See *Ramban, Shemos* 28:2, Introduction to *Parashas Terumah.*
2. *Berachos* 7a.
3. *Shemos* 19:9.
4. Ibid. 19:18.
5. *Bamidbar Rabbah* 2:3.
6. *Tehillim* 68:18. The *Ibn Ezra* interprets the word שִׁנְאָן as *Shenayim,* two — thus, 2,000.
7. *Midrash Aggadah Bereishis 28:11.* See also "2: Opposite and Equal."
8. *Maharal, Gur Aryeh, Bamidbar 10:36* [34].
9. *Bamidbar Rabbah* 2:3. See also *Ramban, Bamidar* 2:2 citing *Bamidbar Rabbah* 2:10.
10. *Bava Kamma* 83a; *Yevamos* 63b-64a. See "600,000: The Jewish Nation," for an opinion that the *Shechinah* rests among 600,000 Children of Israel. For how the holiness of the *Shechinah* relates to the number 10, see also "9: Where to Turn?" and "10: Top Ten."
11. *Bamidbar* 10:36.
12. See *Rashi, Bamidbar* 10:36.
13. *Bamidbar* 3:39 and *Rashi* ad loc.
14. *Shemos* 32:26.
15. *Bamidbar* 3:5-13.
16. *Maharal, Gur Aryeh, Bamidbar* 10:36 [34]; see also *Maharsha, Yevamos* 63b and *Ibn Ezra, Tehillim* 68:18.
17. See "22: The Sacred Letters."
18. See "1000: A Thousand to One."
19. *Maharal, Chiddushei Aggados, Bava Kamma* 83a (Vol. 3, p. 13).
20. See *Bava Basra* 14a-b cited in *Rashi, Devarim* 31:26.
21. Prayer at conclusion of *Shemoneh Esrei.*
22. *Shemoneh Esrei.*

24,000

THE FALLEN ONES

24,000 is the number of Israelites
who tragically died in a plague at Shittim and
of the students of Rabbi Akiva
who died in a plague
between Pesach and Shavuos.

TWO HORRIFIC OCCURRENCES MAKE MENTION OF THE NUMBER 24,000. There were 24,000 Israelites who died in Shittim following the debacle with the Moabite women. Many generations later, 24,000 disciples of the famous Talmudic sage Rabbi Akiva similarly perished in a plague.

The iDeAL TRANSFORMATION

Should man deviate from the ways of Torah, he can remedy the situation by effecting a complete transformation. Something that is negative can be turned into something positive. Evil can and must be transformed into good. Impurity must similarly be transformed into purity. And whatever was originally cursed must now turn to become a source of blessing.

The Jewish People would escape their lowly state in Egypt[1] to transform themselves into a purified state through their 49-day journey to Sinai en route to embrace Torah.

Such a metamorphosis was seen on a national scale following the Exodus. Despite being on the 49th level of impurity, the Jewish People would escape their lowly state in Egypt[1] to transform themselves into a purified state through their 49-day journey to Sinai en route to embrace Torah.[2] Indeed, this transformation is destined to be repeated in the Final Redemption where Mashiach will transform the contaminated world of sin into a purified world that reveals the knowledge of G-d.

Conversely, where this situation is revoked or this process is put into reverse, the inevitable result is one of devastation and disaster. This is found in the appearance of the number 24,000.

24,000: The FALLEN OF ShiTTIM

Bilaam's proposed curses were Divinely transformed into blessings.

Invited by Balak king of Moav to curse Israel, Bilaam's efforts were thwarted. The gentile prophet's proposed curses were Divinely transformed into blessings.[3] Rather than deride and denigrate the Children of Israel, Bilaam could only praise and bless them. It is possible to deduce from these blessings what was really in Bilaam's heart; this is because they were the diametric opposite of his intended curses.[4]

Despite Israel's temporary salvation, Bilaam devised a cunning scheme for their downfall. Aware that G-d detests harlotry, Bilaam advised Balak to send Moabite maidens into the Jewish camp to entice the Jewish men into immorality and the idol worship of Baal Peor. This evil ploy succeeded. A plague erupted that claimed the lives of 24,000 men, all from the Tribe of Shimon. It abruptly came to an end through the zealotry of Pinchas, who grabbed a spear and put to death two of the most prominent perpetrators.[5] Consequently, all of Bilaam's blessings — with one notable exception[6] — now reverted back into curses.[7]

24,000: DISCIPLES OF RABBI AKIVA

Rabbi Akiva had an academy of 24,000 disciples (12,000 sets of pairs) who were all accomplished Torah scholars. But tragedy struck as they all died in a single time span during the period from Pesach to Shavuos. The reason attributed for their death was that they did not properly honor each other.[8]

Many of the commentaries address the timing of this plague during the historic 49-day interval bridging the Exodus and Israel's acceptance of Torah at Sinai. In truth, this period of the Jewish calendar should have been a particular joyous time. It was meant to mark the transformative journey from the spiritual impurity of Egypt toward the spiritual purity of Sinai, from being an accursed slave to a blessed, free man.

Parallel to Rabbi Akiva's personal transformation from ignorant shepherd[9] to outstanding Jewish leader,[10] this 49-day period would have been perfect for the transformative power toward the ultimate level of Torah. Regrettably, there was the tragic failure by his disciples to realize this. Consequently, the 49-day period that was originally intended to be a path of life and a blessed state now reverted to become a path of death, thus entering into an accursed state.

The 49-day period originally intended to be a path of life now reverted to become a path of death.

24,000: BLESSINGS TO CURSES

On a deeper level, the two groups of 24,000 are linked. Rabbi Akiva's 24,000 disciples were supposed to rectify the sin of the 24,000 men from Shimon who consorted with the daughters of Moav.[11]

Spiritual decline is frequently identified with Moav, as the national epitome of spiritual contamination, depths of immorality,[12] and accursed status.[13] Moav often reflects a descent to the lowest, 49th level of impurity, as alluded to in its numerical value of 49.[14] Consequently, the influence of Moav was responsible for a complete reversal.

Bilaam's efforts to curse Israel had earlier miraculously turned into blessing.

Bilaam's efforts to curse Israel had earlier miraculously turned into blessing. He subsequently tried to undo this by luring the Children of Israel into sin through the maidens of Moav. So instead of a process going from impurity to purity or from cursing to blessing, sin removed the level of protection offered by blessing. It now exposed Israel to Bilaam's original plans — so that his blessings reverted back into curses. This resulted in the death of 24,000 men from the Tribe of Shimon. Of the 12 Tribes, Shimon was cursed and subsequently would not receive a blessing from Moshe before his death.[15]

The tragedy of Rabbi Akiva's 24,000 fallen disciples can be attributed to a failure to turn impurity into purity.

The tragedy of Rabbi Akiva's 24,000 fallen disciples can similarly be attributed to a failure to turn impurity into purity or to transfer curses into blessings through the 49-day journey between Pesach and Shavuos. Rabbi Akiva's disciples did not manage to revoke the curse and impurity of Moav that led to the downfall of 24,000 from the Tribe of Shimon. Their failing in the area of honoring others finds its parallel in the idolatry of Baal Peor at Shittim, whose repugnant worship entailed denigration of any semblance of honor.[16] Thus the period between Pesach and Shavuos would remain the longest extended mourning period in the Jewish calendar

24,000: CURSES TO BLESSINGS

It is possible to ascend from the lowliest level and to ultimately rise up until reaching the highest position.

Despite these tragedies of the 24,000, the historic passage of the Jewish People from Pesach to Shavuos shows that it is nevertheless possible to ascend from the lowliest level and to ultimately rise up until reaching the highest position. This applies even where dealing with Moav, which reached the depths of impurity on the 49th level. Turning the world from "impurity" to "purity" and from "curses" to "blessings" is what Mashiach is destined to achieve in the Final and Ultimate Redemption.

King David, who was born and died on Shavuos,[17] descended from Ruth the Moabite.[18] It is Mashiach, a scion of the Davidic royal dynasty, who will reverse the contaminated world of sin into a purified world that reveals knowledge of G-d.[19] The lineage of Mashiach going back to Moav enables him to overturn all curses and return the world into a blessed state where they return to G-d.

This will reverse the tragedies of 24,000 who died at Shittim and the 24,000 disciples of Rabbi Akiva. The journey from Pesach to Shavuos will once again depict the ascent of life to fully embrace the Torah ideal. Bilaam's curses will then be neutralized forever — to be replaced with blessings.

NOTES

1. See 210: The Iron Furnace."
2. See "49: The Full Measure."
3. *Devarim* 23:6.
4. *Sanhedrin* 105b.
5. *Bamidbar* 25:1-15 See *Bamidbar Rabbah* 14:17 for how the 24 groupings of the priests in the service of the *Mishkan* atones for the 24,000 who died because of the sin of Baal Peor.'
6. This refers to the blessing, "How goodly are your tents O Yaakov, the dwelling place of Yisrael" (*Bamidbar* 24:5), which refers to the beauty of Jewish synagogues and study houses.
7. *Sanhedrin* 105b.
8. *Yevamos* 62b.
9. *Yalkut Shimoni, Mishlei* 948.
10. *Avos deRabbi Nassan* 6.
11. *Megaleh Amukos* 86. One additional association mentioned is the 24,000 inhabitants of the town of Shechem killed by Shimon (together with his brother Levi) in retribution for the assault and violation of his sister Dinah at the hands of Shechem son of Chamor. Years later, an equivalent 24,000 men fell from the Tribe of Shimon (*Megaleh Amukos* 86, in name of *Arizal*).
12. The conception of Moav, the patriarch of this nation, shamefully resulted through the union between Avraham's nephew Lot and his daughter, whose naming of the child (*moav*, derived from *mei'av*, "from [the] father") did not even try to mask his disgraceful origins (*Bereishis* 19:31-37).
13. Moav's father was Lot, whose name implies *lit,* accursed. See *Targum Onkelos, Bereishis* 3:14.
14. *Rabbeinu Bachya, Devarim* 34:6. See "49: The Full Measure."
15. *Devarim* 33:6-29. Furthermore, the 11 curses [on the twin mountains, Gerizim and Evel] correspond to 11 tribes — to the exclusion of Shimon, who was not blessed by Moshe before his death. Since Shimon was not included in the blessing, neither did he want him to be associated with the curse. (*Rashi, Devarim* 27:24). See also *Rashi Devarim* 33:7; quoting *Midrash Haggadah Tehillim*.
16. The idolatry of Baal Peor was the antithesis to honor (*Sanhedrin* 64a).
17. *Tosafas, Chagigah* 17a citing *Yerushalmi*. See *Kiddushin* 38a, that the pious die on the same date as their birthday.
18. *Rus* 4:17-22.
19. *Tzefaniah* 3:9.

600,000

The Jewish NATION

600,000 is the number
commonly associated
with the Jewish People
in its entirety.

THE NATION

The number
600,000
describes Klal
Yisrael, the
Congregation of
Israel.

THE NUMBER 600,000 IS THE CELEBRATED NUMBER THAT DESCRIBES *Klal Yisrael*, the Congregation of Israel.

600,000: MEMBERS OF ISRAEL

The formation of the Jewish people began when Yaakov's household of 70 souls migrated to Egypt. During the 210 years of the Egyptian Exile, the Children of Israel proliferated to emerge at the Exodus as an independent, newly formed Jewish nation.

At the time of their departure, the Jewish people numbered "about 600,000 men on foot, aside from children."[1] Later, during their 40-year trek in the Wilderness, the national census would calculate the sum of the Israelites as variations of this 600,000 figure (as 603,550 people[2] or 601,730 people[3]).

600,000 is the designated number who were essential for the national definition of the Jewish people.

In truth, the figure 600,000 does not reflect the total Jewish population. The segment it refers to is exclusively those Jewish men between the ages of 20 to 60 years old.[4] It did not include any Jewish women, children, or elders. Nevertheless, 600,000 is the designated, all-encompassing number who were essential for the national definition of the Jewish people.

600,000: THE WHOLE NATION

The symbolism of the number 600,000 is ideal to depict the Jewish nation in its entirety. We have discussed that the number 6 is the epitome of *sheleimus*, completion, in the physical world.[5] This can be extended to encompass the 3 primary numeric denominations: single units (**1** x 600,000 = 600,000), hundreds (**100** x 6000 = 600,000) and thousands (**1000** x 600 = 600,000). Accordingly, 600,000 is the number that conceptually represents the most complete level possible.[6]

600,000 is the number that conceptually represents the most complete level possible.

Once the Jewish people had reached this complete level of perfection and maturity, they would be in the position to be liberated.

They proudly left Egypt "complete," as a people of 600,000, ready to be classified as an independent nation. The repeated association Israel has to this number illustrates that Israel, as a nation, is meant to exemplify a state of perfection through having their fullest expression in the physical world.[7] Additionally, the Jewish People would be led by their leader Moshe, whose individual greatness was equivalent to all 600,000 members of Israel that he represented.[8]

600,000: IN puBLIC

The joining of individuals into a communal unit starts with the number 10.[9] Nevertheless, the classic definition of what constitutes a צִיבּוּר, *multitude* or *public*, lies within the number 600,000 which defines the Jewish nation in its entirety. In a sense, 600,000 is the broadest determinant of a כְּלָל, *congregation*, in the "nationhood" of Israel.

There is a special blessing to be recited upon seeing a gathering of 600,000 Jews: *Baruch ... chacham harazim*, Blessed are You [G-d] ... the wise One of secrets.[10] This refers to the fact that G-d knows the innermost thoughts of each individual and knows of each person's uniqueness within the greater context of 600,000 — the number associated with the Jewish people in its entirety. Another well-known application in halachah is found in the laws of transporting on Shabbos. An area at least 16 cubits wide that is in use by a multitude of 600,000 people or that serves a city with a population of 600,000 is universally agreed to meet the definition of a *reshus harabbim*, public domain.[11]

600,000: spiRITUAL ROOTS

The number 600,000 is used to depict a full generation. On the verse "A generation goes, a generations comes,"[12] the Midrash notes that there is no day on which there are not 600,000 that are born and 600,000 that die.[13] There is a tradition that the Jewish nation in any given generation would never number fewer than 600,000 people.[14] In truth, the importance of this number is because 600,000 *signifies the whole nation in its perfected state*. There are 600,000 "spiritual roots" within Israel. They are the "general souls" that are the central core of the unified Jewish people.[15] In turn, these then separate into individual sparks that become the soul that is implanted into each and every living Jew.

There are 600,000 "spiritual roots" within Israel.

The formation of Israel began with their first forefather. Avraham is compared to a tree whose trunk then divides into 600,000 main branches. Here the 600,000 members of Israel would take on the task to realize the purpose of creation as G-d originally intended it.[16] Together, they collectively represent the spiritual makeup of the Chosen Nation.

The 600,000 members of Israel collectively represent the spiritual makeup of the Chosen Nation.

600,000: RESIDING OF DIVINE PRESENCE

The spiritual composition of Israel, as the Chosen Nation, means that G-d wills His *Shechinah*, Divine Presence, to reside among them. G-d chooses to associate Himself with His people, and, by extension, to their number of 600,000 which symbolizes their completeness. According to one opinion, "G-d does not choose to rest His *Shechinah* on fewer than 600,000 people."[17]

G-d chooses to associate Himself with His people, and, by extension, to their number of 600,000 which symbolizes their completeness.

THE TORAH

ONCE THE JEWISH CONGREGATION CAME TOGETHER AS ONE collective nation, the 600,000 spiritual roots of Israel would perfectly align themselves with the holy words of Torah that were given at Sinai.

The 600,000 spiritual roots of Israel would perfectly align themselves with the holy words of Torah.

600,000: WITNESSES AT SINAI

The completion of the Exodus was the acceptance of Torah at Sinai.[18] The 600,000 as the number of the Jewish nation departing from Egypt were the same number of participants present at the Divine Revelation. They would constitute the "root souls" of Israel for time immemorial. The national state of completion synonymous with 600,000 meant that every single member of the Jewish nation had to be present at this momentous event.

This degree of completion extended to ensuring that every one of the congregation be physically "perfect" at Sinai — in concert with the perfection of Torah[19] — such that they were healed of any physical blemishes.[20]

When the Jewish people said their famous pronouncement, נַעֲשֶׂה וְנִשְׁמָע, *We will do and we will understand*,[21] placing action before comprehension, a corresponding 600,000 Heavenly Administering angels descended to adorn each individual Jew with crowns from the glow of the *Shechinah*.[22]

600,000: LETTERS OF TORAH

There is a close correlation between the 600,000 members of Israel who accepted the Torah and the 600,000 letters that are said to be included within a Torah Scroll. (Several resolutions are offered by the classic commentators of how exactly to compute the 600,000 letters.[23]) This relationship is alluded to in the name יִשְׂרָאֵל, *Yisrael*, that can be read as an acrostic for the phrase, יֵשׁ שִׁשִּׁים רִבּוֹא אוֹתִיוֹת לַתּוֹרָה, *There are 600,000 letters in the Torah*.[24]

Each of 600,000 letters represents a particular life-force that animates the existence of the parallel 600,000 Jews. In other words, *the individual's letter is the spiritual root of his existence.* The crowns conferred upon the members of Israel by the 600,000 Administering Angels similarly convey the idea of the Jew being readily identifying through his connection to a Heavenly source.[25]

Part of the symbolism of the Jewish census was to sensitize the Jew to his unique spiritual root and relate to his unique area of Torah. This is because each Jew rightly has a claim to his specific, individual portion in Torah.[26] Therefore, just as all 600,000 letters must be incorporated into a Torah Scroll or it is invalid, the presence of all 600,000 members of Israel was similarly essential — without a single exception — for the revelation of Torah at Sinai.

Together, the 600,000 become the fullest comprehensive expression of Torah. The whole Torah would be taught by and named after Moshe ("Remember the Torah of Moshe my servant"[27]), reflecting his position as the Jewish leader who internally encompassed all facets of Torah within him. Furthermore, Moshe integrated Israel into one nation, and who was himself on par with all 600,000 members of Israel.

600,000: TORAH EXPLANATIONS

We have seen that every soul in Israel is rooted in the Torah. Just as there are 600,000 general souls to the nation, so is there a grand

Every soul in Israel is rooted in the Torah.

total of 600,000 different Torah explanations. "A hammer that splits a rock into many fragments"[28] is the analogy used to explain how 600,000 explanations of Torah similarly emerge out of the 600,000 souls — such that each elicits his individualistic spark and connection to the Holy Torah.[29] It was specifically in the presence of 600,000 members of Israel that the Torah was given.

So the number 600,000 reflects the full community of Israel as the perfect nation to leave Egypt and receive the Torah at Sinai such that the *Shechinah* would rest in their midst. The collective Jewish nation in its composition of 600,000 reflects the wholeness of Torah in its entirety. Together, the number of 600,000 different Torah explanations finds its parallel in the spiritual roots of Israel.

The number 600,000 reflects the full community of Israel as the perfect nation to leave Egypt and receive the Torah.

NOTES

1. *Shemos* 12:37. See also *Bamidbar* 11:21.
2. Ibid. 1:46.
3. Ibid. 26:51.
4. See "20: Manhood" and "60: In Principle."
5. See "6: It's Only Natural"
6. See *Maharal, Gevuros Hashem* 3 for why the non-inclusion of 600,000 is no usage of the two other numeric denominations of 10 or 10,000.
7. *Maharal, Gevuros Hashem* 12.
8. There was a woman in Egypt who gave birth to 600,000 children; this was Yocheved who gave birth to Moshe, who was equivalent to all the members of the Jewish people (*Mechilta, Beshalach*). See *Maharal, Gevuros Hashem* 19.
9. See "9: Where to Turn?" and "10: Top Ten."
10. *Shulchan Aruch, Orach Chaim* 224:5, based on *Berachos* 58a. See also the discussion about saying a blessing upon seeing a similar gathering of idol worshipers.
11. See *Shulchan Aruch, Orach Chaim* 345:7; *Mishnah Berurah*, 345:24; and *Sha'ar HaTziyun* 25.
12. *Koheles* 1:4.
13. *Koheles Rabbah* 1:5.
14. *Rabbeinu Gershom, Aruchin* 32b.
15. See *Koheles Rabbah* on *Koheles* 1:4; *Shir HaShirim Rabbah* 6:15. See also *Tanya* 37 (48b). See R' Tzadok HaKohen, *Pri Tzadik, Vayigash* 12, who interprets the Midrash (*Bereishis Rabbah* 73:11) that Yaakov had a flock of 600,000 animals as an allusion to the 600,000 Jewish souls that would later become the full flock of the Children of Israel.
16. *Ramchal, Derech Hashem* 2:4:5.
17. *Midrash HaGadol, Vayishlach* 32:3. The other opinion is that the *Shechinah* resides among 22,000 people. See *Yevamos* 64a and "22,000: The Divine Presence."
18. See "50: All the Way."
19. *Tehillim* 19:8.
20. *Mechilta, Yisro* 9. See *Maharal, Derashah L'Shabbos Shuvah*, pp.74-75.

21. *Shemos* 24:7.
22. *Shabbos* 88a.
23. The 600,000 letters cannot be referring to the simple letters within our Torah Scrolls, as these have a total of 304,805 letters. Some suggestions for the computation of 600,000 include the fact that many letters are themselves comprised of 2 or 3 other letters (e.g., מ is constructed of a כ and a ו; the 600,000 includes the unwritten letters of a Scroll (e.g., the letter ב is enveloped within the letter פ; spaces between letters); the total sum includes vowel letters are not included in the text, but implied in the word pronunciation. See *Pnei Yehoshua Kiddushin* 30a and R' Reuven Margoliyos' *HaMikrah VeHaMesorah*, Ch. 12.
24. *Zohar Chadash*, end of *Shir HaShirim, Megaleh Amukos, Va'eschanan* 186. See also R' Gedaliah Schorr, *Ohr Gedalyahu, Shavuos,* p. 84.
25. R' Gedaliah Schorr, ibid., p. 84-5.
26. R' Chaim Volozhin, *Nefesh HaChaim* 4:32. See *Chullin* 7a.
27. *Malachi* 3:22.
28. *Yirmiyah* 23:29.
29. *Ramchal, Derech Eitz HaChaim.*

GLOSSARY

Achav — Ahab, King of Israel

Adam (HaRishon) — Adam, (first) man

Aharon — Aaron, brother of Moshe; first High Priest

ahavah — love

Ahavas Hashem — love of G-d

amah (pl. *amos*) — cubit, a unit of measure

Amalek — archenemy of the Jewish nation; descendants of Eisav

Amidah — literally "Standing [Prayer]," referring to the *Shemoneh Esrei*, the silent, central prayer of all services

Ananei HaKavod — Clouds of Glory

Arbah Minim — Four Species (*esrog*, *lulav*, *hadas*, and *aravah*) taken on the Festival of Succos

Aron — Holy Ark (of the Covenant)

avodah zarah — idolatry

Avodas Hashem — service of G-d

Avos — the Patriarchs

Avraham — Abraham, the first Jew

Bamidbar — Book of *Numbers*, fourth of the Five Books of Moses

bar/bat mitzvah — a boy who turns 13 or girl who turns 12 who becomes obligated to observe Jewish law as an adult

bechirah — free choice; man is endowed with the ability to choose between good and evil

bechor — firstborn male offspring.

beis din — courthouse; court of Jewish law

Beis HaMidkash — Holy Temple in Jerusalem

berachah (pl. *berachos*) — blessing

Bereishis — Book of *Genesis*, first of the Five Books of Moses

bikkurim — the first-ripening fruits of the seven species with which the Holy Land is blessed, which were brought to the Temple and given to a *Kohen*

Binyamin — Benjamin, youngest of the Patriarch Jacob's twelve sons

Birchas Kohanim — Priestly Blessings

Bnei Yisrael — Children of Israel

bris milah — the covenant of circumcision

challah — portion removed from dough of the five grains and given to a *Kohen*; if *challah* is not taken, the rest of the dough may not be eaten

chametz — fermented or leavened bread forbidden on Pesach

Chanah — Hannah

Chanukah — Festival of Lights

Chavah — Eve, the first woman

chesed — kindness

Chevron — Hebron

Chillul Hashem — desecration of G-d's Name

Chiram — Hiram, King of Tyre

chol — mundane

Chumash — Five Books of the Torah, the Pentateuch

chupah (pl. *chuppot*) — marriage canopy

Devarim — Book of *Deuteronomy*, fifth of the Five Books of Moses

din — judgement; strict justice

Divrei HaYamim — Book of *Chronicles*, the final book of *Tanach*

Edom — empire descended from Eisav

Eichah — Book of *Lamentations*

Eigel HaZahav — Golden Calf

Eisav — Esau, the Patriarch Jacob's twin

Eliyahu HaNavi — Elijah the Prophet

Elokim — (*Elo-him*) — G-d's holy Name

emunah — faith; faithfulness

Eretz Yisrael — Land of Israel

galus — exile

Gan Eden — Garden of Eden

gashmiyus — materialism

Gehinnom — Purgatory

Gemara — the Talmud / Talmudic tractate

gematria — numerical equivalencies of Hebrew alphabet (**aleph**=1; **beis**=2, etc.)

geulah — redemption

Gidon — Gideon, a prophet

Haftarah — a section of the Prophets read in conjunction with the public Torah reading on Shabbos, Festivals, and fast days.

Halachah (adj. *halachic*) — Jewish law (literally, "the way" of living)

Hoshana Rabbah — the last day of Succos, so called because of the many special prayers of salvation (*hoshana*) recited on that day

Hashem — literally, "the Name"; a reference to G-d and His Ineffable 4-Letter Name, the Tetragrammaton

Hevel — Abel, son of Adam and Chavah, brother of Cain

Imahos — the Matriarchs

Iyov — Book of *Job*

Izevel — Jezebel, wife of King Ahab

Kabbalah (kabbalistic) — "Tradition"; the esoteric or mystical dimension of Torah

Kabbalas HaTorah — receiving of the Torah at Mount Sinai

kadosh — holy

Kayin — Cain

kedushah — holiness; sanctity

Kehunah — the Priesthood

Keser Torah — Crown of Torah

Keser — crown

ketores — incense-offering

Kiddush Hashem — sanctification of G-d's Name

klal — (a) general principle (b) group; community

Kodesh HaKodashim — Holy of Holies; inner sanctum of the *Beis HaMikdash*

kodesh — holiness

Koheles — Book of *Ecclesiastes*

Kohen (pl. *Kohanim*) — a priest, a descendant of Aaron

Kohen Gadol — High Priest

Korban Pesach — Paschal lamb

korban (pl. *korbanos*) — sacrificial offering brought in the Sanctuary/Temple

Lashon HaKodesh — the Hebrew language (literally, "the holy tongue")

Lavan — Laban, father of the Matriarch Rivkah

Levi (pl. *Leviim*) — Levite (descendants of the Tribe of Levi)

Luchos — tablets; the Two Tablets upon which the Ten Commandments were inscribed

Maariv — evening prayer service

Makkos Bechoros — The 10th plague, "Death of the Firstborn"

makkos — plagues, refers to the 10 plagues in Egypt

Mashiach — the Messiah

Matan Torah — Giving of the Torah at Mount Sinai

matzah (pl. *matzos*) — unleavened bread eaten on festival of Pesach

Megillas Esther — Scroll of *Esther* read on holiday of Purim

Melachim — Book of *Kings;* (l.c.) angels

Menashe — Manasseh, son of Yosef, one of the Twelve Tribes

Menorah — the 7-branched candelabrum within the Sanctuary/Temple

mezuzah — small scroll containing the passages of **Deuteronomy** 6:4-9 and 11:13-21, that is affixed to the right door post

middah (pl. *middos*) — (a) character trait (b) measure

Midrash — homiletic or hermeneutic Torah sources of the Oral Law.

mikveh — a body of naturally collected standing water (ritual bath) of 40 *se'ah*, into which a person or object is immersed to attain ritual spiritual purity

Minchah — afternoon prayer service

Mishkan — Sanctuary; portable *Beis HaMikdash* (Temple) that accompanied the Israelites through their 40-year sojourn in the Wilderness

Mishlei — Book of *Proverbs*

Mishnah — the central, primary text of Oral Law redacted by Rabbi Yehudah the Prince shortly after the destruction of the second Holy Temple. These laws were elaborated by later scholars in the Talmud.

Mitzrayim — Egypt

mitzvah (pl. *mitzvos*) — commandment

Mitzvos Asei — Positive Commandments

Mitzvos Lo Saaseh — Prohibitive Commandments

Mizbei'ach — Altar

Moav — Moab

Moshe — Moses, leader of the Jews in their 40-year sojourn in the Wilderness

mussaf — (a) (l.c.) additional sacrifice offered on Shabbos, Festivals, and Rosh Chodesh (b) (cap.) additional prayer service recited in lieu of this sacrifice

navi — prophet

Ne'ilah — special prayer recited on Yom Kippur

nefesh — the lowest level of the soul

neshamah — the third level of the soul

niddah — a woman who has menstruated or has given birth and who is therefore ritually impure until she has completed her purification process and has immersed in a *mikveh*

Noach — Noah, builder of the Ark, survivor of the Great Flood

Ohel Moed — Tent of Meeting, the **Mishkan**

Olam HaBa — the World to Come

Olam Hazeh — This World

parashah (pl. *parshios*) — weekly Torah portion

Pelishtim — Philistines

Pesach — Festival of Passover

Purim — Festival of Purim (Feast of Lots)

rachamim — mercy

Rivkah — Rebecca, one of the Four Matriarchs

Rosh Chodesh — first day of the new Jewish month

Rosh Hashanah — Jewish New Year

ruach — the second level of the soul

Rus — Ruth

Sanhedrin — High Court of Israel; the Supreme Court

Seder — (literally "Order") festive ceremony of proceedings on the first night of Pesach

Sefer Torah — Torah Scroll

Sha'kkai (*Shad-ai*) — One of the Divine Names of God

shaatnez — forbidden mixture of wool and linen

Shabbos — Sabbath, the day of rest

Shacharis — morning prayer service

shalom — peace

Shalosh Regalim — Three Pilgrimage Festivals (Pesach, Shavuos, and Succos)

Shamayim — the heavens

Shavuos — Festival of Weeks, Pentecost

Shechinah — the Divine Presence of G-d as it is manifest in the world

shekel (pl. *shekalim*) — a unit of monetary currency

sheker — falsehood

sheleimus — completion

Shem HaMeforash — the Ineffable 4-Letter "Explicit Name" of G-d

Shema Yisrael — Jewish credo and statement of Hashem's Unity

Shemini Ateres — the eighth and concluding festival day of Succos (includes a second day of Simchas Torah in the Diaspora); in many respects, it constitutes a *Yom Tov* in its own right

shemittah — the Sabbatical (7th) year, during which the Holy Land may not be cultivated

Shemoneh Esrei — literally 18 blessings, the term for the silent standing prayer called *Amidah*; the central prayer of all services.

Shemos — Book of *Exodus*, second of the Five Books of Moses

Shes — Seth

shevatim — tribes (of Israel)

Shimon — Simeon

Shimshon — Samson, a prophet

Shir HaShirim — Book of *Song of Songs*

Shlomo — Solomon, king of Israel

Shmuel — Samuel, the first prophet

Shnei Luchos HaBris — Two Tablets of the Covenant

shofar — (ram's) horn blown on Rosh Hashanah

Simchas Torah — celebration of the completion of the yearly cycle of reading the Torah

succah — temporary dwelling, "booth" or "hut" used during the Festival of Succos (Tabernacles)

Succos — Festival of Tabernacles

taharah — ritual purity

Talmud — Oral Law (literally, "Learning") as the primary texts of the discussions of Jewish law based upon the Mishnah; they include the Babylonian Talmud (*Talmud Bavli*) and Jerusalem Talmud (*Talmud Yerushalmi*)

tamei — ritually impure

Tanach — Scripture; an acronym for Torah (5 Books of Moses), *Neviim* (Prophets), and *Kesuvim* (Writings)

tefillah — prayer

tefillin — phylacteries, the black leather boxes bound upon the (weaker) hand and on the head by adult men during weekday morning prayers

Tehillim — Book of *Psalms*, composed by King David

terumah — the first portion of the crop separated and given to a **Kohen**

teshuvah — repentance

Tishah B'Av — Ninth of Av, national day of mourning for the destruction of the Holy Temples in Jerusalem

Torah SheBa'al Peh — the Oral Torah

Torah SheBichsav — the Written Torah

Torah — the Law; also a reference to the 5 Books of the Torah, the Pentateuch

Trei Aser — the Books of the *Twelve Prophets*

tumah — ritual impurity

tzaddik (pl. *tzaddikim*) — righteous person

tzedakah — charity

tzitzis — fringes placed on the corners of 4-cornered garments

Tzor — Tyre

Vayikra — Book of *Leviticus*, third of the Five Books of Moses

viduy — confession

Yaakov — Jacob, the Patriarch, son of Isaac

Yalkut — Midrashic anthology covering the Torah

Yamim Noraim — Days of Awe (Festivals of Rosh Hashanah and Yom Kippur)

Yechezkel — Book of **Ezekiel**

Yehoshua — Joshua, leader after the demise of Moses; Joshua brought the Jewish nation into the Promised Land

Yehudah — Judah, fourth son of Jacob

Yericho — Jericho

Yeshayah — Book of *Isaiah*

Yetzer Hara — Evil Inclination; personification of evil influence

Yetzer Tov — Good Inclination

Yetzias Mitzrayim — Exodus; departure from Egypt

yirah — fear or reverence

Yiras Shamayim — fear of Heaven

Yirmiyah — Book of *Jeremiah*

Yishai — Jesse, father of King David

Yishmael — Ishmael, son of the Patriarch Avraham

Yisrael — Israel, the entire Jewish Nation; this term is derived from another name of Yaakov

Yisro — Jethro, father-in-law of Moses

Yitzchak — Isaac, the Patriarch, son of Abraham

Yom Kippur — Day of Atonement

Yom Tov (pl. *Yamim Tovim*) — lit., good day; i.e., a Festival day

Yosef — Joseph, firstborn son of the Matriarch Rivkah

Yovel — Jubilee, fiftieth year

zecher — a remembrance

zivah, *zivus* — flow or type of discharge which renders a person spiritually impure with the ritual impurity of a *zav* (male) or *zavah* (female)

This volume is part of
THE ARTSCROLL® SERIES
an ongoing project of
translations, commentaries and expositions on
Scripture, Mishnah, Talmud, Midrash, Halachah,
liturgy, history, the classic Rabbinic writings,
biographies and thought.

For a brochure of current publications
visit your local Hebrew bookseller
or contact the publisher:

Mesorah Publications, ltd

313 Regina Avenue
Rahway, New Jersey 07065
(718) 921-9000
www.artscroll.com